5

THE JOURNAL
OF
PHARMACOLOGY
AND
EXPERIMENTAL THERAPEUTICS

FOUNDED BY JOHN J. ABEL

VOLUME 120
MAY - AUGUST 1957

OFFICIAL PUBLICATION
OF THE AMERICAN SOCIETY FOR PHARMACOLOGY AND
EXPERIMENTAL THERAPEUTICS INCORPORATED

BALTIMORE, MARYLAND

CONTENTS

Number 1, May, 1957

I. A Fluorometric Method for the Measurement of 4-amino-10-methyl Pteroylglutamic Acid (Amethopterin) in Plasma. M. V. Freeman.... 1

II. Effects of Ribosides and Related Compounds on Cation Transport in Cold-Stored Human Erythrocytes. J. B. Kahn, Jr. and Shelby B. Cohen.... 9

III. Effects of LSD 25, BOL 148, Bufotenine, Mescaline and Ibogaine on the Potentiation of Hexobarbital Hypnosis Produced by Serotonin and Reserpine. Gian Carlo Salmoiraghi and Irvine H. Page.............. 20

IV. A Spectrophotofluorometric Study of Organic Compounds of Pharmacological Interest. Sidney Udenfriend, Daniel E. Duggan, Bruno M. Vasta and Bernard B. Brodie.. 26

V. Effects of *Dextro*-amphetamine upon Judgment. G. T. Hauty and R. B. Payne.. 33

VI. Auricular Fibrillation by Acetylcholine Injection During Hypopotassemia. Phillip E. Leveque.. 38

VII. The Influence of Various Spatial Groups on Cholinolytic Activity. J. P. Long and A. M. Lands.. 46

VIII. Distribution and Fate of Nalorphine in the Dog and Rat. L. A. Woods and H. E. Muehlenbeck.. 52

IX. Comparative Distribution of Morphine and Nalorphine in Dog Brain. L. A. Woods.. 58

X. Studies on Veratrum Alkaloids. XXV. Veratrine Response and Antiveratrinic Action in Frog Sartorius Muscle. Peter N. Witt and Charles R. Swaine.. 63

XI. Enzymatic Oxidation of Pentobarbital and Thiopental. Jack R. Cooper and Bernard B. Brodie.. 75

XII. The Distribution of Gold Following the Injection of Obesity-inducing Doses of Aurothioglucose in the Mouse. Gerald Friedman and Jay Tepperman.. 84

XIII. Bioassay for Cardiac Active Principles Based on the Staircase Phenomenon of the Frog Heart. Stephen Hajdu.............................. 96

XIV. The Isolation of a Cardiac Active Principle from Mammalian Tissue. Stephen Hajdu, Herbert Weiss and Elwood Titus...................... 99

Number 2, June, 1957

XV. Hemodynamic Effects of Levarterenol Infusion During Induced Pulmonary Stenosis. Noble O. Fowler, E. R. Duchesne and R. H. Franch.... 115

XVI. Bioassay of *Rauwolfia* Roots and Alkaloids. Bernard Rubin, Marvin H. Malone, Margaret H. Waugh and John C. Burke...................... 125

XVII. A Study of Substances Which Alter Intraventricular Conduction in the Isolated Dog Heart. Henry H. Swain and Charles L. Weidner...... 137

XVIII. Central and Peripheral Components of the Action of "Ganglionic" Blocking Agents. A. S. Dontas and Mark Nickerson...................... 147

XIX. Action of Eserine and Amphetamine on the Electrical Activity of the Rabbit Brain. V. G. Longo and B. Silvestrini...................... 160

XX. The Toxicology of Potassium and Sodium Iodates: Acute Toxicity in Mice. Stewart H. Webster, Mary E. Rice, Benjamin Highman and W. F. von Oettingen.. 171

XXI. Some Observations on the Interaction of Reserpine and LSD. M. Taeschler and A. Cerletti.. 179

XXII. Objective Comparison of Primidone and Phenobarbital in Epileptics. Charles M. Gruber, Jr., Jack M. Mosier and Phyllis Grant 184

XXIII. Biochemical and Pharmacological Studies on *O*-Tyrosine and its *Meta* and *Para* Analogues. A Suggestion Concerning Phenylketonuria. Chozo Mitoma, Herbert S. Posner, Donald F. Bogdanski and Sidney Udenfriend 188

XXIV. The Effect of 6-Mercaptopurine on Nucleic Acid Biosynthesis in *Escherichia coli*. H. George Mandel, Joseph K. Inscoe, Harriet M. Maling and Paul K. Smith 195

XXV. The Relation Between Dose of Succinylcholine and Duration of Apnea in Man. W. Kalow and D. R. Gunn 203

XXVI. Antagonism of Tubocurarine III. Time Course of Action of Pyridostigmin, Neostigmine, and Edrophonium *In Vivo* and *In Vitro*. Cedric M. Smith, James C. Mead and Klaus R. Unna 215

XXVII. Distribution and Metabolic Fate of S^{35}-Labeled Myleran (Busulfan) in Normal and Tumor-Bearing Rats. Chin-Tzu Peng 229

XXVIII. Effects of Ribosides and Related Compounds on Phosphate Transport in Incubated Fresh and Cold-Stored Human Erythrocytes. J. B. Kahn, Jr. 239

XXIX. A Comparative Study of the Effects of Four Different *Rauwolfia* Preparations Administered Parenterally. Ralph V. Ford, Richard E. Borreson, Gene R. Lindley and John H. Moyer 247

XXX. Effect of Iproniazid on Serotonin Metabolism *In Vivo*. Sidney Udenfriend, Herbert Weissbach and Donald F. Bogdanski 255

XXXI. The Effect of Certain Central Nervous System Depressants on Pituitary-Adrenal Activating Agents, P. F. Dirk Van Peenen and E. Leong Way 261

NUMBER 3, JULY, 1957

XXXII. Relation of Peripheral Vasodilator Activity to Chemical Structure of 1,2,3,4-Tetrahydroisoquinoline Derivatives. Donald L. Cook, Coleta A. Lawler and John W. Cusic 269

XXXIII. Pyridine-2-aldoxine Methiodide in the Treatment of Sarin and Tabun Poisoning, with Notes on its Pharmacology. Robert V. Brown, Anne M. Kunkel, Lea M. Somers and J. Henry Wills 276

XXXIV. The Effects of some Acetylcholine Derivatives on the Cholinesterases of Chick Embryo Intestine Cultured *in Vitro*. Alan Burkhalter, R. M. Featherstone, F. W. Schueler and Marion Jones 285

XXXV. Enzymatic Reduction of Prontosil and Other Azo Dyes. James R. Fouts, Jerome J. Kamm and Bernard B. Brodie 291

XXXVI. Effects of Diphenylhydantoin on Synaptic Transmission in Cat Spinal Cord and Stellate Ganglion. Don W. Esplin 301

XXXVII. Frequency-force Relationship in the Rabbit Auricle and its Modification by some Metabolic Inhibitors. B. Katzung, H. Rosin and F. Scheider 324

XXXVIII. Release of Serotonin from Blood Platelets by Reserpine *in Vitro*. Arvid Carlsson, Parkhurst A. Shore and Bernard B. Brodie 334

XXXIX. Pharmacology of *d*-Lysergic Acid Morpholide (LSM). John H. Gogerty and James M. Dille 340

XL. Prevention of Experimental Polyarthritis with Sodium Aurothiomalate. Gaëtan Jasmin 349

XLI. Studies of Analgesic Drugs: Dihydrocodeine. Arthur S. Keats, Jane Telford and Yoshio Kurosu 354

XLII. Comparative Effects of Epinephrine and Levarterenol (*l*-Norepinephrine) on Left Ventricular Performance in Conscious and Anesthetized Dogs. Theodore C. West and Robert F. Rushmer 361

XLIII. A Study in the Dog of the Renal Clearance of Morphine and the Effect of Morphine on *p*-Aminohippurate Clearance. W. P. Baker and L. A. Woods. 371

XLIV. A Comparison of some Phenothiazine Derivatives in Inhibiting Apomorphine-Induced Emesis. Herbert Rosenkilde and William M. Govier.... 375

XLV. The Effect of Chlorpromazine on Fear-motivated Behavior in Rats. Robert E. Miller, John V. Murphy and I. Arthur Mirsky.................... 379

XLVI. Use of Differential Bar-pressing Rates of Rats for Screening Analgesic Drugs. I. Techniques and Effects of Morphine. Harris E. Hill, Frank T. Pescor, Richard E. Belleville and Abraham Wikler................. 388

NUMBER 4, AUGUST, 1957

XLVII. Chemoreflex Activity of Dextromethorphan (Romilar), Dextrorphan, Codeine and Morphine in the Cat and the Dog. Carl C. Gruhzit....... 399

XLVIII. Influence of pH and Atropine on the Response of Superfused Tissues to 5-Hydroxytryptamine and Acetylcholine. James L. Leitch, D. Maryn, V. G. Debley and Thomas J. Haley.................................... 408

XLIX. Studies on Veratrum Alkaloids XXVI. Comparison of the Cardiac Action of Various Tertiary Amine Ester Alkaloids. J. M. Benforado.......... 412

L. The Effects of Relaxin-containing Ovarian Extracts on Various Types of Smooth Muscle. Jack W. Miller, Anthony Kisley and William J. Murray.. 426

LI. Pharmacology of some new Unsymmetrical Bisquaternary Hypotensive Agents—Substituted Pyridine and Piperidine Derivatives. Thomas B. O'Dell and Martha D. Napoli... 438

LII. The Absorption and Metabolism of Anileridine, Ethyl-1-(4-aminophenethyl)-4-phenylisonipecotate. Curt C. Porter......................... 447

LIII. The Curariform Action of Streptomycin. Oswaldo Vital Brazil and Alexandre Pinto Corrado... 452

LIV. The Differential Effect of Quinidine and Pyrilamine on the Myocardial Action Potential at Various Rates of Stimulation. E. A. Johnson and M. G. McKinnon.. 460

LV. Tolerance to some Effects of Barbiturates. Richard E. Belleville and H. F. Fraser.. 468

LVI. Some Factors Affecting the Biological Disposition of Small Doses of Morphine in Rats. T. K. Adler, H. W. Elliott and R. George............. 475

LVII. Histochemical Demonstration of Reversible Anticholinesterase Action at Selective Cellular Sites *in Vivo*. George B. Koelle..................... 488

LVIII. *In Vitro* Oxidation of Morphine by Rat Tissue Homogenates. Eikichi Hosoya and Theodore M. Brody.................................. 504

LIX. Effects of Sympathomimetic Drugs on Pulmonary Circulation: With Special Reference to a New Pulmonary Vasodilator. Domingo M. Aviado, Jr. and Carl F. Schmidt.. 512

LX. Absorption of Drugs from the Stomach I. The Rat. Lewis S. Schanker, Parkhurst A. Shore, Bernard B. Brodie and C. Adrian M. Hogben..... 528

LXI. Absorption of Drugs from the Stomach II. The Human. C. Adrian M. Hogben, Lewis S. Schanker, Dominick J. Tocco and Bernard B. Brodie... 540

A FLUOROMETRIC METHOD FOR THE MEASUREMENT OF 4-AMINO-10-METHYL PTEROYLGLUTAMIC ACID (AMETHOPTERIN) IN PLASMA[1]

M. V. FREEMAN

Clinical Pharmacology and Experimental Therapeutics Section, National Cancer Institute, Bethesda, Maryland

Received for publication November 16, 1956

The method currently in use for the determination of 4-amino-10-methyl pteroylglutamic acid (amethopterin) is a bacteriological bioassay. In view of the length of time involved in a bioassay, the possibility of utilizing chemical means to measure the concentration of amethopterin in plasma was investigated. That pteridines fluoresce has been known ever since their extraction from butterfly wings by Hopkins (1894). Recently, it has been shown that the oxidation product of pteroylglutamic acid is more fluorescent than the original compound and that the increase in fluorescence is proportional to the amount of parent compound in solution (Allfrey *et al.*, 1949). Zakrewski and Nichol (1953) have shown that this principle could be used in the determination of amethopterin in aqueous solution. The purpose of the present study has been to examine the fluorescent properties of amethopterin and their applicability to the assay of the drug in plasma. Since the normally occurring fluorescent compounds in plasma do not show increased fluorescence upon oxidation, the enhanced fluorescence of amethopterin upon oxidation is able to serve as a measure of the drug in plasma against a background of fluorescence.

METHODS. *Materials.* The reference standard used was the disodium salt of 4-amino-10-methyl pteroylglutamic acid, a Lederle product, which upon paper chromatography indicated that 90 per cent was a component which, when eluted, had the spectroscopic properties of the pure compound as recorded in the literature (Seeger, 1949).

Instruments. The fluorescent spectrum of amethopterin was determined in an Aminco-Bowman Spectrophotofluorometer (Bowman *et al.*, 1955). Measurements of intensity of fluorescence were made in a Farrand fluorometer, Model A. The filter used for incident light was Corning #5860; and the filter for emitted light a combination of Corning #4308, Wratten gelatin 2B and Corning #3389 in this order, with #3389 facing the phototube.

Procedure. The amount of amethopterin in aqueous solution was determined by Method I of Allfrey *et al.* (1949) for pteroylglutamic acid. Three reference points of instrument sensitivity were used to cover three ranges of concentration. The reference point of instrument sensitivity for the range 10 millimicrogm./ml. to 70 millimicrogm./ml. (standard #1) was obtained by setting the galvanometer deflection due to an oxidized sample containing 70 millimicrogm./ml. of amethopterin at 56 on the 100 unit galvanometer scale; for the range 100 millimicrogm./ml. to 900 millimicrogm./ml. (standard #2) an oxidized sample containing 300 millimicrogm./ml. of amethopterin was used to set the galvanometer deflection at 30; for the range 1 microgm./ml. to 7 microgm./ml. (standard #3) an oxidized sample containing 3 microgm./ml. of amethopterin was used to set the galvanometer deflection at 70.

In chromatographic procedures, samples were applied to one quarter inch wide Whatman #1 filter paper. Descending chromatograms were developed using 0.1 *M* phosphate buffer, pH 7.4.

[1] A preliminary report appeared in Fed. Proc., **15:** 424, 1956.

EXPERIMENTAL. *Spectra.* Amethopterin was observed to have two activating maxima (fig. 1), one at 280 mμ and one at 370 mμ, both producing maximum fluorescence at 450 mμ (fig. 1). When activated at 370 mμ the fluorescence was three times as intense as when activated at 280 mμ. Thus, the filters listed in the section on methods appeared to be the best ones for measuring the fluorescence of amethopterin. The fluorescent spectrums of the oxidized compound were five times as great as those of the unoxidized compound but the shape of the curves was identical.

Linearity. The increment (Δ) in fluorescence intensity due to oxidation of amethopterin was observed to be directly proportional to the concentration of amethopterin present (fig. 2) over a wide range of concentrations. This is in agreement with Zakrewski and Nichol's observations.

Reproducibility. Four representative points were selected on the curve of Standard #1, the most sensitive curve, and the reproducibility of these measurements determined. The measurements were highly reproducible as shown by the following data on fifteen replicates of each point.

The least squares regression line calculated from these determinations, having subtracted the fluorescence increment of the blank sample (distilled water plus reagents) is

$$y = 0.5621x,$$

where y is the fluorescence increment and x is concentration in millimicrogm./ml.

The 95 per cent confidence limits for all values predicted from this line are:

$$0.5621\,x \pm 3.037\sqrt{0.0167 + \frac{(x-30)^2}{45000}}.$$

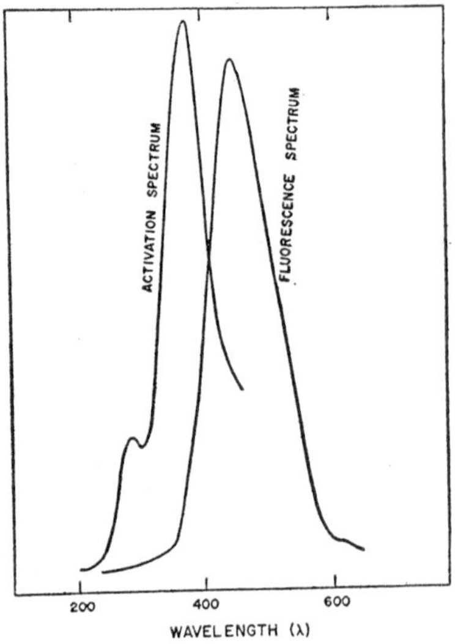

FIG. 1

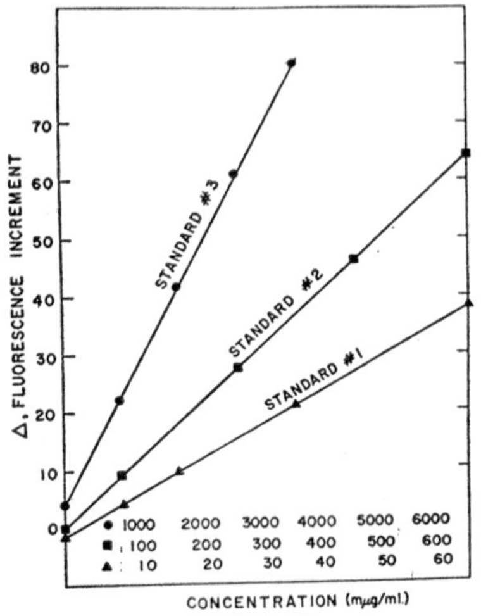

FIG. 2

FIG. 1. Activation and fluorescence spectra of amethopterin.

FIG. 2. Correlation between fluorescence increment and concentration of amethopterin.

TABLE 1
Stability of amethopterin solutions

Variable	Solution	Number of experiments	Retained original oxidizable fluorescence for
Time	5 mgm. % in H_2O at room temp.	3	55 days
	1 mgm. % in H_2O at room temp.	9	16–18 days
	frozen	9	16–18 days
	0.1 mgm. % in H_2O at room temp.	9	5–9 days
	frozen	9	5–9 days
	0.01 mgm. % in H_2O at room temp.	6	<24 hours
	frozen	9	<24 hours
Light	1 mgm. % in H_2O	2	13 days
pH	1 mgm. % in 4% TCA	2	10 days
	1 mgm. % in 4% NaOH	2	0 days*
Temperature	0.3 mgm. % at 100° for 10 min.	2	entire time heated
Air	1 mgm. % in water aerated 30 minutes	2	entire time aerated

* This may be a quenching effect. Only about 50 per cent of the oxidizable fluorescence can be measured in this solution.

That is, a sample containing 10 millimicrogm./ml. would give a Δ of 5.62 with 95 per cent confidence limits of ±0.48 while a sample containing 70 millimicrogm./ml. would give a Δ of 39.3 with 95 per cent confidence limits of ±0.69.

Stability. The stability of solutions of amethopterin under various conditions was investigated. Solutions were prepared and placed in dark bottles except when the stability in the presence of laboratory light was being examined. The fluorescence of an aqueous solution of amethopterin was measured as soon as it was prepared and at hourly intervals for eight hours thereafter. When this showed no change, the solution was then measured daily. The results are tabulated in table 1. No change in fluorescence increment was accepted as the criteria of stability. The deterioration of amethopterin upon standing appeared to be slow and to have two components. The fluorescence increment decreased a few units at a time for seven or eight days, then began to increase. This might be expected since it is well known that slight changes in a molecule may materially enhance or decrease the fluorescence of that molecule. The data in table 1 show that the stability of aqueous solutions of amethopterin varied with the conditions under which the samples were stored. Concentrated solutions were more stable than dilute ones. Storage in the frozen state did not preserve the stability of dilute solutions.

Length of time of oxidation. The variation in fluorescence increment with time of oxidation is shown in table 2. Ten-ml. aliquots of a standard amethopterin solution (3 microgm./ml.) were buffered with 0.1 ml. of acetate buffer, pH 4. The initial intensity of fluorescence was determined. Five hundredths of a ml. of 4 per cent potassium permanganate was added. After the times indicated in the table, 0.1 ml. of 3 per cent hydrogen peroxide was added to reduce the remaining permanganate and the intensity of fluorescence again measured. These measurements were made at an instrument sensitivity corresponding to that used for standard 3. The results tabulated in table 2 show that oxidation occurred rapidly and the solution appeared to be stable for ten minutes. The fluorescence increment then began to decrease, indicating that oxidation should be terminated within ten minutes after commencement.

Amount of permanganate. The increment in fluorescence of duplicate samples containing 0, 10 and 70 millimicrogm./ml. of amethopterin was measured, varying the amount of permanganate used. To one of each duplicate was added 0.05 ml. of the 4 per cent potassium permanganate. To the other was added 0.10 ml. The increment in fluorescence of each set of duplicates was the same.

Amount of sodium hydroxide. The variation in fluorescence increment with the amount of sodium hydroxide added to trichloroacetic acid solutions of amethopterin is shown in fig. 3. To 4-ml. aliquots containing 0.30 microgm./ml. and 1 ml. of 15 per cent trichloroacetic acid were added the indicated amounts of 5 per cent sodium hydroxide in a final volume of 5 ml. One-tenth ml. acetate buffer pH 4 was added and the fluorescence intensities determined in the usual procedures at an instrument sensitivity corresponding to that used for standard 2. The fluorescence increment under these conditions was directly related to the amount of sodium hydroxide added except in the very low ranges. The addition of larger amounts of sodium hydroxide caused the precipitation of manganese dioxide at a later step in the procedure.

Effect of pH at which oxidation is carried out. The variation in fluorescence increment with pH of solution at time of oxidation was determined. To aliquots containing 30 millimicrogm./ml. were added 0.7 ml of 5 per cent sodium hydroxide to a final volume of 5 ml. One-tenth ml. of buffer ranging from pH 2 to 8 was added and the fluorescence intensities determined in the usual procedures at an instrument sensitivity corresponding to that used for standard 2. Up to pH 5 the fluorescence increments were directly proportional to the pH, the increment at pH 5 being the largest. Above pH 5 manganese dioxide precipitated and interfered with fluorescence measurements.

Application to determination of amethopterin in plasma. Reagents: 15 per cent trichloroacetic acid; 3.24 per cent sodium hydroxide; 5 *M* acetate buffer pH 5,

TABLE 2

Effect of time of oxidation upon the fluorescence increment of an amethopterin solution containing 3 microgm./ml.

Time	Fluorescence increment
min.	
2	60
5	60
8	60
10	60
15	58
30	53
60	48
90	46

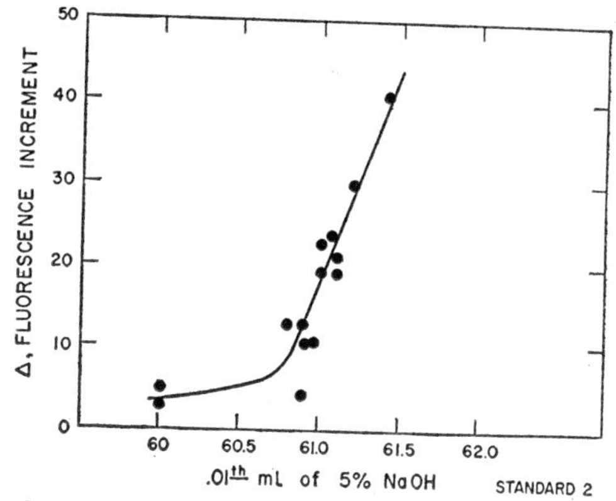

FIG. 3. Effect of amount of NaOH added to TCA solution of amethopterin.

prepared by adding 700 ml. of 5 *M* sodium acetate to 300 ml. of 5 *M* acetic acid; and 3 per cent hydrogen peroxide, prepared as needed by 1:10 dilution of 30 per cent hydrogen peroxide.

Procedure: Collect whole blood in oxalated tubes and separate plasma by centrifugation. Siphon plasma into clean test tube. To 1 ml. of plasma, add 7 ml. of distilled water. Mix thoroughly. Add 2 ml. 15 per cent trichloroacetic acid dropwise, with continuous stirring. Centrifuge. To 5 ml. of the supernatant add 1.0 ml. of 3.24 per cent sodium hydroxide. Add 0.1 ml. 5 *M* acetate buffer pH 5 and mix. Measure fluorescence (fluorescence A). Add 0.05 ml. 4 per cent potassium permanganate. Wait 5 minutes. Add 0.1 ml. 3 per cent hydrogen peroxide and mix. Wait 3 minutes. Measure fluorescence (fluorescence B).

This procedure is carried out on a blank blood sample; that is, one which is withdrawn before any drug is administered, as well as on samples after drug is administered (treated samples).

Calculations: Fluorescence B—Fluorescence A = Δ (Fluorescence increment)
Δ of the treated sample − Δ of blank sample = Δ due to amethopterin.
Read Δ amethopterin from the standard curve in concentration per ml. plasma.

Recovery and reproducibility: Aliquots containing 0, 10, 20, 40, 60 and 70 millimicrogm. of amethopterin per ml. were added to 1 ml. samples of plasma. The proteins were precipitated and the determination carried out as described. The line which resulted from plotting the concentration vs. the fluorescence increment obtained was superimposable on that of the determination in water (standard 1 in fig. 2).

The reproducibility of four representative points (0, 10, 40, and 70 millimicrogm./ml.) on this curve was determined. The measurements were reproducible as shown by the following data on five replicates of each point.

The least squares regression line calculated from these data, having subtracted the fluorescence increment of the blank sample, is:

$$y = 0.5637\,x,$$

where y is the fluorescence increment and x is concentration in millimicrogm./ml.

The 95 per cent confidence limits for all values predicted from this line are:

$$0.5637\ x \pm 2.93 \sqrt{0.05 + \frac{(x - 30)^2}{15{,}000}}.$$

That is, a sample containing 10 millimicrogm./ml. would give a Δ of 5.64 with 95 per cent confidence limits of ± 0.81, while a sample containing 70 millimicrogm./ml. would give a Δ of 39.46 with 95 per cent confidence limits of $\pm$ 1.16.

Specificity: The presence of other materials in plasma which might increase in fluorescence after oxidation was investigated. Blood was withdrawn from ten fasting patients bearing miscellaneous tumors who had not received amethopterin. The fluorescence of these samples was measured before and after oxidation. The values obtained varied from -4 to 0 units on standard 1, the most sensitive standard. Other materials which might be present in plasma under various conditions were examined to determine whether or not they had any effect on the present determination. These are listed in table 3. Heparin, tungstate and diacetamidotri-iodobenzoate (Hypaque), a radio-opaque medium used in doing intravenous pyelograms, appeared to have a marked quenching effect on the fluorescence of amethopterin.

Protein-free filtrates of control blood samples had no fluorescent spectrum when measured in the spectrophotofluorometer, while those collected after amethopterin therapy showed the typical amethopterin spectrum.

Certain of the protein-free filtrates made from the blood of patients receiving amethopterin were lyophilized, put on paper strips and chromatographed. The paper was cut in inch pieces, eluted with distilled water and the amethopterin

TABLE 3

Effect of possible interfering substances on the amethopterin determination

Amethopterin		Possible interfering substance	Fluorescence increment
			Std. #3
μgm./ml.			
3	+	0.1 ml. distilled H_2O	60
3	+	0.1 ml. 0.1 *M* sodium oxalate	60
3	+	0.1 ml. 0.1% heparin	46
3	+	0.1 ml. 1.5% sequestrene	51
3	+	0.1 ml. 0.9% sodium chloride	55
3	+	0.1 ml. 1 mgm. % methyl paraben	56
3	+	0.1 ml. 1 mgm. % propyl paraben	58
3	+	0.1 ml. 0.25% ACTH	60
3	+	0.1 ml. 50% hypaque (diacetamide triiodobenzoate)	3
			Std. #1
mμgm./ml.			
70	+	0.1 ml. distilled H_2O	60
70	+	0.1 ml. 0.1 *M* sodium oxalate	60
70	+	0.1 ml. 1 mgm. % 6-mercaptopurine	60
70	+	0.1 ml. 10% sodium tungstate	20

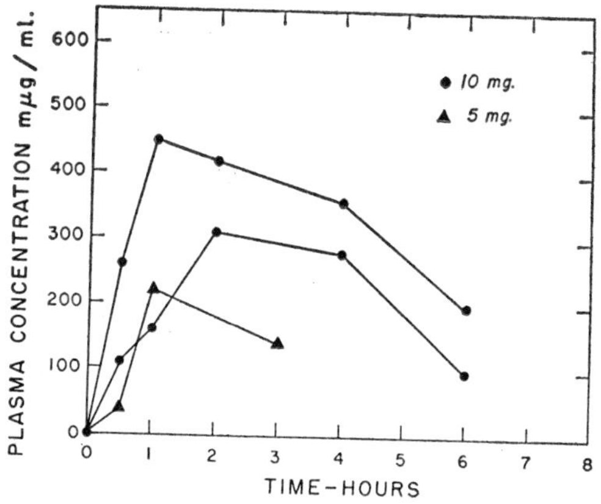

FIG. 4. Amethopterin plasma levels after oral administration.

measured. The plasma filtrates showed only one spot and this had an R_f of 0.64. Standards using amethopterin showed the same R_f.

Plasma levels in patients after the administration of amethopterin: Using this procedure to measure the plasma levels of amethopterin, sample curves are shown in fig. 4 obtained on patients receiving 5 and 10 mgm. doses of amethopterin orally. There are measurable amounts of drug present 30 minutes after oral administration; the peak level being reached at one to two hours. These findings are similar to those of Burchenal *et al.* (1951) which were determined using a bacteriological method.

SUMMARY AND CONCLUSIONS

A fluorometric method for the measurement of amethopterin has been studied and applied to the determination of the drug in plasma.

The reproducibility was such that the actual readings were found to vary about a regression line of Δ F (fluorescence) vs. concentration with a standard deviation of less than 1 Δ F unit.

The sensitivity was such that 5 millimicrogm./ml. in final dilution could be detected.

It is specific in that it measures a material whose fluorescence is activated at approximately 370 mμ, which fluoresces at approximately 450 mμ, and which which will increase in fluorescence in this range upon oxidation. Fasting plasma blank samples have not shown an increase in fluorescence upon oxidation. Chromatographic and spectrophotofluoroscopic analyses indicate that the oxidizable fluorescence in plasma after administration of the drug is amethopterin.

The limits of stability of amethopterin under a variety of conditions have been determined. Concentrated solutions keep very well for two months.

The method described has been used to measure plasma levels of amethopterin in patients.

ACKNOWLEDGMENT. The author is deeply indebted to Mary Wilkinson and Robert Taylor for the statistical analyses of the determinations and to Gilbert D. Press for his excellent technical assistance.

REFERENCES

ALLFREY, V., TEPLY, L. J., GEFFEN, C., AND KING, C. G.: J. Biol. Chem., **178:** 465, 1949.

BOWMAN, R. L., CAULFIELD, P. A., AND UDENFRIEND, S.: Science, **122:** 32, 1953.

BURCHENAL, J. H., WARING, G. B., ELLISON, R. R., REILLY, H. C.: Proc. Soc. Exp. Biol. & Med., **78:** 603, 1951.

HOPKINS, F. G.: Proc. of the Royal Soc., **57:** 5, 1894–1895.

SEEGER, D. R., COSULICH, D. L., SMITH, J. N., JR., AND HULTQUIST, M. E.: J. Am. Chem. Soc., **71:** 1753, 1949.

ZAKREWSKI, S. F., AND NICHOL, C. A.: J. Biol. Chem., **205:** 361, 1953.

EFFECTS OF RIBOSIDES AND RELATED COMPOUNDS ON CATION TRANSPORT IN COLD-STORED HUMAN ERYTHROCYTES[1]

J. B. KAHN, JR.[2] AND SHELBY B. COHEN

Department of Pharmacology, University of Cincinnati College of Medicine, Cincinnati 19, Ohio

Received for publication November 17, 1956

In a paper in which Gabrio *et al.* (1955a) demonstrated that added adenosine or inosine can replenish organic phosphate levels in cold-stored red cells, they noted that these compounds also affect the levels of intracellular potassium. Clarkson (1956) reported that 5 *mM* adenosine increased the rate constant of sodium efflux from incubated cold-stored erythrocytes, but not from fresh cells. This evidence raised the question of the role of ribosides and related compounds in the active transfer of cations by red cells incubated after cold storage, in which intracellular potassium is depleted. We have investigated the relationships between the concentration of various purines, purine ribosides and ribotides, and pyrimidine ribosides and ribotides, and their effects on cation transport. We also determined the effects of purine ribosides on the block of transport induced by ouabain (Kahn and Acheson, 1955). As a consequence of these experiments, we are able to report some data concerning the disappearance of purine ribosides exposed to incubated cold-stored blood. It should be understood that our results pertain only to cold-stored blood, not to fresh blood. Clarkson's evidence (1956) indicates that fresh cells respond differently to purine ribosides.

MATERIALS AND METHODS. Blood was procured, stored, and incubated as previously described (Kahn and Acheson, 1955). Hematocrits were measured in duplicate by the technic of Guest and Siler (1934). Plasma, red cell and whole blood potassium and sodium were quantified as described earlier. Since changes of plasma potassium could be measured with greater accuracy and precision, data for plasma potassium only will be reported. In at least one experiment with each compound, determinations of red cell sodium were also performed. In all cases, whenever a net transfer of potassium occurred in one direction, there was a corresponding net change of sodium in the opposite direction (*cf.* Kahn and Acheson, 1955).

Amounts of compounds required to give desired concentrations were dissolved in not more than three ml. (usually one ml. or less) of 0.9 per cent NaCl; this was added to 12 ml. of cold blood. Zero time (t_0) samples were withdrawn, and the remaining (t_4) aliquots incubated at 37° ± 0.2°C. for four hours. Each sample of blood thus served as its own control. Blood from different donors varied in μEq. of potassium transferred per ml. of red cells per hour by as much as twenty per cent. To eliminate this variability, results are expressed in terms of per cent of control activity for each blood sample.

---

[1] This work was supported in part by Grant #H-1506 (C and C2) from the National Heart Institute, National Institutes of Health, U. S. Public Health Service. A preliminary report was given at the April, 1956, meeting of the Am. Soc. for Pharm. & Exper. Therap., Atlantic City (Fed. Proc., **15:** 443, 1956).

[2] John and Mary R. Markle Scholar in Medical Science, 1954–59.

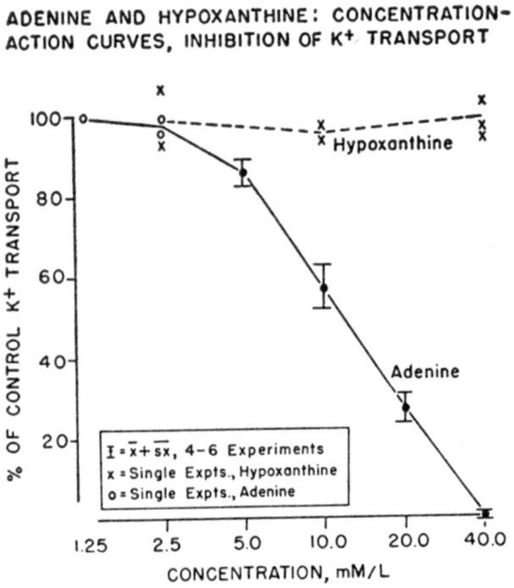

FIG. 1. Effects of the purines, adenine and hypoxanthine, upon potassium transport in the incubated cold-stored human erythrocyte.

Question has arisen as to the constancy of biochemical preparations from one batch to another. Most of the compounds used were obtained from two different sources,[3] and identical experiments performed with each batch. In no case was there any difference between the two batches of compounds from the two suppliers.

Quantifications of ribosides in plasma were done with a Beckman DU ultraviolet spectrophotometer. After removal from the incubation vessel, blood was centrifuged for three minutes at approximately 8000 *g*, and the plasma removed. Each t_0 and t_4 sample of plasma was read against a plasma blank at the λ_{max} of the compound being studied. Plasma was diluted with distilled water to bring the optical densities within the range of the DU, and to reduce blanks to low levels. This method does not distinguish between adenine and its ribosides or ribotides, nor between hypoxanthine and its ribosides or ribotides. Such differentiations can be made by paper chromatography (Prankerd, 1955).

RESULTS. *A. Effects of purines upon potassium transport.* Adenine inhibited potassium transport in all concentrations from 2.5 to 40.0 *mM*, while hypoxanthine in similar concentrations did not appreciably affect the transfer of potassium (fig. 1).

B. Effects of purine ribosides. Adenosine increased potassium transport to a degree dependent upon its concentration between 0.3 and 5.0 *mM* (fig. 2). Above the latter level the slope of the curve was reversed, and concentrations above 10.0 to 20.0 *mM* inhibited potassium influx. Inosine produced its maximum augmentation of potassium influx at 2.5 to 5.0 *mM*; potassium transfer remained at this high level with inosine concentrations up to 40.0 *mM*. Guanosine also increased potassium transport. It was insoluble in concentrations higher than about 1 *mM*. Below this level its concentration-action curve was similar to that for inosine or adenosine.

[3] Compounds used were obtained from the California Institute for Biochemical Research, Los Angeles, and the Nutritional Biochemicals Co., Cleveland. All were "chromatographically pure", and their u-v spectra were consistent with those previously published for the pure compounds as to λ_{max} and molecular extinction coefficients.

C. Effects of purine ribotides. Concentration-action curves for adenosine monophosphate (AMP), the sodium salt of adenosine diphosphate (NaADP), the disodium salt of adenosine triphosphate (Na_2ATP), inosine monophosphate (IMP), and the disodium salt of inosine triphosphate (Na_2ITP) are shown in fig. 3. AMP produced some augmentation of potassium transport in concentrations up to 2.5 *mM*; above this level there was increasing inhibition up to 40.0 *mM*. NaADP and Na_2ATP were inhibitory in all concentrations used. The slopes of their curves are similar. IMP had no detectable effects on potassium transfer in concentrations up to 20.0 *mM*, thus differing from its adenine analog, AMP. Na_2ITP had only inhibitory effects, but these differed from those

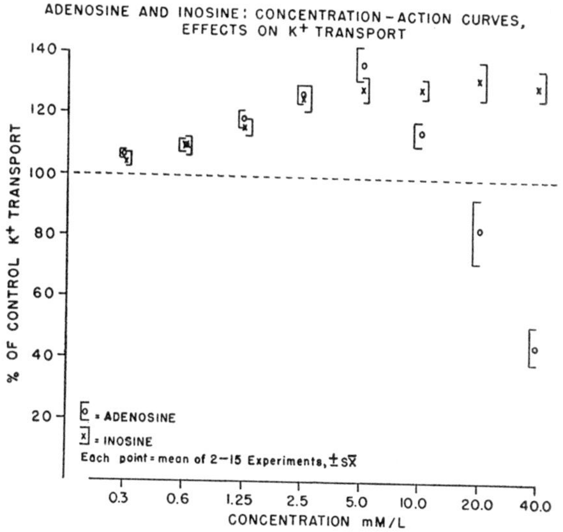

FIG. 2. Effects of the purine ribosides, adenosine and inosine, upon potassium transport.

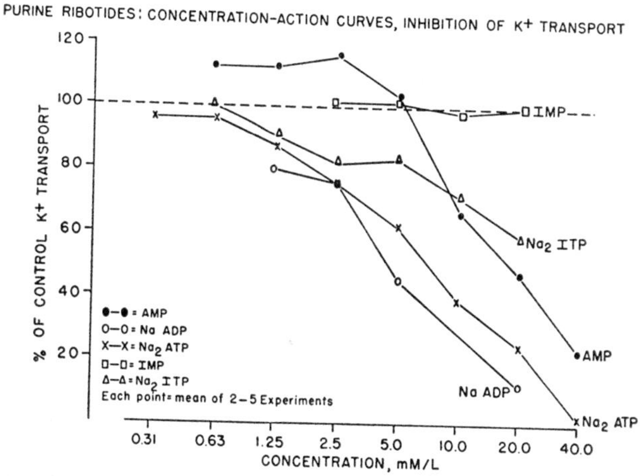

FIG. 3. Effects of purine ribotides upon potassium transport. For meaning of abbreviations, see text.

of its adenine analog, Na_2ATP. The slope of the concentration-action curve for Na_2ITP is less steep than that for Na_2ATP, and the former is less potent in inhibition of potassium transport. It may be concluded that the ribotides of hypoxanthine affect potassium transport differently from the corresponding ribotides of adenine. The monophosphates differ in that one has no effect on potassium transport, while the other augments or inhibits, depending upon its concentration. The triphosphates differ in potency and in the slopes of their curves.

Addition of 10.0 *mM* Na_2ATP to blood resulted in a fall of pH of 0.2 unit. Flynn and Maizels (1949) found net uptake of potassium to vary relatively little between pH 7.0 and 7.6. Similar findings have been reported by Raker *et al.* (1950) and by Ponder (1950). Inhibition of potassium uptake by this concentration of Na_2ATP amounted to 60 per cent. The pH change must have contributed but little to this amount of inhibition.

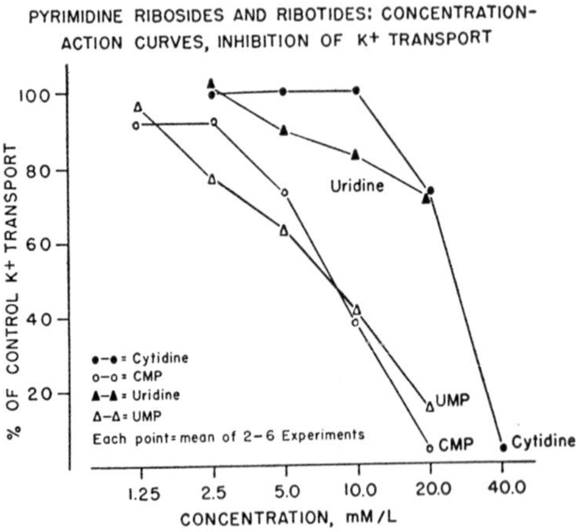

FIG. 4. Effects of pyrimidine ribosides and ribotides upon potassium transport. For explanation of abbreviations, see text.

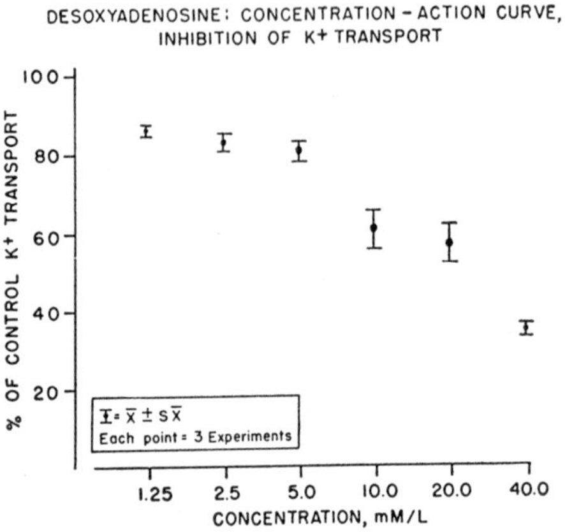

FIG. 5. Effects of the purine desoxyriboside, desoxyadenosine, upon potassium transport.

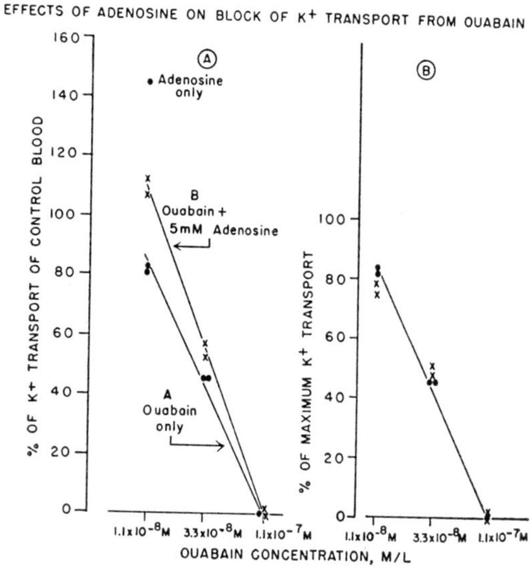

FIG. 6. Effects of the purine riboside, adenosine, upon the block of potassium transport from ouabain.

The concentration of adenosine which was used was that which produced maximal augmentation of potassium transport in cells incubated without ouabain. Each point represents the mean of duplicate experiments performed upon the same sample of blood.

The highest concentration of the disodium salts of the ribotides could have increased external sodium concentration to 80 *mM* above the control level. In two experiments, we have added 80 *mM* sodium to the cold-stored blood, in the form of NaCl; this produced no detectable change in potassium disappearance from plasma in four hours. Hence the maximum possible increase of external sodium attendant upon the use of high concentrations of sodium salts of ribotides could not account for the inhibition of potassium transport produced by these compounds.

D. Effects of pyrimidine ribosides and ribotides. Cytidine, cytidine monophosphate (CMP), uridine and uridine monophosphate (UMP) had only inhibitory effects upon potassium transport (fig. 4).

E. Effects of desoxyadenosine. Desoxyadenosine, the desoxyriboside of adenosine, had only inhibitory effects upon potassium transport (fig. 5). The slope of its concentration-action curve is different from those for adenine and the adenine ribotides; it resembles that for Na_2ITP.

F. Effects of purine ribosides upon the block of transport from ouabain. To determine whether the purine ribosides would affect the block of transport induced by a cardiac glycoside, 5.0 *mM* adenosine was added to blood containing concentrations of ouabain inhibiting potassium transport by about 20, 50, and 100 per cent. Results are shown in fig. 6. In fig. 6A, the transport in the presence of ouabain or adenosine is expressed as per cent of that of the control blood, which had neither adenosine nor ouabain added. This percentage is plotted against glycoside concentration. The single point at 145 per cent of control activity represents the effects of adenosine alone. Line A represents the effects of ouabain alone, and line B those from ouabain in the presence of added adenosine. Plotting the data in this way makes it appear that the addition of adenosine partially reversed the block from ouabain. This agrees with the conclusions of Harris and Prankerd (1955). However, if the data are considered differently, another conclusion is necessary. Blood with added adenosine should not be compared with the control blood. Rather, blood with ouabain plus adenosine should be compared with blood with adenosine only, and blood with ouabain only should be compared with the control blood. If the latter is capable of transporting 100 units of potassium per cell per unit time, blood with added adenosine is capable of transporting 145 units per cell per unit time. If these two values are considered as 100 per cent activity for the two kinds of blood (that with and that without added adenosine), and a graph is constructed of per cent inhibition of maximum potassium transport by a given concentration of ouabain, the two curves are indistinguishable (fig. 6B). For example, addition of 3.3×10^{-8} *M* ouabain reduces potassium transport to one-half of the maximum level in both instances, indicating that adenosine is without effect on the ouabain-induced block of transport.

A similar series of experiments was performed with 5.0 *mM* inosine, with the same results. With inosine concentrations up to 40.0 *mM*, the riboside had no more effect on the block from ouabain than did the lowest maximally effective concentration (5.0 *mM*). When ouabain was added with inhibitory concentrations of adenosine (20 to 40 *mM*), the block from adenosine was additive with the block from ouabain. For example, when cells were exposed to a concentration of ouabain which blocked potassium transport 50 per cent, in the presence of 20 *mM* adenosine (which by itself blocked transport 20 per cent) the total inhibition of potassium transport was 70 per cent.

G. Effects of ouabain upon the disappearance of adenosine and of inosine from the plasma of incubated blood. Adenosine or inosine was added to blood at t_0, and its concentration in plasma measured at t_0 and at four hours. Determination of the concentration in plasma five to ten minutes after its addition to whole blood showed that over 90 per cent of either compound was in the plasma. Hence there is little rapid binding of the ribosides to cells. When the compounds were incubated for four hours in plasma without erythrocytes, disappearance was less than five per cent of that seen in the presence of cells. The cells are therefore necessary for most of the disappearance of ribosides from the plasma.

Plotting μM loss per ml. of packed red cells against the t_0 concentration of riboside in plasma yielded the curves of fig. 7 for the two ribosides. The disappearance of the purine ribosides from plasma was unaffected by ouabain in concentrations up to three times that required for complete inhibition of cation transport. Hence the glycosides do not inhibit cation transport by interfering with the uptake of ribosides by the cells.

Prankerd (1955) studied the disappearance of adenosine incubated with fresh cells, and found that after addition of 1.93 *mM* adenosine the average rate of disappearance of the riboside was 0.22 μM/ml. red cells/hour after 4.75 hours of incubation. From fig. 7, the average rate for incubated cold-stored cells at a

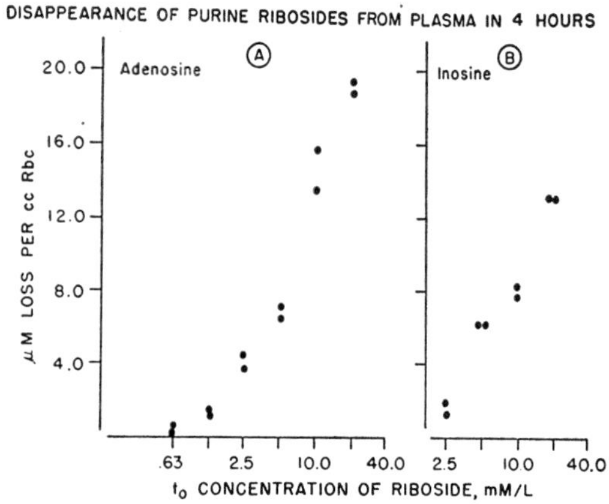

FIG. 7. Effects of the initial concentration of the purine ribosides, adenosine and inosine' upon their disappearance from the plasma of incubated blood.

Each point represents the mean of duplicate experiments performed upon the same sample of blood.

similar adenosine concentration would be about three times as fast, or 0.75 μM/ml. cells/hour, and 2 mM inosine would disappear at the average rate of about 0.25 μM/ml. cells/hour, a figure close to that reported for adenosine in fresh cells. The increased rate of disappearance of adenosine in the presence of cold-stored cells as compared with fresh cells indicates that there is a difference between the two systems. Other evidence for difference between them is seen in the work of Clarkson (1956) dealing with sodium extrusion, and in the fact noted in our laboratory that fresh and cold-stored cells have different responses of their phosphate-transferring systems to ribosides and ribotides.

DISCUSSION. We cannot now state in what form any of the compounds discussed enter the red cell, and therefore we do not know whether the effects observed are the result of the presence of the compounds added or of their metabolites. It is widely believed that the charged ribotide molecules do not enter the cell. Clarkson and Maizels (1952) and Herbert (1952) found enzymes in red cell stromata capable of converting ATP to AMP. Herbert found the apyrase also active on ADP. The possibility therefore exists that even though ADP or ATP be added to blood, the compound gaining access to the cells is not what was added, but a product of the action of phosphatases upon the ribotides. There is no direct evidence pertaining to the entry of purines or purine ribosides into the cell, nor of any enzymes in the stroma capable of acting on them.

Possible role of enzymes. Several hypotheses can be advanced to account for the behavior of the purine ribosides (Section B). Earlier investigators demonstrated the presence and activity of two relevant enzymes within the human red cell. Dische (1941), Prankerd and Altman (1954a, b), and Gabrio *et al.* (1955a, b, c) found a purine riboside phosphorylase in red cells which phosphorylyzes the purine ribosides to form ribose phosphate and a purine. Prankerd and Altman (1954a) have shown that the ribose phosphate formed in the reaction can furnish energy for phosphate transport in fresh human erythrocytes. Implicit in their reports is the assumption that this enzyme can phosphorylyze the purine ribosides regardless of the purine moiety. Gabrio and Huennekens (1955), on the other hand, using a partially purified enzyme preparation, found that it would phosphorylyze inosine but not adenosine, and they therefore assume that adenosine must be deaminated to inosine before being phosphorylyzed. This implies the presence of an enzyme in red cells capable of deaminating adenosine. Adenosine deaminase has been isolated from erythrocytes (Drury *et al.*, 1938; Schaedel and Schlenk, 1948). Hence the enzymatic machinery is present in red cells to furnish substrate for the phosphorylase, whether this substrate is inosine only, or purine ribosides as a group.

If the assumption is made that the ribose phosphate formed from phosphorolysis of purine ribosides can furnish energy for cation transport as it does for phosphate transport, the results of fig. 2 can be explained. After phosphorolysis adenosine yields adenine, which is inhibitory to potassium transport (Section A and fig. 1), while inosine yields hypoxanthine, which has no effect on potassium transfer. The curve for adenosine in fig. 2 can be interpreted as being the resultant of two curves of opposite slopes, one with positive slope, from 0.3 to 5.0 *mM* representing primarily the effects of ribose phosphate, and the other, of negative slope above 5.0 *mM* representing inhibitory effects of adenine formed in the same enzymatic reaction. Inosine, on the other hand, produces a curve which reaches a maximum and stays there. According to this hypothesis the curve for inosine reaches a plateau because the hypoxanthine formed simultaneously with the ribose phosphate would have no effect on potassium transport, and the curve would reflect only the effects of the ribose phosphate.

The present findings can also be explained if, as Gabrio and Huennekens state (1955), inosine is the substrate for the phosphorylase, and if no adenine is formed from adenosine. This requires the added assumption that adenosine *per se* be inhibitory to potassium transport. The rising portion of the adenosine curve would be the result of the deamination of adenosine by the deaminase, and consequent increase of potassium transport by the ribose phosphate split from the formed inosine by the phosphorylase. When the amount of adenosine became greater than that which the enzyme can deaminate, the action of adenosine would become evident, and potassium transport would be inhibited.

A third possible explanation is that both enzymatic pathways are open to added adenosine simultaneously. This does not require the assumption that adenosine *per se* inhibits potassium transfer. Part of the riboside might be acted upon by the deaminase to form inosine, and part by the riboside phosphorylase to form ribose phosphate and adenine. If the deaminase activity became rate-limiting before the phosphorylase activity, it would explain the curve for adenosine in fig. 2. At concentrations of adenosine of 2.5 to 5.0 *mM* the deaminase may become saturated, while the phosphorylase does not. This would limit the production of inosine to the level at which it is formed at adenosine concentrations of 2.5 to 5.0 *mM*, while adenine formation would still be increasing, making more and more inhibition from the latter in the presence of a constant amount of inosine.

Some quantitative evaluation of the first hypothesis can be made. Comparison of the curve for adenine in fig. 1 with that for adenosine in fig. 2 shows that the latter departs from the inosine curve at the point at which the adenine concentration-action curve (fig. 1) begins its steeper slope, at 5 *mM*. Below this concentration the curves for adenosine and inosine are indistinguishable, as would be expected in the absence of amounts of adenine producing inhibition.

The maximum possible value for the ratio (*mM* adenine formed/*mM* adenosine disappearing) is 1.0. Prankerd (1955) has shown that this value is nearly reached in fresh cells after addition of 1.93 *mM* adenosine. If the first hypothesis is valid, inhibition from higher concentrations of adenosine cannot be greater than that which would be produced by an amount of adenine equimolar with the amount of adenosine disappearing during the period of incubation. Our measurements of adenosine concentration before and after incubation revealed that four hours after addition of 10 and 20 *mM* adenosine, loss of the riboside was 6.5 and 11.0 *mM* respectively (*cf.* Section G and fig. 7). If these amounts of adenosine had been quantitatively converted to adenine at zero time, inhibition of transport would have amounted to 25 and 48 per cent (from fig. 1). Inhibition actually found was 12 and 36 per cent (fig. 2). On the curve of fig. 1, the values found correspond to an average adenine concentration over the four hours of 4 and 8 *mM*. The inhibition from the amount of adenosine which disappeared was therefore not greater than that which could be produced by an equimolar amount of adenine, and the first hypothesis is grossly possible.

The second hypothesis is less satisfactory in that it requires the added assumption that adenosine *per se* be inhibitory to potassium transport. At concentrations of adenosine below 5.0 *mM* its effects are indistinguishable from those of inosine. For the second hypothesis to be valid it would be necessary that low concentrations of adenosine augment transport, while higher concentrations inhibit the same process. Parallel situations exist with other substances in different systems, but there is no evidence to support this view in the present case. Furthermore, it does not seem to be necessary for adenosine to be deaminated to inosine before phosphorolysis. The data of Prankerd (1955) from fresh cells show a mole-for-mole correspondence between adenosine disappearing and adenine appearing. Deamination before phosphorolysis would produce hypoxanthine rather than adenine.

The third hypothesis combines features of the first two. It has the teleologic advantage of furnishing a use for another enzyme which has been found in red cells. It is consistent with the suggestion of Gabrio and Huennekens (1955) that inosine is the substrate for the phosphorylase. On the basis of the third hypothesis energy for augmentation of transport would come indirectly from inosine, while the inhibitory part of the adenosine curve would be the result of the presence of formed adenine. There is no good reason for preferring the third hypothesis to the first at the present time. The former involves additional assumptions having to do with rate-limiting concentrations of adenosine, for which there is no evidence yet. In order to make a sounder choice between these alternative hypotheses it would be necessary to have more information about the kinetics of the enzymes involved, and to study in detail the biochemical transformations undergone by added purine ribosides as they enter the cells and act there.

If it is assumed that desoxyadenosine is split by the purine riboside phosphorylase to adenine and desoxyribose, it can be inferred that desoxyribose phosphate is not an effective energy source for cation transport. Two findings make it unlikely that adenine plays a role in the inhibition of transport produced by desoxyadenosine. The first is the difference in the slopes of the concentration-action curves for the purine and the desoxyriboside. The second is the fact that at 1.25 *mM* adenine has no effect on potassium transfer, while desoxyadenosine is already inhibitory. It seems more likely that the inhibition from desoxyadenosine is an effect of the whole molecule rather than of phosphorolysis by the purine riboside phosphorylase, with subsequent inhibition by adenine.

Other considerations. The experiments discussed here give no positive evidence to elucidate the mechanism of the block of transport produced by glycosides. It has been postulated that the glycosides may block an adenyl deaminating system in the guinea pig heart (Rand, Stafford and Thorp, 1955). If this were the case in red cells, inosine, but not adenosine, should have circumvented the ouabain block. Since inosine was ineffective in reversing the block from ouabain, it must be concluded that ouabain does not influence the adenosine deaminase present in red cells in such a way as to interfere with the production or utilization of energy for cation transport.

Discussion such as that above raises the question of the applicability of results with red cells to other tissues. We have referred (Kahn and Acheson, 1955) to the danger of extending findings in the red cell to a supposedly similar system in another tissue. Evidence is accumulating, however, that the potassium transfer systems in red cells and in hearts are similar in many ways. For example, veratridine is without effect on potassium reentry into red cells and without effect on the same process in the isolated guinea pig heart (Vick and Kahn, 1956), though the same compound does affect potassium reentry into stimulated peripheral nerve (Shanes, 1952). Glycosides prevent potassium reentry into the guinea pig heart in the same concentration range required to prevent potassium reentry into cold-stored red cells (Vick and Kahn, 1956). The potency ratio of ouabain to dihydro-ouabain is the same for inhibition of potassium reentry into red cells as it is for production of ventricular fibrillation in the dog heart-lung preparation (Vick, Kahn and Acheson, 1957). Rand *et al.* (1955) found ouabain and adenosine to potentiate each other in the production of irregularities in the guinea pig heart. If adenosine were present in the heart in concentrations preventing potassium reentry, it would be expected to act additively with ouabain. The same sort of enzymatic machinery seems to be present in hearts as is present in erythrocytes. For instance, the existence of an adenosine deaminase in heart muscle has been demonstrated (Ostern and Mann, 1933). Such data, though they are isolated and sparse, suggest that the potassium transport systems in red cells and the heart have several features in common.

SUMMARY AND CONCLUSIONS

Adenine inhibits the transport of potassium by incubated cold-stored red cells to a degree dependent upon its concentration between 1.25 and 40.0 *mM*. Hypoxanthine in similar concentrations has no effect on potassium transport.

Adenosine augments potassium transport in concentrations between 0.3 and 5.0 *mM*. Above the latter level it is inhibitory. Inosine reaches a plateau of augmentation at 2.5 to 5.0 *mM*. Further increases in concentration are without further effect. Possible explanations of the actions of these two ribosides and of the differences between them are discussed. It is suggested that cation transport, like phosphate transport, can utilize purine ribosides as a source of energy.

Desoxyadenosine, adenosine diphosphate, adenosine triphosphate and pyrimidine ribosides and ribotides inhibit cation transport in all concentrations tested between 0.3 and 40.0 *mM*. Inosine monophosphate has no effect on transport. The concentration-action curves of inosine triphosphate and desoxyadenosine are less steep than those of the other effective compounds.

Adenosine and inosine are without effect on the block of transport of potassium induced by ouabain. Conversely, ouabain does not interfere with the uptake of purine ribosides by red cells. The disappearance of adenosine from plasma in contact with incubated cold-stored red cells is three times as rapid as its reported disappearance in the presence of fresh cells. Inosine disappears from the plasma of incubated cold-stored cells at the same rate as that reported for the disappearance of adenosine in the presence of fresh cells.

Parallels are presented between the potassium transport systems in red cells and in the heart.

REFERENCES

Clarkson, E. M.: J. Physiol., **131**: 34P, 1956.

Clarkson, E. M., and Maizels, M.: J. Physiol., **116**: 112, 1952.

Dische, Z.: Symposium on Phosphorous Metabolism, Johns Hopkins Press, Baltimore, 1951.

Drury, A. N., Lutwak-Mann, C., and Solandt, O. M.: Quart. J. Exp. Physiol., **27**: 215, 1938.

Flynn, F., and Maizels, M.: J. Physiol., **110**: 301, 1949.

Gabrio, B. W., Hennessey, M., Thomasson, J., and Finch, C. A.: J. Biol. Chem., **215**: 357, 1955a.

Gabrio, B. W., Donohue, D. M., and Finch, C. A.: J. Clin. Invest., **34**: 1509, 1955b.

Gabrio, B. W., and Huennekens, F. M.: Biochim. Biophys. Acta, **18**: 585, 1955c.

Guest, G., and Siler, V.: J. Lab. & Clin. Med., **19**: 757, 1934.

Harris, E. J., and Prankerd, T. A. J.: Biochem. J., **61**: 705, 1955.

Herbert, E.: Ph.D. Dissertation, Dept. of Physiology, University of Pennsylvania, 1952.

Kahn, J. B., and Acheson, G. H.: This Journal, **115**: 305, 1955.

Ostern, P., and Mann, T.: Biochem. Ztschr., **260**: 326, 1933.

Ponder, E.: J. Gen. Physiol., **33**: 745, 1950.

Prankerd, T. A. J.: Brit. J. Haematol., **1**: 406, 1955.

Prankerd, T. A. J., and Altman, K. I.: Biochem. J., **58**: 622, 1954a.

Prankerd, T. A. J., and Altman, K. I.: Biochim. Biophys. Acta, **15**: 158, 1954b.

Raker, J. W., Taylor, I. M., Weller, J. M., and Hastings, A. B.: J. Gen. Physiol., **33**: 691, 1950.

Rand, M., Stafford, A., and Thorp, R. H.: This Journal, **114**: 119, 1955.

Schaedel, M. L., and Schlenk, F.: Texas Rep. Biol. & Med., **6**: 176, 1948.

Shanes, A. M.: This Journal, **105**: 216, 1952.

Vick, R. L., and Kahn, J. B.: Fed. Proc., **15**: 494, 1956.

Vick, R. L., Kahn, J. B., and Acheson, G. H.: This Journal, **119**: 190, 1957 (Abst.).

EFFECTS OF LSD 25, BOL 148, BUFOTENINE, MESCALINE AND IBOGAINE ON THE POTENTIATION OF HEXOBARBITAL HYPNOSIS PRODUCED BY SEROTONIN AND RESERPINE

GIAN CARLO SALMOIRAGHI AND IRVINE H. PAGE

Research Division of The Cleveland Clinic Foundation and The Frank E. Bunts Educational Institute, Cleveland, Ohio

Received for publication November 29, 1956

Lysergic-acid-diethylamide (LSD 25), a potent hallucinogen (Stoll and Hofmann, 1943), is also a potent antagonist on smooth muscle of serotonin (Gad dum, 1953), a substance normally present in the brain (Twarog and Page, 1 53 Amin, Crawford and Gaddum, 1954). It has recently been suggested (Gadd9um, 1953; Woolley and Shaw, 1954) that serotonin antagonism may be important in the mechanism of LSD-induced psychosis. Against this hypothesis, however, is the finding that brom-lysergic-acid-diethylamide (BOL 148), a lysergic acid derivative with a bromine group in the 2 position, while an even more potent serotonin antagonist than LSD (Cerletti and Rothlin, 1955; Sollero, Page and Salmoiraghi, 1956), does not readily produce mental changes in man (Cerletti and Rothlin, 1955). Another possibility (Woolley and Shaw, 1954) is that the hallucinogenic effect of LSD may not be due to inhibition but to potentiation of the effects of serotonin in the brain. Supporting this hypothesis are the recent observations (Costa, 1956) that the smooth muscle stimulant action of serotonin on the rat's uterus is a) enhanced by concentrations of LSD lower than the minimal effective concentrations necessary for blockade; b) enhanced by mescaline, another hallucinogen, and c) antagonized by the tranquillizing agents reserpine, chlorpromazine and azacyclonol HCl (Frenquel).

Serotonin prolongs the hypnotic effect of hexobarbital (Fornaroli and Koller, 1954), probably by a central potentiating action (Shore, Silver and Brodie, 1955). This effect is also produced by reserpine (Brodie *et al.*, 1955), presumably through release of free serotonin from body depots (Pletscher, Shore and Brodie, 1955, 1956). The effects of both serotonin and reserpine on hexobarbital hypnosis were found to be blocked by relatively large doses of LSD (Shore, Silver and Brodie, 1955) and BOL (Cerletti and Rothlin, 1955; Salmoiraghi, Sollero and Page, 1956).

In view of the fact that BOL does not produce mental disturbances, except possibly in very large doses, and of the suggestion that enhancement of central effects of serotonin may be responsible for the hallucinogenic property of LSD, it seemed important to compare the effect of small doses of the two lysergic acid derivatives and of large and small doses of the potent hallucinogens bufotenine and mescaline and of the mild hallucinogen ibogaine on the potentiation of hexobarbital hypnosis produced by serotonin and reserpine.

METHODS. Unfasted adult white male mice[1] weighing from 20 to 35 gm. were used only once. "Sleeping time" was measured by the same person as the time interval between loss

---

[1] Rockland Farm, N. Y. mice were kept in our laboratory one week before use.

and return of the righting reflex following intraperitoneal injection of hexobarbital sodium (Evipal, 70 mgm./kgm.).

LSD (Delysid, 0.5 to 2 microgm./kgm.) or BOL 148 (1 to 5 microgm./kgm.) was given in a single dose two hours before hexobarbital; bufotenine creatinine sulfate (0.5 microgm./kgm. as base), mescaline sulfate (10 microgm./kgm. to 10 mgm./kgm.) and ibogaine (Su-3772 Ciba, 10 microgm./kgm. to 2.5 mgm./kgm.) one hour before hexobarbital. Serotonin (20 mgm./kgm. as serotonin creatinine sulfate) was injected 10 minutes before the hypnotic and reserpine (Serpasil, 5 mgm./kgm.) one hour before hexobarbital. All drugs were injected intraperitoneally. Results were analyzed statistically and the P values determined by conventional methods.[2]

Each experiment was done on two lots of 6 mice each. If the means of the two lots did not clearly agree, the experiment was repeated on a third group of 6 mice and these were included in the calculation.

Theoretically, control groups of mice given hexobarbital alone, hexobarbital plus serotonin or reserpine, and hexobarbital plus hallucinogen might have been run with each experimental group. This seemed unnecessary because control groups of 8 to 12 mice each, treated with hexobarbital alone, hexobarbital plus serotonin or reserpine were run 3 times as spot checks during the study. Each time hexobarbital alone produced a mean sleeping time of about 10 minutes and the latter two groups about 20 minutes. Two experiments, one with a high dosage of hallucinogen and one with a very low dose were usually run on the same day. The consistency of the results led us to believe that daily use of 36 control mice was unnecessary.

RESULTS. Preliminary experiments indicated that the effect of small doses of LSD and BOL on the prolongation of hexobarbital hypnosis produced by serotonin and reserpine was best seen when the dosage of hexobarbital was 70 mgm./kgm. With higher dosage of hexobarbital (100 and 150 mgm./kgm.) results did not show a clear trend. We did not continue with high doses as the experiment seemed more a toxicological than a pharmacological one. The dose of 70 mgm./kgm. of hexobarbital was therefore chosen to produce hypnosis and was used throughout this study.

Serotonin doubled sleeping time of hexobarbital treated mice ($P < 0.01$). When LSD or BOL (2 microgm./kgm.) was given prior to administration of serotonin, mice slept about one-third longer than those given serotonin plus hexobarbital only. This increase was found to be statistically significant at a probability level of less than 1 per cent (table 1).

Reserpine also increased sleeping time ($P < 0.01$). This increase, however, was not enhanced, rather it was blocked by LSD at 2 microgm./kgm. ($P < 0.02$) and BOL at 5 microgm./kgm. ($P < 0.01$). Smaller amounts (0.5 microgm./kgm. of LSD or 2 microgm./kgm. of BOL) were without significant effect ($P > 0.05$). Thus neither LSD nor BOL in doses of from 0.5 to 5 microgm./kgm. enhanced the prolongation of sleeping time produced by reserpine. On the contrary, both compounds blocked this potentiation, LSD being the more potent of the two drugs (table 1).

The effects of large and small doses of the hallucinogens bufotenine, mescaline

[2] BOL, LSD and serotonin were kindly supplied by Dr. R. Bircher of Sandoz Pharmaceuticals, Hanover, N. J.; Serpasil and ibogaine by Dr. Wm. Wagner of Ciba Pharmaceutical Products, Summit, N. J.; bufotenine by Dr. M. E. Speeter of The Upjohn Company, Kalamazoo, Michigan.

TABLE 1

Duration of hypnosis in mice

Drugs	Duration
	min.
Serotonin + hexobarbital	20.9 ± 2.0 (15)
LSD (2 microgm./kgm.) + serotonin + hexobarbital	33.6 ± 3.4 (11) $P < 0.01$
BOL (2 microgm./kgm.) + serotonin + hexobarbital	32.1 ± 3.5 (10) $P < 0.01$
Resperine + hexobarbital	20.9 ± 2.2 (12)
LSD (2 microgm./kgm.) + reserpine + hexobarbital	13.6 ± 1.8 (12) $P < 0.02$
BOL (2 microgm./kgm.) + reserpine + hexobarbital	21.0 ± 2.2 (12) $P > 0.9$
BOL (5 microgm./kgm.) + reserpine + hexobarbital	12.3 ± 2.1 (12) $P < 0.01$
Hexobarbital alone	10.0 ± 1.1 (11)
Serotonin + hexobarbital	20.9 ± 2.0 (15) $P < 0.01$
Reserpine + hexobarbital	20.9 ± 2.2 (12) $P < 0.01$
LSD (2 microgm./kgm.) + hexobarbital	11.1 ± 1.0 (15) $P < 0.5$
BOL (2 microgm./kgm.) + hexobarbital	10.8 ± 1.0 (16) $P < 0.6$

Values for duration of hypnosis are means ± standard error of the mean. Numerals in parentheses indicate the number of animals in each series. Hexobarbital 70 mgm./kgm. Serotonin 20 mgm./kgm. as serotonin creatinin sulfate. Reserpine 5 mgm./kgm.

and ibogaine on the serotonin- and reserpine-induced prolongation of hexobarbital hypnosis and respective P values are summarized in table 2.

Bufotenine was found to block in large doses and to enhance in small doses the effect of serotonin while both large and small doses of mescaline and ibogaine constantly enhanced the effect of serotonin. On the other hand, and similarly to the results with LSD and BOL, large or small doses of bufotenine, mescaline and ibogaine always blocked the potentiating effect of reserpine.

Discussion. These results show that LSD enhances the potentiating effect of serotonin on hexobarbital hypnosis in mice when it is given in very small dosage, dosage (microgm./kgm. equivalent) that produces hallucinations in man. Similarly to LSD, bufotenine also has a dual effect on serotonin: blockade in large doses and enhancement in small doses; mescaline and the mild hallucinogen ibogaine, on the other hand, have only an enhancing effect. These results, then, show that the hallucinogens LSD, bufotenine, mescaline and ibogaine, given to mice in the dosage range used in human experimentation, have the common property of enhancing the potentiating effect of serotonin on hexobarbital hypnosis, an effect of serotonin which is thought to be centrally mediated (Shore, Silver and Brodie, 1955). This finding, thus, would seem to indicate that potentiation of central effects of serotonin (Woolley and Shaw, 1954) rather than blockade (Gaddum, 1953) may be responsible for the hallucinogenic effects of certain drugs.

The potentiating effect is all the more remarkable because the LSD was given 2 hours before the hexobarbital hypnosis and LSD has been shown by Axelrod *et al.* (1957) to have a biological half-life in mice of only 7 minutes. Enhancement

TABLE 2

Duration of hypnosis in mice

Values for duration of hypnosis are means ± standard error of the mean. Numerals in parentheses indicate the number of animals in each series. Hexobarbital 70 mgm./kgm. Serotonin 20 mgm./kgm. as serotonin creatine sulfate. Reserpine 5 mgm./kgm.

Drugs	Duration
	min.
Serotonin + hexobarbital	20.9 ± 2.0 (15)
Bufotenine (5 mgm./kgm.) + serotonin + hexobarbital	13.1 ± 2.0 (12) $P < 0.02$
Bufotenine (100 microgm./kgm.) + serotonin + hexobarbital	31.2 ± 3.3 (14) $P < 0.02$
Bufotenine (10 microgm./kgm.) + serotonin + hexobarbital	24.3 ± 3.2 (12) $P < 0.4$
Bufotenine (2 microgm./kgm.) + serotonin + hexobarbital	23.5 ± 3.1 (12) $P < 0.5$
Mescaline (10 mgm./kgm.) + serotonin + hexobarbital	18.1 ± 2.0 (12) $P < 0.4$
Mescaline (1 mgm./kgm.) + serotonin + hexobarbital	33.0 ± 4.1 (11) $P < 0.02$
Mescaline (100 microgm./kgm.) + serotonin + hexobarbital	28.6 ± 3.0 (12) $P < 0.05$
Mescaline (10 microgm./kgm.) + serotonin + hexobarbital	28.0 ± 3.5 (12) $P < 0.1$
Ibogaine (2.5 mgm./kgm.) + serotonin + hexobarbital	34.8 ± 3.4 (16) $P < 0.01$
Ibogaine (100 microgm./kgm.) + serotonin + hexobarbital	33.0 ± 4.0 (11) $P < 0.02$
Ibogaine (10 microgm./kgm.) + serotonin + hexobarbital	34.6 ± 3.2 (12) $P < 0.01$
Reserpine + hexobarbital	20.9 ± 2.2 (12)
Bufotenine (5 mgm./kgm.) + reserpine + hexobarbital	9.2 ± 0.8 (12) $P < 0.01$
Bufotenine (10 microgm./kgm.) + reserpine + hexobarbital	9.0 ± 1.4 (12) $P < 0.01$
Bufotenine (1 microgm./kgm.) + reserpine + hexobarbital	13.0 ± 1.7 (14) $P < 0.01$
Bufotenine (0.5 microgm./kgm.) + reserpine + hexobarbital	15.9 ± 2.3 (13) $P < 0.2$
Mescaline (10 mgm./kgm.) + reserpine + hexobarbital	13.5 ± 1.0 (12) $P < 0.01$
Mescaline (1 mgm./kgm.) + reserpine + hexobarbital	12.0 ± 1.3 (13) $P < 0.01$
Mescaline (100 microgm./kgm.) + reserpine + hexobarbital	14.1 ± 1.0 (12) $P < 0.01$
Mescaline (10 microgm./kgm.) + reserpine + hexobarbital	19.4 ± 1.7 (12) $P < 0.6$
Ibogaine (2.5 mgm./kgm.) + reserpine + hexobarbital	10.4 ± 1.0 (18) $P < 0.01$
Ibogaine (100 microgm./kgm.) + reserpine + hexobarbital	10.0 ± 1.1 (11) $P < 0.01$
Ibogaine (10 microgm./kgm.) + reserpine + hexobarbital	23.2 ± 3.1 (12) $P < 0.6$
Hexobarbital alone	10.0 ± 1.1 (11)
Bufotenine (5 mgm./kgm.) + hexobarbital	14.0 ± 2.3 (12) $P < 0.3$
Bufotenine (100 microgm./kgm.) + hexobarbital	9.7 ± 1.3 (12) $P < 0.9$
Mescaline (10 mgm./kgm.) + hexobarbital	7.8 ± 0.9 (12) $P < 0.2$
Mescaline (100 microgm./kgm.) + hexobarbital	10.1 ± 1.2 (11) $P > 0.9$
Ibogaine (2.5 mgm./kgm.) + hexobarbital	6.1 ± 0.9 (12) $P < 0.02$
Ibogaine (10 microgm./kgm.) + hexobarbital	9.5 ± 0.9 (12) $P < 0.8$

of the potentiation must then be due to almost incredibly small amounts provided LSD does not initially cause an irreversible reaction.

This phenomenon may have its counterpart in the persistence of the action of reserpine for several days even though Hess, Shore and Brodie (1956) could find none of it in brain after about eight hours. It has a maximum concentration within 10 to 15 minutes following intravenous administration and its level declines rapidly.

Our findings with BOL need special consideration. Previous studies (Cerletti and Rothlin, 1955; Sollero, Page and Salmoiraghi, 1956; Salmoiraghi, Sollero and Page 1956) have shown that BOL, like LSD, readily blocks serotonin-induced contractions of isolated smooth-muscle preparations and, in large doses, blocks the potentiating effect of serotonin on hexobarbital hypnosis in mice. Like LSD, BOL crosses the blood-brain-barrier and can be detected in brain tissue (Stoll *et al.*, 1955; Rothlin and Cerletti, 1956). Our present data show that similarly to the effect of small doses of the hallucinogens LSD, bufotenine, mescaline and ibogaine, small doses of BOL also enhance the potentiating effect of serotonin on sleeping time of hexobarbital treated mice. Yet BOL was not found to produce signs of mental disturbance when given (presumably *per os*) to volunteers in single doses of from 1 to 20 microgm./kgm. (Cerletti and Rothlin, 1955). This finding, in view of the similarities of the agonistic and antagonistic effects of BOL and LSD on serotonin, would seem to discredit the hypothesis that interference with central effects of serotonin may be responsible for the hallucinogenic effects of LSD. Recent studies in our laboratory (Schneckloth, Dustan and Page, unpublished), however, have shown that when BOL is given to humans by intravenous infusion, rather than orally, in doses of from 5 to 7 microgm./kgm./min., some mental disturbances do occur and become even more pronounced if an intravenous infusion of serotonin, ineffective alone, is given together with the intravenously infused BOL. It seems possible, then, that failure of orally administered BOL to produce mental disturbance in man is not due to its complete lack of hallucinogenic effects; rather it may be due to its failure to reach the brain in sufficient concentrations to have an effect on brain-serotonin.

Our findings on the effects of LSD, BOL, bufotenine, mescaline and ibogaine on the reserpine-induced potentiation of hexobarbital hypnosis suggest that this effect of reserpine is not directly mediated by free serotonin released from body depots (Pletscher, Shore and Brodie, 1955, 1956). If this were the case, enhancement of the potentiating effect of reserpine by small doses of LSD, BOL, bufotenine, mescaline or ibogaine could be expected since all these compounds enhanced the effect of serotonin. Yet none of them was found to do so.

SUMMARY

Lysergic-acid-diethylamide (LSD), a potent serotonin-blocking agent on isolated organs, is shown here to enhance, rather than to block, the potentiating effect of serotonin on hexobarbital hypnosis in mice when given in the small dosage range (microgm./kgm. equivalent) that produces hallucinations in man.

A similar enhancing effect is also produced by small doses of other hallucinogens (bufotenine, mescaline and ibogaine) and also by small doses of brom-lysergic-acid-diethylamide (BOL), a lysergic acid derivative that does not produce mental changes in man when given orally but may do so when given by intravenous infusion together with large doses of serotonin.

The enhancing effect of small doses of LSD, BOL, bufotenine, mescaline and ibogaine does not extend to the reserpine-induced prolongation of hexobarbital hypnosis in mice; all these compounds, in large and small doses, block this effect of reserpine.

REFERENCES

Amin, A. H. T., Crawford, B. B., and Gaddum, J. H.: J. Physiol., **126:** 596, 1954.

Axelrod, J., Brady, R. O., Witkop, B., and Evarts, E. V.: Ann. N. Y. Acad. Science, **66:** 435, 1957.

Brodie, B. B., Shore, P. A., Silver, S. L., and Pulver, R.: Nature, **175:** 1133, 1955.

Cerletti, A., and Rothlin, E.: Nature, **176:** 785, 1955.

Costa, E.: Proc. Soc. Exper. Biol. & Med., **91:** 39, 1956.

Fornaroli, P., and Koller, M.: Farmaco.—ed. sc. (Pavia), **9:** 546, 1954.

Gaddum, J. H.: J. Physiol., **121:** 15 P, 1953.

Hess, S. M., Shore, P. A., and Brodie, B. B.: Fed. Proc., **15:** 437, 1956.

Pletscher, A., Shore, P. A., and Brodie, B. B.: Science, **122:** 374, 1955.

Pletscher, A., Shore, P. A., and Brodie, B. B.: This Journal, **116:** 84, 1956.

Rothlin, E., and Cerletti, A.: "Pharmacology of LSD"—Lysergic Acid Diethylamide and Mescaline in Experimental Psychiatry, Grune & Stratton, Inc., 1956.

Salmoiraghi, G. C., Sollero, L., and Page, I. H.: This Journal, **117:** 166, 1956.

Shore, P. A., Silver, S. L., and Brodie, B. B.: Experientia, **11:** 272, 1955.

Sollero, L., Page, I. H., and Salmoiraghi, G. C.: This Journal, **117:** 10, 1956.

Stoll, A., and Hofmann, A.: Helv. chim. acta, **26:** 944, 1943.

Stoll, A., Rothlin, E., Rutschmann, S., and Schalch, W. R.: Experientia, **11:** 396, 1955.

Twarog, B. M., and Page, I. H.: Am. J. Physiol., **175:** 157, 1953.

Woolley, D. W., and Shaw, E.: Brit. med. J., **2:** 122, 1954.

A SPECTROPHOTOFLUOROMETRIC STUDY OF ORGANIC COMPOUNDS OF PHARMACOLOGICAL INTEREST

SIDNEY UDENFRIEND, DANIEL E. DUGGAN[1], BRUNO M. VASTA AND BERNARD B. BRODIE

Laboratory of Chemical Pharmacology, National Heart Institute, National Institutes of Health, Public Health Service, U. S. Department of Health, Education, and Welfare, Bethesda, Maryland

Received for publication December 1, 1956

Detection and quantitative assay of drugs by fluorometric methods have been the subject of considerable investigation (Radley and Grant, 1954). The majority of such studies, however, have been confined to spot tests based upon the non-specific and vaguely defined visible fluorescence exhibited by solid samples of pure materials or by paper strips treated with standard solutions when irradiated by the total output of a mercury vapor lamp. However, a relatively small number of useful fluorometric procedures have been evolved for the estimation of drugs in tissues utilizing their fluorescence in solution. Fluorometric methods may be classified according to whether the fluorescence measured is that of the drug in its native state or is induced by chemical transformations which are often time consuming and rarely quantitative. Typical of the former are the methods for quinine (Brodie and Udenfriend, 1943a) and atabrine (Brodie and Udenfriend, 1943b; Craig, 1943); of the latter class, which comprises a large percentage of fluorometric methods, the estimation of barbiturates (Pesez, 1938) and penicillin (Scudi and Jelinek, 1946) are typical.

The relatively few existing fluorometric procedures are possible because of the intense visible fluorescence characteristic of these materials, and because the wavelengths of maximum absorption of the fluorophor fortuitously coincide with one of the few available lines in the mercury emission spectrum.[2] Although fluorescence attachments for commercial spectrophotometers have been available, their application has still been limited to materials whose absorption peaks correspond to one of the mercury lines.

A spectrophotofluorometer recently developed in this Institute (Bowman *et al.*, 1955) permits of high intensity monochromatic activation corresponding to the exact peak of maximum absorption at any wavelength throughout the quartz-ultraviolet and visible regions of the spectrum[3] and of automatic spectral analysis of resulting fluorescence throughout this same range. Two commercial modifications of this instrument have subsequently become available.[4] These instruments are routinely employed in this laboratory for the determination in tissues of serotonin (Udenfriend *et al.*, 1955; Bogdanski *et al.*, 1956), tryptophan

[1] American Instrument Company, postdoctoral research fellow.

[2] Mercury vapor lamps ordinarily used in fluorometers emit utilizable lines at 313, 366, 405, and 436 mμ.

[3] For practical purposes this includes the region from 220 mμ to about 650 mμ.

[4] The Aminco-Bowman Spectrophotofluorometer and Farrand Spectrofluorometer.

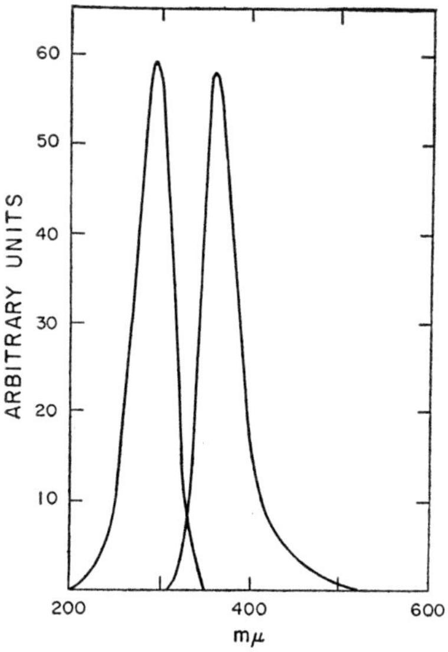

FIG. 1. Activation and fluorescence spectra of procaine (1.0 microgm. per ml. in *N* NH_4OH). Activation maximum at 290 mμ; fluorescence max. at 360 mμ.

and tyrosine (Duggan and Udenfriend, 1956), and various other compounds of biochemical and pharmacological importance.[5]

In the course of a broad investigation of the potential utility of spectrophotofluorometry as an analytical tool for both qualitative and quantitative applications at the sub-microgram level, useful fluorescence was revealed by many drugs, most of which have not hitherto been reported to fluoresce. More detailed study of the fluorescence characteristics of these compounds indicated that, in many cases, spectrophotofluorometry provides the basis for specific assays at levels obtained in pharmacological studies.

For a representative group of these compounds, simple double extraction procedures suitable for their extraction from tissues for spectrofluorometric assay have been devised.

METHODS. *Instrumentation.* The components of the two commercial instruments are essentially those of the experimental spectrophotofluorometer which is described in detail elsewhere (Bowman *et al.*, 1955). These consist of a xenon arc source emitting a continuum from 200 to 800 mμ, a monochromator to select activating light of the proper wavelength and focus it on the sample, a rectangular quartz cuvette,[6] a second monochromator at right angles to the first to analyze the fluorescent spectrum, and an appropriate photosensitive detector.[7] The photomultiplier signal may be read directly on a galvanometer (for routine quantitative analyses) or supplied to the Y input of an oscilloscope or pen and ink recorder. In the latter cases, the X signal is obtained from an appropriate device coupled to the wavelength scale of the fluorescence monochromator. The resulting two coordinate plot is the fluorescence spectrum. An activation spectrum may be obtained in a similar manner by

[5] Tocopherol, 5-hydroxyindole acetic acid, barbital, chlorpromazine, lysergic acid diethylamide and reserpine.

[6] 1 x 1 x 4 cm. silica absorption cuvettes with all four sides optically polished.

[7] RCA IP21 photomultiplier for visible fluorescence, and IP28 for ultraviolet.

taking the X signal from the activating monochromator with the fluorescence monochromator fixed at the wavelength of peak fluorescence. Activation and fluorescence spectra are typified by those of procaine as shown in fig. 1.

Determination of fluorescence characteristics. Pure samples of each drug were obtained from the manufacturer of the pharmaceutical preparation except in the case of those drugs which were available as reagent grade chemicals. Solutions for analysis were freshly prepared by the dilution of aqueous or alcoholic stock solutions (1 mgm. per ml.) to a concentration of 1.0 microgm. per ml. in each of the following media: 0.1 *N* sulfuric acid, phosphate[8] buffer pH 7.0, 1 *N* ammonium hydroxide, 0.1 *N* sodium hydroxide, and 95 per cent ethanol. The fluorescence spectra of each solution were rapidly scanned on the oscilloscope while manually changing the activating monochromator setting, 10 to 20 mμ per scan, until all of the range 200 to 700 mμ had been covered. Upon the appearance of a fluorescence peak, the scan was stopped at the peak and the wavelength of maximum activation accurately determined by manipulation of the activating monochromator. With this value determined precisely and the instrument properly set, fluorescence spectra were obtained in each of the media cited above. The minimum concentration at which useful fluorescence was obtainable was determined by successive dilution in that medium in which maximum fluorescence was observed.[9]

Partition studies. For the preliminary determination of the partition of a drug between any two phases, equal volumes (10 ml.) of each phase, previously saturated with the other, were shaken mechanically for ten minutes in tightly stoppered shaking tubes and the concentration of drug remaining in the aqueous phase determined spectrophotometrically. To determine the overall transfer of a compound throughout a double extraction procedure, a 10-ml. aliquot of a standard solution of the drug in aqueous medium I was shaken as above with 20 ml. of solvent. A 10-ml. aliquot of the solvent phase was then shaken with 5.0 ml. of aqueous medium II, and a sample of this aqueous phase withdrawn and compared to a second aliquot of the original standard solution, the pH and ionic composition of both solutions being made identical.

RESULTS: *Fluorescence characteristics.* The wavelengths of peak activation and fluorescence, the medium in which fluorescence intensity is maximal, and the practical lower limits of concentration at which each drug may be measured are summarized in table 1.

The fluorescent compounds for which data are presented represent a surprisingly large percentage of those drugs tested which absorb light in the region 250 to 500 mu. Drugs which did not fluoresce in any of the media at concentrations up to 10 microgm. per ml. included acetanilid, acetylsalicylic acid, antipyrine, atropine, diphenhydramine (Benadryl), caffeine, meperidine (Demerol), bishydroxycoumarin (Dicumarol), Diparcol, histamine, isoniazid, iproniazid (Marsilid), pentylenetetrazol (Metrazol), heptabarbital (Medomin), methadone, nicotine, nicotinamide, phenolphthalein, pilocarpine, caramiphen (Panparnit), tolazoline (Priscoline), prostigmine, aminopyrine (Pyramidon), phentolamine (Regitine), theobromine and theophylline.

The relationship of structure to fluorescence as indicated by the qualitative results of this survey are in agreement with the structural requirements for

[8] For fluorometric applications, absolute ethanol must be twice redistilled to minimize the fluorescence blank.

[9] Since sensitivity is determined by many instrumental variables in addition to the absolute fluorescence intensity of the fluorophor itself (see Duggan *et al.*, 1956), this is a purely arbitrary value representing that concentration at which the fluorescence intensity is twenty times that of the blank fluorescence.

TABLE 1

Compound	Activation max.	Fluorescence max.	pH	Practical sensitivity
	mμ	*mμ*		*μgm./ml.*
Tetracycline (Achromycin)	390	515	11	0.02
Allylmorphine	285	355	1	0.1
Amobarbital (Amytal)	265	410	14	0.1
p-Aminosalicylic acid	300	405	11	0.004
Aminopterin	280, 370	460	7	0.02
Chlortetracycline (Aureomycin)	355	445	11	0.02
Azaguanine	285	405	7	0.03
Brom LSD	315	460	1	0.005
Chloroquin	335	400	11	0.05
Chlorpromazine	350	480	11	0.1
Chlorpromazine sulfoxide	335	400	7	0.02
Cinchonidine	315	445	1	0.01
Cinchonine	320	420	1	0.01
Dromoran	275	320	1	0.05
Epinephrine	295	335	1	0.07
Eserine	300	360	1	0.04
Zoxazolamine (Flexin)	280	320	11	0.1
Harmine	300, 365	400	1	0.002
LSD	325	465	7	0.002
Menadione*	335	480	*	0.07
Methotrexate	280, 375	460	7	0.02
Neocincophen	275, 345	455	7	0.004
Phenylephrine (Neosynephrin)	270	305	1	0.04
Levarterenol (norepinephrine)	295	335	1	0.06
Oxychloroquin	335	380	11	0.08
Hydroxyamphetamine (Paredrine)	275	300	1	0.05
Pentobarbital	265	440	13	0.1
Thiopental (Pentothal)	315	530	13	0.1
Phenobarbital	265	440	13	0.5
Piperoxan	290	325	7	0.05
Pamaquine (Plasmoquin)	300, 370	530	13	0.06
Podophyllotoxin	280	325	11	0.005
Procaine	275	345	11	0.01
Procaine amide	295	385	11	0.01
Quinacrine	285, 420	500	11	0.02
Quinine	250, 350	450	1	0.002
Rescinnamine	310	400	1	0.008
Reserpine	300	375	1	0.008
Salicylic acid	310	435	11	0.01
Thiamylal (Surital)	310	530	13	0.1
Synephrin	270	310	1	0.08
Oxytetracycline (Terramycin)	390	520	11	0.05
Thymol	265	300	7	0.1
Mephenesin (Tolserol)	280	315	1	0.05
Yohimbine	270	360	1	0.01

* 95% ethanol.

TABLE 2

Compound	Concentration	Aqueous medium I	Organic solvent	Aqueous medium II
	μgm./ml.			
Chlorpromazine	0.5	phosphate buffer pH 11	heptane*	0.1 *N* HCl
Dromoran	0.2	phosphate buffer pH 11	benzene*	0.1 *N* HCl
Neocincophen	0.2	0.1 *N* NaOH	heptane*	0.1 *N* HCl
Pentobarbital	0.5	phosphate buffer pH 5.5	heptane 1.5% isoamyl alcohol	phosphate buffer pH 11
Thiopental	1.0	phosphate buffer pH 5.5	heptane 1.5% isoamyl alcohol	1 *N* NaOH
Podophyllotoxin	0.4	citrate buffer pH 5.5	n-butanol**	0.1 *N* NaOH
Reserpine	0.2	phosphate buffer pH 11	heptane*	0.1 *N* HCl
Yohimbine	0.2	0.1 *N* NH_4OH	ethylene dichloride	0.1 *N* HCl

* Approximately 0.1 ml. of isoamyl alcohol added after the initial extraction as described by Brodie *et al.* (1947).

** One volume heptane added to organic phase after initial extraction.

fluorescence in solution as proposed elsewhere (Duggan *et al.*, 1956) on the basis of a more detailed study of the fluorescence of naturally occurring compounds. The primary requisite for fluorescence is, of course, the ability of a molecule to absorb light. The one outstanding structural requirement for fluorescence over and above those for absorption appears to be the presence on the resonating nucleus of at least one electron donating substituent. Thus, while benzene is non-fluorescent within the scope of these instruments, phenol and aniline are strong fluorophors. Acetylation of aromatic amino or phenolic groups results in a total loss of fluorescence, while alkylation has little or no effect, indicating that the substituent requirement is for a group capable of increasing the electron density of the aromatic nucleus. Polycyclic aromatic systems and aliphatic conjugated polyenes comprise a second general classification of fluorophic structures. These require no additional substituents.

Extraction procedures. The partition characteristics of a representative group of the compounds studied were determined at concentrations sufficient to follow the course of extraction by spectrophotometric methods (20 to 50 microgm. per ml.). The optimum pH for quantitative extraction from an aqueous to an organic phase, the least polar solvent[10] effecting such extraction, and the op-

[10] n-Butanol, ether, ethylenedichloride, benzene and heptane were the only solvents considered because they constitute a sufficient range of polarities to cover all solvent requirements in this respect, and because convenient solvent purification procedures were available. Absorption of fluorescence impurities on silica gel columns following appropriate washing procedures with acid and alkali was found to be a convenient and effective means of removing the major part of blank fluorescence which was even found in reagent grade samples of solvents.

timum pH for returning the extracted material to a second aqueous phase were determined for each compound. Using the media indicated by these preliminary studies, the same double extraction procedures were repeated using concentrations suitable for fluorometric assays.[11] The overall recoveries as determined by fluorescence measurements were found to be as nearly close to quantitative as were the corresponding procedures at high concentrations, if a trace of isoamyl alcohol were added to the organic phase to minimize losses due to adsorption onto glass (Brodie *et al.*, 1947). The optimum conditions for reproducible double extraction procedures are given in table 2.

DISCUSSION. Spectrophotofluorometry affords a number of advantages over conventional fluorometric procedures and over other physical methods utilizing light absorption. In the case of almost every fluorescent compound studied in the course of this survey, spectrophotofluorometry offers a sensitivity at least two orders of magnitude greater than spectrophotometry, and the additional specificity inherent in two spectral requirements instead of one. As compared to conventional fluorimeters, the spectrophotofluorometer offers a greaty extended scope of utility. The activating monochromator can select activating light of any wavelength from the continuum of the xenon arc source, as compared to the few mercury lines available in fluorometers. The detection of fluorescence is not limited to the visible range, but is extended into the ultraviolet. Additional specificity is provided by the high resolving power of monochromators as compared to filters, and the analysis of unknown samples requires no prior knowledge of absorption or fluorescence data as is necessary for the selection of proper primary and secondary filter systems. The ready availability of full activation and fluorescence spectra provides excellent criteria for evaluating specificity and for detecting the presence of interfering substances.

A detailed discussion of the instrumental variables affecting the qualitative data cited in table 1, the possible sources of error in quantitative procedures due to light scattering, blank fluorescence, and extraneous materials absorbing either activating or fluorescent light, and appropriate corrective procedures are presented elsewhere (Duggan *et al.*, 1956).

SUMMARY

A large number of drugs have been subjected to spectrophotofluorometric study. For each compound the wavelengths of maximal activation and fluorescence, the optimum medium, and relative sensitivity are reported. A large number of these compounds fluoresce in regions of the ultraviolet which have heretofore not been amenable to study due to limitations in instrumentation.

For a representative group of these compounds, partition characteristics at the sub-microgram level have also been determined spectrofluorometrically and quantitative double extraction procedures have been evolved which should be applicable to tissue homogenates and body fluids.

[11] Concentrations used were ten times the value given under "practical sensitivity" in table 1.

REFERENCES

Bogdanski, D. F., Pletscher, A., Brodie, B. B., and Udenfriend, S.: Science, **122:** 972, 1955.
Bowman, R. L., Caulfield, P. A., and Udenfriend, S.: Science, **122:** 32, 1955.
Brodie, B. B., and Udenfriend, S.: This Journal, **78:** 154, 1943a.
Brodie, B., and Udenfriend, S.: J. Biol. Chem., **151:** 299, 1943b.
Brodie, B. B., Udenfriend, S., and Baer, J. E.: J. Biol. Chem., **168:** 299, 1947.
Craig, L. C.: J. Biol. Chem., **150:** 33, 1943.
Duggan, D. E., and Udenfriend, S.: J. Biol. Chem., **223:** 313, 1956.
Duggan, D. E., Bowman, R. L., Brodie, B. B., and Udenfriend, S.: Arch. Biochem. and Biophys., **68:** 1, 1957.
Pesez, M.: J. Pharm. Chim., **27:** 247, 1938.
Radley, J. A., and Grant, J.: Fluorescence Analysis in Ultraviolet Light, 4th Ed., London, 1954.
Scudi, J. V., and Jelinek, V. C.: J. Biol. Chem., **164:** 195, 1946.
Udenfriend, S., Clark, C. T., and Weissbach, H.: J. Biol. Chem., **215:** 337, 1955.

EFFECTS OF *DEXTRO*-AMPHETAMINE UPON JUDGMENT

G. T. HAUTY AND R. B. PAYNE

School of Aviation Medicine, USAF, Randolph Air Force Base, Texas

Received for publication December 3, 1956

The uncertainty concerning the effects of amphetamine upon the exercise of judgment is due, certainly not to lack of opinions, but to their divergence. On the one hand, there are the popular and, in many cases, dramatic claims of induced euphoria, irrationality, and other extremes of emotional and attitudinal behavior likely to affect judgmental processes adversely. In addition to these popular notions are findings obtained from laboratory studies of the effects of amphetamine upon psychomotor performance (Davis, 1947). From these, Davis is inclined to infer that the benefits which are derived from the relatively large dosages are not sufficient to compensate for the induced impairment of judgment. Contrary to this are the results of recent investigations designed to determine the efficacy of various analeptic preparations in mitigating fatigue-induced deterioration of proficiency in tasks which may be presumed to require a continuous exercise of judgment. The results leave little doubt as to the efficacy of standard dosages of the amphetamines. Amphetamine counteracted proficiency decrement in simple vigilance tasks (Mackworth, 1950), and, in the case of more complex tasks, *d*-amphetamine was found to sustain proficiency for as long as seven hours (Hauty and Payne, 1955), to restore proficiency following the onset of decrement (Payne, Hauty and Moore, 1957), and to produce the most favorable attitudes toward the prolonged work situation (Payne and Hauty, 1954).

In view of the practical significance of the demonstrated gains to be realized from *d*-amphetamine, the question of risks inherent in the use of this preparation would seem to warrant further study. Accordingly, an investigation was designed to appraise the effects of a standard dosage of *d*-amphetamine upon judgment where appropriateness of judgment would be quantitatively and objectively measured and where integrity of judgment would be taxed by different experimental techniques.

PROCEDURE. *Task.* Following random assignment to the experimental conditions, subjects were administered the appropriate drug and, 1 hour later, were required to perform the AF SAM Pursuit Confusion Test, Model A (Payne, 1949). In this test, a target proceeds at a variable rate around a diamond-patterned pathway. The subject's task is to maintain contact on the target with a stylus. His proficiency is indexed by "time on target" which is electrically accumulated for each trial. A cycling system meters out alternate 1-minute trials and 15-second rest periods. Following certain trials which might be designated as "test" trials, subjects were told the proficiency score that they had attained, then asked to estimate the proficiency score they expected to attain in the next "test" trial. By computing the discrepancy between the estimated and actually attained proficiencies, an error of estimation is obtained which is quantitatively expressed and which indicates the direction of error. To achieve the necessary degree of uncertainty, since it is this which compromises the integrity of judgment, the task was performed with *mirror vision*. In such a task, successful performance is dependent upon the ability to overcome the interfering effects of habitual perceptual-motor behavior so as to effect the newer and different behavior now required. As the subject proceeds with the task, he is provided with a meaningful and valid basis for estimation, namely, his actual progress; but, due to the operation of habit interference, he is subject, nonetheless, to considerable doubt as to how much his next score will differ from his last score and whether it will be better or worse.

Experimental conditions. The pharmacological treatments, which were orally administered in capsule form, consisted of: D_1, a control group receiving no capsule; D_2, placebo (lactose); D_3, 5 mgm. of *d*-amphetamine sulfate; and D_4, for purpose of contrast, 0.65 mgm. of scopolamine plus 50 mgm. of diphenhydramine hydrochloride.

Two psychological variables were also included. These made provision for the possibility that impairment in judgment attributable to the drugs concerned might not occur until the psychological stresses imposed upon the subjects reach a sufficiently high level. These variables involved the following:

T. Task difficulty which was varied by interpolating different activities between the point of test trial completion and the time when the subject was required to estimate the proficiency he exptected to attain on the next test trial. T_1, 15 mirror vision test trials alternating with 15 mirror vision practice trials (MV–MV–MV, etc.). T_2, 15 mirror vision test trials alternating with 15 direct vision trials (MV–DV–MV, etc.). T_3, 15 mirror vision test trials alternating with 90-second rest periods (MV–. . . .–MV, etc.).

R. Standard referents with which the subject compared his performance at the end of each test trial. Designed to induce feelings of either success or failure, these referents consisted of two differently derived performance curves but which were represented to the subject as the "average scores made by most people at this task." R_1, the levels of performance plotted for each successive trial were so low (approximately 3 σ below the means of normative data) that they could be expected to be exceeded by nearly all the subjects. R_2, the plotted levels of performance were so high (approximately 3 σ above normative means) that they were likely to be attained by extremely few subjects.

These experimental conditions were arranged in accordance with conventional factorial design so as to permit an appraisal of the single and joint effects of the factors concerned.

Subjects. The 96 subjects were volunteer, experimentally naive, basic airmen.

RESULTS AND DISCUSSION. *Effects of drugs.* For each estimation, the differences between the estimated proficiency and the proficiency actually attained were algebraically summed and the means computed. These values, representing the degree to which proficiency is over- and/or underestimated, were plotted to give the curves seen in figure 1. Inspection of these yield several interesting observations. At the beginning of this task, the tendency on the part of the subject is to underestimate considerably the proficiency that he actually does attain. As he acquires more experience the degree of underestimation is reduced, as would be expected, of course, on rational grounds. Finally, differences attributable to drugs are not evident save, possibly, for the first estimation. This initial difference, however, must be conceded to chance because when the variation attributable to the different drug conditions is analyzed (Edwards, 1950), it can be seen in table 1 that neither the variance attributable to drugs nor the variance attributable to the interaction, Drugs $\times$ Estimations, approaches a level of significance.

Another important index of estimation error is that which concerns the absolute magnitude of error. When the absolute differences between estimated and attained proficiencies were summed and means plotted, magnitude of error was seen to decrease as successive estimations were made and, again, when the varia-

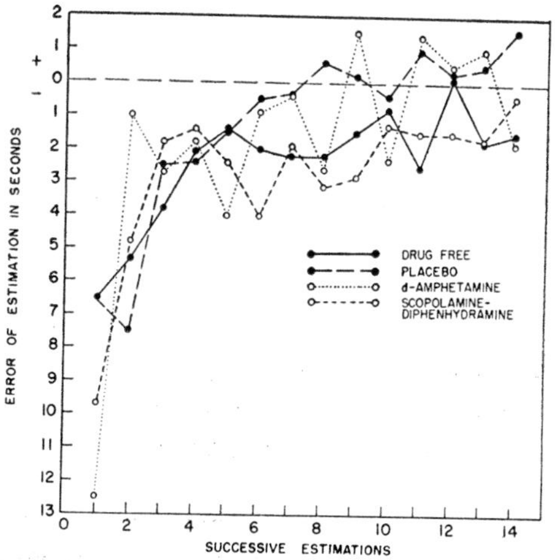

FIG. 1. Means of algebraic differences between estimated and attained proficiencies for the different drug groups.

TABLE 1

Analysis of variance (algebraic differences)

Source	df	Mean square	F
Drugs	3	132.50	0.41
Tasks	2	740.39	2.29
Referents	1	147.34	0.46
D × T	6	649.46	2.01
D × R	3	70.55	0.22
T × R	2	29.98	0.09
D × T × R	6	125.04	0.39
Subjects treated alike	72	323.71	
Total between subjects	95		
Estimations	13	497.65	9.09*
E × D	39	54.91	1.00
E × T	26	109.25	1.99*
E × R	13	56.74	1.04
E × D × T	78	37.83	0.69
E × D × R	39	50.37	0.92
E × T × R	26	63.11	1.15
E × D × T × R	78	52.51	0.96
Pooled error	936	54.77	
Total within subjects	1,248		
Total	1,343		

* Significant at the 0.01 level of confidence.

tion attributable to drugs at successive estimations was analyzed, magnitude of error was not found to be significantly influenced at any point by either of the drugs concerned.

Having discussed the separate effects of the *d*-amphetamine and scopolamine-diphenhydramine preparations upon a judgmental process, it is now necessary to examine their interaction with the respective conditions of the other two experimental variables.

Effects of task difficulty. Inspection of the appropriate curves revealed, for the first estimation, marked differences which were indicated by statistical tests to be significant at the 0.01 level of confidence. Additional tests of significance indicated further that the T_1 and T_2 conditions did not differ significantly from each other but did differ from the most favorable condition, T_3, at the 0.05 and 0.01 levels of confidence respectively. As the subject continues at the task, however, the effect of task difficulty upon the error of estimation is surprisingly shortlived. For the major portion of the task, appreciable, consistent differences do not exist. Consequently, when the variance attributable to the different conditions of difficulty is analyzed over all estimations (table 1), the variance is not found to be significant.

It was expected that both T_1 and T_2 conditions would lead to greater inaccuracy of estimation since in both conditions, the activities which preceded the act of estimation were expected to have a disruptive effect upon the prime basis of estimation, *i.e.*, the experiential referents given by the test trial completed. Accordingly, these conditions were included in the investigation on the grounds that the psychological stress likely to be engendered might bring out latent drug effects to the point of unmistakable detection. This expectation is not realized since table 1 does not reveal the interaction, Drugs × Task Difficulty, to be significant.

Effects of standard referents. It was thought that those subjects who saw their own proficiency scores being consistently plotted above the score made by "most people" (R_1) would be somewhat inclined to overestimate the proficiency they expected to attain while those subjects who observed their proficiency to be consistently inferior to "most people" (R_2) would be more apt to underestimate. If, therefore, these induced feelings of success and failure are relevant conditions for manifestation of the drug effects concerned, such would be revealed. Again, inspection of the appropriate curves gave indication of the expected difference for the first estimation. However, this initial difference, as well as the subsequent differences must be attributed to chance. Table 1 indicates that neither the variance attributable to the different standard referents nor their interaction with successive estimations can be considered to be significant.

It would appear that the subject's estimation of his expected proficiency is predominantly determined by the referents provided by his own past performance at the task and is particularly resistant to extrinsic referents such as were employed. Further, as is indicated by the F-ratios for the Drug × Standard Referents interactions in table 1 this resistance to the extrinsic referents concerned is in no way significantly reduced by either of the drugs administered.

Finally, although this investigation is concerned primarily with the effects of *d*-amphetamine upon judgment, it may be of some interest to consider the extent to which actual proficiency at this mirror vision task was influenced by the single and joint effects of the different experimental variables. Of these three variables, only Drugs failed to modify actual proficiency to a statistically significant degree.

Returning now to the question occasioning this investigation, the following appears evident: Neither *d*-amphetamine nor scopolamine-diphenhydramine when administered in standard dosages had any significant effect upon the judiciousness of the estimations required of the subjects. Furthermore, the effects of these preparations remained undetectable despite the single and joint imposition of psychological stresses which might be presumed to be induced by increased task difficulty and the manipulation of feelings of success and failure.

SUMMARY

Ninety-six male basic airmen volunteers were randomly assigned to the 24 combinations of experimental conditions given by 4 pharmacological treatments, *d*-amphetamine (5 mgm.) scopolamine (0.65 mgm.) plus diphenhydramine hydrochloride (50 mgm.), placebo and no drug; 3 task conditions which permitted variation in the difficulty of the task assigned to the subjects; and 2 standard referents which were expected to induce feelings of success and failure. One hour following administration of the appropriate drug, they were then required to learn a mirror vision task. Before beginning each of the 14 test trials, they were told their proficiency score attained on the test trial just completed, saw that score plotted against a referent curve which was represented as "the average score made by most people", and then were asked to estimate the proficiency score they expected to attain in the test trial about to be performed. The absolute and algebraic differences between the proficiency estimated and the proficiency actually attained were computed and these measures of estimation error, as well as measures of actual performance, were then analyzed.

d-Amphetamine sulfate (5 mgm.) and diphenhydramine hydrochloride (50 mgm.) plus scopolamine (0.65 mgm.) did not influence significantly the judiciousness with which estimations were normally made despite the imposition of experimental conditions designed to elicit or augment whatever adverse effects may be inherent in these pharmacological preparations. Also unaffected was the actual mirror vision performance.

The different conditions of task difficulty did effect significant differences in the error of estimation during the very beginning of the task and in mirror vision performance throughout the task.

The different standard referents did not produce significant differences in error of estimation but did effect significant differences in mirror vision performance during the early part of this task.

REFERENCES

Davis, D. R.: Brit. Med. Bull., **5:** 43, 1947.

Edwards, A. L.: Experimental Design in Psychological Research, Chap. 15, Rinehart and Company, Inc., New York, 1950.

Hauty, G. T., and Payne, R. B.: J. Exper. Psychol., **49:** 60, 1955.

Mackworth, N. H.: Medical Research Council Special Report Series No. 268, His Majesty's Stationery Office, London, 1950.

Payne, R. B.: The AFSAM Pursuit Confusion Test, Model A., USAF SAM Proj. No. 21-02-011, Rep. No. 1, Apr., 1949.

Payne, R. B., and Hauty, G. T.: J. Exper. Psychol., **47:** 267, 1954.

Payne, R. B., Hauty, G. T., and Moore, E. W.: J. Comp. & Physiol. Psychol., in press, 1957.

AURICULAR FIBRILLATION BY ACETYLCHOLINE INJECTION DURING HYPOPOTASSEMIA

PHILLIP E. LEVEQUE

Department of Pharmacology, Medical College of Georgia, Augusta, Georgia

Received for publication December 3, 1956

Auricular fibrillation and flutter have been produced with a high degree of reproducibility in thyrotoxic dogs by the intravenous injection of acetylcholine (Leveque, 1956). Others have been successful with acetylcholine injection by pretreatment of the experimental animal with organic phosphorus anticholinesterases (Loomis and Krop, 1955) and by momentary electrical stimulation to the auricle during acetylcholine infusion (Burn *et al.*, 1956). These arrhythmias may be arrested or prevented by the intravenous administration of potassium chloride (Leveque, Dick and McCawley, unpublished observations, 1953; Burn *et al.*, 1956).

These observations suggested a more important role of potassium in auricular arrhythmias than had been previously suspected. To investigate this further, hypopotassemia was induced in dogs with insulin and glucose. The resulting condition was found to sensitize the auricles to fibrillation and flutter. These arrhythmias were induced by intravenous doses of acetylcholine which during control observations produced much less effect on auricular rhythmicity.

METHODS. Male or non-pregnant female mongrel dogs selected only on the basis of good health and weighing more than 10 kgm. were anesthetized with 35 mgm./kgm. of sodium pentobarbital administered intraperitoneally. The dogs were placed prone on an animal board with a support under the hips and tied securely by the paws. The mouth was blocked open with the tongue out. A 20-gauge needle attached by a 3-way stopcock to a 30-ml. syringe filled with a dilute solution of heparin in saline was introduced into the saphenous vein. The entire injection setup was supported by a clamp on a rigid stand. All injections and withdrawals were made from the sidearm of the stopcock. ECG records were obtained with a Sanborn cardiette. Control records were made with Standard leads I, II, and III. If no arrhythmia was noted the experiment proceeded immediately. Recordings after this were made with lead II.

Acetylcholine chloride solution, 10 mgm./ml. in saline, was injected as rapidly as possible via the stopcock sidearm at about 5 to 10 minute intervals, to a maximum dosage of 1 mgm./kgm. It was found that acetylcholine in a dosage of 0.5 mgm./kgm. would induce auricular fibrillation and flutter in some susceptible normal dogs (three of this series which were omitted from the report). Examination of the ECG of "non fibrillators" after this dosage often gave the impression that this dosage was near a fibrillatory dose (slight vacillation of the isoelectric line) but experience of the author has established that if fibrillation cannot be attained with 0.5 mgm./kgm., greater doses or repetition after a short recovery interval will provide no additional information. In this series usually one or two doses of 0.5 mgm./kgm. were administered prior to other treatment. If no auricular fibrillation was induced, insulin (Iletin U-40 Lilly) was injected at a dosage of from 0.12 to 1.25 unit per kilogram of body weight. After an interval of about ten minutes, acetylcholine was again administered. No serious attempt was made to determine the "minimal fibrillatory dose" of acetylcholine or insulin. Glucose, at a dosage of 200 to 1200 mgm./kgm., usually as an aqueous 10 per cent solution, was administered after insulin in several cases and before the insulin in several other cases.

In most cases the serum potassium was determined to confirm that both insulin and glucose were producing a lowered serum potassium. The potassium determinations were made by diluting heparinized serum 1 to 25 and comparing to known potassium standards with a Beckman model DU flame spectrophotometer.

A series of eighteen dogs weighing from 13 to 30 kgm. was investigated in a total of twenty-two separate experiments.

RESULTS. Because of the wide variety of arrhythmias induced by acetylcholine in this series of experiments, clarification is necessary to avoid confusion. Normal untreated dogs under pentobarbital anesthesia will show a variety of cardiac irregularities when the vagus nerve is stimulated or when cholinergic drugs are injected intravenously. Progressive increases in stimulation or dosage, in the experience of the author, will produce the following successively severe irregularities: 1) bradycardia, 2) momentary asystole (about 1 second), 3) 2:1 atrioventricular block, which may be solitary, or frequently several interspersed episodes of 2:1 A-V block with normal PQRST complexes, 4) prolonged A-V block (any ratio seems possible and the longest observed has been 38:1, 5) prolonged asystole, and 6) more severe arrhythmias such as the ones which were sought and gained in this series. These arrhythmias were interpreted as auricular fibrillation and flutter by employing the following criteria as shown in figure 1: 1) the ventricular rate is irregular, it may be slow in the case of recently initiated arrhythmia which immediately follows an episode of asystole or it may be rapid in the case of rapid flutter, 2) the R wave voltage appears variable, and 3) the P waves are low and indistinct. (Very rapid small waves, about 0.1 mV, frequently occur between or interspersed with distinct P waves. In this series absence of distinct and regular P wave is a fundamental criterion.) Impure or variable flutter appeared consistently after the fibrillation as a transitory phenomenon before conversion to normal. Because the episodes of the various arrhythmias "run together", it appears impossible in most cases to delineate the precise point on the ECG that one arrhythmia stops and another starts. (See figure 1.)

Four dogs of the pretreatment control series were predisposed to acetylcholine-induced auricular fibrillation. This was induced by a dosage of 0.5 mgm./kgm. in all four and in three by 0.25 mgm./kgm. These latter three were omitted from further study. In all of the other cases, auricular fibrillation was not provoked during the control period.

The experimental series may be divided into four superficial categories; those animals which were administered only insulin, those which were administered only glucose, those which were administered glucose and then insulin and those which were administered insulin and then glucose. Suggestive trends appear in each of the categories.

Insulin and glucose both provoked a depression of serum potassium. In the case of intravenously administered insulin, the effect was noticable in five minutes, but susceptibility to fibrillation was very rare in less than ten minutes.

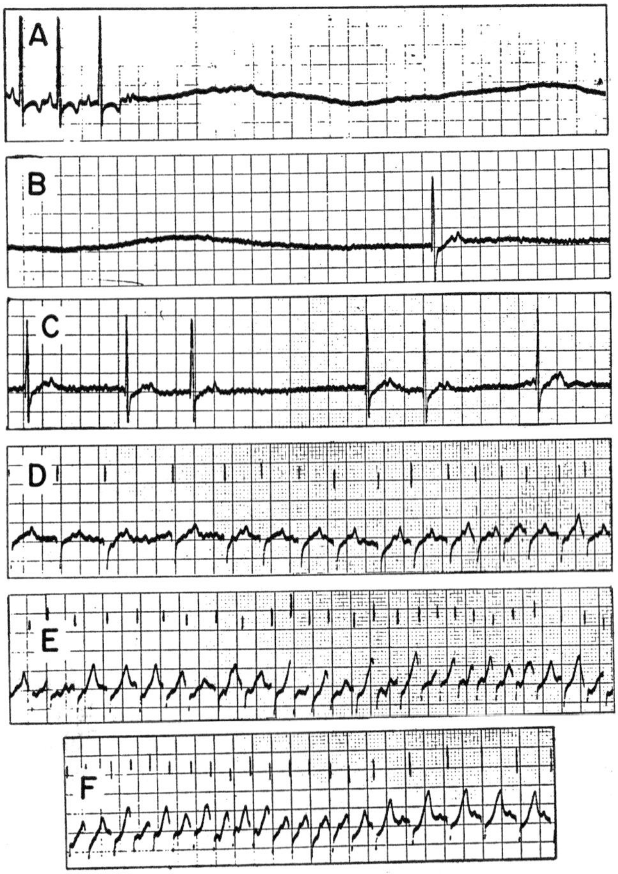

Fig. 1. The effect of intravenous acetylcholine (0.5 mgm./kgm.) on the insulin-pretreate dog.

The ECG shown is a continuous Standard lead II record with 0.2 second lost on the end of each section for mounting purposes. QRS complexes are darkened by redrawing with a pencil. Vertical bold lines are 0.2 second apart. Acetylcholine was administered about 5 seconds before the onset of ventricular asystole.

(A) Normal record and onset of auricular fibrillation with ventricular asystole, (B) the first ventricular complex apparently dissociated from the auricular activity, (C) increased activity of the ventricle, the T wave though irregular remains distinct, (D) steadily increasing ventricular rate but decreasing auricular rate, (E) continuation indicating increasing ventricular rate to more than 300 per minute with auricular rate and activity becoming normal, (F) conversion to a normal appearing ECG with all features of the PQRST distinct.

In view of this observation, ten minutes became a standard interval to obtain a blood specimen and inject acetylcholine. Maximum serum potassium depression did not always occur at the end of this first ten-minute period. Similarly, acetylcholine-induced fibrillation did not always occur at this time. (See table 1.)

Intravenously administered glucose requires more time than insulin to cause depression of serum potassium. Frequently the level of fibrillatory susceptibility was not attained in an hour. After this, small doses of insulin were injected to

TABLE 1

Auricular fibrillation by acetylcholine during hypopotassemia

Dog number	Control		Insulin dose	Glucose dose	Experimental		
	Serum K	Acetylcholine maximuum dose			Serum K Percentage of control	Minimum dose acetylcholine	Duration of arrhythmia
	mEq./l.	*mgm./kgm.*	*units/kgm.*	*mgm./kgm.*	*%*	*mgm./kgm.*	*seconds*
1	*	1.0	0.5		*	0.25	30
2	*	0.54	0.5		*	0.2	10
3	4.4	0.5	1.0		52	0.25	54
4	3.8	0.5	1.0		57	0.5	60
5A†	6.3	0.33	0.5		56	0.33	200
6A	4.4	0.5	0.5		68	0.25	50
6B	5.0	0.5	0.5		68	0.06	30
7A	5.5	0.5	0.5		75	0.125	30
8	5.2	0.5	0.5		67	0.25	20
7B	4.4	0.5		800	73	0.125	27
9	4.9	0.5		400	76	0.5	55
10	4.5	0.5		1200	84	0.5	95
11	5.85	0.5		800	88	0.25	170
12a‡	*	1.0	1.00		*	0.25	83
12b				840		0.06	15
13a	*	0.5	0.25		*	0.125	33
13b				300		0.125	60
14a	3.5	0.5	1.0		71	0.5	NF
14b				200	41	0.5	90
5Ba	4.3	0.5		600	93	0.5	NF
5Bb		0.5	0.12		81	0.5	NF
6Ca	5.0	0.5		400	76	0.5	NF
6Cb		0.5	0.25		62	0.25	60
15a	*	0.5		200	*	0.25	35
15b		0.5	0.5			0.25	40
16a	3.9	0.5		300	95	0.5	NF
16b			1.25		80	0.5	30
17a	4.7	0.5		1200	72	0.5	NF
17b		0.5	1.0		51	0.125	36
18a	5.4	0.5		200	80	0.5	NF
18b			0.5		57	0.25	30

* No analysis made.

† A—B—C large letter; separate experiments on the same dog.

‡ a—b small letter; single experiment divided into two portions for analysis.

provoke greater serum potassium depression and fibrillatory susceptibility. This is indicated in table 1 by separation of an experiment into two parts. These parts are labeled a and b. This label indicates that the two agents were employed to lower the serum potassium. In general, the serum potassium concentration was determined after the administration of each agent. In all cases in which potassium concentration was determined after the two agents, the second agent was shown to further depress the serum potassium. In eight of nine cases attempted, the use of the second agent was required to provoke susceptibility to fibrillation.

In the cases in which insulin was administered initially or alone, 1.0 unit/kgm. provoked susceptibility to fibrillation in three of four cases, the failure was the only female of the series. Fibrillation was provoked in nine of eleven cases after 0.5 unit per kilogram. One of these failures became susceptible after 1.0 unit/kgm. The other was administered a total of 1.0 unit/kgm. without such an effect. Initial dosage 0.25 unit/kgm. was attempted only once. This was adequate to provoke susceptibility to fibrillation in this case. In some of these cases fibrillation was provoked only one time after the administration of the insulin. At this time the serum potassium was at its lowest. Thereafter rising serum potassium levels seemed to accompany an increased or apparently complete resistance to acetylcholine-induced fibrillation. Some of the animals listed on the table were administered more than the 0.5 unit/kgm. indicated, but this increased dosage did not provoke greater serum potassium depression or greater susceptibility to fibrillation by acetylcholine. Larger doses seemed to prolong the period of serum potassium depression.

In the cases in which glucose was administered alone or initially, a dosage of 200 mgm./kgm. provoked susceptibility in one of four cases. When the dosage was increased to 400 mgm./kgm. one of seven was susceptible. Increasing the dosage to 800 mgm./kgm. apparently increased the susceptibility so that two out of four became susceptible. Only one of these latter dogs was resistant after 1200 mgm./kgm. It became apparent during the experimentation that the serum potassium depression after glucose occurred much more slowly than after insulin. It did not seem worth-while to allow greater time for the serum potassium to become depressed as the relationship of glucose was considered a side-issue.

The nine cases in which glucose and insulin were utilized together enabled the provocation of fibrillation in all but one of the cases previously mentioned. The one failure was initially administered glucose, first at a dosage of 400 mgm./kgm., which was later increased to 600 mgm./kgm. This depressed the serum potassium to 93 per cent of control without apparent sensitization. After this, insulin at a dosage of 0.12 unit/kgm. caused a serum potassium depression to 81 per cent of control level but fibrillation could not be provoked. It is interesting to note that on a previous occasion this dog was administered insulin at a dosage of 0.5 unit/kgm. and during a serum potassium level of 56 per cent of control, acetylcholine at a dosage of 0.33 mgm./kgm. provoked fibrillation and flutter for 200 seconds.

The greatest observed decrease in serum potassium was to 41 per cent of the control concentration. This was induced by the administration of insulin at a dosage of 1.0 unit/kgm. (which lowered the serum potassium to 71 per cent of control without fibrillatory susceptibility) followed by the administration of glucose at a dosage of 200 mgm./kgm. When the serum potassium was at 41 per cent of control concentration, acetylcholine at a dosage of 0.125 mgm./kgm. provoked fibrillation and flutter for ninety seconds.

The lowest dose of acetylcholine to produce fibrillation was 0.06 mgm./kgm. This dosage was administered after an insulin dosage of 0.5 unit/kgm. which lowered the serum potassium to 68 per cent of control. The auricular fibrillation and flutter lasted thirty seconds. The usual dose of acetylcholine to provoke fibrillation after insulin was 0.25 mgm./kgm. but threshold dosage was not sought and the values presented may be valid only in the case of a given experiment.

DISCUSSION. Potassium ion has long been known to have a depressing effect on the heart. A study of the effects of potassium on clinical patients in whom cardiac arrhythmias had been induced by excessive dosage of digitalis indicated that oral and intravenous potassium ion would arrest many of these arrhythmias including auricular fibrillation (Sampson *et al.*, 1943). More recent studies indicate that intravenous potassium ion will arrest experimental auricular fibrillation in the dog heart-lung preparation (Burn *et al.*, 1956). It seemed plausible to expect that if increasing the serum potassium level would arrest cardiac arrhythmias that acute depression of serum potassium might provoke cardiac arrhythmias or might sensitize the myocardium so that arrhythmias might be more easily induced or prolonged in the otherwise susceptible animal.

Serum potassium depression along with serum glucose depression was discovered quite early in the investigation of insulin (Harrop and Benedict, 1923). The employment of this well known standardized hormone, insulin, to produce reliable and consistent serum potassium depression appears to be a useful method by which variations in serum potassium concentration can be utilized to investigate this effect on cardiac irritability and arrhythmias.

Intravenous acetylcholine occasionally will provoke auricular fibrillation in the normal dog (Nahum and Hoff, 1935; Surtshin and Rucknagel, 1953; Leveque, 1956). Experimentally induced thyrotoxicosis increased the rate of susceptibility to fibrillation from 30 per cent (7 of 23 untreated dogs) to 81 per cent (13 of 16 thyroid-extract-fed dogs) (Leveque, 1956). A combination of these two effects, acute hypopotassemia and acetylcholine-induced auricular fibrillation, appeared to be a possible method by which cardiac irregularities and the more serious arrhythmias could be investigated.

Early in this investigation it was suggested that the overall effect resulting from insulin injection might be mediated through hypoglycemia or epinephrine release provoked by the hypoglycemia. In an effort to eliminate such a possibility, glucose was injected before, with and after insulin to assure normal or even supernormal blood glucose concentrations. Although blood glucose was not determined in this series, it seems unlikely in view of the results with glucose administration that hypoglycemia could be a factor for consideration.

It is felt that there is no real difference in the cases in which glucose or insulin was administered alone. In the case of insulin administration, glucose is already in the blood of the animal, and cellular deposition of glycogen is a natural result of such a situation. Similarly, when glucose is administered in appreciable amounts, normal physiological mechanisms will provoke the release of insulin from the pancreas and the ultimate result will be identical. A few animals appear to be relatively resistant to treatment but repetition of these experiments allowing greater time of increasing the dosage might alter the results significantly.

Superficial examination of the data indicates that a serum potassium depression of about 20 per cent induced susceptibility to arrhythmia and in general that the greater the potassium depression the more sensitive the animal to acetylcholine-induced fibrillation.

The fate or site of deposition of the potassium was not investigated. The greatest depression occurs in about thirty minutes after intravenous infusion which minimizes renal loss as a factor for consideration.

Concentration of serum potassium from the cases in which it was obtained are presented in table 1. The effect of insulin on blood glucose and potassium is known in a general way so that exhaustive investigation of this effect was considered unnecessary. Direct and reflex activity after acetylcholine injection caused moderate fluctuations in the serum potassium level. For this reason the trends seem more important than any single analysis or experiment. The results given are those found but are not stable for a long period of time. It was observed in some experiments in which many specimens were obtained that after intravenous insulin injection the serum potassium would start to fall immediately and descend to a level characterized by susceptibility to auricular fibrillation in ten to twenty minutes. This level would remain fairly stationary for about ninety minutes after which the serum potassium level would rise concurrently with resistance to fibrillation.

After treatment with insulin and glucose, serum potassium levels often fell precipitously. With this fall, the dogs became extremely sensitive to small doses of acetylcholine and moderate doses would provoke prolonged and alarming asystole and arrhythmia. Extra caution seemed necessary to avoid accidental death of the trained animals. For this reason, after insulin and glucose, very small doses of acetylcholine were administered initially and increased later in an effort to delineate a threshold. This caution, at the expense of more precise data, seemed worth-while in that very few animals were lost during the experimentation.

Several successful attempts were made to prolong the arrhythmias by infusing acetylcholine after the fibrillation had started. In one case flutter was continued for thirty minutes by this procedure. Greater prolongation was not attempted. This method has been reported previously (Burn *et al.*, 1956). With pretreatment of the dog with an anticholinesterase, another group was able by acetylcholine infusion to perpetuate the arrhythmias 90 minutes (Loomis and Krop, 1955).

In several cases potassium chloride solution was administered via the intravenous set-up to the animals during fibrillation and flutter. This procedure uniformly arrested the arrhythmia with less than 10 ml. of 10 per cent KCl. This is an observation which has been reported previously (Burn *et al.*, 1956) and this information is offered as verification of their results. It was also noted that flutter and fibrillation could not be induced in these dogs while the serum potassium level was elevated. After an interval of several minutes, the serum potassium level would often return to a low level after which fibrillation could again be provoked.

SUMMARY

Insulin in dosages of 0.25 to 1.0 unit/kgm. when administered intravenously to pentobarbital-anesthetized dogs lowered the serum potassium concentration to 75 to 52 per cent of control value. This depression began within five minutes of administration and was maximal in about thirty minutes. The depression with higher doses lasted about ninety minutes after which it began to return to control values.

In similar experiments, glucose in dosages of 200 to 1200 mgm./kgm. when administered intravenously produced a serum potassium depression to 95 to 72 per cent of the control value. This depression occurred at a slower rate than with insulin.

The combination of glucose and insulin, regardless of which was administered first, lowered the serum potassium concentration to a greater degree than either agent alone. After a combination of these agents, serum potassium concentration was lowered to 80 to 41 per cent of the control value.

When the serum potassium concentration was depressed by these means to about 80 per cent of control value, auricular fibrillation and flutter were provoked by the intravenous administration of dosages of acetylcholine which were ineffective during the control period.

In general, it was observed that the greater the serum potassium depression the greater the sensitivity or susceptibility to acetylcholine-induced auricular fibrillation and flutter.

A series of eighteen dogs was investigated in a total of twenty-two separate experiments. Fibrillation and flutter were provoked in twenty-one of these experiments. In the sole failure, fibrillation had been induced in a previous experiment.

Several attempts, all successful, were made to perpetuate the acetylcholine-induced flutter by an infusion of acetylcholine. The arrhythmia was perpetuated thirty minutes, at which time the infusion was terminated. A normal rhythm ensued within a few minutes.

Potassium chloride was infused into several dogs during flutter. This uniformly arrested the arrhythmia. Fibrillation and flutter could not be induced during a short period of hyperpotassemia following this infusion.

REFERENCES

Burn, J. H., Gunning, A. J., and Walker, J. M.: Circulation Res., **4:** 288, 1956.
Harrop, G. A., and Benedict, E. M.: Proc. Soc. Exp. Biol. & Med., **20:** 430, 1922–23.
Leveque, P. E.: Circulation Res., **4:** 108, 1956.
Loomis, T. A., and Krop, S.: Circulation Res., **3:** 390, 1955.
Nahum, L. H., and Hoff, H. E.: J.A.M.A., **105:** 254, 1935.
Sampson, J., Alberton, E. C., and Kondo, B.: Am. Heart J., **26:** 164, 1943.
Surtshin, A., and Rucknagel, D. L.: Am. Heart J., **45:** 781, 1953.

THE INFLUENCE OF VARIOUS SPATIAL GROUPS ON CHOLINOLYTIC ACTIVITY

J. P. LONG[1] AND A. M. LANDS

Pharmacology Section, Sterling-Winthrop Research Institute, Rensselaer, New York

Received for publication December 8, 1956

Cholinolytic specificity, and presumably other drug receptor interactions, are dependent on the reacting compound being complementary to the receptor surface in both charge and stereochemical aspects. Numerous papers by Lands and collaborators from this laboratory (1946, 1949, 1951, 1954 and 1956) as well as other laboratories (Blicke, 1944; Ing *et al.*, 1945; Levy, 1948; Pfeiffer, 1948) have outlined carefully the structural specificity for cholinolytic action. In a previous paper we discussed the most probable points of attachment for cholinolytic agents (Long *et al.*, 1956). They were 1) a cationic head, 2) a hydrogen donor group, 3) a large planar ring and, if present, 4) a negative charge on the ester component. To extend the evaluation of the above proposed points of attachment and to study more fully the influence of spatial variations on cholinolytic activity we have evaluated several classes of compounds. It is the hope of the authors that basic concepts derived from the activity of cholinolytic compounds may be applied to other pharmacological agents and this may lead to a better understanding of drug-receptor interactions.

METHODS. The cholinolytic activity was evaluated in mice by use of the mydriasis test (Pulewka, 1932; Ing *et al.*, 1945). Activity has been expressed as per cent atropine sulfate (per cent of the potency of atropine sulfate) following a log dose-probit plot of the results. The compounds were administered intraperitoneally in regular 0.3 log dose intervals to four groups of ten mice each.

The compounds used in this investigation have been synthesized by Ruddy and Buckley (No. 1 and 2; 1950), Adamson *et al.* (No. 3; 1951), Blicke and Tsao (No. 5 through 10; 1944), Blicke and Raffelson (No. 11, 13, 15 and 17; 1952), Blicke and Cox (No. 12, 14, 16 and 18; 1955) and Blicke and Abcede (No. 19 through 27; 1955).

RESULTS AND DISCUSSION. There have been suggestions in the literature that asymmetric substitution on the terminal carbon atom may lead to an increase in cholinolytic activity (Meier and Hoffmann, 1941; Lands *et al.*, 1956). To study this aspect more fully, the activity of both ester and non-ester cholinolytics has been evaluated.

The activity of the non-ester cholinolytics shown in table 1 yields some divergent results. The phenyl-cyclohexyl compound (No. 2) is considerably more active that either diphenyl or dicyclohexyl analogs (Compounds No. 1 and 3). In this series, optimal activity is obtained when there is an asymmetric carbon present. However, the 2-thiophene analog (No. 4) is relatively low in activity and appears to be less favorable for activity than phenyl substitution (No. 2).

[1] Present address: Department of Pharmacology, College of Medicine, State University of Iowa, Iowa City.

TABLE 1

Influence of asymmetry on cholinolytic activity of alkanol derivatives

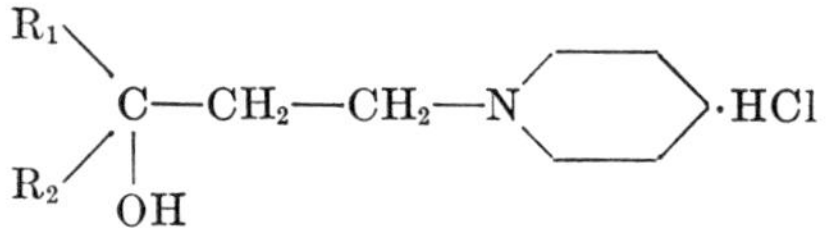

Compound no.	R_1	R_2	Mouse mydriasis ED_{50}	Per cent atropine sulfate
			mgm./kgm.	
1	phenyl	phenyl	11.0	2.2
2	phenyl	cyclohexyl	3.3	7.7
3	cyclohexyl	cyclohexyl	10.5	2.4
4	2-thiophene	cyclohexyl	7.6	3.3
Atropine sulfate			0.25	100.0

TABLE 2

Influence of asymmetry on cholinolytic activity in glycolate derivatives

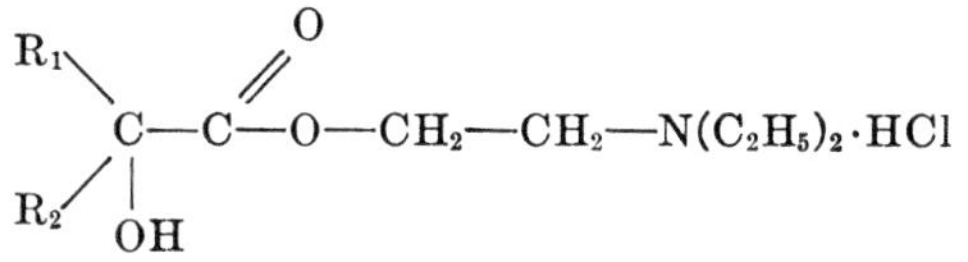

Compound no.	R_1	R_2	Mouse mydriasis ED_{50}	Per cent atropine sulfate
			mgm./kgm.	
5	2-thiophene	cyclohexyl	1.1	24
6	phenyl	cyclohexyl	1.2	21
7	phenyl	phenyl	5.2	4.8
8	cyclohexyl	cyclohexyl	23	1.1
9	2-thiophene	2-thiophene	6	4.2
10	2-thiophene	phenyl	1.8	13.9

Table 2 lists the activity of substituted glycolate derivatives. The highest activity is found in compounds containing asymmetric substitution (No. 5 and 6). In contrast to the compounds shown in table 1, the 2-thienyl-cyclohexyl compound (No. 5) is optimal in this series for activity with the phenyl-cyclohexyl compound (No. 6) approximately equal to it. When there is no asymmetric carbon present, the cholinolytic activity is relatively weak (illustrated by No. 7, 8 and 9). In compound No. 10, where there is an asymmetric carbon substituted with two aromatic planar rings there is a definite decrease in activity.

In an effort to determine the relative importance of the phenyl or cyclohexyl ring for cholinolytic activity, and hence, presumably favorable for binding on the receptor surface, the paired compounds shown in table 3 were evaluated. In this series, the phenyl and cyclohexyl rings are the only variables. In each case, there is increased activity when the compound contains a phenyl ring in place

TABLE 3

The relationship between phenyl and cyclohexyl ring systems

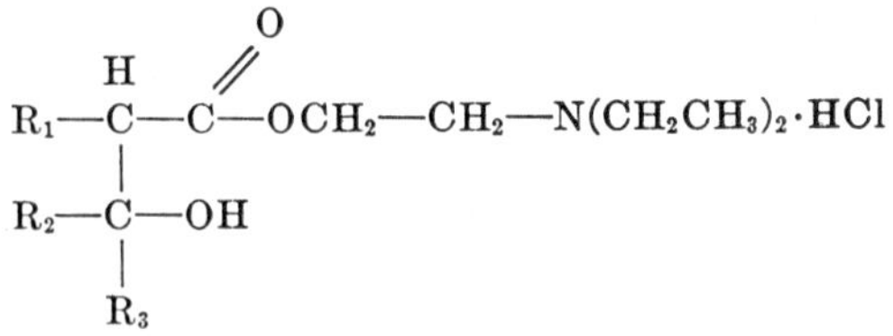

Compound no.	R_1	R_2	R_3	Per cent atropine sulfate
11	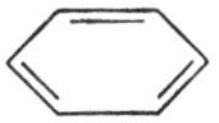	$—CH_3$	$—CH_3$	10.5
12	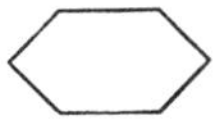	$—CH_3$	$—CH_3$	2.3
13	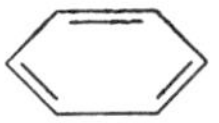	H	$CH_3—\underset{H}{\overset{\vert}{C}}—CH_3$	4.2
14	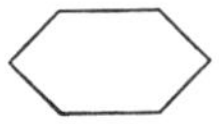	H	$CH_3—\underset{H}{\overset{\vert}{C}}—CH_3$	0.6
15		$—CH_2—CH_3$	$—CH_2—CH_3$	3.3
16	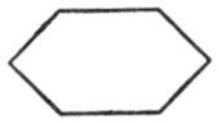	$—CH_2—CH_3$	$—CH_2—CH_3$	0.8
17	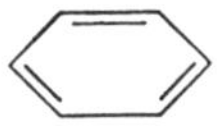	H	$—CH_2—CH_2—CH_3$	3.0
18	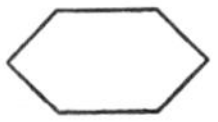	H	$—CH_2—CH_2—CH_3$	1.1

of a cyclohexyl ring (compare No. 11 with 12; 13 with 14; 15 with 16; 17 with 18). The results obtained indicate that the phenyl ring is the preferred group for attachment. Perhaps a relatively flat surface on the receptor is involved. The cyclohexyl ring cannot exist as a flat ring and must be oriented in either the so-called boat or chair form, the chair form being the more probable.

Various series of reported cholinolytic compounds containing alkyl substitution have shown spatial specificity, as far as the cationic head is involved (Burtner and Cusnic, 1943; Ing *et al.*, 1945; Ehrenberg *et al.*, 1952; and de Jongh *et al.*, 1955). Table 4 illustrates the influence on cholinolytic activity of cyclic amines larger than the piperidine ring. These data along with others (Ing *et al.*, 1945; de Jongh *et al.*, 1955) indicate that there is a definite limit in the size of the cationic

TABLE 4

Activity of the higher homologs of piperidine

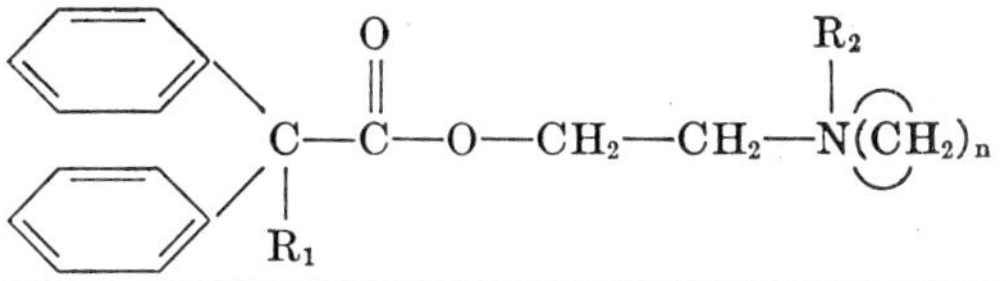

Compound no.	R_1	R_2	n	Per cent atropine sulfate*
19	—OH	CH_3Cl	5	16**
20	—OH	HCl	7	<0.3
21	—OH	CH_3Br	7	1.1
22	—OH	HCl	8	0.3
23	—OH	CH_3Br	8	0.8
24	—H	HCl	7	<0.3
25	—H	CH_3Br	7	<0.3
26	—H	HCl	8	<0.3
27	—H	CH_3Br	8	<0.3

* As determined by the mouse mydriasis test method.
** Datum from Ing *et al.* (1945).

TABLE 5

Cholinolytic activity of various N-oxide derivatives

Compound	Per cent atropine sulfate
Scopolamine·HBr	700
Genoscopolamine·HBr	95
Atropine sulfate	100
Genoatropine	44

head acceptable to the receptor site. Perhaps spatial specificity about the cationic head is to be expected. If the bulk of the head is too large and thus prevents close approach to an anionic receptor site, the attraction may not be sufficient to hold the compound (Lands and Cavallito, 1954; Lands and Luduena, 1956).

The N-oxide derivatives of cholinolytic agents present some interesting problems in charge distribution on the cationic head. A comparison of scopolamine and atropine with the corresponding N-oxides discloses a distinct reduction in potency with this change in structure (table 5). Similar observations have been reported previously (reviewed by von Oettingen, 1936). However, the structural change might be considered somewhat analogous to a methyl quaternary, with which potency is usually increased. This suggests that a change in the charge distribution on the cationic head is responsible for the decreased cholinolytic activity. Since the N-oxide derivatives may be regarded as internally compensated compounds (Ferguson, 1952) having a charge distribution as N^+ -O^-, this effect may reduce affinity for the anionic spot in the receptor site. However, a specific conductance measurement of the hydrobromide salts of genoscopolamine and scopolamine in water failed to show any difference in conductance, as estimated from extrapolation to infinite dilution. This would tend to indicate that the difference in activity shown by these agents may be more likely related to some steric factor. However, presently it is difficult to visualize a mechanism in which the N-oxide would be less favorable for activity than the corresponding methyl quaternary salt.

SUMMARY

The influence of various sterical and spatial factors on cholinolytic activity has been considered.

Asymmetry on the terminal carbon atom is optimal for cholinolytic activity in compounds with or without an ester component. The symmetric molecules are less effective.

In a series of paired compounds where the interchange of a phenyl or cyclohexyl ring was the only variable, compound containing the phenyl rings are definitely more effective as cholinolytic agents.

Some higher homologs of the piperidine ring substituted in the cationic head have been studied and these are clearly less potent.

Selected gen (N-oxide) derivatives have been compared with the tertiary analogs. The N-oxide substitution is not favorable for cholinolytic activity.

The possible influences of the above spatial variations have been discussed in light of a multiple-point attachment hypothesis.

ACKNOWLEDGMENTS. The authors wish to express their thanks to Dr. A. C. White, Burroughs-Wellcome Ltd., Kent, England for a generous sample of 1, 1-dicyclohexyl-3-piperidino-1-propanol·HCl and to Mr. N. Wishnefsky, American Roland Corporation, 16 Hudson Street, New York 13, New York for the N-oxides of scopolamine and atropine.

REFERENCES

ADAMSON, D. W., BARRETT, P. A., AND WILKINSON, S.: J. Chem. Soc., p. 52, 1951.
BLICKE, F. F.: Ann. Rev. Biochem., **13:** 549, 1944.
BLICKE, F. F., AND TSAO, M. U.: J. Am. Chem. Soc., **66:** 1645, 1944.
BLICKE, F. F., AND RAFFELSON, H.: J. Am. Chem. Soc., **74:** 1730, 1952.
BLICKE, F. F., AND COX, R. H.: J. Am. Chem. Soc., **77:** 5401, 5403, 1955.
BLICKE, F. F., AND ABCEDE, J. B.: Doctoral Thesis of J. B. Abcede, University Michigan, February, 1955.
BURTNER, R. R., AND CUSIC, J. W.: J. Am. Chem. Soc., **65:** 262, 1943.
DEJONGH, D. K., VAN PROOSDIJ-HARTZEMA, E. G., AND JANSSEN, P.: Arch. int. Pharmacodyn., **103:** 100, 1955.
EHRENBERG, M. H., RAMP, J. A., BLANCHARD, E. W., AND TREVES, G. R.: THIS JOURNAL, **102:** 141, 1952.
FERGUSON, L. N.: Electron Structures of Organic Molecules, Prentice-Hall, Inc., New York, 1952.
ING, H. R., DAWES, G. S., AND WAJDA, I.: THIS JOURNAL, **85:** 85, 1945.
LANDS, A. M., NASH, V. L., AND HOPPER, K. Z.: THIS JOURNAL, **86:** 129, 1946.
LANDS, A. M., ANENENKO, E., JONES, G., HOPPE, J. O., AND BECKNER, T. J.: THIS JOURNAL, **96:** 1, 1949.

LANDS, A. M.: THIS JOURNAL, **102**: 219, 1951.
LANDS, A. M., AND CAVALLITO, C. J.: THIS JOURNAL, **110**: 369, 1954.
LANDS, A. M., AND LUDUENA, F. P.: THIS JOURNAL, **116**: 177, 1956.
LEVY, J.: J. Physiologie, **40**: 23, 1948.
LONG, J. P., LUDUENA, F. P., TULLAR, B. F., AND LANDS, A. M.: THIS JOURNAL, **117**: 29, 1956.
PFEIFFER, C. C.: Science, **107**: 94, 1948.
PULEWKA, P.: Arch. f. exper. Path. u. Pharmakol., **168**: 307, 1932.
RUDDY, A. W., AND BUCKLEY, J. S., JR.: J. Am. Chem. Soc., **72**: 718, 1950.
VON MEIER, R. AND HOFFMANN, K.: Helv. Med. Acta., **7**: 106, 1941.
VON OETTINGEN, W. F.: The Therapeutic Agents of the Pyrrole and Pyridine Group, Edward Bros., Inc., Ann Arbor, Michigan, 1936.

DISTRIBUTION AND FATE OF NALORPHINE IN THE DOG AND RAT[1, 2]

L. A. WOODS AND H. E. MUEHLENBECK

Department of Pharmacology, University of Michigan Medical School, Ann Arbor

Received for publication December 8, 1956

The therapeutic applications of the remarkable morphine-antagonistic effects of nalorphine have made the investigation of the distribution and fate of this drug very desirable. Accordingly, studies on plasma levels, urinary excretion, and tissue distribution of free and conjugated nalorphine in the dog and rat were initiated. The results of these experiments are described herein.

METHODS. *Estimation of nalorphine.* Free and conjugated nalorphine are estimated in biological materials using the procedure described previously for morphine (Woods *et al.*, 1954). For maximum sensitivity, especially for the determination of nalorphine in plasma, 0.8 ml. microcells are used in the Beckman model DU spectophotometer to measure the optical density of the acid extract of the methyl orange. Standards having concentrations of nalorphine in the range of the unknown samples are analyzed parallel with each set of unknown concentrations. Duplicate determinations are performed on each sample of biological material and the results averaged. The procedure is less reliable for the estimation of nalorphine than for morphine. With minimal concentrations in plasma and tissue, the recovery of added nalorphine is 110 ± 25 per cent and with higher concentrations in these biological materials is 100 ± 12 per cent. Recovery of added nalorphine in urine is in the range of 100 ± 10 per cent.

The specificity of the estimation of nalorphine was appraised by buffer solvent distribution studies comparable to those described for morphine (Woods *et al.*, 1954). The results are presented in table 1 and indicate that the procedure is specific for the estimation of nalorphine. Morphine, but not normorphine, interferes in the procedure for nalorphine as performed routinely. However, the buffer solvent distribution pattern is different for morphine and nalorphine, a buffer of lower pH being required for extraction of the latter drug from the solvent into the aqueous phase.

Animal experiments. Female mongrel dogs were used for the experiments on plasma levels and excretion of nalorphine. Each dog was hydrated with one liter of water by stomach tube about one hour before the administration of the drug. Urine samples were withdrawn from the bladder with the aid of a Foley-bag indwelling catheter. A dose of 30 mgm./kgm.[3] (as free base) of nalorphine hydrochloride[4] was injected subcutaneously and plasma and urine samples obtained at desired intervals. The indwelling catheter was removed at the end of about nine hours and the urine collected in a metabolism cage until the end of the 24 hour period. The dog was then catheterized and the urine so obtained added to the cage-collected urine of the 9- to 24-hour period. Subsequent urine samples were collected in the cage.

---

[1] Supported in part by the research grant B-625 from the Division of Research Grants, National Institute of Health, United States Public Health Service.

[2] A preliminary report describing some of the results of these experiments appears in THIS JOURNAL, **113:** 40, 1955.

[3] All doses are reported as the free base but the nalorphine was administered as the aqueous solution of the hydrochloride salt.

[4] The authors are indebted to Drs. Charles A. Winter and Frederick K. Heath, Merck and Company, Inc., Rahway, N. J., for supplying the nalorphine (Nalline) hydrochloride used in these studies.

TABLE 1

*Distribution of authentic nalorphine and apparent nalorphine from autoclaved dog urine between an 8:10 ratio of $EtCl_2$: Skellysolve D and 0.1 M citrate buffers of varying pH**

pH of buffer**	Per cent extraction of Nalorphine†	
	Authentic nalorphine	Apparent nalorphine
2.1	82	85
2.4	71	73
2.7	61	59
3.0	36	39

* Procedure exactly as described for specificity tests for morphine (Woods *et al.*, 1954) except that 0.5 *N* HCl, instead of 0.2 *N*, was used to extract the nalorphine from the 15 ml. aliquot mixture of $EtCl_2$: Skellysolve D which had been shaken with the respective buffers.

** The extractions of authentic and apparent nalorphine were performed in parallel for each pH value.

† Each figure represents an average of triplicate determinations.

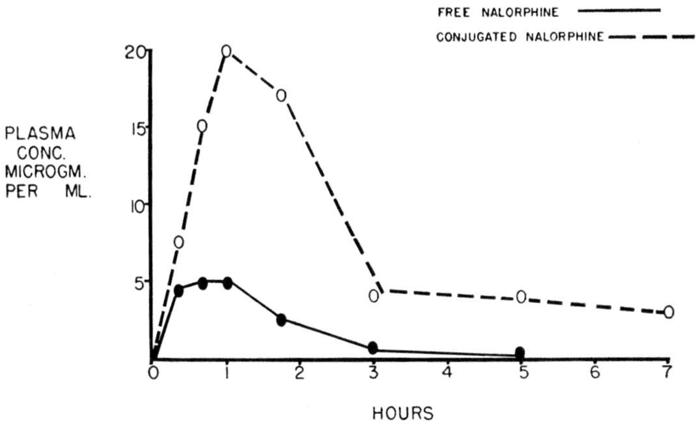

FIG. 1. Plasma levels of free and conjugated nalorphine in the dog following the subcutaneous administration of 30 mgm./kgm. of nalorphine.

Dogs of both sexes were injected subcutaneously with 30 mgm./kgm. of nalorphine and the animals sacrificed at desired intervals by exsanguination under ether anesthesia. The tissues were removed, frozen on solid carbon dioxide, and stored in a freezer until analyzed.

Rats were injected subcutaneously with doses of 150 mgm./kgm. of nalorphine and sacrificed at desired intervals by decapitation. The tissues were removed, frozen as above, and stored in a freezer until analyzed. In a few experiments the site of administration of the nalorphine was excised and analyzed in comparison with animals receiving morphine in the same dosage.

RESULTS: *Plasma levels.* The plasma levels of free and conjugated nalorphine in a typical experiment following the subcutaneous administration of 30 mgm./kgm. of nalorphine to the dog are illustrated in figure 1. The biologic half-life of free nalorphine is approximately one and one-half to two hours and of conjugated nalorphine approximately two and one-half hours. Free nalorphine is detectable in the plasma for approximately three hours after the administra-

TABLE 2

Percentage recovery of free, conjugated, and total nalorphine in the urine of dogs injected subcutaneously with 30 mgm./kgm. (as free base) of drug

Dog no.	Percentage recovery		
	Free	Conjugated	Total
N-1	4	56	60
N-2	1	46	47
N-3	2	42	44
average	2.3	48	50

tion of the drug. Following the administration of the same dose (30 mgm./kgm.) by the same route (subcutaneous), plasma levels of free nalorphine are lower and conjugated nalorphine higher than those observed for free and conjugated morphine (Cochin *et al.*, 1954). Apparently the dog is able to conjugate nalorphine more rapidly and more completely than morphine.

Urinary excretion. The per cent recovery of free, conjugated and total nalorphine in the urine of dogs injected subcutaneously with 30 mgm./kgm. of drug is summarized in table 2. One to four per cent of the administered dose of nalorphine is recovered as free nalorphine and 42 to 56 per cent as conjugated nalorphine, the total recovery being 44 to 60 per cent. The average per cent recovery of administered nalorphine as conjugated drug is in the same range as that described for morphine (Cochin *et al.*, 1954). However, a striking difference is observed between the recovery of free nalorphine in urine as compared with free morphine, the per cent recovery of the former being one-sixth that of the latter.

The urinary excretion of free nalorphine is substantially complete four hours after the injection of a single dose of drug, although 30 to 40 per cent of the conjugated nalorphine to be excreted appears in the urine of the seven to twenty-four hour period. Very little conjugated nalorphine is eliminated in the urine after the first twenty-four hours.

Tissue distribution. The distribution of free and conjugated nalorphine in 2 dogs, each, ninety minutes and four hours after the subcutaneous administration of 30 mgm./kgm. of nalorphine is summarized in table 3. In most tissues and fluids the concentration of both forms of nalorphine is quite low with the exception of gall bladder bile. The levels of conjugated nalorphine in bile are much higher than those found in other fluids or in tissues. Total nalorphine in gall bladder bile ranges from 1.5 to 6 per cent of the administered dose of drug.

Preliminary results from the estimation of nalorphine in dog brain indicated higher levels than observed for morphine. A comparison of the concentration in dog brain of these two drugs is the subject of another report (Woods, 1957).

The values for the concentration of free or conjugated nalorphine in the tissues and fluids removed from rats ninety minutes and four hours after the subcutaneous injection of 150 mgm./kgm. of drug are presented in table 4. Since the figures are lower than those observed for morphine (Woods, 1954), a com-

TABLE 3

Distribution of free and conjugated nalorphine in two dogs, each, ninety minutes and four hours after the subcutaneous administration of 30 mgm./kgm. of nalorphine

Tissue of fluid*	Concentration of nalorphine (microgm./gm. or ml.)**			
	Ninety minutes		Four hours	
	Free	Conjugated	Free	Conjugated
Gall bladder bile†	6	450	12	1020
Kidney	18	34	<5	<5
Spleen	20	0	<5	0
Lung	5	10	10	<5
Liver	5	11	<5	<5
C. muscle	5	<5	<5	<5
S. muscle	12	0	<5	0
Pancreas	16	0		
Jejunum	5	25	<5	96
Colon	10	<5	<5	35
Blood	<5	15	<5	5

* Levels of free and conjugated nalorphine for adrenal gland, cerebrospinal fluid and fat were less than 5 microgm./gm. or ml.

** Each figure represents the average of the results for two animals.

† The recovery of total nalorphine in gall bladder bile ranged from 1.5 to 6 per cent of the administered dose of nalorphine.

TABLE 4

Distribution of free and conjugated nalorphine in rats ninety minutes and four hours after the subcutaneous administration of 150 mgm./kgm. (as free base) of drug

Tissue or fluid*	Concentration of nalorphine† (microgm./gm.)			
	Ninety minutes		Four hours	
	Free	Conjugated	Free	Conjugated
Kidney	30	8	<5	8
Spleen	60	0	9	0
Lung	40	0	<5	0
Liver	<5	40	<5	5
C. muscle	13	20	5	<5
S. muscle	25	0	6	0
Brain	7	<5	<5	0
Fat	10	<5	12	0

* The concentration of free or conjugated nalorphine in the blood of animals ninety minutes and four hours after injection was less than 5 microgm./ml.

† Each figure is an average of two determinations, each analysis being performed on the pooled tissues of 5 to 6 rats.

parison was made of the absorption of morphine and nalorphine from the site of injection. Three rats, each, were injected subcutaneously with 150 mgm./kgm. (as free base) of morphine or nalorphine. The injection area of the skin, having a diameter of about 4 cm. and including subcutaneous tissue and underlying muscle, was removed from each animal. This tissue was minced and shaken mechanically with 0.5 *N* HCl for several hours. Four hours after the administration of the drug, the per cent of administered dose recovered at the site of injection in each animal was as follows: For nalorphine, 0.3, 0.2, and 4.2; for morphine 16, 17, and 15.

DISCUSSION. Following the subcutaneous injection of identical doses of drug (30 mgm./kgm.), nalorphine is conjugated more rapidly and more completely by the dog than morphine (Cochin *et al.*, 1954) whether plasma levels or urinary excretion are considered. Only one-sixth as much nalorphine is excreted in the free form in urine as compared with morphine. A possible explanation of the differences in the extent of conjugation of nalorphine and morphine is that the dose of 30 mgm./kgm. of morphine has a very profound pharmacological action on the dog, whereas that dose of nalorphine has very little effect. It would be necessary to assume that the mechanisms of conjugation are depressed by morphine but not by nalorphine. *In vitro* studies have shown (Seibert and Huggins, 1953) that at similar concentrations of drug, dog liver slices conjugate nalorphine at approximately the same rate as morphine. However, this *in vitro* study does not preclude the possibility of vascular effects, etc., of morphine which *in vivo* might alter the pattern of conjugation in a manner not observed with nalorphine.

The concentration and the per cent of administered dose of nalorphine, especially the conjugated form, found in the gall bladder bile of the dog are much lower than those described for morphine (Woods, 1954). It is apparent that the route of biliary excretion is of less importance for nalorphine than for morphine. Although the fecal excretion of nalorphine was not determined directly, the indirect evidence based on presence in the gall bladder bile, colon, and jejunum, would suggest this route as a minor avenue of elimination.

The concentrations of free and conjugated nalorphine in tissues and fluids of dogs and rats are in most instances significantly lower than the values obtained for morphine (Woods, 1954). These differences probably result from the greater rate of conjugation and elimination of nalorphine. That these differences are not due to a slower rate of absorption of nalorphine as compared with morphine has been shown in rats. Indeed, the rate of absorption of nalorphine from the site of injection is considerably more rapid than that of morphine.

Since no more than 50 to 60 per cent of the administered dose of nalorphine has been recovered as free and conjugated drug, additional routes of chemical alteration must exist in the dog.

SUMMARY

Following the subcutaneous administration of 30 mgm./kgm. of nalorphine to dogs, the biologic half-life of the free drug in plasma is about one and one-half to two hours and that of conjugated nalorphine about two and one-half hours. In the same animal species the urinary recovery of the administered dose of drug is one to four per cent as free nalorphine, 42 to 56 per cent as conjugated nalorphine, and 44 to 60 per cent as total nalorphine. Essentially all of the free nalorphine appears in the urine three to four hours after injection. Very little total nalorphine is found in the urine after twenty-four hours. Nalorphine is conjugated more quickly and more completely by the dog than morphine.

The concentrations of free and conjugated nalorphine in most tissues and fluids of dogs and rats are lower than those described for morphine. Compared with other tissues, the concentration of conjugated nalorphine in gall bladder bile is very high but still accounts for no more than a few per cent of the administered drug.

In rats the rate of absorption of nalorphine following subcutaneous injection is more rapid than that of morphine.

ACKNOWLEDGMENT. The authors are greatly indebted to Miss Beverly Waterman for invaluable technical assistance in performing many of the analytical procedures described in this report.

REFERENCES

COCHIN, J., HAGGART, J., WOODS, L. A., AND SEEVERS, M. H.: THIS JOURNAL, **111:** 74, 1954.
SEIBERT, R. A., AND HUGGINS, R. A.: Proc. Soc. Exper. Biol. and Med., **82:** 518, 1953.
WOODS, L. A.: THIS JOURNAL, **112:** 158, 1954.
WOODS, L. A.: THIS JOURNAL, **120:** 58, 1957.
WOODS, L. A., COCHIN, J., FORNEFELD, E. G., AND SEEVERS, M. H.: THIS JOURNAL, **111:** 64, 1954.

COMPARATIVE DISTRIBUTION OF MORPHINE AND NALORPHINE IN DOG BRAIN[1, 2]

L. A. WOODS

Department of Pharmacology, University of Michigan Medical School, Ann Arbor

Received for publication December 8, 1956

Suggestive evidence was obtained during tissue distribution studies on nalorphine that the free form of this drug was concentrated in dog brain to a significantly greater extent than morphine, while simultaneously the concentrations of free nalorphine in plasma and most other tissues were lower than those of free morphine (Woods and Muehlenbeck, 1957). Since the concentrations of nalorphine and morphine in the brain were at the borderline of detectability using the described method of estimation, the procedure was modified especially for the analysis of larger quantities of brain tissue thus markedly increasing sensitivity. It became possible to estimate reliably as little as 0.5 to 1 microgm. of nalorphine or morphine per gm. of brain tissue. Subsequently, the comparative distribution of morphine and nalorphine was studied in dog brain at intervals following the subcutaneous administration of varying doses of drug. The results are reported in this communication.

METHOD. Mongrel dogs weighing 7 to 12 kgm. were injected subcutaneously in the dorsum a few inches from the mid-line with 1 ml./kgm. of the appropriate aqueous solution of morphine[3] or nalorphine.[3, 4] At the desired interval following injection, the animals were sacrificed by the rapid intravenous administration of 40–50 mgm./kgm. of sodium thiopental followed by the immediate opening of the chest and incision of the left ventricle and superior vena cava. After hemorrhage had ceased, the descending aorta was clamped and a catheter was introduced through the ventricular incision and aortic valve into the ascending aorta. The head of the animal was perfused for 90 seconds with physiological saline under a pressure of 100 to 120 mm. of Hg. The calvarium was removed and the brain excised and promptly frozen on solid carbon dioxide and stored in a freezer until analysis.

A 10-gm. sample of cerebral tissue was mixed with 20 ml. of 0.5 *N* HCl and homogenized with a Waring blendor using the monel-metal, semi-micro container (25 to 250 ml. capacity). The container was cooled on ice prior to the homogenizing of the tissue, and care was exercised to prevent the container and homogenate from becoming warm. The homogenate was transferred to a glass-stoppered 50-ml. centrifuge tube and shaken 25 minutes at a frequency of 300 oscillations per minute by an International shaker machine using bottle holders made from wooden blocks as described previously (Woods *et al.*, 1951). Then 10 ml. of a 20 per cent aqueous solution of trichloroacetic acid were added, and the mixture was shaken vigorously by hand for one minute and then centrifuged for five minutes. The supernatant liquid was filtered. Twenty ml. of this filtrate were shaken three times with 20 ml. of ethyl acetate, each of the three ethyl acetate extracts being shaken with the same

[1] Supported in part by research grant B-625 from the Division of Research Grants, National Institutes of Health, United States Public Health Service.

[2] A preliminary report of these experiments appears in Fed. Proc., **15:** 502, 1956.

[3] Throughout this paper the dose of each drug is indicated as the free base although aqueous solutions of morphine sulfate or nalorphine hydrochloride were administered.

[4] The author is indebted to Drs. Charles A. Winter and Homer K. Heath, Merck and Co., Rahway, N. J., for supplying the nalorphine (Nalline) hydrochloride.

5.0 ml. of 0.5 *N* HCl, and the acid extract analyzed in a manner described for the estimation of morphine in urine (Woods *et al.*, 1954). Analyses of the cerebral tissue of each animal were performed in triplicate. Triplicate parallel standards were carried through all of the dilutions and manipulations exactly as described for brain tissue, the concentrations of the standards being in the range of the levels found in tissue.

Recovery of added amounts of drug from brain tissue of the dog varied from 70 ± 10 per cent at the lower concentrations to 95 ± 10 per cent at the higher concentrations. Accordingly, recoveries of known drug were determined at the various concentrations found in the tissue and these figures used to correct the observed readings in cerebral tissue to the 100 per cent value.

RESULTS. The values for the concentrations of morphine or nalorphine in cerebral tissue of the dog at intervals following the subcutaneous injection of 30 mgm./kgm. (as free base) of drug are summarized in table 1. Figure 1 illustrates these data in comparison with plasma levels following the administration of the same dose of drugs by the same route. The concentration of free nalorphine in brain tissue ninety minutes after administration is three to four-fold greater than that observed for morphine. Conversely, free morphine persists in brain for a much longer period than that observed for nalorphine. In the dose administered to these dogs, morphine shows a significant pharmacological effect twelve hours after administration and a slight effect sixteen hours after administration. It would appear that the threshold concentration of morphine in dog brain for exhibiting demonstrable pharmacological effects is in the range of 0.5 to 1 microgm./gm. Nalorphine produces very little, if any, pharmacological action when administered to the dog in a dose of 30 mgm./kgm.

TABLE 1

Concentration (microgm./gm.) of free drug in cerebral tissue of the dog at intervals following the subcutaneous injection of 30 mgm./kgm. (as free base) of morphine or nalorphine

Interval after injection	Number of dogs used for each drug	Mean concentration of free drug* *Microgm./gm. tissue* (Range of results)	
		Morphine	Nalorphine
Ninety minutes	6	4.3 (3.7–5.6)	14 (10–18)
Four hours	2	4.6 (4.1–5.1)	2.6 (1.9–3.3)
Eight hours	2	3.8 (3.3–4.2)	Approx. 0.2 (0.0–0.4)
Twelve hours	2	1.5 (1.3–1.6)	—
Sixteen hours	2	0.9 (0.8–1.0)	—

* Triplicate determinations of free drug were performed on the brain tissue of each animal, the results averaged, and corrected to 100 per cent recovery.

The mean concentrations of nalorphine and morphine in brain tissue of two dogs, each, ninety minutes after the subcutaneous injection of 10 mgm./kgm. of drug were 3.8 (range, 3.7 to 3.9) and 1.1 (range, 0.94 to 1.3) microgm./kgm., respectively. Thus, the relative concentration of nalorphine vs. morphine holds for 10 mgm./kgm. as well as for 30 mgm./kgm.

That the concentration of morphine or nalorphine is proportional to the dose of drug is demonstrated in figure 2 which shows concentration of drug ninety minutes after subcutaneous administration plotted against dose.

Nalorphine was also administered to the dog together with morphine in a dosage ratio of 1:10. The dose of morphine was 30 mgm./kgm. combined with 3 mgm./kgm. of nalorphine, the mixture being administered subcutaneously. Ninety minutes after the administration of the drugs, the animals were sacrificed. The results were as follows: The mean apparent concentration of morphine in brain tissue was 4.2 microgm./gm. (range, 3.1 to 5.0 in 3 dogs), as compared with 4.3 microgm./gm. (range, 3.7 to 5.6 in 6 dogs) after the same dose of morphine alone (table 1). No attempt was made to separate the nalorphine from the morphine in the estimation of morphine so that undoubtedly both nalorphine and morphine were detected in the brain of the animals receiving the mixture. If one estimates from figure 2 the brain concentration of nalorphine at the dosage level of 3 mgm./kgm. as being 1.2 microgm./gm., then the actual concentration of morphine (estimated at 3.0 microgm./gm.) in the brain of the animals receiving the mixture would be significantly lower than the concentration of morphine (4.3 microgm./gm.) in the brain of animals injected with morphine.

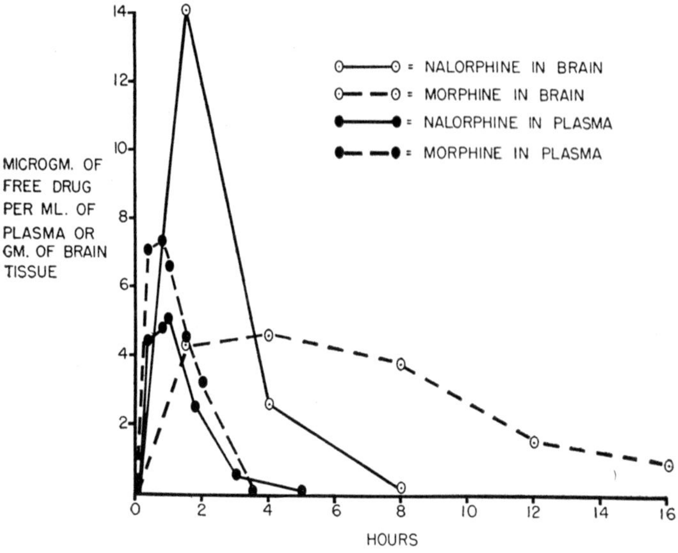

FIG. 1. Brain and plasma concentration (microgm./ml. or gm.) in the dog of morphine or nalorphine at various intervals following the subcutaneous injection of 30 mgm./kgm. (as free base) of drug.

Plasma levels and brain concentration were obviously not determined on the same animals. The values for plasma levels represent typical experiments performed previously.

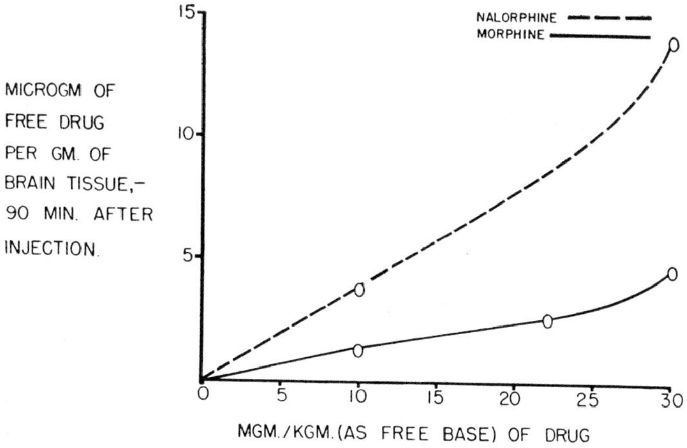

FIG. 2. Brain concentration (microgm./gm.) of morphine and nalorphine ninety minutes after the subcutaneous injection of various doses of drug.

The only value not presented elsewhere in this report is that for 22 mgm./kgm. of morphine, the mean concentration in two dogs being 2.5 (range, 2.3–2.7).

Regardless of which calculation is used, the concentration of morphine in the brain tissue of dogs receiving the mixture was well above the level for pronounced pharmacological effects. At the time of sacrifice the dogs injected with the mixture of nalorphine with morphine exhibited very slight, if any, narcotic action. However, salivation was very prominent in all animals, being much more striking than that observed if the animals would have received just morphine.

DISCUSSION. It is a well-known fact that the pharmacological actions of morphine outlast those of nalorphine. Such has been demonstrated by the nalorphine antagonism of morphine in morphine-tolerant and non-tolerant animals including man. Likewise, the onset of the nalorphine antagonism of morphine is known to be very rapid. The results on the comparative brain distribution of nalorphine and morphine described in this report explain the rapid effect and short duration of action of nalorphine.

The brain-plasma distribution ratio is obviously much higher for nalorphine than for morphine (figure 1). In addition, brain and plasma levels of nalorphine parallel each other more closely than do those of morphine.

Since the technique of perfusion utilized in these studies would reduce the intravascular content of drug to zero or near zero, any drug present in brain tissue must be located either in the interstitial fraction of the extracellular compartment or in the intracellular compartment, or both. If all the drug in the brain were in the interstitial compartment, one would expect a rate of disappearance from brain similar to the rate of disappearance from plasma. Such is true for nalorphine but not for morphine suggesting that morphine persists in brain tissue because of a significant intracellular distribution. It has been postulated (Seevers and Woods, 1953; Seevers, 1954) that nalorphine occupies primarily an extracellular site whereas morphine occupies both extracellular and intracellular sites. The results noted in this report are not inconsistent with this hypothesis.

It is quite surprising that the relatively slight difference in chemical structure between morphine and nalorphine would alter so markedly the nature of the distribution pattern. There is evidence for a difference in the ionization of the amino group in the two drugs, nalorphine (Woods and Muehlenbeck, 1957) being less basic than morphine (Woods *et al.*, 1954) on the basis of buffer distribution studies. However, this difference alone is not likely to offer a complete explanation of the marked differences in the cerebral distribution of the two agents.

Nalorphine, in a 1:10 ratio, may decrease slightly the gross concentration of morphine in brain tissue. Since the resulting concentration of morphine is well above the threshold concentration for overt pharmacologic actions of morphine, it appears that this slight reduction of the gross concentration of morphine by nalorphine does not explain the effective antagonism by the latter drug. However, that this small reduction in gross concentration may represent most of the morphine associated with extracellular receptors cannot be excluded completely at the present time.

SUMMARY

The levels of nalorphine and morphine in brain tissue of the dog have been determined at various intervals after the subcutaneous injection of doses of drug ranging from 10 to 30 mgm./kgm. (as free base). Nalorphine penetrates into brain tissue much more rapidly and attains a concentration three- to four-fold greater than that observed for morphine. The rate of egress of nalorphine from dog brain is much more rapid than that of morphine. These results have been correlated with the known duration of pharmacological actions of the two drugs. The effect of nalorphine upon the gross concentration of morphine in brain is not particularly striking and does not appear to offer an explanation of its antagonistic action.

ACKNOWLEDGMENT. The author is greatly indebted to Miss Beverly Waterman for technical assistance in carrying out the analytical procedures required for this investigation.

REFERENCES

SEEVERS, M. H.: Fed. Proc., **13:** 672, 1954.

SEEVERS, M. H., AND WOODS, L. A.: Amer. J. Med., **14:** 546, 1953.

WOODS, L. A., COCHIN, J., FORNEFELD, E. J., MCMAHON, F. G., AND SEEVERS, M. H.: THIS JOURNAL, **101:** 188, 1951.

WOODS, L. A., COCHIN, J., FORNEFELD, E. J., AND SEEVERS, M. H.: THIS JOURNAL, **111:** 64, 1954.

WOODS, L. A., AND MUEHLENBECK, H. E.: THIS JOURNAL, **120:** 52, 1957.

STUDIES ON VERATRUM ALKALOIDS. XXV. VERATRINE RESPONSE AND ANTIVERATRINIC ACTION IN FROG SARTORIUS MUSCLE[1]

PETER N. WITT[2,3] AND CHARLES R. SWAINE

Department of Pharmacology, Harvard Medical School, Boston, Massachusetts

Received for publication December 11, 1956

The veratrine response of the amphibian muscle is caused by the ester alkaloids, veratridine and cevadine, from *Schoenocaulon officinale*. Since these ester alkaloids are now available it seems advantageous to abandon the use of the ill-defined mixture "veratrine" and employ one of the ester alkaloids. In previous work from this department veratridine was used and has been found suitable to reproduce the veratrine response (Krayer and George, 1951; Arora and Krayer, 1952; Arora, 1953; Fuentes, 1957).

In the characteristic myogram of the frog sartorius muscle treated with veratridine the initial twitch-like contraction resulting from a single electrical stimulus is followed by a more or less pronounced relaxation; this is followed again by a slow secondary rise and fall of tension. Sometimes with high concentrations of the alkaloid the secondary rise is superimposed upon the initial twitch without any intervening relaxation. It is the secondary rise and fall of tension which is referred to in this paper as the veratrine response (VR).

The secondary alkamines among the veratrum alkaloids, such as veratramine from *Veratrum album* or *Veratrum viride*, do not possess veratrinic action, rather they abolish the VR and restore the normal twitch. In this regard they are similar to quinine and quinidine (Krayer and George, 1951). The term "antiveratrinic action" was introduced by Krayer to characterize substances which, in appropriate dosage range, are capable of antagonizing, in the presence of veratridine (or a similarly acting substance), the secondary rise of tension without reducing the initial twitch.

An aid in the investigation of the VR was the application of the intracellular microelectrode technique as described by Nastuk and Hodgkin (1950). This method enabled us to study the fast electrical changes of the veratrinized muscle in the single cell. The combination of this technique with simultaneous recording of tension of a small group of fibers should clarify the question whether there exists a close connection between the electrical changes in the cell membrane (seen as repetitive discharges and negative afterpotential) and the characteristic VR.

METHODS. Frog sartorius muscle was prepared so that no fiber was impaired. For most of the experiments reported here the size of the muscle was reduced by cutting a certain

[1] This work was supported in part by funds from the Eugene Higgins Trust and in part by a research grant (H-2205) from the U. S. Public Health Service.

[2] Rockefeller Fellow.

[3] Present address: Department of Pharmacology, State University of New York, Upstate Medical Center, Syracuse, N. Y.

number of fibers in the middle, pulling the cut ends back to their respective insertions at both ends, and eliminating them carefully. The connective tissue which surrounds the muscle was removed as completely as possible. Nearly all of the experiments were made with approximately 100 intact fibers. The number of intact fibers could be roughly estimated by the tension developed in response to a supramaximal stimulus.

The buffered Ringer solution used was prepared according to Nastuk and Hodgkin's "Normal Ringer" (1950). Pure oxygen, air or the gases indicated under the respective experiments were bubbled through the bathing solution during the experiments.

The dissected muscle was fixed with its proximal end near one side of the bottom of the vessel containing the Ringer solution in an angle of 45° to the horizontal. The distal one-sixth of the muscle was not immersed, but was kept wet with Ringer solution, and was connected by a glass rod to a strain gauge. The stimulating platinum electrodes were fixed to the distal end. By adjusting initial tension it was possible to determine that tension which produced a maximal twitch after a supramaximal stimulus. Smaller variations in initial tension showed no detectable change in the sensitivity to veratridine and the form of the VR.

Tension was recorded by means of a Grass strain gauge, amplifier, demodulator and inkwriter (especially adapted for this purpose). The inertia of this transmitting system was found low enough to give a full sized excursion with a 1 msec. sine wave. The calibration was not fully linear as can be seen from figures 1 and 2. The amplification which remained the same throughout the experiment could be regulated for each experiment according to the tension which the muscle developed. The speed of the recording paper could be increased up to 60 mm./sec., allowing tension measurements every 0.0166 sec. This recording device did not enable us to measure the latency period between the stimulus and the development of tension. It is assumed that for figures 1 and 2 the latency is of the order determined by Sandow (1952).

Supramaximal stimuli of 0.1 msec. duration were delivered from a Grass stimulator, model 4. As intensity was never increased, our results include only experiments with muscles in which the excitability was not markedly decreased. As a control, each stimulus transmitted to the muscle was recorded simultaneously on the inkwriter. Stimulus duration was kept at 0.1 msec. to minimize the stimulus artifact. As the recording microelectrode was placed into a distant part of the muscle, only conducted impulses were measured.

Microcapillaries prepared as described by Ling and Gerard (1949), with a tip diameter of two micra or smaller and filled with saturated KCl solution, were lowered into a fiber by means of a de Fonbrune micromanipulator (de Fonbrune, 1949) under optical control through a stereoscopic microscope. The microelectrode was connected through a 25 mm. long piece of polyethylene tubing filled with KCl and an unpolarizable silver-silver chloride electrode to the grid of a cathode follower. The cathode follower with the tube 5800 from the Victoreen Instrument Company was set up as described by Nastuk and Hodgkin (1950). Its input valve had a grid current of 6.8×10^{-11} amp. The second electrode was a saturated KCl-agar filled glass tube which dipped into the Ringer solution. It was connected through another silver-silver chloride electrode. The voltage was called zero when both electrodes dipped into the Ringer bath. The voltage was amplified through a two channel DC amplifier[4] and connected to the plates of a Dumont flatfaced cathode ray oscilloscope. The movements of the ray were recorded with a Grass Kymograph Camera[5]. The film speed was 10 cm./sec. and figures 1 and 2 show the original records in low magnification. Each microelectrode was checked for its resistance and the whole apparatus for its ability to transmit the expected changes of voltage undistorted in time. When a voltage step was introduced in series with the microelectrode the new potential was reached with a time constant of 0.1 msec.

[4] Lent to us by the Department of Pharmacology, University of Bern, Bern, Switzerland, through the kindness of Dr. W. Wilbrandt.

[5] We wish to express our gratitude to Mr. A. M. Grass of the Grass Instrument Co., Quincy, Mass. for kindly lending us the oscilloscope and the camera.

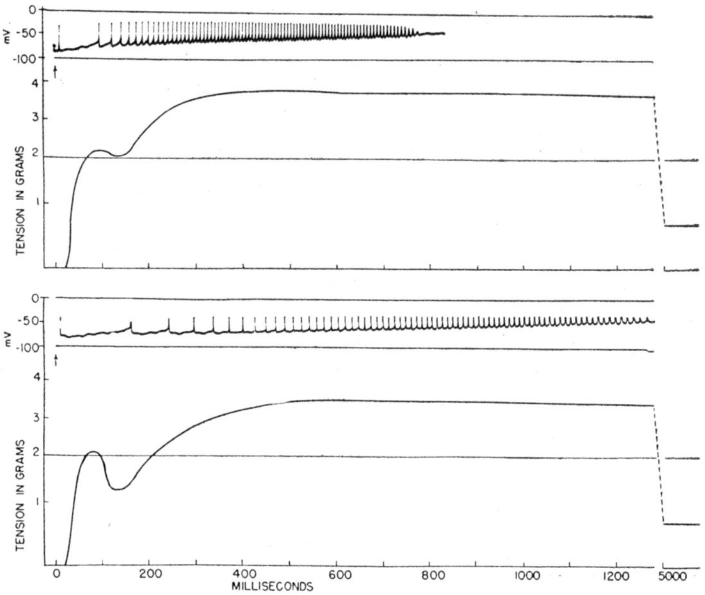

FIG. 1. Effects of veratridine upon electrical and mechanical events in striated muscle. *Rana pipiens*, male. Fiber bundle of sartorius muscle. Two records of veratrine responses are shown: both electrograms are from the same single fiber; the corresponding myograms are from the whole fiber bundle. The upper response was obtained by a stimulus (at the arrow) given to the fiber bundle after a two-minute rest period. The stimulus (at the arrow) of the lower response was given one minute later.

The veratridine used was the free base prepared from veratrine[6] by Deliwala and Kupchan. It had a rotation of $[\alpha]_D^{25} + 6°$ (c = 2.00 in ethanol). Stock solutions containing 1 mgm./ml. were prepared by dissolving the alkaloid in distilled water with an equimolar amount of hydrochloric acid. The veratramine, which was generously supplied by O. Wintersteiner of E. R. Squibb & Sons, was dissolved in the same way as veratridine to produce a stock solution of 10 mgm./ml. In most experiments appropriate amounts of the stock solution were added to the bath to obtain the concentration desired. In some experiments the whole bathing solution was replaced.

In the beginning of the experiments the microelectrode was often broken or pulled out of the cell by the movement of the muscle during a VR. Later on this difficulty was largely overcome by choosing an electrode with a thin, elastic tip and by reducing the number of muscle fibers which led to a reduction in pull during the twitch. If after a VR the membrane potential returned to the old value and the cell had shown action potentials, the photograph was used for evaluation. However, from time to time strange forms of potential changes appeared and it could not be decided whether they were artifacts due to our recording method or real potential changes in the cell membrane. These photographic records were not included in our evaluation.

RESULTS. *The activity of a muscle fiber during a VR.* Figures 1 and 2 represent typical tracings of the photographs obtained during a VR. Shortly after the stimulus was given (represented by the stimulus artifact above the arrow) the action potential rose sharply, fell approximately to the preceding membrane potential, and was followed by a number of repetitive discharges which arose from a slowly decreasing membrane potential, the *negative afterpotential*. The repolar-

[6] Generously supplied by J. B. Penick & Co., New York, N. Y.

ization of the membrane is not shown in these pictures as it took place at a relatively late time; no measurements of its time course were made.

The *membrane potential* in a veratrinized muscle seemed less stable than in a muscle in normal Ringer especially after a VR. Frequently undulations of the potential were observed for some time after the negative afterpotential was over. There is no indication for the assumption that this was an artifact brought about by the electrode moving in the cell.

Depending on the preparation, but constant for each muscle, the *action potential* began 6.8 ± 0.6 msec. (N = 34)[7] after the stimulus artifact. This distance was not measurably influenced by antagonists or differences in the length of the preceding stimulus interval. The resting potential in the veratrinized muscle was found to be 73.9 ± 9.6 mV (N = 35)[8], the action potential 47.2 ± 1.8 mV (N = 35); this is to be contrasted to the normal resting potential of 86 to 88 mV and the normal action potential of 119 mV. This means that the action potential was about 64 per cent of the membrane potential and did not show an overshoot, except directly after the addition of veratridine or after the antiveratrinic action was fully developed. No relationship was found between the height of the membrane potential and that of the action potential.

While the action potential showed a rather constant time distance from the stimulus, the *repetitive discharges* began after a widely varying time interval (see example in figure 1). The most frequently used stimulus interval of two minutes showed an average time between the stimulus artifact and the first discharge of 109 ± 21 msec. (N = 43). The repetitive spontaneous electrical discharges following a four-minute stimulus interval showed an average time of 38.6 ± 32.9 msec. (N = 3); and the discharges following the one minute interval came after an average time of 128.8 ± 9.8 msec. (N = 13). The three values are not significantly different which probably can be attributed to the relatively small number of observations.

The *time interval* between the individual discharges in one VR was—with very few exceptions—regularly decreasing, sometimes constant, seldom irregular. The average distance between the discharges in one VR was measured as the distance between two potentials which lay in the middle of the total number. This seemed again dependent on the preceding stimulus interval, being 19.5 ± 5.0 msec. (N = 10) for the one-minute interval, 13.4 ± 4.1 msec. (N = 42) for the two-minute stimulus interval, and 7.2 ± 0.7 msec. (N = 5) for the four-minute interval. The results varied widely from fiber to fiber but records from the same fiber consistently showed a shorter average distance after a longer resting period. An example is shown in figure 1.

The *average height* of the first action potential of a group of repetitive discharges measured from its take-off level was 39.0 ± 2.3 mV (N = 74)[9], being

[7] In this paper the first figure is the mean: the figure following ± is the standard error of the mean; N is the number of observations; the concentrations are in w/v.

[8] For evaluation we used records of all fibers that showed action potentials and in which the membrane potential had the same height before and after a VR.

[9] This figure includes some measurements of veratrine responses soon after the antiveratrinic substance was given since the height was not measurably influenced at first.

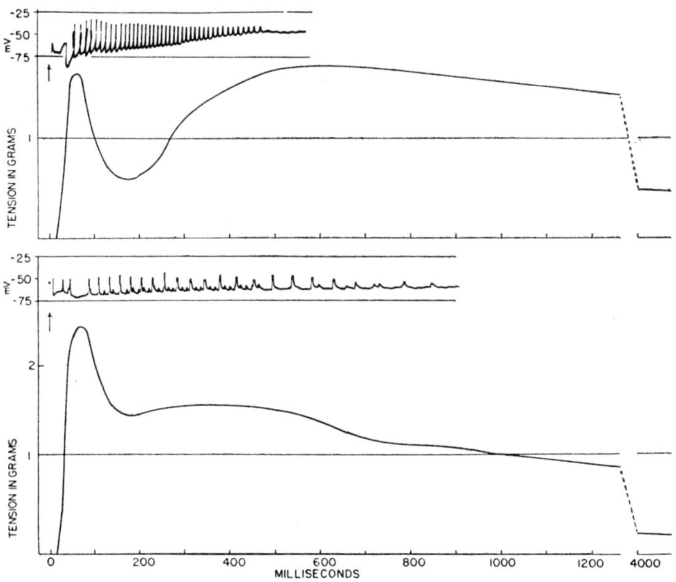

FIG. 2. Effect of veratramine on the electrical and mechanical events of the veratrine response.

Rana pipiens, male. Fiber bundle of sartorius muscle. The electrograms are from two different fibers in the same fiber bundle; the corresponding myograms are from the same whole fiber bundle. Both responses were obtained after a two-minute rest period. The veratrine response shown in the lower tracing was obtained 13 minutes after veratramine had been added in a concentration of 10^{-5}.

nearly always lower than the preceding action potential. The following discharges in one VR always showed a decrease in height, mostly regularly decreasing. Discharges increasing in height were never observed by us. That the discharges decreased in height was partly due to the decrease in membrane potential —which means a decreasing level of the take-off voltage—and partly due to a lower amplitude of the discharge.

The total *number of discharges* varied widely and up to 166 were recorded by us. There was some difficulty in obtaining exact figures of the total number as during many veratrine responses the height of the discharges continuously decreased until only a damped oscillation of the membrane potential was discernible, and it was sometimes impossible to decide which discharge should be considered the last one. In other veratrine responses the discharges ended abruptly. The average figure for the total number of discharges in our experiments was 33.4 ± 3.2 (N = 64). The number showed no relationship to the preceding stimulus interval. In each muscle some fibers showed no discharges at all, but our technique did not enable us to decide how far these fibers took part in the VR.

The effect of stimulus frequency, temperature and drug concentration on the VR. The influence of the *resting period* preceding a stimulus on the VR was investigated in 59 experiments. As is well known, a change in the frequency of stimulation is followed by a change in the VR: by applying the stimulus with shorter interval (1, 0.5, 0.25 minutes) the twitch was not affected but the second tension rise was comparatively lower. At a relatively low frequency of stimulation (4-, 8-, 16-minute intervals) the second contraction was higher. An example of this behavior of the muscle is shown in figure 1 and the left part of figure 3. Figure 1 shows the influence of a long (2-minute) and a short (1-minute) stimulus interval on the following VR; in addition the simultaneous electrical activity is recorded. The VR after one minute shows a smaller second tension rise as well as a delay in time in the beginning of repetitive discharges; besides, the latter are more widely spaced. With a stimulus interval of 0.25 minute, action potentials without following discharges were observed in many fibers.

When the stimulus interval was held constant at two minutes the concentration of veratridine with which a VR could be obtained depended upon the *temperature* of the bath. At 6°C. the concentration necessary to produce a VR was 1.3×10^{-6}, while at 31.5°C. the necessary concentration was 1.3×10^{-8}. The relationship between temperature and veratridine concentration was found to be the same as the one represented in the figure of Miyake (1939).

The antiveratrinic action. Twenty-two experiments were performed with *veratramine* added to the bath after veratridine had acted for at least ten minutes at a time when the muscle showed its characteristic VR. The substance was added to the bath in an amount to obtain an end concentration of 10^{-5}. Stimuli were applied to the muscle regularly every two minutes. After an average time of 26 minutes in a whole sartorius muscle and an average time of 8.3 minutes in a 100 fiber preparation, the VR reached only one-half of its initial height. The difference in time between the whole muscle and the 100 fiber preparation is significant below the 5 per cent probability level with $t = 2.87$. The influence of different stimulus frequencies, as described in the last paragraph, could be obtained at any time during the veratramine antagonism. This means a second tension rise in a VR reduced by veratramine action could be brought back again to its full initial height after waiting 4 or 8 minutes between stimuli instead of 2. The addition of veratramine has an effect which can be described as equal to that of shortening the stimulus interval. This is illustrated in figure 3.

The antagonized VR, the short muscle twitch without a second tension rise, often looked electrically like an action potential rising from a higher membrane potential. A few records of the electrical behavior of the cell were obtained during the transient period in which the second tension rise was already smaller but not yet totally abolished. At this time only a small number of fibers showed repetitive discharges and these were changed in shape as shown in figure 2. The discharges were irregular in height and some spikes showed an abnormally slow time course.

After having obtained an antagonized VR with veratramine the concentration of neither veratridine nor veratramine could be increased without suppression of the activity of the muscle. There was no indication for competition between the two substances. While the concentration of veratridine necessary to elicit a full VR changed with the temperature, as soon as a VR was obtained at a certain temperature, it could always be antagonized with veratramine at 10^{-5}. Only the effective veratridine concentration was temperature-dependent, not the antiveratrinic veratramine concentration.

Strophanthin K (ampules Strophosid Sandoz) was used in 9 experiments. The final concentration in Ringer was between 2×10^{-6} and 3×10^{-6}. The strophanthin had been added 14 minutes before the veratridine was given and a stimulus was given every two minutes, as described by Arora (1953). The results were similar to those obtained with veratramine. The influence of muscle diameter, temperature and the electrical behavior of the cells were not investigated.

Quinine and *quinidine* (12 experiments) showed an antiveratrinic action in a concentration of 10^{-6}, and the effect had the same characteristics described in the veratramine and strophanthin experiments. After the quinine had begun to act on the VR, a large action potential with overshoot and without repetitive discharges could be recorded. However, in two photographs taken during the

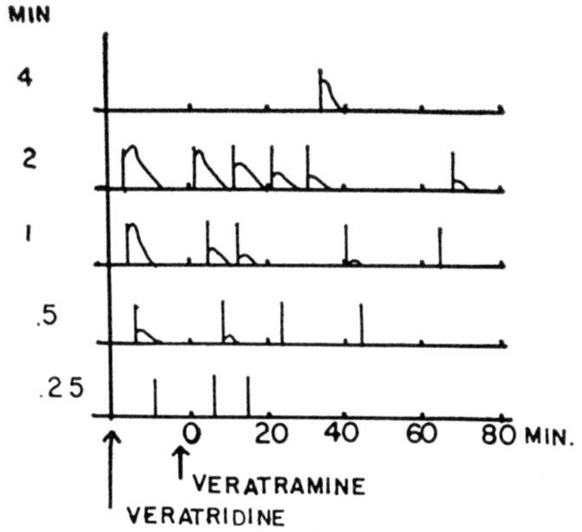

FIG. 3. Influence of rate of stimulation and veratramine on the veratrine response. *Rana pipiens*, male. Sartorius muscle. Ordinate: tension. The figures refer to the stimulus interval preceding each veratrine response. Abscissa: time in minutes after the addition of veratramine. The veratrine responses are traced from the original records.

transient decline of the VR the electrical activity of the cell could be shown to be the same as that observed after veratramine shown in figure 2.

Iodoacetic acid (18 experiments) was shown to act on the VR in a manner different from that of veratramine, strophanthin and quinine. After having added iodoacetate 10^{-4} to the Ringer-veratridine bath, the VR remained unchanged for several minutes then both—the first quick rise of tension and the VR—gradually declined in height. The rate of the tension decrease was dependent on the initial height of the VR and was not always equal for both parts; but in no case was only the VR affected. According to our definition therefore iodoacetic acid has no antiveratrinic activity.

The influence of *dinitrophenol* (7 experiments in concentrations between 10^{-8} and 10^{-6}), *sodium cyanide* (9 experiments at 10^{-4}) and *nitrogen* (3 experiments) on the VR followed the pattern described for iodoacetate. The time constant of the effect varied with different concentrations and different substances. By varying the concentration and stimulus frequency no indication could be found that any one of these substances had antiveratrinic activity. A representative experiment is plotted in figure 4B.

The influence of *sodium excess* in the Ringer solution (120 per cent to 135 per cent as compared to normal Ringer 100 per cent) on the VR was investigated

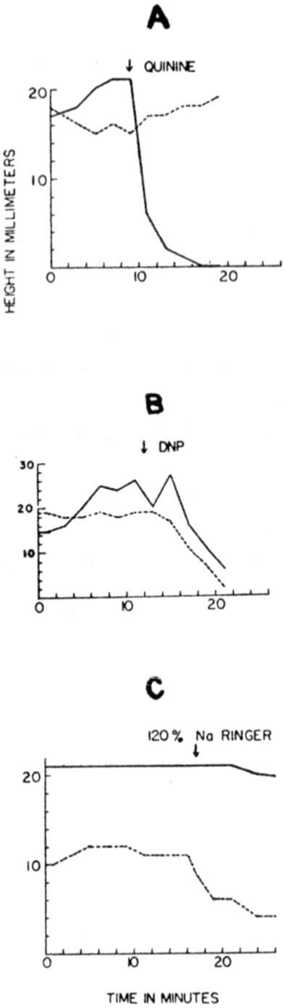

FIG. 4. Three ways in which substances influence the veratrine response.
Rana pipiens, male. Sartorius muscle. Ordinate: tension as measured in mm. on the original record. Abscissa: experimental time. Solid line: height of second tension rise. Broken line: height of twitch. A: In A, quinine abolished the second tension rise while the twitch remained constant. B: In B, dinitrophenol caused both the twitch and the second tension rise to decrease simultaneously. C: In C, excess sodium caused the twitch to decrease while the second tension rise remained relatively constant.

in 5 experiments. The pattern of the influence of sodium excess on the VR was found different from both patterns described earlier. Figure 4C shows a representative experiment. It can be seen that the known decrease of twitch height in Ringer with excess sodium does not coincide with a decrease of the VR. On the other hand, in some experiments the VR increased simultaneously with the decrease in twitch height. This effect lasted only 15 minutes; and no systematic studies were made over a long period of time. Only in one experiment electrical records were obtained from the muscle fibers. The variation of the data obtained from different fibers was too great to make valid statements about the height of the membrane potential, the action potential, or the repetitive discharges. However, the increase of the VR under sodium excess corresponded electrically to a higher number of repetitive discharges per unit time and a decrease in distance between the stimulus artifact and the first action potential when compared to the control VR in the same muscle.

Decamethonium bromide was added in 4 experiments in which the muscle preparation under veratridine was stimulated alternately through the nerve and directly at the muscle tissue. At a concentration of 5×10^{-5} decamethonium inhibited the effect of indirect stimulation while direct stimulation still produced an unchanged VR. In two of the four experiments, exchanging the bathing solution for normal Ringer resulted in a restoration of the VR when the muscle was stimulated through the nerve. Electrical records taken after the addition of decamethonium 10^{-4} in one experiment showed that repetitive discharges occurred.

DISCUSSION. In our veratridine experiments the average membrane potential was 73.9 ± 9.6 mV as compared to 88 ± 1 mV found by other authors in the normal frog sartorius muscle (Nastuk and Hodgkin, 1950). We have no measurements of our own with unpoisoned muscles. Straub (1956) found the same effect of veratridine on the resting potential of myelinated nerve fibers of the frog. The membrane potential in each cell showed a stable value to which it returned after a VR. However, a wide variation existed in height of membrane potential from cell to cell, and some abnormally high and low values were observed. There seemed to be no relationship of the height of the resting potential to either the VR or the ability of the cell to produce repetitive discharges. Similar findings in nerve fibers were reported by Guttman (1940), Acheson and Rosenblueth (1941) and Hodler, Staempfli and Tasaki (1950). It may indicate that not the height of the membrane potential but its instability is characteristic for the action of veratridine in low concentrations.

The amplitude of the action potential appeared distinctly decreased under the conditions of our experiments: 47.2 ± 1.8 mV as compared to 119 ± 1 mV (Nastuk and Hodgkin, 1950). This is also confirmed by measurements on the nerve by Graham and Gasser (1931) and Schmitt and Gasser (1933). The height of the action potential seems independent of the increased twitch height under veratridine as was found already by Rosenblueth *et al.* (1941). It seems the more probable that the low action potentials which we found are attributable to the veratridine, since development of the full antiveratrinic action sometimes brought back overshooting action potentials on a higher membrane potential.

If the correlation between frequency of repetitive discharges, stimulus interval, and steepness of second tension rise, as shown in figure 1, could be confirmed in further experiments (possibly the two first properties also in nerve fibers) it would mean that immediately after a VR the muscle becomes refractory to a second VR, but not to a single action potential. The longer the interval between stimuli the greater the VR. The membrane of the veratrinized muscle behaves like that of the nerve when stimulated with alternating current (Schaefer and Goepfert, 1937). The characteristic of the membrane which determines the frequency of conducted impulses would be dependent on the rest period which the muscle had after the last VR. That the repetitive discharges become smaller and at last cease is also consistent with the findings of Schaefer and Goepfert (1937) on the normal nerve membrane. They describe a slowly developing inhibition of conducted stimuli at high frequency stimulation.

No definite statements about excitation-contraction coupling in the VR can be made on the basis of our experiments since our tension records are not from single fibers. However, the parallelism between the steepness of tension rise and density of repetitive discharges appears striking enough (figure 1). There seem to be no parallel measurements about the phenomenon of dependence of frequency of discharges and the preceding resting period in nerve fibers. If this relationship could be found consistently it would be a further indication that veratridine acts on the excitable mechanisms of the membrane, and the contractile processes only follow the changes in the membrane without dissociation. This statement does not refer to the relaxation of the muscle in the VR, as we did not register the negative afterpotential in its end phase.

If the assumption is correct that veratridine acts on the excitable mechanisms of the cell membrane it should be inactive when applied to the isolated contractile substance. Robb (personal communication) made such experiments with actomyosin threads with a technique described previously (Robb and Mallov, 1953). Robb found that "veratridine in a concentration which affects the whole muscle fiber does not enhance shortening of weighted threads to a degree which is statistically valid."

The old observation could be confirmed that neither the nerve nor the endplate are necessary for the VR of skeletal muscle. The result of the decamethonium experiments seems of interest since this substance blocks neuromuscular transmission at the endplate in a different way from that of curare (Paton and Zaimis, 1952). The depolarization of the membrane in the endplate region by decamethonium obviously did not interfere with the origination of a VR in muscle fiber.

Considering the substances which show no antiveratrinic activity, several metabolic processes become unlikely as being directly affected by varatridine. It is improbable that veratridine interferes primarily with the oxidative processes, because lack of oxygen (experiments in nitrogen atmosphere) and blocking of oxygen transport (sodium cyanide experiments) do not interfere specifically with the VR. Likewise there seems no direct interference with the acetylcholine metabolism (Grupp, 1951). The experiments of Sandow and Kiebel (1952) can be interpreted in the same way if the antiveratrinic action is defined as strictly not affecting the twitch height. The results of the experiments with iodoacetic acid and dinitrophenol would seem to indicate that veratridine affects neither the formation of lactic acid nor the oxidation-phosphorylation coupling in muscle.

The group of antiveratrinic substances is chemically not homogeneous. The cellular mechanism of action of cardiac glycosides as well as of quinine and veratramine is unknown and consequently little can be said concerning the mechanism of their antiveratrinic action. Recent work done with strophanthin on erythrocytes (Schatzmann, 1953) and frog skeletal muscle (Schatzmann and Witt, 1954) suggests that digitalis glycosides interfere with an active ion transport mechanism in the cell membrane. As strophanthin is an antagonist of veratridine the ion transport mechanism across the cell membrane might be the point of attack of both substances, however, the data indicate that such an antagonism would not be competitive in nature.

The change in the VR after antiveratrinic substances seemed not to be brought about only by a participation of fewer and fewer fibers in the VR. Our single cell records indicated that there existed, at least in many fibers, a transient state in which the VR in each fiber is diminished through a diminished frequency of repetitive discharges from each cell. If the lower parts of figures 1 and 2 are compared there seems to be a certain similarity in the action of a short stimulus interval and antiveratrinic action. In both cases the frequency of repetitive discharges is diminished. The antiveratrinic substances may also increasingly prolong the period in which the muscle is refractory to a VR, as was suspected in the discussion of the result of a small stimulus interval. The action of veratridine appears to be coupled to a mechanism which is active in the restoration period after activity. There exists another indication that the veratridine action is coupled to a process in connection with the frequency of muscle activity. Benforado and Witt (1954) observed that the lethal dose of veratridine infused into a heart was dependent on the heart rate; faster beating hearts went into fibrillation at an earlier time, *i.e.*, after the administration of a smaller lethal dose.

An unstable membrane potential, a low action potential, repetitive discharges depending probably in their frequency on the length of the preceding recovery period, the indications for a close parallelism between excitation and contraction, the probable indifference of the contractile substance itself to veratridine, the influence of sodium excess on the VR, and antiveratrinic activity—all these seem to indicate that veratridine affects a mechanism related to the excitation of the cell membrane. This mechanism would be responsible for maintaining the right concentrations of ions on both sides of the membrane and would be responsible for the renormalization of the concentrations after an activity. Consequently, more direct data than electrical records, namely measurements of ionic flux into and out of the cell, should provide the information necessary to elucidate the mechanism of action of veratridine on the muscle cell.

SUMMARY

Simultaneous records were made of the isometric tension developed by about 100 fibers of the frog sartorius muscle and the electrical activity of a single fiber.

Administration of veratridine 10^{-7} resulted in a state of the muscle where a single stimulus was followed by the characteristic two-peaked tension response simultaneous with a series of electrical discharges; these were superimposed on a negative afterpotential. The second tension rise (VR) and the frequency of firing was higher (7.2 msec. average distance) when the muscle had been allowed to rest for four minutes instead of for only one minute (19.5 msec. average distance). The membrane potential under veratridine was found relatively low (73.9 mV) and unstable, the action potential without an overshoot (47.2 mV).

Addition of veratramine 10^{-5}, strophanthin 3×10^{-6}, quinine or quinidine 10^{-5} to the veratrinized muscle normalized the situation in that a single stimulus was again followed by a single action potential and twitch. In the transient period when the full antiveratrinic action had not yet developed, unusually slow repetitive discharges were observed together with a small second tension rise.

At lower temperatures (6°C.) higher veratridine concentrations (1.3×10^{-6}) were necessary to elicit a VR, but the antiveratrinic action of veratramine was at all temperatures fully developed at 10^{-5}.

Lack of oxygen, addition of sodium cyanide, iodoacetic acid, and dinitrophenol reduced the amplitude of both parts of the mechanical response simultaneously; they had no antiveratrinic action.

Sodium excess in the Ringer bath diminished the twitch before it influenced the VR.

Like curare, decamethonium did not affect the VR and repetitive discharges in a concentration which blocked neuromuscular transmission.

A mechanism influencing the ionic flux into and out of the muscle cell in connection with excitation is discussed as a possible site of action of veratridine.

REFERENCES

ACHESON, G. H., AND ROSENBLUETH, A.: Am. J. Physiol., **133:** 736, 1941.
ARORA, R. B.: THIS JOURNAL, **108:** 26, 1953.
ARORA, R. B., AND KRAYER, O.: THIS JOURNAL, **106:** 37, 1952.
BENFORADO, J. M., AND WITT, P. N.: THIS JOURNAL, **110:** 334, 1954.
DE FONBRUNE, P.: Monographies de l'Institut Pasteur: Paris, 1949.
FUENTES, J.: THIS JOURNAL, **119:** 225, 1957.
GRAHAM, H., AND GASSER, H.: THIS JOURNAL, **43:** 163, 1931.
GRUPP, M.: Arch. f. exper. Path. u. Pharmakol., **212:** 221, 1951.
GUTTMAN, R.: J. Gen. Physiol., **23:** 343, 1940.
HODLER, J., STAEMPFLI, R., AND TASAKI, I.: Helv. Physiol. Acta, **8:** C 62, 1950.
KRAYER, O., AND ACHESON, G. H.: Physiol. Rev., **26:** 381, 1946.
KRAYER, O., AND GEORGE, H. W.: THIS JOURNAL, **103:** 249, 1951.
LING, G., AND GERARD, R. W.: J. Cell. Comp. Physiol., **34:** 383, 1949.
MIYAKE, Y.: Arb. a. d. Med. Fakultaet, Okayama, **6:** 237, 1939.
NASTUK, W. L., AND HODGKIN, A. L.: J. Cell. Comp. Physiol., **35:** 39, 1950.
PATON, W. D. M., AND ZAIMIS, E.: Pharmacol. Rev., **4:** 219, 1952.
ROBB, J. S., AND MALLOV, S.: THIS JOURNAL, **108:** 258, 1953.
ROSENBLUETH, A., WILLS, G., AND HOAGLAND, H.: Am. J. Physiol., **133:** 724, 1941.
SANDOW, A.: The Yale J. Biol. & Med., **25:** 176, 1952.
SANDOW, A., AND KIEBEL, G.: Am. J. Physiol., **169:** 649, 1952.
SCHAEFER, H., AND GOEPFERT, H.: Pflüg. Arch. ges. Physiol., **238:** 684, 1937.
SCHATZMANN, H. J.: Helv. Physiol. Acta, **11:** 346, 1953.
SCHATZMANN, H. J., AND WITT, P. N.: THIS JOURNAL, **112:** 501, 1954.
SCHMITT, F. O., AND GASSER, H.: Am. J. Physiol., **104:** 320, 1933.
STRAUB, R.: Helv. Physiol. Acta, **14:** 1, 1956.

ENZYMATIC OXIDATION OF PENTOBARBITAL AND THIOPENTAL[1]

JACK R. COOPER[2, 3] AND BERNARD B. BRODIE

Laboratory of Chemical Pharmacology, National Heart Institute, National Institutes of Health, Public Health Service, U. S. Department of Health, Education, and Welfare, Bethesda, Maryland

Received for publication December 19, 1956

Barbiturates are generally metabolized *in vivo* by pathways involving oxidation of the alkyl sidechain; and a number of oxidized products, including alcohols, ketones and acids have been isolated from the urine of animals and man receiving various barbiturates (Maynert 1952; Bush *et al.*, 1953; Brodie *et al.*, 1950; Titus and Weiss, 1955).

Gould and Shideman (1952) were the first investigators to study the requirements of tissue homogenates in barbiturate metabolism. They demonstrated that there is little disappearance of thiopental in a rat liver homogenate unless it is fortified with nicotinamide, adenosinetriphosphate, cytochrome c and a Krebs cycle intermediate. Kidney, brain, skeletal muscle, heart and intestines were also found capable of metabolizing the drug. The conclusion was drawn that the system catalyzing the metabolism of thiopental is dependent on the tricarboxylic acid cycle.

More definite information concerning the metabolism of a barbiturate resulted from studies (Cooper and Brodie, 1955) demonstrating that hexobarbital is oxidized to keto-hexobarbital by the action of an enzyme system in liver microsomes and that this system requires both reduced triphosphopyridine nucleotide (TPNH) and oxygen.

The present paper compares the enzyme systems in rabbit that catalyze the sidechain oxidation of pentobarbital, and its thio-analogue, thiopental. It will be demonstrated that both barbiturates are oxidized by enzyme systems that require oxygen and TPNH, and are localized in microsomes of liver cells. Furthermore, pentobarbital is only oxidized by microsomes of liver whereas thiopental is metabolized by microsomes of kidney and by other tissues as well.

MATERIALS AND METHODS. *Materials.* A mixture of two diastereoisomeric pentobarbital alcohols 5-ethyl-5-(3-hydroxy-1-methylbutyl) barbituric acid was kindly donated by Dr. Elwood Titus of the National Heart Institute. Triphosphopyridine nucleotide (TPN), diphosphopyridine nucleotide (DPN) and glucose-6-phosphate dehyrdogenase were obtained from the Sigma Chemical Company. TPNH was prepared by the method of Kaplan *et al.* (1952).

Preparation of tissue samples. The preparation of tissue samples was carried out at 0 to 3°C. Male albino rabbits were stunned, exsanguinated, and the tissues quickly removed

---

[1] Presented in part before the American Society for Pharmacology and Experimental Therapeutics, New Haven, Connecticut, 1953.

[2] Smith, Kline and French Research Fellow.

[3] Present address, Department of Pharmacology, Yale University School of Medicine, New Haven, Connecticut.

and chilled. Homogenates were prepared in 2 volumes of 0.1 *M* phosphate buffer, pH 7.4, with a Waring blendor. Liver supernatant fractions (9000 × *g* supernate), liver microsomal and liver soluble fractions (78,000 × *g*) were prepared by differential centrifugation of liver homogenates as described previously (Cooper and Brodie, 1955).

The barbiturates were incubated with the various preparations in a Dubnoff metabolic shaking incubator at 37°C. using oxygen as the gas phase. Enzyme activity was determined by measuring the disappearance of barbiturate. In most experiments, barbiturate substrate was incubated for 1 hour with 2 ml. of enzyme preparation, 50 micromoles of nicotinamide, 25 micromoles of $MgCl_2$, 0.26 micromole of TPN, and 0.1 *M* phosphate buffer, pH 7.4, to a final volume of 4 ml.

Chemical methods. Pentobarbital and thiopental were determined by methods previously described (Brodie *et al.*, 1953; Brodie *et al.*, 1950).

Paper chromatography. Samples were chromatographed on Whatman No. 3 paper with butanol saturated with 1 per cent aqueous ammonium hydroxide as the ascending solvent. The paper was dried in air and examined under an ultraviolet lamp (No. V4 mineralight lamp). The products showed up as dark spots on a purplish-blue background. The sensitivity of the test permitted the detection of about 0.2 micromole of pentobarbital, pentobarbital alcohol or thiopental.

RESULTS. *Distribution of enzyme activity in various tissues.* The barbiturates were incubated for three hours with slices of various rabbit tissues in Krebs-Ringer phosphate buffer, at pH 7.4. Pentobarbital was metabolized only by the liver whereas thiopental underwent biotransformation in a number of tissues with liver being the most active, kidney and brain being less active and heart showing a slight but measurable activity (table 1). Similar results were obtained with rat tissues. These observations were in general agreement with those of other workers who reported that thiopental but not pentobarbital is metabolized by liver, kidney and brain (Dorfman and Goldbaum, 1947; Gould and Shideman, 1952).

Requirements of enzyme systems in liver homogenates. Pentobarbital and thiopental were metabolized to only a small extent in a rabbit liver homogenate. Enzyme activity was markedly increased by the addition of nicotinamide and either TPN or DPN. Nicotinamide was needed to protect the pyridine nucleotides from enzymatic hydrolysis (Mann and Quastel, 1941). It could not be concluded which of the two pyridine nucleotides was needed for activity since DPN can be converted to TPN in crude liver homogenates. The homogenate

TABLE 1

Metabolism of barbiturate in various rabbit tissues

Three hundred and fifty mgm. tissue slice, 2 micromoles of barbiturate and 3 ml. of Krebs-Ringer phosphate buffer, pH 7.4, were incubated for 3 hours at 37°C. with oxygen as the gas phase.

Tissue	Barbiturate metabolized	
	Pentobarbital	Thiopental
	μmoles	*μmoles*
Liver	0.70	0.73
Kidney	0.0	0.38
Brain	0.0	0.24
Heart	0.0	0.14
Skeletal muscle	0.0	Trace

TABLE 2

Requirement for TPN by dialyzed rabbit liver homogenate

To 2 ml. of dialyzed liver homogenate were added 1 micromole of barbiturate, 50 micromoles of nicotinamide, 25 micromoles of $MgCl_2$ and phosphate buffer to a final volume of 4 ml.

Additions	Barbiturate metabolized	
	Pentobarbital	Thiopental
	μmoles	*μmoles*
None	0.05	0.0
0.2 micromole DPN	0.05	0.0
0.2 micromole TPN	0.30	0.31

TABLE 3

Intracellular distribution of enzyme activity

Various cell fractions equivalent to 0.66 gm. of rabbit liver were incubated with 1 micromole of barbiturate as described under METHODS.

System	Barbiturate metabolized	
	Pentobarbital	Thiopental
	μmoles	*μmoles*
Whole homogenate	0.24	0.30
Supernatant fraction (9000 × *g* supernate)	0.32	0.28
Microsomes	0.0	0.0
Soluble fraction (78,000 × *g* supernate)	0.0	0.0
Microsomes + soluble fraction	0.35	0.29

was therefore dialyzed for 10 hours at 0°C. against 0.1 *M* phosphate buffer, pH 7.4, to remove the pyridine nucleotides as well as ATP, which is a cofactor in the conversion of DPN to TPN. The barbiturates were no longer metabolized by the dialyzed homogenates, but the activity could be restored, in part, by the addition of nicotinamide and catalytic amounts of TPN, but not by DPN (table 2). Mg^{++} and glucose-6-phosphate also increased the activity of the dialyzed homogenates. The metabolism of the barbiturates did not occur under anerobic conditions, but equal activity was observed with air or oxygen as the gas phase. These requirements were similar to those found necessary for the metabolism of hexobarbital (Cooper and Brodie 1955).

The amount of pentobarbital or thiopental oxidized after various periods of incubation showed that no further oxidation took place after 1 hour with amounts of substrate ranging from 1 to 2 micromoles. At this time about one-third of the substrates had disappeared. The addition of fresh homogenate resulted in further metabolism of the barbiturates indicating that the enzyme had been inactivated during the incubation period. Further evidence of this was found by preincubating the homogenate for 1 hour and then adding barbiturate; no activity was observed.

Intracellular localization of enzyme activity. Almost all the enzyme activity of a liver homogenate was found in the 9000 × *g* supernate which contained the microsomes and soluble fraction of the cell (table 3). The supernatant fraction

TABLE 4

Requirement for TPNH

Microsomes equivalent to 0.66 gm. liver were incubated with 1 micromole of barbiturate as described under METHODS.

Additions	Barbiturate metabolized	
	Pentobarbital	Thiopental
	μmoles	*μmoles*
Microsomes + 1.0 micromole TPN	0.0	0.0
Microsomes + 1.0 micromole TPN and 0.5 ml. soluble fraction (78,000 × *g* supernate)	0.35	0.44
Microsomes + 1.0 micromole TPN + 4 micromoles glucose-6-phosphate + glucose-6-phosphate dehydrogenase	0.28	0.38
Microsomes + TPNH*	0.30	0.44

* Eight-tenths micromole of TPNH was added at 10-minute intervals to the incubation system since TPNH disappeared rapidly even in the absence of substrate. The addition of an equivalent amount of TPN did not result in barbiturate metabolism.

was separated into microsomes and the soluble portion of the cell by centrifugation at 78,000 × *g*. Neither of these fractions alone demonstrated activity but when added together activity was restored.

The requirement for TPN and oxygen and the recovery of virtually all the enzyme activity of the homogenate in the 9000 × *g* supernate suggested that as with hexobarbital (Cooper and Brodie 1955), the enzyme that oxidized the barbiturates was present in microsomes and that the role of the soluble fraction was to maintain the actual coenzyme TPNH in a reduced form. This was shown to be so, as indicated in table 4.

Identification of reaction products. Pentobarbital: Maynert and Dawson (1952) isolated from dog urine two diastereoisomeric forms of 5-ethyl-5-(3-hydroxy-1-methylbutyl) barbituric acid with almost identical solubility characteristics. These metabolites are subsequently referred to as pentobarbital alcohols. One of these, a *d*-isomer, was found by Brodie *et al.* (1953) to be a major metabolite of pentobarbital in man. Titus and Weiss (1955) administered pentobarbital-2-C^{14} to dogs and isolated an additional metabolite from the urine, 5-ethyl-5-(3-carboxyl-1-methylpropyl) barbituric acid, referred to subsequently as pentobarbital carboxylic acid.

To identify the metabolites of pentobarbital in liver homogenate, 200 micromoles of pentobarbital, 50 micromoles of TPN, 750 micromoles of $MgCl_2$, 500 micromoles of nicotinamide and 200 ml. of rabbit liver supernatant (9000 × *g*) were incubated for 75 minutes at 37°C. Analyses of an aliquot of the mixture indicated that about 50 per cent of the pentobarbital had been metabolized. Extraction of another aliquot, substituting the more polar solvent ether for petroleum ether, indicated the presence of not only pentobarbital but considerable amounts of material which also absorbed light at 255 mμ in 1 *N* NaOH. The total optical density of the extracted material accounted for about 100 per cent of the incubated pentobarbital. Since the ultraviolet absorption of pentobarbital depends on the intact malonylurea ring, this result indicated that the barbituric acid ring had not been cleaved.

The bulk of the incubation mixture was acidified and extracted several times with ether. The ether extracts were pooled, an equal volume of petroleum ether added, and the barbiturate material returned to an aqueous phase by shaking with dilute NaOH. The aqueous phase was separated, acidified and dried by lyophilization. The lyophilized material was dissolved in 0.1 *M* pyrophosphate buffer, pH 9.3, and subjected to an eight transfer countercurrent distribution using 5 ml. volumes of butanol and aqueous phase. Tubes 1 to 3, 4 to 6, and 7 to 9 were pooled. The aqueous phase of each of the three pools was adjusted to a pH of about 11.5 and 15 ml. of petroleum ether added to each organic phase. The material in each pool was returned to the aqueous phase by shaking. The aqueous phases were separated, acidified and each one extracted with 5 volumes of ether. The ether extracts were evaporated to a small volume at room temperature in a current of nitrogen and chromatographed using the solvent system described in METHODS. Pentobarbital and the two diastereoisomeric forms of pentobarbital alcohol,[4] were chromatographed simultaneously but no reference standard of pentobarbital carboxylic acid was available. The material from tubes 1 to 3 chromatographed as pentobarbital (R_f 0.8), tubes 4 to 6 as pentobarbital alcohol (R_f 0.5). Tubes 7 to 9 contained mainly material having the same R_f, 0.15, as that reported by Titus and Weiss (1955) for pentobarbital carboxylic acid but also contained a trace of pentobarbital alcohol. The spots were cut out and eluted with 80 per cent methanol. Ultraviolet absorption measurement indicated that the alcohol and acidic metabolites had the same spectrum as the parent compound and were formed in about equal amounts.

Since no pentobarbital carboxylic acid was available as a reference standard, further proof of the proposed acidic metabolite was undertaken by determination of the pKa of the apparent acid using the partition coefficient method of Butler (1953). The partition coefficients were determined from the distribution of the material between chloroform containing 5 per cent isoamyl alcohol and aqueous solutions at various pH values (0.1 *M* acetate buffer pH 4.53, 0.1 *M* citrate buffer pH 3.58 and 0.1 *M* HCl). The pKa of the apparent pentobarbital carboxylic acid was calculated from the observed partition coefficients as 4.4. This indicates that the substance is a carboxylic acid and the pKa value corresponds closely to the value of 4.5 for the authentic compound reported by Titus and Weiss (1955).

Thiopental: Brodie *et al.*, (1950) have shown, following thiopental administration to man, that there is excreted in the urine a carboxylic acid (thiopental carboxylic acid). This substance was identified as 5-ethyl-5-(3-carboxy-1-methylpropyl) thiobarbituric acid (Wood and Horning, 1953).

Seven hundred ml. of rabbit liver supernatant were incubated for 90 minutes with 200 micromoles of thiopental, 50 micromoles of TPN, 500 micromoles of nicotinamide, and 750 micromoles of $MgCl_2$. Using an aliquot of the mixture it

[4] The two diastereoisomeric forms have almost the same R_f values and cannot be distinguished by the chromatographic procedure used.

was shown as with pentobarbital that the metabolism of thiopental did not involve cleavage of the thiobarbituric acid ring. The bulk of the mixture was acidified and extracted several times with ether. An aliquot of the ether extract was shaken with 0.1 *N* NaOH. The aqueous phase was separated, adjusted with HCl to about pH 7 and then extracted with petroleum ether to remove the major part of unchanged thiopental. The aqueous phase was then acidified and extracted several times with ether. The ether was reduced to a small volume at room temperature under a stream of nitrogen and chromatographed as described in METHODS. Three spots were noted under ultraviolet light; one with the same R_f as thiopental (0.80), one with an R_f of 0.56 and the third with an R_f of 0.15. No thiopental metabolites were available as reference standards but by analogy with pentobarbital it might be assumed that the spot with R_f 0.56 was thiopental alcohol and the material with R_f 0.15 was thiopental carboxylic acid. The major metabolic product was the presumed carboxylic acid, for the material with an R_f of 0.56 always showed up as a very faint spot both in this and other experiments involving both liver slices and homogenates. On spraying the paper with a copper sulfate reagent[5] which reacts with thiobarbiturates (Raventos, personal communication), the spots turned green, indicating that the metabolites contained the thioketo linkage.

To isolate the thiopental carboxylic acid, the remainder of the ether extract of the incubation mixture was shaken with 0.1 *N* NaOH. The aqueous phase was adjusted to pH 7 and extracted with petroleum ether to remove the main portion of the unchanged thiopental. The aqueous phase was lyophilized and the residue subjected to an 8 transfer countercurrent distribution using 10-ml. volumes of 1 *M* phosphate buffer, pH 5.9, and petroleum ether containing 56 per cent isoamyl alcohol. The contents of tubes 2 to 6 which contained material with almost identical partition ratios were pooled. The pooled aqueous phase was adjusted to pH 11 to 12 by the addition of NaOH solution and the barbiturate material taken into the aqueous phase by shaking. The aqueous phase was removed, acidified, and extracted twice with 3 volumes of ether. The ether extracts were pooled, dried with anhydrous sodium sulfate and evaporated to dryness in a warm water bath under a stream of nitrogen. The material was taken up with a small volume of 0.1 *N* NaOH. On addition of 1 *N* HCl, crystals formed overnight at 3°C. These were dried *in vacuo* and found to melt at 171 to 179°C. The melting point of pure thiopental carboxylic acid has been reported to be 185 to 187°C. There was not enough of the material to attempt recrystallization. Instead, the pKa of the material was determined as described for pentobarbital carboxylic acid. The material was dissolved in ethylene dichloride containing 1.5 per cent isoamyl alcohol and partition coefficients determined between this solvent and 0.1 *N* HCl and 0.1 *M* acetate buffer, pH 5.0. The pKa calculated from the partition coefficients was 4.4 indicating that the metabolite was a carboxylic acid. In addition, its ultraviolet absorption spectrum was identical with that of the parent compound.

[5] Three ml. of 4 per cent cupric sulfate plus one ml. of pyridine in 36 ml. of water.

Thiopental metabolism in kidney homogenates. The enzyme system in rabbit kidney which catalyzes the metabolism of thiopental was investigated. This system was shown to have the same requirements as the one in liver, and to also be localized in microsomes. The main product of thiopental metabolism in the kidney supernatant was probably the carboxylic acid as indicated by its R_f on a paper chromatogram. No thiopental alcohol was demonstrated to be present but this may merely reflect the small degree of metabolism of thiopental in kidney relative to liver.

DISCUSSION. The present investigation on the metabolism of pentobarbital in rabbit tissues, *in vitro*, the previously reported study on hexobarbital, and unpublished results with secobarbital indicate that the oxygen barbiturates are oxidized only in liver, whereas the thiobarbiturate, thiopental, as well as thiamylal (unpublished), are also metabolized by kidney and brain. In general, barbiturate metabolism by microsomes appears to involve sidechain oxidation rather than ring cleavage, though in experiments with C^{14}-pentobarbital in dogs, Titus and Weiss (1955) demonstrated a slight amount of ring cleavage.

Pentobarbital forms two products in about equal amounts, as follows:

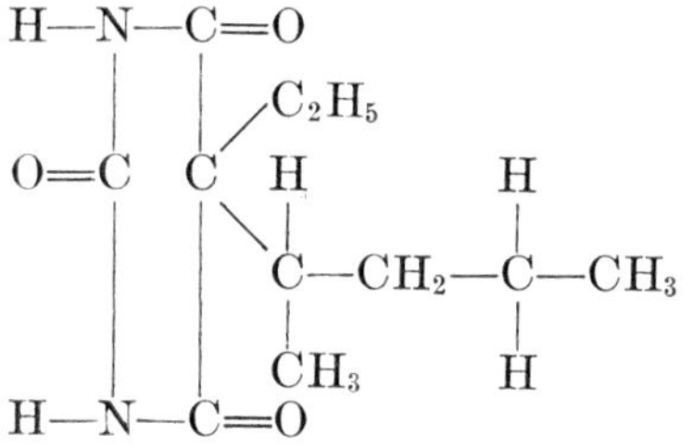

Pentobarbital

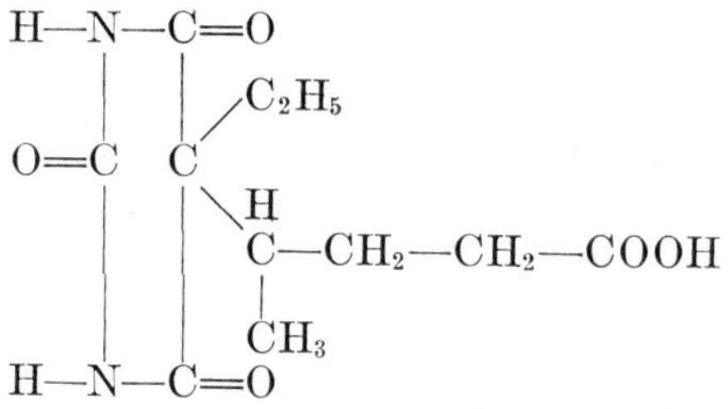

Pentobarbital carboxylic acid

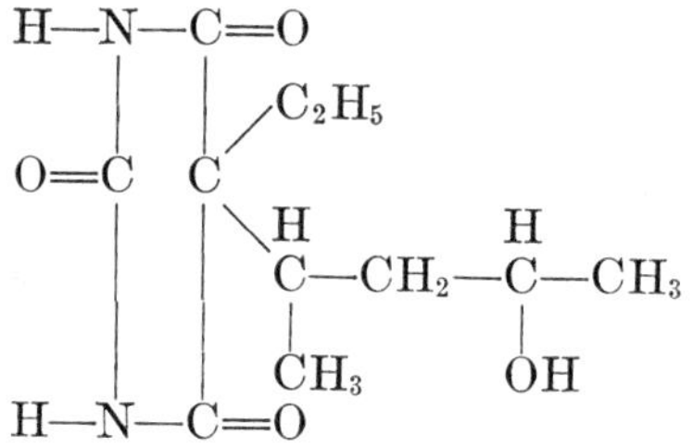

Pentobarbital alcohol

Thiopental is converted to the corresponding thio compounds, but the major metabolite appears to be the acid. The alcohol forms in only minor amounts and has not been identified with certainty because of the lack of a reference compound.

It is not yet known whether a single or a multiplicity of enzyme systems are involved in the oxidation of the various barbiturates. Evidence at hand suggests that more than one enzyme is involved. Thus, pentobarbital (and probably thiopental) is oxidized to both an alcohol and an acid. The carboxyl group of the acidic metabolite is on the terminal carbon atom whereas the alcohol metabolite represents an oxidation in position three. It would be surprising to find that the same enzyme system catalyzed the formation of both these metabolites. There is rather definitive evidence that oxygen barbiturates and thiobarbiturates are metabolized by different systems in the finding that the former compounds are oxidized only by liver whereas thiobarbiturates are also metabolized by kidney and brain.

The present studies indicate that the enzyme systems responsible for the side-chain oxidation of oxygen and thiobarbiturates are localized in liver microsomes and have the requirements for both TPNH and oxygen. A number of recent reports on drug metabolism have shown that a variety of drug metabolic transformations are catalyzed by enzyme systems in microsomes and require TPNH and oxygen (Brodie *et al.*, 1955). These reactions include N-dealkylation (La Du *et al.*, 1955), ether cleavage (Axelrod, 1956), hydroxylation of aromatic rings (Mitoma *et al.*, 1956), deamination of primary amines (Axelrod, 1954), and formation of sulfoxides from sulphur containing compounds (Brodie and Kamm, unpublished).

The mechanism of these microsomal oxidations still remains elusive. The role of TPNH is being studied in this laboratory. It has been shown that a step common to the various oxidative drug pathways is the oxidation of TPNH to TPN by an enzyme in microsomes. This oxidation is not blocked by cyanide and therefore does not involve the cytochrome c–cytochrome oxidase system. A product of the reaction is a substance with peroxidase-like properties which is possibly a common intermediate in the various types of drug oxidation (Gillette *et al.*, 1957).

Some of the observations of Gould and Shideman (1952) on the metabolism of thiopental by rat liver homogenates may be explained in the light of our observations. As mentioned in the introduction, these workers found a requirement for nicotinamide, ATP, cytochrome c and a Krebs cycle intermediate in their homogenate preparation. It may be inferred that succinate, the Krebs cycle intermediate, and cytochrome c served to generate ATP, which in turn was utilized in the conversion of DPN to TPN.

Winters *et al.* (1955) have reported the presence of an enzymatic mechanism in rat liver that converts thiopental to pentobarbital. Under our experimental conditions the conversion of thiopental to pentobarbital was not observed. This suggests that the requirements or the cellular localization of the two systems are different.

SUMMARY

Pentobarbital and its thio-analogue thiopental are oxidized in rabbit liver homogenates. Thiopental, in addition, is metabolized to a lesser extent in other tissues, especially kidney and brain.

Pentobarbital is converted to an alcohol with the hydroxyl group on carbon three of the sidechain and an acid with the carboxyl group on carbon four. These metabolites are formed in about equal amounts. Thiopental appears to yield mainly the corresponding acid and a small amount of the alcohol.

As with the oxidation of a number of other drug metabolic transformations, the oxidative system for the barbiturates occurs in the microsomes and requires TPNH and oxygen. The microsomal systems cause little or no splitting of the malonylurea ring.

The oxidation of pentobarbital and thiopental seems to be carried out by different catalytic mechanisms.

REFERENCES

AXELROD, J.: THIS JOURNAL, **110:** 2, 1954.
AXELROD, J.: Biochem. J., **63:** 634, 1956.
BRODIE, B. B., MARK, L. C., PAPPER, E. M., LIEF, P. A., BERNSTEIN, E., AND ROVENSTINE, E. A.: THIS JOURNAL, **98:** 85, 1950.
BRODIE, B. B., BURNS, J. J., MARK, L. C., LIEF, P. A., BERNSTEIN, E., AND PAPPER, E. M.: THIS JOURNAL, **109:** 26, 1953.
BRODIE, B. B., AXELROD, J., COOPER, J. R., GAUDETTE, L., LA DU, B. N., MITOMA, C., AND UDENFRIEND, S.: Science, **121:** 603, 1955.
BUTLER, T. C.: THIS JOURNAL, **108:** 474, 1953.
BUSH, M. T., BUTLER, T. C., AND DICKISON, H. L.: THIS JOURNAL, **108:** 104, 1953.
COOPER, J. R., AND BRODIE, B. B.: THIS JOURNAL, **114:** 409, 1955.
DORFMAN, A., AND GOLDBAUM, L. R.: THIS JOURNAL, **90:** 330, 1947.
GILLETTE, J., BRODIE, B. B., AND LA DU, B. N.: THIS JOURNAL, **119:** 532, 1957.
GOULD, T. C., AND SHIDEMAN, F. E.: THIS JOURNAL, **104:** 427, 1952.
KAPLAN, N. O., COLOWICK, S. P., AND NEUFELD, E. F.: J. Biol. Chem., **195:** 107, 1952.
LA DU, B. N., GAUDETTE, L., TROUSOF, N., AND BRODIE, B. B.: J. Biol. Chem., **214:** 741, 1955.
MANN, P. J. G., AND QUASTEL, S. H.: Biochem. J., **35:** 502, 1941.
MAYNERT, E. W., AND DAWSON, J. M.: J. Biol. Chem., **195:** 389, 1952.
MAYNERT, E. W.: Fed. Proc., **11:** 2, 625, 1952.
MITOMA, C., AND UDENFRIEND, S.: THIS JOURNAL, **113:** 40, 1955.
TITUS, E. O., AND WEISS, H.: J. Biol. Chem., **214:** 807, 1955.
WINTERS, W. D., SPECTOR, E., WALLACH, D. P., AND SHIDEMAN, F. E.: THIS JOURNAL, **114:** 343, 1955.
WOOD, H., AND HORNING, E.: J. Am. Chem. Soc., **75:** 5511, 1953.

THE DISTRIBUTION OF GOLD FOLLOWING THE INJECTION OF OBESITY-INDUCING DOSES OF AUROTHIOGLUCOSE IN THE MOUSE[1]

GERALD FRIEDMAN[2] AND JAY TEPPERMAN

Department of Pharmacology, State University of New York, Upstate Medical Center, Syracuse, New York

Received for publication December 19, 1956

Following the injection into mice of a single LD_{50} dose of aurothioglucose (ATG) about a third of the survivors regularly show an increased spontaneous food intake and, subsequently, varying degrees of obesity (Brecher and Waxler, 1949). Since the gold portion of the molecule appears to be involved in the production of the obesity (Drachman and Tepperman, 1954) and because the early deaths may have been due to heavy metal intoxication, it was pertinent 1) to study the tissue and body fluid distribution of gold in mice injected with obesity-inducing doses of aurothioglucose within 24 hours after injection, 2) to compare the gold distribution patterns of ATG-injected obese mice and those of ATG-injected non-obese mice months after injection; and 3) to compare the metal distribution patterns in acutely injected groups of mice in which marked toxicity differences had previously been noted; *i.e.*, mice injected in the fed and fasted state. The last part of the study was included because Brecher (personal communication), Owen (1953) and Drachman and Tepperman (1954) had all described reduction of mortality in previously starved mice injected with ATG.

METHODS AND MATERIALS. Approximately 300 female Albino mice (Albino Farms) were used in this study. Prior to each experiment they were maintained at about 26°C. and were permitted free access to water and Purina Dog Chow. All animals weighed between 17 and 25 grams at the time of injection.

Aurothioglucose[3] was used as a freshly prepared solution of a water soluble powder. Injections were made intraperitoneally in a dose of 0.8 mgm. of ATG per gram of body weight.

Organs were weighed on a Roller-Smith torsion balance. Blood samples were obtained directly from the right auricle in mice deeply anesthetized with pentobarbital sodium. The heparinized blood was centrifuged immediately and the separated plasma was stored in the frozen state until it was analyzed.

A staggered time schedule of injection and sacrifice permitted sample collections from complete groups of 10 animals on each of five successive days. After the organs were weighed they were placed on saline-moistened filter paper in petri dishes and stored in a freezer until they were analyzed for gold.

Unless it is specifically stated that pooled organs were used, all of the samples were analyzed individually for gold by a modification of the method of Block and Buchanan

---

[1] Taken fom a thesis written by Gerald Friedman in partial fulfillment of the requirements for a Ph.D. degree in pharmacology.

[2] Present address: Department of Pharmacology, University of Buffalo, School of Medicine, Buffalo, N. Y.

[3] The authors are grateful to Dr. Norman Heminway and the Schering Corporation for generous supplies of aurothioglucose.

(1940), which, in turn, was modified from the procedure of Pollard (1937). This method, which is based on the color produced by the reaction of *ortho*-dianisidine and auric chloride in a slightly acid solution buffered with potassium bifluoride, permits accurate and specific analysis for gold in quantities as low as 5 micrograms per sample. A series of experiments in which known amounts of gold were added to mouse liver, kidneys and gastrocnemius muscle showed recoveries of 90 to 103 per cent.

The modification of the original method consisted of two procedures: 1) the amount of *o*-dianisidine recommended by Block and Buchanan was doubled, but the amount of 1:4 HCl was the same; 2) it was found that losses of gold occurred in attempts at recovering 50 micrograms or less, as intense heating to dryness tended to volatilize not only the sulfuric acid but also the gold. To avoid this, approximately one ml. of sulfuric acid was left in the tube following strong heating. The remainder of the acid was removed by means of less intense heat from a microburner and by water-pump suction.

Probabilities were estimated according to student's test of "t" (Fisher, 1946).

EXPERIMENTAL DESIGN AND RESULTS. *Distribution of gold within 3 hr. after injection of ATG.* Female mice which weighed between 17 and 25 grams were injected intraperitoneally with 0.8 mgm. of ATG per gram of body weight, and groups of animals were sacrificed 15, 30, 60, 120 and 180 minutes after injection. Tissues analyzed in this experiment included: the entire liver, both kidneys, the gastrocnemius muscle, the whole brain and 0.1 ml. of plasma. The results of this experiment are shown in table 1.

It is evident that the peak plasma level occurred between 30 and 60 minutes after injection. Clearly, the concentration of gold in the kidney is very much higher than that in liver and muscle, and the concentrations in the latter organs, were, in turn, higher than that in brain. The brain concentrations were very close to the lowest concentrations that would have permitted analysis by this method, and thus the differences in brain concentration over the three hour period of observation have no real significance. It is of some interest that the gold concentration in the liver remained reasonably constant over the entire period studied.

TABLE 1

Tissue concentration of gold (mgm./gm.) after injection of ATG

Means ± S.D.; no. of mice per group in parentheses.

Organs	Minutes after injection				
	15	30	60	120	180
Liver	0.076 ± 0.01 (10)	0.082 ± 0.010 (9)	0.079 ± 0.007 (6)	0.058 ± 0.008 (9)	0.072 ± 0.004 (9)
Kidney	0.396 ± 0.04 (10)	0.732 ± 0.104 (9)	0.404 ± 0.061 (6)	0.184 ± 0.046 (9)	0.231 ± 0.033 (8)
Muscle	0.057 ± 0.006 (7)	0.082 ± 0.021 (5)	0.07 ± 0.021 (5)	0.019 ± 0.009 (10)	0.015 ± 0.005 (9)
Brain	0.006 ± 0.0004 (6)	0.005 ± 0.001 (5)	0.009 ± 0.002 (5)	0.002 ± 0.001 (9)	0.003 ± 0.001 (8)
Plasma	0.350 ± 0.05 (3)	0.546 ± 0.224 (6)	0.950 ± 0.336 (5)	0.148 ± 0.079 (6)	0.184 ± 0.047 (9)

TABLE 2

A comparison of hepatic gold content in ATG-obese and ATG-injected non-obese mice
Means of groups and standard deviations.

Type	No.	Time after injection	Body weight	Liver weight	Total liver gold	Gold conc.
					mgm.	*mgm./gm.*
Obese	10	2 mo.	52 ± 7.4	2.83 ± 0.49	0.054 ± 0.005	0.020 ± 0.008
ATG-N.O. (fed)	10	2 mo.	31 ± 3.1	1.64 ± 0.28	0.038 ± 0.006 *	0.025 ± 0.015
Obese	5	3 mo.	53 ± 5.4	2.23 ± 0.015	0.045 ± 0.024	0.021 ± 0.014
ATG-N.O. (fed)	5	3 mo.	29 ± 4.0	1.66 ± 0.003	0.012 ± 0.014 **	0.004 ± 0.005
Obese	6	1 mo.	48 ± 1.8	2.69 ± 0.008	0.07 ± 0.010	0.026 ± 0.004
ATG-N.O. (fed)	8	1 mo.	35 ± 1.4	1.74 ± 0.008	0.08 ± 0.005	0.047 ± 0.003 **
Obese	7	1 mo.	49 ± 2.6	2.94 ± 0.198	0.086 ± 0.014	0.030 ± 0.006
ATG-N.O. (fasted)	6	1 mo.	34 ± 2.0	2.01 ± 0.011	0.078 ± 0.016	0.038 ± 0.009

* $P < 0.05$.
** $P < 0.01$.

A comparison of gold recoveries from obese and non-obese ATG-injected mice 2 and 3 months after injection. About 65 mice were injected with 0.8 mgm. of ATG/gm. body wt. and were permitted free access to food and water. Approximately two and three months after injection representative groups of obese and non-obese mice were selected for study. In the two month group the obese animals had a mean body weight of 52 ± S.D. 7.4 grams (range 44 to 66), while the ATG-injected non-obese had a mean weight of 31 ± S.D. 3.1 grams (range 27 to 35).

The only organ which showed readily demonstrable amounts of gold was the liver. Repeated attempts to demonstrate gold in pooled tissues of several mice in both the obese and non-obese groups were unsuccessful, aside from certain pooled spleen samples which contained the smallest perceptible trace of gold.

Table 2 contains a summary of the figures for gold concentrations and total gold in the two groups. The amounts of gold recovered were very small in comparison with those found in the livers of acutely injected animals: 0.02 mgm./gm. versus 0.8 mgm./gm. of liver. In neither experiment was there a significant difference in gold concentration between the livers of obese and non-obese mice but in both of them there was a difference in total hepatic gold in favor of the obese mice, which, in confirmation of previous experiments (Drachman and Tepperman, 1954) showed a substantial hepatomegaly. In the 2 month experiment the difference was significant at the 5 per cent level of confidence, while in the 3 month experiment it was significant at the 1 per cent level.

Subsequent experiments done only one month after injection revealed a total

TABLE 3

Gold concentrations in livers and kidneys of fed and fasted mice 120 minutes after injection with ATG, 0.8 mgm./gm.

Condition	No.	Liver gold	Kidney gold
		mgm./gm.	*mgm./gm.*
Fed	10	0.064 ± S.D. 0.004	0.277 ± 0.021
24-Hr. fasted	11	0.111 ± 0.010	0.538 ± 0.087
P		<0.01	<0.01

gold content of about 0.08 mgm. per liver in both obese and non-obese mice, approximately twice the amount found at two and three months. There was no difference in total hepatic gold between the two groups in spite of the fact that the degree of hepatic enlargement seen in these obese animals one month after injection was fully as large as that seen in the experiments described above.

Gold distribution patterns in fed and fasting mice injected with ATG. It had been observed repeatedly that ATG was substantially more toxic to mice injected in the fed state than it was to mice fasted for 24 hours before injection and 22 hours after injection. It was of interest, therefore, to ascertain whether or not differences in tissue concentrations could be demonstrated in fed and fasting mice. For this purpose estimations of gold concentration in the livers and kidneys of ATG injected mice were made on tissues obtained 120 minutes after injection. The results are given in table 3.

The concentration of gold in both liver and kidneys of fasted mice was approximately twice that found in the corresponding organs of fed mice. These results are significant at a confidence level of less than one per cent.

DISCUSSION. *Acute gold distribution experiments.* When these studies were planned there had been no convincing demonstration of the hypothalamic etiology of ATG obesity. It was the hope of the experimenters that large enough concentrations of gold could be detected in the brain to make possible a study of brain gold concentration in a number of circumstances in which both toxicity and obesity incidence following ATG injection had been shown to vary. Thus, from one point of view, the most significant finding in the acute injection experiments is the fact that the concentrations of gold in the brain approach the lower limit of effectiveness of the method used.

This observation must be examined in the light of the recent findings of Marshall *et al.* (1955) who discovered that mice injected with obesity-inducing doses of ATG regularly show rather sharply delimited hemorrhagic, edematous and inflammatory lesions in the region of the ventromedial nuclei, the supra optic nuclei, the median eminence, the arcuate nuclei and the lateral hypothalamic area. The remarkably selective damage produced by ATG and demonstrated in their photographs suggests that gross chemical analytical methods are not equal to the task either of establishing the anatomical basis of injury or of elucidating the variability in susceptibility to the injury seen in various experimental cirsumstances. It would seem much more appropriate to use histochemical methods, either for gold or for SH groups, for the study of these problems.

The distribution of injected ATG in the mouse as reported above is very similar to that reported for the rat by Freyberg *et al.* (1942). The greatest concentration of gold occurs in the kidneys and the next highest occurs in the liver.

Gold recoveries from obese and gold-injected non-obese mice. At 2 and 3 months after injection there appeared to be slightly more gold in the obese mice than in the lean ones. The liver was the only organ in which measurable amounts were found, and even in that organ the concentrations were very low. It is not permissable to extrapolate these findings back to the acute period immediately after injection, since even the one-month series showed no differences in total hepatic gold. The finding of an increased concentration of gold in the livers of non-obese mice in one experiment one month after injection is duly noted, but not understood, by the authors.

Gold distribution in fed and fasting mice injected with ATG. Brecher (1950), Owen (1953) and Drachman and Tepperman (1954) all reported that prior starvation reduces mortality from ATG. It can be assumed either that, in the fasted mouse, the critical cells whose injury results in death are comparatively invulnerable to the toxic effect of ATG or that less of the compound reaches them.

The only significant findings were in the liver and kidneys, and in both of those organs the concentration of the compound was markedly higher in the fasted mice than in the fed ones. This occurred in spite of the fact that the fed animals were given an excess of the compound per unit of active metabolic mass, since the dose was calculated on the basis of body weight. The finding of strikingly higher tissue concentrations in the fasted mice, which were destined to survive the fed ones in larger numbers, suggests the possibility that fasting somehow permits the accumulation or "sequestration" of gold in indifferent tissues, and that vulnerable tissues are thereby protected from the toxic effects of the compound.

SUMMARY

The concentration of gold in the liver, kidneys, muscle, brain, and plasma was estimated within 180 minutes after the injection of obesity-producing doses of aurothioglucose (ATG) into mice. The peak plasma concentration occurred between 30 and 60 minutes after injection. The largest tissue concentrations were found in the kidneys and liver, and extremely small quantities were detected in brain.

The only organ in which small quantities of gold were detected one, two and three months after injection of ATG was the liver.

Fasted mice, which have been shown to be more resistant to the toxic action of ATG than fed mice, show almost twice the liver and kidney gold concentrations seen in similarly injected fed controls.

REFERENCES

Block, W. D., and Buchanan, O. H.: J. Biol. Chem., **136:** 379, 1940.

Block, W. D., Buchanan, O. H., and Freyberg, R. H.: This Journal, **76:** 355, 1942.

BRECHER, G., AND WAXLER, S. H.: Proc. Soc. Exp. Biol. & Med., **70:** 489, 1949.
DRACHMAN, R. H., AND TEPPERMAN, J.: Yale J. Biol. and Med., **26:** 394, 1954.
FISHER, R. A.: Statistical Methods for Research Workers, Hafner Publishing Co., 10th Ed., New York, 1946.
MARSHALL, N. B., BARRNETT, R. J., AND MAYER, J.: Proc. Soc. Exper. Biol. & Med., **90:** 240, 1955.
OWEN, J. A., JR., FALK, L. J., JR., CRISPELL, K. R., AND PARSON, W.: Am. J. Med., **14:** 521, 1953.
POLLARD, W. B.: Analyst., **62:** 597, 1937.

BIOASSAY FOR CARDIAC ACTIVE PRINCIPLES BASED ON THE STAIRCASE PHENOMENON OF THE FROG HEART

STEPHEN HAJDU

National Heart Institute, National Institutes of Health, Bethesda, Maryland

Received for publication December 24, 1956

It has been suggested in a previous paper that the staircase phenomenon of the frog heart can be used to assay cardiac glycosides (Hajdu and Szent-Györgyi, 1952b). Since then the action of glycosides and other substances on the staircase phenomenon has been worked out in detail (Hajdu, 1953) so that it is now possible to describe a refined assay method.

The results of previous experiments (Hajdu, 1953) suggest that the contractile matter of the heart is very sensitive to the sum of intracellular Na^+ and K^+. If the level is as high as 107 mEq./liter of fiber water there is no contraction on electric stimulation (diastolic arrest). A net loss of 3 per cent of the intracellular cations is associated with an alteration of the tension, registered isometrically, from zero to that of a maximal tension. With a further 6 to 7 per cent loss the contractile protein becomes maximally contracted even without an electric stimulus (systolic arrest). Thus the tension is a sensitive indicator of intracellular ion content.

It was also found that the heart muscle loses approximately 130 microequivalents of K^+ per liter of fiber water during each contraction and that the K^+ reenters the fiber during rest between contractions. The longer the rest, the more will reenter. If the stimulation frequency is high enough, there is insufficient time for the K^+ lost during contraction to reenter the fiber, and the K^+ content of the muscle falls (tension rises). At low frequencies the time between stimuli is longer than required for the reentry of all the K^+ which left the fiber and an additional amount will enter the cell. The muscle gains K^+ and tension decreases. There is only one stimulation frequency, at any chosen tension, for which the time interval between contractions is exactly sufficient for the reentry of the same amount of K^+ as that which left the fiber during contraction. At this frequency the intracellular K^+ content, and with it the tension, will remain constant. This time interval, indicated by a steady maintenance of tension will be referred to as a the *critical frequency interval* (CFI). If, then, the interval is increased, there is a net gain in fiber K^+ and a fall in tension until a new steady state is reached. Thus, every steady state level of K^+ and tension is characterized by a specific CFI. We may refer then, to a CFI for every tension, *e.g.* for maximum tension CFI_{100}, for 50 per cent of maximum, CFI_{50}, etc. (fig. 1).

The potassium movement hypothesis (Hajdu, 1953) was suggested to account for the Bowditch staircase phenomenon only. Other investigators however attempted to apply it to other phenomena like "rest contraction" and post stimulation potentiation without success (Rosin and Farah, 1955; Katzung and Farah, 1956; Penna and Garb, 1956).

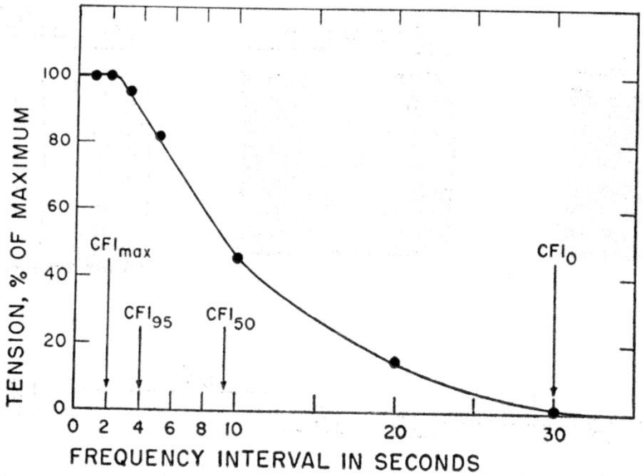

FIG. 1. Tension, expressed in percent of the maximum, plotted against frequency interval in seconds. CFI values, read on the abscissa, are indicated by arrows.

METHODS. The method was essentially the same as in earlier work (Hajdu and Szent-Györgyi, 1952a) with the following modifications: Since the glass cannula used for the perfusion of the heart proved to be very fragile, with the exception of the cannula proper, all other parts were made of stainless steel tubing similar to that used in hypodermic needles. The straight part entering the heart cavity was made of 16 gauge tubing, while the central rod was composed of 21 and 26 gauge tubing. The tension produced by the heart was measured with a transducer (Statham Lab. Inc. G 1-4-225) coupled with an amplifier (Brush Universal Analyser Model BL 320) connected to an ink recorder (Brush Oscillograph BL 202/931). The central rod of the cannula was coupled to the transducer by means of a soft rubber pad in order to reduce vibration originating from oxygenation and friction. The chart speed was 250 mm. per hour. For the cauterization of the auricle, a General Electric midget (⅛″ tip) soldering iron was used, the temperature of which was regulated by a Variac (type V-5). Boyle-Conway solution (Boyle and Conway, 1941) was used for perfusion with the modification that Ca^{++} was kept at 1.6 mM. except in one series of experiments (fig. 5). Frogs (*Rana pipiens*) were kept in a refrigerator at 10° to 12°C. for at least 6 weeks before use, to minimize seasonal changes (Hajdu, 1951). To prevent "red leg" the frogs were treated with chloramphenicol (Smith, 1950), but treatment was terminated two weeks prior to experiments. It was found that during the winter months (December-March) spontaneous rhythm sometimes occurred even after cauterization unless the frogs were kept at room temperature for at least one week after refrigeration. Hearts were equilibrated for half an hour to one hour by repeated changes of the perfusion fluid. The cannula always contained 3 ml. of solution.

EXPERIMENTAL. *Determination of the critical frequency interval.* The CFI is the time just sufficient for the reentry of the K^+ which leaves the fiber during contraction. The following procedure was used to determine CFI_{95}. First the stimulation frequency which produced maximal tension was determined, frequencies above this causing no further increase in tension. The frequency was then reduced stepwise until the tension showed a decrease to a level of about 95 per cent of the maximum. To be certain that the decrease in tension was the result of the lowered frequency and not due to some other change, a higher frequency was used again, to ascertain that the tension level would return to the original 100 per cent. The simplicity of detecting fortuitous tension changes by

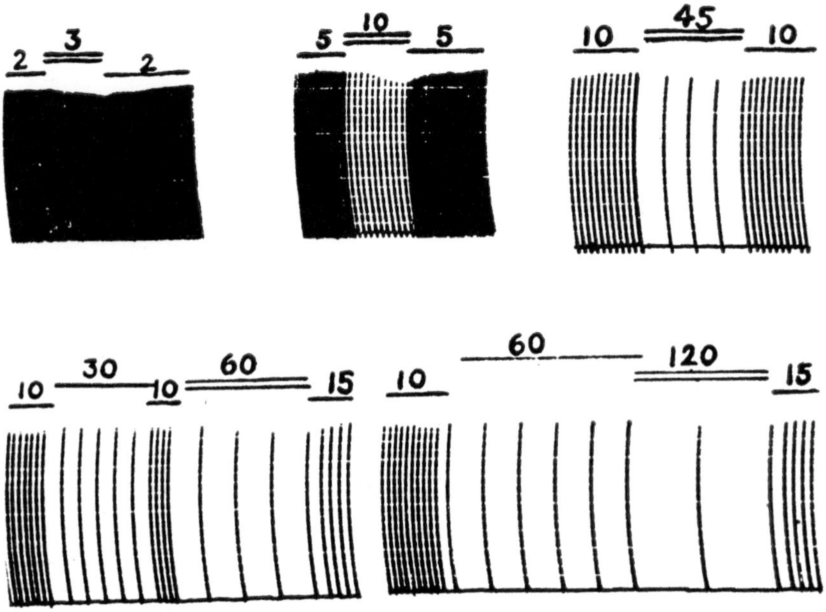

FIG. 2. Original tracings from one heart in which the shift in CFI_{95} caused by strophanthidin is demonstrated.

First record: control. Each of the following records was made at a progressively higher concentration of strophanthidin (1, 2, 2.5, 3 microgm./3 ml.). = marks the frequency interval which produces the first drop of tension to the approximate 95 per cent level. Numbers above the lines refer to frequency interval in seconds. Note how a shorter interval brings the tension back to the maximum again.

this method makes it advantageous to measure CFI_{95} rather than to work at a lower tension. The CFI_{95} value is influenced by environmental factors so that it can vary from a fraction of a second to 10 to 15 minutes. It is most convenient to choose the experimental conditions which will result in a CFI_{95} range of 2 to 120 seconds.

Examples of the measurements of CFI are given in fig. 2. The smaller the steps in stimulation frequency, the more accurate the measurement of CFI_{95}. In using the CFI_{95} in bioassay, the bath concentration of the substance in question bears a roughly linear relationship to the logarithm of CFI_{95} (fig. 3), and therefore the steps in the high frequency range should be much smaller than in the low frequency range. The following series of stimulation frequency intervals has proved to be practical in bioassay: 2, 3, 5, 7.5, 10, 15, 20, 30, 45, 60, 90 and 120 seconds.

Factors influencing CFI. Cardiac glycosides: The *critical frequency interval* for any tension has a seasonal variation in frog hearts. It is much shorter for the same tension in summer frogs than in winter frogs. However, keeping the frogs at 12° C. during the summer and at least for one or two weeks at room temperature (21° C.) after refrigeration during the winter decreases, or abolishes, this seasonal variation. In fig. 3 the points at zero strophanthidin concentration demonstrate

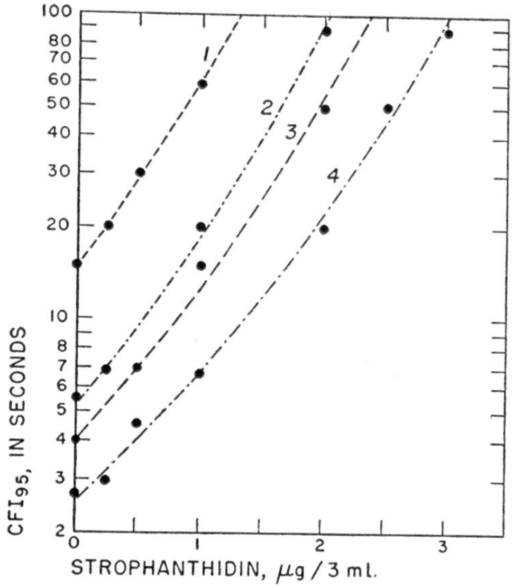

FIG. 3. Typical examples of the effect of strophanthidin on the CFI_{95}. Hearts from frogs under different experimental conditions.

Curve 1: winter frog refrigerated at 12°C. Curve 2: winter frog kept at 21°C. for 2 weeks. Curve 3: summer frog, 12°C. for 6 weeks. Curve 4: summer frog, 21°C. for 2 weeks.

these differences. Curve 1 gives the CFI_{95} value (15 sec.) for a winter frog kept under refrigeration, while curve 4 represents the CFI_{95} value (2.5 sec.) of a summer frog kept at 21° C. for two weeks before the experiment. Curves 2 and 3 show how these two extreme groups slowly move towards each other as a result of the temperature treatment. The CFI_{95} of most of the summer frogs brought into the laboratory and used without any pretreatment was so low that it could not be measured at all, since 100 and 95 per cent tension can not be achieved with the highest frequency (60 per minute) at which the heart can be stimulated. Fig. 3 further shows how the CFI_{95} changes upon the addition of strophanthidin. Strophanthidin was chosen as the standard with which the effect of other drugs on CFI_{95} was compared, since it is potent, but at the same time can be washed out of the preparation easily because of its weak binding to the heart. The curves for the variously pretreated frogs are roughly parallel. It should be noted that they are not straight lines, but have a tendency toward an upward swing. Since the strophanthidin sensitivity of the frogs pretreated in the same way is very similar, in routine assay a check of the normal CFI_{95} and the effect of one strophanthidin concentration is enough to establish the CFI_{95} concentration curve. A large variety of cardiac glycosides and aglycones, including many of the toad poisons, had an activity on the assay system similar to that of strophanthidin. Cardiac-active principles of different structure exhibit quantitative differences in activity. For example on an equimolar basis strophanthidin is 1.5 times more active than digitoxin and 20 times more active than periplogenin. Telocinobufagin, an aglycone isolated from toad poison, had 4 times the activity of

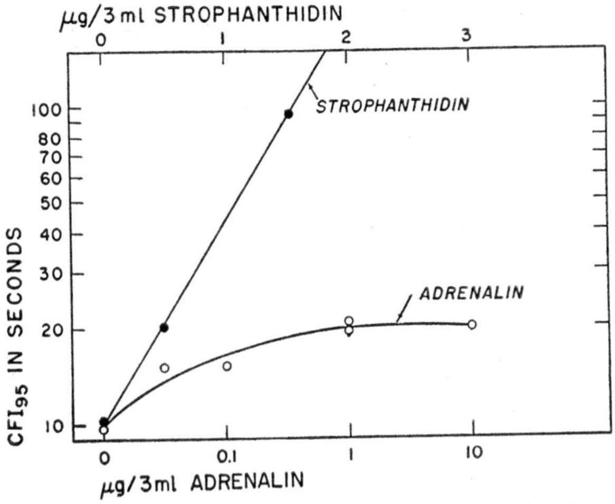

FIG. 4. Comparison between the effects of strophanthidin and epinephrine (adrenalin) on the same heart.

periplogenin. The significance of these differences will be considered in the discussion.

Suprarenal steroids and progesterone: Among these, desoxycorticosterone (DOC) and progesterone are effective, with an action very similar to that of strophanthidin. Corticosterone has an effect resembling that of cardiac glycosides, but is much weaker than DOC. Aldosterone which elicits an effect similar to DOC in other biological systems has no DOC-like activity on the frog heart. Steroids with an hydroxyl group in the C-17 position (Compounds E, F, Reichstein S and 17 OH progesterone) elicit an effect on CFI in the opposite direction to DOC and cardiac glycosides.

Epinephrine is the most active member of a group of miscellaneous substances: ATP, ADP, fatty acids, lecithins, bile acids and catecholamines. Fig. 4 shows the effect of epinephrine which at very low concentrations (0.05 microgm./3 ml.) acts like strophanthidin. However, the curve flattens out so that further increases in epinephrine concentration have no more effect on the CFI_{95}. The effect of epinephrine on the CFI has a wide seasonal and individual variation.

Temperature: It has been shown that the speed of transfer of potassium into cells is very sensitive to changes in temperature (Raker *et al.*, 1950; Love and Burch, 1953). Therefore it was of interest to test the effect of the temperature on the CFI_{95}. In order to determine this effect the temperature was lowered from 20°C. to 10°C. in four experiments. The measurements showed that a ten degree drop in temperature results in a more than twofold increase in the CFI_{95}. In terms of the theory outlined in the introduction this is thought to reflect a comparable decrease in the speed of transfer of potassium (Q_{10} 2.46 ± 0.17) as that reported earlier on red cells (Q_{10} 2.2–2.35).

Ca^{++} and K^{+} in the extracellular medium: Both ions have a very strong effect on the CFI (fig. 5) as was pointed out by Moulin and Willbrandt (1955) in their

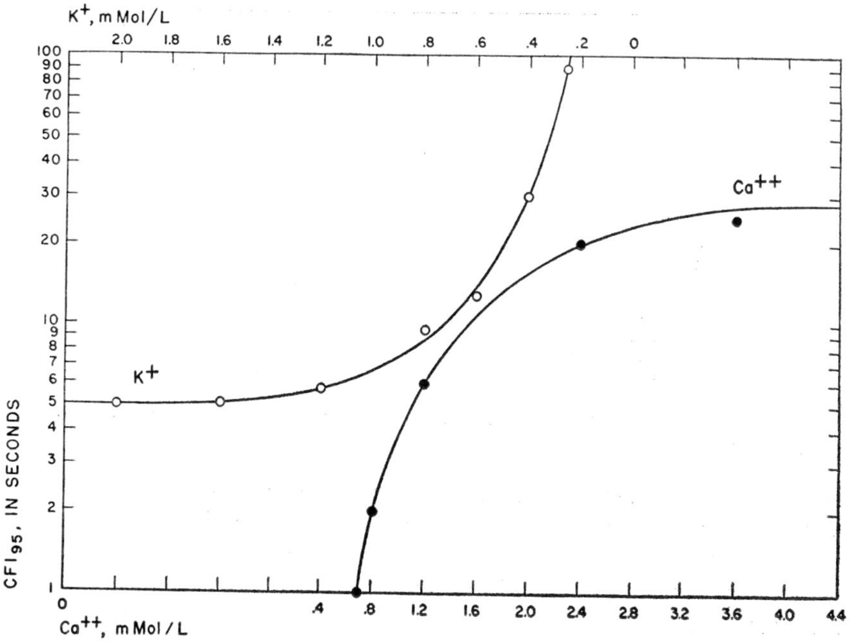

FIG. 5. The effect of Ca^{++} and K^{+} concentration on the CFI_{95}. Both curves were obtained on the same heart.

work on the staircase phenomenon of the frog heart. As the Ca^{++} is decreased below the normal of 1.6 *mM*, the CFI_{95} is markedly decreased. If calcium is increased above normal, the CFI_{95} is lengthened, but this is a much less impressive effect, and the flattened curve resembles that obtained with adrenalin.

The effect of K^{+} is the opposite, in that lowering the concentration of this ion *increases* the CFI_{95}. Below 1 *mM*/l. the effect of decreasing K^{+} becomes progressively more marked, the slope of the curve swinging upwards in a fashion similar to that observed with strophanthidin.

The effect of binding: Comparison of the binding of a cardiac glycoside with its corresponding aglycone can be demonstrated in the following experiment. Strophanthin, a strongly binding substance, was compared to strophanthidin, which is bound very weakly. At the beginning of the experiment the heart cannula was emptied. A 1.2 micromol. per liter solution of the drug in Ringer was then added to the heart in 0.5 ml. steps, so that the concentration of drug remained constant and only the volume of solution bathing the tissue increased. The time for the muscle to reach a steady state after each addition was 6 to 7 minutes. Figure 6 shows that with strophanthidin the CFI_{95} reached a constant value with the first sample added, whereas a progressive change in CFI_{95} occurred as the volume of strophanthin-Ringer increased up to a level of 3.0 ml. The fact that the effect of strophanthin depends not simply on the concentration but also on the total amount of the drug can be adduced as evidence that the material is bound by the cardiac muscle.

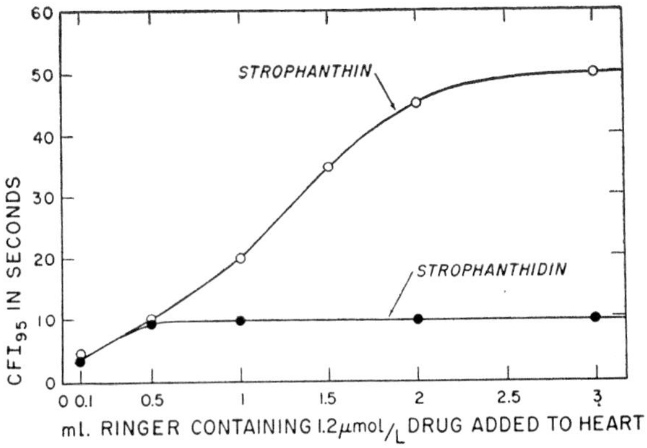

FIG. 6. A typical example demonstrating the binding of strophanthin. See text for experimental details.

None of the aglycones is bound appreciably to the frog heart, since the activity disappears within a few minutes after the drug is washed out of the cannula. The glycosides, on the other hand, are bound to some extent, since the activity persists up to half an hour after washing. Four of them (strophanthin, ouabain, convallatoxin and scillarin A) are bound strongly, with activity still evident 12 to 24 hours after washing.

Differential assay using toad heart. The heart of the toad (*Bufo marinus*) can be used in the same fashion as was described in the method for frogs. It exhibits the same type of staircase phenomenon, but as has been known for a long time (Issekutz, 1923) it is practically unresponsive to cardiac glycosides. This quality of the toad heart was used as a further means of differentiating between substances which change the CFI values. As was described earlier, the substances having a marked effect on the CFI values are first, the cardiac glycosides with a lactone ring, secondly, certain steroids without a lactone ring (DOC, progesterone), and thirdly, miscellaneous substances such as epinephrine, with a structure not related to steroids. Although some differentiation can be made among these groups with the frog heart alone, the difference becomes more pronounced by using the toad heart in addition. The group of glycosides with a lactone ring has no action on the toad CFI. However the action of the other two groups of compounds is similar for both toad and frog heart. Thus, a substance which acts on the frog, but not on the toad, is presumed to have a structure similar to that of cardiac glycosides.

There is a group of substances, the erythrophleum alkaloids, which is not related chemically to the cardiac glycosides (Blount, Openshaw and Todd, 1940), but has the same type of activity on mammalian hearts (Chen, 1945; Maling and Krayer, 1946). A representative of this group, coumingine HCl, was found to have strong activity, comparable to that of strophanthin on the frog heart, but in contrast to the cardiac glycosides, it was also highly effective in the toad. This experiment substantiates the specificity of the combined assay for cardiac active lactones.

DISCUSSION. If all the factors (temperature, Ca^{++}, K^{+}) influencing the CFI are kept constant, the method described proves to be very useful and highly reproducible for measuring the concentration of cardiac active principles. DeSalva *et al.* (1955), using 2.75 microgm. of digitoxin per heart, obtained a standard error of ± 0.052 microgm. ($P = 0.001$) in 32 measurements. This method has the advantage necessary to any biological assay but not always available, that the unknown substance can be compared to the standard on the same heart. One heart can be used for many assays unless a drug is bound so strongly that it cannot be washed out within a reasonable time.

The action of the glycosides depends on two factors. First, the chemical structure of the steroid nucleus itself. For example, strophanthidin, with an aldehyde on the C-10 position, is 20 times more active than the corresponding molecule without the C-10 aldehyde (periplogenin). Similar results have been obtained in mammals (Chen, 1945). It has also been shown that an aglycone with a 6-membered lactone ring (telocinobufagin) has 4 times the activity of the corresponding compound with a 5-membered lactone (periplogenin).

The other factor which will decide the activity is the binding of the cardiac active principle. Conjugation with a sugar increases the binding (Chen *et al.*, 1938) to an extent determined by the structure of the sugar residue. For the frog heart, cymarose or rhamnose insure the strongest binding (strophanthin, ouabain, convallatoxin, scillaren A). The difference in sensitivity of the hearts of various species to the same glycoside may reflect differences in response to the chemical structure of the steroid nucleus or differences in the firmness of binding or both. This may explain the findings of DeSalva *et al.* (1955) that the staircase assay and generally the frog heart assay can not be directly used for clinical purpose, and bears no direct quantitative relation to cardiotonic activity in mammals. However this system described is well suited for the separate study of the effects of binding and structure of the steroid nucleus on cardiotonic activity in frogs.

Among steroids other than cardiac glycosides, DOC, progesterone and to a smaller extent corticosterone, have a similar activity on the frog heart. Their activity however is about 50 to 100 times smaller in the same molar concentration, and as with the aglycones, binding is negligible. As was mentioned earlier they act on the toad heart in the same way and at the same concentrations as on the frog heart. The same three molecules with the addition of an OH group in the C-17 position exert the opposite effect, that is, they increase the rate of reentry of K^+ lost during contraction. This effect, however, is subject to seasonal variation and fails to appear in winter or refrigerated frogs. Epinephrine has a very marked action which resembles that of digitalis on the staircase phenomenon of the frog heart, but in the final analysis (see fig. 4) its activity, together with the action of Ca^{++} ions (see fig. 5) is quantitatively different from that of the glycosides. This observation is somewhat against the concept that digitalis acts by affecting the movement of Ca^{++} across the membrane (Moulin and Willbrandt, 1955). On the other hand, the striking similarity in action of epinephrine and Ca suggests the possibility that adrenalin acts on the heart by affecting the transport of Ca^{++}.

The main purpose of setting up this bioassay was not to provide a new method for assaying digitalis preparations, but to measure minute amounts of cardiac active substances in tissue extracts at physiological concentration levels. This is rather a difficult problem in view of the fact that extracts prepared from biological materials contain a minute amount of activity in huge quantities of tremendously varied types of "impurity." This type of work requires that the bioassay provide high specificity, good quantitation at the microgram level and speedy performance. This method has had a long trial during the past years in thousands of assays on one unknown principle which has cardiac activity in the frog and it has been found to meet these requirements (Hajdu *et al.*, 1957).

SUMMARY

A bioassay using the isolated frog ventricle for the measurement of cardiac active principles is described. It is based upon the effect of such substances on the staircase phenomenon; from this it is inferred that the effect is probably exerted upon the reentry of potassium lost by the fiber during contraction. Since the reentry of potassium across the cell membrane is influenced by calcium, potassium, temperature and seasonal variations, these effects are also discussed.

If the assay is made with both frog and toad hearts, it is possible to distinguish cardiac glycosides with a lactone ring specifically among several groups of substances with activity in the frog preparation.

ACKNOWLEDGMENT. I wish to express my gratitude to Dr. K. K. Chen for a generous gift of coumingine HCl from the original batch isolated by G. Dalma.

REFERENCES

BLOUNT, B. K., OPENSHAW, H. T., AND TODD, A. R.: J. Chem. Soc., **143:** 286, 1940.
BOYLE, P. J., AND CONWAY, E. J.: J. Physiol., **100:** 1, 1941.
CHEN, K. K., ROBBINS, E. B., AND WORTH, H.: J. Am. Pharm. A., **27:** 189, 1938.
CHEN, K. K.: Ann. Rev. Physiol., **7:** 677, 1945.
DESALVA, S., DERTINGER, B., AND ERCOLI, N.: Proc. Soc. Exper. Biol. & Med., **89:** 99, 1955.
HAJDU, S.: Arch. internat. Physiol., **59:** 58, 1951.
HAJDU, S., AND SZENT-GYÖRGYI, A.: Am. J. Physiol., **168:** 159, 1952a.
HAJDU, S., AND SZENT-GYÖRGYI, A.: Am. J. Physiol., **168:** 171, 1952b.
HAJDU, S.: Am. J. Physiol., **174:** 371, 1953.
HAJDU, S., WEISS, H., AND TITUS, E. O.: THIS JOURNAL, **120:** 99, 1957.
ISSEKUTZ, B.: Pfluegers Arch. ges. Physiol., **198:** 429, 1923.
KATZUNG, B., AND FARAH, A.: Am. J. Physiol., **184:** 557, 1956.
LOVE, W. D., AND BURCH, G. E.: J. Lab. and Clin. Med., **41:** 337, 1953.
MALING, H. M., AND KRAYER, O.: THIS JOURNAL, **86:** 66, 1946.
MOULIN, M., AND WILLBRANDT, W.: Experientia, **11:** 72, 1955.
PENNA, M., AND GARB, S.: Am. J. Physiol., **184:** 572, 1956.
RAKER, J. W., TAYLOR, I. M., WELLER, J. M., AND HASTINGS, A. B.: J. Gen. Physiol., **33:** 691, 1950.
ROSIN, H., AND FARAH, A.: Am. J. Physiol., **180:** 75, 1955.
SMITH, S. W.: Science, **112:** 274, 1950.

THE ISOLATION OF A CARDIAC ACTIVE PRINCIPLE FROM MAMMALIAN TISSUE

STEPHEN HAJDU, HERBERT WEISS[1] AND ELWOOD TITUS

Laboratory of Kidney and Electrolyte Metabolism and Laboratory of Chemical Pharmacology, National Heart Institute, National Institutes of Health, Public Health Service, U. S. Department of Health, Education, and Welfare, Bethesda, Maryland

Received for publication December 24, 1956

It has long been known that the mammalian heart, even though well supplied with oxygenated blood, loses efficiency when separated from the rest of the body in a heart-lung preparation. Its contractile force gradually but inevitably weakens and the heart eventually goes into a failure which in some respects is comparable to chronic congestive heart failure. This mechanical failure has been attributed to denervation of the heart (Gollwitzer-Meier and Krüger, 1938; Gremels, 1936), to absence of metabolic control resulting from the depletion of known hormones (Gremels, 1940) and to the absence of unknown substances normally supplied by the liver (Pinotti, 1941; Rein, 1942). Since the contractile force of such a failing heart may be restored to normal if the liver and spleen are again included in the circulatory pathway, it has been concluded that these organs supply a factor with physiological effects closely resembling those of strophanthin (Rein *et al.*, 1949; Bücherl and Rein, 1949; Mertens and Rein, 1949).

A somewhat similar failure occurs upon perfusion of the frog heart with Ringer's solution. This has been ascribed by Clark (1913–14) to a loss of lipids from the surface of the muscle cells. He has shown that the contractility of the heart can be restored by the addition of serum or of alcoholic extracts of serum. The active principle in his opinion was probably a lipid, since lecithin or sodium oleate could act in similar fashion.

Kutschera-Aichenberger (1929) reported a decrease in the phospholipids of the hearts of patients with congestive heart failure and in experimental myocardial injury produced by chloroform or by acute bacterial infections. He also observed that digitalis intoxication in rabbits resulted in an increased phospholipid content of the heart.

These reports reinforced the findings of Rubow (1905) who noted that the phospholipid content of the heart decreased in experimental myocardial insufficiency. More recently Schulze and Südhof (1953) have observed that in experimetal heart failure produced by enforced exercise there is a decrease in the amount of phospholipid although the total lipid content remains unchanged.

Hajdu and Szent-Györgyi (1952), while working on the Bowditch staircase phenomenon of the frog heart observed that the first drop of tension occurred when the interval between stimuli exceeded twenty seconds. As the hearts were

[1] A portion of this work has been submitted by Herbert Weiss in partial fulfillment of tne requirements for the degree of Doctor of Philosophy in Biochemistry at the George Washington University.

perfused with Ringer's solution, however, the interval at which the staircase phenomenon could be demonstrated gradually became shorter. After prolonged washing the heart became unable to develop its normal tension when stimulated at frequencies approximating the normal rhythm (1- or 2-sec. intervals). This condition was equivalent to the hypodynamic state produced by Clark (1913–14) whose experiments were carried out without altering the normal rhythm of the heart. He observed decreases in tension which amounted to 10 to 20 per cent after 4 hours of perfusion and which increased with longer washing.

Hajdu and Szent-Györgyi (1952) found, as had Clark (1913–14), that the effects of prolonged perfusion could be reversed by substituting serum for the perfusion fluid. After repeated additions of serum to the heart, the interval at which the first drop in tension could be demonstrated increased to a normal value. A heart thus restored could again be made hypodynamic by perfusion with fresh Ringer's solution, but only after prolonged washing, indicating that the serum factor was firmly bound to the cells. This behavior could also be produced by minute amounts of cardiac glycosides such as strophanthin and ouabain which are firmly bound in the heart. Use of the staircase phenomenon, in fact, has provided a convenient method for the quantitative estimation of these substances (Hajdu, 1957). Although soaps and lecithin could increase the tension developed by a hypodynamic heart stimulated at a normal frequency, these substances could not duplicate the effect of serum on the staircase phenomenon. Furthermore they could be readily removed from the heart by washing with fresh Ringer's solution for a few minutes.

Since these experiments indicated the presence in serum of a factor whose effects resembled more those of digitalis than those of the lipids mentioned by Clark (1913–14), the staircase assay was used to guide a search for an active principle.

This paper reports the isolation of such a substance from mammalian tissue and its characterization as palmitoyl lysolecithin.

When extracts from blood which had been deproteinized with acetone were fractionated by solvent extraction, a preparation was obtained which exhibited the characteristic action of serum on the staircase. As had been observed with the original serum, this activity persisted in the heart for several hours after repeated washings with fresh Ringer's solution.

Examination of several other tissues revealed similar activity in heart muscle, liver and adrenal medulla. Skeletal muscle had no detectable activity.

Preliminary fractionation was carried out by chromatography on Florisil. Elution of the columns with solvents of gradually increasing polarity partially resolved two active components, the first of which emerged with ethanol and the second of which predominated in 70 per cent ethanol-eluates. These two components were separable by paper chromatography. Since the more polar component occurred in quantities approximately twenty times greater than the earlier emerging material, it was decided to concentrate our effort on the characterization of the more abundant substance.

METHODS. *Materials.* Methylene chloride was passed over a column of activated silica gel to remove impurities and redistilled before use.

The lyophilized venom of *Crotalus adamanteus*, used as a source of phospholipase A, was obtained from Ross Allen's Reptile Institute, Silver Springs, Florida.

Florisil (60–100 mesh), obtained from the Floridin Company, Warren, Pa., was washed with water, ethanol, methylene chloride and again with ethanol. After decantation of the final ethanol wash, the adsorbent was sucked dry on a Buchner funnel, then spread out to dry in air at 100°C. The material was allowed to stand in a muffle furnace at 300°C. for several hours just prior to use.

Biological assay. The cardiotonic activity of serum and other tissue extracts was determined by the frog heart assay based on the staircase phenomenon. Details of this method are described by Hajdu (1957). The activities of unknown samples were compared to strophanthidin standards and expressed as microgm. equivalents of strophanthidin.

Certain qualitative biological tests were occasionally performed with other isolated tissue systems. These included: 1) the isolated carotid strip described by Leonard (1956), 2) the right ventricular wall of the squab used under conditions similar to those described for the rat ventricle by McDowall and Zayat (1952) except that the tension was recorded isometrically and 3) the hypodynamic frog heart as prepared by Clark (1913–14).

Paper chromatography. Two systems were used in the examination of active extracts. The first was prepared by mixing tertiary butanol, normal butanol and 0.001 *N* HCl 3:1:1 v/v. Samples of about one mgm. were applied directly to Whatman No. 3 paper without prior treatment and developed for 18 to 24 hours with the solvent mixture.

The second was prepared by shaking together toluene, ethanol and water, 1.5:4:2 v/v, and allowing the mixture to stand until the phases had completely separated (Pechet, 1955). In order to saturate the atmosphere of the chromatographic cylinder with the solvents, the apparatus was lined with a cylinder of filter paper which had been moistened with the aqueous phase and which was allowed to stand in a pool of aqueous layer covering the bottom of the chromatographic cylinder and provided with a small filter paper wick to aid evaporation.

In order to prepare the chromatogram, a sheet of Whatman No. 1 paper was immersed in the lower layer, allowed to drain in air for 8 minutes and blotted dry between two sheets of Whatman No. 3 paper. After application of the samples, the paper was suspended from a trough in the sealed chromatographic cylinder for 1 hour. The organic layer was then added to the trough through a small hole in the cover of the apparatus, the hole was resealed, and the chromatogram was allowed to develop for 12 to 18 hours.

Since the chromatograms were often analyzed by bioassay the chromatographic papers were washed to remove toxic substances by allowing the solvent to pass through the paper by capillary adsorption for several days as in descending chromatography. The papers were routinely washed with 0.01 *N* hydrochloric acid, distilled water, ethanol and the solvent system to be used for development of the chromatogram. After final washings with ethanol and water the papers were air dried and set aside until used.

Identification of chromatographic spots. Ester-containing spots were identified by conversion to hydroxamic acids. Alkaline hydroxylamine reagent and ferric chloride were prepared as described by Bagget *et al.* (1955). Papers were sprayed with the hydroxylamine, heated at 90°C. for 1 minute and immersed in the ferric chloride reagent until the initial pink color was washed out leaving the true violet-pink of the hydroxamate ferric chloride complex.

Hydrolysis of esters with phospholipase A of rattlesnake venom. Lecithin or lysolecithin was made up to a concentration of 20 micromoles of ester per ml. in a 0.005 *M* solution of calcium acetate which had been adjusted to pH 7.0. One mgm. of dried venom of *Crotalus adamanteus* was added, and the solution was incubated at 37°C. Samples of 0.1 ml. of the reaction mixture were withdrawn as required and pipetted directly into test tubes containing 0.2 ml. of hot ethanol to stop the enzyme reaction. The tubes were heated on a water bath at 100°C. for 30 seconds, then placed under a stream of nitrogen to remove solvents. The residues were assayed for ester content as described by Rapport and Alonzo (1955a).

Preparation of crude tissue extracts. The extraction procedure as outlined below for adrenals was generally applicable to most tissues. The ratio of 3 liters of acetone per kgm. of tissue was the minimum which would permit adequate coagulation of the protein and allow a reasonable rate of filtration. For best results with blood, 4 liters of acetone were added with good stirring over a period of 30 minutes to 4 liters of citrated blood. A second volume of acetone was added over the next ten minutes. Subsequent treatment was the same as that described below for other tissues. Refrigerated blood which was received from the slaughterhouse at 0 – 5°C. about two hours after slaughter was brought to 18°C. before addition of the acetone.

In an extraction from adrenals which may be considered as representative of the general procedure, 500-gm. batches of the frozen glands were homogenized in one liter of acetone in a large Waring blendor. The homogenates were collected in a glass-lined reaction kettle and maintained at 0°C. by the occasional addition of dry ice until a total of 18 kgm. of adrenals had been processed. Eighteen liters of acetone were then added and the mixture was stirred vigorously for one hour during which time the temperature rose gradually to 25°C. The mixture was filtered through Buchner funnels, and after reagent grade NaCl was added to the filtrate to a concentration of 18 gm. per liter, the solution was extracted with an equal volume of petroleum ether. This was conveniently accomplished by placing the propellor of a heavy duty stirrer at the water-petroleum ether interface and agitating for about ten minutes. The petroleum ether extraction of the salt-treated residues removed not only fat, but a large proportion of the acetone, thus avoiding the necessity for prolonged distillations[2]. The aqueous phase (20.2 liters) was drawn off, adjusted to pH 2.0 by the gradual addition of HCl and allowed to stand overnight at room temperature. The solution was then saturated by the addition of 170 gm. per liter of reagent grade NaCl and extracted with 4 liters of chloroform. The upper phase consisting of about 12 liters of a chloroform-acetone mixture was separated, dried over anhydrous Na_2SO_4 and evaporated under vacuum at room temperature.

Chromatography of active extracts. Columns were prepared by pouring a slurry of Florisil in methylene chloride-ethanol, 1:1 v/v, into chromatographic tubes. The adsorbent was allowed to settle and the solvent was slowly drained off at the bottom, until the meniscus just reached the top of the column.

The brown oily residue obtained by extraction of 18 kgm. of tissue was taken up in 8 to 10 ml. of methylene chloride-ethanol, 1:1, and placed on a column 2.1 cm. in diam. x 15.5 cm. The column was eluted with solvents of gradually increasing polarity as follows: 1) methylene chloride-ethanol, 1:1, 300 ml.; 2) ethanol, 150 ml.; 3) 90 per cent ethanol, 350 ml.; 4) 80 per cent ethanol, 500 ml.; 5) 70 per cent ethanol, 500 ml.; and 6) 50 per cent ethanol, 500 ml.

Small aliquots were evaporated for bioassay (table 2). The active material in fractions 4, 5 and 6 was recovered by extracting each ethanol-water eluate with an equal volume of chloroform. After a second extraction with the same volume of chloroform the combined organic phases were dried over anhydrous Na_2SO_4 and evaporated to dryness under vacuum.

Colored fatty impurities which still remained in this preparation were eliminated by rechromatographing the residue on a 1.2 cm. diam. x 12 cm. Florisil column. After elution with approximately 200 ml. of methylene chloride-ethanol, followed by 200 ml. of 70 per cent ethanol, all of the activity was found in the aqueous ethanol. Extraction of the latter with chloroform as before and evaporation of the dried extract yielded an amorphous waxy residue. In a typical preparation from 18 kgm. of adrenals this residue weighed 360 mgm. and was equivalent in activity to approximately 3.5 mgm. of strophanthidin.

---

[2] In occasional preparations from livers with very high fat contents some of the active substance was removed by the petroleum ether, but this was not ordinarily observed.

TABLE 1

Concentration of the cardiac active principle in different tissues

Tissue (beef)	Total microgm. activity*/kgm. wet tissue
Plasma	180
Red cells	0
Liver	100
Heart muscle	330
Skeletal muscle	10
Adrenal cortex	0
Adrenal medulla	1000

* Expressed as microgm. equivalents of strophanthidin.

Countercurrent distribution. A mixture of methanol, ether, chloroform and 0.001 *N* HCl, 2:1:1:1 v/v, was shaken and allowed to stand until the heat of mixing had been dissipated, shaken again and allowed to stand until the two phases separated. Active material obtained by Florisil chromatography was made up to a concentration of 10 mgm./ml. in the upper phase. Countercurrent distribution between equal volumes of the two phases was then carried out in separatory funnels as described by Craig *et al.* (1945).

RESULTS. *Tissue distribution of the active substance.* In order to select a suitable source for the isolation of the active factor, crude concentrates from several beef tissues were prepared for bioassay by the solvent extraction and acidification procedure as described. The content of active substance in these tissues is recorded in table 1. Active material has also been found in rabbit liver and serum and in human serum.

The chromatographic properties of the active principles from all these sources were similar to those of the substance obtained from beef adrenals. Eluates from Florisil columns were examined by paper chromatography in both the butanol-tertiary butanol-water system and the toluene-ethanol-water system. In the former the active substance was uniformly associated with a component of R_f 0.75 which gave a positive test for ester when sprayed with hydroxylamine. Since the solvent overran the paper in the second system, the mobility of the active principle was compared to that of hydrocortisone, which was used as a reference standard. In all cases the activity was associated with an ester which moved with approximately three-tenths of the mobility of the standard.

Isolation and characterization. The crude extracts prepared from 18-kgm. batches of tissue by the solvent extraction procedure were obtained as dark brown oils containing several grams of lipid. Chromatography on Florisil as summarized in table 2 removed most of the colored and lipoidal contaminants in the methylene chloride-ethanol eluates. Catechol amines which were present in the extracts appeared in the ethanol and early ethanol-water eluates. Although these affect the staircase phenomenon, they were readily distinguishable both biologically and by paper chromatography from the digitalis-like activity which followed in the later ethanol-water fractions.

After rechromatographing the material obtained in fractions 4, 5 and 6 of table 2 in order to remove traces of lipoidal contaminants which persisted from the

TABLE 2

Chromatography on Florisil of extracts from 18 kgm. of adrenal

Fraction no.	Eluent	Ml.	Activity	
			Unwashable*	Washable*†
1	CH_2Cl_2-EtOH	300	0	0
2	EtOH	150	0	2.0
3	90% EtOH	350	0.5	0.5
4	80% EtOH	500	1.0	0
5	70% EtOH	500	3.0	0
6	50% EtOH	300	0.5	0

* Measured by effect on the staircase in frog heart and expressed as mgm. equivalents of strophanthidin.

† This activity which was rapidly removed from the heart by washing with Ringer's solution, was associated with a catechol amine chromatographically similar to epinephrine. It was not further investigated.

first separation, the active material was obtained as a pale yellow grease. On a weight basis this substance was roughly one-seventieth to one one-hundredth as active as strophanthidin. This specific activity could not be improved by further chromatography on Florisil or alumina. Chromatography on silica gel caused extensive destruction of activity. The material was strongly adsorbed on silicic acid from which it could be eluted by 70 per cent ethanol. It was, however, quite unstable in the presence of silicic acid and aqueous solvents, and chromatography on this adsorbent caused destruction of from 80 to 90 per cent of the activity.

Some further purification was achieved by countercurrent distribution by the method of Craig *et al.* (1945). This removed 3.3 per cent of impurity (figure 1).

A sample of 334 mgm. obtained from fractions 4, 5 and 6 of the distribution illustrated in figure 1 was taken up in 0.5 ml. of an anhydrous mixture of acetone and ethanol 1:3 v/v and cooled to −10°C. overnight. The solution deposited 120 mgm. of white, needle-like crystals. The substance was recrystallized by adding dry acetone to a solution of the material in ethanol and cooling to −10°C. When observed on a hot stage under a polarizing microscope the hygroscopic product sintered at about 110°C. then formed translucent droplets which gradually darkened and coalesced with decomposition at about 255–7°C.

Elemental analysis revealed the following composition:

Found	C 56.35	H 9.34	N 2.64	P 5.91
Calculated for $C_{24}H_{52}O_8NP$	56.09	10.21	2.73	6.02

The one to one molar ratio of phosphorus to nitrogen and the high ratio of hydrogen to carbon suggested that the material was a phospholipid. The ratio of moles of ester to moles of phosphorus was 0.99.

A portion of the compound was dissolved in 1 *N* HCl and hydrolyzed by heating at 100°C. for one hour. The choline content of the resulting solution as measured by the method of Appleton *et al.* (1953) accounted quantitatively for all of

and biological tests were carried out. Impurities in a preparation from adrenals might be expected to contain unknown catecholamines or steroids. Any action of the former was eliminated chemically by permitting the preparation to stand for several hours in 0.01 *N* nitrous acid. This treatment, which completely destroyed the effect of epinephrine on the heart, was without effect on the activity of the lysolecithin preparation.

Using the carotid strip preparation described by Leonard (1957) it is possible to differentiate biologically between catecholamines and cardiac glycosides. The former causes a rapid contraction of the strip, whereas the cardiac glycosides produce no contraction, but in small concentrations increase the amplitude of contractions induced by electrical stimulation. In high concentrations they increase the tone of the muscle and eventually put the strip into contracture. The isolated lysolecithin produced no catecholamine-like contraction in this preparation, but exerted effects similar to those of the cardiac glycosides.

To eliminate the cardiac lactones as possible active impurities, differential assay of a sample was carried out with both frog and toad hearts. It has been noted by Hajdu (1957) that the heart of *Bufo marinus* is insensitive to all the cardiac glycosides which have thus far been tested, but that it responds in a manner identical to that of the frog heart to other cardiotonic substances such as epinephrine, desoxycorticosterone and coumingine. This preparation of lysolecithin was active on the toad heart in the same manner as on the frog, and was so firmly bound to the heart as to resist repeated washing with Ringer's solution.

As a final test for the absence of active steroids, a sample of the preparation in ethanol solution was treated with hydrogen in the presence of palladium catalyst. Although the activity of a 2-mgm. sample of the cardiac lactone, Scillaren A, was completely destroyed, this treatment was without effect on the lysolecithin activity. It was concluded that the activity could not be due to the presence of either a cardiac lactone or a cortical steroid, since reduction of the double bonds in either structure would produce inactive molecules.

Isomeric forms of lysolecithin. Although the isolated substance appeared to be chemically pure it exhibited two types of biological activity (figure 3). One of these was the characteristic digitalis-like staircase activity which developed slowly, reaching a maximum in about six to ten minutes. The second was a rapid rise in tone (contracture) which became maximal within the first minute and which was not associated with any effect on the staircase.

In crude extracts the contracture-causing activity was usually minimal or nonexistent, but it became increasingly apparent during the course of the chromatographic separations and on recrystallization. While some slight enrichment of the contracture-causing substance could be achieved by countercurrent distribution in a system prepared by mixing chloroform, ether, water and methanol, 1:1:1:2 v/v, or by chromatography on Florisil, it was never possible to separate the two principles.

To provide further assurance that lysolecithin was responsible for the biological activity and to clarify the relationship between the contracture-causing activity and the true staircase activity, attention was turned to lysolecithins from other

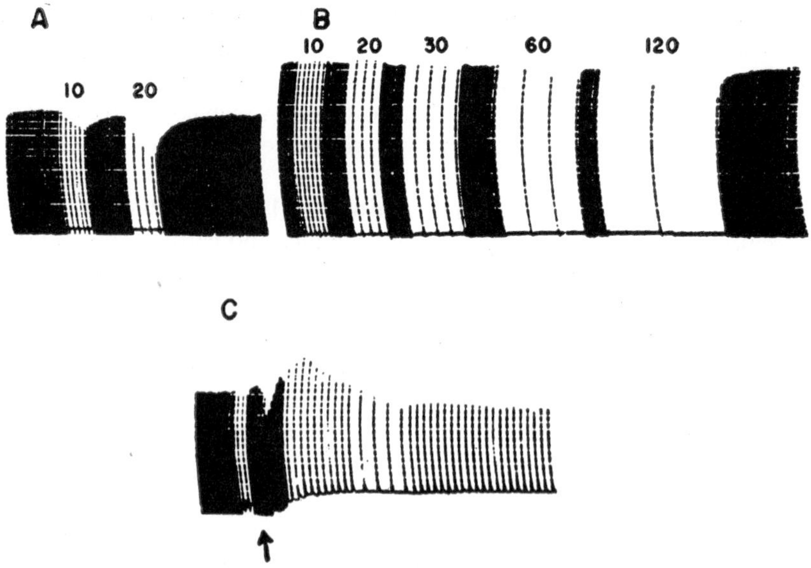

FIG. 3. Tension developed by frog heart stimulated at intervals as shown by superscripts.

Interval is 5 seconds when not otherwise indicated. A. Frog heart after several hours of washing with Ringer's solution. B. Same heart 10 minutes after addition of 200 microgm. of β-lysolecithin from adrenal in 3 ml. of Ringer's solution. Note first appearance of staircase at 60 second-intervals. C. Normal frog heart after addition (at arrow) of 3 ml. of Ringer's solution containing 150 microgm. of mixed lysolecithin (approximately 50 per cent α-lysolecithin). Note rapid onset of contracture.

sources. A sample of crude, mixed lysolecithins prepared by incubation of commercial vegetable lecithin with the venom of *Crotalus adamanteus* was tested. The biological activity was qualitatively indistinguishable from the digitalis-like effect of the adrenal substance.

Similar results were obtained with myristyl lysolecithin prepared by incubation of crystalline synthetic *l*-di-myristyl lecithin with snake venom.

When, however, a sample of synthetic mono-oleyl lysolecithin with an ester to phosphorus ratio of 1.08 was tested, it exhibited very marked contracture causing activity. Since the method of synthesis used (Baer, Buchnea and Newcombe, 1956) would be expected to yield a mixture of lysolecithins esterified on the α and β positions of glycerol, it was considered that the α-lysolecithin might account for the contracture causing effect, and that the β isomer would have the digitalis-like activity. Since it has been shown (Hanahan, 1954) that the phospholipase A of *C. adamanteus* venom affects only the α position of lecithin, the lysolecithins prepared from vegatable sources and from myristyl lecithin, which were free of contracture-causing activity, were presumably β-lysolecithins.

Although there have been no published reports of the action of phospholipase A on lysolecithins, it was considered possible that the enzyme might catalyze the hydrolysis of the α ester bond regardless of whether the β hydroxyl was esterified or free. This was confirmed by incubation of the synthetic oleyl lysolecithin with

C. adamanteus venom. A rapid reaction was observed which stopped when exactly half of the ester bonds had disappeared. The lysolecithin recovered from the reaction mixture was now devoid of the rapidly appearing contracture-causing activity, and only the digitalis-like response could be observed.

These observations indicated that the presence of α-lysolecithin in quantities which varied with the method of handling probably accounted for the contracture-causing effects of the adrenal preparations. In order to demonstrate this, a sample of beef adrenal lysolecithin which had been partially purified by Florisil chromatography and which caused marked contracture was treated with snake venom phospholipase. In this experiment the reaction ceased when 14 per cent of the total ester bonds had been hydrolyzed, and as before, the product exhibited only the staircase effects.

It is possible that the contracture-causing activity may also be a property of lysolecithins with longer aliphatic side chains regardless of the position of esterification since one sample of β-stearoyl lysolecithin exhibited some contracture-causing activity in addition to its effects on the staircase.

Inactive precursor and activation. It was noted in preliminary observations that the biological activity of crude tissue extracts could be preserved and markedly enhanced by treatment with dilute acids.[3] Preparations allowed to stand at room temperature at pH 3 required approximately six days to reach maximal activity. At pH values of 1 or less, destruction of the active substance was so rapid that it obscured the effects of activation. It was found most practical to carry out the acid treatment at pH 2.0 and room temperature, and these conditions were routinely used in treating the defatted tissue extracts. In preliminary experiments to determine the optimal time of activation a defatted acetone extract of beef blood was allowed to stand at pH 2.0. At intervals aliquots equivalent to 45 ml. of the original blood were extracted by shaking with an equal volume of chloroform-methanol 1:1 v/v followed by a second extraction with an equal volume of chloroform. The per cent of maximal activity (about 3 microgm. equivalents of strophanthidin) found in the organic extracts at various times was as follows: 0 min., 0 to 20; 10 min., 40; 2 hrs., 70; 3 hrs., 85; 24 hrs., 100; 48 hrs., 100; 10 days, 40.

On the basis of these data 18 hours was chosen as convenient time for acid treatment in routine isolations.

The values of table 1 record the total amount of activity measured after acidification. The relative amounts occurring free and as inactive precursor varied with the tissue, however. In blood and liver from 0 to 20 per cent, and in adrenal medulla approximately 50 per cent of the total activity usually occurred as free lysolecithin.

The inactive precursor appeared to be chemically very similar to lysolecithin, since it could be quantitatively extracted by the procedures used for the isolation of the latter. It appeared to be somewhat less polar than lysolecithin, since it was eluted from Florisil columns in ethanol and 90 per cent ethanol rather than in the later fractions containing higher concentrations of water. The great

[3] The effect of acid on the active principle was observed in preliminary studies by Drs. W. Frick and S. Hajdu at the Institute for Muscle Research, Woods Hole, Mass. in 1952.

ease with which very dilute acid converts the precursor into the more polar lysolecithin and the appearance of a petroleum ether extractable long chain aldehyde in the medium suggest that the precursor may be a hemiacetal of the lysolecithin with a fatty aldehyde.

Efforts to isolate the precursor in chemically pure form have not been successful. Preparations have been obtained, however, which were estimated to be from 50 to 70 per cent pure on the basis of the biological activity produced by acid treatment. The aldehyde content of these preparations as measured by the Rapport and Alonzo (1955b) modification of the Feulgen procedure was roughly in agreement with that to be expected if a hemiacetal were the precursor. Quantitative estimations were untrustworthy, since the Feulgen procedure does not provide an absolute measure of tissue aldehydes. Evidence for the existence of hemiacetals in which the fatty aldehyde is bound to the α position of lysolecithin has recently been published by Klenk and Debuch (1955). It has been suggested by Klenk that a similar structure may represent the naturally occurring form of the acetal phospholipids, isolated by Feulgen and Bersin (1939) and that the acetal which these authors reported may have arisen during isolation by degradation of the hemiacetal form.

Although our data offer no information concerning the possible natural occurrence of the acetal form, they are consistent with the existence of the hemiacetal structure. In order to avoid ambiguity in future reference to the two types of aldehyde-containing phospholipids it is suggested that the hemiacetal structure containing both esterified fatty acid and fatty aldehyde be referred to as *aldolecithin.*

DISCUSSION. It has been observed that two components of mammalian tissue can exert effects very similar to those of digitalis in the frog heart assay. These occur in very minute amounts in plasma and liver and it is at present difficult to say which, if either, may account for the digitalis-like effects which have been observed in liver by Rein *et al.* (1949), Mertens and Rein (1949) and Bücherl and Rein (1949), and in serum by Hajdu and Szent-Györgyi (1952).

One of these substances has been characterized as palmitoyl lysolecithin. The toxic, contracture-causing α isomer which accompanied it in some preparations is probably an artefact arising by intramolecular migration of the ester bond during manipulation. Such migrations are commonly observed with glycol esters (Fischer, 1920).

It is possible that lysolecithin may have an important physiologic role. Our observations indicate that it can affect the heart and vascular muscle *in vitro* and its hemolytic effects are well known. It is possible that the hemiacetal precursor provides a convenient non-hemolytic form in which lysolecithin may be transported to a site of action, perhaps a muscle membrane, where it can be released as needed by enzymes which detach the fatty aldehyde.

The much more abundant lecithins could also, of course, serve as precursors of lysolecithins. In this case ester hydrolysis by tissue phospholipase A would release the active principle. In view of the number of fatty acids of different molecular weight and varying degrees of unsaturation found in lecithin, it might

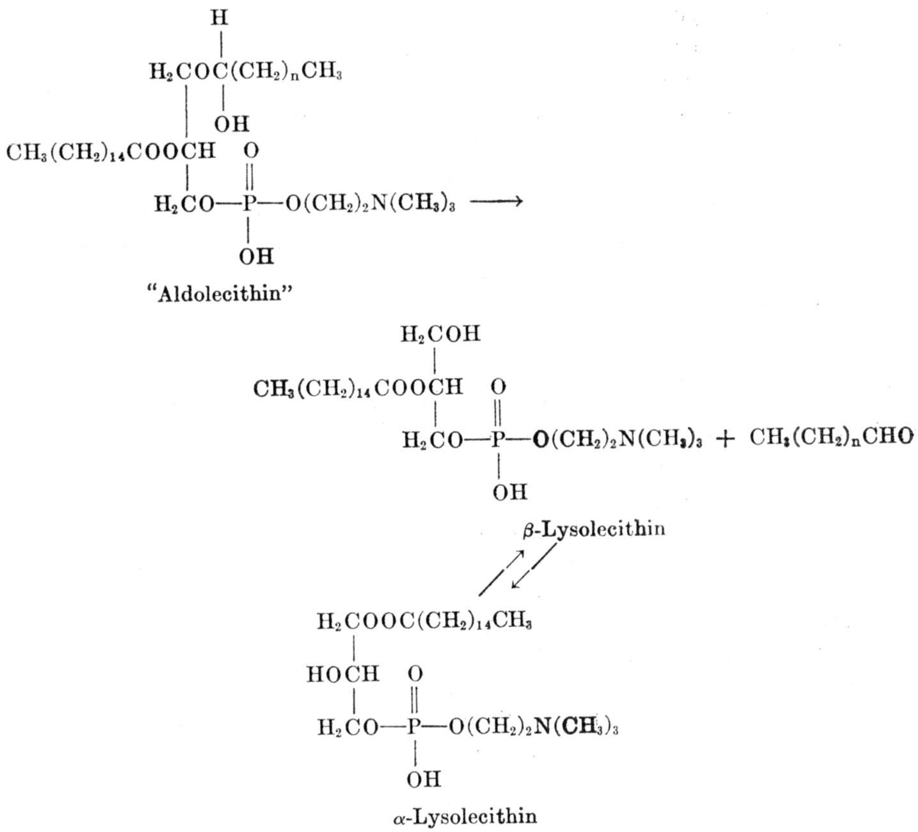

FIG. 4. Conversion of "Aldolecithin" to active β-lysolecithin and transformation of the latter to the contracture-causing α-lysolecithin.

be expected that the resulting product would be a complex mixture of lecithins. Since all of the free lysolecithin of the adrenal was palmitoyl (C_{16}, saturated), and since the same substance was the only product obtained on acid hydrolysis of the precursor it is tempting to speculate that removal of aldehyde from the hemiacetal may be the only way of providing lysolecithin at the site where it is to be used physiologically.

The precursor of the lysolecithin has no biological activity on the heart. Palmitoyl lysolecithin which has been isolated from biological fluids has the following activities: it increases the tension of the hypodynamic frog heart, abolishes the staircase of the frog heart, increases the tension of the hypodynamic squab ventricular muscle, and causes contracture of the isolated carotid artery strip. In all these respects the action of digitalis is similar. Furthermore, the lysolecithin resembles the glycosides by virtue of its strong binding to the membrane, a quality not shared by other cardiotonic substances.

Although our experiments indicated that the digitalis-like effects on the staircase are a general property of lysolecithins, too few of these substances have been examined to permit adequate correlation of effectiveness with the length and degree of unsaturation of the fatty acid side chain. In general the other lysolecithins which have been tested were approximately one-half to one-fourth as active on a weight basis as the adrenal substance.

Since the identification of palmitoyl lysolecithin was carried out by chemical degradation, the possibility that the active molecule is a polymeric form containing more than one lysolecithin unit has not been rigorously excluded.

The isolation of this compound was followed by the comparison of its action on the frog heart to that of strophanthidin, which has been previously proposed to act by slowing the rate of K^+ reentry into the muscle cells after contraction (Hajdu, 1953). Direct evidence that lysolecithin may similarly affect K^+ reentry has not yet been obtained.

The active material is unevenly distributed in the body, occurring in the highest concentration in the adrenal medulla. It is of interest that it is present in the heart in high concentration, about forty times that in skeletal muscle. It is possible that phospholipid is synthesized in chromaffin tissue, transported in inactive form and concentrated in the heart.

α-Lysolecithin is regarded as an artefact of chemical handling, and there is no evidence that it occurs physiologically. It has no digitalis-like effect on the staircase phenomenon of the heart, but causes a sudden contracture, a toxic action which resembles that of the saponins such as digitonin.

The main purpose of this work was to isolate a substance which has biological activity similar to that of digitalis. Whether β-lysolecithin is involved *in vivo* in cardiac function is a question which remains to be answered.

SUMMARY

A substance with digitalis-like activity occurring in mammalian blood and tissues has been isolated and identified as β-palmitoyl lysolecithin.

Much of the lysolecithin occurs as an inactive precursor, presumably in the form of a hemiacetal derivative of a fatty aldehyde. The substance is unevenly distributed in the body occurring in highest concentration in adrenal medulla and in the heart. Little or none occurs in skeletal muscle.

Its digitalis-like activity has been shown by its effect on the hypodynamic frog heart, on the staircase phenomenon in the isolated frog ventricle, on the tension developed by the right ventricular wall of the squab and the isolated carotid strip of the rabbit.

Two forms of lysolecithin, esterified at the α and β positions of glycerol were isolated. Of these, the α isomer was presumed to be an artefact arising by intramolecular rearrangement of the β form during isolation.

α-Lysolecithin, which has no digitalis-like activity, was found to be readily hydrolyzed by the phospholipase A of snake venom.

Acknowledgments. The authors wish to thank Dr. Maurice Pechet for his assistance in the paper chromatographic experiments, Professor Erich Baer for generous gifts of synthetic lecithins and lysolecithins, and Dr. D. J. Hanahan for a sample of stearoyl lysolecithin.

REFERENCES

APPLETON, H. D., LA DU, B. N., LEVY, B. B., STEELE, J. M., AND BRODIE, B. B.: J. Biol. Chem., **205:** 803, 1953.
BAER, E., BUCHNEA, D., AND NEWCOMBE, A. G.: J. Am. Chem. Soc. **78:**, 232, 1956.
BAGGET, B., ENGEL, L. L., AND FIELDING, L. L.: J. Biol. Chem., **213:** 87, 1955.
BÜCHERL, E., AND REIN, H.: Naturwissenschaften, **36:** 260, 1949.
CHARGAFF, E., LEVINE, C., AND GREEN, C.: J. Biol. Chem., **175:** 67, 1948.
CLARK, A. J.: J. Physiol., **47:** 66, 1913–14.
CRAIG, L. C., GOLUMBIC, C., MIGHTON, H., AND TITUS, E.: J. Biol. Chem., **161:** 321, 1945.
FEULGEN, R., AND BERSIN, T.: Hoppe-Seyler's Z. physiol. Chem., **260:** 217, 1939.
FISCHER, E.: Ber. deut. chem. Ges., **53:** 1621, 1920.
GOLLWITZER-MEIER, K., AND KRÜGER, E.: Arch. f. d. ges. Physiol., **240:** 89, 1938.
GREMELS, H.: Arch. f. exper. Path. u. Pharmakol., **182:** 1, 1936.
GREMELS, H.: Arch. f. exper. Path. u. Pharmakol., **194:** 629, 1940.
HANAHAN, D. J.: J. Biol. Chem., **207:** 879, 1954.
HANAHAN, D. J., RODBELL, M., AND TURNER, L. D.: J. Biol. Chem., **206:** 431, 1954.
HAJDU, S.: Amer. J. Physiol., **174:** 371, 1953.
HAJDU, S.: THIS JOURNAL, **120:** 90, 1957.
HAJDU, S., AND SZENT-GYÖRGYI, A.: Am. J. Physiol., **168:** 159, 1952.
HOUGH, L.: Nature, **165:** 400, 1950.
KLENK, E., AND DEBUCH, H.: Hoppe-Seyler's Z. physiol. Chem., **299:** 66, 1955.
KUTSCHERA-AICHENGERGER, H.: Wien Arch. f. inn. Med., **18:** 209, 1929.
LEONARD, E.: Am. J. Physiol., in press.
McDOWALL, R. J. S., AND ZAYAT, A. F.: J. Physiol., **117:** 75p, 1952.
MERTENS, O., AND REIN, H.: Naturwissenschaften, **36:** 237, 1949.
MICHEEL, F., AND SCHWEPPE, H.: Angew. Chem., **66:** 136, 1954a.
MICHEEL, F., AND SCHWEPPE, H.: Mikrochim. Acta, 53, 1954b.
MORTIMER, D. C.: Can. J. Chem., **30:** 653, 1952.
PECHET, M.: Science, **121:** 39, 1955.
PINOTTI, O.: Arch. di fisiol., **42:** 160, 1941.
RAPPORT, M., AND ALONZO, N.: J. Biol. Chem., **217:** 193, 1955a.
RAPPORT, M., AND ALONZO, N.: J. Biol. Chem., **217:** 199, 1955b.
REIN, H.: Klin. Wchnschr., **21:** 873, 1942.
REIN, H., MERTENS, O., AND BÜCHERL, E.: Naturwissenschaften, **36:** 233, 1949.
RUBOW, V.: Arch. f. exper. Path. u. Pharmakol., **52:** 173, 1905.
SCHULZE, G., AND SÜDHOF, H.: Pflügers Arch. ges. Physiol., **258:** 211, 1953.

HEMODYNAMIC EFFECTS OF LEVARTERENOL INFUSION DURING INDUCED PULMONARY STENOSIS[1]

NOBLE O. FOWLER, E. R. DUCHESNE AND R. H. FRANCH

Georgia State Heart Association Cardiovascular Research Laboratory, Grady Memorial Hospital, and the Department of Medicine, Emory University, Atlanta

Received for publication November 15, 1956

Studies of the cardiac effects of levarterenol have led to conflicting interpretations. Goldenberg *et al.* (1948) found no significant increase of cardiac output in eight human subjects given an infusion of 0.11 to 0.4 micrograms/kgm./minute of levarterenol. Shadle, Moore, and Billig (1955) found in the dog no consistent increase of cardiac output attendant upon the infusion of levarterenol, 0.5 to 2.5 micrograms/kgm./minute.

On the other hand, Hellems *et al.* (1953) found an increase in cardiac output of anesthetized dogs upon the infusion of arterenol, 19 to 43 micrograms/minute. Also DeLaunois and Vandenberghen (1954) and Brewster *et al.* (1956) found an increase in cardiac output following levarterenol infusion in dogs.

The purpose of the present study is to observe the hemodynamic effects of levarterenol upon the heart with an increased work load.

METHOD. Studies were performed upon mongrel dogs of both sexes, anesthetized with sodium pentobarbital, 30 mgm./kgm. intravenously and weighing 13.6 to 30.9 kilograms. Supplemental doses of sodium pentobarbital were administered at intervals of twenty minutes to one hour in order to keep the level of anesthesia constant. A total of 23 dogs was studied.

Systemic arterial pressures were recorded from a cannula placed in the common carotid artery. Right atrial and pulmonary arterial pressures were recorded through #7 to #9 cardiac catheters. Five centimeters above the animal board was used as a zero reference point for pressure measurements. Pressures were recorded upon a four channel direct-writing oscillograph using electromanometers. Mean pressures were determined by electrical integration. The electromanometers were calibrated with mercury manometers before and after each experiment. The baseline was checked before and after each pressure recording for balance shift and electrical drift, the combined total of which was not permitted to exceed 1.25 per cent of full scale. In most experiments, the electrocardiogram was recorded. Cardiac outputs were measured by the Fick principle. Expired air was collected from an indwelling endotracheal tube over a three-minute period in a Douglas bag, measured in a wet-test meter and analyzed in the Scholander 0.5 ml. gas analyzer. The endotracheal tube was checked for leaks before each output. Duplicate samples were required to check within 0.04 vol. per cent. Midway during the collection of expired air, simultaneous samples of pulmonary and systemic arterial blood were collected over a one-minute period. Blood samples were analyzed for oxygen in the Van Slyke manometric apparatus. Duplicate samples were required to check within 0.2 ml. per 100 ml.

In ten dogs, experimental procedure was as follows: Respirations were maintained by positive pressure. The chest was opened on the left side. The main pulmonary artery was dissected free of the aorta, and was progressively constricted by means of an umbilical tape

[1] Supported by a grant from the Georgia State Heart Association and by grant H2161, United States Public Health Service.

passed through a rubber cuff until one of the following occurred: 1) fall in systemic arterial pressure; 2) elevation of systolic pulmonary arterial pressure proximal to the constriction to 55 to 60 mm. mercury; or 3) dilatation of the right ventricle. Pulmonary arterial constriction was maintained at this degree throughout the remainder of the study. After a period of 15 to 20 minutes, 3 to 7.7 micrograms/kgm./minute (expressed as base) of levarterenol were given. Measurements were made of pressures and cardiac outputs during a control period (period 1); 10 to 15 minutes after pulmonary artery constriction (period 2); during the first levarterenol infusion (period 3); 10 to 15 minutes after discontinuance of the first levarterenol infusion (period 4); and during a second levarterenol infusion (period 5). The foregoing studies were done in eight animals.

In two animals, pulmonary artery constriction was not tolerated by the heart. In these animals some degree of persistent right ventricular dilatation followed pulmonary arterial constriction. The effect of levarterenol infusion upon cardiac dynamics was studied after discontinuing pulmonary artery constriction in these two dogs since it was apparent that cessation of effectual cardiac contraction would occur if constriction were continued. In 13 intact anesthetized dogs, the effect of levarterenol infusion upon hemodynamics was observed. Seven dogs received infusion of 0.5 microgram of levarterenol/kgm./minute; six received large dose infusions of 3.6 to 7.3 micrograms/kgm./minute. In four dogs observation was made of the effect during pulmonary arterial constriction of increasing aortic pressure by clamping the aorta and left subclavian artery.

RESULTS. The following results were obtained in the eight dogs in which repeated studies during pulmonary artery constriction were made.

External effects. The infusion of levarterenol was in each instance associated with increase in the vigor of cardiac contraction, decrease in cardiac size, usually increase in heart rate, and often the appearance of premature contractions. After cessation of levarterenol infusion, cardiac contraction often appeared more feeble than during the control period.

The effects of levarterenol infusion upon cardiac output and arteriovenous oxygen difference in eight animals with pulmonary arterial construction are shown in table 1. It may be seen that cardiac output fell during pulmonary artery constriction in seven of the eight animals. Cardiac output rose during the first levarterenol infusion in seven of eight animals. This was associated with a decrease in arteriovenous oxygen difference in each animal having an increase in cardiac output. There was a striking decrease in cardiac output and marked increase in arteriovenous oxygen difference in each of seven animals studied following discontinuance of levarterenol infusion. During the second levarterenol infusion, there was a definite increase in cardiac output and decrease in arteriovenous oxygen difference. In table 2, it may be seen that arteriovenous oxygen difference increased significantly over control during pulmonary artery constriction from a mean of 7.3 to 8.39, $p < 0.01$[2]. During the first levarterenol infusion, the arteriovenous difference decreased from 8.72 to 5.78, $p < 0.05$. After discontinuing the drug, arteriovenous oxygen difference increased significantly from 5.78 to 11.18, $p < 0.001$. During a second levarterenol infusion, arteriovenous oxygen difference decreased significantly from a mean of 11.18 to 6.77 in six animals, $p < 0.01$, table 2.

[2] Student t test as described in Snedecor, G. W., *Statistical Methods*, Iowa State College Press, 1946, is used here and in all other tests of significance in this paper.

Effect upon cardiac output of levarterenol infusion during pulmonary artery constriction

Dog weight; Dose Levarterenol, micrograms/kgm./minute—1st and 2nd Infusion	Period 1 Control			Period 2 P.A. Constricted			Period 3 1st Levarterenol			Period 4 After 1st Levarterenol			Period 5 2nd Levarterenol		
	O_2 Cons. *ml./min.*	A-V O_2 diff.	C.O. *ml./kgm./min.*	O_2 Cons. *ml./min.*	A-V O_2 diff.	C.O. *ml./kgm./min.*	O_2 Cons. *ml./min.*	A-V O_2 diff.	C.O. *ml./kgm./min.*	O_2 Cons. *ml./min.*	A-V O_2 diff.	C.O. *ml./kgm./min.*	O_2 Cons. *ml./min.*	A-V O_2 diff.	C.O. *ml./kgm./min.*
6-A 20 kgm. 5.0 micrograms 4.2 micrograms	165	19.5–15.2* 4.3	191	130	210–14.9 6.1	106	137	21.7–17.0 4.7	147	123	19.3–11.3 8.0	78	152	19.4–13.1 6.3	120
7-A 29 kgm. 3.0 micrograms 3.9 micrograms	149	14.7–9.0 5.7	97	149	17.0–11.4 5.6	99	177	17.8–12.7 5.1	129	158	16.3–7.8 8.5	69	148	17.0–11.7 5.3	103
8-A 13.6 kgm. 4.7 micrograms 5.2 micrograms	96	20.9–14.5 6.4	110	81	17.5–9.4 8.1	74	61	18.9–14.4 4.5	99	59	15.0–6.5 8.5	51	132	15.4–10.5 4.9	197
10-A 16.8 kgm. 7.7 micrograms 6.5 micrograms	150	23.5–9.3 14.2	63	104	24.0–9.7 14.3	43	129	23.9–16.9 7.0	110	102	21.0–7.2 13.8	44	112	20.9–14.7 6.2	108
13-A 17.7 kgm. 5.3 micrograms 5.6 micrograms	181	18.6–11.1 7.5	136	28	18.0–8.4 9.6	17	176	19.4–12.2 7.2	139	73	16.0–2.1 13.9	29	176	15.7–6.7 9.0	111
14-A 26.4 kgm. 3.9 micrograms 4.9 micrograms	171	22.5–15.9 6.6	98	162	24.2–16.3 7.9	77	164	24.3–14.2 9.6	64	118	22.5–6.1 16.3	27	159	20.9–12.0 8.9	67
15-A 30.9 kgm. 3.1 micrograms	190	18.5–13.8 4.7	132	190 177†	20.0–15.1 4.9 19.0–12.7 6.3†	125 90†	246	20.3–15.8 4.5	178	178	18.4–9.1 9.3	62	—	—	—
16-A 20.5 kgm. 4.9 micrograms	145	23.1–14.1 9.0	79	149 117†	22.0–11.4 10.6 21.4–9.5 11.9†	69 48†	213	22.2–18.7 3.6	291	—	—	—	—	—	—

* The first figure represents systemic arterial oxygen content, the second represents pulmonary arterial oxygen content, each expressed in ml./100 ml. of blood.

† Second observation during pulmonary artery constriction after aortic constriction.

The effects of levarterenol upon cardiac output stroke volume, heart rate, systemic arterial pressure, and total peripheral resistance are summarized in table 2.

Cardiac output (*table 2*). The cardiac output in ml./kgm./minute declined significantly from a control mean of 113 to a mean of 76 with constriction of the pulmonary artery, $p < 0.05$. During the first levarterenol infusion, cardiac output rose significantly to a mean of 145, $p < 0.05$. After discontinuance of the drug, cardiac output fell significantly to a mean of 51, $p < 0.001$. With a second

TABLE 2

Hemodynamic effects of infusion of levarterenol during pulmonary artery constriction

	Period 1 Control	Period 2 PA Constricted	Period 3 1st Levarterenol	Period 4 After 1st Levarterenol	Period 5 2nd Levarterenol
C.O., ml./kgm./min.	63–191	17–125	64–291	27–78*	67–197†
Mean	113	76	145	51	118
Change ± S.E.		−37 ± 15	+75 ± 28	−72 ± 11	+68 ± 17
p value		$p < 0.05$	$p < 0.05$	$p < 0.001$	$p < 0.02$
Arteriovenous oxygen diff., ml./100-ml.	4.3–14.2	4.9–14.3	3.6–9.6	8.0–16.3	4.9–9.0
Mean	7.3	8.39 (8.72)‡	5.78	11.18	6.77
Change ± S.E.		+1.1 ± 0.31	−2.95 ± 1.19	+5.1 ± 0.61	−4.7 ± 0.98
p value		$p < 0.01$	$p < 0.05$	$p < 0.001$	$p < 0.01$
Heart rate/min.	125–187	133–167	144–220	125–176	128–255
Mean	157	152	188	151	183
Change ± S.E.		−6 ± 5.2	+41 ± 9.2	−31 ± 11	
p value		$p = 0.3$	$p < 0.01$	$p < 0.05$	
Stroke vol., ml./min.	7–21	5–27	8–33	4–15	7–16
Mean	16	13	21	9	13
Change ± S.E.		−3 ± 0.87	+8 ± 4.27	−11 ± 3.9	−6 ± 2.07
p value		$p < 0.02$	$p = 0.1$	$p < 0.05$	$p < 0.05$
Mean systemic pressure, mm. Hg	58–155	38–125	90–190	19–75	86–190
Mean	109	82	147	42	134
Change ± S.E.		−27 ± 14.1	+70 ± 15.6	−110 ± 13.2	+94 ± 12.9
p value		$p < 0.1$	$p < 0.01$	$p < 0.001$	$p < 0.001$
Total peripheral resistance, dynes sec./cm.$^{-5}$	1982–4707	1927–8392	1247–7401	919–3980	2302–6865
	3713	4294	4105	2617	4851
Change ± S.E.		−580 ± 596	−237 ± 914	−1861 ± 875	+2083 ± 670
p value		$p < 0.4$	$p = 0.8$	$p < 0.1$	$p < 0.05$

* 7 animals in this group.

† 6 animals in this group.

‡ Second mean value indicates two animals restudied prior to levarterenol infusion

TABLE 3

Effect of levarterenol infusion upon pulmonary arterial systolic pressure during pulmonary artery constriction*

Dog	Control	Immed. After Constriction	20 Min. After Constriction	During 1st Levarterenol	After 1st Levarterenol	During 2nd Levarterenol
6-A	46	68	63	139	54	131
7-A	22	63	39	90	39	100
8-A	19	42	29	57	25	44
10-A	20	63	35	136	30	120
14-A	20	60	60	55	19	30
15-A	25	50	50	95	39	—
16-A	21	29	29	88	—	—

Mean increase in P.A. systolic pressure of 51 ± 12.8 mm. mercury was significant, $p < 0.01$, during first infusion of levarterenol.

* Pressure proximal to constriction.

levarterenol infusion, cardiac output again rose significantly to a mean of 118 $p < 0.02$. Cardiac outputs were significantly lower, $p < 0.05$, after discontinuing the first levarterenol infusion than before it.

Heart rate (table 2). Heart rate did not change significantly following pulmonary arterial constriction. Mean heart rate increased significantly from 152 to 188/minute, $p < 0.01$, during the first levarterenol infusion, and decreased significantly after the drug to 151, $p < 0.05$.

Stroke volume (table 2). Stroke volume decreased significantly, $p < 0.02$, following constriction of the pulmonary artery. The increase in stroke volume during the first levarterenol infusion was not significant, $p = 0.1$. However, stroke volume declined significantly, $p < 0.05$, after discontinuance of the first levarterenol infusion, and rose significantly during the second infusion, $p < 0.05$.

Mean systemic arterial pressure (table 2). Average mean systemic blood pressure fell from 109 to 82 mm. mercury upon constricting the pulmonary artery. The decline was not significant, $p < 0.1$. During the first levarterenol infusion, mean pressure rose significantly to 147 mm., $p < 0.01$. After stopping the first infusion, mean systemic blood pressure declined significantly to 42 mm., $p < 0.001$. During the second levarterenol infusion, systemic pressure rose significantly to 134 mm., $p < 0.001$. Systemic pressures were significantly lower, $p < 0.01$, after stopping the drug than before its administration.

Total peripheral resistance (table 2). Total peripheral resistance changed significantly only during the second infusion of levarterenol, at which time there was a significant increase, $p < 0.05$.

In table 3, may be seen the effect of pulmonary artery constriction and of levarterenol infusion on pulmonary arterial pressure proximal to the constriction in seven dogs. In animals 7-A, 8-A and 10-A systolic pressure rose with constriction of the pulmonary artery, but fell after 20 minutes because of weakening of right ventricular contraction. In six of the seven animals the pulmonary artery systolic pressure rose strikingly with levarterenol infusion (table 3). The increase was significant ($p < 0.01$). It may be seen that pulmonary artery systolic pres-

TABLE 4

Effect on cardiac output in normal dogs of infusion of levarterenol, 0.5 micrograms/kilogram/minute

Dog No.	Control			During Inf.			15 Minutes After Inf.		
	O_2 cons. *ml./min.*	A.V. O_2 diff.* *ml./100ml.*	C.O.† *ml./kgm./min.*	O_2 cons. *ml./min.*	A.V. O_2 diff. *ml./100 ml.*	C.O. *ml./kgm./min.*	O_2 cons. *ml./min.*	A.V. O_2 diff. *ml./100 ml.*	C.O. *ml./kgm./min.*
39-A	103	3.2	219	119	5.2	154	—	—	—
40-A	120	3.6	231	115	3.2	214	—	—	—
41-A	104	5.3	121	114	5.1	138	111	4.5	150
42-A	136	9.4	66	161	8.0	9.2	134	11.2	55
43-A	96	4.2	160	99	5.0	96	140	5.2	131
44-A	110	5.9	100	132	4.7	151	129	4.3	160
45-A	94	2.7	243	94	3.4	145	95	3.8	176
Mean.....	—	4.9	163	—	5.0	141	—	—	—

* Arteriovenous oxygen difference expressed as ml./100 ml. of blood.

† Cardiac output expressed in ml./kgm./minute.

sure fell following discontinuation of the drug and rose again with the second infusion. Significance was not calculated because of the small number of animals.

In tables 4 and 5 are shown the effects of levarterenol infusion upon the arteriovenous oxygen difference and cardiac output in 13 dogs without pulmonary artery constriction. It may be seen in table 4 that the infusion of 0.5 microgram/kgm./minute of levarterenol was associated with an increase in cardiac output in only one dog—#42-A. This animal had an abnormally low cardiac output with a wide arteriovenous oxygen difference in the control period. However, it is shown in table 5 that infusion of larger doses of levarterenol (3.6 to 7.33 micrograms/kgm./minute) was associated with a significant increase in cardiac output in each of six animals. The mean cardiac output rose from 162 ml./kgm./minute to 227 ml./kgm./minute during levarterenol infusion. The mean increase of 65 ± 11.3 was significant, $p < 0.01$. Following discontinuation of the infusion the mean output fell to 137 ml./kgm./minute. The mean decrease of 90 ± 16 was significant, $p < 0.01$. Cardiac output rose again during a second infusion of levarterenol in each of five animals. Not included in the tables are dogs 9-A and 11-A who received large doses of levarterenol. These animals were in shock at the beginning of the study and did not tolerate pulmonary arterial constriction. In dog 9-A arteriovenous oxygen difference narrowed from 17.9 ml./100 ml. of blood to 2.3 ml./100 ml. during infusion of levarterenol, and increased to 14.3 ml./100 ml. following discontinuation of the drug. Oxygen consumption was too low during the initial shock for accurate calculation of cardiac output. Dog 11-A showed an increase in cardiac output from 61 ml./kgm./minute in the control period to 154 ml./kgm./minute during infusion, with a decline to 36 ml./kgm./minute after stopping the drug, and a rise to 123 ml./kgm./minute during a second infusion of levarterenol.

Table 6 shows the effect upon cardiac output, arteriovenous oxygen difference,

TABLE 5

Effect on cardiac output of normal dogs of infusion of large doses of levarterenol

Dog No. and Dose Levarterenol *micrograms/kgm./min.*	Control			During Inf.			15 Minutes After Inf.			During 2nd Infusion			15 Minutes After 2nd Infusion		
	O_2 cons. *ml./min.*	A.V. O_2 diff.*	C.O.†	O_2 cons. *ml./min.*	A.V. O_2 diff.	C.O.	O_2 cons. *ml./min.*	A.V. O_2 diff.	C.O.	O_2 cons *ml./min.*	A.V. O_2 diff.	C.O.	O_2 cons. *ml./min.*	A.V. O_2 diff.	C.O.
12-A 5.2	235	6.3	173	196	4.6	199	131	13.0	47	—	—	—	—	—	—
19-A 5.4	77	5.7	100	90	3.8	174	80	5.5	108	99	4.0	182	84	6.6	95
4.0															
20-A 3.8	126	5.3	109	171	3.8	206	128	5.4	107	155	4.0	179	—	—	—
3.6															
46-A 7.33	116	4.3	183	129	3.4	253	113	4.7	163	126	3.6	240	—	—	—
7.33															
47-A 7.33	107	4.2	186	128	3.4	273	104	3.3	239	113	3.2	262	—	—	—
7.33															
48-A 7.33	77	3.5	220	89	3.4	259	83	5.2	159	99	5.6	177	90	6.6	136
7.33															
Mean	—	4.9	162	—	3.7	227	—	4.23	137	—	4.1	208	—	—	—
Change ± S.E.						+65 ± 11.3			−90 ± 16						
p value						p < 0.01			p < 0.01						

* Arteriovenous oxygen difference expressed in ml./100 ml. of blood.

† Cardiac Output expressed in ml./kgm./minute.

TABLE 6

Effect of aortic occlusion upon hemodynamics during pulmonary artery constriction

Dog	Control			P. A. Constriction			Aortic Const.			After Aortic Const.			Levarterenol		
	C.O., *ml./kgm./min.*	A-V O_2 diff. *ml./100 ml.*	Systemic B.P. *mm. mercury*	C.O., *ml./kgm./min.*	A-V O_2 diff. *ml./100 ml.*	Systemic B.P. *mm. mercury*	C.O., *ml./kgm./min.*	A-V O_2 diff. *ml./100 ml.*	Systemic B.P. *mm. mercury*	C.O., *ml./kgm./min.*	A-V O_2 diff. *ml./100/ml.*	Systemic B.P. *mm. mercury*	C.O., *ml./kgm./min.*	A-V O_2 diff. *ml./100 ml.*	Systemic B.P. *mm. mercury*
15-A	132	4.7	105	125	4.9	125	77	4.9	155	90	6.3	88	178	4.5	115
16-A	79	9.0	90	69	10.6	40	78	7.2	90	48	11.9	35	291	3.6	116
17-A	—	5.3	105	89	6.0	92	84	7.9	100	—	—	—	128	5.1	185
18-A	—	—	—	134	6.2	105	135	3.2	155	—	—	—	166	3.3	180

and systemic blood pressure in 4 dogs of occluding the left subclavian artery and the aorta distal to the left subclavian artery. In dogs 15-A and 16-A, aortic occlusion was released prior to levarterenol infusion. In dogs 17-A and 18-A, levarterenol infusion was given while aortic occlusion was maintained. It may be seen that although aortic occlusion increased systemic pressure proximal to the occlusion, there was an increase in cardiac output only in dog 16-A. Levarterenol infusion increased cardiac output greatly in dogs 15-A and 16-A in whom aortic occlusion was not maintained, and moderately in dogs 17-A and 18-A, in whom aortic occlusion was maintained.

The effect of levarterenol infusion upon right atrial mean pressure in the acutely dilated heart merits a comment. Because of the rapid onset of ventricular fibrillation during the acute right ventricular dilatation following severe pulmonary artery constriction, it was difficult to follow acute right atrial pressure changes during the initial infusion of levarterenol.

The effect of levarterenol infusion upon right atrial pressure and heart size was observed in two dogs in whom severe acute right heart dilation occurred during pulmonary artery constriction. In one dog, upon stopping the first levarterenol infusion, there occurred marked dilatation of the right ventricle and elevation of right atrial pressure from 4 to 10.5 cm. of water. During reinstitution of levarterenol infusion, the right ventricle became definitely smaller, although still dilated; right atrial pressure fell to 6.5 cm. of water. In a second dog with right heart dilatation, right atrial mean pressure rose from 5.5 mm. mercury during levarterenol infusion to 13 mm. mercury following infusion and fell again to 7 mm. mercury during a second infusion of levarterenol. The right heart dilated greatly as levarterenol was discontinued, and decreased in size when the drug was reinfused.

In the non-dilated heart, the effect of levarterenol upon right atrial mean pressure was variable, the change not exceeding 2 mm. mercury in either direction.

Discussion. The foregoing results indicate that large dose infusions of levarterenol have considerable cardiac effect in the anesthetized dog. It seems clear that cardiac output was increased by levarterenol infusion under conditions of the experiment, both in the failing dilated heart and in the heart not under stress. The results suggest, under conditions of the experiment, that cardiac contraction is, at least temporarily, weaker after discontinuing levarterenol infusion than before it under conditions of acute pulmonary artery constriction. Whether this is due to deterioration of the preparation or exhaustion of cardiac sources of energy by levarterenol cannot be stated with certainty. Another possible cause of this effect is that of peripheral venous pooling following discontinuation of the drug.

These studies show also that large dose levarterenol infusions produce cardiac acceleration, and auricular and ventricular premature contractions. Further evidence of cardiac action is the decrease in the size of the heart during levarterenol infusion. This is especially striking if the heart is dilated. The minimal changes in total peripheral resistance during the first levarterenol infusion suggest that the increase in cardiac output was the principal reason for the elevation of systemic blood pressure occurring at this time.

Although it has been postulated that pressor drugs combat acute right ventricular failure by increasing coronary perfusion pressure (Salisbury, 1955), no striking increase in cardiac output was seen when proximal aortic pressure was elevated by aortic constriction, although the heart was still capable of increasing its output when levarterenol was infused. In this connection, Lu and Melville (1951) found in the isolated rabbit heart that arterenol infusion increased the strength of cardiac contraction before increasing coronary flow. The latter effect was observed only as the effect on cardiac contraction subsided.

Many studies in recent years have shown that levarterenol has important cardiac effects. Garb (1950) using an isolated papillary muscle preparation, found more increase in contractile force produced by *d,l*-arterenol than by epinephrine. Luedena *et al.* (1949) found that infusion of levarterenol in animals increased the amplitude of cardiac contraction from 40 per cent to 300 per cent. Gazes, Goldberg and Darby (1953) and Cotten and Pincus (1955) found that the force of cardiac contraction in the dog, measured by a strain gauge arch sutured to the ventricle, was increased by levarterenol. Ebert *et al.* (1955) found that levarterenol increased the cardiac output of dogs with shock due to meningococcus toxin. Zanetti and Opdyke (1953) found no difference between *l*-epinephrine and levarterenol in the dog with regard to acute changes in cardiac cycle length, aortic systolic and diastolic pressures, and calculated stroke index.

The difference between our results and those reported by Goldenberg and co-workers in man (1948) insofar as the effect of levarterenol upon cardiac output is concerned may be due to several factors. One is the dose of drug used. In our present studies, the dose of levarterenol per unit weight was approximately ten times the maximal dose employed by Goldenberg. A second factor is the possible modifying effect of the anesthesia used in our study. A third possible factor is the species difference. Our failure to find consistent increase in the cardiac output of anesthetized dogs receiving a dose of levarterenol in the range used by Goldenberg, together with the observation of significant increase in cardiac output of animals receiving larger doses of the drug, suggests that the large dose of levarterenol used in the study, in part explains the difference between our observations and those of Goldenberg.

SUMMARY

In anesthetized dogs with pulmonary artery constriction, infusion of levarterenol, 3 to 7.7 micrograms/kgm./minute produced the following effects:

1) A significant increase in cardiac output—the cardiac output after discontinuing levarterenol declined to a figure below that before the drug; 2) significant cardiac acceleration; 3) significant increase in systemic arterial pressure without increase of total peripheral resistance during the first infusion; 4) decrease in cardiac size, especially if dilated; 5) reduction in right atrial pressure if elevated because of right heart dilation; and 6) a significant increase in pulmonary arterial systolic pressure.

Levarterenol infusion was also observed to increase cardiac output in the intact animal without pulmonary artery constriction when doses of 3.6 to 7.33 micrograms/kgm./minute were infused. No consistent increase in cardiac output was observed when the dose infused was 0.5 microgram/kgm./minute.

Acknowledgment. The technical assistance of Miss Mary Elizabeth Shannon and Mrs. Bonnie Covell is acknowledged.

REFERENCES

Brewster, W. R., Jr., Isaacs, J. P., Osgood, P. F., and King, T. L.: Circulation, **13:** 1, 1956.

Cotten, M. deV., and Pincus, Sylvester: This Journal, **114:** 110, 1955.

DeLaunois, A. L., and Vandenberghen, C.: Arch. internat. de Pharmacodyn. et de Therap., **99:** 435, 1954.

Ebert, R. V., Borden, C. W., Hall, W. H., and Gold, D.: Circulation Research, **3:** 378, 1955.

Garb, S.: Proc. Soc. Exper. Biol. & Med., **73:** 134, 1950.

Gazes, P. C., Goldberg, L. I., and Darby, T. D.: Circulation, **8:** 883, 1953.

Goldenberg, M., Pines, K. L., Baldwin, E. deF., Greene, D. G., and Roh, C. E.: Am. J. Med., **5:** 792, 1948.

Hellems, H. K., Leight, L., Clifford, G. O., Heinrich, C., and Snider, T. H.: Clinical Research Proc., **1:** 6, 1953.

Lu, F. C., and Melville, K. I. J. Physiol., **113:** 365, 1951.

Luedena, F. P., Ananenko, E., Siegmund, O. H., and Miller, L. C.: This Journal, **95:** 155, 1949.

Salisbury, P. F.: Circulation Research, **3:** 633, 1955.

Shadle, D. W., Moore, J. C., and Billig, D. M.: Circulation Research, **3:** 385, 1955.

Zanetti, M. E., and Opdyke, D. F.: Am. J. Physiol., **109:** 107, 1953.

BIOASSAY OF *RAUWOLFIA* ROOTS AND ALKALOIDS[1]

BERNARD RUBIN, MARVIN H. MALONE, MARGARET H. WAUGH
AND JOHN C. BURKE

The Squibb Institute for Medical Research, New Brunswick, New Jersey

Received for publication November 23, 1956

Oral preparations of *Rauwolfia serpentina* have come into widespread use in the therapy of hypertension and neuropsychiatric disorders. These preparations have included powdered whole root, various extracts thereof, and the alkaloid reserpine. It is not yet clear whether the total activity of the natural preparations is attributable solely to their reserpine content. Clinical estimates of the ratio of therapeutically equivalent dosages of reserpine and powdered whole root of *R. serpentina* have varied widely. These include 1:1000 (Wilkins, 1954), 1:500 (Tuchman and Crumpton, 1955), and 1:250 (Moyer *et al.*, 1955) in the treatment of hypertension, and 1:500 (Kline, 1954) and 1:100 (Holt *et al.*, 1955) in the treatment of mental disorders. These reported variations in equivalence of dosages are not surprising in view of the flat dose-response relationships obtained with either short term or chronic courses of therapy.

Cronheim *et al.* (1953) and Kohli and Mukerji (1955) suggested that reserpine did not account for all the potency found in *R. serpentina* or an extract thereof in laboratory studies with dogs and monkeys. Neither report, however, cited quantitative details to support these conclusions.

It is the purpose of this report to compare quantitatively the reserpine-like activity of single doses of the whole roots of *R. serpentina*, *R. heterophylla*, and *R. canescens* in the mouse, rat, and dog with their respective reserpine contents. The ptotic responses were ascertained in each of the 3 animal species, the hypotensive responses were measured in rats and dogs, the changes in body weight were determined in rats, and the degrees of sedation, miosis and relaxation of nictitating membrane were ascertained in dogs. The alkaloids rescinnamine, 11-desmethoxyreserpine and methyl reserpate were also compared with reserpine in one or more of the 3 animal species.

MATERIALS AND METHODS. *Materials*. Each of the 3 species of *Rauwolfia* root was a blended root batch which had been identified pharmacognostically; the same root batch of each *Rauwolfia* species was used for all comparative studies reported herein. The batches of *R. serpentina* root and of *R. canescens* root were of Indian origin; the batch of *R. heterophylla* was of Central American origin.

Samples of reserpine, rescinnamine, and *Rauwolfia* roots were obtained from Drs. O. P. Wintersteiner and R. F. Varney of the Organic Chemistry and Quality Control Divisions, respectively, E. R. Squibb & Sons. Samples of rescinnamine and 11-desmethoxyreserpine were made available by Dr. G. E. Cronheim of Riker Laboratories and Dr. W. G. Bywater of S. B. Penick and Company.

---

[1] A preliminary report was presented at the meeting of The American Society for Pharmacology and Experimental Therapeutics held at Iowa City, Iowa, in September, 1955 (THIS JOURNAL, **116:** 50, 1956).

Preparation of solutions and suspensions. Each *Rauwolfia* root was ground until the total sample passed a 200 mesh screen and was then suspended on the day of test by trituration in 0.25 per cent agar solution at concentrations of 80 mgm./ml. or less. The crystalline alkaloids were dissolved in glacial acetic and then diluted with distilled water to yield stock concentrations of 10 mgm. alkaloid/ml. of 10 per cent acetic acid. These stock solutions were stored at 7°C. and utilized within two weeks. Fresh daily working dilutions of the alkaloids were prepared with distilled water (for parenteral) or with 0.25 per cent agar solution (for *peroral* use) to yield alkaloidal concentrations of 0.08 to 0.64 mgm./ml. in 0.08 to 0.64 per cent acetic acid. Equivalent dose-volumes of all test materials were administered in all tests or assays with a given animal species.

Mice. In mice only the ptotic assay (Rubin *et al.*, 1953; Rubin and Burke, 1954) was employed as an index of reserpine-like activity. White male mice, ranging in body weight from 16 to 24 grams, were fasted 2 to 4 hours. Each mouse received a single oral dose of reserpine or of *Rauwolfia* root. Maximal ptotic effects were apparent 5 to 7 hours later at which time each eye was given a ptotic score of 0-4 according to the scale shown in figure 1. The test response, which ranged from 0-8 for each mouse, was the sum of the scores for the

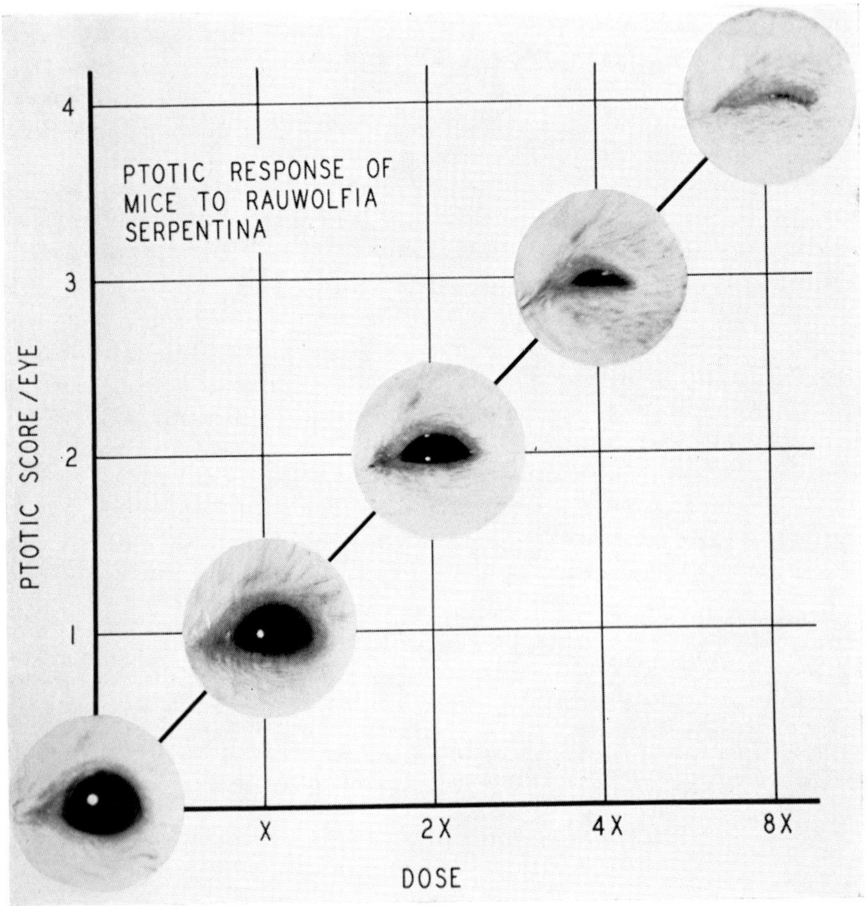

FIG. 1. Schematic relationship between graded ptotic score and increasing dosage of *Rauwolfia serpentina* whole root or of reserpine-containing substance.

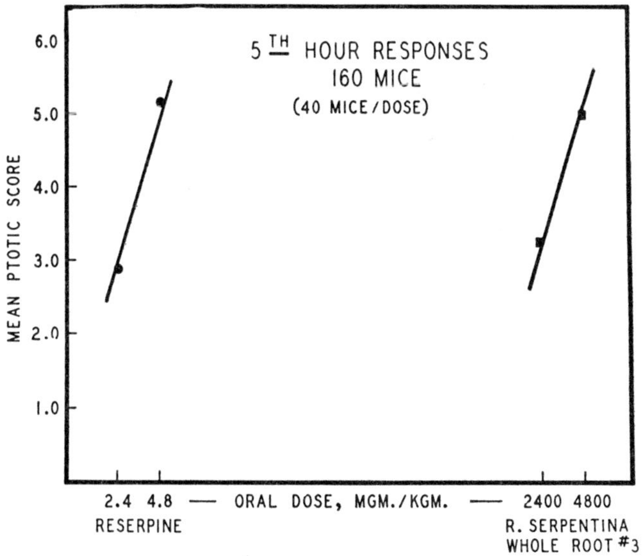

FIG. 2. Dose-response relationships in a comparative assay of *Rauwolfia serpentina* whole root and reserpine in mice.

2 eyes. At least 2 or 3 dose levels were employed in factorially designed assays with a dose interval of 2 × and generally with 30 to 40 mice at each dose level. The oral dose ranges employed were 1.2 to 4.8 mgm./kgm. for reserpine and 1200 to 4800 mgm./kgm. for each *Rauwolfia* root. A representative assay of *R. serpentina* whole root versus reserpine is shown in figure 2. An average λ (s/b) value of 0.24 was obtained in the first 21 ptotic assays in mice, *i.e.*, the standard deviation (s) about the dosage-response line was nearly one-fourth the slope (b) of this line. λ or (s/b) represents the inherent precision of an assay and can be used to estimate the number of animals or responses required for a given level of assay error (Bliss, 1952). Accordingly at least 120 mice were used in each comparative assay of *Rauwolfia* root with reserpine in order to obtain confidence limits of ±20 per cent or better.

The method of assay of the several alkaloids by either the oral or intravenous route was essentially identical to that described above except for adjustments in dosage as needed for the production of the typical graded effects.

In the intravenous assays 0.2 ml./20 gm. body weight were ordinarily administered via a lateral tail vein to each mouse during a 20-second period.

Rats. In rats the criteria of reserpine-like activity employed were ptosis, hypotension and body weight change within a 24-hour period after dosage. The ability of these agents to produce inanition and weight loss in laboratory animals has been previously described (Rubin *et al.*, 1953; Gaunt *et al.*, 1954). Male albino rats of from 200 to 300 grams were fasted 18 to 24 hours and then dosed with alkaloid or whole root. After dosage, food and water were given *ad libitum*. In addition to a control group of rats dosed with acetic acid and agar solution, at least 2 or 3 dose levels were employed for each preparation in factorially designed assays with a dose interval of 2 ×. Groups of 16 to 28 rats were employed per dose in the assays of whole roots and 7 to 20 rats per dose in the assays of the alkaloids. The oral dose ranges commonly employed were 9.6 to 38.4 mgm./kgm. for reserpine and 2400 to 9600 mgm./kgm. for *Rauwolfia* whole root. Because of the high dose volumes required with whole root in the rat, each dose (of whole root or of reserpine) was subdivided equally into two portions administered 30 minutes apart.

The degree of ptosis was evaluated in rats in a manner similar to that employed in mice.

The peak ptotic effects of these agents occurred 10 to 24 hours after oral dosage and the latter time was ordinarily selected for measurements. With intravenous administration of the alkaloids, the peak ptotic effects occurred closer to the 10th hour; in some instances determinations were also made at the 5th and 24th hours.

After the ptotic effects had been recorded, if blood pressure measurements were to be made, each rat was anesthetized with pentobarbital sodium 50 mgm./kgm. intraperitoneally. A small incision was then made in the neck, a carotid artery was isolated, and mean blood pressure was determined by direct arterial puncture with a 22 gauge needle. A mercury manometer with connecting polyethylene tubing and glass bore of 2 mm. internal diameter was employed which required a maximum blood displacement of approximately 0.25 ml. The tubing leading from the mercury reservoir to the needle was filled with 0.02 per cent heparin in 0.9 per cent sodium chloride solution. Blood pressure was recorded at 1, 2, and 3 minutes after puncture and the average of these 3 values was used for calculation. In preliminary studies factorial analysis had shown that there were no significant differences in the mean blood pressure readings at ("O" time plus) 10 seconds, 1, 2, 3, 4, or 5 minutes after arterial puncture for groups of 8 to 12 rats. In one such test, however, the first reading was lower by several mm. of Hg than the next three readings ($P = 0.10$ to 0.20), whereas among the latter, the mean values were essentially similar to each other ($P > 0.20$). Accordingly, the readings obtained at 1, 2, and 3 minutes were adopted as satisfactory indexes of blood pressure under these test conditions. Each rat was sacrificed upon completion of the blood pressure determination.

An 8 point assay for *R. serpentina* whole root *versus* reserpine has been shown graphically in figure 3; dose-response curves for ptotic and hypotensive effects as well as for reduced gain in body weight have been illustrated therein. In the order of test responses named the average λ (s/b) values were 0.20, 0.50, and 0.37 respectively.

Dogs. A total of 117 trained, unanesthetized, normotensive mongrel dogs of either sex, ranging in body weight from 7 to 12 kgm. were employed. The overall average initial blood pressure for these dogs was 115.2 mm. Hg by auscultation; for each drug group (12 to 30 dogs per group), the average initial pressure ranged from 112.9 to 117.2 mm. Hg, whereas

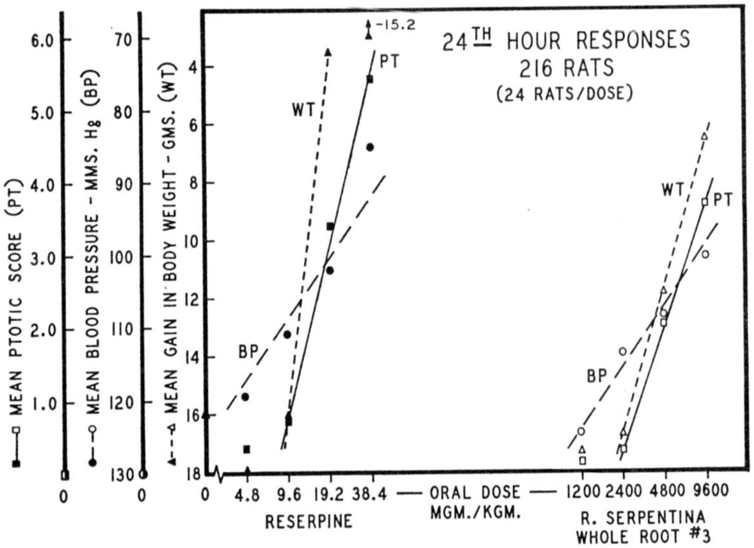

FIG. 3. Dose-response relationships in a comparative assay of *Rauwolfia serpentina* whole root and reserpine in rats. Mean responses of control rats (no drug) are shown on the lower portion of each ordinate.

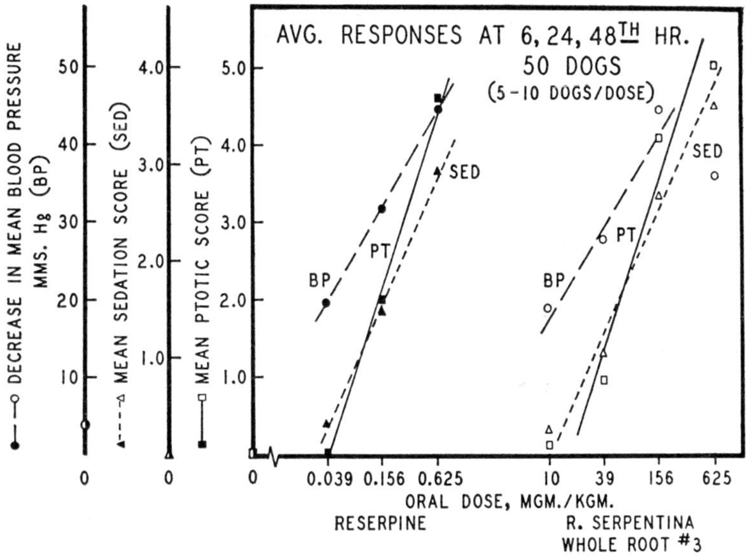

FIG. 4. Dose-response relationships in a comparative assay of *Rauwolfia serpentina* whole root and reserpine in dogs. Mean responses of control dogs (no drug) are shown on the lower portion of each ordinate.

the total range for the individual dogs was 105 to 128 mm. Hg. These animals were given single oral doses of alkaloid or of *Rauwolfia* whole root and were examined at 0, 6, 24, and 48 hours after each dose for changes in pupil diameter, femoral blood pressure (auscultatory), and pulse rate. Blood pressure decreases of about twenty to forty mm. Hg were obtained after dosage with reserpine or whole root. Scores of 0-4 were assigned for ptosis, relaxation of nictitating membrane and sedation. As in the mouse and rat, the ptotic response was the sum of the scores for the 2 eyes. Relaxation of nictitating membrane was rated maximal (4) when the lateral margin of the membrane was immediately adjacent to the medial arc of the pupil, with decreasing scores assigned for ¾, ½, and ¼ this degree of relaxation. Reserpine-like sedation was rated according to the following schedule: 0 = normal posture and activity; 1 = head lowered, little or no tendency to assume sleep position, dog stands and walks, slight reduction in activity; 2 = position of sleep assumed when undisturbed, animal stands up when disturbed (as by gentle tapping on cage), marked reduction in activity; 3 = position of sleep assumed, but animal only opens eyes and raises head, does not stand up when disturbed; 4 = as in 3, but neither opens eyes nor raises head when disturbed. The incidence of diarrhea was also noted at each of the test times. For assay purposes the values obtained for each animal at 6, 24, and 48 hours were averaged for each response, since they differed but little due to the drugs' long duration of action.

At least 2 or 3 dose levels were employed with each preparation with a dose interval of 4 × and with 5 to 10 dogs at each dose level. The oral dose ranges employed were 0.039 to 0.625 mgm./kgm. for reserpine and 10 to 625 mgm./kgm. for *Rauwolfia* whole root. The responses evaluated biometrically were ptosis, hypotension, and sedation; their average λ (s/b) values respectively were 0.30, 0.43, and 0.27. Representative dose-response curves for hypotension, ptosis and sedation obtained with reserpine and *R. serpentina* whole root have been illustrated in figure 4. Linear (log) dose-response relationships for bradycardia and diarrhea were not apparent and potency estimates based thereon have not been included. For other test responses such as miosis and relaxation of nictitating membrane, only graphical estimates of potency were made. Twenty to 45 dogs were employed in the comparative evaluation of each *Rauwolfia* root with reserpine. Five dogs given a placebo demonstrated the stability of each of the functions measured over the period of the experiment.

In addition to the whole root-reserpine comparisons by the oral route, a total of 12 dogs was used for reserpine alone by the intravenous route in ¼ the dose range employed orally and a group of 15 dogs was used to evaluate rescinnamine orally.

Biometrical evaluation. In all assays or comparisons reported herein orally administered reserpine (in dilute acetic acid) was employed as a working standard unless otherwise indicated. Relative potencies and per cent limits of error at P = 0.05 were calculated according to the methods of Bliss (1952) and Bliss and Marks (1939) for graded response assays. In those instances in which repeated assays were conducted, the potency estimates were combined after appropriate tests for homogeneity (Bliss, 1952).

In those few instances in which the test material was not assayed concurrently with the working standard or when combined slope significance was not obtained (at P = 0.05), graphical estimates of potency were made in order to yield an approximate order of activity.

Determinations of reserpine content of Rauwolfia whole root by isotope dilution analysis. 3,4,5-Trimethoxybenzoyl (carboxyl-carbon 14)-methyl reserpate (Numerof *et al.*, 1955) was added to "total alkaloid" extracts of each whole root and the extracts were fractionated to isolate crystalline reserpine. The content of reserpine in the "total alkaloid" extract was calculated using the isotope dilution equation. These determinations were conducted by Dr. Paul Numerof of the Analytical Division, Squibb Institution for Medical Research.

RESULTS. The potencies of each *Rauwolfia* root relative to reserpine as determined by bioassays in the 3 animal species as well as the reserpine content of each root as determined by isotope dilution technique have been expressed as equivalence-ratios in table 1.

Each of the 3 *Rauwolfia* roots was about 1/850 as active as reserpine in the mouse and about 1/340 as active as reserpine in the rat. In the dog, however, *R. serpentina* was about 1/350 as active as reserpine; each of the other 2 roots, *R. heterophylla* and *R. canescens*, was no more than 1/1000 as potent as reserpine.

The reserpine contents of these 3 roots, as obtained by isotope dilution technique, were about 1 part per 1100 for *R. serpentina* and for *R. heterophylla* and about 1 part per 1400 for *R. canescens*.

When potency of a root was calculated on the basis of more than one test response in the rat or dog, essentially the same activities were found.

Comparisons of intravenous and oral potencies of the several reserpine-like alkaloids have been summarized in table 2. By either route, rescinnamine was

TABLE 1

Oral dose equivalence-ratios of reserpine to Rauwolfia whole root

Animal	Test Response: Type	Test Response: Time *hr.*	*R. serpentina*	*R. heterophylla*	*R. canescens*	No. of Animals Per Assay
			Dose equivalence-ratio (range at P = 0.05)			
Mouse	Ptosis	5	1:862 (1:767–1:965)	1:877 (1:762–1:1008)	1:833 (1:666–1:1041)	240–320
Rat	Ptosis	24	1:401 (1:345–1:465)	1:387 (1:310–1:484)	1:258 (1:222–1:299)	96–224
	Blood pressure		1:310 (1:217–1:440)	1:296 (1:207–1:423)	1:172 (1:113–1:260)	144–336
	Body weight		1:412 (1:333–1:506)	1:436 (1:266–1:710)	1:389 (1:280–1:544)	144–288
Dog	Ptosis	6, 24, 48*	1:365 (1:215–1:616)	1:1780 (1:836–1:3756)	1:1320 (1:700–1:2455)	20–30
	Blood pressure		1:299 (1:150–1:598)	1:1100 (1:583–1:2046)	1:1130 (1:497–1:2576)	30–45
	Sedation		1:324 (1:207–1:502)	1:1660 (1:896–1:3088)	1:1150 (1:748–1:1759)	20–45
Isotope dilution			1:1100	1:1140	1:1430	

* Readings pooled for each animal at 6, 24, and 48 hours.

TABLE 2

Oral and intravenous relative potencies of reserpine-like alkaloids in mice, rats and dogs

Animal	Test Response		Alkaloid(s) U × S	Route(s) U × S	Potency, U × S (Range at P = 0.05)	No. Animals
	Type	Time *hr*				
Mouse	Ptosis	5	R × R	i.v. × p.o.	16.3 (14.0–18.9)	180
			MR × R	i.v.	0.024*	
			MR × R	p.o.	0.34 (0.28–0.39)	160
			MR × MR	i.v. × p.o.	1.14 (0.96–1.34)	240
			Rc × R	i.v.	0.13†	113
			Rc × R	p.o.	0.13 (0.11–0.16)	180
			Rc × Rc	i.v. × p.o.	16.0*	
			D × R	i.v.	0.82 (0.66–1.02)	60
			D × R	p.o.	1.03 (0.88–1.20)	120
			D × D	i.v. × p.o.	14.0*	
Rat	Ptosis	5			>100†	32
		10	R × R	i.v. × p.o.	128 (90–146)	72
		24			20†	72
		5			0.0057†	48
		10	MR × R	i.v.	0.072 (0.0048–0.0105)	48
		24			⩽0.0038†	48
		10	MR × R	p.o.	0.50†	48
		24			0.32 (0.24–0.42)	48
		10	MR × MR	i.v. × p.o.	1.24 (0.80–1.90)	48
		24			1.0†	48
		5			0.49 (0.41–0.59)	120
		10			0.31 (0.21–0.45)	36
		24	Rc × R	i.v.	0.22	36
	Blood pressure	5			0.25†	80
	Ptosis	10	Rc × R	p.o.	0.40 (0.24–0.67)	28
		24			0.49 (0.35–0.68)	28
		5			>100†	48
		10	Rc × Rc	i.v. × p.o.	70†	48
		24			20†	48
Dog	Ptosis	6, 24, 48‡			3.6†	28
	Blood pressure		R × R	i.v. × p.o.	2.0†	38
	Sedation				3.4†	28
	Miosis				2.4†	42
	Ptosis	6, 24, 48‡			indeterminate	45
	Blood pressure		Rc × R	p.o.	1.4†	45
	Sedation				3.1†	45
	Miosis				4.8†	45

* Calculated from accompanying potency relationships.

† Graphical estimate

‡ Readings pooled for each animal at 6, 24, and 48 hours.

U = test alkaloid.

S = reference alkaloid = 1.00.

R = reserpine; MR = methyl reserpate; Rc = rescinnamine; D = 11-desmethoxy-reserpine.

about $\frac{1}{8}$ as potent as reserpine in the mouse and about $\frac{1}{4}$ to $\frac{1}{2}$ as potent in the rat. In the dog, however, orally administered rescinnamine appeared to at least equal, if not exceed, the activity of reserpine.

11-Desmethoxyreserpine appeared to be equipotent to reserpine in the mouse by either the oral or intravenous route.

Methyl reserpate, administered intravenously, was about $\frac{1}{50}$ as potent as reserpine in the mouse and no more than $\frac{1}{100}$ as potent in the rat. When administered by the oral route, however, methyl reserpate was $\frac{1}{3}$ to $\frac{1}{2}$ as potent as reserpine in the mouse and in the rat.

Reserpine was about sixteen or more times as active intravenously as orally in the mouse and in the rat, but only about three times as active in the dog. Similar route-activity relationships were found with rescinnamine in the mouse and in the rat and with 11-desmethoxyreserpine in the mouse. In contrast, methyl reserpate was as active orally as intravenously in the mouse and in the rat.

DISCUSSION. *Alkaloid activity.* Cronheim and Toekes (1955) previously reported that rescinnamine was about twice as potent as reserpine in the dog but considerably less potent in mice and our results tend to agree with theirs.

A series of other studies (Schneider *et al.*, 1955; Cronheim *et al.*, 1955; Slater *et al.*, 1955; Cerletti *et al.*, 1955; Packman *et al.*, 1956) indicated that 11-desmethoxyreserpine was approximately equipotent to reserpine in the rat and in the dog as well as in other animal species. Our tests in mice also indicated equipotency for these 2 alkaloids.

Plummer *et al.* (1954) found methyl reserpate to be considerably less active than reserpine in the dog. Our results with methyl reserpate in the unanesthetized dog were quite similar in that methyl reserpate was rated no more than $\frac{1}{50}$ as active as reserpine after parenteral administration (Rubin and Burke, unpublished).

Alkaloid absorption. When ratios of intravenous to oral activity were used as an index of absorption, each of the reserpine-like alkaloids appeared to be absorbed to varying degrees in the several animal species. Reserpine, rescinnamine, and 11-desmethoxyreserpine appeared to be absorbed in the mouse to the extent of about six per cent (as reserpine or reserpine-equivalents). In the rat, in which species assays were conducted with the 2 first-named alkaloids, possibly only one to two per cent of an oral dose was absorbed. In the dog, however, reserpine appeared to be absorbed to the extent of about thirty-five per cent; with the broader limits of error applicable to the tests in this animal species, however, this value could range from about eighteen to seventy per cent. Methyl reserpate, in contrast with these three 18-ester alkaloids, appeared to be almost completely absorbed from the gastrointestinal tract of either the mouse or rat.

Alkaloid hydrolysis and metabolic fate. Intestinal enzymatic hydrolysis of reserpine appears to play a role in determining its oral effectiveness in the several animal species. Such hydrolysis ordinarily results in the formation of the very weakly active methyl reserpate and the inactive trimethoxybenzoic acid. Intestinal hydrolysis of reserpine was found in the mouse and rat *in vitro* and *in vivo* (Glazko *et al.*, 1955; Numerof *et al.*, 1955; C. I. Smith, personal communication) but little or none was found in either the dog *in vitro* (Glazko *et al.*, 1955; C. I. Smith, personal communication) or in the monkey *in vitro* and *in vivo* (Glazko *et al.*, 1955). Furthermore, when reserpine is absorbed, considerable variations are apt to occur amongst the several animal species in the demethylation or hydrolysis of this alkaloid by hepatic tissue (Sheppard and Tsien, 1955; Sheppard *et al.*, 1955). Whether other reserpine-like alkaloids are similarly altered by the intestine or liver is not known; the similar order of intravenous to oral effectiveness of rescinnamine and 11-desmethoxyreserpine in the mouse and the rat suggests that the intestinal fate of these two orally administered alkaloids may not be too different from that of reserpine in either or both of these animal species.

Alkaloid distribution in Rauwolfia whole root. Reserpine is present in each of the 3 whole root species studied but rescinnamine (Klohs *et al.*, 1954, 1955) and 11-desmethoxyreserpine (Stoll and Hofmann, 1955) have been isolated only from *R. serpentina* and *R. canescens* respectively. Little or no rescinnamine was found by Banes and Carol (1955 a,b) in *R. heterophylla* or in *R. canescens*. Only one report has appeared (Hofmann, 1954) indicating the presence of very small quantities of methyl reserpate in *R. serpentina* whole root.

Experience in these laboratories with a large series of *R. serpentina* whole roots batches has shown that the isotope dilution technique consistently detected a reserpine content nearly equal (±twenty per cent) to that found as reserpine-equivalents by the mouse ptotic assay (P. Numerof, personal communication); in this series the average reserpine content was about one part per thousand. The batch of *R. serpentina* employed in this study yielded typical results in agreement with previous experience as to reserpine content.

In the case of either *R. heterophylla* or *R. canescens* whole root, agreement between these two methods of assay has not been as consistent as in the case of *R. serpentina*. Isotope dilution analyses applied to *R. heterophylla* or *R. canescens* have detected an average of about sixty-five per cent of the reserpine content indicated by the mouse ptotic assay; for individual root batches of either of these 2 root species, this value has ranged from about fifty to one hundred per cent. Of the root batches of *R. canescens* and *R. heterophylla* included in this study, isotope dilution analyses detected about sixty and eighty per cent respectively of the reserpine-equivalent content indicated by ptotic assays in mice. In those instances in which the reserpine content found by isotope dilution assay was less than about eighty per cent of that indicated by ptotic assay in mice, there could be a) incomplete extraction of reserpine in the preparation of the "total alkaloid extract" for isotope dilution analysis b) contributions to total ptotic activity by other alkaloids, especially those reserpine-like in nature, *e.g.*, equi-active 11-desmethoxyreserpine in *R. canescens*.

Unlike *R. canescens*, *R. serpentina* whole root contains at least one other reserpine-like alkaloid, rescinnamine, which on an additive basis alone would appear to offer negligible contributions to total ptotic activity of this root in mice. This is supported by the following points: a) the consistent agreement between (reserpine) isotope dilution assay and mouse ptotic assay as to reserpine content b) the lesser order of activity of rescinnamine in mice and c) the occurrence of rescinnamine only to the extent of about ½ the content of reserpine (Banes and Carol, 1955 a, b).

If a small amount of the weakly active methyl reserpate occurs in *R. serpentina* whole root, its contribution to total ptotic activity in mice would appear to be negligible.

Whole root activity vs. reserpine content. The comparative studies of the 3 types of *Rauwolfia* root have indicated that although each of these roots possessed equal or nearly equal reserpine-equivalent content of the order of 1:1000, considerable quantitative differences in activity were found among the several animal species. Whereas the mouse ptotic assay indicated activity in general agreement with reserpine content (or reserpine plus possible 11-desmethoxyreserpine content in the case of *R. canescens*), the rat and dog tests indicated significant departures quantitatively from reserpine content. In the rat each of these roots was about 1/200 to 1/450 as active as reserpine, indicating total activity about 2 to 4 times greater than reserpine content. In the dog, only *R. serpentina* manifested the increased order of activity also found in the rat, whereas *R. heterophylla* and *R. canescens* were no more than 1/1000 as potent as reserpine in the dog.

In the case of the dog, a large part of the greater activity seen with *R. serpentina* whole root may have been accounted for by its content of rescinnamine. The other 2 root species, lacking rescinnamine, apparently manifested actively attributable largely, if not entirely, to reserpine or to reserpine plus 11-desmethoxyreserpine. Even if about ⅓ the total ptotic activity of *R. canescens* whole root in mice were due to its content of 11-desmethoxyreserpine, this alkaloid would be indistinguishable from reserpine by its effect in the dog.

In the rat, however, each of the 3 types of *Rauwolfia* root manifested activity several times greater than that expected from its reserpine content alone. In the rat, as in the mouse, the contribution of rescinnamine to the total activity of *R. serpentina* would also appear to be minimal; furthermore, neither of the 2 other *Rauwolfia* species contain rescinnamine (Banes and Carol, 1955 a,b). It would appear that some common factor(s) present in each of the 3 roots was in some unknown manner increasing the oral effectiveness of the reserpine-like material present in each root. Thus, there could be substances (alkaloidal or non-alkaloidal) present in each root which either inhibited intestinal hydrolysis or promoted absorption of reserpine-like substances present in powdered whole root. Even more speculatively, there could be substances in one or more of the 3 types of root which augmented or potentiated reserpine-like action.

The quantitative differences in activity of the several *Rauwolfia* roots as well as the quantitative differences in activity of reserpine and related alkaloids in the several animal species indicate the difficulty of establishing biological equivalence between a *Rauwolfia* whole root (or possibly an extract thereof) and reserpine. Since biological assays are not practicable in man, because of the slow mild nature of the response(s) and the relatively flat dose-response relationships, it would appear safest to standardize natural or semi-purified preparations of *Rauwolfia* on the basis of *multiplicity* of criteria such as pharmacognostic identification, chemical or biological estimates of total or specific alkaloidal composition, as well as biological assays for total hypotensive, sedative and related activity in two or more appropriate animal species. It would be desirable to include all of these procedures until such time as the total activity of *R. serpentina* whole root can be explained in terms of pure component substances. Appropriate specific assay procedures for such substances could then be developed and applied as amended control procedures for standardization.

SUMMARY AND CONCLUSIONS

After single oral or intravenous dosing, rescinnamine had about ⅛ the ptotic activity of reserpine in mice and about ½ to ¼ its ptotic activity in rats. In dogs, however, rescinnamine was at least equipotent to reserpine in hypotensive, sedative and miotic activity. 11-Desmethoxyreserpine was equipotent to reserpine in respect to ptotic activity in the mouse.

The dog was most sensitive to single oral doses of reserpine or of 3 types of *Rauwolfia* powdered whole root (*serpentina*, *heterophylla*, and *canescens*), the rat was least sensitive, and the mouse was intermediate in sensitivity.

Each of the 3 whole roots was about 1/1000 as potent as reserpine in the mouse, which value agrees with isotope dilution estimates of the reserpine content of these 3 roots.

Unlike the results in the mouse, each of the 3 roots was about 1/200 to 1/450 as potent as reserpine in the rat. *R. serpentina*, however, was about 1/300 as potent as reserpine in the dog; *R. heterophylla* and *R. canescens* were each no more than 1/1000 as potent as reserpine.

These differences indicate that the total hypotensive and sedative activities present in a *Rauwolfia* whole root are not necessarily definable in terms of reserpine content alone. In 2 of the 3 animal species employed, reserpine content accounted for only ¼ to ½ the total ptotic, hypotensive or sedative activity of *R. serpentina* whole root.

ACKNOWLEDGMENT. The authors are indebted to Mrs. Margaret L. Carter and Mr. Arnold J. Boyce for their valuable technical assistance.

REFERENCES

BANES, D., AND CAROL, J.: 69th Annual Meeting, Ass. Offic. Agr. Chemists, Washington, D. C., October 10–12, 1955a.

BANES D., AND CAROL, J.: J. Ass. Offic. Agr. Chemists, **38:** 866, 1955b.

BLISS, C. I.: The Statistics of Bioassay, Academic Press Inc., New York, 1952.

BLISS, C. I., AND MARKS, H. P.: Quart. J. Pharm. and Pharmacol., **12:** 182, 1939.

CERLETTI, A., KONZETT, H., AND TAESCHLER, M.: Experientia, **11:** 98, 1955.

CRONHEIM, G., ORCUTT, J. A., AND TOEKES, I. M.: Proc. Soc. Exper. Biol. & Med., **89:** 21, 1955.

CRONHEIM, G., STIPP, C., AND BROWN, W.: Evans Memorial Research Conference, Symposium on Hypotensive Drugs, Boston, Mass., "Hypotensive Agents from *Rauwolfia serpentina;* Reserpine and Other Alkaloids", p. 84, September 14-15, 1953.

CRONHEIM, G., AND TOEKES, I. M.: THIS JOURNAL, **113:** 13, 1955.

GAUNT, R., RENZI, A. A., ANTONCHAK, N., MILLER, G. J., AND GILMAN, M.: Ann. N. Y. Acad. Sci., **59:** 107, 1954.

GLAZKO, A. J., DILL, W. A., WOLF, L. M., AND KAZENKO, A.: Fed. Proc., **14:** 58, 1955.

HOFMANN, A.: Helv. Chim. Acta, **37:** 849, 1954.
HOLT, E. K., WARD-DUNN, G., NEDILSKY, B. T., AND NISWANDER, G. D.: Dis. Nerv. System, **16:** 222, 1955.
KLINE, N. S.: Ann. New York Acad. Sc., **59:** 107, 1954.
KLOHS, M. W., DRAPER, M. D., AND KELLER, F.: J. Am. Chem. Soc., **76:** 2843, 1954.
KLOHS, M. W., DRAPER, M. D., AND KELLER, F.: J. Am. Chem. Soc., **77:** 2241, 1955.
KOHLI, J. D., AND MUKERJI, B.: Current Sc., **24:** 198, 1955.
NUMEROF, P., GORDON, M., AND KELLEY, J. M.: THIS JOURNAL, **115:** 427, 1955.
MOYER, J. H., DENNIS, E., AND FORD, R.: A.M.A. Arch. Int. Med., **96:** 530, 1955.
PACKMAN, E. W., ABBOTT, D. D., AND HARRISSON, J. W. E.: J. Amer. Pharm. A. (Scient. Ed.), **45:** 89, 1956.
PLUMMER, A. J., BARRETT, W. E., AND RUTLEDGE, R. A.: Fed. Proc., **13:** 395, 1954.
RUBIN, B., AND BURKE, J. C.: Fed. Proc., **13:** 400, 1954.
RUBIN, B., DIASSI, P. A., BURKE, J. C., AND WINTERSTEINER, O. P.: Evans Memorial Research Conference, Symposium on Hypotensive Drugs, Boston, Mass., "Chemical and Pharmacological Studies on *Rauwolfia serpentina*", p. 91, September 14-15, 1953.
SCHNEIDER, J. A., PLUMMER, A. J., EARL, A. E., BARRETT, W. E., RINEHART, R., AND DIBBLE, R. C.: THIS JOURNAL, **114:** 10, 1955.
SHEPPARD, H., AND TSIEN, W. H: Proc. Soc. Exper. Biol. & Med., **90:** 437, 1955.
SHEPPARD, H., LUCAS, R. C., AND TSIEN, W. H.: Arch. internat. pharmacodyn., **103:** 256, 1955.
SLATER, I. H., RATHBURN, R. C.. HENDERSON, F. G., AND NEUSS, N.: Proc. Soc. Exper. Biol. & Med., **88:** 293, 1955.
STOLL, A., AND HOFFMANN, A.: J. Am. Chem. Soc., **77:** 820, 1955.
TUCHMAN, H., AND CRUMPTON, C. W.: Am. Heart J., **49:** 742, 1955.
WILKINS, R. W., JUDSON, W. E., STONE, R. W., HOLLANDER, W., HUCKABEE, W. E., AND FRIEDMAN, I. H.: New England J. Med., **250:** 477, 1954.

A STUDY OF SUBSTANCES WHICH ALTER INTRAVENTRICULAR CONDUCTION IN THE ISOLATED DOG HEART[1]

HENRY H. SWAIN AND CHARLES L. WEIDNER[2]

Department of Pharmacology, University of Michigan Medical School, Ann Arbor

Received for publication December 7, 1956

The transmission of the cardiac impulse to the various parts of the ventricles involves both the regular myocardial fibers and the specialized or so-called Purkinje network. When the ventricles are driven electrically and conduction times are measured to several epicardial electrodes, it is possible to estimate the conduction velocities in these two conductile tissues.

Thus Lewis and Rothschild (1915) demonstrated that conduction between electrodes close to the site of stimulation is relatively slow. They assumed that an impulse arising at the epicardium would have to travel a certain distance through the slowly conducting myocardial fibers before it could reach and utilize the more rapidly conducting Purkinje fibers. Therefore transmission for short distances along the epicardial surface of the heart would involve only the slow system, and conduction times to near-by electrodes would reflect this slow conduction velocity. They estimated that the regular myocardial fibers in the dog ventricle conduct at a rate of 300 to 500 mm./sec.

When these investigators drove the ventricle at a greater distance from the recording electrodes, they noted that the intraelectrode conduction time became much shorter. This, they believed, reflected the conduction time in the Purkinje network between their electrodes. Their estimate of Purkinje conduction velocity was 3000 to 5000 mm./sec.

Moe and Mendez (1951) used a somewhat similar technique to demonstrate that strophanthin K in toxic doses slows Purkinje conduction at a time when myocardial conduction is not significantly altered. They related this preferential effect of strophanthin K on the high-speed system to the ability of the drug to induce ventricular fibrillation.

Many investigators have measured the effects of drugs upon ventricular conduction velocity, but in the main, they have not differentiated between effects on myocardial conduction and effects on Purkinje conduction. Because some agents alter conduction in the two systems to different degrees or even in different directions, it seemed germane to observe both the myocardial and Purkinje effects of conduction-altering substances.

[1] This investigation was supported in part by a grant from the Michigan Heart Association and in part by Grant H-2466 from the National Institutes of Health, Public Health Service.

[2] Summer Research Fellow, National Fund for Medical Education, June-August, 1955, Medical Student Research Fellow, United States Public Health Service, Grant #FG-154, December 1955–May 1956.

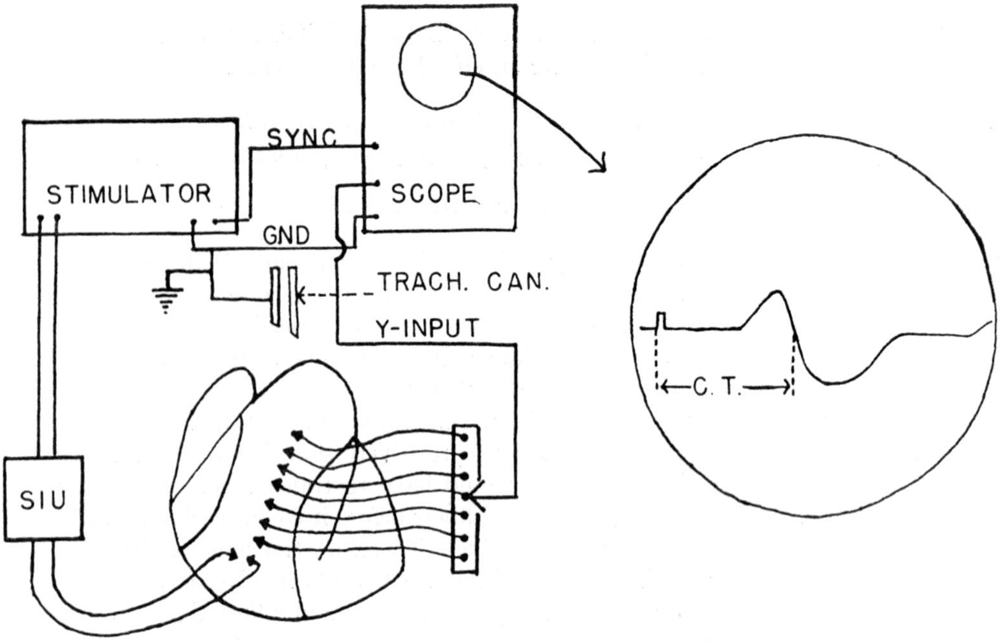

FIG. 1. Circuit diagram.

Stimulator with stimulus isolation unit (SIU) drives right ventricle through bipolar clip electrode. Synchronization lead (SYNC) connects stimulator to oscilloscope (SCOPE). A common ground connects stimulator, oscilloscope, and the metal tracheal cannula (TRACH. CAN.) of the heart-lung preparation. Alligator clips fastened to the epicardium are connected to a terminal block. The Y-input lead connects one recording electrode at a time to the oscilloscope. Sketch at right shows the square-wave stimulus artifact, upward and downward deflections, and at far right, the beginning of the T-wave. Conduction time (C.T.) is measured in milliseconds.

METHODS. The dog heart-lung preparation was employed in these studies. Subject dogs weighed between 8 and 12 kgm. and were anesthetized with intravenous sodium pentobarbital, 30 mgm./kgm. Donor dogs received no general anesthetic agent but were exsanguinated from an arterial cut-down performed under local procaine anesthesia. The blood of both subject and donor dogs was rendered non-coagulable with Mepesulfate,[3] 20 mgm./kgm.

After the pericardium was opened, a bipolar clip electrode was fixed onto the epicardial surface of the right ventricle toward its apical end, as shown in figure 1. This bipolar electrode was driven by a Grass (Model 3-C) square-wave stimulator through a stimulus isolation unit (SIU). Occasionally the parameters of stimulation were changed for specific reasons as mentioned, but unless otherwise stated the heart was driven at a rate of 192 beats per minute with 20 volt square-wave shocks 1 millisecond in duration. After the stimulating electrode was affixed to the heart, the S-A node was crushed in a large hemostat to slow the spontaneous rate of the heart.

Local electrograms were obtained from a row of seven small alligator clips placed as indicated in figure 1. Wires were passed from the alligator clips to a terminal block, and

---

[3] Mepesulfate 'Roche' is the registered trade mark of Hoffmann-LaRoche Inc. for the sodium salt of sulfated polygalacturonic acid methyl ester methyl glycoside.

from there each electrode was connected in turn to the Y-input of a cathode ray oscilloscope. The circuit was completed by grounding the oscilloscope to the metal tracheal cannula of the heart-lung preparation. The sweep of the oscilloscope was triggered by the Grass stimulator, and the X-amplitude was adjusted so that the one-tenth inch horizontal scale division was equal to 4 msec. With such a sweep speed, the entire depolarization complex can be observed on the oscilloscope at one time, and the arrival of the propagated impulse at a given electrode can be timed to 1 msec. Although only one recording electrode is in the circuit at any one time, readings from all seven can be obtained in less than half a minute.

The typical unipolar electrogram as sketched in figure 1 includes a stimulus artifact at the left, an upward deflection, a downward deflection, an isoelectric segment, and, off the screen to the right, an upright T wave. The time of arrival of the propagated impulse at the recording electrode was taken as that point between the upward and downward deflections where the tracing crosses the base-line.

Early in an experiment local injury caused by the clip electrodes is manifested by an elevation of the S-T segment. This local effect disappears within ten to fifteen minutes, and control readings are not taken until the S-T segment has returned to the base-line.

Distances from the stimulating electrode to the several recording electrodes were measured with a pair of dividers and a millimeter ruler. Repeat measurements on the beating heart check within 2 mm.

Conduction times to the several recording electrodes were plotted against the distances of these electrodes from the stimulating electrode. Control readings consistently form two straight lines. Readings from electrodes within the first 20 to 25 mm. determine a line with a slope corresponding to a conduction velocity of 450 to 650 mm./sec. Readings from more distant electrodes determine a second line with a slope corresponding to a conduction velocity of 1500 to 4000 mm./sec. The former is assumed to be a reflection of myocardial conduction velocity and the latter a reflection of Purkinje conduction velocity.

With this preparation we can measure changes in myocardial and Purkinje conduction velocities. In addition we can see an indication of any marked increase in automaticity which may be induced by the agents studied. After the S-A node was crushed the hearts had spontaneous rates in the range of 100 to 120 beats per minute. Such hearts will follow electrical stimulation of the ventricle at rates of 130 to 160 beats per minute without the appearance of spontaneous beats. Since our preparations were driven at the rate of 192 beats per minute, spontaneous beats rarely were seen under control conditions. However, certain substances in addition to their effects upon conduction increase the automaticity of the heart to the point that the usual driving frequency will no longer maintain control. Under these circumstances increasing the driving frequency to 220 to 250 beats per minute may eliminate spontaneous beats. By noting the driving frequency required to suppress spontaneous beats, we have a rough indication of the automaticity of the heart.

The preparation is quite stable, after the first fifteen minutes during which the local injury effects are disappearing. If no drugs are given and temperature is constant, no conduction time changes of more than 2 msec. are observed during the next hour.

RESULTS. *Effects of the parameters of stimulation.* Voltage: The threshold for ventricular driving was found to be between 2 and 6 volts in the various preparations. At these lower voltages there appears to be an appreciable latency between the application of the stimulus and the initiation of a propagated response, as indicated by an intercept on the X-axis of the conduction graphs (see figure 2). With increasing voltage, the curve is shifted to the left and shows an intercept on the Y-axis. This suggests that the shocks of greater intensity are capable of initiating a propagated impulse at some small distance removed from the stimulating electrode. A stimulus of 20 volts was employed routinely because at this value small voltage changes have little effect upon conduction times.

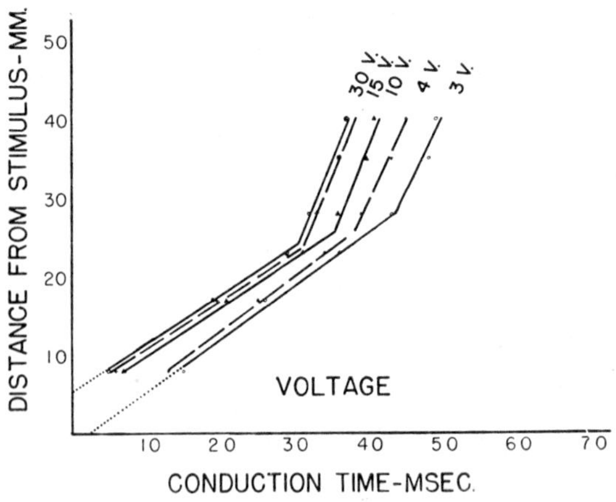

FIG. 2. Effect of variation of voltage.

Slope of left hand portion of each curve is myocardial conduction velocity. Greater slope at right is Purkinje conduction velocity. Dotted extrapolation of 3 V curve intercepts X-axis, indicating a latency between application of minimal stimulus and initiation of propagated impulse. Dotted extrapolation of 30 V curve intercepts Y-axis, indicating that at higher voltage, propagated impulse is started several millimeters away from stimulating electrode.

Duration: Shocks of less than 0.1 msec. duration were found to be ineffective for driving the ventricle. Variation of shock duration from 0.1 to 20 msec. produced no change in conduction times to the several recording electrodes. A shock of 1 msec. duration was used in these studies.

Frequency: Conduction times were found to be constant though the heart rate was varied from 120 to 250 beats per minute. This agrees with the findings of Lewis and Rothschild (1915). At very high rates of stimulation the cardiac output is markedly decreased, as would be expected.

The effect of temperature. As would be expected, conduction velocities are a function of temperature. The circulating blood can be cooled to about 30° C., and this procedure slows both myocardial and Purkinje conduction, as shown in figure 3. Below 30° C. the cardiac output of the preparation is so low that there is no necessary relationship between the temperature of the blood in the inflow cannula (where we measure it) and the temperature of the blood in contact with the heart. Elevating the blood temperature to 42° C. produces a corresponding increase in the two conduction velocities.

Since conduction is temperature-sensitive, results were discarded when the temperature of the circulating blood changed as much as 0.5° C. between control and experimental observations.

Effects of cations. The chloride salts of sodium, calcium, and magnesium prolong intraventricular conduction times. The doses required for this effect are large and the myocardial and Purkinje systems are both depressed. With sufficiently large doses of any of these three salts, the ventricles may fibrillate. On the estimate that our average heart-lung preparation has 500 ml. of circulating

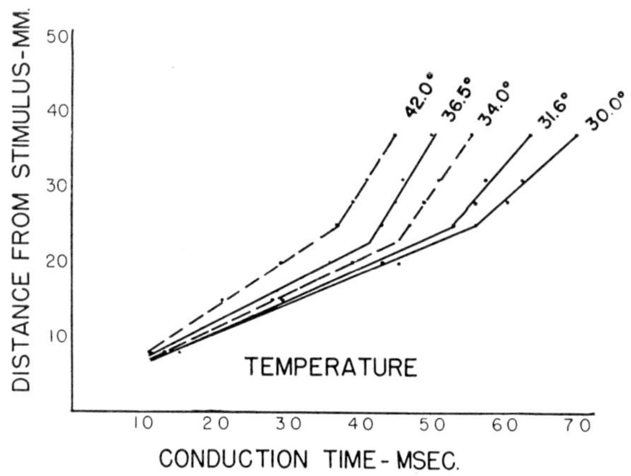

FIG. 3. Effect of blood temperature on myocardial and Purkinje conduction velocities.

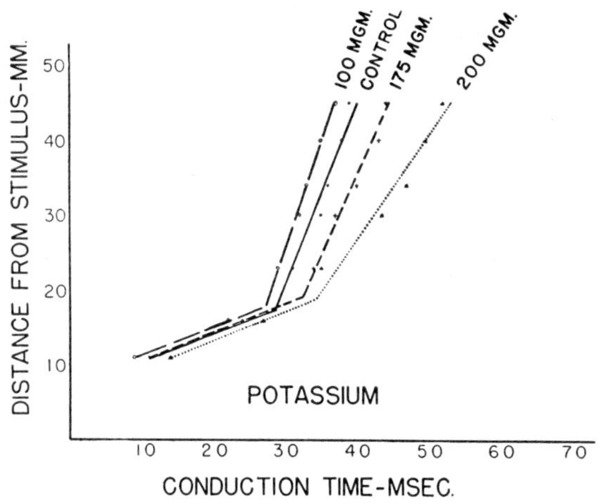

FIG. 4. Effect of potassium chloride on conduction.
Addition of 100 mgm. of KCl (approximately 2.6 mEq./l. of K ion) shortened conduction times to all electrodes. A total of 175 mgm. (approximately 4.5 mEq./l.) added prolonged conduction times moderately, and further addition of 25 mgm. slowed conduction markedly. The 200 mgm. total dose is approximately 5.2 mEq./l. added to the preparation.

plasma, we calculate that an additional 70 mEq./l. of sodium ion will prolong conduction times markedly, and when 340 mEq./l. is added the ventricles fibrillate. The addition of 11 mEq./l. of calcium ion produces a conspicuous prolongation of conduction times and 40 mEq./l. added causes fibrillation. Doses of magnesium are approximately the same, 10 mEq./l. added to prolong conduction times and 36 mEq./l. to produce fibrillation.

Potassium chloride produces a biphasic effect upon intraventricular conduction, as shown in figure 4. When 2.5 to 3.0 mEq./l. are added, conduction times are shortened to all electrodes. Further additions of potassium ion then prolong

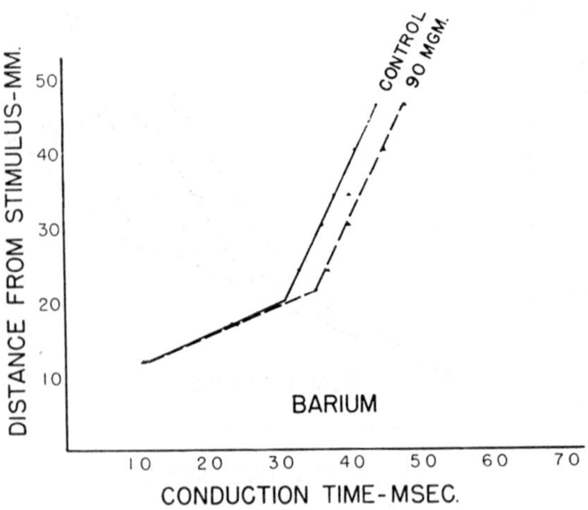

FIG. 5. Effect of barium acetate.

Addition of 90 mgm. (approximately 0.6 mEq./l of Ba ion) prolonged conduction times slightly. Further addition had little effect upon conduction times but produced a marked increase in automaticity in the heart. Ventricular fibrillation followed a total dose of 240 mgm. of barium acetate (approximately 2.0 mEq./l.).

conduction times so that after the addition of 6 to 7 mEq./l. conduction is slowed markedly, and when 10 to 12 mEq./l. have been added, the preparation usually fibrillates. These calculated values for potassium ion agree well with the measurements of Winkler *et al.* (1938).

Barium ion will cause ventricular fibrillation, but it has little effect upon conduction times. A dose of 90 mgm. of barium acetate, which is calculated to give a plasma level of approximately 0.6 mEq./l. of barium ion, prolongs conduction times by the small amount shown in figure 5. Conduction times remain essentially constant from that point until the ventricles fibrillate at approximately 2 mEq./l.

The more striking effect of barium ion is to increase the automaticity of the heart. This action of the ion necessitates increasing the driving frequency of the stimulator to maintain control of the heart rate. Prior to ventricular fibrillation from barium, the heart may show a spontaneous rate faster than 250 beats per minute.

Effects of epinephrine, levarterenol, and acetylcholine. Myocardial and Purkinje conduction are not altered by infusions of epinephrine at rates which shorten markedly the conduction time through the A-V system from right auricular appendage to epicardium of the right ventricle. When epinephrine is infused into the inflow cannula at a rate of 0.5 microgm. per minute for five minutes, A-V conduction time is decreased by about 10 per cent. Epinephrine infusions at 3.0 microgm. per minute decrease A-V conduction time by as much as 40 per cent, and more rapid infusions have no further effect upon auricle-to-ventricle conduction time. These values agree with the observations of Krayer *et al.* (1951). Only at far higher rates of epinephrine infusion is there a change in the intraventricular conduction times. At 80 microgm. per minute we frequently see

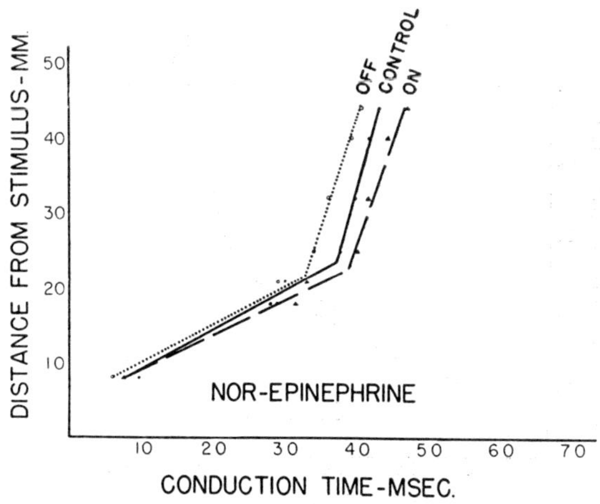

FIG. 6. Levarterenol infusion.

ON indicates conduction times after six minutes of infusion of a 1:25,000 solution of levarterenol at a rate of 2 ml. per minute. OFF indicates conduction times 10 minutes after infusion was stopped.

small changes, but even these changes are not consistent from experiment to experiment.

Levarterenol shares with epinephrine this lack of conspicuous effect upon intraventricular conduction. Very high rates of infusion may alter conduction slightly. Figure 6 shows the effect of infusion of 80 microgm. per minute of levarterenol. During infusion, conduction times were somewhat prolonged; after the infusion was stopped, conduction times became somewhat shorter than control.

Both epinephrine and levarterenol caused an increase in automaticity of the heart which occasionally necessitated an increase in the driving frequency to maintain control.

Acetylcholine had little or no effect upon intraventricular conduction when infused at rates as high as 2 mgm. per minute.

Effects of ouabain and quinidine. Ouabain exerts qualitatively different effects upon the two conduction systems. It slows Purkinje conduction at a time when myocardial conduction is unchanged or actually speeded. The onset of action of ouabain is slow, so the usual procedure was to administer a single dose of the drug to the preparation. Changes in conduction time were recorded at intervals during the period while the drug was exerting a progressively greater effect. Figure 7 shows the conduction values 13 and 28 minutes after a dose of 100 microgm. of the glycoside. In some experiments, just prior to ventricular fibrillation the values for the seven conduction times fall on a single straight line, suggesting that the Purkinje system is no longer conducting impulses more rapidly than is the myocardium. In ouabain experiments we see some increase in automaticity but it is not as pronounced as in experiments with barium ion, epinephrine and levarterenol.

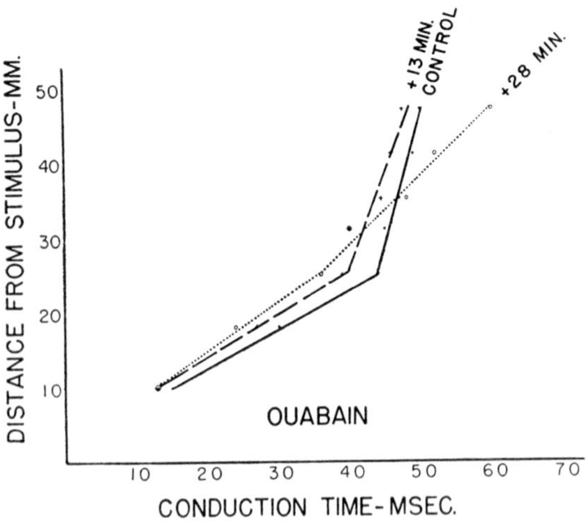

FIG. 7. Ouabain effect.

Conduction times 13 and 28 minutes after a dose of 100 microgm. of ouabain are shown. Ventricular fibrillation occurred 41 minutes after administration of the ouabain in this particular preparation.

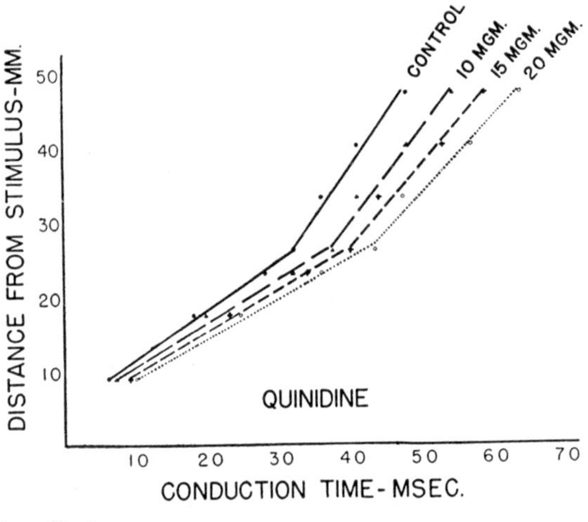

FIG. 8. Quinidine effect.

Successive doses of 10, 5, and 5 mgm. of quinidine sulfate were administered at 10-minute intervals.

Quinidine sulfate, shown in figure 8, slows conduction in both systems.

Veratrine, protoveratrine, and andromedotoxin. A dose of 750 microgm. of veratrine causes a conspicuous slowing of Purkinje conduction, while the myocardial conduction in the ventricle is normal or moderately accelerated. Protoveratrine differs from veratrine in some of its actions but has somewhat similar effects upon intraventricular conduction. A dose of 40 microgm. of protoveratrine is sufficient to slow Purkinje and speed myocardial conduction. After 75 to 100 microgm. of protoveratrine, the Purkinje slowing is profound. Similar in action to protoveratrine is andromedotoxin, a non-nitrogenous substance from *Rhododendron maximum* (Moran *et al.*, 1954). Andromedotoxin[4] in doses of 300 to 500 microgm. slows Purkinje conduction without depressing myocardial conduction. Thus veratrine, protoveratrine, and andromedotoxin share with ouabain the ability to differentially depress Purkinje conduction in the ventricle of the dog heart-lung preparation. All four substances are able to induce ventricular fibrillation in the preparation when administered in microgram quantities.

DISCUSSION. *Interpretation of conduction graphs.* When large changes in the slopes representing the two conduction systems are seen (as with changes in temperature or following administration of quinidine) or when the two slopes are altered in opposite directions (as seen after ouabain administration), conclusions are easy to draw. On the other hand, when individual conduction times are changed by only a few milliseconds, it may be difficult to pin-point the site of change.

Conduction to a more distant electrode involves at least three variable components. First is the "instantaneous" conduction from the stimulating electrode to the point where the propagated impulse is actually initiated, represented by the intercept on the Y-axis. Increased stimulating voltage or small doses of potassium ion, for instance, increase this Y-intercept. Second is the transmission of the impulse from epicardium to Purkinje system and back again through the slowly conducting myocardium. Third is the usually rapid conduction along the Purkinje system. The conduction velocities in the myocardium and in the Purkinje network may be altered, and not necessarily in the same direction.

Following the administration of small doses of potassium salts, conduction times to the more distant electrodes are decreased by several milliseconds. The Y-intercept is definitely increased and velocities in the two conduction systems appear to be increased slightly. We are working so close to the limit of our measurements that the apparent increase in the two slopes may not be significant. The same situation exists for the slight prolongation of conduction times after barium ion. The conduction times are longer after the drug than they were during the control period, but one cannot say with assurance whether the change is primarily one of myocardial conduction, Purkinje conduction, or Y-intercept.

When conduction in both systems is altered in the same direction we have made no attempt to quantitate the relative changes in the two components. Thus after quinidine, for example, it is sufficient to say that both myocardial and Purkinje conduction are slowed. We could calculate percentage changes in the two slopes, but it is doubtful that such calculations would be meaningful.

The relationship between conduction velocity and ventricular fibrillation. We feel that it is profitable to think of rapid intraventricular conduction as a mechanism for integrating ventricular activity and preventing ventricular fibrillation. As long as the depolarizing impulse can travel from one spot in the ventricles to any other spot in the ventricles in a time less than the effective refractory period of the ventricular muscle, there can be no more than one impulse in the tissue at

[4] Andromedotoxin was kindly supplied by Dr. Neil C. Moran.

a given time. However if the total conduction time becomes long with respect to the refractory period, it then becomes possible to start a second impulse before the first is extinguished. We believe that an essential criterion of fibrillation is the co-existence of more than one impulse in the ventricular muscle mass at a given instant.

When conduction time becomes long with respect to refractory period, it becomes possible for the ventricles to fibrillate. Whether or not they do fibrillate will depend upon whether an impulse is initiated in the critical interval before the previous impulse is extinguished. It should make little difference in the hypothesis whether this new impulse arises from a stimulating electrode, from an ectopic focus, or from a re-entry mechanism.

We believe that in our preparation the ventricular fibrillation from potassium salts is the result of profound slowing of intraventricular conduction to the point that the electrical stimulus arrives at the heart before the previous impulse has completed its journey through the myocardium. Fibrillation from barium ion, on the other hand, is more likely the consequence of the increased automaticity which supplies impulses at an increased rate at a time when conduction is slightly depressed. Fibrillation from ouabain or protoveratrine seems to be an intermediate case, combining some increase in automaticity with marked slowing of Purkinje conduction. Drugs of this latter group demonstrate the importance of the Purkinje network, for it appears that even augmented myocardial conduction is insufficient for maintaining coordination of widely separated areas in the ventricles.

SUMMARY

A method is described for estimating the myocardial and Purkinje conduction velocities in the right ventricle of the dog heart.

The effects upon these conduction velocities of changes in the parameters of stimulation, of changes in temperature, and of the addition of several chemical substances were investigated.

Ouabain, veratrine, protoveratrine and andromedotoxin share the property of depressing Purkinje conduction while leaving myocardial conduction unchanged or even augmented. All four agents can produce ventricular fibrillation in the heart-lung preparation when administered in microgram quantities.

The relationship between changes in intraventricular conduction and the development of ventricular fibrillation is discussed.

ACKNOWLEDGMENT. The authors would like to thank Mr. Allan Stephan who voluntarily assisted us in the surgical preparations for our experiments.

REFERENCES

KRAYER, O., MANDOKI, J. J., AND MENDEZ, C.: THIS JOURNAL, **103:** 412, 1951.
LEWIS, T., AND ROTHSCHILD, M. A.: Phil. Trans. Royal Soc., **206 B:** 181, 1915.
MOE, G. K., AND MENDEZ, R.: Circulation, **4:** 729, 1951.
MORAN, N. C., DRESEL, P. E., PERKINS, M. E., AND RICHARDSON, A. P.: THIS JOURNAL, **110:** 415, 1954.
WINKLER, A. W., HOFF, H. E., AND SMITH, P. K.: Am. J. Physiol., **124:** 478, 1938.

CENTRAL AND PERIPHERAL COMPONENTS OF THE ACTION OF "GANGLIONIC" BLOCKING AGENTS[1]

A. S. DONTAS[2] AND MARK NICKERSON[3]

Departments of Internal Medicine and Pharmacology, University of Michigan, Ann Arbor

Received for publication December 24, 1956

Despite an overwhelming volume of literature on ganglionic blocking agents since interest in these compounds was renewed by the study of tetraethylammonium by Acheson and Moe (1946), we know of no attempts to study the effects of these drugs on the spontaneous or induced activity of preganglionic sympathetic fibers. Heymans, Delaunois and Martini (1954), using a perfused, isolated dog's head, reported that large doses of hexamethonium administered intraarterially did not interfere with direct or indirect excitation of the cardioinhibitory center of the vagus, but they did not study other autonomic activity.

The "selectivity" of these agents for autonomic ganglia is only relative. They are known to have both excitatory and inhibitory effects on afferent structures, chemoreceptors and somatic sensory endings (Gollwitzer-Meier and Witzleb, 1953; Douglas, 1952; Dontas and Nickerson, 1956), and to inhibit axon reflexes (Janowitz and Grossman, 1949). In addition, O'Dell and coworkers (1955a, b) have noted that a number of unsymmetrical bisquaternary compounds have a hypotensive action which is greater in proportion to their peripheral ganglionic blocking activity than that of hexamethonium. These authors suggested that an action on the central nervous system was involved, but presented no more direct evidence to support this conclusion.

The present study was undertaken with the hope of detecting by electrophysiological methods possible actions of ganglionic blocking agents on preganglionic structures, and of correlating such actions with responses to afferent discharges from the carotid area and with overall circulatory responses to the blocking agents.

METHODS. Thirty-two cats, anesthetized with chloralose (60 mgm./kgm.) and urethane (300 mgm./kgm.) administered intravenously following ether induction, were used in this study. All animals were artificially ventilated with air at a rate just sufficient to abolish spontaneous respiratory movements. In the majority of experiments, neuromuscular blockade was produced by the intravenous administration of small amounts of decamethonium to eliminate artifacts from skeletal muscle and for the "asphyxia" test. The *right* carotid and *right* greater splanchnic nerves were sectioned and dissected free. Electrical activity in the distal stump of the carotid nerve and the proximal stump of the splanchnic nerve was recorded after removal of the sheath as previously described (Dontas, 1955). Activity of the splanchnic was usually recorded from an intrathoracic portion of the nerve, always proximal to the point of entry into the celiac or any other

[1] This work was supported in part by grants from the American Heart Association, the Michigan Heart Association and the Horace H. Rackham School of Graduate Studies.

[2] Research Fellow of the American Heart Association.

[3] Present address: University of Manitoba Faculty of Medicine, Winnipeg, Canada.

macroscopically visible ganglion. Mean femoral arterial pressure was recorded with a mercury manometer and a smoked drum. In several experiments, carotid artery pressure and right atrial pressure were recorded by means of strain-gauge transducers with the nerve action potentials on a multichannel recorder.

The response of the nictitating membrane to preganglionic nerve stimulation with rectangular pulses (5 or 10 msec. duration, 1.0 to 10/sec.) was determined before and after the administration of blocking agents by isotonic mechanical recording on a smoked drum. In 6 animals splanchnic action potentials and responses of the nictitating membrane to preganglionic stimulation were studied simultaneously. In the remaining experiments the two determinations were made on separate animals.

Reflex excitation of splanchnic activity was induced by injecting small doses of lobeline, acetylcholine or sodium cyanide into the circulation of the *left* (innervated) carotid body. "Asphyxia" tests were performed on some animals treated with decamethonium by stopping the artificial ventilation for periods of 15 to 45 seconds, constant in each experiment.

The quaternary ganglionic blocking agents tetraethylammonium chloride (TEA) and hexamethonium dichloride, and the tertiary amines tris(diethyl-aminoethyl)amine trihydrochloride (SU-1194) and 1-[bis(2-diethylaminoethyl)amino]-3-diethylamino-2-propanol trihydrochloride (SU-2704) were injected intravenously to total doses of 0.5 to 5.0 mgm./kgm. of the salts.[4]

RESULTS. A. *Spontaneous splanchnic activity.* The normal pattern of splanchnic nerve activity, correlated with carotid pressoreceptor fiber activity, carotid pressure and right atrial pressure, is shown in Fig. 1. Although the "normal" pattern differed somewhat from animal to animal, a majority had a roughly pulse-synchronous pattern, frequently with maximal splanchnic activity near the end of systole. The upper strip in this figure shows a cyclic change in carotid and right atrial pressures induced by the artificial respiration. Maximal splanchnic activity occurred during the arterial and atrial pressure minima. A similar effect of respiration on efferent sympathetic nerve activity has been observed in recordings from branches of the stellate ganglion (Marguth, Raule and Schaefer, 1951). This slow variation in splanchnic activity probably is entirely due to cyclic changes in arterial pressure.

Near the end of the first strip the abdominal aorta was clamped just above the renal arteries and changes resulting from the acute hypertension are shown in the lower strips, which are consecutive. As the carotid pressure rose, splanchnic activity decreased, but retained a cyclic relation to the arterial pressure. The right atrial pressure was not altered significantly.

B. *Effects of ganglionic blocking agents on spontaneous splanchnic activity.* Splanchnic nerve activity always decreased following the administration of moderate doses (1.0 mgm./kgm.) of the blocking agents tested. The first effect, which was usually apparent before the onset of hypotension, was a reduction in the pulse-synchronous activity. This was followed by a disorganization of splanchnic activity, *i.e.*, continuous low-voltage activity unrelated to pulse replaced the pulse-synchronous pattern (fig. 2, first part of middle strip). Following the administration of minimal doses of blocking agent, some disorganization of

[4] The authors are indebted to Dr. E. J. de Beer of the Wellcome Research Laboratories for supplies of hexamethonium and decamethonium and to Dr. A. J. Plummer of Ciba Pharmaceutical Products for supplies of SU-1194 and SU-2704.

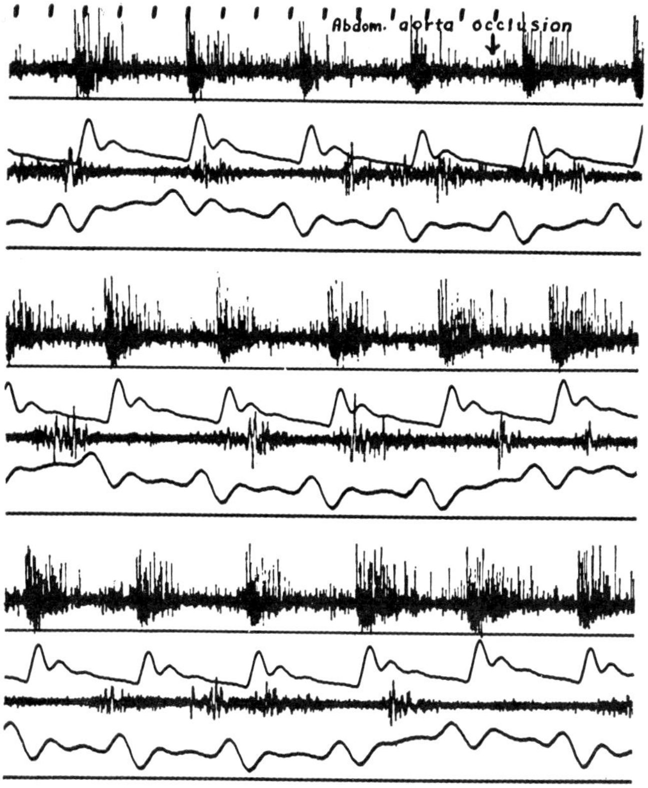

FIG. 1. Consecutive strips; time 1/10 second. In each from above: Right carotid nerve action potentials, carotid pressure, right greater splanchnic nerve action potentials and right atrial pressure. Horizontal lines indicate levels of 0 and 160, and 0 and 20 mm. Hg for arterial and right atrial pressures respectively. At the interruption of the timer in the upper strip, the abdominal aorta was clamped just above the renal arteries. Discussion in text.

splanchnic activity may occur without significant arterial hypotension. Larger doses of blocking agent (2.0 mgm./kgm. or more) caused almost complete cessation of splanchnic nerve activity (fig. 2, bottom strip). Limited splanchnic activity frequently reappeared before the end of the period of maximal hypotension.

Quantitative comparison of the inhibitory effects of the various blocking agents on splanchnic activity was difficult because of variability in the control activity, the difficulty in quantitating changes in activity recorded from a large number of fibers and the persistent effect of some agents which precluded giving repeated test doses in a single preparation. However, a limited comparison of maximal inhibition during the first 5 minutes after injection was attempted. Essentially complete inhibition was obtained with *initial* intravenous injections of 1.5 to 2.5 mgm./kgm. of hexamethonium, 2.0 to 3.0 mgm./kgm. of TEA or SU-1194 or 3.0 to 4.0 mgm./kgm. of SU-2704. Although inhibition of splanchnic

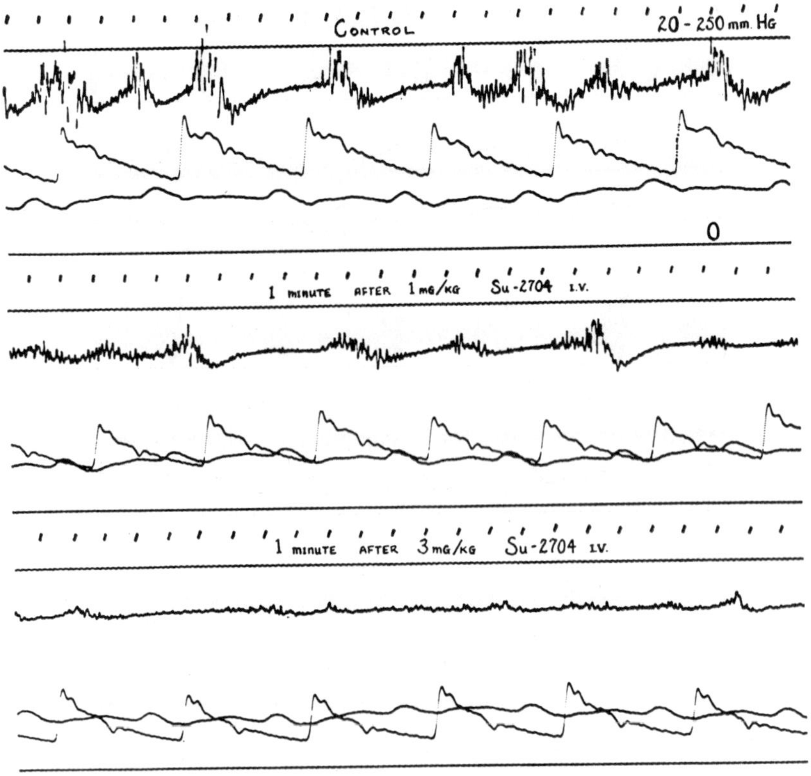

FIG. 2. In each strip from above: Time (1/10 second), splanchnic nerve action potentials, carotid and right atrial pressures. Horizontal lines indicate levels of 0 and 250, and 0 and 20 mm. Hg for arterial and right atrial pressures respectively. See text for details.

activity was obtained with nearly equal doses of hexamethonium and TEA, the duration of action of the former was much greater. In general, the duration of inhibition of splanchnic activity with the various agents was parallel to that of the induced hypotension. The duration of the hypotension and altered splanchnic nerve activity resulting from an injection of 1.0 mgm./kgm. of blocking agent was approximately 40 minutes after hexamethonium, 20 minutes with TEA or SU-1194 and 10 minutes with SU-2704.

In contrast to the decreased splanchnic activity associated with hypotension induced by the ganglionic blocking agents, hypotension following the injection of peripheral vasodilators (acetylcholine or histamine) or Dibenzyline was accompanied by a marked increase in activity. Fig. 3 illustrates responses to the intravenous injection of 1.0 mgm./kgm. of Dibenzyline. A considerable increase in high-voltage, synchronous splanchnic activity appeared concomitant with the hypotension, probably as a component of attempted reflex compensation. Subsequent administration of TEA sharply reduced the splanchnic activity, but caused little further decrease in carotid pressure.

C. *Effects of ganglionic blocking agents on reflexly induced splanchnic activity.*

Injection of chemoreceptor stimulants into the carotid artery induces hyperpnea and an increase in systemic blood pressure, both arising reflexly as shown by the classical work of Heymans. In our preparations, injection of 10 to 50 microgm. of lobeline hydrochloride or 20 to 100 microgm. of NaCN into the *left* carotid artery (innervated carotid body) elicited strong splanchnic nerve discharges with latencies of 1.5 to 3 and 5 to 7 seconds respectively. This activity (fig. 4) con-

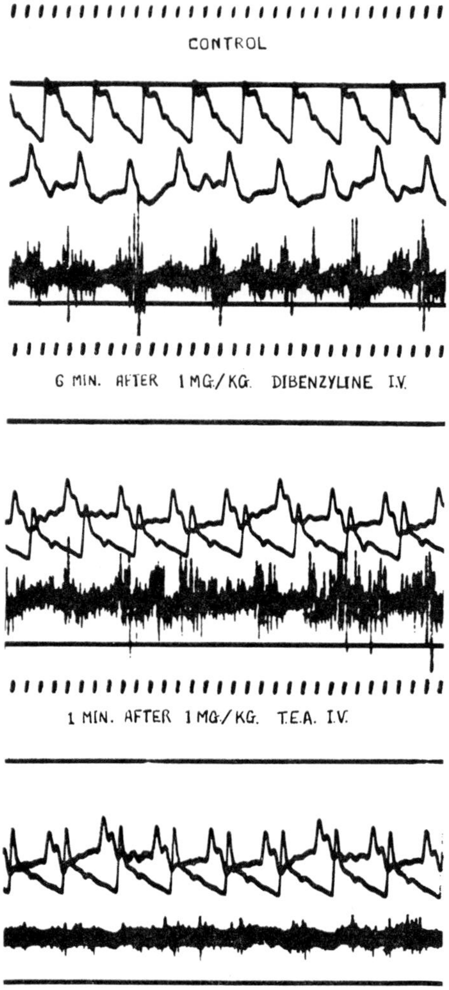

FIG. 3. In each strip from above: Time (1/10 second), carotid and right atrial pressures and splanchnic nerve activity. Horizontal lines indicate levels of 0 and 130 and 0 and 20 mm. Hg for arterial and right atrial pressures respectively. Upper strip: Control record. Middle strip: Six minutes after 1 mgm./kgm. Dibenzyline. Significant drop in arterial and no change in right atrial pressure; splanchnic activity much increased. Lower strip: Ten minutes after middle strip, 1 minute after 1 mgm./kgm. TEA. No further change in either arterial or atrial pressures; considerable decrease in splanchnic activity. (Note that these records were taken at a slower speed than those in the other figures.)

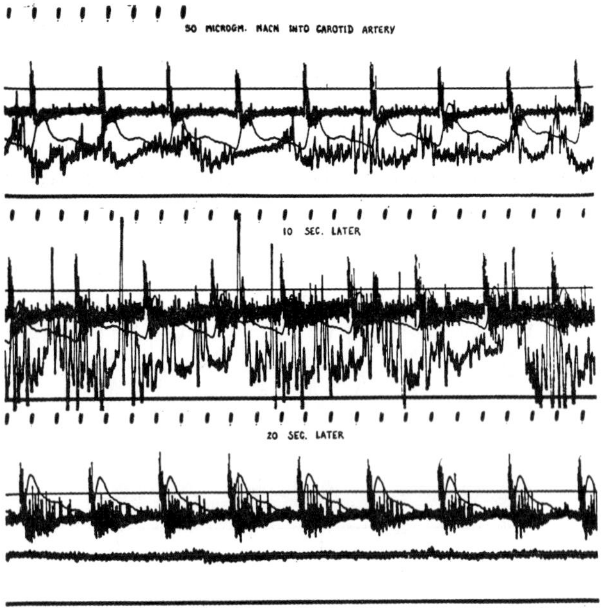

FIG. 4. In each strip from above: Time (1/10 second), right carotid nerve action potentials, carotid pressure and greater splanchnic nerve action potentials. Horizontal lines indicate levels of arterial pressure of 0 and 150 mm. Hg. Upper strip: Control, interruption of timer indicates beginning of left intracarotid injection of 50 microgm. NaCN. Middle strip: 10 seconds later; chemoreceptor discharge in the sinus nerve; blood pressure steadily increasing; splanchnic activity maximal. Lower strip: 20 seconds after injection; carotid chemoreceptors quiescent, but many pressoreceptors active; blood pressure maximal; splanchnic activity almost entirely absent.

sisted of highly synchronized high voltage discharges. Increased activity appeared 5 to 10 seconds before the blood pressure started to rise. The increased activity induced by the chemoreceptor discharge probably represents vasoconstrictor impulses to the splanchnic vascular bed. Increased chemoreceptor activity in the *right* carotid nerve appeared 8 to 12 seconds after the end of the left intracarotid injection, the time necessary for recirculation of the drug. Splanchnic activity usually decreased during the peak of the pressor response, but increased again as soon as the blood pressure started to fall toward normal.

After the administration of 1.0 to 2.0 mgm./kgm. of the blocking agents tested, the reflex splanchnic nerve discharge in response to NaCN appeared with the same latency, but the intensity of the response was diminished and grouped discharges appeared only infrequently (fig. 5). This reduction in induced splanchnic activity is significant because the doses of ganglionic blocking agents employed do not decrease the intensity of the chemoreceptor response to cyanide and actually prolong it (Dontas and Nickerson, 1956). The residual splanchnic response may not be followed by a rise in blood pressure, probably because of the additional effects of blockade of ganglia distal to the point of recording. Administration of higher doses of the blocking agents delayed or completely inhibited the

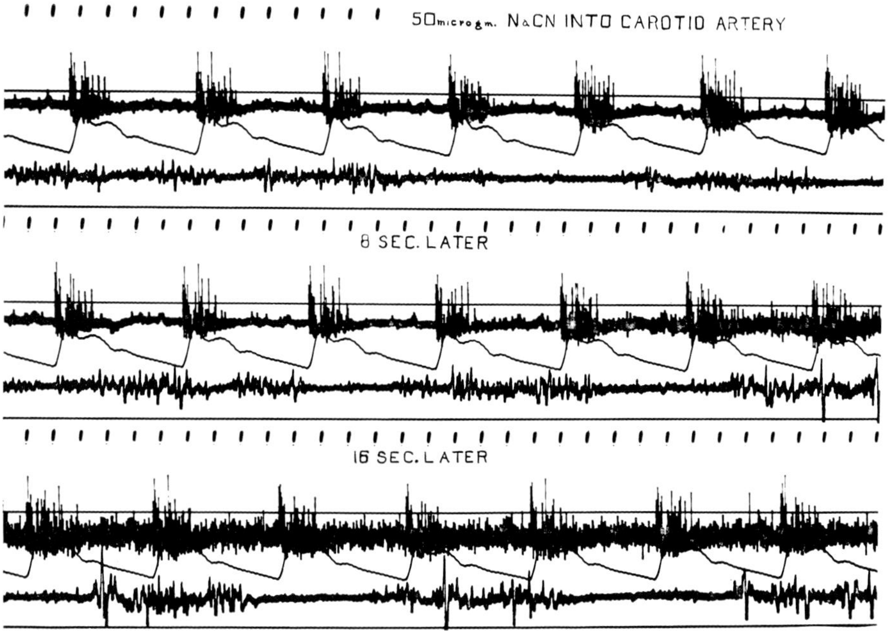

FIG. 5. Records the same as in figure 4, but two minutes after 2.0 mgm./kgm. SU-2704 injected intravenously. The moderate increase in splanchnic activity shown in the middle and lower strips is not accompanied by a significant change in blood pressure.

reflex response to the doses of NaCN employed, despite the fact that a small amount of spontaneous splanchnic nerve activity persisted (fig. 6). Both the increase in splanchnic nerve activity and the rise in arterial pressure resulting from a period of asphyxia were partially or completely prevented by suitable doses of blocking agent (2.0 mgm./kgm. of hexamethonium or TEA). This occurred despite the markedly increased chemoreceptor discharge, which lasted up to two minutes after artificial ventilation was resumed.

Reflex splanchnic activity elicited by cholinergic agents (acetylcholine, lobeline) was also decreased, delayed and eventually abolished by the ganglionic blocking agents. However, stimulation of the carotid body by cholinergic drugs is inhibited by these blocking agents, and it is impossible to evaluate the significance of the decreased splanchnic response in the presence of a decreased afferent stimulus.

D. *Effect of varied preganglionic stimuli on "apparent" ganglionic blockade.* Ganglionic blockade was studied by delivering shocks to the cervical sympathetic trunk and recording contractions of the nictitating membrane. Initially, maximal stimuli at a rate of 10/sec. for 10 seconds were employed and a recovery period of at least ninety seconds was allowed between periods of stimulation. Under these conditions doses of the blocking agents which caused a considerable reduction in preganglionic splanchnic activity appeared to have very little effect on

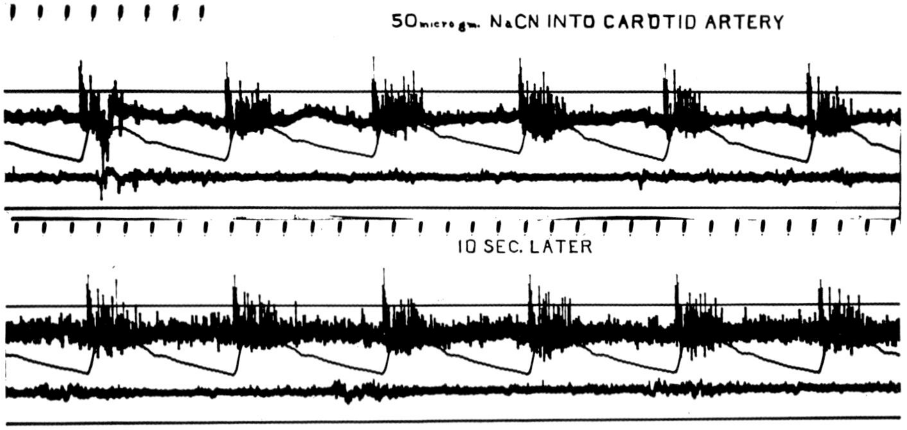

FIG. 6. Records from the same experiment as figures 4 and 5 after an additional 2.0 mgm./kgm. of SU-2704. Little spontaneous splanchnic activity, and no splanchnic response to the NaCN injection despite good chemoreceptor activation.

ganglionic transmission in 4 of 6 experiments; in the remaining 2, the only effect observed was a prolongation of relaxation. Only when longer periods of stimulation were employed was ganglionic transmission significantly impaired, an observation previously reported by Paton (1952).

We therefore tested the blockade of responses to submaximal shocks to approximate the situation arising when preganglionic activity is converted from a high-voltage synchronous type to a lower amplitude diffuse type by the blocking agents. (See section B of results.) Under these conditions, ganglionic blockade was quite apparent with 1.0 to 2.0 mgm./kgm. of blocking agent. Inhibition of the response was most prominent when contractions were elicited by stimuli close to threshold. Calculation of the areas of the myograms reproduced in fig. 7 (left) showed that 1.0 mgm./kgm. of hexamethonium reduced the first (0.5 volt stimulus) to 73 per cent of its control, the second (0.4 volt) to 59 per cent and the third (0.3 volt) to 42 per cent. It is obvious that responses to weak, close to threshold stimuli were more completely blocked than those to stronger stimuli. This dose of hexamethonium does not inhibit and may potentiate responses of equal magnitude elicited by maximal shocks of low frequency (fig. 7, right).

These experiments indicate that the extent to which moderate doses of a blocking agent inhibit ganglionic transmission is to a large extent dependent upon the choice of the parameters of excitation. To obtain a more complete picture of the effect of blocking agents on transmission through the superior cervical sympathetic ganglion under varied conditions of stimulation, "ganglionic summation" was studied in three experiments. Voltage-number curves for threshold responses to definite numbers of preganglionic shocks were constructed from data obtained by delivering a known number of shocks to the preganglionic trunk at a frequency of 3/sec. every 90 seconds and progressively decreasing the voltage until a just detectable response of the nictitating membrane was obtained. Such

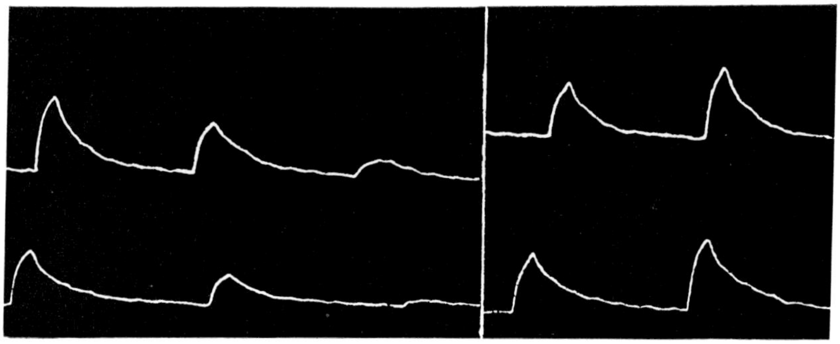

FIG. 7. Responses of nictitating membrane to 10-second periods of preganglionic cervical sympathetic stimulation. Above: Left, submaximal stimuli (10/sec., 5 msec. duration), applied voltages from left to right were 0.5, 0.4 and 0.3. Right, maximal stimuli (1.5 V, 5 msec. duration), frequency 1/sec. and 2/sec. (left and right respectively). Below: Responses to the same stimuli 4 minutes after 1.0 mgm./kgm. of hexamethonium administered intravenously. The areas of the lower myograms are 73, 59 and 42, and 125 and 114 per cent of the corresponding controls.

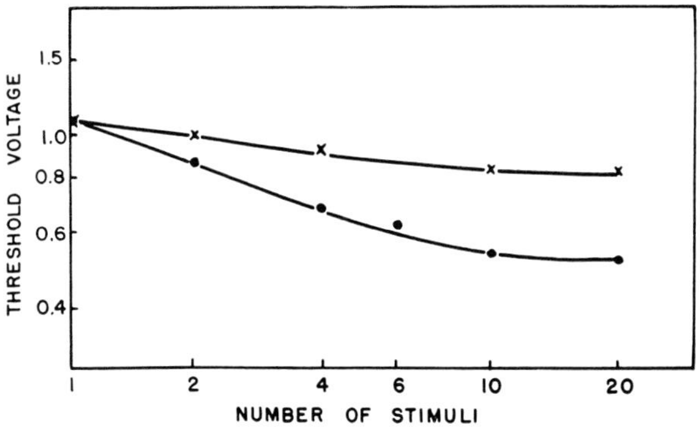

FIG. 8. Voltage-number curves for threshold responses of the nictitating membrane in response to preganglionic stimuli. ●——● control; X——X after 1.0 mgm./kgm. of hexamethonium injected intravenously.

curves are shown in fig. 8. The curve approximates the formula $V = A \frac{1}{1 - e^{-Bn}}$, where V is applied voltage; n is the number of stimuli; and A is equal to the voltage when the denominator becomes 1, *i.e.*, when n is large. As the value of B increases, the curve becomes flatter and eventually the linear equation V = A is reached, *i.e.*, no temporal summation occurs. The curves were redetermined after the intravenous administration of 0.5 to 1.5 mgm./kgm. of hexamethonium, and in all experiments threshold voltages for the higher numbers of stimuli were significantly increased, whereas there was no increase in the threshold for a single shock. B increased from approximately 0.45 to 0.80 in the experiment shown in fig. 8. The results indicate that this dose of hexamethonium would much more effectively inhibit responses to repetitive, low intensity stimuli than those to fewer impulses of high intensity. This "metachronosis" of the voltage-number curve can be obtained only with moderate doses of a ganglionic blocking agent. Larger doses (2.0 mgm./kgm. or more of hexamethonium) increase the threshold voltages for all numbers of stimuli and the curve becomes very flat.

Discussion. The results presented above indicate that the flow of efferent impulses in the preganglionic splanchnic nerves of cats can be decreased or abolished by hypotensive doses of the "ganglionic" blocking agents tetraethylammonium, hexamethonium, SU-1194 and SU-2704. Interpretation of the change from high-voltage, synchronized bursts of activity to continuous low-voltage activity as a decrease requires clarification. This interpretation appears to be justified by the fact that desynchronized activity always appeared as an intermediate stage between normal activity and complete quiescence, and by a comparison of the present records of splanchnic activity with those from experiments in which an increase or decrease in vasomotor outflow is known to occur. Relevant observations include: 1. The fast, desynchronized type of discharge always precedes complete quiescence when splanchnic activity is inhibited reflexly by agents such as protoveratrine or serotonin (Dontas, 1955). 2. During the early states of hemorrhagic shock sympathetic activity is greatly enchanced and this is expressed as high-voltage, synchronized bursts of impulses in the splanchnic nerves. Only during the stage of "automatic reinfusion" does the splanchnic discharge become desynchronized or disappear. 3. Chemoreceptor stimulants injected into the circulation to the carotid body induce extremely high voltage, synchronized splanchnic potentials just preceding the reflex rise in blood pressure. At the peak of the blood pressure rise and during the first part of the slow return to normal levels, splanchnic activity is either totally absent or of the desynchronized, low-voltage type. 4. In contrast to the changes observed with ganglionic blocking agents, hypotension induced by peripheral vasodilators such as histamine or acetylcholine or by adrenergic blocking agents such as Dibenzyline (phenoxybenzamine) is associated with an increase in the high voltage, synchronized bursts of splanchnic activity. Hypotension induced by ganglionic blocking agents is clearly associated with a pattern of splanchnic activity qualitatively different from that which accompanies hypotension due to agents acting peripherally. This comparison also helps to rule out artifacts associated with the hypotension as the cause of the changes in splanchnic activity.

The possibility that the observed changes in electrical activity might be due to recording from postganglionic fibers running in the preceliac portion of the greater splanchnic nerve must be considered. Anatomical evidence indicates that this area of the nerve is composed almost entirely of preganglionic fibers, the only postganglionic component being a few fibers running to the mediastinal blood vessels (Kuntz, 1953, and personal communication). In addition, certain physiological observations support the assumption that the fibers under study are predominantly preganglionic. 1. If a sufficiently large dose of blocking agent is injected intravenously, the recorded activity of the splanchnic nerve is almost completely abolished (fig. 2). Electrical activity would not be expected to disappear completely if the nerve under study contained significant numbers of both pre- and postganglionic fibers, and only the latter were affected. 2. Recovery of the blood pressure following the hypotensive response to moderate doses of a ganglionic blocking agent may not occur until some time after considerable return of activity in the fibers under study. Presumably the hypotension persists because ganglia distal to the point of recording are still blocked. Such records appear to dissociate the preganglionic or central from the true ganglionic inhibitory effects. This dissociation is also evident when the splanchnic nerves are excited reflexly following the administration of intermediate doses of a ganglionic blocking agent. Here the splanchnic activity may increase moderately without a concomitant rise in blood pressure.

Heymans *et al.* (1954) reported that they were unable to detect in dogs any "interference with reflex transmission and direct excitation" of the cardio-inhibitory center of the vagus by large doses of hexamethonium. Their observations are superficially contrary to the present findings. However, it is not unusual for responses of the sympathetic and parasympathetic centers to drugs to be qualitatively different. It is well known that most agents which act centrally to decrease sympathetic outflow (ergot and *Rauwolfia* alkaloids, *etc.*) actually tend to increase parasympathetic activity.

In the experiments reported herein, injections of 0.5 to 2.5 mgm./kgm. of the ganglionic blocking agents tested resulted primarily in desynchronization of splanchnic activity and replacement of the rhythmical high-voltage pattern by continuous low-voltage activity. As shown in section D of the results, this disruption of the pattern of preganglionic sympathetic activity may contribute to the effectiveness of the blockade at ganglia. Moderate doses of a blocking agent may reduce ganglionic transmission of near-threshold preganglionic impulses considerably, whereas they cause little or no impairment of the transmission of maximal or submaximal volleys (comparable to the synchronous high-voltage discharges).

Little can be said regarding the locus of the central or preganglionic inhibitory action of the agents studied. This could be exerted at one or more of the numerous brain-stem or spinal-cord synapses involved in vasomotor center discharge. It is also possible that the central connections of afferent components of vasomotor reflexes may be inhibited. Although hexamethonium and most other ganglionic blocking agents inhibit ganglionic transmission by competition with acetylcholine, the locus and mechanism of action of these agents in reducing preganglionic nerve activity are too poorly understood for the present data to be considered reliable evidence for a transmitter role of acetylcholine at central synapses involved in vasomotor activity. However, they are compatible with such an interpretation.

The temporal relation of the central and ganglionic components of the action of the agents studied is difficult to define. It appears that not only do different ganglia recover from blockade at different rates, but also that the "blockade" of any one ganglion may or may not be effective depending upon the type of impulses reaching it. Central inhibition disappears before the most sensitive tests indicate the return of ganglionic transmission to normal, but it lasts longer than the blockade of ganglionic transmission of maximal, intermittent volleys.

The relative importance of central and ganglionic blockade in hypotensive responses to the ganglionic blocking agents in intact animals or man cannot be stated precisely. However, it appears probable that following the administration of large doses hypotension results predominately from the central action. If no impulses reach the ganglia, blockade at this locus is of no importance. Following moderate doses, both actions are probably involved, the central inhibition facilitating the ganglionic blockade.

SUMMARY

Extraganglionic actions of ganglionic blocking agents were studied in cats by the simultaneous recording of action potentials of the carotid nerve (afferent) and of the preganglionic portion of the greater splanchnic nerve (efferent).

Moderately hypotensive doses of hexamethonium, tetraethylammonium, SU-1194 or SU-2704 administered intravenously decreased blood pressure and splanchnic outflow concomitantly. Continuous low-grade activity replaced the synchronized, high-voltage discharge seen prior to drug administration. Larger doses of the blocking agents (2.0 mgm./kgm. or more of hexamethonium) largely or completely abolished splanchnic activity. Carotid nerve activity was not changed significantly. In contrast, hypotension induced by peripheral vasodilators (acetylcholine or histamine) or by Dibenzyline was associated with a marked increase in splanchnic nerve activity.

Activity in the splanchnic nerves induced reflexly by excitation of carotid chemoreceptors by either cholinergic or hypoxic (NaCN) stimuli was considerably reduced by the ganglionic blocking agents. The moderate increase in splanchnic activity which often persisted was of the desynchronized type and no high-voltage bursts, which characteristically followed chemoreceptor activation prior to administration of a ganglionic blocking agent, occurred. This mild increase in splanchnic activity did not cause a rise in blood pressure, probably because of an element of true ganglionic blockade peripheral to the point of recording.

Ganglionic transmission of maximal stimuli applied to preganglionic cervical sympathetic neurons was unaltered or only minimally decreased by hypotensive doses of the ganglionic blocking agents. However, responses to near-threshold or prolonged stimulation were more effectively inhibited. These observations suggest that the major effect of moderate doses of these agents on ganglia is to impair temporal summation, and that the continuous, low-voltage activity of preganglionic neurons which follows the administration of the blocking agents would be inhibited more readily at peripheral ganglia than would the normal synchronized high-voltage activity.

The relative importance of central and ganglionic blockade in determining responses to ganglionic blocking agents in the intact animal cannot be stated definitely, but it appears probable that the former is of major importance in the response to large doses, and that both actions are involved, the former facilitating the latter, in the response to moderate doses.

Acknowledgment. The authors wish to acknowledge the help of Dr. Leonard Procita during a part of this investigation.

REFERENCES

ACHESON, G. H., AND MOE, G. K.: THIS JOURNAL, **87:** 220, 1946.
DONTAS, A. S.: Circulation Res., **3:** 363, 1955.
DONTAS, A. S., AND NICKERSON, M.: Arch. internat. pharmacodyn., **106:** 312, 1956.
DOUGLAS, W. W.: J. Physiol., **118:** 373, 1952.
GOLLWITZER-MEIER, K., AND WITZLEB, E.: Arch. ges. Physiol., **256:** 381, 1953.
HEYMANS, C., DELAUNOIS, A. L., AND MARTINI, L.: Arch. internat. pharmacodyn., **97:** 313, 1954.
JANOWITZ, H., AND GROSSMAN, M. I.: Science, **109:** 16, 1949.
KUNTZ, A.: The Autonomic Nervous System. Lea & Febiger, Philadelphia, 1953.
MARGUTH, H., RAULE, W., AND SCHAEFER, H.: Arch. ges. Physiol., **254:** 224, 1951.
O'DELL, T. B., LUNA, C., AND NAPOLI, M. D.: THIS JOURNAL, **114:** 306, 1955a.
O'DELL, T. B., LUNA, C., AND NAPOLI, M. D.: THIS JOURNAL, **114:** 317, 1955b.
PATON, W. D. M.: Brit. M. Bull., **8:** 310, 1952.

ACTION OF ESERINE AND AMPHETAMINE ON THE ELECTRICAL ACTIVITY OF THE RABBIT BRAIN

V. G. LONGO AND B. SILVESTRINI

Laboratory of Therapeutical Chemistry, Istituto Superiore di Sanitá, Roma

Received for publication December 24, 1956

Significant differences in the electroencephalograms (EEG) between the state of rest and alertness have been recorded in man and also in experimental animals. The resting EEG is characterized by large slow waves interrupted by "spindles" of fast waves of high amplitude, whereas alertness may be distinguished by fast waves of low voltage. The change from sleep to alertness in the EEG is abrupt when men or animals are subjected to an external stimulus. This response has been called: blocking reaction (Berger, 1934), activation pattern (Rheinberger and Jasper, 1937), and desynchronization (Adrian and Matthews, 1934). Moruzzi and Magoun (1949) have described a similar response following the electrical stimulation of the gray matter (reticular formation) in the central core of the brain stem. An increased attention is given to this afferent extralemniscal "activating" system through which external stimuli are conducted to the cortex and which is essential for the maintenance of the alertness of the brain (French *et al.*, 1953).

A pattern similar to the activation after arousal reaction to external stimuli may be observed following the administration of certain drugs. EEG activation has been obtained with small doses of acetylcholine injected into the carotid artery (Bonnet and Bremer, 1937; Bremer and Chatonnet, 1949; Longo, 1955). Eserine when given by intravenous injection had the same action (Funderburk and Case, 1951; Bradley and Elkes, 1953). These observations have recently been confirmed by Rinaldi and Himwich (1955), in a series of experiments on the action of DFP and acetylcholine on the cortical electrical activity involving the use of such preparations as the "cerveau isolé" and the "isolated hemisphere". These authors claim that cholinergic drugs act upon the reticular formation of the mesencephalon. Desmedt and La Grutta, however, (1955a, b) believe that an action of these drugs on the cortex is more likely, as they observed that the desynchronization produced by an anticholinesterase (dimethylcarbamate 2-hydroxy-5-phenyl benzyl trimethylammonium, RO2-0683) injected into the carotid artery persisted even in the "cerveau sans reticulée" preparation. On the other hand, anticholinergic drugs such as atropine and scopolamine produce synchronization of the EEG that cannot be interrupted by external stimulation (Funderburk and Case, 1951), by the injection of acetylcholine into the carotid artery (Rinaldi and Himwich, 1955), or by means of electric stimulation of the reticular formation (Longo, 1956).

These data suggest a cholinergic mechanism for the arousal reaction. However, a similar pattern of cortical activation may be obtained with drugs of a completely different mode of action. In the curarized cat and in the "encéphale isolé" preparation of the same animal, Bonvallet *et al.* (1954) were able to obtain, with epinephrine, a desynchronization similar to that obtained by means of external stimuli. The same results have been obtained by Elkes *et al.* (1954) with amphetamine. Schallek and Walz (1953) have described in dogs a pattern of cortical activation after amphetamine, and have drawn attention to the similarity between this pattern and that observed in the alert animal. Hiebel *et al.* (1954), using curarized cats, "encéphale isolé", and "cerveau isolé" preparations, have shown that the activation due to amphetamine diminishes and disappears with the removal of rostral portion of the reticular formation. These authors have suggested that the activation effects of epinephrine and of amphetamine take place through the reticular formation.

Evidence limited to EEG tracings can offer only an approximate indication of the activating action of different drugs and can lead to contradictory interpretations as those found in the literature regarding cholinergic drugs and amphetamine (*cf.* Rinaldi and Himwich, 1955; Hiebel *et al.*, 1954).

The present study was designed to provide evidence for differences in the EEG activation obtained with a cholinergic drug (eserine) or with an adrenergic drug (amphetamine). In the course of these experiments, the action of amphetamine and eserine was observed on the electrical activity of the cortex and of subcortical structures of normal animals and of "cerveau isolé" preparation. Observations were also made on the effects of these drugs on EEG activation obtained either by means of external stimulations or by electrical stimulation of the reticular formation, and on the recruitment obtained by electric stimulation of the anteromedial nuclei of the thalamus. In addition, a number of antagonistic actions of the two drugs on the EEG effects of pentylenetetrazol and of scopolamine have been studied.

METHODS. The experiments were performed on 70 rabbits of an average weight of 2.0 kgm. The animals were anesthetized with ether and prepared in the following manner: a tracheotomy was performed, the skull bone was laid bare, electrodes were screwed through the bone with their tips on the dura mater for bipolar recordings of the electrical potentials of the cortex. Stimulation of and recordings from the deep structures were made by means of concentric electrodes measuring 0.5 mm. in diameter and fixed according to the method of Hess, modified by Monnier and Laue (1953). In a few animals the blood pressure was recorded from the femoral artery with a mercury manometer. After the operation, the animals were placed in a box which, while restricting their movements, allowed them to rest in a normal crouching position. The recordings were taken in the unanesthetized uncurarized animal at least one hour after the surgical procedures. At the end of the experiments the animals were killed, and the position of the electrodes was determined histologically in serial sections.

"Cerveau isolé". In a second group of animals a complete transverse section of the brain stem from the intercollicular line to the rostral end of the pons was performed by means of a blunt lancet introduced through an opening in the occipital bone (part of the cerebellum had previously been removed). This operation was performed following a technique slightly modified from the original method of Bremer (1936). In the rabbit an ossified *tentorium cerebelli* is not present and thus can not be followed by the blunt lancet. Furthermore, a better view of the field of operation can be obtained by removing part of the cerebellum. Edema is avoided since the cerebrospinal fluid is allowed to flow from the ventricles. The recordings were obtained in the same manner as has been described for the first group.

The level of the section was verified after each experiment. The blood pressure was always measured during the experiments.

Recordings were made with a Grass electroencephalograph, Model IIID, and with a Cossor oscillograph, Model 1049. In order to activate the tracing, two types of external stimulation were used and care was taken to obtain stimuli of equal intensity and duration throughout the experiment. Auditory stimuli were applied through a buzzer and tacticle stimuli through a hammer falling from a fixed distance on the same place on the back of the animal. Electrical stimulation was performed with an electronic generator furnishing a rectangular pulse of varying frequency, duration, and amplitude; the stimuli reached the brain through a transformer. Both eserine and amphetamine were injected in the form of salicylate and sulphate salts respectively, diluted in physiological solution; the doses are expressed as weights of the free bases.

RESULTS. *Cortical and subcortical electrical activity in the normal animal.* The electrical activity of the cortex of an unanesthetized rabbit during rest varies from area to area. In recordings taken from the frontal lobes three different types

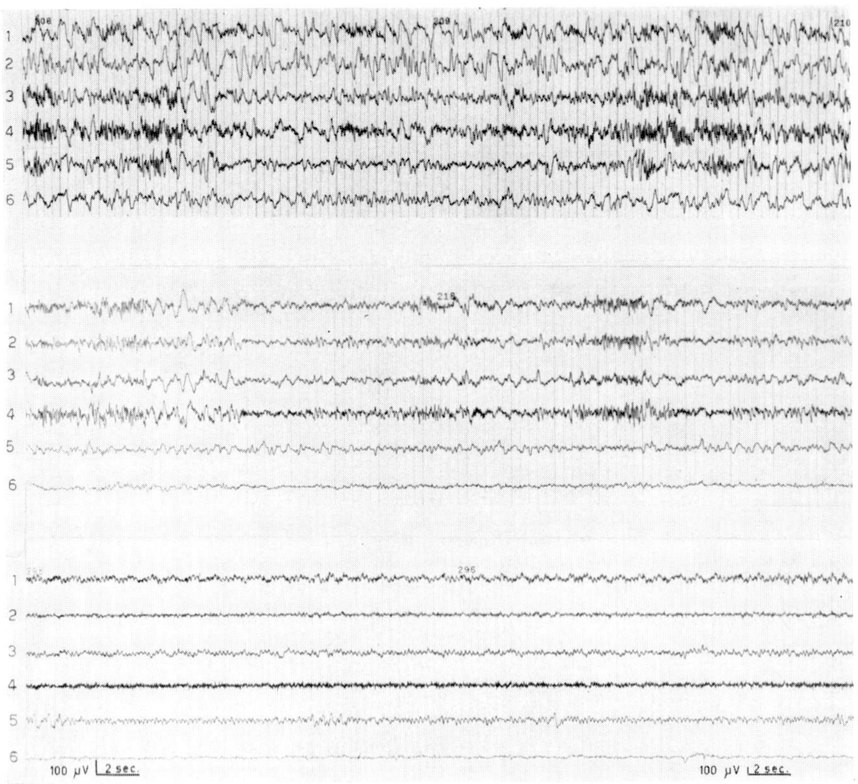

FIG. 1. Action of eserine on the cortical and subcortical electrogram of the normal rabbit. Progressive disappearance of the slow waves and diminution of spindles activity (middle tracing), which ends in a complete activation (lower tracing).

Rabbit 2.2 kgm., 12/7/55. First tracing, normal; second tracing, 3 minutes after 0.05 mgm./kgm. of eserine i.v.; third tracing, 10 minutes after. Leads: 1—L fr.-occ.; 2—R. fr.-par.; 3—R.par.-occ.; 4—L.fr.-R.fr.; 5—medial nucleus of the thalamus; 6—mesencephalic reticular substance. The calibration at the right is for all the cortical tracings; at the left is for all the subcortical leads.

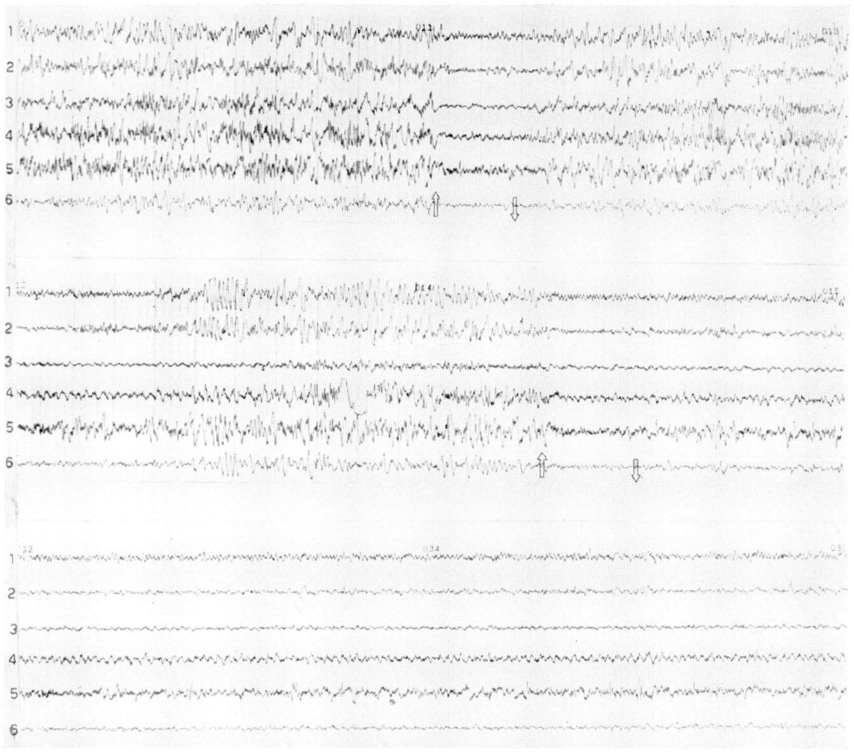

FIG. 2. Action of amphetamine on the EEG of the normal rabbit. Trains of slow waves in occipital leads and activation confined mainly to the left frontal lead can be noticed after small doses (middle tracing). Further administration of the drug produces a picture of general activation (lower tracing).

Rabbit 2.0 kgm., 23/11/55. First tracing, normal; between arrows short activation elicited by means of acoustic stimulation. Second tracing, two minutes after 1 mgm./kgm. of amphetamine. Absence of enhancement of the activation after acoustic stimuli. Third tracing, after 4 mgm./kgm. the EEG is completely activated. Leads: 1—L. occipital; 2—L. parietal; 3—L. frontal; 4—R. frontal; 5—R. parietal; 6—R. occipital.

of activity can be distinguished, which are always found together, though one type may predominate over the others: 1) waves at 4 to 7 c/sec. and 60 to 150 μV, 2) bursts of waves at 10 to 15 c/sec. and of 200 to 500 μV which may appear scattered in the tracings or organized as "spindles", *i.e.*, as a succession of waves of a progressively increasing and decreasing amplitude, and 3) large slow waves at 1.5 to 3 c/sec. and of 300 to 700 μV. In the parietal leads the rhythm of 4 to 7 c/sec. waves and the large waves clearly predominate, while the bursts of "spindles", although present, have a lower voltage. In the occipital lobes no "spindles" can be seen, and the large slow waves only occasionally appear; the normal occipital activity consists in irregular waves at 5 to 8 c/sec. of a relative low voltage. This state of synchronization was prevalent under the conditions of our experiments and is referred to as the normal electrical activity of the rabbit brain (upper tracings of fig. 1 and 2).

External stimulation abruptly changes the normal activity to the "activation" pattern, consisting of rapid waves (25 to 35 c/sec.) of low voltage (40 to 60 μV), especially evident in the tracing from the frontal lobe. In recordings from the parietal lobe a pattern may be obtained of waves at 5 c/sec. and of 80 to 100 μV with a superimposed rapid activity which is the same as the one obtained from frontal recordings. Occipital leads show a widespread lowering of the voltage of the tracings or sometimes an activity at 5 to 6 c/sec. similar to the one observed in the parietal area, but the rapid waves are absent. The activation pattern normally lasts only a few seconds after the end of the stimulation and the spindles and the slow waves return on the tracing.

The tracings obtained by means of deep electrodes were generally taken from the areas which were subsequently stimulated, *i.e.*, from the antero-medial nuclei of the thalamus and from the reticular formation of the mesencephalon at the level of the *anterior colliculus*. From the thalamus an activity characterized by "spindles" may be recorded. This spindling is similar to the activity of the cortex, though not always synchronous with it. Slow potentials and waves of lower voltage and of irregular frequency can also be recorded. Following external stimulation the thalamic activity is replaced by 5 to 6 c/sec. waves. Recordings from the reticular formation of the mesencephalon are generally characterized by an irregular activity with a poor tendency to the formation of "spindles"; external stimulation causes the appearance of a 5 to 6 c/sec. rhythm with superimposed waves of low voltage and high frequency. There is a close resemblance between tracings from the cortex and those taken from the thalamus and the reticular formation during rest and during activation provoked by external stimuli.

Action of eserine and amphetamine on the EEG of normal rabbits. Eserine: Within 2 to 3 minutes following the injection of small doses (0.025 to 0.05 mgm./kgm.), the slow waves disappeared and the number of spindles per unit time decreased (fig. 1). These modifications lasted for about 30 minutes. In many animals, the activation response to acoustic or tactile stimuli was prolonged; it outlasted the stimulus two or three minutes.

Larger doses of the drug (0.05 to 0.1 mgm./kgm.) gave rise to desynchronization similar to the one obtained by means of external stimuli but of longer duration (fig. 1). The acceleration of the waves also appeared in tracings from the thalamus and from the reticular formation, the response to the drug being uniform from all the leads. The animal was generally calm. This sharp activation of the tracing often lasted 15 to 30 minutes and was then followed by a pattern similar to the one obtained with smaller doses. Normal electrical activity returned only after hours.

The drug in doses up to 0.1 mgm./kgm. administered by slow intravenous injection caused no significant alterations of blood pressure, in some cases slight but transient depressions were recorded.

Amphetamine: The blood pressure did not show a significant alteration on slow intravenous injection of doses up to 2 mgm./kgm. With larger doses (2 to 5 mgm./kgm.), a diphasic action was observed, characterized by a slight lowering of the blood pressure followed by a somewhat prolonged increase. The action of amphetamine on the EEG appeared after a short latent period (30 to 60 sec.). With small doses (0.25 to 0.5 mgm./kgm.), the slow waves disappeared and the number and amplitude of "spindles" diminished. In contrast to the eserine, the desynchronized activity frequently appeared in the frontal leads, sometimes first in one side, then spreading to the other, while normal activity was still present in the tracings from parietal and occipital lobes. In about 50 per cent of the experiments, trains of slow waves of 2 to 4 per second and of high voltage (300 to 500 μV) appeared in the occipital leads. With larger doses (1 to 2 mgm./kgm.), a generalized desynchronization in all leads was noticed and the slow occipital waves disappeared (fig. 2). Tracings from deep electrodes were much less modified than the tracings from superficial electrodes. The behaviour of the animals was substantially changed; spontaneous excitement, tachypnea, and mydriasis were always observed.

Attention should be drawn to the fact that the desynchronized EEG tracings of the animal injected with amphetamine could always be further modified by external stimuli. The response to external stimulation consists in an increased desynchronization in the superficial and especially in the deep leads. However, no prolongation of the arousal reaction after external stimulation was observed.

Action of eserine and amphetamine on the spike-waves produced by pentylenetetrazol. It is well known that after the injection of pentylenetetrazol in doses of 5 to 10 mgm./kgm. spike-waves appear in the electrical tracings of the cortex which progressively take the place of the "spindles" characteristic of the normal EEG (Toman *et al.*, 1946). These spike-waves occur also in thalamic and reticular leads. These are blocked by external stimuli. Eserine in producing a general desynchronization of the tracing also abolished the characteristic potentials due to pentylenetetrazol in all leads.

Amphetamine in doses of 1 to 2 mgm./kgm. desynchronized the pattern of electrical activity but did not affect the spike-waves caused by pentylenetetrazol. Indeed, these complexes appeared very distinctly on the background of the rapid waves of the tracing. Even larger doses (3 to 5 mgm./kgm.) did not modify the spike-waves in parietal and occipital leads, although they sometimes abolished the complexes in the frontal tracings.

The EEG "grand mal" patterns produced by larger doses (15 to 20 mgm./kgm.) of pentylenetetrazol were not influenced by either eserine or amphetamine.

Antagonism of scopolamine to eserine and amphetamine. The administration of 0.03 to 0.05 mgm./kgm. of scopolamine produced a marked increase in the slow waves and spindles of the cortical tracings and a block of the activation response to external stimuli. The desynchronization obtained with 0.05 to 0.1 mgm./kgm. of eserine, which usually lasted for a period of 30 to 40 minutes, quickly disappeared after intravenous injection of 0.1 to 0.2 mgm./kgm. of scopolamine, and was substituted by a pattern consisting of only slow waves and spindles which did not respond to external stimuli. By injecting first 0.1 mgm./kgm. of scopolamine and subsequently 0.2 to 0.3 mgm./kgm. of eserine, the opposite phenomenon may be observed, *i.e.*, the change from a synchronization to a prolonged desynchronization of the tracing.

Scopolamine also antagonized the effects of amphetamine on the EEG. Following the administration of 0.05 to 0.1 mgm./kgm. of scopolamine, the desynchronization produced by amphetamine completely disappeared. The opposite phenomenon, however, could not be demonstrated; the cortical synchronization produced by scopolamine persisted unchanged even after 5 mgm./kgm. of amphetamine, although the animal became markedly agitated.

Action of eserine and amphetamine on recruitment obtained by stimulation of the antero-medial nuclei of the thalamus. In resting normal rabbits, a recruiting response could be elicited over wide cortical areas by stimulation of the antero-medial nuclei of the thalamus at a frequency from 5 to 15 c/sec. (fig. 3). The cortical recruiting response consisted of a complex of waves (at least two) which appeared after a latency of 15 to 25 msec. and were preceded by smaller deflections. External stimulation blocked the recruiting response. Eserine (0.05 to 0.1 mgm./kgm.) inhibits the recruiting response in the frontal leads, as shown in fig. 3. The inhibition of the recruiting response by external stimulation and also by eserine was obtained regularly with appropriate voltage of stimulation in the frontal lead, then the frontal lobe was chosen for the oscillographic recordings. In other parts of the cortex the recruiting response was less sensitive to external stimulation and to eserine. After the administration of amphetamine the recruitment was not significantly changed, even after large doses of the drug (3 to 4 mgm./kgm.).

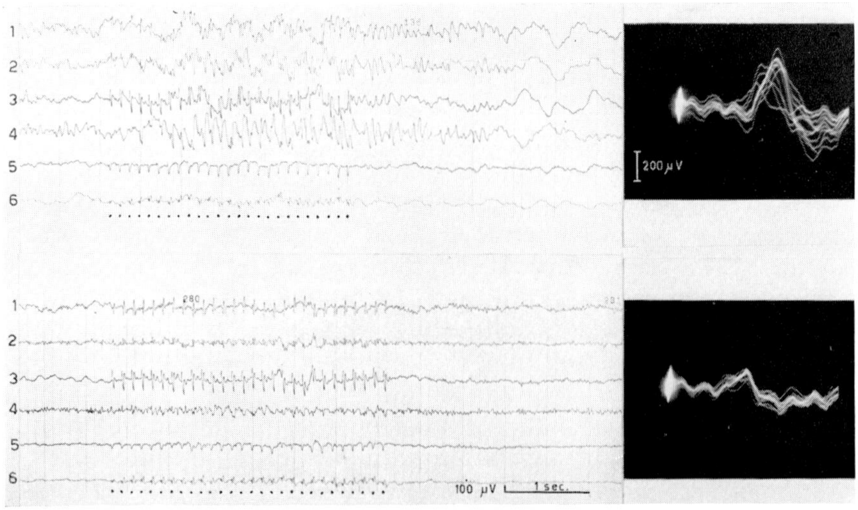

FIG. 3. Action of eserine on the recruiting response after thalamic stimulation.

Rabbit 2.3 kgm. 11/10/55. First tracing, the recruiting response to the stimulation of the thalamic antero medial nucleus is particularly evident in the frontal leads, a train of waves follows the end of stimulation. Second tracing, 10 minutes after administration of 0.1 mgm./kgm. of eserine. Activation of the tracing, the recruiting response is inhibited. In the oscillographic record (L.fr.-R.fr.) the disappearance of the response is better noticed. Leads: 1—L.fr.-occ.; 2—R.fr.-par.; 3—R.par.-occ.; 4—L.fr.—R.fr.; 5—L. occ.—R. occ.; 6—mesencephalic reticular substance.

Stimulation (black spots) 1 msec., 12 V, 9 c/sec. Sweep duration 50 msec.

Action of eserine and amphetamine on the activation produced by electrical stimulation of the reticular formation. High frequency stimulation applied to the reticular formation in the periaqueductal gray at the level of the *anterior colliculus* produced a generalized desynchronization of the cortex and of the nuclei of the thalamus similar to the desynchronization produced by external stimuli. With the appropriate regulation of the intensity of the stimulation, a threshold response not lasting beyond the period of stimulation was obtained. With stimuli of greater intensity and of short duration, a prolonged activation could be observed, the duration of which is fairly constant in the same animal. The action of drugs was studied on both threshold and duration of activation followed reticular stimulation. In 6 out of 10 animals, eserine in doses of 0.025 to 0.050 mgm./kgm., which produced incomplete desynchronization of the tracing, prolonged the duration (two or three times the original values) of the activation. No significant effect on the threshold was observed. Larger doses (0.075 to 0.1) gave no further information because they produced by themselves complete desynchronization of the tracing.

It was always possible to obtain by stimulation of the reticular formation an additional desynchronization to the activation produced by large doses of amphetamine (3 to 4 mgm./kgm.). A lowering of the threshold of the activation or a prolongation of the duration of the EEG arousal were not observed in the animals treated with amphetamine.

Action of amphetamine and eserine on the electrical activity of the "cerveau isolé" preparation. The electrical activity of the "cerveau isolé" preparation of the rabbit consisted of spindles alternating with slow waves of varying amplitude. The spindles occurred at rather regular intervals but were not synchronous at the different leads.

The administration of eserine by intravenous injection (0.025 to 0.05 mgm./kgm.) produced a desynchronization of the tracing similar to the one observed in the normal animal with the exception that it commenced in the occipital lobes. The effects of the electrical stimulation of the reticular formation were sometimes prolonged. Scopolamine had a marked antagonistic action of the desynchronization produced by eserine. The pattern of synchronized activity after injection of scopolamine differed from that of the normal "cerveau isolé" in that the slow waves at high voltage were markedly prevalent over the spindles.

For eliciting a desynchronization similar to that observed in the intact animal, the dosage of amphetamine had to be raised up to 2 to 3 mgm./kgm. However, the distinct localization of the activation in the frontal tracing which occurred in the intact animal could not be observed in the "cerveau isolé" preparation. At the same time amphetamine accentuated the decerebrate rigidity, provoked tachypnea, and increased movements of the extremities. Scopolamine antagonized the desynchronization produced by amphetamine.

Discussion. Detailed studies on the effects of eserine and amphetamine on the electrical activity of the brain have demonstrated that their desynchronizing effects differ and that these differences are not only quantitative, since by increasing the dose of amphetamine it has never been possible to reproduce the same effects obtained with eserine. The more significant data on the actions of these two drugs are shown in table 1.

The EEG picture produced by eserine consists of desynchronization similar to the pattern elicited by external stimuli. In fact, external stimuli produced no additional activation of the eserine tracing. Other evidence which suggests that the EEG changes obtained with eserine are closely related to the activation pattern following external stimuli was found in: a) the enhancing action of eserine on the activation after sensory stimulation and after electrical stimulation of the reticular system, and b) the similarity between the inhibition produced by external stimuli and by eserine on recruitment provoked by thalamic stimulation and on subconvulsive dysrythmia elicited by pentylenetetrazol. Eserine also provoked desynchronization in the "cerveau isolé" preparation in which the greater part of the reticular formation is excluded. It is also possible to demonstrate a desynchronizing action of anticholinesterase drugs in the "cerveau sans reticulée" (Desmedt and La Grutta, 1955). Thus, the available information indicates that the action of this drug is widespread and not limited to the reticular substance.

TABLE 1

Comparison of the effects of eserine and amphetamine on the electrical activity of the brain

	Eserine	Amphetamine
Cortical recordings	With small doses (0.025 mgm./kgm.) disappearance of slow waves and spindles. With large doses (0.5–0.1 mgm./kgm.) complete and diffuse activation.	With small doses (0.5 mgm./kgm.) disappearance of slow waves and spindles; trains of waves of the subconvulsive type in occipital recordings. With large doses (1–3 mgm./kgm.) activation especially in frontal recordings.
Deep recordings (Medial nuclei of the thalamus; reticular formation of the mesencephalon.)	Activation with an identical or slightly smaller intensity compared to cortical recordings.	Activation with a definitely smaller intensity compared to cortical recordings.
Spike-wave complexes due to pentylenetetrazol	Complete block.	No action.
Synchronization due to scopolamine	Desynchronization of the tracings and return of the "arousal" reaction. Scopolamine produces synchronization of tracings activated by eserine.	Amphetamine does not desynchronize the scopolamine tracings. Scopolamine produces synchronization of tracings activated by amphetamine.
Recruitment	Block	No action.
Activation due to external stimuli or electrical stimulation of the reticular formation	Prolonged (not constant)	No effect.
"Cerveau isolé" preparation	Activation, stronger in occipital recordings.	Diffuse activation.

On the other hand, the EEG picture produced by amphetamine resembled the spontaneous patterns of activation which may be noted in the normal alert animal. It was always possible to superimpose the activation provoked by external stimuli on the background of desynchronization of the alert animal as well as on that provoked by amphetamine. The lack of antagonism against the synchronization produced by scopolamine can also be referred to an action of amphetamine restricted to one part of the activating mechanisms, as opposed to the widespread action of eserine and scopolamine which mutually antagonize each other. Amphetamine still provokes activation in the "cerveau isolé"; these results are in agreement with those of Hiebel *et al.* (1954) but differ from those obtained by Elkes *et al.* (1954), who claim that amphetamine does not produce any desynchronization of tracings in this preparation. Variations in the plane of sectioning may explain such different results. In fact, there is no precise anatomical indication regarding the level of the section made by the English authors, whereas it is known from the results of Hiebel *et al.* (1954) that a more rostral section, passing through the posterior third of the thalamus to reach the base in front of the mammillary bodies, leads to complete ineffectiveness of amphetamine. Hiebel *et al.* (1954) suggested that activation due to the amphetamine is mediated through the hypothalamus. This hypothesis can be related to the results of Starzl *et al.* (1951) who have shown that alternative routes are available for the conduction of the reticular activating influence to the cortex: a thalamic path (through the diffuse thalamic projection system) and an extra-thalamic path involving sub- and hypo-thalamus by direct passage to the internal capsule.

The high voltage 3 to 4 c/sec. waves that can be observed on the occipital leads after amphetamine strictly resemble those obtained with subconvulsive doses (5 to 7 mgm./kgm.) of pentylenetetrazol; but as the latter spreads to the whole cortex, the slow waves caused by amphetamine always remained localized in the posterior leads. However, in other instances it has been observed that the desynchronizing effect of amphetamine is accompanied by inhibition of the spikes induced by the topical application of diluted (0.1 per cent) solution of strychnine on the frontal cortex (Longo and Silvestrini, in press). Thus, amphetamine possesses both synchronizing and desynchronizing actions which may be reflected on some conflicting clinical observations. In fact, amphetamine was found to greatly reduce the EEG pattern of pyknolepsy (Golla *et al.*, 1937; Livingstone *et al.*, 1948) whereas other authors (Blum *et al.* 1948) have found that it may reveal the presence of latent epileptic foci.

Although the EEG effects of eserine and amphetamine are very similar, they have different actions on the behaviour of the animals. Amphetamine not only produces modifications of the tracings but also gives rise to a characteristic excitement with hyperpnea, mydriasis, and increase in the spontaneous activity. After the administration of eserine, even in large doses (up to 0.3 mgm./kgm.), excitation has never been observed. In most cases a complete dissociation between the electrical pattern and the behaviour was noted, *i.e.*, complete desynchronization of the electrical activity while the animal was calm. This dissociation may be compared to that described by Wikler (1952) in the dog after the administration of atropine, which produces synchronization of the EEG and marked agitation of the animals.

SUMMARY

The influence of eserine and of amphetamine on the cerebral electrical activity was studied on unanesthetized non-curarized rabbit, and on the "cerveau isolé" preparation of this animal.

Both eserine and amphetamine produce acceleration and desynchronization of the EEG waves. However, certain significant differences in their action on electrical potentials of the brain have been demonstrated.

Eserine produces a more intense and widespread desynchronization than amphetamine, blocks the cortical recruiting response obtained by stimulation of the antero medial nuclei of the thalamus, and also the spike-wave complexes which follow the injection of pentylenetetrazol. It antagonizes the synchronization due to scopolamine.

Amphetamine exerts its desynchronizing influence mainly in the frontal cortex, the occipital leads showing slow waves of high voltage. It does not block the recruiting response; it does not abolish the spike waves due to pentylenetetrazol; and it does not influence the synchronization after the administration of scopolamine.

Possible loci of action of the two drugs are discussed.

REFERENCES

ADRIAN, E. D., AND MATTHEWS, B. C. H.: Brain, **57:** 355, 1934.
BERGER, H.: Arch. Psychiat. Nervenkr., **106:** 165, 1934.
BLUM, R. A., BLUM, J. S., AND CHOW, L. K.: Science, **108:** 460, 1948.
BONNET, V., AND BREMER, F.: C. R. Soc. Biol., **126:** 1271, 1937.
BONVALLET, M., DELL, P., AND HIEBEL, G.: EEG Clin. Neurophysiol., **6:** 119, 1954.
BRADLEY, P. B., AND ELKES, J.: J. Physiol., **120:** 14p, 1953.
BREMER, F.: C. R. Soc. Biol., **122:** 460, 1936.
BREMER, F., AND CHATONNET, J.: Arch. Internat. Physiol., **57:** 106, 1949.
DESMEDT, J. E., AND LA GRUTTA, G.: Boll. Soc. It. Biol. Sper., **31:** 913, 1955a.
DESMEDT, J. E., AND LA GRUTTA, G.: J. Physiol., **129:** 46p, 1955b.
ELKES, J., ELKES, C., AND BRADLEY, P. B.: J. Ment. Sci., **100:** 125, 1954.
FRENCH, J. D., VERZEANO, M., AND MAGOUN, H. W.: Arch Neurol. Psychiat., **69:** 519, 1953.
FUNDERBURK, H. W., AND CASE, T. J.: EEG Clin. Neurophysiol., **3:** 213, 1951.
GOLLA, F., GRAHAM, S., AND WALTER, W. G.: J. Ment. Sci., **83:** 137, 1937.
HIEBEL, G., BONVALLET, M., HUVÉ, P., AND DELL, P.: Sémaine des Hopitaux, **30:** 1880, 1954.
LIVINGSTON, S., KAJDI, L., AND BRIDGE, E.: J. Pediat., **32:** 490, 1948.
LONGO, V. G.: Experientia, **11:** 76, 1955.
LONGO, V. G.: THIS JOURNAL, **116:** 198, 1956.
MONNIER, M., AND LAUE, H.: Helv. Physiol. Acta, **11:** 73, 1953.
MORUZZI, G., AND MAGOUN, H. W.: EEG Clin. Neurophysiol., **1:** 455, 1949.
RHEINBERGER, M. B., AND JASPER, H. H.: Am. J. Physiol., **9:** 33, 1937.
RINALDI, F., AND HIMWICH, H. E.: Arch. Neurol. Psychiat., **73:** 387, 1955.
SCHALLEK, W., AND WALZ, D.: Proc. Soc. Exp. Biol. Med., **82:** 715, 1953.
SILVESTRINI, B., AND LONGO, V. G.: Rendiconti Ist. Sup. San., in press.
STARZL, T. E., TAYLOR, C. W., AND MAGOUN, H. W.: J. Neurophysiol., **14:** 461, 1951.
TOMAN, J. E. P., GOODMAN, L. S., AND SWINYARD, E. A.: Federation Proceedings **5:** 208, 1946.
WIKLER, A.: Proc. Soc. Biol. Exp. Med., **79:** 261, 1952.

THE TOXICOLOGY OF POTASSIUM AND SODIUM IODATES: ACUTE TOXICITY IN MICE

STEWART H. WEBSTER, MARY E. RICE, BENJAMIN HIGHMAN AND W. F. VON OETTINGEN

National Institute of Arthritis and Metabolic Diseases, National Institutes of Health, Public Health Service, Department of Health, Education, and Welfare, Bethesda, Maryland

Received for publication December 24, 1956

Interest in the toxicology of iodates apparently stemmed from the work of Melsens (1865) and of Rabuteau (1869), both of whom recognized the danger of administering iodide contaminated with iodate. Binz (1878) and Ruhemann (1894), and subsequently, others, proposed to use iodates therapeutically after a series of investigations concerning their pharmacologic and toxic actions. However, the suggested uses were not widely adopted.

A renewed interest in potassium iodate, KIO_3, resulted from the proposal by Johnson and Herrington (1927) to substitute the more stable iodate for potassium iodide, KI, in so-called iodized salt and in dairy-feed mixtures. Iodide used for this purpose requires the addition of one or more substances to increase its stability. More recently, the use of KIO_3 has again received serious consideration (Mendez *et al.*, 1953). However, the earlier toxicity studies cited above, as well as more recent ones by Crespolani (1908) and by Macciotta (1916), are inadequate to evaluate the possible dangers involved in using iodates in salt for the seasoning of food.

The purpose of this investigation was to study the action of KIO_3 on experimental animals and to measure its toxicity when given orally as well as by other routes. Due to the toxicity of the potassium ion, some work was carried out with the corresponding sodium salt. Finally, since a substitute for iodide was being tested, measurements were made of the relative toxicities of the corresponding iodate and iodides. This paper is limited to a study of acute single-dose toxicity in mice.

METHODS. Female white Swiss mice of the NIH strain were housed in groups of 5 to 7 in glass jars with sawdust bedding. Purina Laboratory Chow Checkers and water were available at all times.

The mice given intraperitoneal and intravenous injections were fasted for 17 to 20 hours previous to the administration of drugs. Three groups were used for the intraesophageal or intragastric injections; one group was fasted on sawdust, a second on wire screens, and a third, following determination of fasted weights, was fed for 24 hours before receiving the drug.

Iodate and iodide dosages, based on fasted body weights, were varied ordinarily by equal logarithmic steps; this facilitated determination of the LD_{50} values by the probit method (Finney, 1952). Usually ten mice were used for a trial of each dosage. Comparable groups, given iodides, water, or normal saline, served as controls.

After the administration of the drug, observations were made for evidence of toxic effects, such as hemoglobinuria, prostration, or convulsions. Tests for hemoglobinuria were made routinely with benzidin, and red blood cell (RBC) counts, hematocrit, and non-protein nitrogen (NPN) determinations were carried out on certain groups.

Survival times were estimated as accurately as possible. Survivors were killed with ether two weeks after injection. A postmortem examination, whenever practicable, was made soon after death. Heart, lungs, liver, stomach, duodenum, spleen, pancreas, adrenals, kidneys, brain, gonads and thyroid of representative mice were studied microscopically after fixation in a 10 per cent aqueous solution of buffered formalin (pH = 7.0).

RESULTS AND CONCLUSIONS. *Acute intraperitoneal toxicity.* The toxicity of sterile 3 per cent solutions of KIO_3, KI, and $NaIO_3$, and of 2.3 per cent NaI, was determined in mice fasted on sawdust overnight. In addition, KIO_3 was administered to one group of non-fasted animals. The solutions used were approximately isotonic. Fasted control mice received normal saline and were killed at intervals thereafter.

Symptoms of intoxication: a) Iodates. Intoxication was manifested by alternate hyperactivity and lassitude, followed by weakness, prostration, and dyspnea. After the higher doses, excitability and convulsions frequently preceded death. Respiration often ceased before the heart stopped beating and paresis of the hind legs was common. Hemoglobinuria occurred in many mice and was observed at levels as low as 115 mgm./kgm. and as early as 2 hours after injection; it was generally absent in those given high doses, presumably because survival was too brief. b) Iodides. The signs and symptoms of iodide intoxication were essentially similar to those of iodate but developed more slowly and hemoglobinuria was never observed. Whereas the iodate mice frequently became ill within an hour after injection, the action of KI in equivalent doses was much slower at the lower dosage levels and became apparent only after several hours. However, at the higher dosage levels, the toxicity of the potassium ion became manifest.

Comparative toxicities of iodates and iodides: Table 1 summarizes the toxicity values for the four compounds studied. At the highest dosage levels causing 100 per cent mortality, the average survival times are nearly identical for the two iodates. Also, these two compounds have similar LD_{50} values and survival times. These facts suggest that the toxicity at these levels depends largely on the iodate ion. However, at the higher dosage levels used with the iodides, the toxicity of the potassium ion becomes of importance.

Comparison of the LD_{50} values (in millimoles/kgm.) in table 1 shows that KIO_3 administered intraperitoneally to mice is about eleven times as toxic as KI; with the corresponding sodium compounds, the iodate is about nineteen times as toxic as the iodide.

Acute intravenous toxicity. Sterile isotonic solutions of $NaIO_3$ and NaI were injected via tail vein. The corresponding potassium compounds were not used, due to the high intravenous toxicity of the potassium ion. Similar amounts of normal saline solution were injected into the control animals.

Symptoms of intoxication: The signs and symptoms of intoxication were similar to those following an intraperitoneal injection. Hemoglobinuria occurred only in the iodate animals and was observed at levels as low as 110 mgm./kgm. The survival times of over half of the iodate mice were less than one day whereas over half of the iodide animals had survival times between two and five days.

TABLE 1

Comparative toxicities of iodates and iodides

Intraperitoneal injection of 15 to 20 gm. female white Swiss mice fasted overnight on sawdust and for 1 hour after injection.

	3% KIO_3	3% $NaIO_3$	3% KI	2.3% NaI
Number of mice used	140	100	110	110
LD_{50} in mgm./kgm.	136 ± 5	119 ± 4	1117 ± 30	1690 ± 85
LD_{50} in millimoles/kgm.	0.635 ± 0.023	0.601 ± 0.020	6.73 ± 0.18	11.27 ± 0.57
Range in survival time (hr.)*	2–47	1–32	16–57	8–52
Average survival time (hr.)*	23	21	36	16
Highest dosage tolerated by 10/10 mice without death (mgm./kgm.)	100	90	756	1200
Dosage range in mgm./kgm.	76–265	81–245	658–2010	1000–3500

* Based on dosage near LD_{50} level.

TABLE 2

Comparative toxicities of iodates and iodides

Intravenous injection of 15 to 20 gm. female white Swiss mice fasted overnight on sawdust and for 1 hour after injection.

	3% $NaIO_3$	2.3% NaI
Number of mice used	90	50
LD_{50} in mgm./kgm.	108 ± 4	>1500
LD_{50} in millimoles per kgm.	0.546 ± 0.020	>10
Range in survival time (hr.)	16–29*	13–61**
Average survival time (hr.)	cir. 24*	cir. 40**
Highest dosage tolerated by 10/10 mice without death (mgm. per kgm.)	70	700
Dosage range in mgm. per kgm.	70–150	700–1500

* Based on dosage near LD_{50} level.
** Based on dosage near LD_{20} level.

Comparative toxicities of sodium iodate and sodium iodide: Table 2 gives the data for the toxicity determinations for $NaIO_3$. The LD_{50} value for intravenous administration, 108 mgm./kgm., is only slightly less than the intraperitoneal LD_{50} value for this same compound. This unusual similarity in LD_{50} values for these two routes of administration perhaps can be explained by the rapidity with which intravenously injected iodate is excreted in the urine (Webster, Rice and Highman, unpublished data); in mice, iodate appears in the urine within five minutes after injection but neither in the stomach nor saliva in appreciable amounts.

The LD_{50} for NaI could not be determined since the dosage corresponding to 100 per cent kill was not found; 1.4 ml. of the solution killed only 7/10 mice and intravenous injection of larger volumes would greatly dilute the blood.

Acute oral toxicity. Six per cent solutions of KIO_3, KI, $NaIO_3$ and NaI were introduced into the esophagus through a special curved hypodermic needle with ball tip (Morris and Thompson, 1940).

Two groups of animals were fasted overnight previous to injection and one hour following injection; one was fasted on screens and the second on sawdust bedding. A third group was allowed to feed *ad libitum* both before and after injection. Similar groups, fasted and non-fasted, served as controls.

Symptoms of intoxication: a) Iodates. The symptoms of intoxication, which included diarrhea in addition to those previously mentioned, were similar in both fasted and non-fasted mice, except that hemoglobinuria was observed only in the former. In some cases it occurred within 4 hours after administration at a dosage level as low as 400 mgm./kgm. b) Iodides. The symptoms of intoxication usually developed slowly; at the LD_{50} level few animals appeared ill during the first 4 to 6 hours. Subsequently, the animals became apathetic and then weak and dyspneic. Hemoglobinuria was never observed.

Comparative oral toxicities of iodates and iodides: Mortality and LD_{50} values for orally-administered iodates and iodides are given in table 3. The marked decrease in toxicity of iodate, but not of iodide, in the presence of food, is of im-

TABLE 3

Comparative toxicities of iodates and iodides

Oral administration to 15 to 20 gm. female white Swiss mice.

	Mice not fasted**	Mice fasted on sawdust***	Mice fasted on screens***		Mice not fasted**	Mice fasted on sawdust***	Mice fasted on screens***	
	6% KIO_3	6% KIO_3	6% KIO_3	6% $NaIO_3$	6% KI	6% KI	6% KI	6% NaI
Number of mice used	90	140	110	140	80	130	90	130
LD_{50} in mgm. per kgm.	1177 ±61	815 ±29	531 ±21	505 ±26	2068 ±140	1982 ±90	1862 ±100	1650 ±90
LD_{50} in millimoles per kgm.	5.50 ±0.29	3.81 ±0.14	2.48 ±0.10	2.55 ±0.13	12.46 ±0.84	11.94 ±0.54	11.22 ±0.60	11.01 ±0.63
Range in survival time (hr.)*	3–16	2–14	2–38	2–14	18–64	10–18	13–39	8–46
Average survival time (hr.)*	9	10	13	7	47	15	23	21
Highest dosage tolerated by 10/10 mice without death (mgm. per kgm.)	819	513	359	—	1780	1420	1260	—
Dosage range in mgm. per kgm.	737–1750	447–1240	316–891	261–824	1590–3500	1120–3500	1120–2820	903–2820

* Based on dosages near LD_{50} level.

** Mice were in non-fasted condition when injection was made. Dose was based on fasted body weight measured 24 hr. before injection.

*** Mice were fasted overnight and 1 hr. after injection.

portance. Based upon the LD_{50} ratios for acute toxicity, expressed in mgm./kgm. and (millimoles/kgm.), KIO_3 is 8.2 times (10.6 ×) as toxic as KI when given intraperitoneally in fasted female mice. When administered orally on an empty stomach, the iodate is only 3.5 times (4.5 ×) as toxic as KI. If the stomach contains a small amount of sawdust, this ratio is lowered to 2.4 (3.1). Finally, when administered on a full stomach, the iodate is 1.8 times (2.3 ×) as toxic as the iodide.

Mice of different weight groups were found to have nearly the same susceptibility to lethal doses of KIO_3 and toxicity was not increased in weanlings. Also, males and females of the same weight group showed nearly identical susceptibility to toxic action with this compound.

Laboratory and gross findings. Blood studies revealed only a slight decrease (about 10 per cent) in hematocrit and RBC during 48 hours following intraperitoneal injection of 3 per cent KIO_3 at 132 mgm./kgm.

Another series of mice received the same dosage of the drug intraperitoneally. Five were sacrificed immediately and two groups of five survivors each were sacrificed 7 and 24 hours later. The NPN values, made on the pooled blood of each of the three groups, were 40.5, 124.3, and 138.6 mgm./100 ml. of blood, respectively.

Determinations were made of the pH of the stomach contents of numerous mice. Values in controls and in animals receiving iodide or iodate intraperitoneally or intravenously, or iodide orally, ranged between 2 and 4. However, the pH was increased to 6 to 7 two to six hours after oral administration of KIO_3 in fasted mice and to somewhat lower levels (5 to 6) in non-fasted mice. The stomach in those receiving iodate orally often showed mucosal hemorrhages and was distended with mucus and fluid or food. However, little material was found in the lower digestive tract. This typical picture of retardation of gastric emptying was shown particularly in non-fasted mice given KIO_3 orally and then killed after fasting for 7 hours. The stomach was consistently distended with food, the pH of the contents was 5.5 to 6.0, and the intestinal tract was nearly empty. However, no significant changes were noted in 2-week survivors.

Although the stomach appeared normal in the mice dying from KI intoxication, pleural effusion was found in one-fourth of the animals. Grossly, the livers of all animals fasted overnight appeared paler (due to fatty changes) than the fed controls. However, the color was normal 24 to 48 hours later.

Histopathologic findings. Effect of intraperitoneal or intravenous administration of iodates: Histopathologic studies of white mice dying in 18 to 26 hours after an intraperitoneal injection of potassium or sodium iodate, whether fasted overnight on sawdust or not fasted, frequently disclosed marked fatty changes in the liver and kidney, depletion of lipoid in the adrenal cortex, and occasionally fatty changes in the myocardium. Sections often revealed extensive necrosis of the renal convoluted tubules with numerous hemoglobin casts. The spleen frequently showed abundant nuclear debris in the white pulp and some cellular depletion. Focal necrosis of liver cells was seen occasionally. Animals surviving 12 to 16 days generally exhibited no unequivocal changes except for occasional deposits of hemosiderin in the kidney. The changes following intravenous injections of sodium iodate were essentially similar to those following intraperitoneal injection.

Effect of intraperitoneal or intravenous administration of iodides: Mice dying within 22 to 26 hours following intraperitoneal injection of KI or NaI showed microscopic fatty visceral changes and changes in the spleen essentially similar to those found after injecting iodates; several revealed liver necrosis focally. However, no significant changes were noted in 2-week survivors. Likewise, the microscopic changes in mice dying within a few days following intravenous injection of NaI were similar to those observed following intraperitoneal injection of this compound. Several 2-week survivors showed foci of liver cell necrosis with an inflammatory reaction.

Effect of oral administration: a) Controls. No significant changes were found in the controls fed *ad libitum*. However, the control mice fasted overnight showed marked fatty changes in the liver, kidney, and, occasionally, in the heart. Intragastric administration of water to these fasted mice did not prevent these fatty changes. However, these changes diminished after feeding was resumed and disappeared within 16 to 48 hours. b) Iodides. Both fasted and non-fasted mice, killed or dying within 26 hours after intragastric administration of iodides, often showed fatty changes similar to those seen in the fasted controls. No fatty or other significant changes were noted in the mice that recovered. c) Iodates. Histopathologic study disclosed degeneration of many parietal cells of the stomach, at 1 to 24 hours after the administration of 6 per cent KIO_3 (501 mgm./kgm.). The changes ranged from slight pyknosis to frank necrosis and exfoliation and were least pronounced at the base of the glands. Some necrotic cells could not be identified. Similar changes in the gastric glands were noted after administration of 463 mgm./kgm. of $NaIO_3$, but not after comparable amounts of NaI, saline, or water. The animals receiving iodates also exhibited severe visceral fatty changes within 24 hours. Hemosiderin deposits in the kidneys were noted in 14-day survivors, particularly in the non-fasted animals that had received more than 1000 mgm./kgm. KIO_3. No other significant changes were observed in mice surviving 48 hours or more after injection.

Discussion. The use of fasted animals made it possible to secure estimates of net body weight based on an essentially empty stomach and gastrointestinal tract, thus eliminating some of the uncertainties in determining LD_{50} values. However, the fasting of mice overnight resulted in fatty visceral changes which disappeared within 1 to 2 days after resumption of feeding. Similar fatty changes were noted within 24 hours after administration of iodates or iodides in non-fasted mice. This suggests that the fatty changes may be caused in part by restriction of nutriment following administration of the drugs, due to anorexia or to delayed gastric emptying.

The action of orally administered iodate in reducing the acidity of the stomach contents has been observed in numerous mice. This appears to be associated histologically with extensive, but rapidly reparable, damage to the parietal cells. Since the changes in the glands were least marked at the base and were not noted after intraperitoneal or intravenous administration, these changes may be due to direct contact of the iodate with the glandular cells. The irritating action of the iodate on the mucosa is evidenced further by an abundance of mucus in the stomach. The high pH of the contents (often 6 to 7) may be due to neutralization by this faintly alkaline mucus and to suppression of HCl secretion resulting from damage to the parietal cells.

The pronounced decrease in oral toxicity of iodate, but not of iodide, in the presence of food, has been demonstrated. If the food acted only mechanically, that is, to reduce the concentration and presumably the rate of absorption of the drugs, then food would be expected to give marked protection against each compound. Since this is not true for iodide, the protection of food for orally-administered iodate appears to involve chemical interaction.

The reduction of iodate to iodide by peptones was shown by Crespolani (1908) who explained the lower toxicity of iodate in the presence of food as due to this reduction in the gastrointestinal tract. After ingestion of moderate amounts of iodate, only iodide appeared in the urine; after excessive amounts of iodate, the urine contained both iodide and iodate. Hence, there is a practical limit beyond which food cannot offer protection.

Although the data from this investigation do not enable one to calculate a safe tolerated dose of KIO_3 for man, it is of interest to note that Rabuteau (1869) reported taking this substance by mouth on two occasions, in the amounts of 1.0 gm. and 2.5 gm., with only minor gastric effects lasting for one day after the larger dose. These amounts are quite comparable with the doses of KI sometimes prescribed for adults.

SUMMARY

Single-dose, acute toxicity experiments, carried out with white Swiss mice, using potassium and sodium iodates and the corresponding iodides, led to the following conclusions:

Administered in sufficient quantities, the iodates cause intoxication and death. In some instances, death is attributed to renal damage with retention of non-protein nitrogen. Hemolytic effects are evidenced by hemoglobinuria and, histologically, by hemoglobin casts and hemosiderin deposits in the kidneys.

Fatty visceral changes, non-specific in nature, appear within 24 hours after ingestion of iodates or iodides. Similar changes occur in fasted animals.

Oral administration of iodates, at levels of 140 to 500 mgm./kgm., often increase the pH of the gastric contents. This is frequently accompanied by degenerative changes in the parietal cells. The damage is transient, as evidenced by restoration to normal in histological appearance of the gastric mucosa and in the pH values after 24 hours. Intraperitoneal and intravenous injections of iodates have little effect on the gastric pH.

The toxicity of potassium iodate varies greatly with the route of administration; the oral LD_{50} for mice fasted on sawdust overnight is six times that of the intraperitoneal LD_{50}. Potassium iodate and sodium iodate have nearly identical oral toxicities and similar intraperitoneal toxicities; the oral toxicity of the potassium compound is nearly the same for heavy and light mice and for both sexes, and is not increased in weanling animals.

Similarly, the relative toxicities of iodates and iodides depend on route of administration and on previous treatment of the mice.

ACKNOWLEDGMENT. Grateful acknowledgment is made to Dr. Sanford M. Rosenthal for interest and help in this investigation and to Mr. Edwin C. Thompson, Laboratory of Physical Biology, for making the NPN determinations.

REFERENCES

BINZ, C.: Arch. f. exper. Path. u. Pharmakol., **13:** 125, 1880.
CRESPOLANI, E.: Boll. chim. farm., **47:** 679, 1908.
FINNEY, D. J.: Probit Analysis: A Statistical Treatment of the Sigmoid Response Curve, Cambridge University Press, Cambridge, 1952.
JOHNSON, A. H., AND HERRINGTON, B. L.: J. Agr. Res., **35:** 167, 1927.
MACCIOTTA, C.: Arch. di farmacol. sper., **22:** 3, 161, 1916.
MELSENS, H. L. F.: Mémoires couronnés, Royal Academy of Science, Brussels, **17:** 44, June, 1865.
MENDEZ, J., CABEZAS, A., CASTILLO, F., AND SCRIMSHAW, N. S.: Fed. Proc., **12:** 423, 1953.
MORRIS, H. P., AND THOMPSON, J. W.: J. Nat. Cancer Inst., **1:** 395, 1940.
RABUTEAU, A. P. A.: Gas. hebd. de méd., Par. **6:** 2nd Ser., 84, 1869.
RUHEMANN, J.: Therap. Monatsh., **8:** 117, 1894.

SOME OBSERVATIONS ON THE INTERACTION OF RESERPINE AND LSD

M. TAESCHLER AND A. CERLETTI

Department of Pharmacology, Sandoz Ltd., Basle, Switzerland

Received for publication December 24, 1956

Central actions of reserpine have been attributed to a liberation of 5-hydroxytryptamine (serotonin) (Brodie, Pletscher and Shore, 1955). The following experimental results support such an interpretation:

1) Reserpine decreases the serotonin content of the brain while increasing the urinary excretion of 5-hydroxyindolacetic acid, a major metabolite of serotonin (Brodie, Pletscher and Shore, 1955; Pletscher, Shore and Brodie, 1956; Shore, Silver and Brodie, 1955a).

2) Serotonin has a slight sedative effect and potentiates barbiturate hypnosis; it exerts in this respect an action similar to that of reserpine. A further parallelism between the two drugs is evident in the finding that a potent inhibitor of serotonin, lysergic acid diethylamide (LSD-25), antagonizes not only the potentiating effect of serotonin on barbiturate hypnosis but also that of reserpine (Shore, Silver and Brodie, 1955a, b). Barbiturate-induced hypnosis itself is not inhibited by LSD (Shore, Silver and Brodie, 1955a, b; Taeschler and Rothlin, 1956).

Although both reserpine and serotonin potentiate barbiturate hypnosis, the two drugs manifest profound differences in central actions, notably regarding the pattern of sedation and regarding EEG effects on the rabbit (unpublished data).

BOL-148 (2-brom-lysergic acid diethylamide) inhibits serotonin at least to the same extent as LSD but differs fundamentally in other peripheral and central effects from LSD (Cerletti and Rothlin, 1955; Cerletti, 1956). A comparison of the action of LSD and BOL on the barbiturate-potentiating effect on serotonin and reserpine was undertaken in an effort to answer the question whether the antagonistic effect of LDS on reserpine is actually due to its anti-serotonin effect and whether the potentiating action of the barbiturate hypnosis by reserpine and serotonin is based on a common mechanism.

METHODS. Barbiturate potentiation was assayed in mice of a uniform strain. In all experiments a threshold dose of thiopental (20 mgm./kgm. intravenously), which induced an average sleeping time of 0.7 minutes, was administered; maximal sleeping time observed after this dose of thiopental was 1.3 minutes. Following pretreatment with the potentiating substances (serotonin and reserpine) alone or together with the inhibitors (LSD and BOL), the hypnotic effect of 20 mgm./kgm. thiopental was determined. The degree of barbiturate potentiation was expressed by the percentage of the total number of mice which show a hypnosis of more than two minutes. Thus the results were evaluated by an "all or none" reaction rather than by the average sleeping time. Drug-induced changes of spontaneous motor activity were measured by means of activity cages according to Aschoff's method (Aschoff, 1951), which was slightly modified.

RESULTS. Fig. 1 illustrates the results with LSD and BOL on the serotonin-induced thiopental potentiation. Both compounds show an equal inhibitory potency with minimal effective doses of 200 microgm./kgm. subcutaneously. Despite equal serotonin antagonism, BOL, however, does not inhibit the reserpine-induced thiopental potentiation (fig. 2). Using a large dose of reserpine the degree of barbiturate hypnosis had to be expressed by the average sleeping time

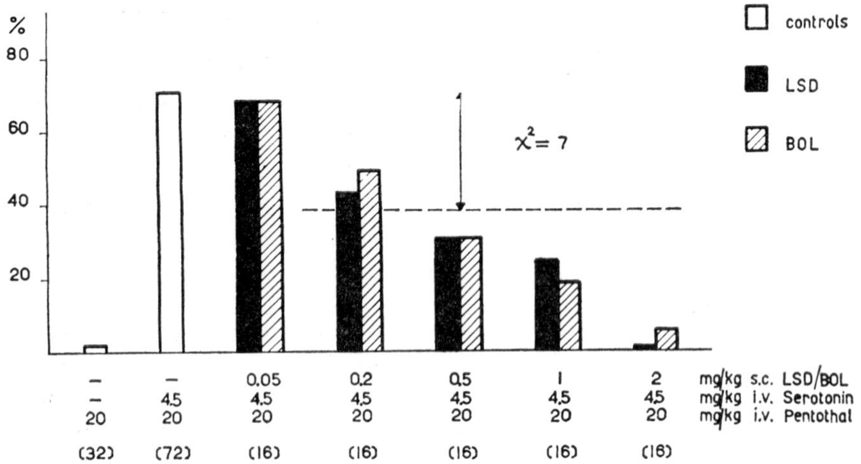

FIG. 1. Effect of LSD-25 and BOL-148 on the potentiation of thiopental by serotonin in mice. Ordinate: percentage of mice which show a hypnosis of more than two minutes. Abscissae: doses of LSD or BOL, respectively, with the corresponding control values. Numbers in parentheses represent the number of animals used with each substance. $\chi^2 = 7$ gives the confidence limit of 99 per cent. LSD and BOL were administered subcutaneously 20 minutes prior to serotonin which was injected intravenously 10 minutes before thiopental.

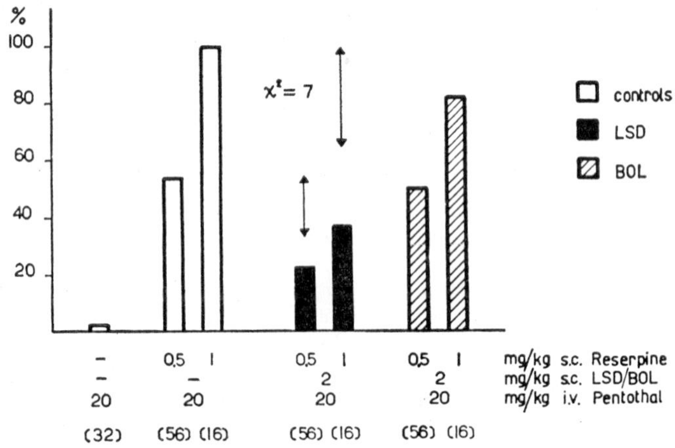

FIG. 2. Effect of LSD-25 and BOL-148 on the potentiation of thiopental by reserpine in mice. Ordinate: percentage of mice which show a hypnosis of more than two minutes. Abscissae: doses of reserpine, LSD or BOL, respectively, and thiopental. Numbers in parentheses represent the number of animals used with each substance. $\chi^2 = 7$ gives the confidence limit of 99 per cent. Reserpine was administered 140 minutes before thiopental. LSD and BOL were injected 120 minutes after reserpine (= 20 minutes before thiopental).

of the mice. Fig. 3 illustrates the pronounced inhibitory effect of LSD on the thiopental potentiation by 2 mgm./kgm. of reserpine. These experiments also suggest that an equal dose of LSD (2 mgm./kgm.) antagonizes larger doses of reserpine more markedly than lower reserpine doses. A dose of 0.7 mgm./kgm. of LSD did not inhibit the potentiating effect of 0.5 mgm./kgm. reserpine. Minimal effective doses of LSD for antagonizing reserpine are, therefore, five to ten times higher than those antagonizing serotonin. Additional experiments showed that the difference between LSD and BOL is not related to the length of time between the administration of LSD (or BOL) and reserpine. These experiments fail to support the assumption that the inhibitory effect of LSD on the reserpine-induced potentiation of thiopental is due to its anti-serotonin activity. It rather appears that this effect of LSD is related to some other mechanism.

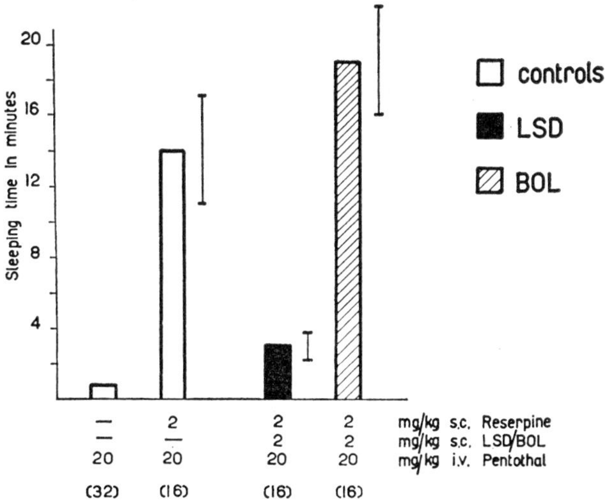

FIG. 3. Effect of LSD-25 and BOL-148 on the reserpine-induced potentiation of thiopental in mice. Ordinate: Average sleeping time in minutes. Abscissae: Doses of reserpine, LSD or BOL, respectively, and thiopental. Numbers in parentheses represent the number of animals. I indicates the standard error. Interval of injections as in fig. 2.

Besides its serotonin antagonism, LSD produces in rabbits a syndrome of central sympathetic excitation consisting of hyperthermia, hyperglycemia, mydriasis, etc. (Rothlin *et al.*, 1956). LSD also elicits in mice a slight stimulation of spontaneous activity, a potentiation of the excitatory effects of amphetamine and a mydriasis which can be inhibited by adrenergic blocking agents. BOL lacks this stimulating action. As a mild sedative it antagonizes the amphetamine-induced excitation and also the mydriatic effects in mice. It does not produce hyperthermia or hyperglycemia in rabbits. The possibility should, therefore, be considered that the antagonistic effect of LSD on the thiopental potentiation by reserpine is not primarily due to its serotonin blocking activity but rather to its central stimulatory effect. Such an assumption is supported by the fact that amphetamine (1 or 3 mgm./kgm. subcutaneously) antagonizes the reserpine-

TABLE 1

Effect of amphetamine on the reserpine-induced thiopental potentiation in mice

Five-tenths mgm./kgm. of reserpine was given subcutaneously in all experiments 100 minutes before amphetamine or saline, which were administered 20 minutes before thiopental (20 mgm./kgm. intravenously).

Number of animals	Dose of amphetamine s.c.	Per cent of mice which show hypnosis of more than two minutes
	mgm./kgm.	
48	—	71*
48	1.0	29*
48	3.0	25
24	Control with thiopental alone	0

* = $\chi^2 > 7$, *i.e.* these values fall outside the 99 per cent confidence limits.

TABLE 2

Effect of LSD-25 (2 mgm./kgm. s.c.) on the activity of mice

Pretreatment	Interval	Total activity per mouse per 30 minutes	Number of animals
	hours		
Reserpine, 5 mgm./kgm. s.c.	20	49	36
Saline = Control	20	7	36

The activity (arbitrary units) was measured 20 minutes after LSD during a period of 90 minutes.

induced thiopental potentiation in the same manner as LSD (table 1) without interfering with the barbiturate hypnosis itself. Since LSD and these low doses of amphetamine do not influence the thiopental hypnosis itself, a specific interference of LDS and amphetamine with reserpine is suggested, namely that reserpine enhances the slight stimulatory effect of LSD or amphetamine. Indeed, pretreatment of mice with a relatively large dose of reserpine administered twenty hours before LSD potentiates greatly the slight excitatory effect of LSD. Table 2 illustrates such results obtained in the activity cage. Amphetamine excitation is not regularly potentiated by reserpine. A slight and short lasting potentiating effect can, however, be obtained if the time of pretreatment is more than twenty hours. This difference could possibly point to a difference in the central site of action of LSD and amphetamine, respectively. The activity of mice receiving BOL is not influenced or further depressed by pretreatment with reserpine.

After the completion of this study, Salmoiraghi *et al.* (1956) reported that BOL inhibits the potentiating effect of serotonin, as well as that of reserpine on hexobarbital hypnosis. The doses of BOL used by these investigators (10 mgm./kgm. i.p.) are considerably higher than the doses used in the present study (2 mgm./kgm. s.c.). In view of the greater toxicity of BOL (LD_{50} = 20 mgm./kgm. i.v. in mice) as compared to LSD (LD_{50} = 67 mgm./kgm. i.v.), high doses of BOL have been avoided in the present study, and emphasis was put on a comparison of the specific activity of LSD and BOL on serotonin- and reserpine-induced barbiturate potentiation. Thus it can be concluded that BOL has in high doses a certain antagonistic action toward the barbiturate potentiating effect of reserpine, but that it is in this respect much weaker than LSD.

SUMMARY

LSD antagonizes the potentiating effect of reserpine on barbiturate hypnosis in mice. This effect of LSD is probably due to its own central stimulatory action. Amphetamine, likewise, antagonizes the effect of reserpine on barbiturate hypnosis.

The excitatory effects of LSD in mice are markedly enhanced by pretreatment with reserpine.

BOL, an equipotent inhibitor of serotonin which lacks the central stimulatory effect of LSD, does not antagonize the sedative- and barbiturate-potentiating action of reserpine although it blocks the serotonin-induced potentiation of barbiturates to the same extent as LSD.

A common mechanism of action of reserpine and injected serotonin in mice regarding their barbiturate potentiation must therefore be questioned.

REFERENCES

Aschoff, J.: Pflüger's Arch. f. d. ges. Physiol., **254:** 262, 1951.

Brodie, B. B., Pletscher, A., and Shore, P. A.: Science, **122:** 968, 1955.

Cerletti, A., and Rothlin, E.: Nature, **176:** 785, 1955.

Cerletti, A.: Neuropharmacology, p. 9, H. A. Abramson, Editor. Trans. Second Conf. Princeton, Josiah Macy, Jr. Foundation, 1955, Madison, N. J., Madison Printing Company, Inc., 1956.

Pletscher, A., Shore, P. A., and Brodie, B. B.: This Journal, **116:** 84, 1956.

Rothlin, E., Cerletti, A., Konzett, H., Schlach, W. R., and Taeschler, M.: Experientia, **12:** 154, 1956.

Salmoiraghi, G. C., Sollero, L., and Page, I. H.: This Journal, **117:** 166, 1956.

Shore, P. A., Silver, S. L., and Brodie, B. B.: Science, **122:** 284, 1955a.

Shore, P. A., Silver, S. L., and Brodie, B. B.: Experientia, **11:** 272, 1955b.

Taeschler, M., and Rothlin, E.: Arch. f. exper. Path. u. Pharmakol., **228:** 184, 1956.

OBJECTIVE COMPARISON OF PRIMIDONE AND PHENOBARBITAL IN EPILEPTICS

CHARLES M. GRUBER, JR.,[1] JACK M. MOSIER[2] AND PHYLLIS GRANT[3]

Lilly Laboratory for Clinical Research, Indianapolis General Hospital, Indianapolis, Indiana

Received for publication December 31, 1956

A previous report (Gruber *et al.*, 1956) described an efficient method for determining the effectiveness of antiepileptic drugs in blocking spontaneous focal and generalized seizures in humans. This study indicated that phenobarbital and diphenylhydantoin were interchangeable in equal amounts and additive when administered together.

Primidone represents a third group of chemical agents (figure 1) of value in the seizures associated with focal brain damage. It is a fairly recent addition to the physician's armamentarium (Handley and Stewart, 1952; Bogue and Carrington, 1953). It was, therefore, decided to compare primidone to phenobarbital or diphenylhydantoin.

METHOD. The method used has been described in detail (Gruber *et al.*, 1956). In summary, the experimental medications were substituted (one dose every eight hours) on three successive days at weekly intervals for the patient's usual medications. Each drug was given in a random order and was given to all patients. The seizures during these three days and on the subsequent day were recorded by attendants who had no knowledge of the medications involved on any particular week. Each focal seizure was scored 1 and each generalized seizure 2; thus a daily seizure score for each patient was obtained.

RESULTS. Two false starts were made. In each the dose of primidone was too large. These doses had a profound effect upon the seizure frequency though neither was completely effective (table 1). Both produced excessive sedation and apparently could not have been given as continuous therapy.

Twenty patients received all of the medications reported in table 2. In this table, the column totals indicate a progressive increase in the frequency and severity of seizures during the three days of substitution therapy. This response was most prominent when the blank was given, but was also evident when 125 mgm. of primidone was used. Statistical analysis (table 3) shows this to be a significant source of variance from a random distribution of seizure scores.

The row totals of table 2 indicate the relative effectiveness of the various medications. The administration of the blank had the greatest score, but a significant difference between the sum of the scores for the two doses of phenobarbital and the sum of the scores for the two doses of primidone was also present.

[1] Lilly Laboratory for Clinical Research, Indianapolis General Hospital, Indianapolis, Indiana.

[2] The Indiana Village for Epileptics, New Castle, Indiana, and Indiana University School of Medicine, Department of Neurology, Indianapolis, Indiana.

The Indiana Village for Epileptics, New Castle, Indiana.

The dose of 50 mgm. of phenobarbital was almost as effective as 250 mgm. of primidone. The difference between the responses to these two medications was not significant. Apparently, therefore, 1 mgm. of phenobarbital is approximately equivalent to 5 mgm. of primidone. The effects of 125 mgm. of primidone with 50 mgm. of phenobarbital was not significantly different from the

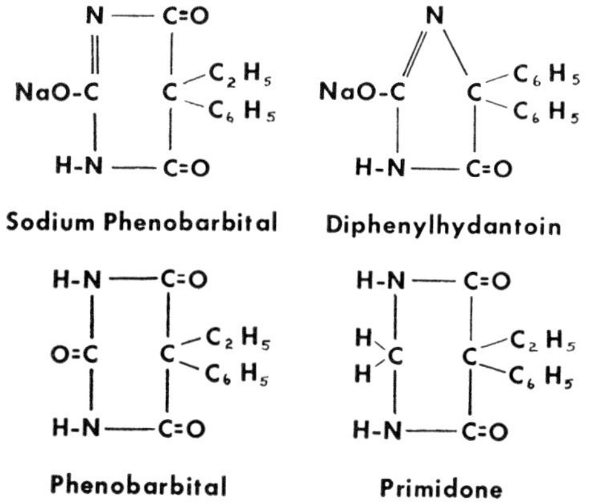

FIG. 1. The structural formulae of diphenylhydantoin, phenobarbital, phenobarbital sodium and primidone showing the differences and similarities among these drugs.

TABLE 1

The results with large doses of primidone

These doses were given at eight-hour intervals for three days. Primidone produced excessive drowsiness in all patients.

Medication	Dose	Seizure score for 9 patients
	mgm.	
Diphenylhydantoin	100	32
Primidone	1000	11
Blank	—	56
		Seizure score for 8 patients
Phenobarbital	50	36
Primidone	500	5
Blank	—	61

mean of the total score for 250 mgm. of primidone plus the total score for 100 mgm. of phenobarbital. Thus, when the two drugs were given together an additive and not a potentiated effect was obtained.

CONCLUSIONS. Doses of 250 mgm. of primidone and 50 mgm. of phenobarbital are equally effective in controlling the seizures of patients with focal brain damage.

TABLE 2

The total seizure scores obtained on substituting experimental medications for the usual medications of twenty patients with focal brain damage

Each generalized seizure was scored 2 and each focal seizure was scored 1. The experimental medications were given every 8 hr. on days 1, 2, and 3 and the patients returned to their former medication on the fourth day.

Code	Experimental medication	Days				
		1	2	3	4	Total
a	Phenobarbital, 100 mgm.	4	10	16	6	36
b	Phenobarbital, 50 mgm.	17	29	29	13	88
c	Blank	38	76	120	26	260
d	Primidone, 125 mgm.	34	36	63	17	150
e	Primidone, 250 mgm.	22	21	18	10	71
f	Primidone, 125 mgm. + Phenobarbital, 50 mgm.	6	22	11	0	39
Total		121	194	257	72	644

TABLE 3

Analysis of the data summarized in table 2

Source of variance	Sum of squares	Degrees of freedom	Mean square
Patients	178.4	19	9.4*
Days	55.0	3	18.3*
1 + 2 vs. 3 + 4		(1)	0.1
1 + 3 vs. 2 + 4		(1)	8.7*
1 + 4 vs. 2 + 3		(1)	46.2*
Medications	152.0	5	30.4*
5 c vs. a, b, d, e, and f		(1)	116.5*
a and b vs. d and e		(1)	9.8*
b vs. e		(1)	0.6
2 f vs. a and e		(1)	0.8
Interaction			
Days × Medication	64.0	15	4.3*
Remainder	1,886.6	1,397	1.35
Total	2,336	1,439	

* Significant effects.

Primidone and phenobarbital, when given together, have an additive and not a synergistic anticonvulsant action.

Doses of 500 mgm. and 1000 mgm. of primidone given three times daily produce excessive sedation. Drowsiness is the principal limiting factor upon increasing the dose of either phenobarbital or primidone, but this factor apparently limits the dose of primidone to a greater extent than it does phenobarbital.

SUMMARY

When patients with focal brain damage and epilepsy are given primidone or phenobarbital at eight-hour intervals for three days, it is possible to determine the relative anticonvulsant activity of these agents. A study of this sort, involving twenty patients who received all medications, indicates that 250 mgm. of primidone and 50 mgm. of phenobarbital are approximately equivalent. When these two drugs are given together an additive and not a potentiated effect is observed.

REFERENCES

Bogue, J. Y., and Carrington, H. C.: Brit. J. Pharmacol., **8**: 230, 1953.
Gruber, C. M., Jr., Mosier, J. M., Grant, P., and Glen, R.: Neurology, **6**: 640, 1956.
Handley, R., and Stewart, A. S. R.: Lancet, **1**: 742, 1952.

BIOCHEMICAL AND PHARMACOLOGICAL STUDIES ON *O*-TYROSINE AND ITS *META* AND *PARA* ANALOGUES. A SUGGESTION CONCERNING PHENYLKETONURIA

CHOZO MITOMA, HERBERT S. POSNER, DONALD F. BOGDANSKI AND SIDNEY UDENFRIEND

Laboratory of Clinical Biochemistry and Laboratory of Chemical Pharmacology, National Heart Institute, National Institutes of Health, Public Health Service, U. S. Department of Health, Education, and Welfare, Bethesda, Maryland

Received for publication January 10, 1957

The demonstration by Fölling (1934) that excretion of phenylpyruvic acid accompanies mental deficiency in the condition now known as phenylpyruvic oligophrenia has suggested that phenylalanine metabolism is in some way connected with the mental defect. The one biochemical defect that has been demonstrated in this disorder is the almost complete inability to convert phenylalanine to tyrosine (Jervis, 1947; Udenfriend *et al.*, 1953b). Since this conversion is normally the major route of phenylalanine metabolism there results a piling up of phenylalanine in the tissues and an increased metabolism of phenylalanine along what are normally minor routes of metabolism. It has been frequently suggested that the mental deficiency might ensue from an overproduction of some metabolites of phenylalanine other than *p*-tyrosine and, indeed, phenylalanine deficient diets have been reported to be beneficial (Bickell *et al.*, 1954; Armstrong *et al.*, 1955a).

One of the urinary metabolic products recently reported in phenylketonuria is *o*-hydroxyphenylacetic acid (Boscott *et al.*, 1953). This phenolic acid was also found in much smaller concentration in normal urine. It has been shown that phenylalanine is the precursor of *o*-hydroxyphenylacetic acid (Udenfriend *et al.*, 1955a; Armstrong *et al.*, 1955b). In considering the intermediates in this conversion two possibilities exist, one, *ortho* hydroxylation of phenylpyruvic acid followed by oxidative decarboxylation; the other, hydroxylation of phenylalanine to form *o*-tyrosine which would then lead to *o*-hydroxyphenylacetic acid. The latter possibility seemed of great interest since it is known that *o*-tyrosine is decarboxylated to *o*-tyramine in mammalian tissues (Blaschko, 1950). and since it has recently been shown in this laboratory that the central actions of another aromatic amino acid, 5-hydroxytryptophan (5HTP), result from its *in vivo* decarboxylation to form the amine, serotonin (Udenfriend *et al.*, 1957).

The present studies on the metabolism and pharmacology of *o*-tyrosine indicate that this amino acid can enter the central nervous system and then be converted to *o*-tyramine. At high concentrations marked excitation is produced in animals, resembling the effects of *d*-amphetamine and having some similarity to effects produced by 5-hydroxytryptophan. A comparison is made with *meta* and *para* tyrosine.

MATERIALS. *d,l-o*-Tyrosine and *d,l-m*-tyrosine were obtained from the California Foundation for Biochemical Research and from H. M. Chemical Company. The *d,l-p*-tyrosine

TABLE 1

Chromatographic properties of the tyrosines and their metabolites

Compound	R_f	2,6-Dichloroquinone Chlorimide	Diazotized Sulfamerazine
o-Tyrosine	0.15	Blue→Purple	Yellow
o-Tyramine	0.71	Blue→Purple	Yellow
o-Hydroxyphenylacetic acid	0.40	Blue	Yellow
m-Tyrosine	0.13	Blue	Yellow
m-Tyramine	0.69	Blue	Yellow
p-Tyrosine	0.11	None	Pink
p-Tyramine	0.65	None	Pink

Ascending chromatography on Whatman # 1 paper using the organic phase of a mixture of n-butanol: conc. NH_3:H_2O (80:1:19).

used in these studies was purchased from the Nutritional Biochemicals Corporation. The 2,6-dichloroquinone chloroimide, technical grade, was obtained from Eastman Kodak. Iproniazid was kindly supplied by Hoffman-LaRoche Inc. as the phosphate salt.

p-Tyramine hydrochloride was obtained from the Nutritional Biochemicals Corporation. However, there were no commercial sources of the *ortho* and *meta* tyramines. These were, therefore, prepared by decarboxylation of the corresponding amino acids with an acetone dried preparation of *S. faecalis*[1] (Udenfriend *et al.*, 1953a) and isolation of the amines by the butanol extraction procedure as described for separation of serotonin from 5-hydroxytryptophan (Udenfriend *et al.*, 1955b). The amine solutions were standardized spectrophotometrically by comparison of their extinctions with those of the corresponding amino acids (290 mμ in alkali). Their purity was also ascertained by chromatography on paper.

METHODS. *Paper chromatography.* The amines and amino acids were separated by ascending chromatography on Whatman # 1 paper, using n-butanol: conc. NH_3:H_2O (80:1:19) as the solvent. The *ortho* and *meta* compounds were detected by spraying with 0.05 per cent 2,6-dichloroquinone chloroimide in alcohol followed by 0.5 *M* borate buffer pH 9.3. The *para* compounds were detected by spraying with diazotized sulfamerazine. The R_f values and colors are summarized in table 1.

Determination of tyrosines and tyramines. Tissues were first homogenized using 5 ml. of 0.1 *N* HCl to 1.6 grams of tissue; 5 ml. of water were added to 1 ml. of blood.[2] Following this, 0.5 ml. of 40 per cent trichloracetic acid was added and the samples were centrifuged. To a 3-ml. aliquot of the supernatant fluid were added 1.0 ml. of 0.5 *M* borate buffer, pH 10 and 0.5 ml. of 20 per cent Na_2CO_3. The solution was then saturated with NaCl and extracted with 25 ml. of ether. In each case the ether was used for tyramine assay and the aqueous phase for tyrosine assay.

For *ortho* and *meta* tyramine 20 ml. of the ether were extracted with 3.0 ml. of 0.2 *N* HCl. Then 2.0 ml. of the acid extract were transferred to a 15-ml. glass-stoppered shaking tube containing 0.4 ml. of 1 *N* NaOH, 2.0 ml. of 0.5 *M* borate buffer, pH 9.3, and 0.1 ml. of 0.05 per cent 2,6-dichloroquinone chloroimide in ethanol. After color formation was complete (20 minutes) 1.5 ml. of n-butanol were added and the tubes shaken. The chromophore in the butanol layer was measured spectrophotometrically (*o*-tyramine, 570 mμ and *m*-tyramine, 600 mμ). Appropriate standards and blanks were carried through the entire extraction procedure. Normal tissues contained no material giving a color with this method.

[1] The decarboxylation of *o*-tyrosine by *S. fecaelis* is contrary to reports of Blaschko (1950).

[2] Siliconized glassware and heparin were used for collection of whole blood.

p-Tyramine was extracted according to the procedure described for serotonin (Udenfriend *et al.*, 1955b) and assayed by the α-nitroso-β-naphthol procedure (Udenfriend *et al.*, 1952).

For *o*- and *m*-tyrosine assay the aqueous layer following the ether extraction (see above) was extracted once, with 25 ml. of n-butanol to remove residual traces of amines and was then acidified by adding 0.5 ml. of 8 *N* HCl. It was then extracted twice with 25-ml. portions of ether to remove any hydroxyphenylacetic acid which might have been formed in the experiment. Two-ml. portions of the residual aqueous phase were then treated with the chloroimide reagent. The *o*-tyrosine chromophore was extracted into butanol as described above for tyramine assay. In the case of *meta* tyrosine the sample was acidified by addition of 0.1 ml. of 8 *N* HCl before butanol extraction.

RESULTS. *Decarboxylation of ortho and meta tyrosine by brain homogenates.* It has already been shown that some mammalian tissues decarboxylate *ortho* and *meta* tyrosine (Blaschko, 1950). Since brain decarboxylates 3,4-dihydroxyphenylalanine (Dietrich, 1954) and 5-hydroxytryptophan (Udenfriend *et al.*, 1957) it was of interest to determine whether it could decarboxylate any of the tyrosine analogues. When rat brain homogenates were incubated with the tyrosines the corresponding amines were formed from the *ortho* and *meta* isomers. These were identified with the specific procedure described above and by chromatography on paper.

In vivo conversion of tyrosines to their respective amines. When *o*-tyrosine was administered to rats *o*-tyramine was formed (table 2), the amine concentration being higher in brain and liver than in blood. Pretreatment with iproniazid, an inhibitor of monoamine oxidase activity in the brain, tremendously increased the amount of *o*-tyramine in the brain and other tissues. Administration of *m*-tyrosine also resulted in the appearance of *m*-tyramine in the tissues. The level

TABLE 2

o-Tyrosine and o-tyramine in rat tissues following administration of the amino acid

Exp.	Tissue	Control		Tyrosine		Tyrosine + Iproniazid	
		Tyramine	Tyrosine	Tyramine	Tyrosine	Tyramine	Tyrosine
a	Brain	—	—	3	—	—	—
a	Brain	0	—	16	12	58	34
b	Brain	0	0	11	—	—	—
c	Brain	0	0	61	29	238	44
a	Blood	0	*	5	29*	42	65*
a	Liver	0	—	4	—	59	—
b	Liver	—	—	13	—	—	—

Values are given in terms of microgm. per gram of tissue or microgm. per ml. of blood.

All agents were administered intraperitoneally. Iproniazid, 150 mgm./kgm., was administered 1 hour before the *o*-tyrosine. In experiments a, b and c, 150, 300 and 450 mgm./kgm. respectively, of *o*-tyrosine were used. The animals either died or were sacrificed within 90 to 120 minutes.

* The limits of detection of *o*-tyrosine in blood with this procedure are not very high. *ca.* 7 microgm./ml.

TABLE 3

Tyrosines and tyramines in rabbit brain

Compound Administered	Exp. #	Control		Experimental	
		Tyramine	Tyrosine	Tyramine	Tyrosine
o-Tyrosine	1	0	0	30	22
	2	0	—	34	—
m-Tyrosine	1	0	0	15	23
	2	0	—	8	—

Values are given in terms of microgm. per gram of tissue. The experimental animals were pretreated with iproniazid, 150 mgm./kgm., 1 hour before administering the amino acid. They either died or were sacrificed 1 to 2 hours following amino acid administration. In these experiments 200 mgm./kgm. of tyrosines were admistered.

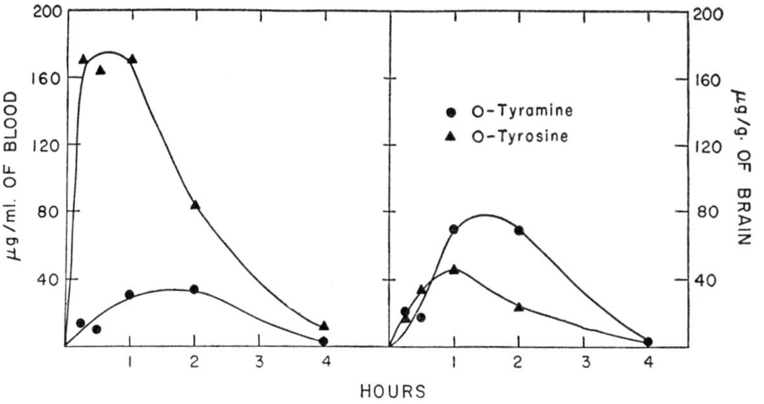

FIG. 1

in brain 90 minutes after giving 450 mgm./kgm. of the amino acid was 4.4 microgm./gm., pretreatment with iproniazid increased it to 15 microgm./gm. No *p*-tyramine was detected even when *p*-tyrosine was administered with iproniazid.

In rabbits, too, *ortho* and *meta* tyrosine penetrated into the brain and were converted to the corresponding amines (table 3).

To determine the sequence of events following the administration of *o*-tyrosine to animals, the following experiment was carried out. *o*-Tyrosine, 450 mgm./kgm. was administered to rats and at intervals several animals were sacrificed and the concentrations of *o*-tyrosine and *o*-tyramine in brain and blood were determined. The results, shown in fig. 1, indicate that *o*-tyrosine rapidly penetrates into the brain and that *o*-tyramine is formed from it, the maximum level of amine being reached in about 70 minutes. The usual precursor product relationship of *o*-tyrosine to *o*-tyramine was followed in blood. In the brain, however, the amine appeared in higher concentrations than the amino acid suggesting that *o*-tyramine may also penetrate and accumulate from peripheral sources.

Pharmacological effects. Both *o*-tyrosine and *m*-tyrosine produced marked pharmacological effects in mice, rats, rabbits and dogs. These effects were markedly potentiated by iproniazid. The effects of *ortho* and *meta* tyrosine were characterized by central excitatory actions and in general were sympathetic in nature resembling those produced by *dextro*-amphetamine. Comparable doses of *p*-tyrosine were without effect in all species investigated.

In mice, doses of 300 mgm./kgm. of either *o*-tyrosine or *m*-tyrosine following pretreatment with iproniazid, produced marked hyperactivity leading to convulsions and death within one to two hours. In rats 450 mgm./kgm. of *o*-tyrosine produced hyperactivity, piloerection and mydriasis. In rats, which had been pretreated with iproniazid these effects were observed at much smaller doses of the amino acid (100 mgm./kgm.) and in addition marked tremors accompanying voluntary movements became evident. At the higher doses convulsions terminating in death, were observed in some animals. However, except in the convulsing animals most reflexes seemed normal.

In rabbits 100 mgm./kgm. of *o*-tyrosine, following pretreatment with iproniazid, produced the following sequence of events. Hyperpnea and piloerection became evident at 45 minutes. At 75 minutes these effects were striking and in addition salivation, hyperactivity and tremors were apparent. Within 90 minutes the animals were prostrate with the head drawn back and the back arched in opisthotonus accompanied by miosis. Death followed within several minutes. Until these animals became moribund, the righting, contact, visual plantar, and the patellar reflexes were normal. The pupillary light reflex was present, although occasionally showing partial inhibition.

Comparable amounts of *m*-tyrosine also produced hyperpnea, hyperactivity and salivation. However, the effects differed from those of *o*-tyrosine in two ways, the pupillary light reflex disappeared relatively early and maximal mydriasis was observed. The *m*-tyrosine-treated animals also gradually lost the ability to right themselves and finally died 2½ to 3 hours after receiving the drug.

The effects produced by 200 mgm./kgm. of *o*-tyrosine in conscious dogs[3] were hyperpnea, tachycardia, hypertension, mydriasis, exophthalmos, retraction of the nictitating membrane and central excitement, characterized by hyperkinesis, tremors and rigidity. These led to an apparent confusion and inability to focus attention. Reflexes, in general, were maintained, except for a depressed pupillary response to light. Righting reflexes and the response to noxious stimuli were maintained and visual and contact plantar reactions were only temporarily depressed. The patellar reflex was also present.

DISCUSSION. These experiments show quite clearly that administration of *ortho* and *meta* tyrosine causes marked central actions. Since both amino acids are decarboxylated *in vivo*, and iproniazid potentiates their pharmacologic effects it is quite likely that the corresponding amines are responsible for their central actions. In this respect they resemble 5HTP. The autonomic effects of *o*-tyrosine resemble grossly those of 5HTP but the central actions are somewhat different. 5HTP-treated animals show a fixed escape response to painful stimuli whereas *o*-tyrosine-treated animals reacted essentially in a normal manner. *o*-Tyrosine does not depress reflexes to the extent that 5HTP does.

[3] *o*-Tyrosine was administered intravenously in doses of 100 mgm./kgm., 90 and 120 minutes following administration of iproniazid 150 mgm./kgm.

The demonstration that *o*-hydroxyphenylacetic acid is derived from phenylalanine strongly suggests that *o*-tyrosine and, therefore, *o*-tyramine may be normal metabolites in mammals. Although *o*-tyrosine has not as yet been found in mammalian tissues it has been reported to be present in insects (Dennell, 1956). The recognized importance of other normally occurring amines in physiological processes suggests that *o*-tyramine, if it exists, may also have some important role.

The increased excretion of *o*-hydroxyphenylacetic acid in phenylketonuria suggests that there may be an overproduction of a potent central agent in this disorder. The excitatory effects of large doses of *o*-tyrosine do not coincide with the retardation seen in patients with phenylpyruvic oligophrenia. However, one must consider that such individuals would have been exposed from birth to the chronic actions of such an agent and that all their learning and behavior could have been influenced by it. It will, of course, be necessary to demonstrate the presence of *o*-tyrosine and *o*-tyramine in the tissues of such patients and attempts to do this are now in progress.

The formation of *o*-tyrosine and *o*-hydroxyphenylacetic acid represents another metabolic route involving aromatic hydroxylation which is obviously distinct from the phenylalanine *para* hydroxylating system (Mitoma, 1956). It will be of interest to purify the *ortho* hydroxylase for comparison with the *para* hydroxylase. From a pharmacological standpoint the demonstration that these amino acids possess central activity suggests that other "amino acid" drugs should be investigated. Such compounds can evidently penetrate readily into the central nervous system and produce pharmacological effects of their own or they may be decarboxylated centrally, as are 5HTP and *ortho* and *meta* tyrosine, and thus act through their corresponding amines.

SUMMARY

It has been shown that ortho and meta tyrosine are taken up by brain and other tissues and are decarboxylated to the corresponding amines. The formation of large amounts of these amines in the central nervous system, produces effects which resemble those of *d*-amphetamine. Since *ortho*-hydroxyphenylacetic acid, the metabolic end product of *o*-tyrosine and *o*-tyramine, is normally excreted in the urine and its excretion is increased in phenylketonuria, it is suggested that *o*-tyramine may be a normally occurring physiologic agent and that its overproduction may lead to the mental defect seen in phenylketonuria.

REFERENCES

Armstrong, M. D., and Tyler, F. H.: J. Clin. Invest., **34:** 565, 1955a.
Armstrong, M. D., Shaw, K. N. F., and Robinson, K. S.: J. Biol. Chem., **213:** 797, 1955b.
Bickell, H., Gerrard, J., and Hickmans, E. M.: Acta paediat., **43:** 64, 1954.
Blaschko, H.: Biochim. et Biophys. Acta, **4:** 130, 1950.
Boscott, R. J., and Bickell, H.: Scand. J. Clin. & Lab. Invest., **5:** 380, 1953.
Dennell, R.: Nature, **178:** 922, 1956.
Dietrich, L. S.: J. Biol. Chem., **204:** 587, 1954.
Fölling, A.: Hoppe-Seyl. Z., **227:** 169, 1934.
Jervis, G. A.: J. Biol. Chem., **169:** 651, 1947.
Mitoma, C.: Arch Biochem. and Biophys., **60:** 476, 1956.

Udenfriend, S., and Cooper, J. R.: J. Biol. Chem., **196:** 227, 1952.
Udenfriend, S., and Cooper, J. R.: J. Biol. Chem., **203:** 953, 1953a.
Udenfriend, S., and Bessman, S. P.: J. Biol. Chem., **203:** 961, 1953b.
Udenfriend, S., and Mitoma, C.: in "Amino Acid Metabolism", The Johns Hopkins Press, Baltimore, 1955a.
Udenfriend, S., Weissbach, H., and Clark, C. T.: J. Biol. Chem., **215:** 337, 1955b.
Udenfriend, S., Weissbach, H., and Bogdanski, D. F.: J. Biol. Chem., **224:** 803, 1957.

THE EFFECT OF 6-MERCAPTOPURINE ON NUCLEIC ACID BIOSYNTHESIS IN *ESCHERICHIA COLI*[1]

H. GEORGE MANDEL, JOSEPH K. INSCOE,[2] HARRIET M. MALING[3] AND PAUL K. SMITH

Department of Pharmacology, The George Washington University School of Medicine, Washington 5, D. C.

Received for publication January 11, 1957

6-Mercaptopurine (6-MP) has been shown clinically to possess valuable carcinostatic properties in cases of acute leukemias and chronic myelocytic leukemia (Burchenal *et al.*, 1953). The close structural similarity of the drug to the purines of nucleic acids, as well as the reversibility of its inhibitory effects by adenine and hypoxanthine in various biological systems (Elion *et al.*, 1954), suggests that 6-MP acts as a purine antimetabolite. This study was initiated to investigate the effect of 6-MP on nucleic acid formation of the growing cell, utilizing a bacterial system partially inhibited by the drug. With such a biological system observations could be made on a well-controlled proliferating system in a relatively short time. Suitable radioactive tracers were employed to study the effects of 6-MP upon the synthesis of nucleic acid from endogenous sources and from exogenously added guanine.

METHODS. *Growth and measurement of bacteria. Escherichia coli*, strain B[4], were grown in the synthetic medium of Cohen, (1949) modified by increasing the glucose concentration to 0.4 per cent. The bacteria were grown in 2-liter Fernbach flasks at 37°C. with aeration. The extent of bacterial growth was determined by optical density measurements on a Coleman Universal spectrophotometer at a wave length of 540 millimicrons. Viable bacterial counts of normal and 6-mercaptopurine-inhibited cultures compared at selected optical densities showed no differences between the two cultures, justifying the use of optical density measurements as criteria of growth. Microscopic examination of stained cells revealed no morphological differences between inhibited and control cultures.

Materials. Guanine-4-C^{14} was previously prepared in this laboratory (Mandel and Carló, 1953); sodium formate-C^{14} was purchased from Isotopes Specialties Co., Glendale, Cal.; 6-mercaptopurine was supplied by the Burroughs Wellcome and Company, courtesy of Dr. G. H. Hitchings.

---

[1] This research was aided by a contract with the U.S. Atomic Energy Commission (AT(30-1)-1107), and by grants from the National Cancer Institute, (C-2326), of the National Institutes of Health, Public Health Service, the American Cancer Society Institutional Grant 24H, and the Damon Runyon Memorial Fund for Cancer Research (DRIR-42). A preliminary report of these investigations has been presented (Mandel *et al.*, 1956).

[2] A portion of this material is from a thesis presented by Joseph K. Inscoe in partial fulfillment of the requirements for the M.S. degree. Present Address: Laboratory of Clinical Biochemistry and Physiology, National Institute of Mental Health, Bethesda, Maryland.

[3] Present Address: Laboratory of Chemical Pharmacology, National Heart Institute, Bethesda, Maryland.

[4] The organisms were obtained originally from Dr. Roger M. Herriott of the Department of Biochemistry, School of Hygiene and Public Health, Johns Hopkins University.

Measurements of total uptake of radioactivity by bacteria. Samples of the cultures at the desired optical density levels were centrifuged at 1000 *g*. The precipitated bacteria were washed with one per cent saline, plated in aluminum cups, and measured for uptake of radioactivity in a proportional gas flow counter.

Isolation and specific activity measurements of DNA and RNA purines from bacteria. Bacteria were harvested by centrifuging and washing with saline and then with 95 per cent ethanol. The precipitated bacteria then were mixed with glass beads, packed into small bottles with absolute ethanol, and vibrated at −10° for 42 hours. The bacterial residue was centrifuged, washed with ethanol and ether and dried in a vacuum desiccator.

The bacterial nucleic acids were extracted and degraded, using methods previously described (Conzelman *et al.*, 1953; Roll and Weliky, 1955). The dried bacterial homogenates were extracted with hot 10 per cent NaCl solution, and the sodium nucleates were precipitated with 95 per cent ethanol and dried. The mixture of desoxyribose nucleic acid (DNA) and ribose nucleic acids (RNA) was dissolved in 1 *N* NaOH at room temperature and was separated by precipitating the DNA with 6 *N* HCl and 10 per cent trichloroacetic acid (TCA) in the cold. The DNA was then washed with alcohol and ether. From the supernatant, the RNA mononucleotides were converted to the barium salts and precipitated with 95 per cent ethanol.

The RNA nucleotides and DNA were hydrolyzed separately to the purine bases and pyrimidine nucleotides by treatment with 1 *N* HCl for one hour in a boiling water bath. The purines then were separated and isolated by use of Dowex-50 cation exchange chromatography, (Cohn, 1949). The purines were identified by the ratios of their ultraviolet light absorption at wave lengths of 250, 280 and 290 millimicrons to their absorption at 260 millimicrons, as determined with a Beckman model DU spectrophotometer. The separated adenine and guanine fractions were evaporated to dryness under reduced pressure and the residue taken up in a small volume of 0.1 *N* HCl. Specific activities of the purines were determined from radioactivity counts of plated aliquots of the solutions and from ultraviolet absorption values. The possibility of exogenously added guanine-C^{14} adsorbing onto the bacteria or of small amounts of the purine remaining undissolved in the bacterial medium and being carried along the isolation procedure as a contaminant needed to be excluded. A separation of the RNA mononucleotides was carried out by use of a Dowex-50-acetate and a Dowex-1-formate system (Cohn, 1950). The separate RNA mononucleotides then were hydrolyzed with 1 *N* HCl for one hour in a boiling water bath, the purine bases separated as described above, and radioassayed. The equivalence of the molar activities of the nucleotides and the purines isolated after complete hydrolysis of the nucleic acids justified elimination of this extra step of analysis.

Isolation of purines from combined nucleic acids. The bacteria were harvested, and extracted with cold TCA solution and alcohol. The purine bases then were extracted with hot 10 per cent TCA according to the procedure of Schneider (1945). To insure complete hydrolysis to the purine bases, the extracts were further hydrolyzed with 1 *N* HCl for one hour in a boiling water bath. The purines were evaporated to dryness under reduced pressure and then resolved by paper chromatography according to the method of Wyatt (1951). The adenine and guanine spots were located with the use of an ultraviolet lamp (Model SL 2537 Mineralight) and by their R_f values. The spots were eluted from the chromatogram with 0.1 *N* HCl and the identity and purity of the compounds confirmed by ultraviolet absorption spectrophotometry. Aliquots were plated in aluminum cups to determine radioactivity, and specific activities were calculated.

RESULTS. *Effect of 6-MP on guanine-C^{14} utilization.* Bacteria were inoculated into two flasks, each containing culture medium plus 5 mgm. of guanine-C^{14} per liter. One of these flasks contained in addition 3 mgm. of 6-MP per liter. This concentration had been shown to cause a significant inhibition of the growth of *E. coli* even in the presence of guanine, although higher concentrations of gua-

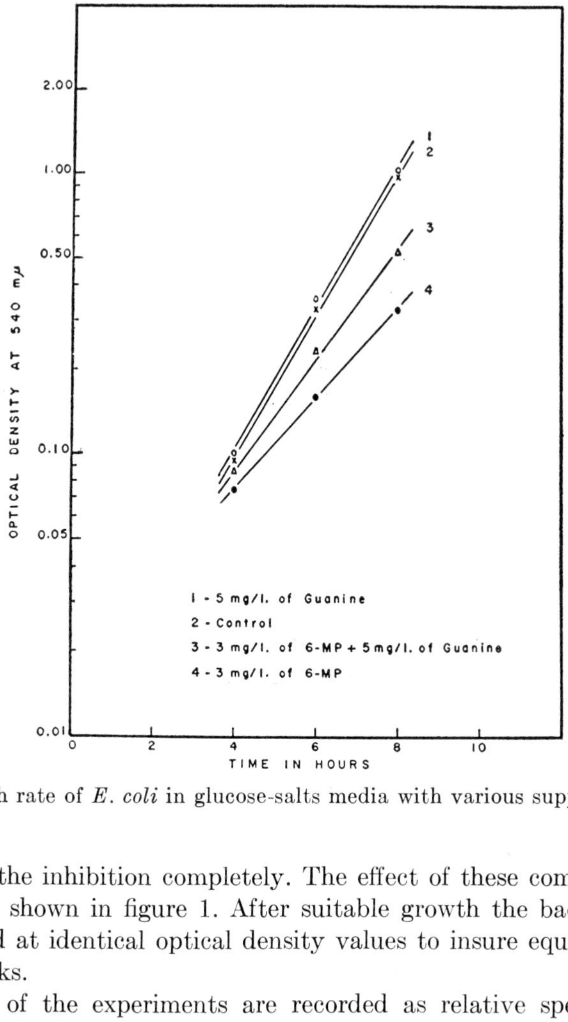

FIG. 1. Growth rate of *E. coli* in glucose-salts media with various supplements as indicated.

nine reversed the inhibition completely. The effect of these compounds on the growth rate is shown in figure 1. After suitable growth the bacterial cultures were harvested at identical optical density values to insure equal proliferation in the two flasks.

The results of the experiments are recorded as relative specific activities (RSA's), using the formula:

$$\text{RSA} = 100 \times \frac{\text{molar activity of isolated purine}}{\text{molar activity of guanine-C}^{14}\text{ added to medium}}.$$

The RSA values of the various purine fractions isolated from the 6-MP-inhibited and the control cultures are shown in tables 1 and 2 for RNA and DNA, respectively. As the bacterial cultures continued to proliferate the RSA values of the purines decreased, reflecting the increased utilization of endogenous sources for purine synthesis after the supply of the exogenous guanine had decreased.

The RSA's of all adenine fractions formed during drug inhibition were approximately 60 per cent higher than those of the corresponding controls, whereas in the case of the guanine fractions there was only a slight increase in RSA. 6-MP affected RNA and DNA similarly.

TABLE 1

Per cent of RNA purines derived from guanine-C^{14}

E. coli were grown in the presence of guanine-C^{14} with and without 6-MP.

OD at harvest	Control culture, Guanine (RSA)	Control culture, Adenine (RSA)	6-MP inhibited culture, Guanine (RSA)	6-MP inhibited culture, Adenine (RSA)	RSA guanine, 6-MP / RSA guanine, control	RSA adenine, 6-MP / RSA adenine, control
0.35	52.4	16.3	62.8	26.5	1.20	1.63
0.74	27.1	7.5	28.6	12.5	1.05	1.67
1.04	16.3	3.4	17.7	5.9	1.08	1.73
1.25	16.0	4.1	15.8	8.2	0.99	2.00

TABLE 2

Per cent of DNA purines derived from guanine-C^{14}

E. coli were grown in the presence of guanine-C^{14} with and without 6-MP.

OD at harvest	Control culture, Guanine (RSA)	Control culture, Adenine (RSA)	6-MP inhibited culture, Guanine (RSA)	6-MP inhibited culture, Adenine (RSA)	RSA guanine, 6-MP / RSA guanine, control	RSA adenine, 6-MP / RSA adenine, control
0.35	48.0	14.8	51.1	21.6	1.06	1.46
0.74	19.5	5.9	22.4	10.9	1.15	1.85
1.04	12.6	2.8	13.9	4.7	1.10	1.68
1.25	11.3	4.4	14.3	5.6	1.26	1.27

In order to account for this observed increase in purine RSA, the following factors which could influence the uptake of labeled guanine were considered: the uptake of labeled guanine by resting cells, the total uptake of labeled purine by growing cells, and the effect of 6-MP on nucleic acid synthesis from endogenous sources.

Resting cell experiments. Because of the slower rate of growth, the microorganisms in a medium containing 6-MP had been exposed for a longer period of time to the radioactive medium than had the control culture, for the same extent of growth. The possibility of this longer exposure time causing an increased uptake of the isotope by the inhibited culture due to exchange between exogenous and endogenous guanine was tested by determining the uptake of labeled guanine by resting cells. Bacteria from the exponential phase of growth were harvested, washed, resuspended and maintained without growth, as confirmed by optical density measurements, in a nitrogen- and glucose-deficient medium containing 5 mgm. of guanine-C^{14} per liter. Determinations of the total uptake of radioactivity by samples of the bacteria harvested after varying exposure times showed that the resting cells did not incorporate the labeled purine. Other investigators also have found that no such simple exchange takes place (Roberts *et al.*, 1955).

Total uptake of radioactivity from guanine-C^{14}. The possibility of 6-MP causing an increased total incorporation of guanine-C^{14} and in particular an enhanced conversion to adenine was tested by determining the total uptake of radioactivity by cultures grown in the presence of guanine-C^{14} with and without 6-MP. The total uptake of radiocarbon was unchanged by the addition of 6-MP. Complementary determinations on the residual radioactivity of the medium during growth of the bacteria confirmed this lack of an effect of the drug on the total uptake of isotope by the bacteria. These experiments indicate that 6-MP does not influence appreciably exogenous purine utilization.

Effect of 6-MP on endogenous nucleic acid synthesis. A third possibility for the increase in purine RSA would be a suppression of endogenous purine synthesis by 6-MP so that the exogenously administered purine would be subject to less dilution with purines synthesized from glucose, the only other carbon source. The inhibition of *de novo* synthesis by 6-MP had been reported by Skipper (1954) in mice and has in the meantime also been confirmed by other studies on *E. coli*. The bacterial cultures inhibited with 6-MP took up less C^{14}-formate, P^{32}-phosphate or C^{14}-uracil for nucleic acid synthesis than did control cultures for the same extent of proliferation, and the bacterial nucleic acid content was similarly decreased (Mandel and Bolton, 1956).

For the present investigation, the utilization of labeled formate by bacterial cultures grown in the presence and absence of 6-MP was measured. Bacteria were allowed to grow to an optical density reading of 0.17 and then a small amount of C^{14}-formate plus carrier sodium carbonate was added to dilute out the conversion to and incorporation of $C^{14}O_2$ (Roberts *et al.*, 1955). Five mgm. of 6-MP per liter were then added to one of the cultures. The cultures were harvested when they had reached optical density values of 0.40. The guanine and adenine fractions from the combined nucleic acids were isolated and specific activities measured as described. It was necessary to introduce the drug and isotope to an already proliferating culture so that specific activity measurements would reflect any altered utilization of the isotope for nucleic acid biosynthesis.

The results are shown in table 3. It is evident that the uptake of C^{14}-formate was depressed by the drug, in conformance with the decrease in nucleic acid content produced by 6-MP. The effect of the drug was essentially identical on both the adenine and guanine fractions.

The increase in RSA of the 6-MP-inhibited cultures as shown in tables 1 and 2 can thus be explained by a decrease in the synthesis of purines from endogenous sources without appreciably influencing the incorporation of the labeled purine for a constant extent of growth.

TABLE 3

Specific activities of nucleic acid purines isolated from E. coli after addition of C^{14}-formate with and without 6-MP to proliferating cultures

	Guanine		Adenine	
	cpm/*mM* × 10^{-6}	Per cent of control	cpm/*mM* × 10^{-6}	Per cent of control
Control culture	10.0	100	9.8	100
6-MP culture	4.5	45	4.3	44

TABLE 4

Specific activities of nucleic acid purines isolated from E. coli grown in the presence of formate-C^{14} and guanine and 6-MP as indicated

	Guanine			Adenine		
	cpm/mM $\times 10^{-6}$	Per cent of		cpm/mM $\times 10^{-6}$	Per cent of	
		a	b		a	b
a. Formate-C^{14}	11.0	100	xxx	11.5	100	xxx
b. Formate-C^{14} plus guanine	4.8	44	100	10.3	90	100
c. Formate-C^{14} plus guanine plus 6-MP	3.7	34	77	7.3	63	70

Effect of 6-MP and guanine on C^{14}-formate utilization. The discrepancy in the apparent selective effect of 6-MP on the RSA of the adenine fractions compared to the corresponding guanine samples, as shown in tables 1 and 2, needed elucidation.

Since the interference with utilization of endogenous material by 6-MP was thought to be responsible for the increase in RSA of purines, shown in tables 1 and 2, an attempt was made to confirm this hypothesis by experiments using labeled formate and unlabeled guanine.

Glucose-salts media were supplemented with a trace of C^{14}-formate plus carrier sodium carbonate solution to dilute out the conversion to and incorporation of $C^{14}O_2$. To one medium 5 mgm. of guanine per liter were added; to another culture 5 mgm. each of guanine and 6-MP were added. Bacterial inocula then were introduced, and the cultures were grown for a constant extent of growth. After harvesting, the purines were isolated and specific activities measured. Results are shown in table 4.

The drop in the specific activities of the purine fractions of table 4 produced by guanine demonstrates the formation of the purines from another source, namely the preformed purine. It is apparent that exogenous guanine produces a sparing action, particularly on the synthesis of this purine from formate. The effect on adenine synthesis under these conditions is relatively minor, in agreement with the limited conversion of guanine to adenine in *E. coli* (Koch *et al.*, 1952). The replacement of nucleic acid guanine biosynthesis from other endogenous sources such as CO_2 by the utilization of exogenously added guanine has been observed (Bolton and Reynard, 1954).

The addition of 6-MP to a guanine-containing medium curtails the endogenous synthesis of both purines by approximately the same relative extent, in agreement with the findings reported in table 3.

Since the synthesis of nucleic acid guanine from endogenous sources has been largely replaced by direct incorporation, the decreased utilization of formate produced by the drug does not result in a very pronounced effect on total polynucleotide guanine synthesis. In the case of adenine, however, only a small portion of which is derived from the exogenous guanine, a proportional decrease in formate utilization would appear to increase considerably the *relative* portion derived from the exogenous guanine. With exogenous guanine-C^{14} the differential effects on the two purines, shown in tables 1 and 2, would therefore be expected.

It may be concluded, therefore, that 6-MP inhibits partially the biosynthesis of purines from endogenous sources without influencing appreciably the utilization of exogenous guanine. The curtailment in the formation of adenine and guanine from endogenous sources is approximately equal. Exogenous guanine spares endogenous synthesis of guanine considerably more than endogenous synthesis of adenine. The dilution of exogenous guanine-C^{14} by a decreased amount of endogenously synthesized purines during growth, as produced by 6-MP, would in effect raise the RSA's of the purine fractions isolated (tables 1 and 2). The increase in RSA would be greater in the case of the adenine fractions since such a relatively large portion of this fraction is derived from endogenous sources.

DISCUSSION. It should be emphasized that comparisons were made in these experiments between bacterial cultures of the same extent of proliferation. The slower growth rate of the microorganisms in the presence of 6-MP would be expected to decrease proportionally all biosynthetic processes related to growth. Thus, utilization of guanine-C^{14}, as in the present experiments, would be slowed down in relation to the decreased growth rate. When total proliferation is equal, however, so that the inhibited culture is allowed more time to reach the same extent of growth as the uninhibited culture, no difference in guanine utilization could be recorded. Bacterial systems of this nature are well suited for obtaining constant proliferation during the pharmacological studies.

An experiment measuring the effect of 6-MP on the uptake of a labeled purine is complicated by the relatively large amount of carrier purines involuntarily introduced with the addition of the isotope. Since high concentrations of the purines reverse all effects of the drug, the use of purines of extremely high specific activity would be advantageous.

The effect of 6-MP upon *E. coli* is analogous to the results reported by Skipper in tumor bearing mice (1954), and by Heidelberger and Keller (1955) with rat spleens and Flexner-Jobling carcinomas. No effort was made in these investigations to study the specific site of inhibition by the drug in various steps of purine biosynthesis.

SUMMARY

The growth of *Escherichia coli* was inhibited partially by the carcinostatic purine analog, 6-mercaptopurine (6-MP), at a concentration of 3 mgm. per liter in a glucose-salts medium, without change in viability or gross morphology of the microorganisms. Simultaneous addition of 5 mgm. of guanine per liter of medium partially reversed this inhibition without the added guanine becoming the sole source of bacterial purines. DNA and RNA purines were isolated from bacteria grown with 5 mgm. of guanine-C^{14} in the presence and absence of 3 mgm. of 6-MP per liter. The relative specific activities (RSA's) of both RNA and DNA adenine obtained from cultures grown in the presence of 6-MP were approximately 60 per cent higher than those of control cultures, whereas the corresponding guanine fractions showed only a slight increase. Utilization of exogenous guanine for the same extent of growth was unaffected by 6-MP. The increase in the RSA's of bacterial purines was due to a lessened dilution of the labeled exogenous purine by endogenous purine since experiments with labeled formate demonstrated a reduction in endogenous purine synthesis produced by 6-MP. Although this curtailment was approximately equal for adenine and guanine, 6-MP affected the RSA's of the nucleic acid adenine fractions more than those of the guanine fractions because a larger proportion of adenine than guanine is endogenously synthesized when guanine-C^{14} is added to the growth medium.

REFERENCES

Bolton, E. T., and Reynard, A. M.: Biochimica et Biophysica Acta, **13:** 381, 1954.
Burchenal, J. H., Murphy, M. L., Ellison, R. R., Sykes, M. P., Tan, T. C., Leon, L. A., Karnofsky, D. A., Craver, L. F., Dargeon, H. W., and Rhoads, C. P.: Blood, **8:** 965, 1953.
Cohen, S. S.: J. Biol. Chem., **177:** 607, 1949.
Cohn, W. E.: Science, **109:** 376, 1949.
Cohn, W. E.: J. Am. Chem. Soc., **72:** 1471, 1950.
Conzelman, G. M., Jr., Mandel, H. G., and Smith, P. K.: J. Biol. Chem., **201:** 329, 1953.
Elion, G. B., Singer, S., and Hitchings, G. H.: Ann. N. Y. Acad. Sciences, **40:** 200, 1954.
Heidelberger, C., and Keller, R. A.: Cancer Research Supplement, No. **3:** 106, 1955.
Koch, A. L., Putnam, F. W., and Evans, E. A., Jr.: J. Biol. Chem., **197:** 105, 1952.
Mandel, H. G., and Bolton, E. T.: Proc. Am. Assn. Cancer Res., **2:** 131, 1956.
Mandel, H. G., and Carlo, P. E.: J. Biol. Chem., **201:** 335, 1953.
Mandel, H. G., Inscoe, J. K., Maling, H. M., and Smith, P. K.: Fed. Proc., **15:** 454, 1956.
Roberts, R. B., Abelson, P. H., Cowie, D. B., Bolton, E. T., and Britten, R. J.: Studies of Biosynthesis in *Escherichia coli*: Carnegie Institution of Washington Publication 607, Washington, D. C., 1955.
Roll, P. M., and Weliky, I.: J. Biol. Chem., **213:** 509, 1955.
Schneider, W. C.: J. Biol. Chem., **161:** 293, 1945.
Skipper, H. E.: Ann. N. Y. Acad. Sciences, **60:** 315, 1954.
Wyatt, G. R.: Biochem. J., **48:** 584, 1951.

THE RELATION BETWEEN DOSE OF SUCCINYLCHOLINE AND DURATION OF APNEA IN MAN

W. KALOW AND D. R. GUNN

Department of Pharmacology, University of Toronto and the Ontario Hospital, New Toronto

Received for publication January 14, 1957

One of the uses of the muscular relaxant succinylcholine is to modify the severity of the convulsions induced by electroshock in the treatment of mental illness (see review by Brücke, 1956). Patients are usually given a series of electroshock treatments and therefore receive a number of injections of succinylcholine at intervals of a few days to a few weeks. In such a situation there arose the opportunity to apply different doses of succinylcholine to the same patients under standardized conditions, and to measure the duration of the resulting apnea. The analysis of dose-duration curves thus obtained is presented in this paper, while further observations and clinical implications of this work will be published elsewhere.

METHODS. *Patients.* The period of this investigation, which lasted for the first half of 1956, was preceded by three years during which the methods were gradually developed and experience gained as to the effects of various doses of succinylcholine. The investigation was carried on during the active treatment of mental illness. It differed from the regular routine treatment only by the presence of a specially trained person with equipment to measure the duration of apnea after an injection, and by the effort to vary the dose of succinylcholine after a schedule which will be described below. In no single instance was it necessary to curtail the dosage because of any physical or emotional ill-effect on the patient. There was no selection of patients; that is, apnea was measured in all of some 118 male patients who arrived consecutively for treatment. However, 61 patients needed less than five treatments during the period of study. The data from these patients were omitted from the analysis because of their incompleteness. On the other hand, data from three further cases were included. That is, two patients with intermediate Dibucaine Numbers (see below) would have been treated ordinarily in the treatment room of another ward of the same hospital, and the data of one of the patients with low Dibucaine Numbers had been obtained before the start of the formal period of investigation (patient E. G., table 3). Altogether, the results could be based on observations on 60 mentally ill adult males. These patients had the common need for a prolonged series of electroshock treatments but their psychiatric diagnosis was not uniform. They had no disease other than their mental condition.

Treatment. The patients received 0.2 to 0.8 gm. of amobarbital sodium one hour prior to treatment. Thus they were drowsy as a result of the sedative but responded to questions. That is, contrary to common practice, the patients were not under general anesthesia. The main purpose of administering a general anesthetic is to prevent fear and apprehension as a result of curarization. This could be achieved by sedation, reassurance, precise timing of the injection, and by inflating the patient with oxygen while the muscular relaxant took effect. Unconsciousness of the patient started with the shock and lasted for some time afterwards, gradually changing into sleep.

The intravenous injection of succinylcholine was timed with a stopwatch. The first 10 mgm. were injected slowly over a period of 30 seconds in order to avoid twitching. The rest of the dose was injected during the next 15 seconds, regardless of the size of the dose. Since apnea usually started about a quarter of a minute after the end of the injection, in all cases the apnea was assumed to have started at exactly 15 seconds after the injection. The electroshock was always administered 75 seconds after the end of the injection.

Oxygen was administered by a positive pressure inhalator, commencing immediately after the completion of the injection. The administration was continued at 5 to 10 second intervals until just before the application of the shock. After the termination of the "convulsion", the patient was given two or three additional inflations. Thereafter, oxygen was given when necessary or advisable. Care was taken to avoid changes in blood pressure, heart rate, and the electrocardiogram. Measurements of the blood gases were not performed in this series.

The number of treatments per patient varied between 5 and 25, with an average of about nine. The standard doses were 30, 62.5, 125, 250, 500, and 1000 mgm. of succinylcholine chloride per person. All patients with the usual type of esterase received 1000 mgm. and, with one exception, 500 mgm. In some cases, 25, 50, 100, and 200 mgm. and other doses were used. Two-thirds of all patients received a dose which induced between nine and eleven minutes of apnea. The extreme doses used were 5 mgm. and 2000 mgm. In 26 patients, some dose or doses were repeated at least once. The various doses were not given in regular order but their sequence was randomized as far as possible.

All the data on doses of succinylcholine refer to the water-free dichloride salt. The commercial preparations used for the treatment were occasionally subjected to the U.S.P. XV assay and found to be of full strength.

Measurements of apnea. To observe the return of spontaneous respiration, a thin latex bag was attached by a special adapter to a face mask and held to the mouth of the patient. The bag was partially inflated so that it fluctuated with each heart beat. The time at which the first definite respiratory movement of the bag occurred, was recorded as the end of apnea. The sensitivity of this method was tested by connecting a syringe of 50-ml. capacity to the closed system of mask and bag. It was found that an exchange of 20 ml. of air produced a movement of the bag corresponding to that caused by the first respiratory movement.

Body weight. The body weight of each patient was routinely measured once a month; the weight determined nearest the time of injecting the highest dose was used for the calculation of correlation coefficients.

Serum cholinesterase activity. Esterase activity was determined by ultraviolet spectrophotometry, using benzoylcholine as the substrate. The determination was made as described by Kalow and Lindsay (1955), except that the measurements were performed in a recording spectrophotometer. This led to a choice of a final serum concentration of 1:100. Automatic pipettes were used, sacrificing some accuracy but gaining speed. To facilitate comparison, all units of esterase activity or "esterase levels" were expressed as micromoles of acetylcholine hydrolysed per hour per ml. of serum at 37°C.

A second portion of the same sample of serum was always investigated at the Ontario Department of Health, Central Laboratories,[1] where esterase activity was measured as described by de la Huerga *et al.* (1952). This method is based on the determination of acetylcholine by the formation of coloured ferric hydroxamic acid. The results of the tests were always made immediately available and hence served throughout the study as a most valuable check on, and confirmation of, the data obtained by ultraviolet spectrophotometry. The correlation coefficient for the two determinations of esterase activity was 0.895 ± 0.028. All further correlation coefficients reported in this paper and involving esterase levels, were also calculated for the data determined by the Central Laboratories. Since both sets of data were statistically indistinguishable, the latter set of data was omitted from this report for the sake of simplification.

Determination of serum cholinesterase characteristics (*Dibucaine Number*). As described in some preliminary reports (Kalow, 1956a, b; Kalow *et al.*, 1956a, b) the enzyme serum cholinesterase is not the same in all people. The different types of enzyme have been demonstrated by measuring the degree of inhibition produced by dibucaine (cinchocaine—TN Nupercaine, Perkain) (Kalow and Genest, 1957). Dibucaine was mixed with a solution of benzoylcholine

[1] We are grateful for these tests to Dr. L. E. Elkerton, Director of the Division of Laboratories, and to Mr. E. J. Fasken, Chief Provincial Analyst, Province of Ontario.

and the mixture added to diluted serum. The esterase activity was then determined by ultraviolet spectrophotometry exactly as was done before without dibucaine. The final concentrations were serum 1:100, benzoylcholine 5×10^{-5} molar, dibucaine 10^{-5} molar, all dissolved in phosphate buffer of 7.4. The degree of inhibition expressed in per cent was called the Dibucaine Number.

The Dibucaine Number is not affected by such pathological conditions as liver disease, which can reduce the esterase level (Kalow and Genest, 1957). Dibucaine Numbers are genetically determined. According to the pattern of inheritance we divide the Dibucaine Numbers into three groups: values above 70 (average 79) are most frequent and therefore considered normal. Values between 45 and 70 (average 60) are considered intermediate; they occur in about 3 per cent of the normal population. Values below 25 (average 16) are rare but indicate a very pronounced change of the esterase.

RESULTS. *Observations on patients with the normal type of esterase.* Of the 60 patients, 51 had a Dibucaine Number above 74 and were therefore regarded as having the usual type of esterase. The average Dibucaine Number in this group was 78.8, with a standard error of ±0.3 and a standard deviation of ±2.1. All the variation around the mean could be accounted for by experimental error. Hence, there was no correlation within this group between Dibucaine Number and esterase level, reaction towards succinylcholine, age, or body weight. The data obtained from this group of 51 patients will be described first.

On these patients, with the usual type of esterase, 482 responses towards succinylcholine have been measured. Of these, 86 were duplicate determinations, that is, the injection of a given dose into a given patient was repeated 43 times. Fourteen patients received one dose in replication and 9 patients received more than one dose in replication. The doses used were 62.5, 125, 250, 500, and 1000 mgm., with 9, 13, 8, 4, and 9 replications respectively. From these data, an analysis of variance has been made. For reasons which will become obvious in the next section, the units for calculation were the logarithms of the duration of apnea, measured in minutes. This analysis gave information which is not directly available from the bulk of the data. First, the experimental error was ±0.062; the antilog of this error term indicated that two-thirds of all responses were within about ±15 per cent of their mean. Second, the replication term was small in comparison with the error; that is, the difference between the two responses did not depend on their sequence. Hence, one can assume that no tolerance, sensitization, or other alteration of susceptibility towards succinylcholine developed during the treatments. Furthermore, the error of the observations in terms of log minutes appeared to be the same for all 5 doses, as evident from a chi-square test for the homogeneity of variance.

All observations, including the replications, were analyzed as follows: The data for each patient were plotted on separate sheets of graph paper, showing the dose as abscissa and minutes of apnea as ordinate. A smooth curve was drawn through the data under the guidance of the eye. From the curves thus obtained, the doses corresponding to an apnea of 10 minutes duration were read. Since many patients had received doses causing close to 10 minutes apnea, only little interpolation was needed in most cases. Probits were calculated from the frequency distribution of these "10-minute doses" and plotted against log dose.

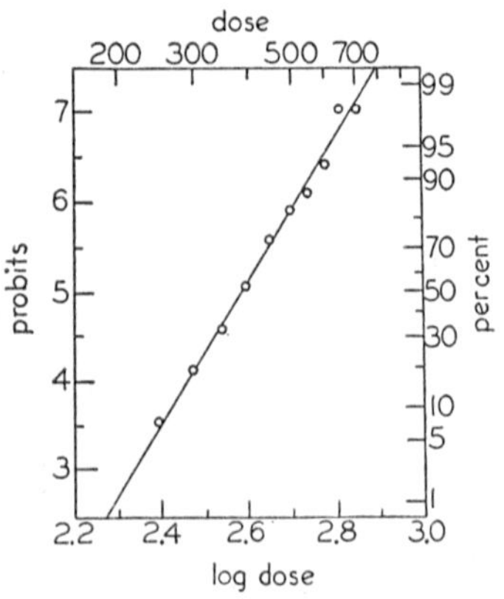

FIG. 1. Doses of succinylcholine chloride (mgm.) necessary to produce an apnea of 10 minutes' duration in 51 patients with normal type of serum cholinesterase.

The "10-minute dose" was determined for each patient and the per cent of patients reacting at each dose level counted. The integrated percentage frequencies were transformed into probits and are shown as the ordinate. The abscissa is log dose in mgm.

The ED_{50} (median 10-minute dose) is 385.6 ± 15.7 mgm. The slope is 7.98 ± 0.11.

If computation of the probits were confined to the 51 data from the patients with the usual type of esterase, the data fell on a straight line (fig. 1), indicating normal distribution of the logarithm of the doses.

The probit method was also used for the analysis of the variation of the duration of apnea after four fixed doses, 1000, 500, 250, and 100 mgm. The first two doses were selected because all 51 patients had received these doses, so that original data could be used without interpolation. The doses, 250 and 100 mgm., were chosen because the duration of apnea could be determined for all patients with a minimum of interpolation and no extrapolation. The variation of the time of apnea from patient to patient was found to be asymetrical but the logarithm of the times of apnea were normally distributed (fig. 2). In addition, the proportional variation was the same after all four doses, as indicated by the fit of the data to four parallel straight lines. The units of time used to calculate the frequency distribution were half-minute intervals. This caused the decreasing number of points with decreasing dose in fig. 2, although there were 51 values at each dose.

The ED_{50} for 10 minutes of apnea, its 95 per cent fiducial limits, and a range corresponding to ±2 SD, were calculated from the data of fig. 1. The data from fig. 2 were treated in the same way. The statistics thus obtained were entered into a graph with log dose as abscissa and log minutes of apnea as ordinate (fig. 3). They fit to a series of parallel lines. The band bordered by the two extreme lines should contain 95 per cent of all data. A recount of the original data showed that 457 of the 482 data of this group of 51 patients fell actually into this range. This includes the responses of those doses which had not been used for the calculation of the limits.

The regression lines in fig. 3 are described by the equation $y = bx + a$, where

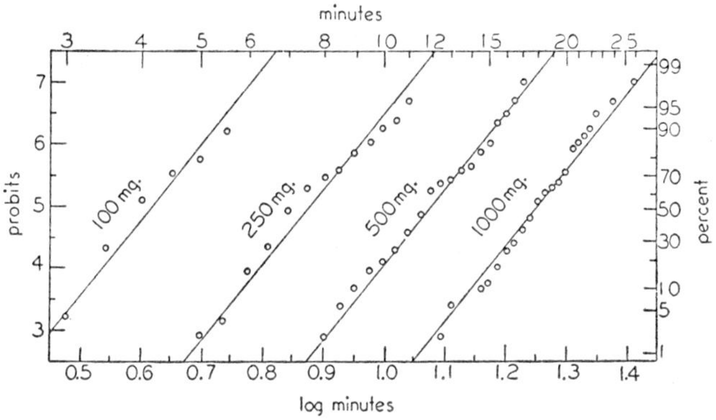

FIG. 2. Durations of apnea in 51 patients with normal type of esterase, after four doses of succinylcholine.

The per cent of patients having an apnea of a given duration were calculated. The integrated percentage frequencies were transformed into probits, as shown. The unit time interval used in this calculation was 30 seconds; hence, there were fewer points in the curve showing the effect of 100 mgm. than in that of 1000 mgm., although there were 51 observations in each case.

The median durations of apnea expressed in minutes and seconds are 4′8″, 7′30″, 11′53″, and 17′45″ after 100, 250, 500, and 1000 mgm. of succinylcholine respectively. The approximate standard error is ±2.5 per cent. The common slope is $b = 12.259$.

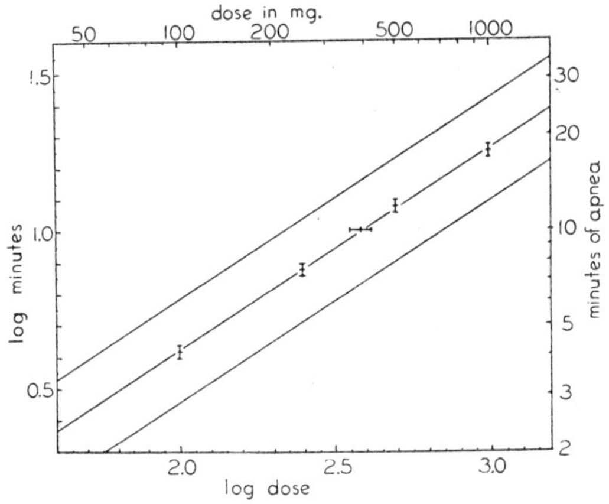

FIG. 3. Relation between dose of succinylcholine chloride (mgm.) and duration of apnea in 51 patients with normal type of esterase.

The short bars picture the median values derived from fig. 1 and 2, and their 95 per cent fiducial limits. The line connecting these bars follows the equation, log minutes = 0.6365 log dose − 0.6525. The two parallel lines indicate the limits for 95 per cent of all responses in patients with normal esterase.

y = log minutes of apnea and x = log dose in mgm. succinylcholine chloride. The constant b expresses the slope and has the numerical value 0.6365 ± 0.154. The constant a represents the ordinate intercept. A change of this constant is graphically represented by a parallel shift of the lines. The numerical value of a

is −0.6525 for the middle or average regression line. For the line representing the upper limit, $a = -0.4894$ and the lower limit $a = -0.8156$.

Individual variation of susceptibility towards succinylcholine appears to find its expression not so much in alterations of the slope of the logarithmic dose-duration curves but primarily in a parallel shift of the curves. That is, the variation between patients can be described shortly as a variation of the constant a. This is suggested by an inspection of individual data when they are fitted to the common slope b. An example (fig. 5) will be discussed below in greater detail because this common slope fits also to the data of patients with atypical esterase.

The validity of the constant a for summarizing the responses of a given patient towards various doses of succinylcholine has been assessed by the following test: The 51 constants have been calculated by the equation $a = \bar{y} - 0.6365\bar{x}$, where $\bar{y}$ is the mean of all responses of a given patient in logarithmic units, and $\bar{x}$ is the mean log dose for the same patient. The values of a thus obtained have been used to compute expected responses, Y, for each dose of succinylcholine administered to each individual, *i.e.* $Y = 0.6365x + a$. The difference between the n expected response Y and the n observed responses y were calculated with $n = 482$. Then, $\sqrt{(Y - y)^2/n - 52}$ = standard deviation of observed from expected responses = 0.061. This value is very similar to the standard deviation 0.062 which was obtained from the replication data. Hence the constants a represent the individual responsiveness as well as an average of paired data.

All the constants a have negative values. Since it is inconvenient to picture the response to a drug in negative terms, one can describe instead the responses of each individual by some expected response Y and thereby avoid the negative sign. For this purpose, an expected response Y_{100} has been arbitrarily chosen to indicate a response in log minutes apnea after 100 mgm. of succinylcholine, that is, $Y_{100} = a + 1.273$, where $1.273 = b \log 100$. The mean value of Y_{100} in this group of patients was 0.6210 with a standard deviation of ±0.0738. The standard deviation of the directly observed responses to given doses (fig. 2) was ±0.0816; this is not significantly different from 0.0738.

The correlation between the values of Y_{100} and other measurable features of this population of 51 patients has been investigated. Available for this study were measurements of age, body weight, and serum cholinesterase level (table 1).

TABLE 1

Four measurements on 51 patients with normal type of esterase

	Mean	Standard Error	Standard Deviation
Age	44.000	2.05	14.619
Body weight	136.72	3.15	22.503
Esterase level	209.39	6.38	45.541
Y_{100} (responsiveness)	0.62104	0.01033	0.073804

Age is given in years, body weight in lbs., esterase level in micromoles of acetylcholine hydrolyzed at 37°C. per ml. serum per hour. Y_{100} is defined as log minutes of apnea after intravenous injection of 100 mgm. of succinylcholine. Each Y_{100} summarizes all responses of a patient to all doses

TABLE 2

Correlation coefficients among four measurements on 51 patients with normal type of esterase

Weight vs. Esterase	r_{12}	0.2004
Weight vs. Age	r_{13}	0.0755
Esterase vs. Age	r_{23}	−0.3230*
Response (Y_{100}) vs. Weight	r_{y1}	−0.3030*
Response (Y_{100}) vs. Esterase	r_{y2}	−0.7493**
Response (Y_{100}) vs. Age	r_{y3}	0.3530*
Response (Y_{100}) vs. Weight + Esterase	$R_{y.12}$	0.7653**
Response (Y_{100}) vs. Weight + Age	$R_{y.13}$	0.4836**
Response (Y_{100}) vs. Esterase + Age	$R_{y.23}$	0.7584**
Response (Y_{100}) vs. Weight + Esterase + Age	$R_{y.123}$	0.7785**

See table 1 for the description of the four measurements.
* $P < 0.05$.
** $P < 0.01$

All three characteristics appeared to be normally distributed in this group, as tested graphically by probit plots. The coefficient of variation of numerous literature data on serum cholinesterase has been described as about 20 per cent (Wolfsie and Winter, 1952). The coefficient in this group is about the same, in spite of the absence of cases with atypical esterase. The results of a study of correlation between these characteristics within the group of 51 patients are shown in table 2. There is no correlation between body weight and esterase level but some correlation between age and esterase level. All three characteristics have a correlation with Y_{100}.

All correlation coefficients with other measures of responsiveness towards succinylcholine than Y_{100}, were smaller than those shown in table 2. For instance, the correlation coefficient between esterase level and the duration of apnea after 1000 mgm. of succinylcholine was 0.570. The correlation coefficients of esterase level with the "10-minute doses" was 0.687; and 0.693 with the logarithm of the "10-minute doses".

The mean responses Y_{100} could have been predicted from body weight, age and esterase level by the following multiple regression equation:

$$Y_{100} = 0.8965 + 0.000776 \times \text{age in years} - 0.000601 \times \text{body weight in lbs.} - 0.001086 \times \text{esterase level.}$$

The standard error of estimate would have been ± 0.048. However, a prediction of almost the same precision could have been made by disregarding both body weight and age and using the equation $Y_{100} = 0.8778 - 0.001266 \times$ esterase level. The standard error of estimate would have been ± 0.050.

Observations on patients with atypical esterase. Figure 4 presents the same type of plot as fig. 1 but the data of fig. 4 were calculated from the observations on all patients, including those with atypical esterase. The points in fig. 4 do not fall on a straight line. This is evidence that the total group of patients is inhomogeneous in their reaction towards succinylcholine; hence the data from patients with the atypical esterase are dealt with in this separate section.

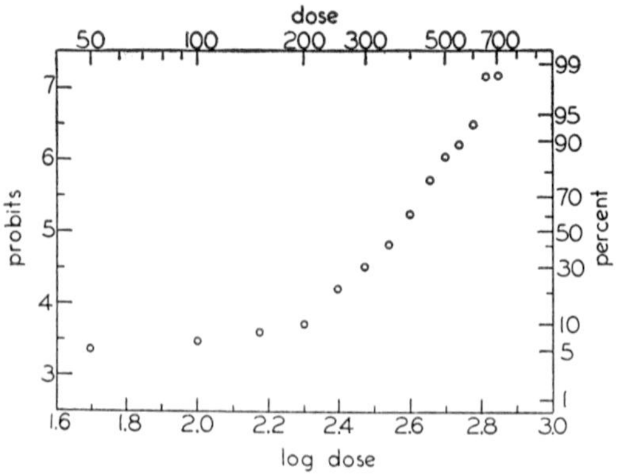

FIG. 4. Doses of succinylcholine chloride (mgm.) necessary to produce an apnea of 10 minutes' duration in 60 patients.

Same plot as fig. 1 but the data obtained on patients with atypical esterase are included. The non-linearity of the plot indicates that this inclusion renders the total group of patients inhomogeneous with respect to reaction towards succinylcholine.

TABLE 3

Data on 6 patients with intermediate, and 3 patients with low Dibucaine Numbers

Patient	Dibucaine Number	Body Wt. in Lbs.	Age	Cholinesterase Level	Antilog Y_{100} in Minutes and Seconds**
Usual Range*...	74.5–83.1	92–182	15–73	118–300	2′59″–5′52″
R.C.	61.2	107	27	153	8′2″
D.F.	46.1	145	50	77	12′24″
L.T.	69.7	143	25	205	5′31″
R.D.	65.2	134	22	164	5′35″
J.J.	63.1	144	32	185	8′44″
S.M.	56.9	150	32	160	6′47″
Average	60.4	137	31	157	7′19″
F.O.	16.7	102	68	70	64′
E.G.	12.0	147	51	111	50′
H.K.	14.0	130	20	37	55′
Average	14.2	126	45	73	56′

* This range was calculated as average values ±2 SD from the 51 patients with normal type of esterase described in the previous section.

** Duration of apnea after 100 mgm. of succinylcholine as calculated from responses to various doses. See text for further definition.

Nine patients with atypical esterase were available for observations on the duration of apnea after succinylcholine. Some data to characterize these patients are presented in table 3. These 9 patients were subdivided into two groups according to their Dibucaine Number. All the Dibucaine Numbers from 46.1 to

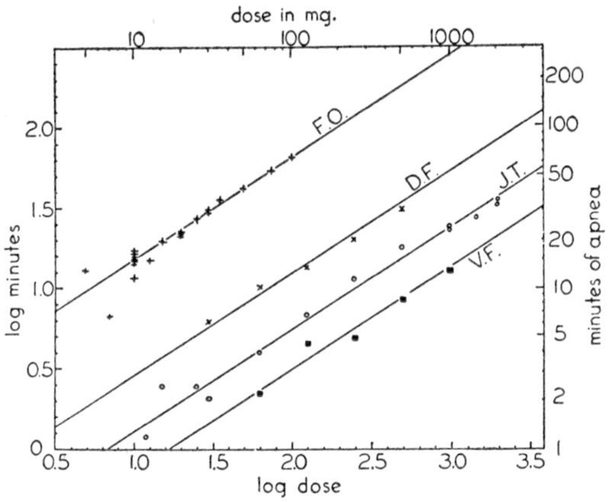

FIG 5. Relation between dose of succinylcholine chloride (mgm.) and duration of apnea in 4 representative patients.

Lines with the slope 0.6365 (*cf.* fig. 3) have been drawn to the data of 4 patients in this logarithmic plot.

Patient V. F. represents a case with a high level of usual type of esterase. Patient J. T.: low level of usual type of esterase. Patient D. F.: low level of intermediate type of esterase. Patient F. O.: atypical esterase. No evidence for any capacity of his serum to hydrolyse succinylcholine.

69.7 are classified as intermediate because they appear to be genetically of one group.

The six cases with intermediate Dibucaine Numbers have a significantly ($P < 0.01$) lower average esterase activity than the normal group but the esterase levels of five of these patients are within the normal range, *i.e.* within $\pm$ twice the standard deviation. On the other hand, only two of these patients have a response towards succinylcholine within the normal range.

The three cases with low Dibucaine Numbers have a low esterase activity. Following succinylcholine, the duration of apnea is far longer than in the normal or intermediate groups.

Full dose-duration curves of some selected patients representing all three esterase types, are shown in fig. 5 in a double logarithmic plot. Lines with the same slope as in fig. 3 are drawn to the individual data. The two "normal" patients were about the most (patient V. F.) and the least (patient J. T.) resistant patients towards succinylcholine from the group of 51 patients described in the first section. Both had a Dibucaine Number of 80, one had an esterase level of 310 units, the other 130 units.[2] The data of patient D. F. were selected for presentation because he is the patient most susceptible to succinylcholine of the group with intermediate Dibucaine Numbers. His Dibucaine Number of 46 is

[2] None of the mentally ill patients receiving succinylcholine had a normal Dibucaine Number and at the same time a pathologically low esterase activity. Hence, we were particularly grateful to Dr. R. Matthews, anaesthetist at St. Michael's Hospital, Toronto, who submitted for investigation the serum of a surgical patient because of prolonged apnea after succinylcholine. This patient was a woman in fair condition three months after having suffered severe burns. Although she had received numerous blood transfusions, her esterase

very rare and may be about the lowest value which can occur in the intermediate group. All the other curves of this group fall between those of patients J. T. and D. F. Patient F. O. received succinylcholine more often than the other two patients with low Dibucaine Numbers and his data are, therefore, presented in fig. 5.

As stated above, apnea in this paper means complete paralysis of the respiratory muscles. The times of the return to a normal or adequate respiration have not been exactly measured. However, it has been the impression by clinical observation that the interval was prolonged between the first signs of the returning respiration and adequate respiration in the patients with low Dibucaine Numbers. For instance, patient F. O. was totally apneic for 63 minutes after 100 mgm. (fig. 5) but it took 3 hours till the administration of oxygen could be entirely stopped. That is, the ratio of these two measurements of apnea was approximately 1:3. In the patients with normal type of esterase, the corresponding ratio was probably close to 3:4, and in the intermediate group 2:3.

Although the patients with low Dibucaine Numbers were grossly sensitive towards succinylcholine, they reacted normally towards decamethonium. This statement is based on the injection of 18 doses of 3 to 7 mgm. of decamethonium iodide into 10 patients with all three types of esterase. In five treatments, an injection of edrophonium was made which did not seem to alter the response towards decamethonium.

Discussion. A linear relationship between log dose of succinylcholine and log duration of action in cats has been described by Thesleff (1952). Thus, the dose-duration curves are logarithmic in at least two species but the slope of these curves is distinctly steeper in man ($b = 0.637 \pm 0.015$) than in cats ($b = 0.416 \pm 0.010$). Espinosa and Artusio (1954) measured the depth of respiratory depression during intravenous infusion of succinylcholine in 50 surgical patients. They described a linear relationship between log dose and per cent respiration.

The four factors—age, body weight, type of esterase, and esterase level—appeared to influence the individual susceptibility towards succinylcholine (*cf.* table 2).

The correlation coefficient of the response Y_{100} with esterase level (r_{y2}) was significantly greater than those with either body weight (r_{y1}) or age (r_{y3}). There was a trend of Y_{100} to be more closely correlated with age (r_{y3}) than with body weight (r_{y1}). However, this trend was reversed if esterase levels were included in these correlations ($R_{y.12}$ and $R_{y.23}$). This could mean that the coefficients for age and response were high only because the coefficient for age and esterase (r_{23}) was relatively high. An analysis of variance in regression, based on the multiple correlation coefficient $R_{y.123}$ and a comparison with $R_{y.12}$ also suggested that age had no independent significant influence upon the duration of action of succinylcholine. Nevertheless, had esterase levels not been known, the responsiveness towards succinylcholine could have been better predicted by regarding both body weight and age than by considering the weight alone (*cf.* r_{y1} and $R_{y.13}$).

level was 40 units, while her Dibucaine Number was 76.2 (*cf.* case IV, fig. 2 of Kalow and Genest, 1957). She was apneic for 12 minutes after the injection of 100 mgm. succinylcholine chloride.

The numerous references on the relation of esterase level and action of succinylcholine have been summarized in a recent review by Brücke (1956). According to this review, the role of age which appeared in these data has not been previously noted. The small influence of body weight upon the duration of action of succinylcholine has been stressed by Evans and Lehmann (1954).

The capacity of human serum to hydrolyse succinylcholine depends on both type and concentration of esterase. The occurrence of different types of human serum cholinesterase has not yet been extensively described; detailed publications are in preparation. The type characterized by Dibucaine Numbers below 20 appears to be of extremely low activity under many, but not all, testing conditions. This type did not readily hydrolyse succinylcholine in the Warburg apparatus (Kalow, unpublished observation). That is, for practical purposes some patients are devoid of serum cholinesterase activity towards succinylcholine, although the esterase is more or less active towards other substances. This explains, for instance, the great difference of susceptibility for succinylcholine between patients F. O. and D. F. (table 3 and fig. 5), although their esterase levels are similar in conventional terms.

Since patient F.O. reacted normally towards decamethonium and edrophonium, the prolonged action of succinylcholine in his case cannot find any other explanation than lack of serum cholinesterase activity. Probably because of his age and low body weight, he reacted even slightly longer towards a given dose of succinylcholine than two other patients with the same type of esterase. It is, therefore, reasonable to assume that the dose-effect curve of this patient (fig. 5) shows the maximum duration of complete apnea which can be caused by succinylcholine and absence of esterase activity in any patient. The cases described by Lehmann and Ryan (1956) as "familial incidence of low pseudocholinesterase level" are most likely of that type.

The cases with intermediate Dibucaine Numbers constitute a rather diverse group. For instance, the reaction of patient R. D. (table 3) towards succinylcholine is within the normal range. On the other hand, patient J. J., a 32 year old man with a normal esterase level and body weight, is more sensitive towards succinylcholine than would be expected from these data. However, his serum did not split succinylcholine in the Warburg apparatus with the rate to be expected from his conventional esterase level. The Dibucaine Number of patient D. F. is the lowest which we believe will be found in this intermediate group. Hence his reaction towards succinylcholine (*c.f.* fig. 5) may represent the extreme which can occur within this intermediate group.

The frequency of atypical forms of esterase reported here (9 in 60) is not representative of the frequency of occurrence in unselected patients (Kalow, 1956b).

SUMMARY

Succinylcholine was repeatedly administered to 60 male patients as an adjuvant to electroshock therapy. Since each patient received between 5 and 25 treatments, the relationship between intravenously injected doses of succinylcholine and duration of complete apnea could be measured.

Of the 60 patients, 51 had the usual or normal type of serum cholinesterase, as defined by inhibition tests with dibucaine. In these 51 patients, there was a normal distribution of the logarithm of the dose of succinylcholine necessary to produce a standard effect. Also, there was a normal distribution of the logarithms of the minutes of apnea after standard doses.

In all 60 patients, there was a linear relationship between log dose and log duration of apnea. The slope of this line seemed to be constant from person to person.

The responsiveness towards succinylcholine was correlated with esterase level, age, and body weight. The correlation with esterase activity was preponderant and tended to obscure the role of body weight. Age was a secondary factor.

The influence of the two atypical forms of serum cholinesterase was demonstrated by some examples. One of these types of esterase does not hydrolyse succinylcholine in vivo. The dose-duration curve from a patient with this type of esterase may, therefore, indicate the limits of duration of apnea which can occur after succinylcholine, due to a lack of esterase activity.

ACKNOWLEDGMENTS. Thanks are due to Dr. T. D. Cumberland, Superintendent, Ontario Hospital, New Toronto, for his encouragement and support of the clinical studies; to Dr. J. K. W. Ferguson, Director, Connaught Medical Research Laboratories, University of Toronto, for his stimulating interest; and to Prof. H. Cullumbine, Department of Pharmacology, University of Toronto, for reading the manuscript.

This work was supported by a Mental Health Grant from the Ontario Department of Health, and the Insulin Fund of the University of Toronto.

REFERENCES

BRÜCKE, F.: Pharmacol. Rev., **8:** 265, 1956.
ESPINOSA, A. M., AND ARTUSIO, J. F.: Anesthesiology, **15:** 239, 1954.
EVANS, F. T., AND LEHMANN, H.: Lancet, **II:** 601, 1954.
DE LA HUERGA, J., YESINICK, G., AND POPPER, H.: Am. J. Clin. Path., **22:** 1126, 1952.
KALOW, W.: Can. Anaesth. Soc. J., **3:** 22, 1956a.
KALOW, W.: Lancet, **II:** 576, 1956b.
KALOW, W., GENEST, K., AND STARON, N.: Fed. Proc., **15:** 444, 1956a.
KALOW, W., AND LINDSAY, H. A.: Can. J. Biochem. and Physiol., **33:** 568, 1955.
KALOW, W., AND LINDSAY, H. A.: THIS JOURNAL, **116:** 34, 1956b.
KALOW, W., AND GENEST, K.: Can. J. Biochem. and Physiol., **35:** In press. 1957.
LEHMANN, H., AND RYAN, E.: Lancet, **II:** 124, 1956.
THESLEFF, S.: Acta Physiol. Scand., **26:** 103, 1952.
WOLFSIE, J. H., AND WINTER, G. D.: Arch. Ind. Hyg. and Ind. Med., **6:** 43, 1952.

ANTAGONISM OF TUBOCURARINE III: TIME COURSE OF ACTION OF PYRIDOSTIGMIN, NEOSTIGMINE, AND EDROPHONIUM *IN VIVO* AND *IN VITRO*

CEDRIC M. SMITH, JAMES C. MEAD AND KLAUS R. UNNA

Department of Pharmacology, University of Illinois College of Medicine, Chicago

Received for publication January 16, 1957

The rapid onset and short duration of action of edrophonium with respect to neostigmine has been noted by a number of investigators (Cowan, 1938; MacFarlane *et al.*, 1950; *cf.* Riker, 1953). Another neostigmine analogue, pyridostigmin (Mestinon), has been reported to have a slower onset and a longer duration of action than neostigmine, both in potentiating the response of rat diaphragm and masseter muscle to nerve stimulation and in the improvement in muscle strength in patients with myasthenia gravis (Bauer and Schmidt, 1953; Osserman *et al.*, 1954; Tether, 1954). The anti-cholinesterase activity of pyridostigmin was found to be one-fifth (Hobbiger, 1950) to one-tenth (Blaschko *et al.*, 1949) the activity of neostigmine, but it was also found to be a less potent antagonist of curare than neostigmine (Blaschko *et al.*, 1949).

It was of interest to compare the time course of action and potency of these compounds *in vitro* and *in vivo*[1], since it has been presumed that the anti-curare and acetylcholine potentiating properties of edrophonium and neostigmine are primarily the result of their anti-cholinesterase activity (Hobbiger, 1952; Pelikan *et al.*, 1954; Nastuk and Alexander, 1954; Smith *et al.*, 1952).

METHODS AND COMPOUNDS. The cholinesterase (ChE) inhibitors used in these studies were neostigmine bromide, edrophonium chloride (3-hydroxyphenyldimethylethylammonium chloride, Tensilon) and pyridostigmin bromide (the dimethyl carbamic ester of 3-hydroxy-1-methylpyridinium bromide, Mestinon). The edrophonium and pyridostigmin were generously supplied by Hoffmann LaRoche Inc. The other compounds used were acetylcholine chloride (ACh) and tubocurarine chloride (TC).

Inhibition of cholinesterase. Determination of activity of ChE inhibitors: The cholinesterase inhibitory activity of the three compounds was studied by the Warburg manometric technique of Ammon (1934), as modified by Bain (1950). The enzyme was a commercially available purified bovine erythrocyte cholinesterase (ChE), specified to be a "true" cholinesterase and inactive toward benzoylcholine, kindly supplied by Dr. M. L. Tainter, Sterling-Winthrop Research Institute.

The control flasks contained enzyme, substrate and buffer. In all experiments the substrate was acetylcholine (ACh) in final concentration of 1.1×10^{-2} *M*. The cholinesterase concentration was selected to produce fifteen to thirty microliters of gas per five minutes and ranged from 0.06 to 0.12 mgm. of the above preparation. The buffer, inhibitor and enzyme were placed in the main compartment of the flasks; the enzyme being added just before joining them to the manometers. The total time elapsing between the addition of the ChE to the flasks and the addition of the ACh from the side arm varied between 30 to 40 minutes. Readings were made at five-minute intervals for at least thirty minutes subse-

[1] A preliminary report has already appeared (Smith and Mead, 1956).

quent to the addition of ACh. The temperature of the bath was 37 ± 0.5°C. in all experiments. Corrections for non-enzymatic hydrolysis of ACh were not required.

The ChE inhibiting activity of the compounds was expressed as:

$$\text{per cent inhibition} = 100 - \frac{\text{mean } \mu\text{l. } CO_2\text{/five minutes/experimental flask} \times 100}{\text{mean } \mu\text{l. } CO_2\text{/five minutes/control flask}}.$$

The per cent inhibition was always calculated from readings taken at five-minute intervals for a total period of thirty minutes following the addition of ACh to the flask. Per cent inhibition of CO_2 production was plotted against the logarithm of the molar concentration of the inhibitor and the concentration required to produce 50 per cent inhibition of enzyme activity (IC_{50}) determined by interpolation. At least five different concentrations of the inhibitors were used in each experiment and the experiment was repeated at least three times. The inhibitory activity of two different compounds was always assayed simultaneously.

Determination of the time course of the development of inhibition: The inhibitor was placed in one side arm of a double arm flask, ACh in the other, and the ChE and buffer in the main compartment of the flask. The final volume of the fluid in the flasks was 2.8 ml. and the final concentration of the inhibitor was the IC_{50} as previously determined. After the flasks had been gassed, the inhibitor was tipped into the main compartment. ACh was tipped into the compartment at various time intervals after the addition of the inhibitor. The time intervals between the addition of inhibitor and substrate varied from 0 to 30 minutes; three time intervals were chosen for use in each experiment. The per cent inhibition for each flask was calculated from the readings taken during the thirty minutes immediately following the addition of the ACh to flask.

Determination of the time course of the inhibition produced by different concentrations of the inhibitors: In these experiments two groups of flasks were used in each experiment. In one group of flasks, the conditions were identical to those described in the section on "determination of activity", with the exception that measurements of CO_2 production were continued at five-minute intervals for a total of at least seventy minutes. In the other group of flasks, both the ACh and various concentrations of the inhibitor were placed in the side arm together. Thus, in one case the inhibitor was in contact with the enzyme from thirty to forty minutes prior to the addition of the substrate, while in the other case the inhibitor and the substrate were added to the ChE simultaneously. The per cent inhibition of CO_2 production for both groups of flasks was calculated as above, except that alternate thirty-minute intervals after the addition of the ACh (0 to 30, 10 to 40, 20 to 50, 30 to 60, and 40 to 70 minutes) were used for calculations.

Isolated frog rectus abdominis muscle preparation. The frog rectus abdominis muscle was prepared for recording as described previously (Smith *et al.*, 1952). The response of the muscle to 40 micrograms/ml. of ACh was considered to be a maximal response. The response of the muscle to at least four other logarithmically spaced concentrations of ACh were determined.

After the initial dose-response curve for ACh was obtained, a concentration of ACh, which produced a response between fifteen and thirty per cent of the maximal response, was chosen and the responses to this concentration again determined. The bath solution was then changed to one containing a ChE inhibitor. Two minutes after the ChE inhibitor was added, the response of the muscle to the single concentration of ACh was determined' Eight minutes later and thereafter at ten-minute intervals, the response of the muscle to this concentration of ACh was measured. The bath solution was changed at least three times between responses to ACh. When the response of the muscle to this concentration of ACh appeared to be approaching a constant value, a dose-response curve for ACh was again determined, employing at least four concentrations of ACh.

The effect of ACh was expressed as the ACh EC_{50}, *i.e.*, that concentration of ACh required to produce a fifty per cent of maximal response as calculated from the probit of per cent of maximal response—log concentration of acetylcholine curve. The ratio of the control ACh EC_{50} to the ACh EC_{50} determined in the presence of varying concentrations of a ChE inhibitor was plotted against the logarithm of the concentrations of the ChE inhibitor and the slope (b), its standard error (s_b), and the concentration of anti-cholinesterase required to halve the amount of ACh required to produce a given effect determined (Smith *et al.*, 1952).

The time course of the development of the potentiation of ACh, as measured by the response of the muscle to a given concentration of ACh, was expressed graphically, plotting the potentiation of ACh vs. time after the addition of the anti-cholinesterase to the bath solution. The potentiation of ACh by the ChE inhibitors was expressed in terms of ACh concentrations as the ratio of the actual concentration of ACh employed to the concentration of ACh which would have been required, in the absence of a potentiator, to produce the observed ("potentiated") response. At least four muscles were employed for each concentration of the ChE inhibitor and the effects of at least four concentrations of the inhibitors were studied.

Rabbits. The anticurare activity and the time course of curare antagonism produced by the three ChE inhibitors were investigated by means of a head drop crossover technique (Pelikan and Unna, 1952). The concentration of the tubocurarine solution was selected in each case to produce head drop within a period of from two to six minutes (0.9 ml. to 2.5 ml. of solution). The dose of tubocurarine which produced a head drop in a rabbit was designated as the head drop dose (HDD) for that rabbit.

Compounds to be tested for anticurare activity were administered to the animal intravenously over a period of one minute in a volume equal to 1 ml./kgm. of body weight. The injection of tubocurarine was begun within ten seconds after the end of the injection of edrophonium. In the case of the other two ChE inhibitors, there was a delay of one minute before the timed intravenous injection of the tubocurarine was begun.

The anticurare activity of a given dose of the ChE inhibitor was expressed as the ratio of the HDD of tubocurarine given after the inhibitor ("Protected HDD") to the HDD of the tubocurarine given alone ("Control HDD"). "Control HDD's" and "Protected HDD's" were obtained on successive days. The ratio was determined for each animal individually and at least three animals were employed at each dose level of a ChE inhibitor.

A number of different doses of each of the ChE inhibitors were tested in order to establish an approximate dose response curve for each compound and to find that dose which produced the maximum anticurare effect.

The time course of the anticurare activity of the compounds was studied by determining the HDD's of tubocurarine at four to eight time intervals after the administration of maximally effective doses of each of the inhibitors.

Statistical methods and terminology, unless otherwise specified, are those used by Snedecor (1946).

RESULTS. *Inhibition of cholinesterase.* The slope and standard error of the slope of the log concentration-per cent inhibition curve and the concentration of the compounds required to produce 50 per cent inhibition of the activity of bovine erythrocyte cholinesterase (IC_{50}) are given in table 1. It can be seen that pyridostigmin is about 1/8 as potent as neostigmine and that edrophonium is 1/60 as effective an anti-cholinesterase as neostigmine. These values agree very well with those previously reported (Blaschko *et al.*, 1949; Hobbiger, 1950) and with a recent report of Randall *et al.*, (1955). The slopes of the log concentration-per cent inhibition curve were approximately the same for neostigmine and pyridostigmin, but that obtained with edrophonium was significantly steeper.

The relationship between the time during which an inhibitor was in contact with the enzyme before the addition of the substrate and the per cent inhibition produced, as measured during the first thirty minutes after the addition of the substrate, is illustrated in figure 1. The concentration of each inhibitor was the IC_{50} as determined previously. (These concentrations are slightly different from those presented in table 1, since the data on table 1 include all experiments,

TABLE 1

Potency of cholinesterase inhibitors

The inhibitors were added to ChE 30–40 minutes prior to the addition of ACh. IC_{50} = concentration required to produce 50% inhibition of enzyme activity. b = slope of log concentration vs. per cent of inhibition curve. s_b = standard error of the slope. n = number of experiments. At least 5 different concentrations of each of the compounds were employed. The number of replications per each concentration varied with the different compounds.

Compound	IC_{50}	b	s_b	n
Neostigmine	0.23×10^{-6} *M*	15.3	4.5	22
Pyridostigmin	1.8×10^{-6} *M*	19.4	2.2	26
Edrophonium	36.9×10^{-6} *M*	43.6	2.7	20

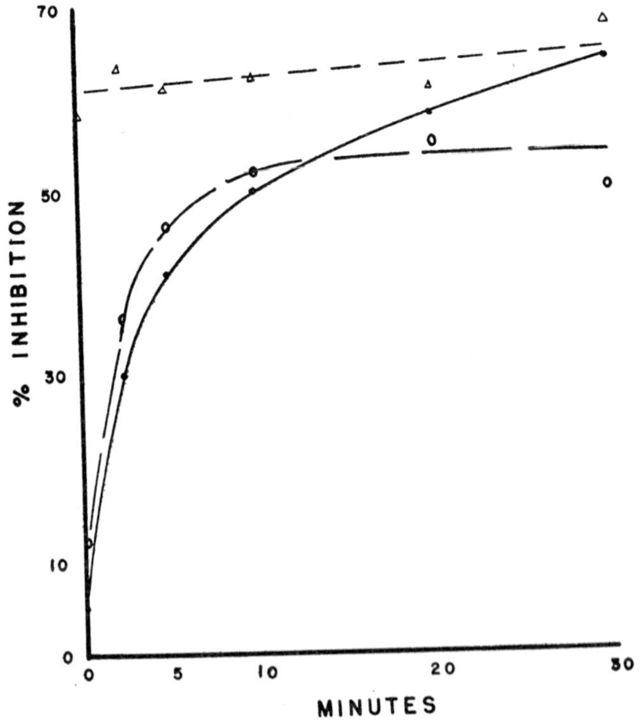

FIG. 1. Time course of the onset of inhibition of cholinesterase.

Ordinate—per cent inhibition of cholinesterase activity. Abscissa—time between the addition of the cholinesterase inhibitor and the addition of acetylcholine to the cholinesterase. ○ — — — Neostigmine 2.5×10^{-7} *M*. ● ——— Pyridostigmin 1.8×10^{-6} *M*. △ - - - - - - Edrophonium 5.0×10^{-5} *M*.

those done prior to and after this study on the time course of anticholinesterase activity.). It is evident that neostigmine reaches its maximum ChE inhibiting activity in about ten minutes, while pyridostigmin continues to produce progressively more inhibition, even after a period of thirty minutes.

The time course of the ChE inhibition produced by the IC_{50} of pyridostigmin, after the addition of the substrate, is shown in figure 2. Each curve represents a different time interval between the addition of the pyridostigmin to the ChE and the addition of the ACh to the ChE in the main compartment of the flask. Similar curves were obtained when neostigmine was employed as the ChE in-

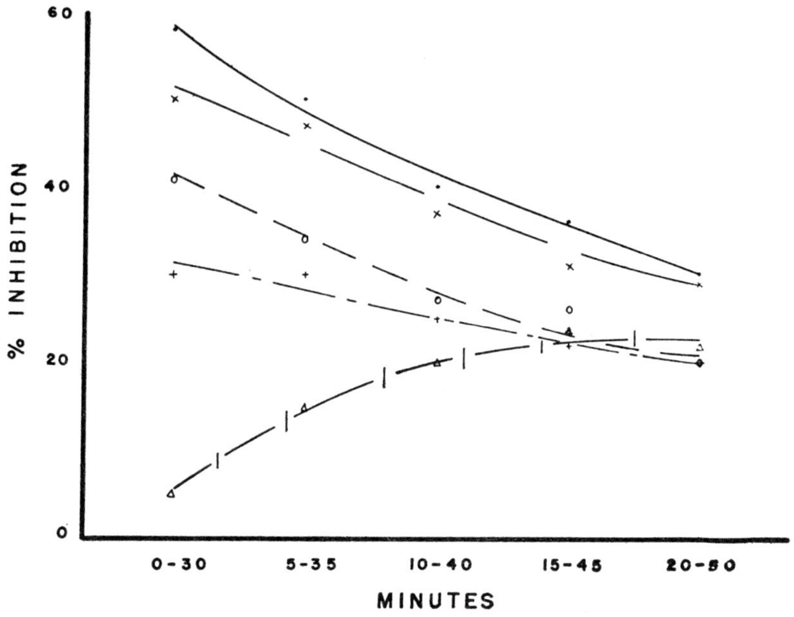

FIG. 2. Time course of cholinesterase inhibition produced by pyridostigmin (1.8×10^{-6} *M*).

Abscissa—time period of measurements after substrate addition. Time interval between addition of pyridostigmin and the addition of substrate to the enzyme varied. △ — — — 0 Minutes between addition of pyridostigmin and substrate. + - - - - - - 2.5 Minutes. ○ — — — — 5 Minutes. × —— —— 10 Minutes. ● —— —— 20 Minutes.

hibitor. It can be seen that the per cent inhibition tends to approach a constant level with the passage of time without respect to the initial level of inhibition. It is evident, therefore, that both the period of incubation of the inhibitor with the enzyme, prior to the addition of the substrate, and the length of time after the addition of the substrate during which observations are made are both critical in the determination of the relative potency of ChE inhibitors.

In contrast to the effects of neostigmine and pyridostigmin as demonstrated in figure 2, the degree of inhibition which was observed with concentrations of edrophonium producing 10 to 100 per cent inhibition of ChE activity did not change appreciably with the passage of time.

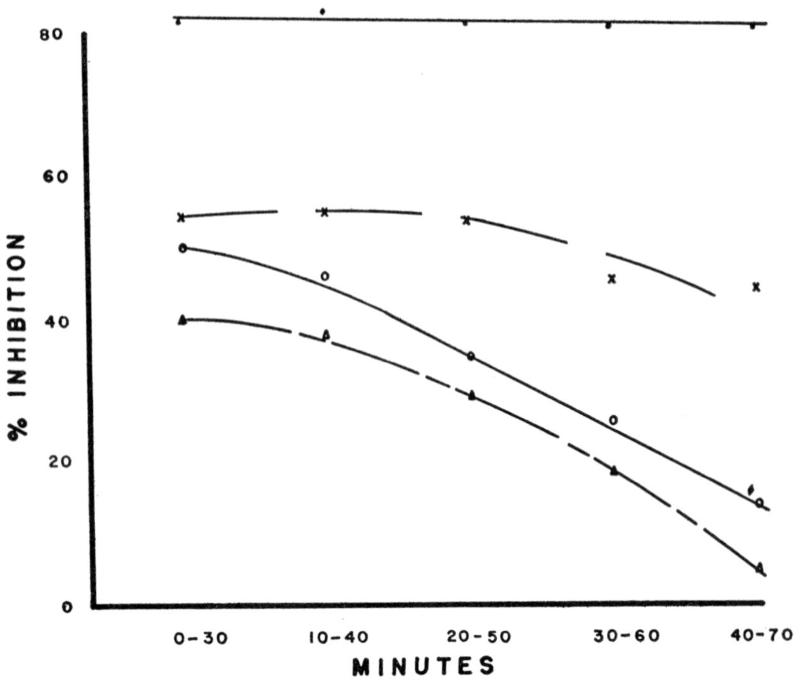

FIG. 3. Time course of cholinesterase inhibition produced by different concentrations of pyridostigmin.

Abscissa—time period of measurements after substrate addition. Inhibitor in contact with the enzyme thirty minutes prior to the addition of acetylcholine. ● ——— 5×10^{-5} *M*. × — — — 1×10^{-5} *M*. ○ ——— 0.3×10^{-5} *M*. △ - - - - - - - - - 0.1×10^{-5} *M*.

The change with time in the degree of inhibition produced by different concentrations of the ChE inhibitors is illustrated for pyridostigmin (figure 3); essentially similar curves were obtained with neostigmine. In this set of experiments, the inhibitor was incubated with the ChE for thirty minutes prior to the addition of ACh. These curves (figure 3) clearly indicate that the degree of inhibition which is observed with the larger concentration of pyridostigmin, as well as neostigmine, tended to remain constant with the passage of time, while the inhibitory activity observed with the lower concentrations decreases after the addition of substrate. Therefore, the log concentration-per cent inhibition curves based on estimates of inhibition obtained only during the 30-minute period after the addition of substrate were found to have a lower slope than such curves which were constructed from data obtained during the 40- to 70-minute period after the addition of substrate. IC_{50}'s for pyridostigmin and neostigmine determined from data obtained the 40- to 70-minute period after addition of substrate were appreciably higher than those obtained during the first 30 minutes—1.1 and 10×10^{-6} *M*, respectively, as compared with 0.23 and 1.8×10^{-6} *M* (table 1). In fact, the slopes of such curves (for neostigmine and pyridostigmin) were not significantly different from the slope of the curve obtained with edrophonium during the first 30-minute period. However, the degree of inhibition produced by different concentrations of edrophonium tended to remain constant over the period of time investigated.

Isolated from rectus abdominis muscle preparation. Data from at least 12 different experiments were pooled and that concentration of the ChE inhibitor which decreased the amount of the ACh required to produce a given response by one-half, and the negative log of such a concentration (pS_2), were calculated from log dose-probit effect curves. The concentrations of the inhibitors required to produce this amount of potentiation and the respective pS_2's are given in table 2. In these experiments, both edrophonium and pyridostigmin were found to be about $\frac{1}{25}$ as potent as neostigmine; pyridostigmin was slightly less potent than edrophonium.

The potentiation of the effects of ACh by edrophonium reached a maximum in two minutes or less and the degree of potentiation decreased with passage of time to approach a constant value in ten to twenty minutes (figure 4). In contrast, neostigmine, and pyridostigmin (figures 5 and 6) approached maximal potentiation of ACh only after thirty to fifty minutes after their addition to the bath solution. The triethyl- and trimethylammonium congeners of edrophonium were also investigated and it was found that the curve for the potentiation of ACh by the *trimethyl* derivative was indistinquishable from that obtained with edrophonium. On the other hand, the *triethyl* derivative produced maximal potentiation of ACh ten to thirty minutes after its addition to the bath solution. The degree of decline of ACh potentiation from a maximum similar to that observed with edrophonium (figure 4) was also obtained with its trimethyl and triethyl analogs, but quantitative comparisons among the ethyl analogs of edrophonium were not made.

The concentrations of the ChE inhibitors employed were well below the concentrations which produce any stimulatory effect when added alone to the isolated frog rectus abdominis muscle preparation. In no case was the resting tension of any of the muscles observed to change with any of the ChE inhibitors in concentrations which produced maximum potentiation of the effects of ACh.

TABLE 2

Potentiation of effects of acetylcholine on the frog rectus abdominis muscle

Time elapsing between the addition of the compound and the determination of the degree of ACh potentiation was 30 minutes with edrophonium, 30–60 minutes with neostigmine, and 60–70 minutes with pyridostigmin. Concentration = concentration of compound required to halve the amount of ACh required to produce a given effect. pS_2 = negative logarithm of the above concentration. b = slope of the probit of the per cent increase in the ACh ED_{50} vs. the logarithm of the concentration of ChE inhibitor. s_b = standard error of the slope. n = total number of muscles.

Compound	Concentration	pS_2	b	s_b	n
Neostigmine	0.25×10^{-6} *M*	6.58	2.2	0.5	10
Pyridostigmin	0.86×10^{-6} *M*	5.16	0.67	0.5	15
Edrophonium	3.65×10^{-6} *M*	5.44	1.4	0.5	18

Rabbit experiments. Figure 7 illustrates dose-effect curves plotting the "HDD ratio" vs. dose of the ChE inhibitors. Neostigmine was the most potent tubocurarine antagonist of the three compounds and also had the steepest dose-response curve; pyridostigmin was less potent and its curve had a lower slope, while edrophonium was the least active and had the lowest slope. It should be

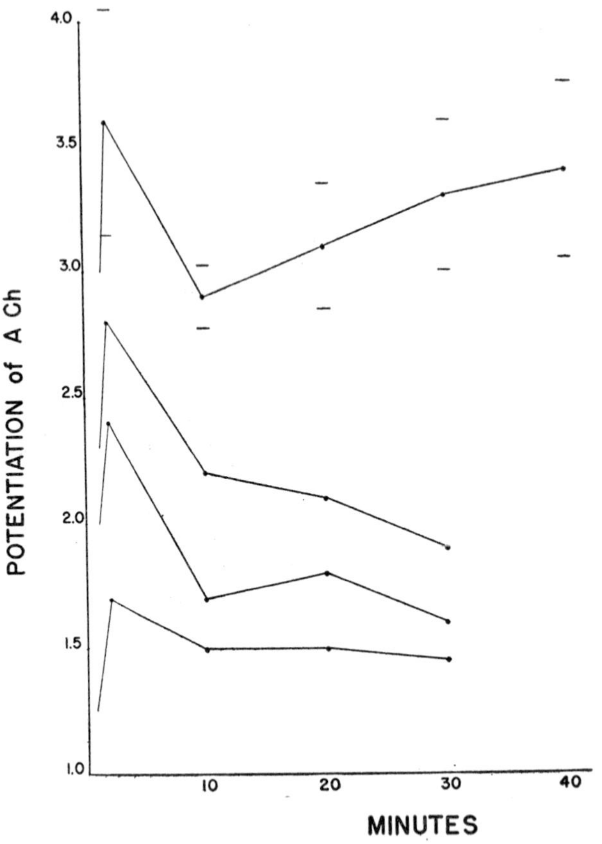

FIG. 4. Time course of potentiation of acetylcholine by edrophonium.

Curves relating potentiation of acetylcholine (see METHODS) with time of the exposure the rectus abdominis muscle of the frog to edrophonium. Concentrations: Top curve, 9.9×10^{-6} *M*, 5.0, 2.5, and bottom curve, 1.25×10^{-6} *M*, respectively. Brackets on top curve denote standard deviation of the mean response. (The variability of responses at this concentration was greater than that obtained with any other concentration or drug in this preparation.)

noted that the effects of optimal doses of neostigmine and pyridostigmin were approximately the same (HDD ratio 1.8 to 2.0), while the largest dose of edrophonium was only capable of increasing the head drop dose of tubocurarine slightly less than 1.5 times.

The duration of the curare antagonism produced by the ChE inhibitors was tested by determining the HDD of the tubocurarine at various time intervals after the administration of the ChE inhibitor (figure 8). The mean HDD ratio after pyridostigmin was found to differ significantly ($P < 0.01$) from the control HDD up to 80 minutes after its administration; HDD ratios after neostigmine were increased significantly up to 60 minutes; but HDD ratios obtained from edrophonium were significantly different from the controls for only 5 minutes. Similar experiments were carried out employing two other doses of each of the

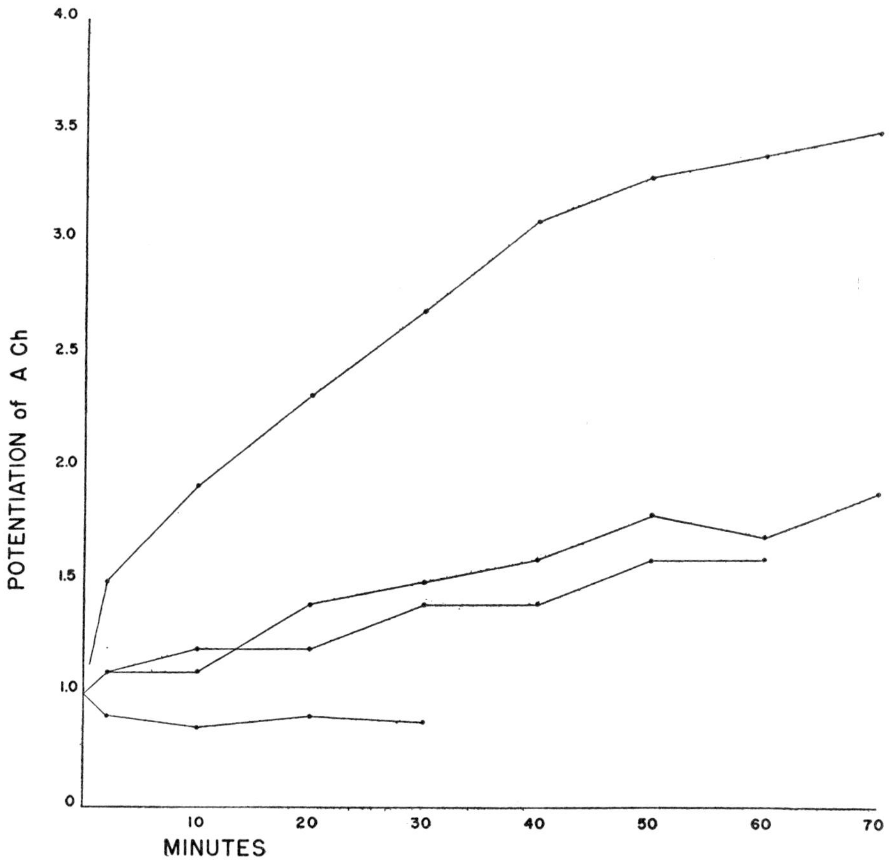

FIG. 5. Time course of the potentiation of acetylcholine by neostigmine (see figure 4). Concentration: Top curve, 0.66×10^{-6} *M*, 0.33, 0.16, 0.08×10^{-6} *M* and bottom curve, a control obtained in the absence of nesotigmine, respectively.

ChE inhibitors and in every case pyridostigmin was found to have a slightly greater duration of action than neostigmine.

The effects of the ChE inhibitors on the duration of head drop was ascertained by measuring the time interval between the beginning of a rapid injection of a ChE inhibitor and the moment at which the tubocurarine was antagonized sufficiently to permit the rabbit to raise its head. The mean time interval for pyridostigmin was found to be 28.9 seconds, for neostigmine 20.1 seconds, and for edrophonium 8.3 seconds (table 3). These values were all significantly different from the mean time for the recovery of the head drop without the injection of ChE inhibitor (382 seconds). All of the means were significantly different from each other (table 3).

DISCUSSION. The time course of action of three inhibitors of cholinesterase has been investigated, using three different techniques, two *in vitro* and one *in vivo*. In the *in vitro* studies there was positive correlation between the rate of production of inhibition of cholinesterase and the rate of production of potentia-

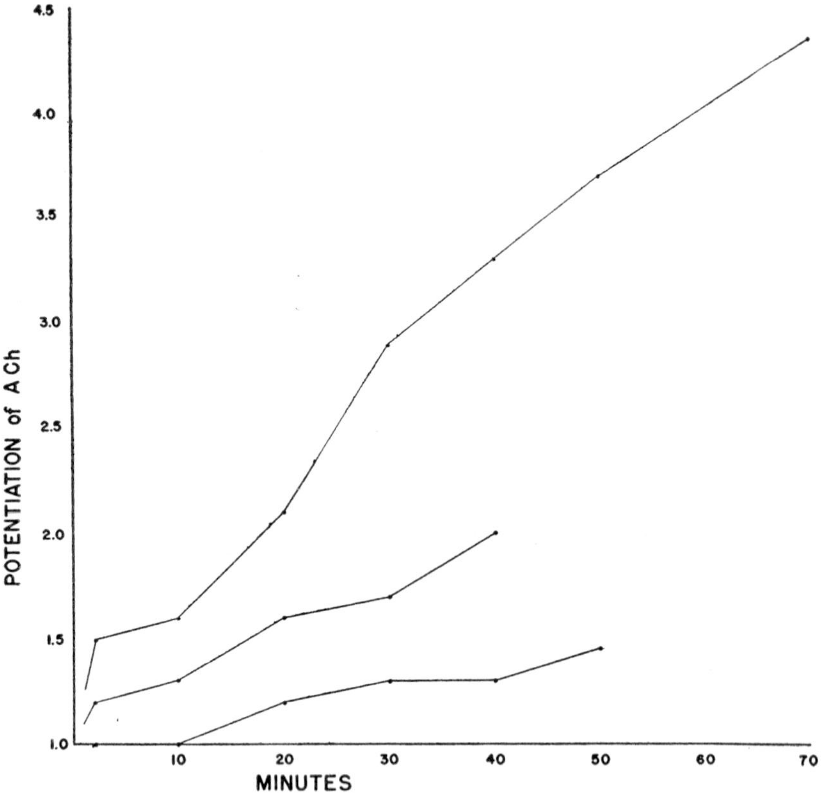

FIG. 6. Time course of the potentiation of acetylcholine by pyridostigmin (see figures 4 and 5).

Concentrations: Top curve, 7.7 × 10^{-6} *M*, 3.8 and bottom curve, 1.9 × 10^{-6} *M*, respectively.

tion of the response of the rectus abdominis muscle to acetylcholine within the series of three compounds. Edrophonium had the most rapid onset of action in the potentiation of acetylcholine and reached equilibrium with the acetylcholine and cholinesterase most rapidly of the three compounds. The recent paper of Wilson (1955), which appeared while this work was in progress, reports that the time required for completion of the association of edrophonium and eel cholinesterase does not exceed 12 seconds, and that the time for one-half dissociation was not more than 30 seconds.

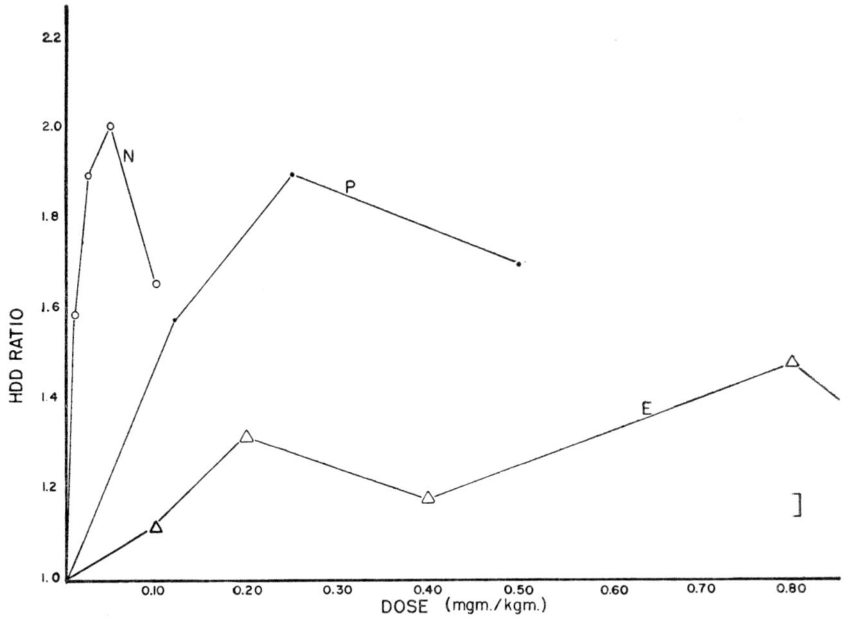

FIG. 7. Dose response curves for neostigmine (N), pyridostigmin (P), and edrophonium (E) Antagonism of tubocurarine in the rabbit.

Ordinate: Mean HDD ratio; HDD Ratio $= \frac{\text{HDD after antagonist}}{\text{HDD of tubocurarine alone}}$. Abscissa: Dose of antagonist in mgm./kgm. Brackets indicates largest standard deviation of a single mean HDD ratio which was obtained.

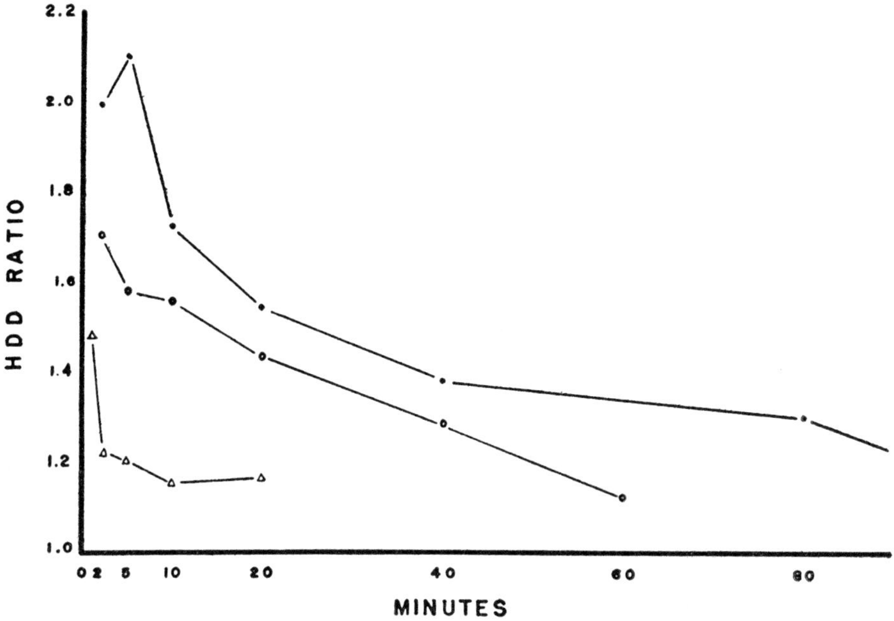

FIG. 8. Duration of antagonism of tubocurarine in the rabbit.

Ordinate: Mean HDD ratio. Abscissa: Time in minutes after intravenous injection of the antagonist. Top curve, pyridostigmin 0.25 mgm./kgm., middle curve, neostigmine 0.05 mgm./kgm., bottom curve, edrophonium 0.80 mgm./kgm.

TABLE 3

Antagonism of tubocurarine by cholinesterase inhibitors in rabbits

Antagonist administered one minute after HDD of tubocurarine. $\bar{x}$ = Mean of time in seconds for recovery from head drop. $s_{\bar{x}}$ = Standard error of mean time. n = Number of animals.

Compounds	n	Recovery time	$s_{\bar{x}}$
		seconds	
Neostigmine	14	20.1	1.3
Pyridostigmine	15	28.0	1.7
Edrophonium	16	8.3	0.5
None (control)	24	382.0	34.0

We have calculated association and dissociation rate constants; however, these values are only approximate, since no consideration could be given to the fact that addition of substrate would shift the equilibrium toward dissociation of the enzyme-inhibitor complex, and the necessary data for enzyme activity with varying concentrations of substrate was not obtained.

It could be pointed out that the slope of the per cent inhibition vs. log concentration curve for edrophonium approaches the theoretical slope expected in competitive inhibition (57.5) in the region of 50 per cent inhibition (Goldstein, 1944). Slopes of such curves obtained with neostigmine and pyridostigmin were found to be not significantly different from slope of curve for edrophonium when enough time was allowed (±40 minutes) for steadystate conditions to be approached.

The curves relating the potentiation of acetylcholine and the time during which the muscle was in contact with edrophonium (figure 4) suggest that this potentiation of acetylcholine has two components. Certainly the speed with which edrophonium inhibits the enzyme in vitro indicates that it could act rapidly enough to account for the initial rapid potentiation. In our previous report (Smith *et al.*, 1952), edrophonium was in contact with the muscle for a period of 20 to 30 minutes prior to determination of acetylcholine potentiation and, therefore, the marked initial potentiation of acetylcholine was not observed. The curves obtained in this study for potentiation of acetylcholine by edrophonium might be explained by postulating that the inhibition of cholinesterase takes place rapidly and that there is a secondary inhibition of acetylcholine-induced depolarization which has a slower time course.

In vivo studies on the rate of onset of anticurare activity and the duration of effects as determined by a rabbit head drop cross-over technique demonstrates similar relationships among the actions of the compounds as was found with the *in vitro* experiments. Edrophonium had the most rapid onset of anticurare action and the shortest duration of effect. Neostigmine and pyridostigmin were similar, but pyridostigmin had a slightly longer duration of action and slightly longer onset time than did neostigmine. These findings are all consistent with the previous reports cited in the introduction.

Both neostigmine and pyridostigmin exert their anticurare effect *in vivo* in much less time than the time required *in vitro* for the production of maximum inhibition of cholinesterase. Consideration of all of the rate-controlling factors, including distribution through the vascular system, diffusion to site of the cholinesterase, and rates of destruction, storage, and elimination of each of the inhibitors, in addition to kinetics of particular muscle enzyme-inhibitor combination, would be required before definitive statements involving causal relationships between *in vivo* and *in vitro* kinetic studies could be made. Riker (1953), among others, has pointed out the hazards of correlating information obtained in "steadystate" systems with that obtained in dynamic systems. On the basis of the present evidence, however, it is postulated that the differences among neostigmine, pyridostigmin, and edrophonium, with regard to rate of onset of anticurare effect and the duration of this effect, are primarily related to the differences in the kinetics of inhibitor-cholinesterase combination.

On the other hand, it should be pointed out that there was no positive correlation between the relative potencies of three compounds as anti-cholinesterases and their potencies as potentiators of acetylcholine on the frog rectus muscle (tables 1 and 2).

SUMMARY

The potency and the time course of action of three reversible ChE inhibitors, neostigmine, pyridostigmin, and edrophonium have been studied *in vivo* and *in vitro*.

The effects of these compounds on the activity of a purified bovine erythrocyte acetylcholinesterase were determined: a) Neostigmine was the most potent of the three compounds in inhibiting the hydrolysis of ACh followed, in order, by pyridostigmin, and edrophonium; b) edrophonium produced its maximum inhibition in the absence of substrate much more rapidly than did neostigmine or pyridostigmin; and c) the inhibition of ChE by edrophonium was reversed by the addition of substrate too rapidly for the time course to be measured with the manometric technique, while the inhibition produced by neostigmine and pyridostigmin was reversed by the addition of substrate much more slowly.

The degree and time course of the potentiation of the effects of ACh on the rectus abdominis muscle of the frog by the ChE inhibitors were characterized: a) Edrophonium and pyridostigmin were approximately equally potent, but only $\frac{1}{25}$ as potent as neostigmine; b) neostigmine and pyridostigmin required from thirty to fifty minutes to produce maximum potentiation, but with edrophonium, an initial maximum potentiation of response was observed two minutes after the inhibitor was added to the bath.

The compounds were compared with respect to their ability to antagonize tubocurarine induced head drop in rabbits: a) Neostigmine was the most potent antagonist, pyridostigmin less active, and edrophonium the least potent of the three compounds; b) the duration of the anticurare effect of edrophonium was less than that of neostigmine and pyridostigmin, $\frac{1}{12}$ and $\frac{1}{16}$ respectively; and c) intravenously administered edrophonium produced the most rapid antagonism of the effects of tubocurarine followed in order by neostigmine and pyridostigmin.

The evidence obtained neither directly confirms nor negates the thesis that the potentiation of acetylcholine and antagonism of tubocurarine produced by these compounds is the result of their inhibition of cholinesterase. It is postulated that the differences in the time-effect curves obtained in the intact animal with respect to antagonism of curare produced by these compounds is causally related to the differences among the compounds with respect to the kinetics in the inhibitor-cholinesterases combination and dissociation.

REFERENCES

AMMON, R.: Pflüger's Arch. f. d. ges. Physiol., **233:** 486, 1934.
BAIN, J. A.: Am. J. Physiol., **160:** 187, 1950.
BAUER, H., AND SCHMID, O.: Deutsche Zeits. f. Nerverheilkunde, **169:** 427, 1953.
BLASCKO, H., BULBRING, E., AND CHOU, T. C.: Brit. J. Pharmacol., **4:** 129, 1949.
COWAN, S. L.: J. Physiol., **93:** 215, 1938.
GOLDSTEIN, A.: J. Gen. Physiol., **27:** 529, 1944.
HOBBIGER, F.: Brit. J. Pharmacol., **5:** 37, 1950.
HOBBIGER, F.: Brit. J. Pharmacol., **7:** 223, 1952.
MACFARLANE, D. W., PELIKAN, E. W., AND UNNA, K. R.: THIS JOURNAL, **100:** 382, 1950.
NASTUK, W. L., AND ALEXANDER, J. T.: THIS JOURNAL, **111:** 302, 1954.
OSSERMAN, K. E., TENG, P., AND KAPLAN, L. I.: J.A.M.A., **115:** 961, 1954.
PELIKAN, E. W., AND UNNA, K. R.: THIS JOURNAL, **104:** 354, 1952.
PELIKAN, E. W., SMITH, C. M., AND UNNA, K. R.: THIS JOURNAL, **111:** 30, 1954.
RANDALL, L. O., CONROY, C. E., FERRUGGIA, T. M., KAPPELL, B. H., AND KNOEPPEL, C. R.: Amer. J. Med., **19:** 673, 1955.
RIKER, W. F., JR.: Pharm. Rev., **5:** 1, 1953.
SMITH, C. M., COHEN, H. L., PELIKAN, E. W., AND UNNA, K. R.: THIS JOURNAL, **105:** 391, 1952.
SMITH, C. M., AND MEAD, J. C.: THIS JOURNAL, **116:** 53, 1956.
SNEDECOR, G. W.: Statistical Methods, 4th Ed., Iowa State College Press, Ames, Iowa, 1946.
TETHER, J. E.: Dis. Ner. System, **15:** 227, 1954.
WILSON, I. B.: Arch. int. pharmacodyn., **104:** 204, 1955.

DISTRIBUTION AND METABOLIC FATE OF S^{35}-LABELED MYLERAN[1] (BUSULFAN) IN NORMAL AND TUMOR-BEARING RATS

CHIN-TZU PENG

Radioactivity Research Center, and School of Pharmacy, University of California Medical Center, San Francisco

Received for publication January 19, 1957

Among the mesyloxy type compounds of the structure $CH_3SO_2O(CH_2)_nOSO_2$-CH_3, reported by Haddow and Timmis (1953) as potential agents against Walker rat carcinoma 256, the most active member is Myleran (1,4-dimethanesulfonoxy-butane or Busulfan) with n = 4. This compound has been applied clinically in the treatment of chronic myelocytic leukemia (Galton, 1953; Petrakis *et al.*, 1954; and Frost and Jackson, 1956). The recommended dose is 4 to 6 mgm. daily although single doses as high as 100 to 150 mgm. have been used (Galton, 1953). Treatment with Myleran is generally continued until maximum hematological and clinical improvement is achieved. This may occur in a period from several weeks to several months after the beginning of therapy. Since lack of data on distribution and fate of Myleran may seriously hamper the optimum therapeutic use of the drug, especially during prolonged therapy, this study has been undertaken to provide information on this subject with normal and tumor-bearing rats.

METHODS. *Synthetic.* The labeled Myleran used in this study was sythesized as follows:

Preparation of sodium (thio-S^{35})-sulfate: Forty-five mgm. of inactive sublimed sulfur was added as carrier to a benzene solution (3 ml.) containing 40 (±20 per cent) millicuries of elemental sulfur-35 (procured from the Oak Ridge National Laboratory, as S-35-P-3 Processed item). The solution was evaporated in an atmosphere of nitrogen. The sulfur was then converted to thiosulfate by heating 200 mgm. of sodium sulfite in 5.0 ml. of 0.05 *N* sodium hydroxide under nitrogen in a sealed glass tube at 100°C. until all traces of unreacted sulfur had disappeared.

Preparation of methanesulfonyl-S^{35} chloride: This compound was prepared according to the method of Douglass and Johnson (1938) with slight modification. Methyl thiosulfate, formed from 10 millimoles of dimethyl sulfate and equimolar radioactive sodium thiosulfate in 10 ml. of water, was chlorinated and the formed sulfonyl chloride was then extracted with diethyl ether. The pooled ether extract was shaken with 20 ml. of 1 per cent sodium bisulfite, washed twice with water, and dried over anhydrous sodium sulfate. The ether was removed by distillation and the crude oil was fractionated by diffusion under high vacuum to yield approximately 0.5 gm. (44 per cent) of pure methanesulfonyl chloride.

Synthesis of S^{35}-labeled Myleran: Five hundred mgm. of the *pure* labeled sulfonyl chloride in 2.0 ml. of anhydrous diethyl ether was reacted with 190 mgm. of redistilled 1,4-butanediol in 0.8 ml. of dry pyridine. A few minutes after mixing the two reagents, a heavy oily phase separated which solidified on standing. The solid was filtered by suction and washed freely with anhydrous ether and then with water. Recrystallization from 95 per cent

---

[1] Myleran has been adopted by the Council on Pharmacy and Chemistry, American Medical Association as a new and non-official remedy under the name of Busulfan (J.A.M.A., **161:** 63, 1956).

ethanol gave 270 mgm. (50 per cent) of pure Myleran, m.p. 115–116° uncor. Mixed melting point with an authentic sample[2] showed no depression.

Anal. (for a cold sample synthesized by the same method): Calcd. for $C_6H_{14}O_6S_2$: C, 29.26; H, 5.73; S, 26.04. Found: C, 29.33; H, 5.59; S, 26.09. It was observed that the course of condensation reaction was markedly affected by the purity of the sulfonyl chloride.

Myleran is completely optically transparent in the region of 220 to 310 mμ when measured in an ethanolic solution at a concentration of 2.32 mgm. per cent employing either 1 cm. or 10 cm. cuvettes. The infrared absorption spectra[3] of the prepared compound and the authentic sample were identical, and gave the following bands when measured with a Perdin-Elmer recording infrared spectrophotometer, Model 21, using the method of solid KBr disc: 1478 cm^{-1} (vw), 1417 (w), 1350 (s), 1240 (w), 1171 (s), 1030 (m), 977 (m), 958 (m), 928 (s), 856 (s), 770 (m), and 721 (w).

Radiopurity of the prepared Myleran was defined by the techniques of paper chromatography and radioautography which revealed a single radioactive spot. The specific activity was 40.2 microcuries per mgm., measured by the method of absolute *beta*-counting using a thin mica, large end-window Geiger-Mueller counter. At this relatively high specific activity, labeled Myleran showed incipient radiolysis, ascertained to be 0.3 per cent in three weeks after initial purification and 0.8 per cent in six months by counting the paper chromatograms in sections, thus indicating that the extent of decomposition is negligible. Nevertheless, most of the following experiments were conducted using freshly recrystallized, labeled Myleran.

Biological. Distribution: A total of 16 animals consisting of 8 normal and 8 lymphosarcoma-bearing rats of the Slonaker strain (Scott and Peng, 1955) were used. Body weights ranged from 115 to 241 gm. and the mean size of tumor was 13.1 per cent body weight (range: 5.9 to 16.8 per cent). Injections were made intraperitoneally[4] with 0.8 to 1.0 mgm. of the labeled Myleran solubilized in 0.2 to 0.3 ml. hot propylene glycol; the solution was cooled to near body temperature for injection, care being taken to avoid crystallization. The animals were kept in individual cages and allowed no food but water *ad lib.* for 4, 8, 16, or 32 hours post-injection. For each experiment, the animals were paired, one normal and one tumor-bearing, and matched for sex and weight. Following intracardial puncture with a heparinized syringe, the animals were sacrificed by etherization. Urine voided during this course of experiments was collected. A tight gauze screen placed between the cage and collecting pan separated the feces from urine. Both the feces and the screen were rinsed with water and the rinsings were pooled with urine. The paws, hind legs and the skin of the ventral side of the animals were also washed and the washings combined with main urine pool.

Preparation of the sample: The tissues were removed, weighed and digested with 4 volumes of concentrated hydrochloric acid. The remainder of the animal was ground in a meat grinder and an aliquot taken for digestion. The digest was evaporated using infrared lamps, care being taken to remove the free acid as completely as possible. The carbonized tissues were treated with four volumes of Benedict's solution (Benedict, 1909) on a hot plate for 5 to 10 minutes and then taken to dryness under gentle heat with constant rotation of the container to avoid sputtering. The dried samples were heated at 100° for approximately three hours and then at 500 to 550° in a muffle furnace for sixteen hours. The samples were dissolved in 2 *N* hydrochloric acid and subsequently precipitated as barium sulfate after adding various amounts of sodium sulfate solution as carrier. In all cases radioactivity was determined with a sample mass of 5 to 10 mgm. per cm^2.

[2] The authentic sample of Myleran was obtained from Dr. N. L. Petrakis for which the author is grateful.

[3] The measurement was made by M. K. Hrenoff of the Spectrographic Laboratory, School of Pharmacy.

[4] Because of the extreme insolubility of Myleran in aqueous medium and the ease of hydrolysis in acid solution, oral administration which is practiced clinically was purposely avoided in this study.

Radioassay: Samples of barium sulfate were used to prepare the self absorption curve and were precipitated from solutions containing identical quantities of radiosulfate but varying amounts of the inert carrier. The obtained curve fits the equation $I_t/I_o = (1 - e^{-ut})/ut$[5] with u = 0.25 which is in accord with the reported value, 0.23 (Kulishenko, 1954). The samples were all counted at a comparable geometry to a probable error of ±2 per cent.

Sulfur-35 incorporation: In this experiment, normal and tumor-bearing rats were repeatedly treated with divided doses of Myleran (total 4.5 mgm.) at 0, 8, 16 and 20 hours. Four hours after the last injection, these animals were sacrificed, and the bone marrow, plasma and spleen, were taken for analysis. The spleen was homogenized and precipitated with an equal volume of 10 per cent trichloroacetic acid and thoroughly washed with 5 per cent trichloroacetic acid. The bone marrow was hydrolyzed with 6 *N* hydrochloric acid, and the hydrolysate was freed of excess acid and chromatographed on filter paper. The plasma was studied using the technique of paper electrophoresis.[6]

Nature of the circulating label: In a separate experiment, blood specimens were taken from the tail vein of the normal and tumor-bearing rats at 4, 8, 16 and 32 hours after Myleran injection and used for spotting the Whatman No. 1 filter paper which was then chromatographed and subsequently counted as described for urine. Blood samples from normal untreated animals with added labeled Myleran or labeled methanesulfonic acid (MSA)[7] were used as controls.

Analysis of inorganic, ethereal, and neutral sulfates in urine: The method used was essentially that described in the literature (Hawk *et al.*, 1947) with certain modification found to be more appropriate for these studies. Thus, approximately one-tenth volume of a 24-hour urine specimen was either concentrated *in vacuo* or diluted with water to a volume of 10 ml. One ml. of 6 *N* hydrochloric acid. 1 ml. of 5 per cent sodium sulfate and 2 ml. of 5 per cent barium chloride solutions were successively added to precipitate the sulfate, which was allowed to stand for one hour before centrifuging. The precipitate, representing inorganic sulfate, was washed four times with water and assayed for radioactivity.

The ethereal sulfate fraction was precipitated as barium sulfate after boiling the supernate for 1 hour with 10 ml. of hydrochloric acid, care being taken to restore the volume lost during boiling with water. The radioactivity which remained in solution and consisted of neutral sulfate, was determined by direct-counting an aliquot after drying or by precipitation as barium sulfate after oxidation. Similar results were obtained by both methods.

Preparation of urine samples for paper chromatography: A 24-hour urine specimen, collected in distilled water saturated with C.P. toluene, was concentrated under reduced pressure to about 10 ml. Ten microliters of this concentrate were used directly for chromatography. Separate aliquots were hydrolyzed with twice the volume of redistilled 6 *N* hydrochloric acid in sealed Pyrex tubes by 1) heating for 2 hours in a boiling water-bath, and 2) autoclaving at 18 lbs. pressure for 6 hours. (Care should be exercised in opening the autoclaved tubes since excessive pressure is developed from decomposition products.) All the hydrolysates were taken to dryness under nitrogen at 60° and reconstituted with water. These unfiltered solutions were used for paper chromatography.

Paper chromatography and radioautography: Characterization of the urinary biotransformed products of labeled Myleran was effected by ascending paper chromatography using 95 per cent ethanol as solvent. The radioautogram was prepared from the paper chromatogram using DuPont Xtra Fast, Type 508, X-ray film. For quantitation, the paper chromatograms were cut in sections and counted in a windowless gas flow counter.

---

[5] In this equation, I_t and I_o represent the transmitted activity at thickness t and original activity, respectively; u is the internal absorption coefficient and t, the thickness of the sample, expressed in mgm. per cm^2.

[6] The paper electrophoresis was performed by Miss Mary Jo Cobb of the Clinical Laboratories, University of California Moffitt Hospital, using a Spinco Model R Series C paper electrophoresis cell.

[7] Labeled MSA was obtained by boiling an aqueous acetone solution of Myleran for one hour.

TABLE 1

*Distribution of radioactivity in rats after a single administered dose of S^{35}-labeled Myleran**

Organ	Normal				Tumor-bearing			
	Hours after injection							
	4	8	16	32	4	8	16	32
Bone**	0.16	0.67	0.048	0.010	0.18	0.85	0.061	0.018
Brain	0.39	0.16	0.025	0.025	0.45	0.22	0.056	0.009
G-I tract†	0.82	0.44	0.11	0.022	0.53	0.45	0.20	0.041
Heart	0.40	0.14	0.042	0.027	0.42	0.12	0.071	0.028
Kidneys	0.52	0.29	0.061	0.021	0.69	0.39	0.14	0.026
Liver	0.44	0.19	0.040	0.018	0.43	0.24	0.073	0.019
Lungs	0.42	0.23	0.072	0.018	0.57	0.34	0.12	0.033
Muscle‡	0.32	0.14	0.063	0.018	0.27	0.20	0.093	0.022
Plasma	0.34	0.16	0.030	0.010	0.44	0.18	0.055	0.014
Red blood cells	0.32	0.15	0.038	0.019	0.45	0.23	0.066	0.020
Skin	0.18	0.16	0.034	0.038	0.22	0.12	0.057	0.041
Spleen	0.90	0.44	0.21	0.15	1.2	0.62	0.63	0.19
Stomach	0.43	0.22	0.057	0.019	0.56	0.25	0.10	0.032
Tumor					0.27	0.17	0.050	0.008
Urine	48.5	73.5	92.3	95.8	39.7	68.4	86.1	95.2
Feces	0.17	0.34	0.96	0.65	0.29	0.40	1.76	0.42
Balance of rat	0.18	0.14	0.050	0.017	0.28	0.19	0.11	0.029

* Figures are expressed as per cent of recovered dose per gram of wet tissue, with the exception of urine. The sample size of these organs varied within the following limits, expressed in terms of gm. of wet weight: Bone, 1.3–2.3; Brain, 0.9–1.1; G-I tract, 6.2–13.8; Heart, 0.4–0.9; Kidneys, 0.9–1.6; Liver, 4.1–7.7; Lungs, 0.7–1.5; Muscle, 4.5–10.7; Skin, 12.6–28.4; Spleen, 0.3–0.7; Stomach, 0.9–1.9; Tumors, 7.5–35.8; Feces, 0.1–2.8; and Balance of rat, 70–157.

† Small intestines, colon and their contents were included.

‡ Gastrocnemius muscles from both legs were used.

** This included femurs and bone marrow of both hind legs of the animal.

RESULTS. *Distribution.* The data tabulated in table 1 represent the average of two rats in terms of percentage of the recovered dose per gram wet tissue; while the value for urine is given in per cent *in toto.* Recovery of the administered dose in each experiment ranged from 90.2 to 108.5 per cent with a mean value of 101.5.

In general, a higher level of activity was observed in some organs of the tumor-bearing animals as compared with those of the normal, probably due to the difference in an early elimination of the label. The tissues of the former group tended to concentrate or retain more label than those of the latter group. For instance, spleen not only showed the highest concentration of activity but exhibited a lower rate of elimination. As a result, in the tumor-bearing rat this organ increased from a two-fold activity at the end of 4 to a ten-fold at the end of 32 hours over the activity of other tissues; whereas, in normal animal the increment was from a two to a seven-fold during the same time interval. The bone samples, including the marrow, showed relatively high content of label but the peak values which exceeded those of the spleen were reached only at the end of 8 hours following injection. The fecal excretion followed a similar pattern with a maximum at 16 hours. In other tissues, such as kidneys, heart, lung, muscle, and the balance of the rat, *etc.*, localization of activity was generally high but elimination of the label from the tissues was apparently limited by a logarithmic function, and was independent of individual organs. This was verified by the close similarity of the slopes of the log-log plots (activity vs. time) of the data in table 1. It is interesting to note that the activity in tumor tissue was among the lowest observed. Values for brain, erythrocytes and plasma were close to one another. The activity of skin disappeared at a rate resembling those of other tissues up to 16 hours post injection at which time the rate was reduced. This decrease in rate may indicate a conversion of the radiosulfur into a sulfur-containing amino acid such as cystine of which the hair protein keratin is largely composed. Utilization of sulfate sulfur in the synthesis of cystine in normal rat has been reported by Dziewiatkowski (1954).

The paper electrophoretic studies of the plasma of the treated animals failed to reveal any stable binding between the labeled Myleran or its metabolites and the various plasma protein fractions. Of the radioactivity present in the spleen of the normal and tumor-bearing rats, the trichloroacetic acid precipitate of the homogenates contained approximately 4.8 and 4.5 per cent, respectively. Indications of radioactive spots with R_f values corresponding to those of cystine and cysteine were obtained from the bone marrow after hydrolysis; however, the levels of activities were so low that further confirmatory tests were not feasible.

Chromatography of whole blood revealed the circulating label at 4-, 8-, 16- and 32-hour periods post injection as predominantly intact Myleran. The amount present when expressed in terms of percentage of activity in blood was far in excess of that found in urine (*vide infra*). However, the unusual retention of activity at the point of application on chromatogram made quantitation difficult. A similar phenomenon was also observed with the blood of a normal untreated rat with labeled Myleran, or labeled MSA added. This retention of label by blood could be explained on the basis of a sorption phenomenon which accompanied the denaturation of blood proteins on drying and on imbibing ethanol. During the process of irrigation, ethanol was able to desorb more of the sorbed MSA but less of the sorbed Myleran, probably because of the poor solubility of the latter in this solvent in the cold.

Urinary excretion and metabolites: As indicated in table 1, excretion of label in normal rat at 4 hours post injection was greater than that in tumor-bearing animal. This difference represents a real difference since additional studies on excretion using two more groups of animals yielded results of similar order of magnitude. In both groups of animals, practically 95 to 96 per cent of the administered dose appeared in the urine by 32 hours. Inorganic, ethereal and neutral sulfates were found in ratios of, respectively, 21.5:9.8:1000 in the normal, and 30.3:10.6:1000 in the tumor-bearing rats. Paper chromatography and radioautography of various urine samples revealed in general the presence of

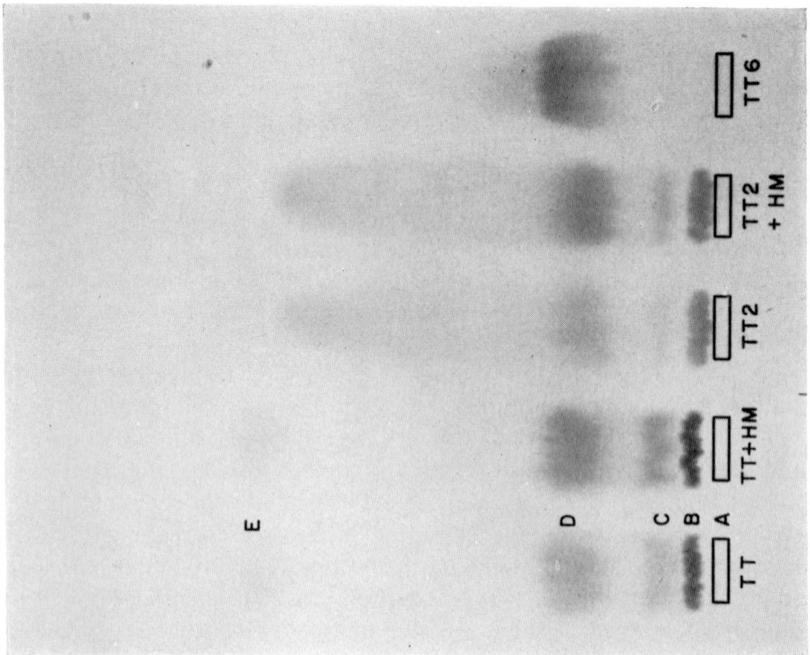

Fig. 1a

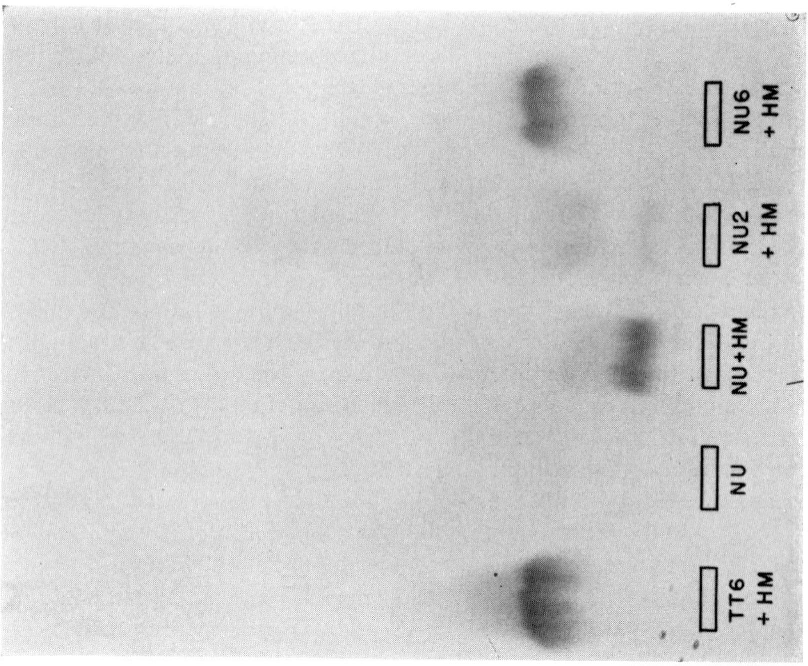

Fig. 1b

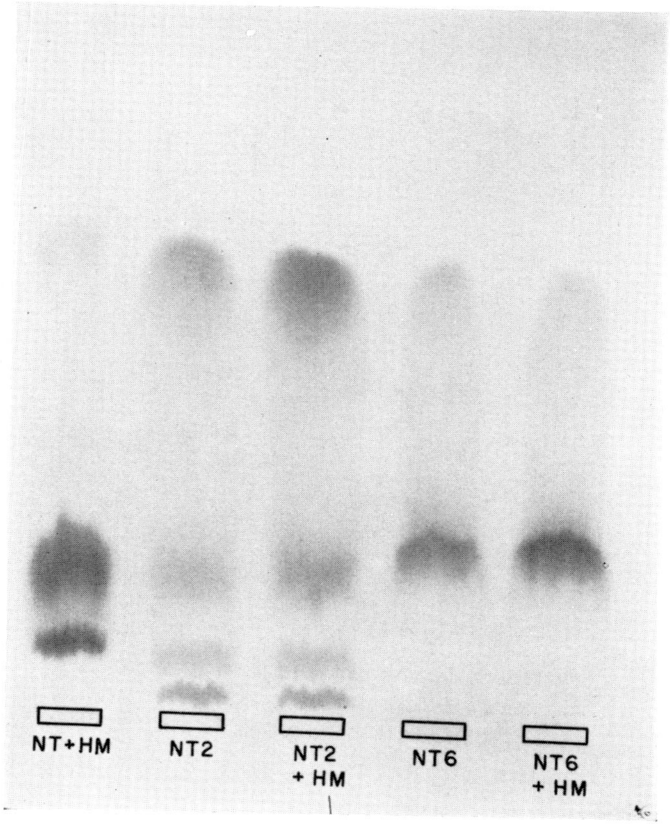

FIG. 1c

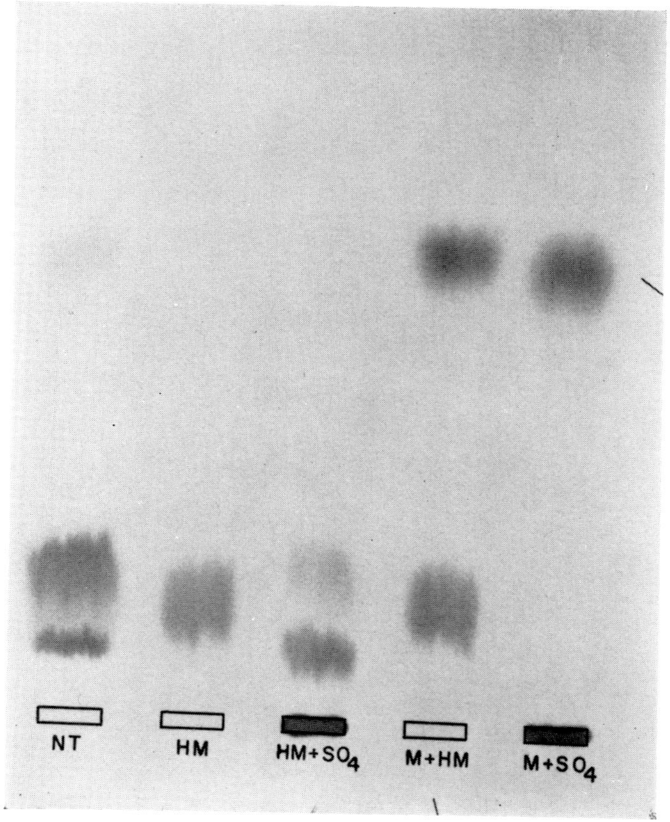

FIG. 1d

FIG. 1. Four radioautograms of paper chromatograms of various rat urine samples.

TT represents urine from treated tumor-bearing animal; NT, that from treated normal animal; NU, that from normal, untreated animal. 2 and 6 represent 2- and 6-hour hydrolysates, respectively, when attached to other letters. M is labeled Myleran; HM, hydrolyzed labeled Myleran or MSA; and SO_4, radiosulfate. For the explanation of A, B, C, D, and E, see text.

five radioactive bands shown in fig. 1 with these R_f values: A(0.00), B(0.05–0.06), C(0.12–0.13), D(0.23–0.27) and E(0.67–0.73). A, C, D, and E were identified as follows: By comparing R_f values and co-chromatographing with known, pure radioactive compounds, both A and E were found to be sulfate and Myleran, respectively. As shown in fig. 1, MSA gave a single radioactive spot when chromatographed alone; on co-chromatographing with radiosulfate, this single spot split into two with approximately seventy per cent of the activity shifted to the new position C leaving thirty per cent behind as a ghost spot at D. It is questionable whether the presence of sulfate in the urine could be entirely responsible for the split two bands of MSA observed since addition of labeled MSA to the urine sample did not result in a similar distribution of radioactivity among the bands as above. This interference of the R_f of one compound by the presence of another was not found with Myleran and sulfate, or Myleran and MSA.

The presence of the radioactive band B to the extent of thirty per cent of urinary radioactivity in tumor-bearing animal, and its absence in the urine of normal rat would appear to be a rather interesting distinction; unfortunately this difference was not sufficiently consistent to permit any generalization. It should be noted that this particular band can be formed by an interaction of the isotopic MSA with some normal constituent of urine from a normal, untreated rat (fig. 1). Subsequent efforts to identify this band as a salt of MSA with some more basic urinary constituents such as creatine and creatinine were unsuccessful.

By counting the paper chromatograms, it was found that unchanged Myleran constituted some six per cent of the total activity excreted by the normal and some ten per cent excreted by the tumor-bearing rats in 24 hours. Judging from their relative isotopic quantities initially present in the urine in comparison with those which would be formed subsequent to an in vitro addition of MSA, it was obvious that the remaining radioactive urinary substances were primarily metabolic products.

On mild acid hydrolysis, both urine samples yielded four identical distinctive radioactive bands, namely, sulfate (A), MSA complex (B), and MSA (C and D) in addition to a frontal trailing caused by residual hydrochloric acid from hydrolysis as proved by a separate experiment. When the urine specimens were hydrolyzed under more drastic conditions by autoclaving, only spots A and D together with some advancing acid smearing, were observed.

Discussion. Structurally, Myleran is an alkane interposed with both sulfone and sulfate ester linkages. The lability of this sulfate-ester linkage may facilitate hydrolysis or degradation of the molecule *in vivo*. Therefore, tracer experiments, using S^{35}-labeled Myleran, measure not only the intact molecule but the degradation product(s) as well. Since Myleran is a radiomimetic agent, its therapeutic action is attributed to its ability to alkylate in the biological system (Haddow and Timmis, 1953). Under these conditions, the degradation product is formed as a result of *in vivo* alkylation and would parallel the therapeutic effect. Hence, barring its rapid elimination from the site of action, the concentration in tissue would correlate well with the localization of the drug.

Similarity between normal and tumor-bearing rats in the distribution of the label following administration of radioactive Myleran lends support to the hypothesis that a common pharmacodynamic action of the drug, most likely alkylation, is affecting these animals, but to varying degrees. The high activity observed in the spleen, especially in tumor-bearing rats, is probably a result of the selective affinity this organ possesses for the chemical. This is in accord with the clinical observation of the regression of the enlarged spleen in leukemic patients undergoing Myleran therapy (Galton, 1953; Petrakis *et al.*, 1954). These workers have also reported that there is a concomitant reduction of the liver size in some clinical cases, but our distribution data in the rat failed to indicate a similar tendency. Myleran in man exerts a depressant action on myelopoiesis (Galton, 1953) which may indicate a local differential accumulation of the drug. These experiments in the rat showing peak activity in the bone marrow would support this view. In order to overcome the adverse concentration gradient existing, the unusually high localization of the label in bone marrow would probably have to be achieved by some form of "active" transport. It is likely that in the process of concentration and transport, the intact Myleran molecule was involved, as indicated by the high content of the compound in blood relative to that in the urine, and also by the greater water solubility of MSA which renders its participation in the process quite improbable.

Considering the simplicity of the molecular structure of Myleran, the nature of its biotransformation products, the high urinary excretion and transient peak levels at the loci of action as shown with the S^{35}-labeled compound, a study of the metabolic fate of the carbon atoms in the alkane moiety of the molecule using isotopic carbon, now in progress in this laboratory, should be fruitful. Additional information made available from such studies may contribute to a better understanding of the mode of action of Myleran and its implication could be of some clinical importance. It would be interesting to observe, for example, when the fate of the *entire* molecule is certain, if Myleran maintains a sustained therapeutic effect between treatments as may be indicated by a steady-state drug concentration in blood or other organs.

SUMMARY

Sulfur-35 labeled Myleran has been synthesized, and its distribution and metabolic fate were studied in normal and tumor-bearing rats.

Spleen and bone-marrow showed selective accumulation of the drug. In the latter organ, a transient maximum radioactivity was observed 8 hours after intraperitoneal injection.

The label was eliminated from various tissues in a manner resembling logarithmic decay; its urinary excretion in the early phase was greater in normal than in tumor-bearing animals, but at 32 hours postinjection approximately 95 to 96 per cent of the dose appeared in both urine specimens.

The main biotransformation product in the urine was methanesulfonic acid, existing mostly in the free form and to some extent in a combined state. In addition, some unchanged Myleran and a small amount of labeled sulfate were also recovered from urine.

ACKNOWLEDGMENT. The author is indebted to Dr. K. G. Scott for his advice and encouragement and for his generosity in making available facilities of his laboratory for this study. Many thanks are due to Dean T. C. Daniels for allocating research funds for this project and to Drs. T. K. Adler and E. L. Way for their helpful comments during the preparation of manuscript.

REFERENCES

BENEDICT, S. R.: J. Biol. Chem., **6:** 363, 1909.
DOUGLASS, I. B., AND JOHNSON, T. B.: J. Am. Chem. Soc., **60:** 1486, 1938.
DZIEWIATKOWSKI, D. D.: J. Biol. Chem., **207:** 181, 1954.
FROST, J. W., AND JACKSON, C. B., JR.: J.A.M.A., **161:** 54, 1956.
GALTON, D. A. G.: Lancet, **1:** 208, 1953.
HADDOW, A., AND TIMMIS, G. M.: Lancet, **1:** 207, 1953.
HAWK, P. B., OSER, B. L., AND SUMMERSON, W. H.: Practical Physiological Chemistry, p. 884, Blakiston, Philadelphia, 1947.
KULISHENKO, A. Z.: Zhur. Fiz. Khim., **28:** 1186, 1954.
PETRAKIS, N. L., BIERMAN, H. R., KELLY, K. H., WHITE, L. P., AND SHIMKIN, M. B.: Cancer, **7:** 383, 1954.
SCOTT, K. G., AND PENG, C. T.: Univ. California Publ. Pharmacol., **2**(22): 345, 1955.

EFFECTS OF RIBOSIDES AND RELATED COMPOUNDS ON PHOSPHATE TRANSPORT IN INCUBATED FRESH AND COLD-STORED HUMAN ERYTHROCYTES[1]

J. B. KAHN, JR.[2]

With the technical assistance of Shelby B. Cohen

Department of Pharmacology, University of Cincinnati College of Medicine, Cincinnati 19, Ohio

Received for publication January 21, 1957

The investigations of Gabrio *et al.* (1955a, b, c) and of Prankerd and Altman (1954a, b) have indicated that the purine ribosides can promote the accumulation of phosphate by human red cells. Gabrio *et al.* used cells which had been stored at 4° C. for relatively long periods of time in acid-citrate-dextrose solution (ACD), while Prankerd and Altman used fresh cells which had been depleted of glucose by several hours of incubation at 37° C. The latter added radioactive inorganic phosphate (P^{32}) to plasma, and measured the rate of disappearance of the radioactivity, while Gabrio *et al.* measured the level of organic phosphate within the cells. Since the two groups of investigators were measuring different things in different systems, comparison of the phosphate-transferring systems in fresh and in cold-stored cells cannot be made on the basis of their data.

We have found (Kahn and Cohen, 1957) that the purine ribosides can also promote cation transport in incubated cold-stored human erythrocytes. This similarity between cation and phosphate transport in the red cell led us to determine how far the parallels between the two systems would extend. To this end we have made two sets of comparisons: a) of phosphate transfer in cold-stored incubated red cells with the same process in fresh cells, and b) of phosphate transfer in incubated cold-stored cells with cation transport in the same system. The test applied to these systems was the addition of varying concentrations of purine and pyrimidine bases, ribosides, ribotides, a purine desoxyriboside, and two lactones. Our results show that fresh cells and cold-stored cells differ in their responses to several of these agents, and that in cold-stored cells their effects upon cation transport differ from those upon phosphate transport.

MATERIALS AND METHODS. Cold-stored blood was procured, stored, and handled as described previously (Kahn and Acheson, 1955). In all experiments with cold-stored blood, measurements of potassium in whole blood and plasma were performed simultaneously with measurements of plasma P^{32}. Not more than 200 microcuries of P^{32} (sodium radiophosphate, Abbott Laboratories) were added to cold blood. The blood was divided into 12-ml. aliquants, and the compound under investigation added in not more than 3.0 ml. (usually 1.0 ml. or less) of 0.9 per cent NaCl. Zero time (t_0) samples were removed, and the remainder of the aliquants incubated at 37° ± 0.2° C. for four hours (t_4 samples). After this time enough whole blood was removed for measurement of the hematocrit and of whole blood

[1] Supported in part by Grants #H-1506 (C2) and H-1506 (C3) from the National Heart Institute, United States Public Health Service.

[2] John & Mary R. Markle Scholar in Medical Science, 1954–59.

potassium, and the remainder was centrifuged at approximately 8000 × g for three minutes. Plasma was removed; part of it was used for determination of the plasma potassium level, and 500 microliters were used for counting P^{32} in the well of a scintillation counter. Correction was made for the background count; since all samples were counted within a thirty-minute period, no correction was made for decay. Counts were of sufficient length to reduce the standard counting error to 1 per cent of the total count. Controls were from blood which was incubated without added compounds, but with P^{32}. The amount of added phosphate was small compared with the total plasma inorganic phosphate. Since the total volume of radiophosphate added was of the order of 0.1 per cent of the total volume of blood, the radioactive solution was not neutralized or buffered. No detectable change of pH occurred (as measured with a Beckman Model G pH meter) upon addition of 1.0 ml. of radiophosphate solution to 100 ml. of whole blood.

When fresh blood was used, it was obtained from healthy volunteers, anticoagulant (Mepesulfate, 20 mgm. per 100 ml. blood) was added, and the blood was shaken for six hours at 37° C. in a Warburg vessel to reduce the blood glucose to a low level (after Prankerd and Altman, 1954b). This blood will be referred to as "incubated fresh blood." After six hours the compound being studied and the P^{32} were tipped in from the sidearm, and incubation was continued for four hours more. Control blood received only the P^{32} solution. After this time the blood was centrifuged for three minutes at approximately 8000 × g, and 500 or 1000 microliters of plasma were counted. Since blood from different donors differed somewhat in the amount of loss of P^{32} from the plasma (the least disappearance was about 15 per cent less than the greatest), results are expressed as per cent of control activity.

RESULTS. *I. Experiments with incubated cold-stored blood.* A. Compounds without effect on the loss of P^{32} from the plasma: The loss of radioactivity from the plasma of control blood during the four hours of incubation was 44.1 per cent ± 1.2 per cent ($s\bar{x}$) in 22 experiments with blood from 12 donors. The following compounds, in the concentration ranges listed, had no detectable effect on the amount of loss of P^{32} from the plasma: adenine, 1.25 to 40.0 mM; hypoxanthine, 1.25 to 40.0 mM; adenosine monophosphate, 2.5 to 40.0 mM; adenosine triphosphate, 1.25 to 40.0 mM; cytidine, 1.25 to 40.0 mM; cytidine monophosphate, 1.25 to 40.0 mM; ouabain, 3×10^{-7} M; β-angelicalactone, 100 mM.

B. Effects of adenosine and inosine: The effects of addition of increasing amounts of the purine ribosides adenosine and inosine upon the disappearance of P^{32} from the plasma during four hours of incubation are shown in the lower (solid line) curves of fig. 1. Both ribosides, in concentrations from 1.25 to 40.0 mM, had only inhibitory effects upon the disappearance of P^{32}. At riboside concentrations of 10 to 20 mM the curves reached a plateau, so that further increase in concentration did not produce greater inhibition of P^{32} loss from the plasma. Maximum inhibition from inosine was about 67 per cent; that from adenosine was about 45 per cent.

II. Experiments with incubated fresh blood. A. Compounds without effect on the loss of P^{32} from the plasma: The loss of P^{32} from the plasma of incubated fresh blood during four hours of incubation was 41.4 per cent ± 1.8 per cent ($s\bar{x}$) in 12 experiments with blood from 7 donors. This is not significantly different, as judged by Student's "t" test (1908) from the disappearance of similar amounts of P^{32} from the plasma of cold-stored blood (Section I, A). The rate of P^{32} disappearance was not affected by adenine or hypoxanthine in concentrations from 1.25 to 40.0 mM, nor by 10^{-6} M ouabain. In two experiments with each, neither

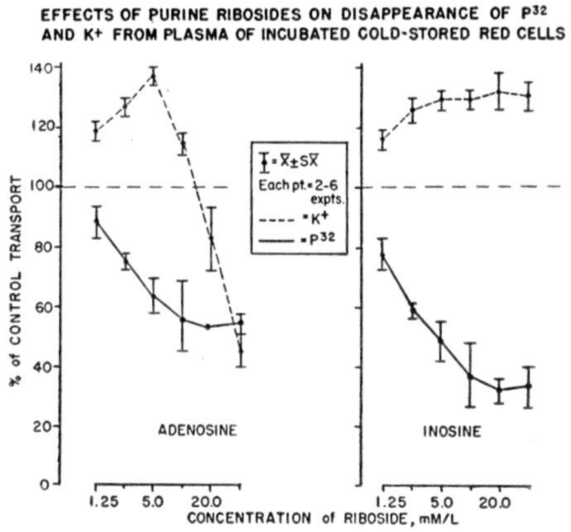

FIG. 1. Effects of purine ribosides on loss of P^{32} (solid line) and potassium (dotted line) from plasma.

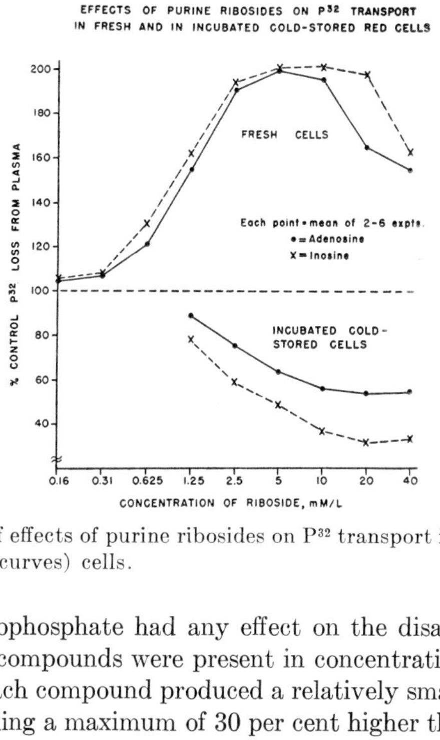

FIG. 2. Comparison of effects of purine ribosides on P^{32} transport in fresh (upper curves) and cold-stored (lower curves) cells.

cytidine nor its monophosphate had any effect on the disappearance of radiophosphate when the compounds were present in concentrations up to 20.0 *mM*. In one experiment, each compound produced a relatively small increase of disappearance of P^{32}, reaching a maximum of 30 per cent higher than the control level at 10 *mM*. What difference in conditions between the blood samples may have accounted for the atypical result is unknown.

B. Effects of adenosine, inosine, and desoxyadenosine: Both purine ribosides could increase the rate of loss of P^{32} from the plasma of incubated fresh cells, as shown in the upper curves of fig. 2. The effect reached its maximum of about double the control rate at riboside concentrations of 5 to 10 *mM*. Above this level

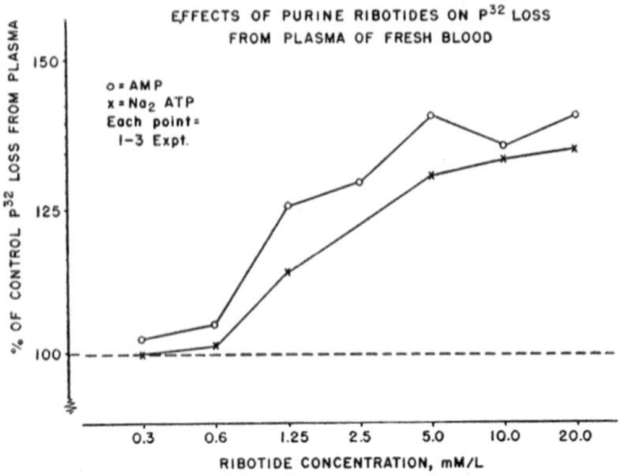

FIG. 3. Effects of adenylic acid and ATP on the loss of P^{32} from the plasma of fresh blood

there was a decrease in the amount of augmentation of transport, but the highest concentration used still produced about a 60 per cent increase relative to the control rate. The effects of desoxyadenosine were similar to those illustrated in fig. 2 for adenosine or inosine.

C. Effects of purine ribotides: Adenylic acid and Na_2ATP augmented the disappearance of P^{32} from plasma, though not as much as the purine ribosides. The maximum increase (by 35 to 40 per cent) of P^{32} disappearance resulted from addition of 5 *mM* ribotide; higher concentrations produced no further increase, nor did they produce the downward trend seen in the curves for higher concentrations of purine ribosides. Concentration-action curves of AMP and Na_2ATP are presented as fig. 3.

DISCUSSION. I. *Cold-stored cells.* Comparison of Columns I and II of Table 1 reveals the observed differences between cation and phosphate transport systems in the incubated cold-stored red cell. Compounds which had purely inhibitory effects on cation transfer in cold-stored cells were without effect on P^{32} transfer in the same system, while the purine ribosides adenosine and inosine, which could augment cation transfer, had only inhibitory effects upon phosphate transfer (upper and lower curves of fig. 1). These data do not support the view that the transfer of potassium may be linked to that of phosphate in the incubated cold-stored human erythrocyte.

The failure of the purine ribosides to inhibit phosphate transport completely in incubated cold-stored cells suggests that two pathways of metabolism may promote the transfer of inorganic phosphate, and that only one of them is inhibited by the purine ribosides under our experimental conditions. The pathway which is unaffected by purine ribosides would be responsible for about one-third to one-half of the phosphate transfer, since the maximum inhibition by these compounds was about 45 to 67 per cent (fig. 1). There are other examples of an active transport process being driven by two separate mechanisms (*cf.* results of Jonas and Gourley on phosphate transport in fresh rabbit cells, 1954; experiments of Foulkes with potassium influx in yeast, 1956).

Gabrio *et al.* (1954) have studied the effects of ribosides and related compounds on the synthesis of organic phosphate in human red cells cold-stored in ACD.

TABLE 1

Comparison of the effects of compounds studied on: potassium transport in cold-stored cells (I); P^{32} transport in cold-stored cells (II); P^{32} transport in fresh cells (III); organic phosphate accumulation in cold-stored cells (IV, data from Gabrio et al. as indicated)

Compound Tested	Class of Compound	Concentration Range. *mM*/l.	Effects on:			
			I $-dK/dt$, cold-stored cells	II $-dP^{32}/dt$, cold-stored cells	III $-dP^{32}/dt$, fresh cells	IV dPo/dt, cold-stored cells
Adenine	Purine	1–40	−	0	0	0[a, b]
Hypoxanthine	Purine	1–40	0	0	0	
Adenosine	Purine riboside	0.3–40	+, ≤5mM −, >10mM	−	++	++[a, b]
Inosine	Purine riboside	0.3–40	+	−	++	++[a, b]
Desoxyadenosine	Purine desoxyriboside	1–20	−		++	+ → ++[b]
Adenylic Acid	Purine ribotide	2.5–40	−	0	+	+[a]
Na ADP	Purine ribotide	1–40	−	0	+	0[a]
Na_2 ATP	Purine ribotide	1–40	−	0	+	0[a]
Cytidine	Pyrimidine riboside	1–40	−	0	0–±	0[b]
Cytidylic Acid	Pyrimidine ribotide	1–40	−	0	0–±	
β-Angelicalactone	Lactone	10–100	−	0		
Ouabain	Lactone	10^{-5}–10^{-3}	−	0	0	

0 = no effect on transport. − = decrease of transport. + = less than 50% increase of transport. ++ = more than 50% increase of transport.

[a] Gabrio *et al.*, 1955b.

[b] Gabrio and Huennekens, 1955c.

Rubinstein *et al.* (1956) have confirmed their results using cells stored in neutral citrate-dextrose solution, thus eliminating pH as a factor which might have affected their data. These workers have shown that the synthesis of organic phosphates in cold-stored cells is markedly increased by adenosine, inosine, and desoxyadenosine, and less markedly so by AMP, but is unaffected by ATP. These data are presented in column IV of table 1. It is striking that the two compounds which most increase the incorporation of phosphorous into organic phosphates (column IV) decrease the transfer of inorganic phosphate into the cell (column II). The amount of inorganic phosphate transferred into the cell might be expected to influence the rate at which inorganic phosphate is synthesized into organic esters. Rubinstein *et al.* (1956) showed, however, that intracellular inorganic phosphate rises during cold storage. This is evidently the source of phosphate for organic phosphate synthesis under the influence of added ribosides, and the inorganic phosphate transferred from outside the cell seems not to be a factor.

II. *Fresh cells.* The two purine ribosides and desoxyadenosine increased phosphate transfer into fresh cells (fig. 2). The purine ribotides did likewise but to a lesser degree (fig. 3). The results with the purine ribosides confirm those reported by Prankerd and Altman (1954b). Differences between the phosphate-transferring systems of fresh and cold-stored cells can be seen by comparing columns II and III of table 1.

The difference in potency between adenosine and inosine (fig. 2, upper curves) is not statistically significant (by Student's "t" test) at any point, yet this difference is consistent throughout the range of nine concentrations used. It is unlikely that random variations would result in the same direction of difference between the two compounds in all concentrations used. We therefore take the view that inosine is slightly more potent than adenosine, but the difference is of the same order of magnitude as the error of our experimental method. The same considerations apply to the differences between AMP and Na_2ATP as expressed in fig. 3. Points on the concentration-action curve of desoxyadenosine were randomly distributed slightly above or below those for adenosine and inosine. Hence we can make no conclusion as to its potency relative to the purine ribosides except that it is similar to both of them.

III. *Some biochemical considerations of differences between fresh and cold-stored cells.* In addition to the differences outlined in table 1, relevant data come from work of other investigators. Prankerd (1955) analyzed fresh cells by paper chromatography, and found that as adenosine disappeared there was an equivalent increase of adenine. This implies that in fresh cells a possible reaction is:

A. Adenosine + phosphate → ribose phosphate + adenine.

Though this reaction has not been proved in fresh cells, it is consistent with the results of Prankerd, and is implied by Prankerd and Altman (1954a).

The situation in cold-stored cells is different. Rubinstein *et al.* (1956) found that as adenosine disappeared, inosine appeared. Later there was disappearance of the formed inosine with concomitant appearance of hypoxanthine. These results support the idea of Gabrio and Huennekens (1954) and of Huennekens *et al.* (1956) that inosine is the substrate for a phosphorylase in incubated cold-stored cells. Thus two reactions are postulated to occur in cold-stored cells:

$$\text{B. Adenosine} \xrightarrow[\text{deaminase}]{\text{Adenosine}} \text{Inosine}$$

$$\text{C. Inosine} + \text{phosphate} \xrightarrow[\text{phosphorylase}]{\text{Purine Riboside}} \text{ribose phosphate} + \text{hypoxanthine}$$

From such considerations, we make the hypothesis that in fresh cells reaction (A) can occur, while in incubated cold-stored cells reactions B and C take place. The shift from reaction A to B + C with cold-storage may perhaps be explained on the basis of loss from the cell, by diffusion or some other process, of some cofactor necessary to reaction A. In the absence of this reaction the deamination (B) could occur, and reaction C could proceed.

In cold-stored cells inosine is significantly more potent as an inhibitor of phosphate transfer than is adenosine (bottom curves of fig. 1 and 2). This would be expected if, as was postulated above, adenosine deaminase was necessary for the production of substrate from adenosine in cold-stored cells, and if this enzyme was not successful in deaminating all the adenosine presented to it under these circumstances. In this case a given concentration of adenosine would produce a less than equimolar amount of inosine, and curves like those of fig. 2 could result. This implies that the inhibitory compound is inosine, not adenosine. Another possibility which the present data do not exclude is that adenosine is *per se* a less effective inhibitor than is inosine.

The processes of organic phosphate accumulation in cold-stored cells and inorganic phosphate influx in fresh cells have similar responses to several of the agents studied (compare columns III and IV of table 1). Studies have not yet been made of the effects of purine ribosides on organic phosphate synthesis in fresh cells. If the assumption is made that this system responds to purine ribosides in the same way it does in cold-stored cells, it can be suggested that perhaps the transfer of inorganic phosphate across the membrane of the fresh cell is linked in some way to the accumulation of organic phosphate. In the cold-stored cells this relationship does not exist, as pointed out in Section A of this Discussion.

SUMMARY AND CONCLUSIONS

The experiments presented here are summarized in table 1. The table permits comparison of the two different pairs of systems considered, *i.e.*, of cation and phosphate transport in the incubated cold-stored human red cell (columns I and II) and of phosphate transport in incubated cold-stored and fresh cells (columns II and III). The actions of the purine ribotides best differentiate the three systems. They inhibit cation transport in the cold-stored cell, have no effect on phosphate transport in the cold-stored cell, and augment phosphate transport in the fresh cell. In addition, the response of the cation-transferring system of the incubated cold-stored cell differs from that of the phosphate-transferring system in the same cell in its response to a purine (adenine), two purine ribosides (adenosine and inosine), a pyrimidine riboside (cytidine), a pyrimidine ribotide (cytidylic acid), and two lactones (ouabain and angelicalactone). The phosphate transport system of cold-stored cells differs from the same system in incubated fresh cells in its response to purine ribosides. We conclude that the three transport systems are different. The meaning of such differences for possible mechanisms of transport has been discussed.

REFERENCES

Foulkes, E. C.: J. Gen. Physiol., **39:** 687, 1956.
Gabrio, B. W., Donohue, D. M., and Finch, C. A.: J. Clin. Invest., **34:** 1509, 1955a.
Gabrio, B. W., Hennessey, M., Thomasson, J., and Finch, C. A.: J. Biol. Chem., **215:** 357, 1955b.
Gabrio, B. W., and Huennekens, F. M.: Biochim. Biophys. Acta, **18:** 585, 1955c.
Huennekens, F. M., Nurk, E., and Gabrio, B. W.: J. Biol. Chem., **221:** 971, 1956.
Jonas, H., and Gourley, D. R. H.: Biochim. Biophys. Acta, **14:** 335, 1954.

KAHN, J. B., AND ACHESON, G. H.: THIS JOURNAL, **115**: 305, 1955.
KAHN, J. B., AND COHEN, S. B.: THIS JOURNAL, **120**: 9, 1957.
PRANKERD, T. A. J.: Brit. J. Haematol., **1**: 406, 1955.
PRANKERD, T. A. J., AND ALTMAN, K. I.: Biochem. J., **58**: 622, 1954a.
PRANKERD, T. A. J., AND ALTMAN, K. I.: Biochim. Biophys. Acta, **15**: 158, 1954b.
RUBINSTEIN, D., KASHKET, S., DENSTEDT, O. F., AND GOSSELIN, S. M.: Can. J. Biochem. and Physiol., **34**: 61, 1956.
"Student": Biometrika, **6**: 1, 1908.

A COMPARATIVE STUDY OF THE EFFECTS OF FOUR DIFFERENT *RAUWOLFIA* PREPARATIONS ADMINISTERED PARENTERALLY[1]

RALPH V. FORD, RICHARD E. BORRESON, GENE R. LINDLEY AND JOHN H. MOYER

Department of Pharmacology, Baylor University College of Medicine, and the Veterans Administration Hospital, Houston, Texas

Received for publication January 24, 1957

It is our purpose to report a study of the comparative hypotensive effects of four *Rauwolfia* compounds administered intramuscularly. One of these drugs, reserpine,[2] is of established clinical usefulness when administered intramuscularly for the treatment of severe hypertension (Dennis and Moyer, 1955) (Griffin Stover and Ford, 1956). The three other drugs, Raunormine (deserpidine),[3] serpentine,[4] and Rescamine (rescinnamine),[4] are compared in effectiveness and toxicity to the effect of reserpine.

METHODS. Twenty-four male patients with severe hypertension were selected for this study. All patients were hospitalized on the hypertensive ward, where conditions were controlled to the extent that all patients received an 800 mgm. sodium diet, 3000 ml. of distilled water, and ward ambulatory privileges. Blood pressures were recorded four times daily in both the supine and upright positions and during periods of drug administration blood pressures were recorded hourly by trained ward personnel. Patients previously receiving digitalis or antibiotics continued on these drugs, but no hypotensive or sedative agents were used during the study. There was an adequate control period of two weeks or more following admission to the hospital to allow for stabilization of the blood pressure before any of the experimental preparations were administered. None of the patients obtained a reduction in blood pressure when a placebo injection of saline was administered intramuscularly. Five of these patients received all four drugs in a randomized fashion but the remaining 19 patients received only one drug with the exception of one patient who received two drugs.

The vital statistics of all patients composing the study are presented in table 1. The ages varied from 22 to 77 with a mean of 53. There were nine Negro and fifteen white patients. The initial blood pressures with the patients supine ranged from 140 to 265 systolic and from 100 to 140 diastolic with a mean of 205 systolic and 123 diastolic. The initial blood pressures with the patient upright ranged from 150 to 243 systolic and from 100 to 150 diastolic with an average of 198 systolic and 122 diastolic. The ocular fundi, renal disease, and electrocardiographic gradings were according to previous criteria (Griffin, Stover and Ford, 1956). After the control determinations were completed, each patient was given an initial dose of one of the experimental hypotensive agents intramuscularly. Reserpine was first administered in a dose of 2.5 mgm. and, if no response was achieved, the next dose was increased to 5 mgm. Ten mgm. were given to one patient. The other three drugs, namely, Raunormine (deserpidine), Rescamine (rescinnamine), and serpentine, were administered in an initial dose of 5 mgm. and, if no response was observed, the dose was increased in 5

[1] With the technical assistance of Ann Alexander.

[2] Supplied by Ciba Pharmaceutical Products as Serpasil.

[3] Supplied by Abbott Laboratories as Harmonyl.

[4] Supplied by Riker Laboratories, Inc.

TABLE 1

Vital statistics of hypertensive patients receiving various forms of Rauwolfia intramuscularly

Patient	Clinical Diagnosis*	Ocular Fundi†	Renal Disease‡	Race	Age	ECG§	Initial Blood Pressure‖			
							Supine		Upright	
							S	D	S	D
1	HCVD	II	+	W	58	III	200	110	190	110
2	HCVD	III	++	N	65	III	180	110	170	100
3	HCVD	III	+	W	56	III	210	130	170	120
4	Chr. Pyl.	II	++	W	22	IV	210	140	200	150
5	HCVD	III	++++	N	48	IV	240	140	210	130
6	HCVD	III	++++	N	29	IV	220	140	190	130
7	HCVD	III	+	W	53	IV	210	120	240	140
8	HCVD	II	+	N	53	IV	140	100	150	110
9	HCVD	III	+	W	65	IV	200	110	210	110
10	HCVD	II	++++	W	77	II	220	120	220	120
11	HCVD	III	++++	W	75	IV	207	123	203	117
12	HCVD	IV	+	W	67	IV	210	140	190	120
13	HCVD	III	++	W	37	IV	190	110	190	110
14	HCVD	III	++++	W	47	IV	220	140	220	150
15	HCVD	III	++	N	54	III	218	127	197	119
16	HCVD	II	+	N	64	II	166	106	172	114
17	HCVD	IV	+++	W	67	IV	190	121	190	120
18	HCVD	III	++	W	37	III	265	132	243	133
19	HCVD	III	++++	N	32	IV	197	131	187	131
20	HCVD	II	++	N	45	III	207	118	194	106
21	HCVD	II	++	W	52	III	175	115	181	116
22	HCVD	III	+++	W	50	IV	200	125	199	123
23	HCVD	II	+	N	54	II	226	109	215	113
24	HCVD	IV	+++	W	56	IV	226	138	226	136

* HCVD—Hypertensive Cardiovascular Disease; Chr. Pyl.—Chronic Pyelonephritis.

† Keith-Wagener classification (grades I–IV).

‡ Grading of renal disease: + normal or occasional albuminuria; ++ albuminuria and elevated blood urea nitrogen; +++ albuminuria, elevated BUN and fixed specific gravity; ++++ renal decompensation (acidosis, formed elements, uremia).

§ Grading of electrocardiograms: IV, hypertrophy of left ventricle with strain and ischemia; III, hypertrophy of left ventricle with strain; II, hypertrophy of left ventricle without strain; I, minimal T-wave changes only.

‖ These are average control figures and are not necessarily the same as the control for any specific drug.

5 mgm. increments to a maximum of 20 mgm. or until an effective reduction in blood pressure was observed. There was always a minimum of 48 hours between doses, at which time the patient's blood pressure had returned to the control level. The blood pressure, pulse rate, and respiration were checked every hour for at least 24 hours following drug administration. Observations were made of the onset of hypotensive action, duration, symptoms, and side effects. The onset of effect is determined by that time in minutes, following administration of the drug, which elapses before there is a decline in mean blood pressure $\left(\text{mean blood pressure} = \text{diastolic} + \frac{\text{pulse pressure}}{3}\right)$ of greater than 20 mm. Hg in the upright position. The duration of effect is determined in hours after the blood pressure is reduced below this point and until the blood pressure rises above this level again. The values

TABLE 2

Responses of hypertensive patients receiving reserpine intramuscularly

Patient	Upright Mean Blood Pressure		Blood Pressure Reduction		Dose	Side Effects
	Control	Drug	Onset	Duration		
	Mm. Hg	*Mm. Hg*	*min.*	*hr.*	*mgm.*	
1	137	117	120	12	5	None
2	123	103	120	18	5	None
3	137	103	120	12	5	None
4	167	100	120	18	5	None
5	157	153	0	0	5	None
6	153	100	300	12	5	None
7	173	130	60	17	10	None
8	123	100	60	18	5	None
9	143	113	60	4	5	None
10	157	113	120	24	5	None
Average....	147	113	120*	15*	6	None

* Includes responsive patients only.

are recorded as mean blood pressure with the patient in the upright position and the side effects are described. The dose is recorded for each patient as the average number of milligrams of the drug required to induce a significant hypotensive effect if such occurred. The maximum dose was 10 mgm. for reserpine and rescinnamine and 20 mgm. for the other drugs.

RESULTS. The responses of the hypertensive patients receiving the various drugs are recorded in tables 2, 3, 4 and 5.

When reserpine (table 2) was administered, there was a decline in the upright mean blood pressure from 147 mm.Hg to 113 mm.Hg ($p < .001$) with an average onset of effect of 120 minutes and a duration of 15 hours. The average dose was 6 mgm. There were no side effects other than mild somnolence noted in any of the patients given parenteral reserpine.

After the administration of Raunormine (deserpidine), (table 3) there was a decline in the upright mean blood pressure from 150 mm.Hg to 115 mm.Hg ($p < .01$) with an average onset of 77 minutes and a duration of 15 hours in those patients in whom a significant reduction in blood pressure was observed. Of the ten patients given an average of 16 mgm. of deserpidine, six reported no side effects, four complained of significant vertigo, and one was nauseated as well. Mild somnolence was observed in a few cases.

After administration of Rescamine (rescinnamine) at an average dose of 10 mgm. (table 4), there was a reduction in the upright mean blood pressure from 148 mm.Hg to 107 mm.Hg ($p < 0.001$). The average delay in onset of action was 3 hours which was one hour longer than was the delay after reserpine administration. This was associated with some side reactions characterized chiefly by dizziness and/or somnolence in 5 patients. The average dose requirement was 10 mgm. Although the blood pressure response to rescinnamine was equivalent to the response to reserpine, the dose requirement was about twice as large.

After administration of serpentine (table 5), there was a reduction in mean

TABLE 3

Responses of hypertensive patients receiving deserpidine intramuscularly

Patient	Upright Mean Blood Pressure		Blood Pressure Reduction		Dose	Side effects
	Control	Drug	Onset	Duration		
	Mm. Hg	*Mm. Hg*	*min.*	*hr.*	*mgm.*	
5	157	90	60	16	5	None
6	153	113	60	18	20	None
7	173	117	60	3	20	None
8	123	90	120	12	20	None
9	143	140	0	0	20	None
10	150	157	0	0	20	None
11	143	150	0	0	20	Vertigo
12	143	90	120	18	20	Vertigo and nausea
13	137	90	60	18	5	Vertigo
14	173	110	60	18	5	Vertigo
Average.......	150	115	77*	15*	16	

* Includes responsive patients only.

TABLE 4

Responses of hypertensive patients receiving rescinnamine (Rescamine) intramuscularly

Patient	Upright Mean Blood Pressure		Blood Pressure Reduction		Dose	Side Effects
	Control	Drug	Onset	Duration		
	Mm. Hg	*Mm. Hg*	*min.*	*hr.*	*mgm.*	
1	145	113	180	24	10	Dizziness, somnolence
2	133	93	150	24	10	None
3	143	105	150	18	10	None
4	170	87	120	6+	10	Dizziness, somnolence and conjunctival injection
5	150	82	60	24+	10	None
6	135	108	240	5	10	Somnolence
7	138	108	300	18	10	Dizziness, weakness
8	148	116	240	7	10	None
9	147	113	180	6+	10	Dizziness, somnolence and conjunctival injection
10	166	145	0	0	10	None
Average.......	148	107	180*	15*	10	

* Includes responsive patients only.

\+ Observations of blood pressure response discontinued after this period of time.

blood pressure from 146 mm.Hg to 130 mm.Hg ($p > 0.1$). When this occurred the average onset of action was 114 minutes and the duration of action was 12 hours at an average dose of 18 mgm. One of these patients became light headed, and one became disoriented. Otherwise, there were no side effects. Serpentine was also given to a limited number of patients (four) intravenously in a dose of 50 mgm. over a 4-hour period. There was no change in blood pressure.

TABLE 5

Responses of hypertensive patients receiving serpentine intramuscularly

Patient	Upright Mean Blood Pressure		Blood Pressure Reduction		Dose	Side Effects
	Control	Drug	Onset	Duration		
	Mm. Hg	*Mm. Hg*	*min.*	*hr.*	*mgm.*	
1	137	113	120	8	20	None
2	123	100	180	9	20	None
3	137	93	90	12	10	None
4	167	123	120	12	10	None
5	157	93	60	18	15	None
6	150	157	0	0	20	None
7	173	227	0	0	20	Vertigo
8	123	113	0	0	20	None
9	143	137	0	0	20	None
11	150	140	0	0	20	Disorientation
Average.......	146	130	114*	12*	18	

* Includes responsive patients only.

Discussion. Reserpine ($C_{33}H_{40}O_9N_2$), the most important of the *Rauwolfia serpentina* alkaloids, was first isolated in Switzerland in 1952 (Schlittler *et al.* 1954). Its pharmacology has been previously reported by others (Plummer *et al.*, 1954), and, in general, there have been influences on the central portion of the autonomic nervous system and on the cardiovascular system, especially on the central nervous system reflexes that ordinarily regulate the blood pressure. Its use in hypertensive emergencies has been previously reported (Griffin, Stover and Ford, 1956) (Hughes, Moyer and Daeschner, 1955). The structural formulae of the experimental preparations are presented in figure 1.

Raunormine ($C_{32}H_{38}N_8O_2$), 11-desmethoxyreserpine (deserpidine), having a structural formula very similar to reserpine, is a newly isolated alkaloid from *Rauwolfia canescens* (Klohs *et al.*, in press), and its pharmacology has been previously reported (Everett, personal communication) (Rubin, and Burke, 1954). In preliminary testing in laboratory animals, no significant differences were observed between this drug and reserpine. Deserpidine is from the same pharmacological group as rescinnamine and reserpine (Cronheim, Orcutt and Toekes 1955). It has been studied as an oral preparation (Kinard *et al.*, 1956) and has been shown to be slightly less potent than comparable alkaloids and extracts of *Rauwolfia serpentina.* However, the side reactions appear to be less annoying and somewhat less frequent.

Rescamine (rescinnamine) is the trimethoxycinnamic ester of methyl reserpate (figure 1). Pharmacologically, it is similar to reserpine. When administered orally it is effective in reducing the blood pressure in patients with hypertension. (Hershberger, Dennis and Moyer, 1956).

Serpentine is a recently isolated compound derived from *Rauwolfia serpentina.* Cronheim (personal communication) has demonstrated that a dose ten times that of reserpine is required to produce similar hypotensive responses and that

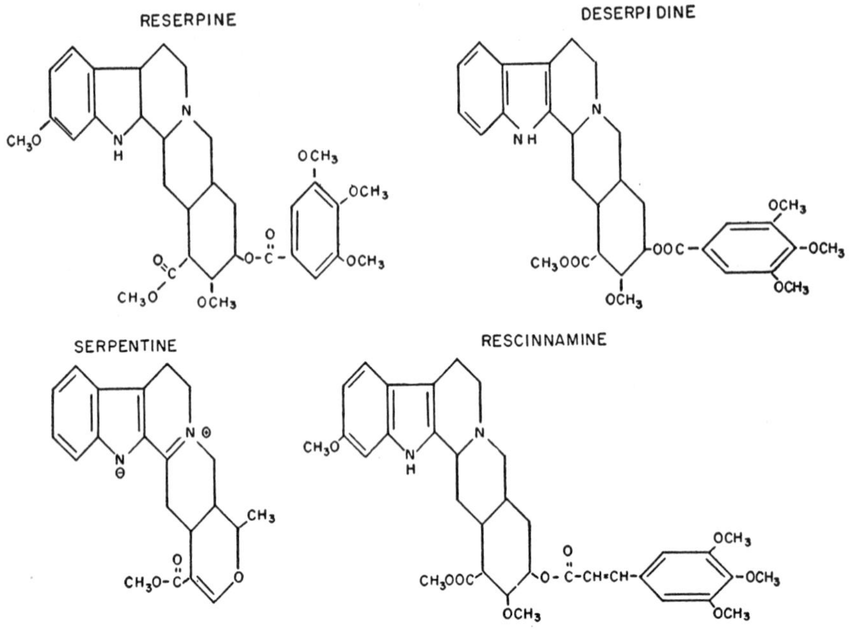

FIG. 1. Structural formulae of the experimental preparations studied.

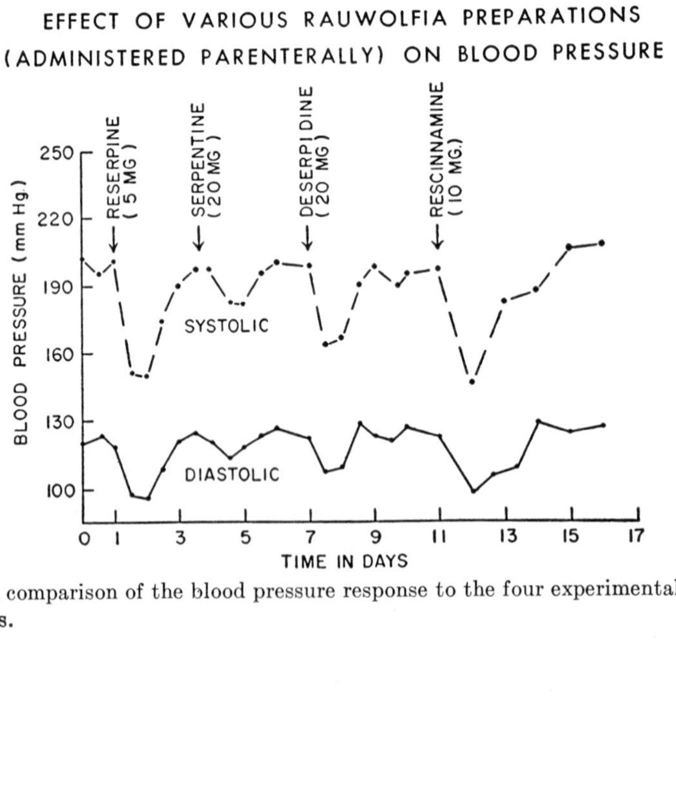

FIG. 2. A comparison of the blood pressure response to the four experimental *Rauwolfia* preparations.

TABLE 6

Average responses to intramuscular administration of various forms of Rauwolfia

Drug	Control Blood Pressure				Maximum Blood Pressure Response				Upright Mean Blood Pressure*		P Value**	Blood Pressure Reduction		Dose	Trials	No. Responding
	Recumbent		Upright		Recumbent		Upright					Onset	Duration			
	S	D	S	D	S	D	S	D	C	Drug						
												min.	*hr.*	*mgm.*	*no.*	
Reserpine....	204	122	196	122	170	98	155	96	147	113	<0.001	120	15	6	10	9
Rescinnamine.	207	122	200	121	163	98	145	90	148	107	<0.001	180	15	10	10	9
Deserpidine..	200	123	200	124	166	102	154	95	150	115	<0.01	77	15	16	10	7
Serpentine....	202	123	194	122	179	108	174	108	146	130	>0.1	114	12	18	10	5

* = Upright Mean Blood Pressure: C = Control; S = Systolic; D = Diastolic.

** P value derived from student "t" test—$t = \bar{x}\sqrt{\frac{n(n-1)}{Sx^2}}$.

Serpentine is best administered by infusion rather than by single injection. Others have reported that, among the *Rauwolfia* alkaloids, serpentine has the lowest toxicity and central depressant action, but a very high peripheral effect. Reserpine was reported to have the greatest toxicity and central depressant action, but hardly any demonstrable immediate peripheral action (Lewis and Gaitonde 1955).

Figure 2 illustrates typical responses to these four drugs when administered to the same patient with hypertension and table 6 summarizes the average responses for all patients studied. It is seen that there was a significant change after the administration of reserpine, rescinnamine, and deserpidine with no significant change following the administration of serpentine intramuscularly. Although there was no significant difference between deserpidine, rescinnamine and reserpine insofar as the degree of blood pressure reduction, it is to be noted that the dose of reserpine was roughly ⅓ that required of deserpidine and ½ that required of rescinnamine to produce a similar degree of reduction in blood pressure.

Finally, the techniques as described in this paper may be applied to the evaluation of other parenterally usable drugs in the treatment of severe hypertensive vascular disease. It is seen that such a drug should have certain qualities, namely significant (and consistent) hypotensive effects with a minimum of adverse side reactions.

SUMMARY AND CONCLUSIONS

Twenty-four male patients with hypertensive disease have been used as the subjects of a study to compare the effects of four parenterally administered hypotensive agents: reserpine, deserpidine, rescinnamine, and serpentine. The results indicate that the reserpine and rescinnamine are the drugs of choice with the least number of side reactions for the treatment of the hypertensive patient who requires a rapidly acting and parenterally administered drug for reduction of blood pressure. The other preparations, deserpidine and serpentine, although generally effective in reducing the blood pressure, have an unpredictable frequency of response and are associated with a greater number of untoward side reactions.

REFERENCES

Cronheim, G. E., Orcutt, J. A., and Toekes, I. M.: Proc. Soc. Exper. Biol. & Med., **89:** 21, 1955.

Dennis, E. W., and Moyer, J. H.: Med. Rec. & Annals, **49:** 342, 1955.

Griffin, R. W., Stover, J. W., and Ford, R. V.: New Engl. Jour. Med., **254:** 8, 1956.

Hershberger, R., Dennis, E., and Moyer, J. H.: Am. J. Med. Sci., **231:** 542, 1956.

Hughes, W. M., Moyer, J. H., and Daeschner, W. C.: Arch. Int. Med., **95:** 563, 1955.

Kinard, S. A., Conner, P. K., Hershberger, R. L., Dennis, E. W., and Moyer, J. H.: Med. Rec. & Annals, **50:** 3, 1956.

Klohs, N. W., Keller, F., Williams, R., and Krisaro, G. W.: J. Am. Chem. Soc., In Press.

Lewis, B. I., and Gaitonde, M. K.: J. Amer. Med. Assoc., **159:** 703, 1955.

Plummer, A. J., Earl, A., Schneider, J. A., Trapold, J., and Barrett, W.: Ann. N. Y. Acad. Sci., **59:** 8, 1954.

Rubin, B., and Burke, J. C.: Federation Proceedings, **13:** 400, 1954.

Schlittler, E., Macphillamy, L., Dorfman, A., Furlenmeier, A., Huebner, C. F., Lucas, R., Mueller, J. M., Schwyzer, R., and St. Andre, A. F.: Ann. N. Y. Acad. Sci., **59:** 17, 1954.

EFFECT OF IPRONIAZID ON SEROTONIN METABOLISM *IN VIVO*

SIDNEY UDENFRIEND, HERBERT WEISSBACH[1] AND DONALD F. BOGDANSKI

Laboratory of Clinical Biochemistry and Laboratory of Chemical Pharmacology, National Heart Institute, National Institutes of Health, Public Health Service, U. S. Department of Health, Education, and Welfare, Bethesda, Maryland

Received for publication January 25, 1957

It is now generally accepted that serotonin (5-hydroxytryptamine) is an important metabolite although its normal functions are still undetermined. What are needed at present are tools and techniques which will make possible the studies required to evaluate the place of serotonin in physiological function. If, as has been suggested, serotonin is a neurohumoral agent, then it may be liberated at nerve endings during appropriate stimulation. It may also be released from various depots to act in other ways. Whatever its functions, it is obvious that it is active at low concentrations (Page, 1954; Erpsamer, 1954). To detect the small amounts of serotonin which may appear during physiological studies it will be necessary to prevent their destruction by tissue catalysts. Since monoamine oxidase is apparently responsible for most of the observed serotonin destruction in tissue (Sjoerdsma *et al.*, 1955) inhibitors of this enzyme will be needed. Such inhibitors should advance our knowledge of serotonin in the same manner that cholinesterase inhibitors have advanced our knowledge of acetylcholine.

The ability of administered iproniazid to inhibit monoamine oxidase activity in homogenates (Zeller *et al.*, 1952) and to potentiate the pharmacological actions of 5-hydroxytryptophan (5HTP) (Udenfriend *et al.*, 1957) and other amines (Rebhun *et al.*, 1954; Schayer and Smiley, 1953) has been taken as evidence that this drug is a potent inhibitor of the actions of this enzyme *in vivo*. For this reason iproniazid is being widely used as a tool in pharmacological studies, particularly with respect to serotonin. However, if iproniazid were as effective *in vivo* as it is in homogenates then one would expect it to produce striking pharmacologic effects when administered alone due to increased levels of unmetabolized amines. Actually, iproniazid produces little pharmacologic effect when administered in quantity sufficient to inhibit almost completely the enzymatic destruction of serotonin and other amines in homogenates. The contradictory nature of these findings led to the following study concerning the efficiency of iproniazid as an inhibitor of monoamine oxidase *in vivo*.

MATERIALS AND METHODS. Iproniazid as the phosphate salt was generously supplied by Hoffmann-LaRoche Inc.

Serotonin in tissues was measured by methods previously described (Udenfriend *et al.*, 1955; Bogdanski *et al.*, 1956). Monoamine oxidase activity was determined by measuring

[1] Part of the work presented here was used by Herbert Weissbach in partial fulfillment of the requirements for the degree of Doctor of Philosophy, Department of Biochemistry, George Washington University, Washington, D. C.

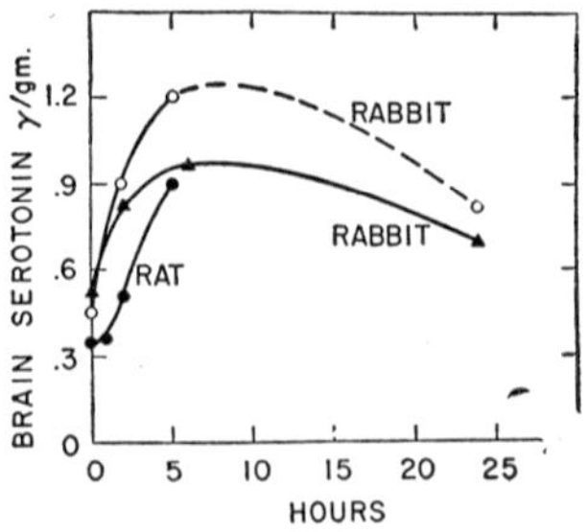

FIG. 1

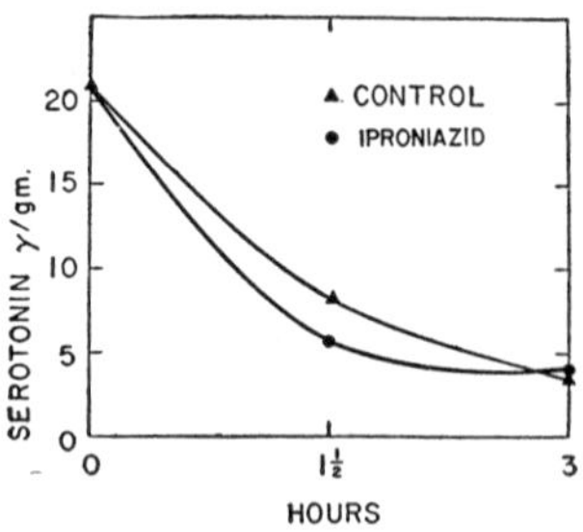

FIG. 2

FIG. 1. Increase in rabbit and rat brain serotonin levels after iproniazid.

Two hundred mgm./kgm. of iproniazid phosphate were administered to rabbits, and 240 mgm./kgm. were administered to rats. At various time intervals the animals were sacrificed and the brains removed and analyzed. Each point represents tissues from two animals.

FIG. 2. Effect of iproniazid on serotonin levels in whole mice after 5HTP.

Mice were pretreated with iproniazid phosphate (300 mgm./kgm.), and after 30 minutes received 80 mgm./kgm. of 5HTP. Control animals received 5HTP alone. At various time intervals the whole mice, including excreta, were assayed for serotonin. Each point represents three animals.

serotonin disappearance, as described by Sjoerdsma *et al.*, (1955). Tyramine was measured using the serotonin extraction procedure followed by colorimetric assay (Udenfriend and Cooper, 1952).

EXPERIMENTAL. *Effect of iproniazid on endogenous brain serotonin.* In previous studies on the biochemistry of 5-hydroxytryptophan it had been shown that administered iproniazid increases endogenous brain serotonin (Udenfriend *et al.*, 1957). Exactly how effective iproniazid is, in this respect, is shown in fig. 1. It is apparent that in both rats and rabbits, iproniazid increased brain serotonin to levels 2 to 3 times normal. Of interest too, is the rapidity with which the effects appeared, the highest level being attained in 3 to 5 hours. However, this increase was not maintained and the levels started to drop within a few hours, although the effects of administered iproniazid, as determined by inhibition of amine oxidation by homogenates, persisted for more than 24 hours (Zeller *et al.*, 1955). When repeated doses of iproniazid were administered over several days, the brain serotonin levels did not rise above the level produced by a single dose.[2] In the same animals in which brain serotonin levels were markedly increased, no increase in any of the other tissue depots was observed, *e. g.*, blood, stomach, intestine.

Effect of iproniazid on administered serotonin. These experiments were carried out with intact mice. Serotonin or its precursor, 5HTP, were administered to mice, both normal and treated with iproniazid. At intervals the mice were sacrificed, homogenized with their excreta and assayed for serotonin. It can be sene in fig. 2 that administration of iproniazid had little, if any, effect on the metabolism of serotonin. This was true whether the compound administered was serotonin or its precursor, 5HTP.

[2] Although a single dose of iproniazid was well tolerated, repeated daily administration produced severe toxicity making it difficult to use the animals for experimental purposes.

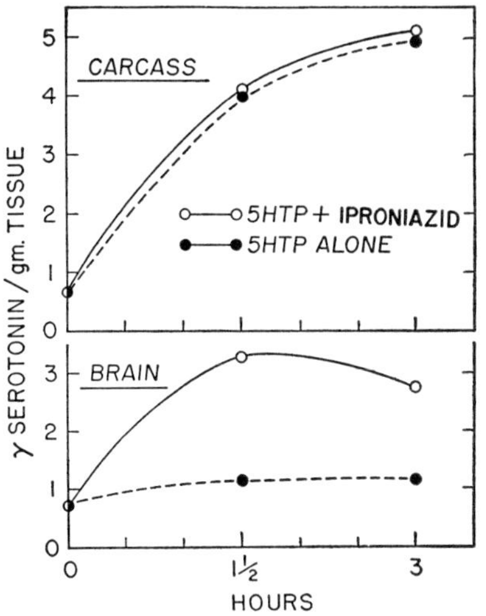

FIG. 3. Effect of Iproniazid on mouse brain and carcass serotonin levels after 5HTP. One set of mice was pretreated with iproniazid phosphate (300 mgm./kgm.) and 5HTP (80 mgm./kgm.) was administered 30 minutes later. Another set of animals received only 5HTP. At various time intervals the animals were sacrificed, and the brain and carcass of each animal homogenized separately. Each point represents the average of the tissues pooled from three animals.

Although the serotonin formed from 5HTP was not significantly increased in the whole animal by administration of iproniazid, the iproniazid-treated animals did show central effects suggesting that metabolism of exogenous serotonin might be inhibited centrally. Accordingly 5HTP was administered to mice following iproniazid and the brains and carcasses were assayed separately. It can be seen in fig. 3 that although iproniazid had no effect on the levels of serotonin in the carcass there was a large increase in brain serotonin.[3] Thus, once again, the ability of iproniazid to influence serotonin metabolism *in vivo* was demonstrable only in the central nervous system.

In rats, too, iproniazid had little effect on the metabolism of administered serotonin. Nine mgm./kgm. of serotonin were injected into control and iproniazid treated rats and the plasma levels were assayed at intervals. Levels of approximately 1 to 2 microgm./ml. of plasma were obtained in 15 minutes and in both cases there was a 70 per cent drop at the end of one hour.

Serotonin metabolism in slices and homogenates of iproniazid-pretreated animals. Although the destruction of injected serotonin in the intact animal was unaffected by iproniazid, homogenates prepared from tissues of these same iproniazid treated animals were practically devoid of any ability to destroy serotonin. Such findings were most puzzling and suggested that either a much more potent catalyst for serotonin destruction existed in intact cells before homogenization, or that iproniazid did not reach the site of monoamine oxidase activity in intact

[3] It should be noted that the amount of serotonin in brain is very small compared to the total body serotonin. Therefore, a substantial increase in brain serotonin would not significantly increase total body serotonin.

cells. There was nothing to support the first possibility since the rate of destruction of serotonin in homogenates appeared to be consistent with its rate of destruction in the intact animal. It has also been shown that 5-hydroxyindoleacetic acid (5HIAA), the expected end product of the action of monoamine oxidase on serotonin, is the major product of serotonin metabolism *in vivo* (Udenfriend *et al.*, 1956). The second possibility, that iproniazid did not reach the site of enzyme action in the intact cells, was therefore considered more likely. To investigate this possibility monoamine oxidase activity was measured in slices and homogenates from iproniazid-treated animals and these values were compared with those obtained on tissues from untreated control animals. The results of these experiments are shown in fig. 4 and 5. It can be seen that both liver and brain slices from iproniazid-treated animals were capable of metabolizing serotonin at virtually the same rates as slices from the untreated controls. On the other hand, homogenates prepared from portions of the same tissues from the iproniazid treated animals were completely devoid of activity.

It should be pointed out that the initial activity of iproniazid slices was comparable to that of controls but started to decrease after 15 to 30 minutes. This decline in rate has been taken to signify disintegration of the tissue slices. For this reason it was difficult to establish a difference in the behavior of slices and homogenates towards iproniazid when the inhibitor was added *in vitro*. For this inhibitor to be effective in the incubation flask, it must be preincubated with the tissues for up to 30 minutes before the substrate is added. Unless such preincubation is carried out little inhibition is observed (Zeller *et al.*, 1955). However, the time required for *in vitro* preincubation is as long as that found to abolish most of the differences between slices and homogenates observed on tissues from animals to which iproniazid had been administered *in vivo*. Even with these difficulties slices were found to be inhibited to a much lesser degree

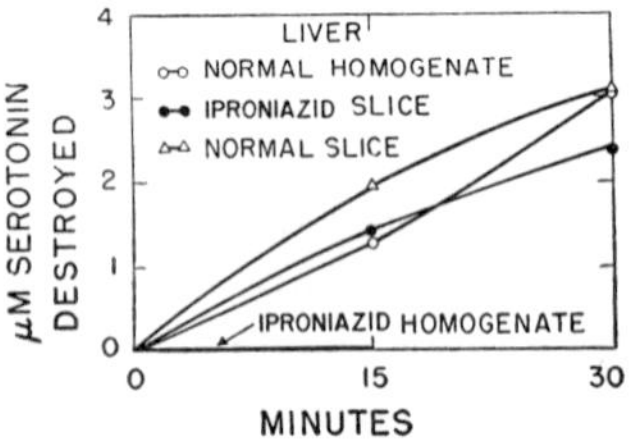

FIG. 4

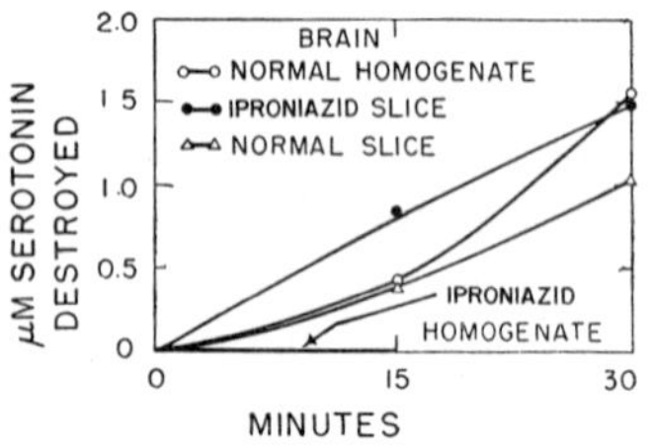

FIG. 5

FIG. 4. Serotonin destruction by liver slices and homogenates from normal and iproniazid treated rats. Rats were pretreated with iproniazid phosphate (100 mgm./kgm.). After one hour the animals were sacrificed and the liver divided into two parts. Half of the tissue was homogenized, while tissue slices were prepared from the other half. Each incubation beaker contained 666 mgm. of tissue, Krebs-Ringer buffer pH 7.4, and 1 mgm. of serotonin.

FIG. 5. Serotonin destruction by brain slices and homogenates from normal and iproniazid-treated rats.

Rats were pretreated with iproniazid phosphate (100 mgm./kgm.). After one hour the animals were sacrificed and the brain divided into two parts. Half of the tissue was homogenized, while tissue slices were prepared from the other half. Each incubation beaker contained 666 mgm. of tissue, Krebs-Ringer buffer pH 7.4, and 1 mgm. of serotonin.

than homogenates by the addition of iproniazid *in vitro*. However, the required preincubation period made these findings difficult to evaluate quantitatively.

Because of the observed effect of iproniazid on brain serotonin levels (fig. 1 and 3 above) it was thought that at least in this tissue there would be a demonstrable effect of iproniazid on the intact cells. However, it is apparent from the data in fig. 4 that brain slices do not differ from liver slices in this respect. The failure to observe such a difference may indicate that only certain areas of the brain are responsible for the observed *in vivo* effects of iproniazid on serotonin in the central nervous system.

Tyramine metabolism in iproniazid-treated animals. Monoamine oxidase can act on a variety of amines and tyramine has been widely used as a substrate in studies on this enzyme. To determine whether the effects described above were unique for serotonin or also occurred with other amines comparable experiments were repeated with tyramine. It was found that iproniazid had little influence on the destruction of parenterally administered tyramine in intact mice. Furthermore, as with serotonin, slices from iproniazid treated rats were able to metabolize tyramine although homogenates prepared from these same tissues were devoid of such activity (table 1).

Discussion. It is apparent from these experiments that iproniazid is a poor *in vivo* inhibitor of serotonin destruction in peripheral tissues. However, the observed effects of iproniazid on brain serotonin do explain earlier experiments indicating a potentiation of the pharmacological effects of 5HTP (Udenfriend *et al.*, 1957) by iproniazid. Thus, although iproniazid does not appear to be an effective inhibitor of serotonin generally, its specific action on brain serotonin makes it an interesting agent nevertheless.

It is probable that even the observed increase in brain serotonin in the central nervous system results from only a partial inhibition of monoamine oxidase and that a more potent inhibitor would produce really striking effects. Experiments now under way are designed to find effective inhibitors of monoamine oxidase in intact animals. Other compounds known to inhibit this enzyme *in vitro* include amphetamine (Blaschko, 1940), choline *p*-tolyl ether (Brown and Hey, 1952), and procaine amide. (Udenfriend *et al.*, unpublished data). However, these too are not effective *in vivo*. Further purification of monoamine oxidase

TABLE 1

Destruction of tyramine by normal liver and liver from iproniazid-treated animals

Tissue	μM of Tyramine Destroyed in 15 Minutes by 1 Gm. of Tissue
Normal slice	1.8
Iproniazid slice	1.1
Normal homogenate	2.4
Iproniazid homogenate	0.1

Animals received 300 mgm./kgm. of iproniazid phosphate 1 hour before the livers were removed. The incubation beakers contained 666 mgm. of tissue, Krebs-Ringer buffer (pH 7.4), and 600 microgm. of tyramine.

and demonstration of its cofactor requirements may explain the non-specific nature of these inhibitors and help in devising more effective agents for *in vivo* studies.

The observations reported here emphasize the caution needed in extrapolating from an experiment carried out on homogenates to the situation prevailing *in vivo*. In this case the drug, iproniazid, was administered to intact animals. When the animals were sacrificed and the tissues homogenized they were found to be devoid of monoamine oxidase activity. The obvious conclusion that iproniazid-treated animals do not metabolize serotonin or other amines was, however, erroneous since iproniazid did not inhibit until the cells were broken by homogenization.

An interesting conclusion that can be drawn from the rapid increase in endogenous brain serotonin following iproniazid administration concerns the rate of formation of serotonin in the central nervous system. If it is assumed that iproniazid is one hundred per cent effective in inhibiting destruction of endogenous serotonin then the observed rate of increase reflects the rate of serotonin synthesis. The data in fig. 1 indicate that in rat and rabbit brain the serotonin content is doubled in 2 to 3 hours. Actually the turnover must be even more rapid than this since iproniazid is apparently not a very effective inhibitor, even in the brain.

SUMMARY

Administration of 1-isopropyl-2-isonicotinyl hydrazide (iproniazid) to animals has been shown to produce a 2- to 3-fold increase in endogenous brain serotonin and to increase the amounts of serotonin appearing in brain following 5HTP. However, iproniazid has little effect on peripheral depots of serotonin or on the metabolism of serotonin or tyramine when they are administered parenterally. This is due to its inability to penetrate to the site of monoamine oxidase in intact cells.

REFERENCES

Blaschko, H.: Nature, **145:** 26, 1940.
Bogdanski, D. F., Pletscher, A., Brodie, B. B. and Udenfriend, S.: This Journal, **117:** 82, 1956.
Brown, B. G. and Hey, P.: J. Physiol., **118:** 15P, 1952.
Erspamer, V.: Pharm. Rev., **6:** 425, 1954.
Page, I. H.: Physiol. Rev., **34:** 563, 1954.
Rebhun, J., Feinberg, S. M. and Zeller, E. A.: Proc. Soc. Exper. Biol. & Med., **87:** 218, 1954.
Schayer, R. W. and Smiley, R. L.: J. Biol. Chem., **202:** 425, 1953.
Sjoerdsma, A., Smith, T. E., Stevenson, T. D. and Udenfriend, S.: Proc. Soc. Exper. Biol. and Med., **89:** 36, 1955.
Udenfriend, S. and Cooper, J. R.: J. Biol. Chem., **196:** 227, 1952.
Udenfriend, S., Weissbach, H. and Clark, C. T.: J. Biol. Chem., **215:** 337, 1955.
Udenfriend, S., Titus, E. O., Weissbach, H. and Peterson, R. E.: J. Biol. Chem., **219:** 335, 1956.
Udenfriend, S., Weissbach, H. and Bogdanski, D. F.: J. Biol. Chem., **224:** 803, 1957.
Zeller, E. A., Barsky, J., Fouts, J. R., Kirchheimer, W. F. and Van Orden, L. S.: Experientia, **8:** 349, 1952.
Zeller, E. A., Barsky, J. and Berman, E. R.: J. Biol. Chem., **214:** 267, 1955.

THE EFFECT OF CERTAIN CENTRAL NERVOUS SYSTEM DEPRESSANTS ON PITUITARY-ADRENAL ACTIVATING AGENTS

P. F. DIRK VAN PEENEN AND E. LEONG WAY

Department of Pharmacology, Schools of Medicine and Pharmacy, University of California, San Francisco

Received for publication January 28, 1957

Numerous pharmacologic agents have been shown to decrease adrenal ascorbic acid but the specific manner in which each agent elicits this effect remains obscure. It is well established that a reduction in adrenal ascorbic acid follows ACTH release by the adenohypophysis and more recent evidence indicates that the integrity of the hypothalamus is also essential (Harris, 1952; Hume, 1952; McCann, 1953; Porter, 1953, 1954; George and Way, 1957). These findings serve to define further the common pathways involved in drug activation of adrenal responses but yield no information as to the effector mechanisms involved.

One approach to this problem has been the use of chemical blocking agents to differentiate the possible modes in which various pharmacologic agents may activate the hypothalamo-pituitary-adrenal axis. Thus, it was recently shown in the rat that nalorphine blocks the adrenal ascorbate depleting effects of morphine and *l*-methadone but not the effects of aspirin and *d*-methadone (George and Way, 1955). As a consequence, it was suggested that different receptors or sites are concerned for mediating the response to morphine and aspirin; likewise for *l*-methadone and *d*-methadone. Contiguous with this hypothesis, Briggs and Munson (1954, 1955) reported that sodium pentobarbital inhibited adrenal ascorbate reduction by morphine in rats but failed to block the effects evoked by histamine and epinephrine. Similarly, Semonsen and Sawyer (1954) reported that in the rabbit 2-benzylaminoethanol blocked eosinopenia induced by histamine but it had no effect on epinephrine-induced eosinopenia. In view of the above findings, a study was initiated to study the effects of some central nervous system depressants on the adrenal ascorbic acid depleting action of four well known activators in the hope that some systematic classification of the mechanisms involved would ensue.

EXPERIMENTAL PROCEDURE. In each series of experiments one of the blocking compounds was tested for its ability to inhibit the adrenal ascorbic acid reducing properties of four activating agents in male Sprague-Dawley rats. The animals, weighing between 70 and 140 grams, were maintained on a diet of Friskies dog chow and tap water, were weighed, and were brought to the laboratory the evening before being used. All drugs were administered intraperitoneally, and with the exception of sodium pentobarbital[1] and reserpine,[2] all were dissolved in distilled water. The activating agents, with their respective doses which were established beforehand to give a comparable degree of adrenal

[1] Dissolved in 5 per cent ethanol and 10 per cent propylene glycol.

[2] Serpasil, Ciba—each ml. contains 2.5 mgm. in a solution of benzyl alcohol, 2 per cent; citric acid, 0.25 per cent; and polyethylene glycol, 10 per cent.

ascorbate depletion, were as follows: aspirin, 150 mgm./kgm.; morphine hydrochloride, 30 mgm./kgm.; epinephrine, 0.4 mgm./kgm.; histamine acid phosphate, 27 mgm./kgm. (equivalent base 10 mgm./kgm.). The blocking agents were used in a dosage previously determined to cause little or no effect on adrenal ascorbic acid. Each blocking agent (distilled water for controls) was administered prior to the activating drug at a time interval estimated to permit its peak action to coincide with the effective period of the activating agent. A summary of the pertinent data is listed below:

Blocking Agent	Dose, mgm./kgm.	Time Before Injecting Activating Drug
Sodium pentobarbital	40	15 minutes
Dibenzyline (N-phenoxyisopropyl-N-benzyl-β-chlorethyl-amine hydrochloride)	2	60 minutes
Nalorphine	5	5 minutes
Reserpine	10	12 to 15 hours
Chlorpromazine	3	60 minutes

One hour after injection of the activating drug (distilled water in control experiments) the animals were sacrificed by decapitation. Both adrenals were removed, dissected free of fat, and analyzed for ascorbic acid content by the Schaffert and Kingsley (1955) modification of the Roe-Kuether method (1943). Control experiments on the activating agent as well as the blocking agent were always made in each set of experiments. The Student t test was used for the statistical evaluation of the results. The level of significance was arbitrarily set at the 5 per cent level (P = <0.05).

RESULTS. *Sodium pentobarbital.* As indicated in figure 1, there was a marked blockade of the adrenal ascorbic acid response to morphine and aspirin. These results are in agreement with those of Cronheim and Hyder (1954) on aspirin and Briggs and Munson (1954) on morphine. Contrary to the findings of Cronheim and Hyder, we observed no consistent difference in the adrenal ascorbic acid concentration of those rats which were fully anesthetized with pentobarbital as

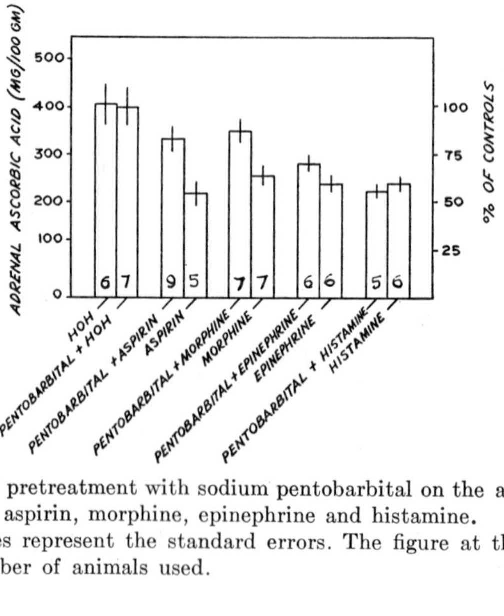

FIG. 1. Effects of pretreatment with sodium pentobarbital on the adrenal ascorbic acid response of rats to aspirin, morphine, epinephrine and histamine.

The vertical lines represent the standard errors. The figure at the base of each bar represents the number of animals used.

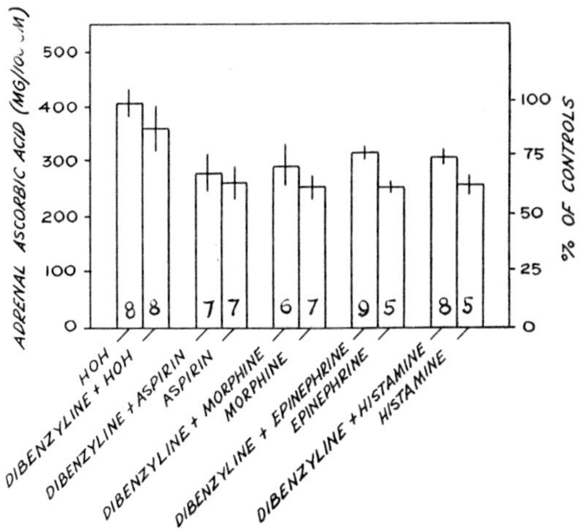

FIG. 2. Effects of pretreatment with Dibenzyline on the adrenal ascorbic acid response of rats to aspirin, morphine, epinephrine and histamine.

compared with those which were not. In confirmation of Briggs and Munson (1954) and Olling and de Wied (1956), no significant inhibition of the effects of epinephrine and histamine were noted.

Dibenzyline. The results, as shown in figure 2, were not as concise as one might wish because of the variations in the adrenal response to Dibenzyline alone. There was a partial blockade of the effect of epinephrine which was statistically significant. The response to aspirin and morphine was not affected. The apparent blockade of the histamine response was not significant ($P = >0.05$). Ohler and Sevy (1953) reported that the depletion of adrenal ascorbic acid caused by epinephrine in the rat was completely blocked by intravenous injections of Dibenzyline but it should be pointed out that these animals had been previously anesthetized with sodium pentobarbital.

Nalorphine. In confirmation of earlier findings (George and Way, 1955) there was a marked inhibition of the effects of morphine (figure 3), but not of aspirin and epinephrine. The apparent slight block in the effects of histamine was not considered to be significant ($P = > 0.05$).

Reserpine. As shown in figure 4, reserpine produced a significant block in the effects of epinephrine and a moderate block of morphine but did not materially influence the depletion caused by histamine and aspirin. This inhibition of the response to epinephrine and morphine by reserpine is perhaps even more significant if one considers that reserpine *per se* caused some reduction of the ascorbic acid in the adrenals.

Chlorpromazine. The results were similar to those obtained with reserpine. The effects of epinephrine and morphine were both blocked but not those of aspirin and histamine. In the case of epinephrine, the blocking effect was quite substantial.[3] This finding is consistent with that reported by Aron, Chambon

[3] Additional experiments on seven chlorpromazine-epinephrine animals yielded similar results.

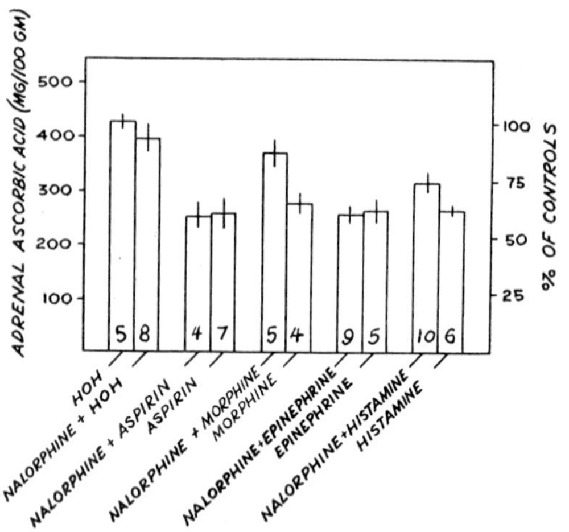

FIG. 3. Effects of pretreatment with nalorphine on the adrenal ascorbic response of rats to aspirin, morphine, epinephrine and histamine.

and Voisin (1953), but not with that of Holzbauer and Vogt (1954) and Nasmyth (1955). In the experiments of Holzbauer and Vogt, a dosage of chlorpromazine (10 mgm./kgm.) was used that caused a very large reduction in the adrenal ascorbic acid by itself and this probably obscured their results. Nasmyth reported on the basis of only three animals in each of the groups in question. Nasmyth also reported blockade of histamine effects by chlorpromazine which the present study fails to confirm. Although his experimental conditions were not identical to ours, the differences in procedure appear to be relatively minor.

DISCUSSION. The results show that certain pharmacological blocking agents can selectively influence the depletion of adrenal ascorbic acid following administration of different drugs. In experiments designed to standardize the doses of the blocking and activating agents, it was found that agents effective in blocking the response to one drug may have no influence on the response to another. It appears reasonable to conclude, therefore, that different effector mechanisms or sites are stimulated by the activating agents and that some degree of selective inhibition is exhibited by the blocking agents.

The results of the blocking agents on the response to epinephrine and histamine are of especial interest in view of their previously postulated role as neurohumoral mediators of the adenohypophysis (Long, 1952; Harris *et al.*, 1952), and the fact that high concentrations of both epinephrine (Vogt, 1954) and histamine (Harris *et al.*, 1952) have been reported in the hypothalamus. Evidence that the two substances act at different receptor sites is indicated by the finding that chlorpromazine, reserpine, and Dibenzyline partially blocked the reduction of adrenal ascorbic acid by epinephrine but not the reduction by histamine. However, it has been reported that the effects of both histamine and epinephrine can be blocked by the combination of sodium pentobarbital plus morphine (Briggs and Munson, 1955) and by sodium pentobarbital plus chlorpromazine (Olling and de Wied, 1956). It is interesting to note that preliminary work shows that the

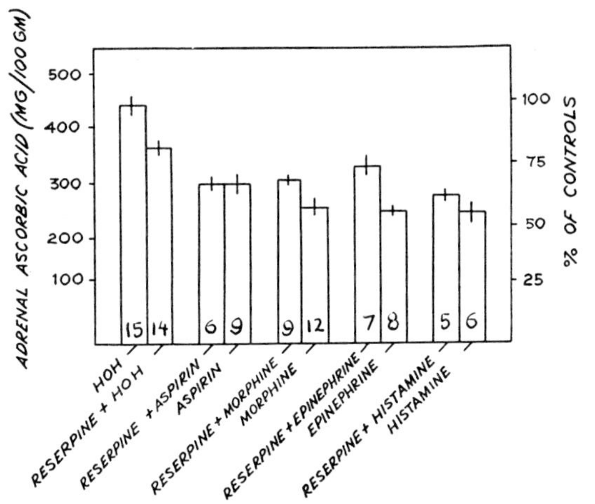

FIG. 4. Effects of pretreatment with reserpine on the adrenal ascorbic acid response of rats to aspirin, morphine, epinephrine and histamine.

action of serotonin, another endogenous activator of the pituitary-adrenal response, does not appear to be blocked by any of the depressants used in this study.

The fact that evidence has been presented to indicate that different drugs act at different sites or receptors to activate the adrenal cortex does not preclude the possibility that such drugs may have their actions mediated through common intermediary systems in addition to the adenohypophysis. It is quite probable that the hypothalamus is the next level intermediary system which is common to many agents known to activate the pituitary-adrenal system, for it has been shown that lesions in the median eminence block the adrenal ascorbic acid reducing effects of aspirin (George and Way, 1957), morphine (George and Way, unpublished data), epinephrine (McCann, 1953), and histamine (Porter, 1953, 1954). That even higher common intermediary systems may exist is suggested by the findings of Sawyer *et al.* (1955). Sawyer found that dosages of pentobarbital, morphine and atropine which blocked neurogenic stimulation of pituitary ovulating hormone release in the rat also depressed the reticular activating system to the extent that a sleep-like electrohypothalamographic record and an elevation of the threshold to electrical arousal of the midbrain reticular formation was produced. He suggested that blockade of pituitary activation by these drugs is related to their demonstrated common effects on the central nervous system and implied that the reticular activating system plays some role to excite hypothalamic centers controlling adenohyphyseal function.

These studies point out that the possible mechanism of adrenal ascorbic acid reduction in the hypothalamo-pituitary-adrenal system by chemical agents can be varied and complex. The theoretical possibility exists that any one organ of this triad is capable of being acted upon directly by pharmacologic agents. In addition, consideration of the indirect effects on this system chould not be neglected. Conceivably, any pharmacologic substance which can evoke a dis-

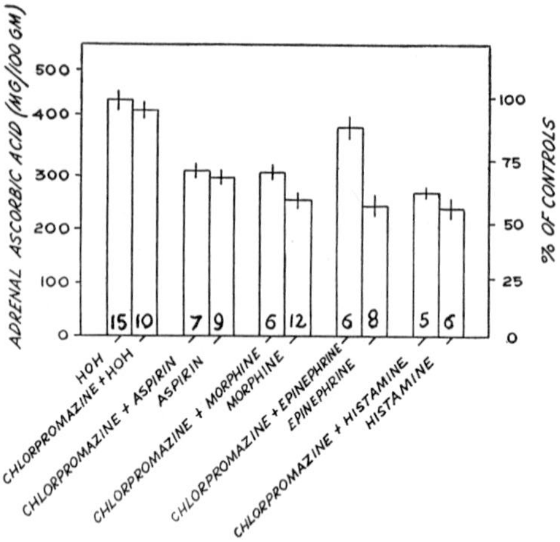

FIG. 5. Effects of pretreatment with chlorpromazine on the adrenal ascorbic acid response of rats to aspirin, morphine, epinephrine and histamine.

charge of naturally occurring neurohumoral substances (*e.g.*, epinephrine, acetylcholine, histamine, 5-hydroxytryptamine, *etc.*) or can increase the rate of destruction or decrease the rate of utilization of the specific humoral agents (hydroxycorticoids, ACTH, or ACTH-releasing substance) released respectively by the adrenals, adenohypophysis or hypothalamus, should effect depletion of adrenal ascorbic acid. In assessing the mode of action of any pharmacologic agents on the hypothalamo-pituitary-adrenal system, all these factors must be considered.

SUMMARY

The effects of five chemical blocking agents were examined in the rat as to ability to inhibit the adrenal ascorbic acid depleting action of four well known pituitary adrenal activators. Pretreatment with sodium pentobarbital significantly blocked the adrenal ascorbic acid reduction effects of aspirin and morphine but not of epinephrine or histamine. Pretreatment with Dibenzyline partially blocked only the response to epinephrine. Nalorphine blocked only the action of morphine. Chlorpromazine and reserpine both significantly blocked the effects of epinephrine and to a lesser degree those of morphine. It would seem, therefore, that a common effector site for the activating drugs cannot be assumed.

ACKNOWLEDGMENTS. This study was supported in part by grants from the Institute of Analgesic and Sedative Drugs and from the Division of Research Grants, National Institutes of Health. We are grateful to Dr. Robert George, Miss Joan Taylor, Dr. Gilbert Gordan and Dr. Ernest Page, for their comments, advice and cooperation.

REFERENCES

ARON, E., CHAMBON, Y., AND VOISIN, A.: Bull. Acad. Nat. Med., **137:** 417, 1953.
BRIGGS, F. N., AND MUNSON, P. L.: THIS JOURNAL, **110:** 7, 1954.

BRIGGS, F. N., AND MUNSON, P. L.: Endocrinol., **57:** 205, 1955.
CRONHEIM, G., AND HYDER, N.: Proc. Soc. Exp. Biol. & Med., **86:** 409, 1954.
GEORGE, R., AND WAY, E. LEONG: Brit. J. Pharmacol., **10:** 260, 1955.
GEORGE, R., AND WAY, E. LEONG: THIS JOURNAL, **119:** 310, 1957.
HARRIS, G. W., JACOBSON, D., AND KAHLSON, G.: Ciba Found. Colloq. Endocrinol., **4:** 186, 1952.
HUME, D. M.: Ciba Found. Colloq. Endocrinol., **4:** 87, 1952.
HOLZBAUER, M., AND VOGT, M.: Brit. J. Pharmacol., **9:** 402, 1954.
LONG, C. N. H.: Rec. Prog. in Horm. Res., **7:** 75, 1952.
McCANN, S. M.: Am. J. Physiol., **175:** 13, 1953.
NASMYTH, P. A.: Brit. J. Pharmacol., **10:** 336, 1955.
OHLER, E. A., AND SEVY, R. W.: Am. J. Physiol., **175:** 285, 1953.
OLLING, CH. C. J., AND DE WIED, D.: Acta Endocrinol., **22:** 283, 1956.
PORTER, R. W.: Am. J. Physiol., **172:** 515, 1953.
PORTER, R. W.: Rec. Prog. in Horm. Res., **10:** 1, 1954.
ROE, J. H., AND KUETHER, C. A.: J. Biol. Chem., **147:** 399, 1943.
SAWYER, C. H., CRITCHLOW, B. V., AND BARRACLOUGH, C. A.: Endocrinol., **57:** 345, 1955.
SCHAFFERT, R. R., AND KINGSLEY, G. R.: J. Biol. Chem., **212:** 59, 1955.
SEMONSEN, C. R., AND SAWYER, C. H.: Am. J. Physiol., **177:** 405, 1954.
VOGT, M.: J. Physiol., **123:** 451, 1954.

RELATION OF PERIPHERAL VASODILATOR ACTIVITY TO CHEMICAL STRUCTURE OF 1,2,3,4-TETRAHYDROISO-QUINOLINE DERIVATIVES

DONALD L. COOK, COLETA A. LAWLER AND JOHN W. CUSIC

The Divisions of Biological Research and Chemical Research, G. D. Searle & Co., Chicago, Illinois

Received for publication January 30, 1957

In the course of studying a variety of compounds for their vascular effects it was found that 1,2,3,4-tetrahydroisoquinoline hydrochloride (THIQ) was an effective vasodilator. Substitutions in the 1, 2 and 3 positions (see table 1) have been shown to modify this activity quantitatively. A series of these substituted tetrahydroisoquinolines was synthesized in order to study the influence of chemical structure on vasodilator activity.

Hjort *et al.* (1940a) studied an homologous series of 2-alkyl derivatives of THIQ. They reported that toxicity increased with the lengthening of straight chain homologs, but there was no consistent trend with similar treatment of branched iso-homologs. Hjort *et al.* (1940b) also demonstrated blockade or reversal of epinephrine vasopressor activity with some of these compounds. Nickerson and Gump (1949) included several N-substituted THIQ compounds in a study of adrenergic blockade. They described activity of short duration for one of the compounds in the present study (table 1, No. III). Some of the compounds discussed below also possess adrenergic blocking action, and this property is discussed for one of the most potent compounds. The present report is concerned primarily with the relationship between chemical structure and peripheral vasodilator activity of substituted THIQ derivatives. Chemically, the compounds are divided into four types: 1) aliphatic, 2) heterocyclic, 3) ester and 4) ether derivatives.

METHODS. *Peripheral vasodilator activity* was determined quantitatively in pentobarbitalized adult mongrel dogs. The rate of blood flow in the right femoral artery was determined with a Shipley (1944) rotameter connected to a Sanborn Electrocardiograph for continuous recording of the flow rate. The femoral artery was cannulated both centrally and distally, and the rotameter placed in direct circuit between the two cannulas. The compounds were administered intraarterially by injection into the tubing connecting the rotameter and the distal artery. Clotting was controlled by using a combination of heparin and pontamine fast pink (Winbury *et al.*, 1950). Blood pressure was recorded routinely; however, since the effects of the intraarterial injections were negligible, blood pressure data are not included.

All doses, ranging from 0.008 to 12.8 microgm. per kgm. depending upon the activity of the compound, were given in 0.25 ml. normal saline adjusted to pH 7. Pairs of geometrically spaced doses of unknown and standard, which gave responses on the linear portion of the dose-response curve, were used in Sherwood's (1947) two-dose assay procedure for determining relative potency. Since maximal flow was found to be directly related to control flow, the values used in the assay procedure were the increase over control flow, *i.e.*, response flow *minus* control flow. Each compound was assayed against the standard in at least two

TABLE 1

Effect on peripheral vasodilator activity of various derivatives of 1,2,3,4-tetrahydroisoquinoline

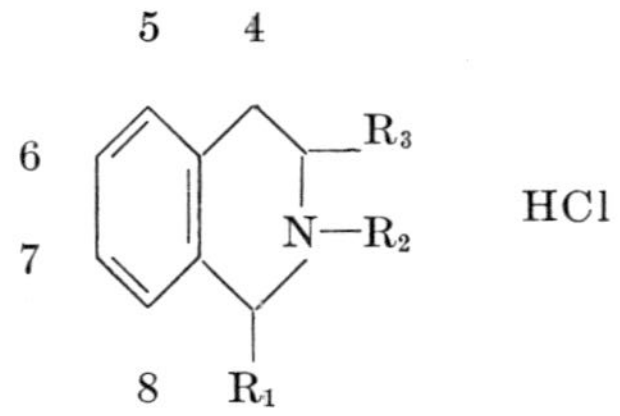

Aliphatic-type Derivatives			Heterocyclic Derivatives		
No.	R_2	Molar potency	No.	R_2	Molar potency
I	H	1.0	VIII	$—CH_2CH_2OOC—$ 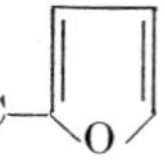	4.8
II	$—CH_2CH_2OH$	0.7	IX	$—CH_2CH_2OOC—$ 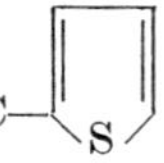	6.9
III	$—CH_2CH_2Cl$	<0.25	X	$—CH_2CH_2OCH_2—$ 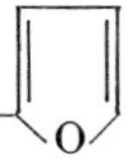	5.1
IV	$—CH_2CH_2Cl$*	<0.25	XI	$—CH_2CH_2OCH_2—$ 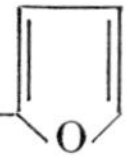	17.2
V	$—CH_2CH_2Cl$**	<0.25	XII	$—CH_2CH_2OCH_2—$ 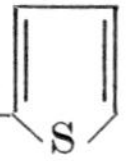	45.4

VI	—$COOCH_2CH_2N(CH_3)_2$	<0.25	XIII	—$CH_2CH_2OCH_2$—  ·HCl	13.9
VII	—$COOCH_2CH_2N(CH_3)_2$†	<0.25	XIV	—CH_2CH_2OOC—  ·HCl	4.4
XV–XXVI Ester Derivatives			**XXVII–XXXIV Ether Derivatives**		
No.	R_2	Molar potency	No.	R_2	Molar potency
XV	—CH_2CH_2OOC— 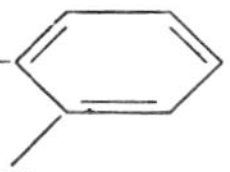 Cl	10.6	XXV	—CH_2CH_2OOC— 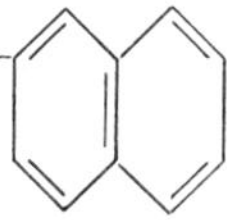	1.2
XVI	—CH_2CH_2OOC—  —Cl	4.6	XXVI	—CH_2CH_2OOC— 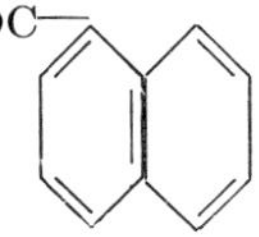	0.3
XVII	—$CH_2CH_2OOCCH_2$— 	1.6	XXVII	—$CH_2CH_2OCH_2$— 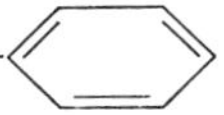	4.7
XVIII	—CH_2CH_2OOC— 	0.7	XXVIII	—$CH_2CH_2OCH_2$—  ‡	3.7
XIX	—$CH_2CH_2OOCCH_2$— 	0.4	XXIX	—$CH_2CH_2OCH_2$— 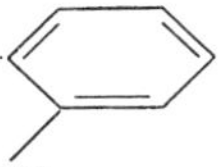 CH_3	8.0

TABLE 1—*Continued*

XV-XXVI Ester Derivatives			XXVII-XXXIV Ether Derivatives		
No.	R_2	Molar potency	No.	R_2	Molar potency
XX	$—CH_2CH_2OOC(CH_2)_2—$ 	5.7	XXX	$—CH_2CH_2OC_2—$ 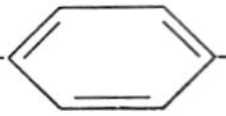 $—OCH_3$	3.7
XXI	$—CH_2CH_2OOC(CH_2)_3—$ 	2.7	XXXI	$—CH_2CH_2OCH_2—$ 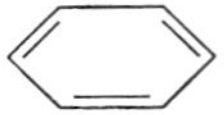 $—Cl$	11.5
XXII	$—CH_2CH_2OOC(CH_2)_4—$ 	1.7	XXXII	$—CH_2CH_2OCH_2—$ 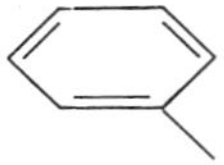 $—Cl$ Cl	1.5
XXIII	$—CH_2CH_2OOCCH_2O—$ 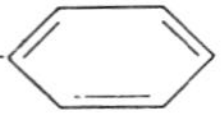	2.8	XXXIII	$—CH_2CH_2OCH_2CH_2—$ 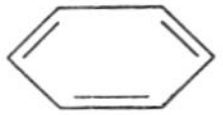	6.7
XXIV	$—CH_2CH_2OOCCHO—$ 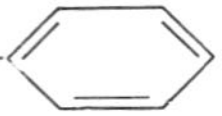	6.1	XXXIV	$—CH_2CH_2OCH_2—$ 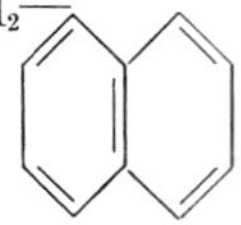	6.3

* No. IV has a CH_3 group at R_3.
† VII is a methoiodide quaternary.
** No. V has a C_6H_5 group at R_1.
‡ No. XXVIII has a CH_3 group at R_3.

dogs and the potency values were averaged. Compounds having less than one-fourth the activity of the parent compound (THIQ) were arbitrarily considered to be inactive.

The normal variability of the assay procedure was studied on potency determinations obtained over a period of time in this laboratory. Statistical analysis of the data indicated that the average potencies of any two compounds, tested in two dogs each, must differ at least fourfold to be significantly different ($P < 0.05$).

Adrenergic blocking activity was determined in cats anesthetized with sodium pentobarbital. Blood pressure was recorded from the right carotid artery. Epinephrine hydrochloride and compounds studied were injected into a cannula in a femoral vein and washed in with two ml. of normal saline.

RESULTS AND DISCUSSION. *Peripheral vasodilator activity.* Typical examples of flow records showing the response of the femoral vascular bed to intraarterial injections of several vasodilator agents are reproduced in fig. 1. The onset of the increase in femoral arterial blood flow is very rapid and the duration of vasodilatation is approximately twenty to fifty seconds. As is indicated, tetrahydroisoquinoline (THIQ) is approximately as active as tolazoline (Priscoline) (2-benzyl-2-imidazoline) and less active than papaverine. One of the most potent derivatives of THIQ, the N-*beta*-hydroxyethyl-2-thenyl ether, is markedly more active than THIQ.

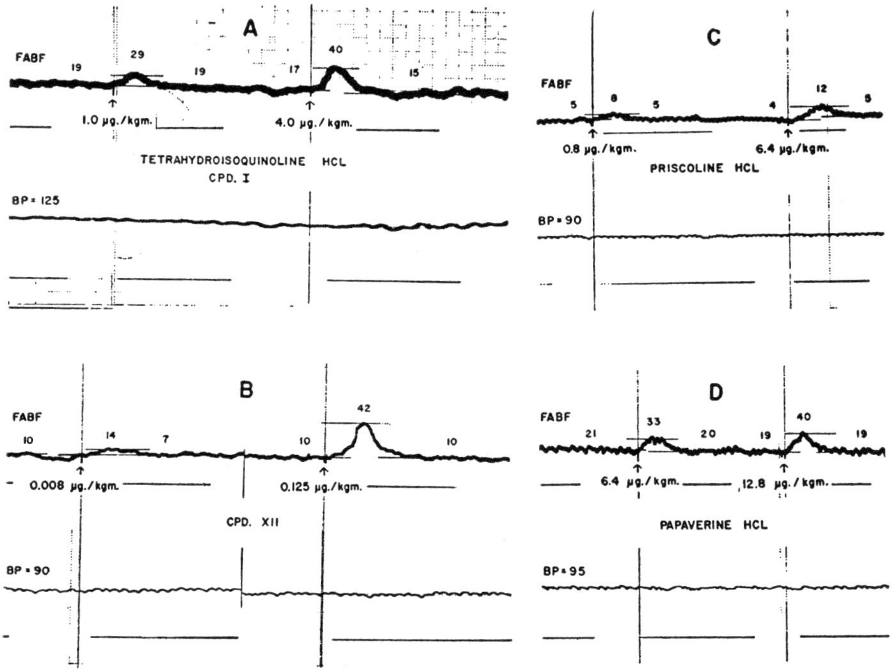

FIG. 1. Blood flow responses in the hind leg of the dog following intraarterial injections: (A) 1, 2, 3, 4-tetrahydroisoquinoline (Cpd. I in the text), (B), Cpd. XII, the N-*beta*-hydroxyethyl-2-thenyl ether derivative of CPD. I, and two standard vasodilator agents, Priscoline (C) and papaverine (D). Figures above the curves are rates of femoral arterial blood flow (FABF) in ml./min. Femoral arterial blood pressures (BP) are indicated in mm. Hg. Time between heavy vertical lines is 10 seconds.

The peripheral vasodilator activity of 34 compounds was measured. The molar potency of each compound relative to THIQ (potency = 1) together with its structural formula is summarized in table 1. Each compound has been assigned a consecutive Roman numeral to facilitate reference to it in the text. The data in the table permit pointing out certain interesting structure-activity relationships.

Aliphatic-type derivatives: The hydroxyethyl derivative (II) has approximately the same activity as the parent compound (I); however, chlorethyl substituted compounds (III) with or without CH_3 (IV) or C_6H_5 (V) on carbon atoms adjacent to the nitrogen are inactive. The carbamate (VI) is inactive and quaternization with methyl iodide does not impart activity.

Heterocyclic derivatives: The most active heterocyclic derivative is the thenyl ether (XII). In general the thiophenes tend to be more active than the corresponding furans. The pyridine compounds (XIII, XIV) have moderate activity.

Ester derivatives: The most active compound of this group is the ortho-chloro substituted benzoate (XV). Among the homologous esters (XVIII through XXII), the cyclohexyl propionate (XX) is the most active, and lengthening of the chain results in a progressive decrease of activity. The *beta*-naphthoate (XXV) is more active than the *alpha*-napthoate.

Ether derivatives: The most active ether derivative is the *para*-chloro substituted benzyl derivative (XXXI). Either the substitution of an additional chlorine (XXXII) or removal of the chlorine (XXVII) results in decreased activity. The *alpha*-naphthyl derivative (XXXIV) has the same order of activity as the benzyl compound (XXVII).

Adrenergic blocking activity. One of the most potent vasodilators, the 2-thenyl ether derivative of N-*beta*-hydroxy-THIQ (cpd. No. XII, table 1.) was also

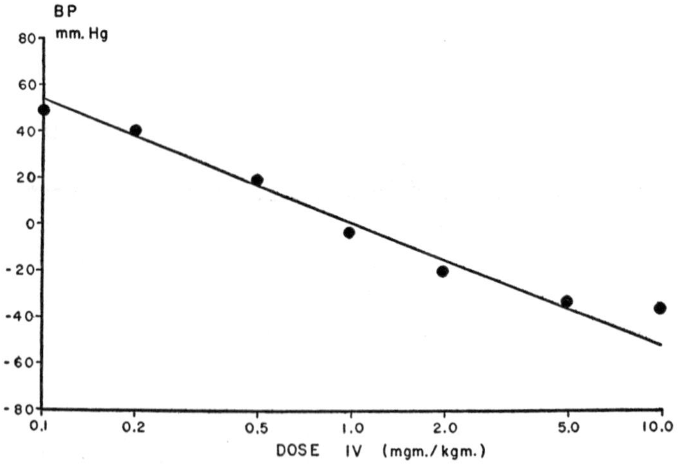

FIG. 2. Blood pressure responses to epinephrine, 5 microgm. per kgm. intravenously, following increasing doses of the 2-thenyl ether derivative of N-*beta*-hydroxyethyl-tetrahydroisoquinoline hydrochloride (Cpd. XII, table 1). Points represent the average results in 2 pentabarbitalized cats.

found to possess potent adrenergic blocking activity in two anesthetized cats. Successive intravenous doses ranging from 0.1 to 10 mgm. per kgm. were given and epinephrine, 5 microgm. per kgm., was injected after each dose. The change in blood pressure produced by this dose of epinephrine, either pressor or depressor, was plotted against dosage of the compound (fig. 2). Doses above 0.2 mgm. per kgm. reduced the height of the epinephrine pressor response. Epinephrine "reversal" occurred with doses above 1.0 mgm. per kgm.

SUMMARY

Peripheral vasodilator activity of a series of 1,2,3,4-tetrahydroisoquinoline (THIQ) derivatives was studied in the dog. The series included four chemical types: aliphatic, heterocyclic, ester and ether. Activity was found in all types. The most active compound was a heterocyclic derivative, N-*beta*-hydroxyethyl-THIQ-2-thenyl ether, which was forty-five times as active as the parent compound (THIQ). This compound was also found to possess potent adrenergic blocking activity.

ACKNOWLEDGMENT. The help of Mr. David Calhoun in the statistical work is gratefully acknowledged.

REFERENCES

HJORT, A. M., DEBEER, E. J., AND FASSETT, D. W.: THIS JOURNAL, **68:** 69, 1940a.
HJORT, A. M., DEBEER, E. J., AND FASSETT, D. W.: THIS JOURNAL, **68:** 73, 1940b.
NICKERSON, M., AND GUMP, W. S.: THIS JOURNAL, **97:** 25, 1949.
SHERWOOD, M. B.: Science, **106:** 152, 1947.
SHIPLEY, R. E., AND CRITTENDEN, JR., E. C.: Proc. Soc. Exper. Biol. & Med., **56:** 103, 1944.
WINBURY, M. M., MICHIELS, P. M., HAMBOURGER, W. E., STOCKFISCH, W. J., AND COOK, D. L.: THIS JOURNAL, **99:** 343, 1950.

PYRIDINE-2-ALDOXIME METHIODIDE IN THE TREATMENT OF SARIN AND TABUN POISONING, WITH NOTES ON ITS PHARMACOLOGY

ROBERT V. BROWN, ANNE M. KUNKEL, LEA M. SOMERS AND J. HENRY WILLS

Physiology Division, Chemical Warfare Laboratories, Army Chemical Center, Maryland

Received for publication January 31, 1957

This report is concerned chiefly with the successful therapy of poisoning produced by intravenous injection of large doses (eight to ten LD_{50}) of the anticholinesterases sarin (isopropyl methylphosphonofluoridate) and tabun (dimethylamidoethoxyphosphoryl cyanide). Holmstedt (1951), DeCandole *et al.* (1953) and Krop and Kunkel (1954) have described the functional alterations produced by these two agents. The principal effects fall into three groups: first, those on the central nervous system; second, the muscarinic effects; third, the nicotinic effects.

Large doses of either agent, when given by vein, produce abrupt respiratory failure and thereby death. With interrupted positive pressure artificial respiration, either dogs or cats can be maintained for some time in moderately good condition; the time is dependent on the size of the dose of either agent. Portions of the central nervous system are stimulated, resulting in convulsions, which are somewhat reduced, but are not abolished, by anesthetic levels of pentobarbital sodium. Similar results after DFP poisoning have been noted by McNamara, Koelle, and Gilman (1946). Atropine sulfate therapy partially abates the convulsions after sarin or tabun; a similar therapeutic effect of atropine sulfate was noted after DFP poisoning by Wescoe *et al.* (1948).

The muscarinic effects correspond to those which would be expected from the anticholinesterasic action of sarin and tabun. The muscarinic component of anticholinesterase poisoning is almost completely abolished by atropine therapy (*cf.:* McNamara *et al.* (1946), Modell *et al.* (1946), Modell and Krop (1946) on DFP; Wright (1954) on sarin and DFP; Loomis and Krop (1956) on sarin; Krop and Kunkel (1954) on sarin and tabun).

The nicotinic actions of chief concern in this paper are the peripheral neuromuscular transmission defects which appear promptly after either agent. In the cat, there is fleeting augmentation of twitch height, quickly followed by complete neuromuscular block (*cf.:* DeCandole *et al.*, 1953; Riker, 1953; Wright, 1954; Kunkel *et al.*, 1956). Responses in the dog are described later. Against neuromuscular block, atropine sulfate (in doses which can be used intravenously) has no significant effect (Kunkel *et al.*, 1956).

METHODS. Cats and dogs were anesthetized with pentobarbital sodium, 32 mgm./kgm. Respiration was recorded from the side arm of an inserted tracheal cannula. Blood pressure was recorded by a bronze bellows manometer from the right common carotid artery. The calcaneous tendon was attached through cord and pulleys to an isotonic muscle lever, recording on the kymograph. The distal end of the ipsilateral sciatic nerve was placed on shielded electrodes activated by a square wave generator. This discharged at a rate of 24 per minute to produce single stimuli; as needed, the frequency was changed to 40 per second to generate a 30-second tetanus. Voltage was just supramaximal, with a shock duration of 0.15 msec. Twitch height and height of the tetanic plateau at 30 seconds (hereafter called "tension" for brevity) were determined from the kymograph record. A 15-second rest was given before and after each tetanus. Except for these periods and the 30-second tetanus, single shocks were given throughout all experiments involving testing of neuromuscular responses.

Two cats, in addition to being prepared as above, were arranged for phrenic nerve-diaphragm recordings as well: one phrenic nerve was crushed centrally and placed on stimulating electrodes wired in parallel to those on the sciatic nerve; a cord was hooked to the exposed under surface of the ipsilateral half of the diaphragm and led through pulleys to a muscle lever.

The amount of each anticholinesterase injected by vein in either species was eight to ten times the intravenous LD_{50}. These doses were prepared by dilution of the agents in anhydrous propylene glycol; from these solutions, working dilutions were made in 0.9 per cent saline such that 0.1 ml. contained the specified dose for one kgm. of animal. Atropine sulfate (hereafter, atropine) was given by vein in dosage of 0.5 mgm./kgm.; the time of injection (whether prophylactic or therapeutic) is specified later. Pyridine-2-aldoxime methiodide[1] (PAM-2) was injected intravenously after being dissolved in 0.9 per cent saline to either 10 or 50 mgm./ml.; such solutions appeared to be somewhat unstable and were never used if over one hour old.

Animals were placed on interrupted positive pressure artificial respiration whenever respiration became inadequate as shown by an asphyxial blood pressure rise, by cyanosis, or by respiratory arrest. Hereafter, "breathing" denotes adequate spontaneous respiration. The sufficiency of breathing was judged by the physical signs in the animal and by the respiration record on the kymograph.

Time is uniformly measured from 0 hours, the time of injection of the sarin or tabun; such times are shown numerically in the text. Temporal relations of drug administrations are given later, in detail.

Where results of tests of significance are shown, the tests were straight variance analyses, with $P < 0.05$ chosen as significant.

RESULTS. 1. *Cats and dogs with prophylactic atropine, with and without PAM-2 therapy.* In four cats poisoned with sarin after receiving 0.5 mgm./kgm. of atropine, breathing returned in 22 ± 12 minutes; in three similar cats which received also therapy with PAM-2 (5 mgm./kgm., at five minutes; dose repeated in two cats) breathing returned in 9.0 ± 2.3 minutes. The difference is not significant, with $P > 0.05$. The second injection of PAM-2 depressed twitch height by about twenty per cent for not over a minute or so. The long-term neuromuscular response to PAM-2 is shown in figure 1. It is apparent that PAM-2 is especially active in restoring the ability of the muscle to generate a sustained tetanus in response to repetitive excitation of the motor nerve.

In three cats poisoned with tabun after atropine administration, breathing returned in 111 ± 21 minutes; in three similar cats treated with PAM-2 (5 mgm./kgm. in 2 cats; 2 mgm./kgm. in one, given at 5 minutes and repeated) breathing returned in 23 ± 2.3 minutes. The difference is significant ($P < 0.05$). Immediate neuromuscular effects of the later PAM-2 injections were similar to

[1] Pyridine-2-aldoxime methiodide has been abbreviated as PAM, PAMI, 2-PAM and PAM-2. Our PAM-2 was synthesized by Drs. G. M. Steinberg and B. E. Hackley, Jr., Directorate of Research of these Laboratories, to whom we are indebted for our supply.

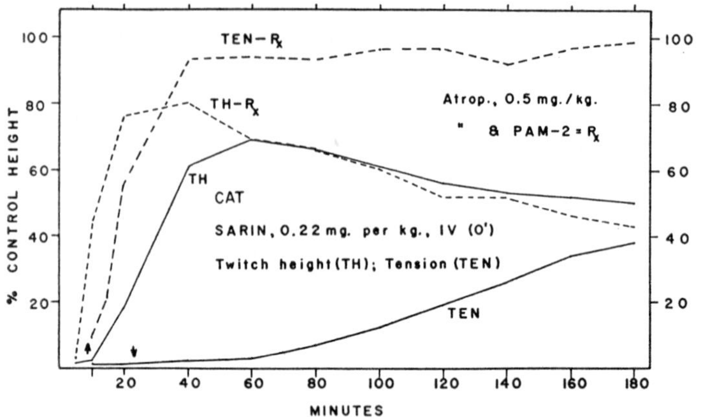

FIG. 1. The effect of PAM-2 therapy on neuromuscular transmission in cats poisoned with sarin at 0 hours following injection of 0.5 mgm./kgm. of atropine sulfate.

The first dose of PAM-2 was given at approximately five minutes. Each point is the mean for four untreated cats or for three PAM-2 treated cats. Arrows indicate the reappearance of breathing.

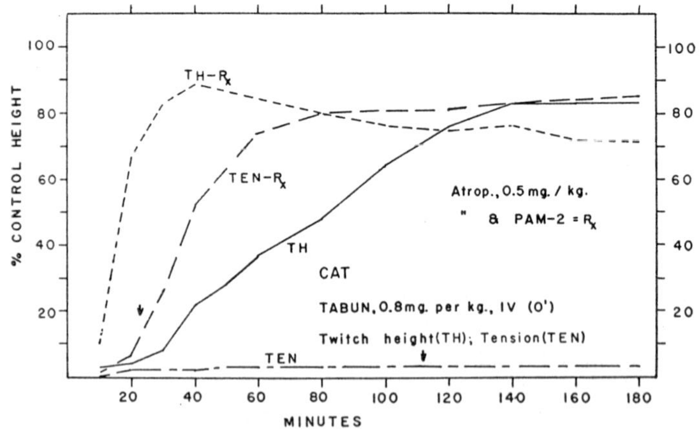

FIG. 2. The effect of PAM-2 therapy on neuromuscular transmission in cats poisoned with tabun at 0 hours after injection of 0.5 mgm./kgm. of atropine sulfate.

The first dose of PAM-2 was given at 5 minutes. Each point is the mean for three cats. Arrows indicate reappearance of breathing.

those described above. The long-term effects are shown in figure 2, where it is evident not only that again PAM-2 had particularly striking effects in restoring the tetanic response but that it also had a marked effect in increasing the rate of recovery of the twitch height.

In four dogs poisoned with sarin after atropine prophylaxis, breathing returned in 23 $\pm$ 5 minutes; of three dogs similarly poisoned but given PAM-2 therapy (5 mgm./kgm. at one to two minutes, repeated later), only two breathed (after the second PAM-2 dose). The remaining dog did not breathe for the 3-hour

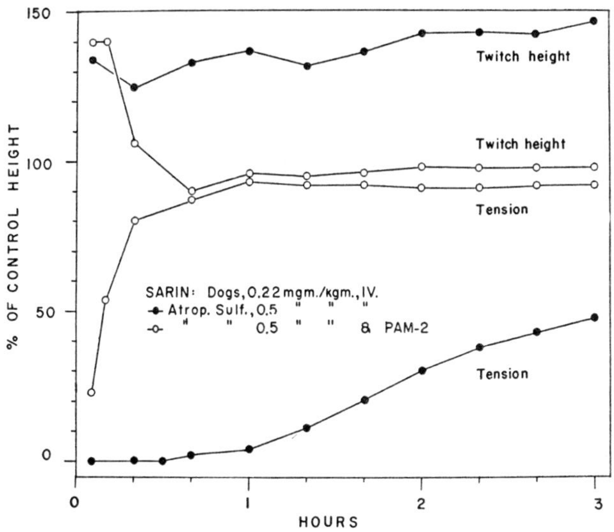

FIG. 3. The effect of PAM-2 therapy on neuromuscular transmission in dogs poisoned with sarin after atropine (0.5 mgm./kgm.) administration.

The first dose of PAM-2 was given at one to two minutes. Each point is the mean for four untreated dogs or for three PAM-2 treated dogs.

duration of the experiment. The neuromuscular effects are shown in figure 3; note especially the persistent augmentation of twitch height after sarin and its return towards control values after PAM-2 therapy.

In three dogs poisoned with tabun following prophylactic administration of atropine, apnea appeared more slowly than in cats; breathing reappeared in 61 $\pm$ 33 minutes. In three dogs similarly poisoned but given PAM-2 therapy (5 mgm./kgm. at 5 minutes, repeated later), respiration did not fail except in one dog; this one breathed at 29 minutes. Neuromuscular effects are shown in figure 4; the augmentation of twitch height in the untreated dogs is ascribable almost entirely to one dog, as the other two showed no such effect.

2. *Cats with simultaneous limb muscle and diaphragm records.* Each of two cats, given prophylactic atropine, was prepared for simultaneous recording from phrenic-diaphragm and sciatic-gastrocnemius-soleus preparations stimulated in parallel from a single stimulator. Neuromuscular dysfunction after tabun was identical in magnitude and time in the two nerve-muscle preparations (*cf.*, figure 5). After PAM-2 (5 mgm./kgm.) the course of neuromuscular recovery was also identical. It appears that sarin produces no differentiation between the muscles of the limbs and of the thorax with respect to response to electric excitation of the motor nerve.

3. *Dogs given PAM-2 (25 mgm./kgm.) at 5 minutes and atropine (0.5 mgm./kgm.) at 30 minutes.* Of three dogs poisoned with sarin and then treated with PAM-2 5 minutes later, but not given atropine until 30 minutes after the poisoning, two breathed before thirty minutes; the third breathed immediately upon getting the atropine. Of three dogs poisoned with tabun and treated similarly, none breathed

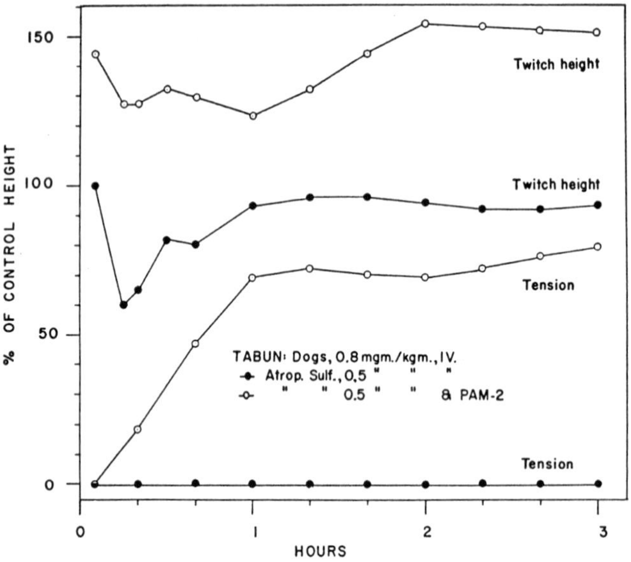

FIG. 4. The effect of PAM-2 therapy on neuromuscular transmission in dogs poisoned with tabun following atropine administration.

The first dose of PAM-2 was given at 5 minutes. Each point is the mean for three dogs. The apparent augmentation of twitch height in the untreated dogs is almost entirely ascribable to the values from a single dog; the other two showed little change from the control value.

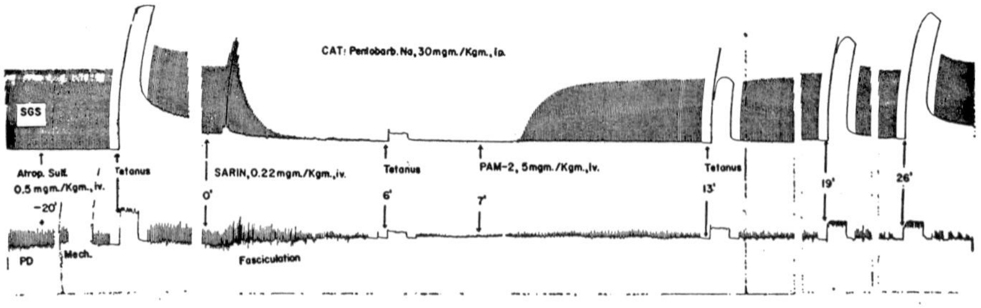

FIG. 5. The neuromuscular response to simultaneous stimulation of a phrenic nerve-diaphragm (PD) and a sciatic nerve-gastrocnemius-soleus (SGS) preparation in a cat, following atropine prophylactically.

Positive pressure artificial respiration was maintained throughout the experiment; the pump strokes show on the tetanus plateaus on PD. Note the rapid and parallel recovery of twitch height and tension after PAM-2 in both preparations.

within the thirty-minute period; all three breathed within one minute after getting the atropine, as shown in figure 6. All six of the dogs breathed for 3 hours, once they started breathing.

4. *Dogs poisoned with sarin or tabun and given atropine (0.5 mgm./kgm.) at 20 minutes and PAM-2 (5 mgm./kgm.) at 25 minutes.* Six dogs were poisoned with

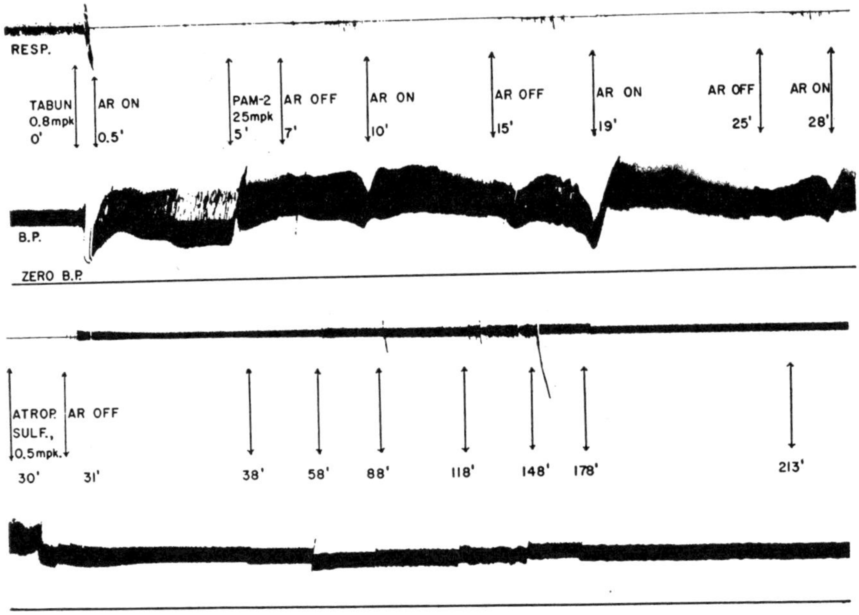

FIG. 6. Respiratory and cardiovascular effects of tabun in the dog.
Note the inability of PAM-2, 25 mgm./kgm., to start and maintain breathing and the abrupt return of breathing after atropine sulfate, 0.5 mgm./kgm., at 30 minutes. Periods of artificial respiration (AR) are marked.

sarin. All six breathed immediately after therapeutic atropine; breathing was improved considerably, within seconds, by PAM-2 therapy. Figure 7 shows the response in a typical experiment; one of the six dogs had excellent breathing before the PAM-2 and showed no improvement from its injection. All six dogs breathed for 3 hours. Six dogs poisoned with tabun and similarly treated showed a response similar to that after sarin, except that all six dogs showed marked improvement after PAM-2. All these dogs also breathed for at least three hours. In similar experiments in which atropine was the only therapeutic drug administered, only 2 of 9 dogs were able to breathe for as long as one hour after treatment. It is clear, therefore, that inclusion of PAM-2 in the treatment has a striking effect on the ability of the dog to maintain adequate respiratory activity.

5. *Cats given atropine sulfate (0.5 mgm./kgm.) before receiving divided doses of PAM-2 (total doses: 10, 12, 18 and 20 mgm./kgm.).* In four cats initial doses of PAM-2 (2 to 10 mgm./kgm.) produced no certain effect no respiration, blood pressure or neuromuscular response. As the cumulative dose became larger, slight bradycardia occurred with correspondingly increased pulse pressure. There were only minor acute effects from PAM-2 in cats as studied.

6. *Dogs given atropine sulfate (0.5 mgm./kgm.) and then PAM-2 (25 mgm./kgm.) three times at 15-minute intervals.* Results were similar to those in cats. The ECG showed no changes other than those related to the observed bradycardia. After the entire 75 mgm. of PAM-2/kgm. had been given, an injection of sarin produced

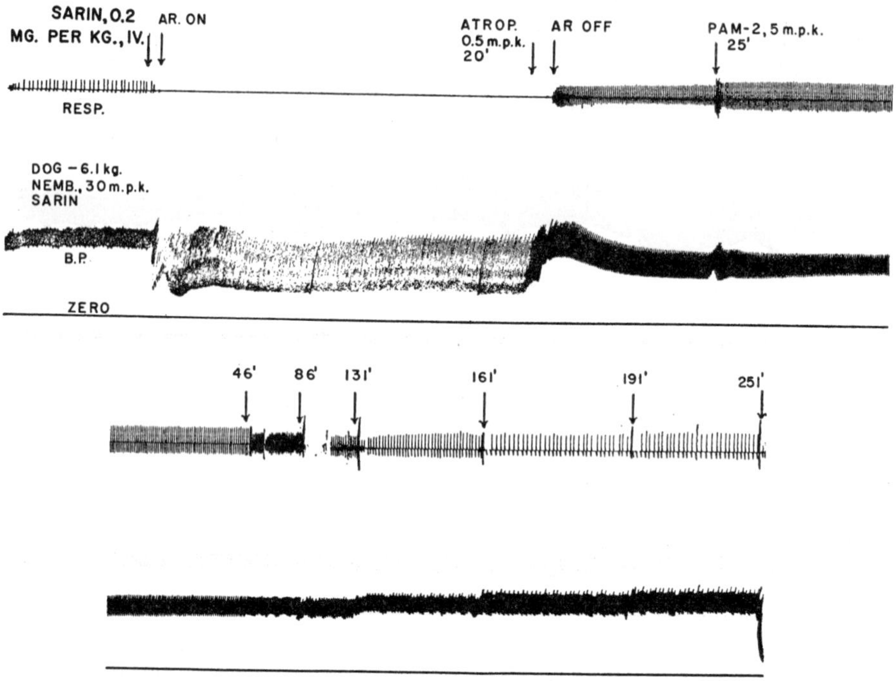

FIG. 7. The respiratory and cardiovascular effects of sarin in the dog.
Artificial respiration (AR) was given for 20 minutes. Breathing started abruptly after atropine sulfate; marked respiratory improvement is shown after PAM-2 at 25 minutes.

abrupt respiratory failure. This experiment shows that PAM-2 has little or no protective action against sarin.

7. *General comparisons and results.* It is evident that PAM-2, in conjunction with either prophylactic or therapeutic atropine, hastens the recovery of neuromuscular transmission in either sarin or tabun poisoning and that it shortens significantly in tabun poisoning the time required for reestablishment of breathing. Comparisons of the times of breathing and of tension recovery in figures 1 through 4 indicate that breathing reappears at a time when only slight recovery of tension has occurred. In the dog, prophylactic atropine plus prompt PAM-2 therapy prevented respiratory failure in two of three tabun-poisoned animals. The response of sarin-poisoned dogs was less favorable.

The results in section 3 indicate that, in the absence of atropine, PAM-2 is not an effective antidote to tabun. The times to breathing after PAM-2 and atropine administrations in this section indicate no certain beneficial effect from PAM-2 therapy *per se.*

The results in section 4 show that if atropine is given therapeutically and is followed by PAM-2, the joint effect is to maintain breathing, which is started by atropine, for the full three-hour duration of the experiments. Neither additional nor larger doses of PAM-2 have improved breathing appreciably.

DISCUSSION. Holmstedt (1951) stated that tabun kills unatropinized rabbits by central paralysis of respiration, which results from the hypoxia caused by poor circulation, bronchoconstriction, and peripheral block of neuromuscular transmission to the respiratory muscles. DeCandole *et al.* (1953) listed several possible causes of death: first, neuromuscular block; second, bronchoconstriction; and third, central respiratory paralysis by direct action of sarin or tabun on the centers. Krop and Kunkel (1954) have pointed out that the severe bradycardia and long-lasting hypotension, *i.e.*, Holmstedt's "poor circulation", may produce sufficiently severe hypoxia to paralyze the respiratory centers, without involving neuromuscular block to any great degree.

Several phenomena reported here throw some light upon the central respiratory effects of sarin and tabun. The failure of respiration after intravenous injection of either agent was abrupt and occurred while twitch height was still little affected. In several groups of animals, therapeutic atropine injection was followed by immediate breathing, although there is known to be no neuromuscular effect from such an injection—a point confirmed in our experiments—and atropine is a central respiratory stimulant *per se*. The rapidity of respiratory failure after the anticholinesterases and the equally rapid recovery after atropine therapy seem to leave little doubt about the central origin of the respiratory failure.

Breathing after PAM-2 therapy occurred at a time when the height of tension was only ten to twenty per cent of the control value. The onset of improvement in breathing, in animals given either sarin or tabun, following the injection of PAM-2 as an adjunct to atropine was almost as abrupt as that after atropine. Holmes and Robins (1955), Wilson and Ginsburg (1955), Childs *et al.* (1955), and Kewitz and Wilson (1956) have shown that certain oximes are potent regenerators of cholinesterase which has been inhibited by organo-phosphorus compounds and Holmes and Robins (1955) have shown that PAM-2 produces the highest rate of regeneration of any of the oximes tested by them. However, the abruptness of respiratory improvement when PAM-2 follows atropine is entirely too rapid to be explained by cholinesterase regeneration. Whether or not the persistence of the respiratory improvement is due to regeneration of cholinesterase is under study at present.

The rate of return of neuromuscular transmission after PAM-2 therapy of sarin or tabun poisoning is considerably lower than is the rate of respiratory recovery. It is entirely possible that the end-plate cholinesterase is sufficiently regenerated by this therapy to account for the diminution of neuromuscular block.

Holmes and Robins (1955), from experiments on isolated nerve-muscle preparations and from close intraarterial injections of PAM-2 into cats, concluded that "...the *in vivo* dose of oximes necessary to reverse block from anticholinesterase is close to the toxic dose. PAM [PAM-2], while very effective as an *in vitro* reactivator, suffers from the disadvantage of having neuromuscular blocking actions of its own." In our experiments, we have found adjuvant doses of PAM-2 to be relatively non-toxic and to have only minor and fleeting neuromuscular blocking actions, of no practical importance.

CONCLUSIONS

Sarin or tabun kill primarily by direct central respiratory paralysis. Both produce neuromuscular block in the cat; recovery is moderately rapid after sarin, slow after tabun. In the dog, both agents augment twitch height, but block sustained tetanus. Recovery from the effects of sarin is rapid, but from those of tabun, recovery is slow.

Prophylactic atropine sulfate conferred little respiratory protection in the cat and only moderate protection in the dog.

Pyridine-2-aldoxime methiodide (PAM-2), 5 mgm./kgm., by vein, is an effective and safe adjunct to atropine sulfate in the therapy of sarin or tabun poisoning. By itself, PAM-2 is a mediocre antidote.

REFERENCES

Childs, A. F., Davis, D. R., Green, A. L., and Rutland, J. P.: Brit. J. Pharmacol., **10**: 462, 1955.

DeCandole, C. A., Douglas, W. W., Evans, C. L., Holmes, R., Spencer, K. E. V., Torrance, R. W., and Wilson, K. M.: Brit. J. Pharmacol., **8**: 466, 1953.

Holmes, R., and Robins, E. L.: Brit. J. Pharmacol., **10**: 490, 1955.

Holmstedt, B.: Acta Physiol. Scandinav., **25**: Suppl. #90, 1951.

Kewitz, H., and Wilson, I. B.: Arch. Biochem. and Biophysics, **60**: 261, 1956.

Krop, S., and Kunkel, A. M.: Proc. Soc. Exper. Biol. & Med., **86**: 530, 1954.

Kunkel, A. M., Wills, J. H., and Monier, J. S.: Proc. Soc. Exper. Biol. & Med., **92**: 529, 1956.

Loomis, T., and Krop, S.: Circ. Research, **3**: 390, 1955.

McNamara, B. P., Koelle, G. B., and Gilman, A.: This Journal, **88**: 27, 1946.

Modell, W., and Krop, S.: This Journal, **88**: 34, 1946.

Modell, W., Krop, S., Hitchcock, P., and Riker, W. K., Jr.: This Journal, **87**: 400, 1946.

Riker, W. F., Jr.: Pharmacol. Rev., **5**: 1, 1953.

Wescoe, W. C., Green, R. E., McNamara, B. P., and Krop, S.: This Journal, **92**: 63, 1948.

Wilson, I. B., and Ginsburg, S.: Biochem. Biophysica Acta, **18**: 168, 1955.

Wright, P. G.: J. Physiol., **126**: 52, 1954.

THE EFFECTS OF SOME ACETYLCHOLINE DERIVATIVES ON THE CHOLINESTERASES OF CHICK EMBRYO INTESTINE CULTURED *IN VITRO*[1]

ALAN BURKHALTER, R. M. FEATHERSTONE, F. W. SCHUELER[2] AND MARION JONES

Departments of Pharmacology and Bacteriology, College of Medicine, State University of Iowa, Iowa City

Received for publication February 1, 1957

Primary explants of chick embryo intestine, cultivated in embryo extract for eight days, lose more than one-half of their cholinesterase (CHE) activity on a weight basis, although the cells grow and multiply well (Jones *et al.*, 1956). This loss of relative enzyme activity can be eliminated by the addition of acetylcholine (ACH) to the incubation medium.

An extension of these experiments has been carried out to evaluate further the structural specificity of the ACH effect, and to characterize the CHE of the chick embryo intestine. The compounds used were acetylcholine (ACH), acetyl-β-methylcholine (MECH), propionylcholine (PRCH), butyrylcholine (BUCH), the "reversed-carboxy" analog of acetylcholine (RC) (Bass *et al.*, 1950) and the N,N-dimethyl derivative of acetylcholine (DIME).

METHODS. Primary explants of 15-day chick embryo intestine were incubated at 37°C. for eight days in roller tubes in 25 per cent embryo extract in a highly buffered salt solution according to methods described by Jones *et al.* (1956). Compounds tested were added to the media in some of the tubes in amounts sufficient to provide an initial concentration of 0.02 molar. Acetylcholine chloride and acetyl-β-methylcholine chloride were purchased from Merck and Company; propionylcholine iodide and butyrylcholine iodide were purchased from the Dajac Laboratories, Leominster, Massachusetts, and benzoylcholine chloride was provided gratis by the Hoffmann-LaRoche Company. The "reversed-carboxy" (RC) analog of acetylcholine and β-dimethylaminoethyl acetate hydrochloride (DIME) were synthesized in our laboratory.

Cholinesterase activity of the cells was measured by a microchemical colorimetric method (Bonting and Featherstone, 1956) in all experiments where tissue culture techniques were used. This enzyme activity was related to protein content of the cells as measured by the method of Bonting and Jones (1957). In experiments comparing the hydrolysis rates of several substrates by different cholinesterases, enzyme activity was measured manometrically using a substrate concentration of 0.02 molar and enough enzyme to give duplicate estimations between 200 to 400 cmm. of CO_2 per hour.

RESULTS. Table 1 summarizes the results of 7 experiments in which ACH or the ACH analogs were added to the incubation media. In each experiment there

[1] This research has been supported by grants from the National Institutes of Health (C-2811 PET and B615), an American Cancer Society Institutional Grant and the State University of Iowa College of Medicine Fund. Part of these data were presented during the 1956 meeting of the American Society for Pharmacology and Experimental Therapeutics in Atlantic City.

[2] Present address: Department of Pharmacology, Tulane University School of Medicine, New Orleans.

TABLE 1

CHE activity of chick embryo intestine expressed in micromoles of substrate hydrolyzed per milligram of protein per hour

Expt.	Substrate Hydrolyzed	Treatment			
		A Not incubated	B Incubated 8 days	C Incubated 8 days with ACH	D Incubated 8 days with other analog ( )
1	ACH	3.56 ± 0.15	1.25 ± 0.06	2.18 ± 0.10	2.11 ± 0.15† (MECH)
	MECH	1.03 ± 0.06	0.47 ± 0.05	0.69 ± 0.06	0.65 ± 0.07† (MECH)
2	ACH	2.94 ± 0.17	0.80 ± 0.06	1.95 ± 0.12	1.99 ± 0.09† (DIME)
	DIME	1.35 ± 0.10	0.29 ± 0.09	0.81 ± 0.09	0.76 ± 0.07† (DIME)
3	ACH	2.85 ± 0.15	1.11 ± 0.06	2.31 ± 0.12	1.57 ± 0.10*† (PRCH)
	PRCH	5.40 ± 0.20	2.39 ± 0.07	3.43 ± 0.08	2.73 ± 0.13*† (PRCH)
4	ACH	3.80 ± 0.10	1.44 ± 0.06	2.46 ± 0.04	2.09 ± 0.12*† (BUCH)
	BUCH	2.81 ± 0.15	0.94 ± 0.14	1.08 ± 0.06	0.86 ± 0.08 (BUCH)
5	ACH	3.38 ± 0.13	1.60 ± 0.12	2.76 ± 0.21	1.68 ± 0.11* (BZCH)
	BZCH	0.21 ± 0.10	0.10 ± 0.04	0.19 ± 0.07	0.20 ± 0.07 (BZCH)
6	ACH	3.03 ± 0.11	1.20 ± 0.15	2.30 ± 0.09	0.94 ± 0.05* (RC)
	RC	0.0	0.0	0.0	0.0 (RC)
7	ACH	3.82 ± 0.20	1.73 ± 0.14	2.92 ± 0.09	1.89 ± 0.17* (CHOLINE)
	ACH				1.85 ± 0.09* (ACETATE)
	ACH				2.36 ± 0.11† (CHOLINE + ACETATE)
	ACH				1.42 ± 0.16* (NaCl)

Each value in experiments 2, 3, 5 and 6 is the mean and standard deviation of the mean hydrolysis value for 8 roller tubes. In experiments 1 and 4 the value is the mean for 12 roller tubes and in experiment 7 the figure is the mean of 6 roller tubes. Differences are considered to be significant when $p < 0.05$. All values in column B are significantly lower than the corresponding values in column A except for the hydrolysis of BZCH (expt. 5). All values in column C are significantly higher than the corresponding values in column B except for the hydrolysis of BZCH (expt. 5) and BUCH (expt. 4). All values in column C are significantly lower than the corresponding values in column A except for the hydrolysis of BZCH (expt. 5). Values in column D that are significantly different than the corresponding values in Column C are marked with an asterisk (*). Values in D that differ significantly from the corresponding values in B are marked with a cross (†).

were four groups of roller tubes containing tissue corresponding to the four following situations: A) explanted—but not incubated, B) explanted and incubated for 8 days, C) explanted and incubated with ACH for 8 days and D) explanted and incubated with an analog for 8 days. At the end of the 8-day incubation period the enzymatic hydrolysis of both ACH and the analog was measured in each group, thus providing comparative rates of hydrolysis by the enzyme and degrees of influence on the enzyme level.

In table 1, experiments 1 and 2, it can be seen that ACH, acetyl β-methylcholine (MECH), and β-dimethylaminoethyl acetate hydrochloride (DIME) were equivalent in their ability to influence the enzyme level. After incubation with ACH or MECH (expt. 1), the enzymatic hydrolysis of both ACH and MECH was significantly higher than the corresponding values in the incubated control group (C and D *vs.* B). However, these higher values were also significantly lower than the corresponding values for the non-incubated group (C and D *vs.* A). Statistical analyses were made using Student's t test according to Mather (1947) and differences were considered significant at the 5 per cent level. It is also apparent that MECH and the DIME analog were enzymatically hydrolyzed at less than one-half the rate of ACH.

In experiment 3 it may be noted that although propionylcholine (PRCH) was hydrolyzed at a greater rate than ACH by this enzyme, addition of PRCH to the incubation medium was less effective than ACH in maintaining a higher rate of hydrolysis of both ACH and PRCH. The addition of butyrylcholine (BUCH) (expt. 4) was only slightly less effective than ACH in maintaining a higher level of ACH hydrolysis, but neither BUCH nor ACH influenced the rate of BUCH hydrolysis.

Results of experiments 5 and 6 show that benzoylcholine (BZCH) and methyl β-trimethylammonium propionate (RC) were not hydrolyzed by this enzyme and that neither of these two compounds had any influence on the enzymatic hydrolysis rate of ACH or of itself. The addition of NaCl, sodium acetate, or choline chloride (expt. 7) had no effect on the CHE content of the incubated cells, while the simultaneous addition of choline and acetate influenced the enzyme level to a lesser extent than ACH. If choline acetylase were present, the ACH synthesized could have produced this effect.

As the relative hydrolysis rates of ACH, PRCH, and BUCH by this enzyme did not support the statement made in the previous paper by Jones *et al.* (1956) that the CHE of the embryonic chick intestine was predominantly the classical specific type, experiments were done in order to characterize the enzyme present. Table 2 presents a summary of these experiments. The hydrolysis rate in cmm. CO_2 per hour of ACH for each enzyme was converted to 100 per cent for comparative purposes. Winthrop-Stearns purified bovine erythrocyte acetylcholinesterase and unpurified dog serum CHE were used as examples of the specific and non-specific types of CHE, respectively. It can be seen that the embryonic chick intestinal enzyme resembled the specific CHE only on the basis of hydrolysis rates of BZCH and MECH, and did not resemble this enzyme on the

TABLE 2

Substrate specificity of 3 cholinesterases

Substrate	Relative Rates of Hydrolysis		
	(W-S) ACHE*	Serum CHE**	CI-CHE†
ACH	100	100	100
MECH	49	12	50
PRCH	73	157	153
BUCH	8	271	77
BZCH	3	68	7

* Winthrop-Stearns acetylcholinesterase.
† Chick embryo intestine cholinesterase.
** Dog serum cholinesterase.

basis of PRCH and BUCH hydrolysis rates. Thus, this CHE had a substrate specificity different from those of the classical specific and non-specific CHE's.

DISCUSSION. As before (Jones *et al.*, 1956), addition of ACH to the incubation media was found to have a profound influence on the CHE level of embryonic chick intestine cultivated *in vitro*. The results of the experiments in which ACH analogs were added to the incubation media allowed some definition of the specificity of the ACH effect. First, rate of hydrolysis *per se* was not a determining factor in the ability of the analogs to influence the CHE level, as MECH and the DIME analog were as effective as ACH in preventing the observed decrease in CHE activity while these two analogs were hydrolyzed enzymatically at less than half the rate of ACH. Also PRCH, which was hydrolyzed enzymatically at a greater rate than ACH, was not as effective as ACH in preventing the observed decrease in CHE level. Second, from the analogs used, it appeared that the acyl chain of ACH was more important in influencing the enzyme level than the choline portion. PRCH, BUCH, the "RC" analog, and BZCH were all less effective than ACH in preventing the observed decrease in CHE activity while MECH and the DIME analog were equally as effective as ACH in this respect.

The type of CHE present in the chick embryonic intestine seemed to be pre-

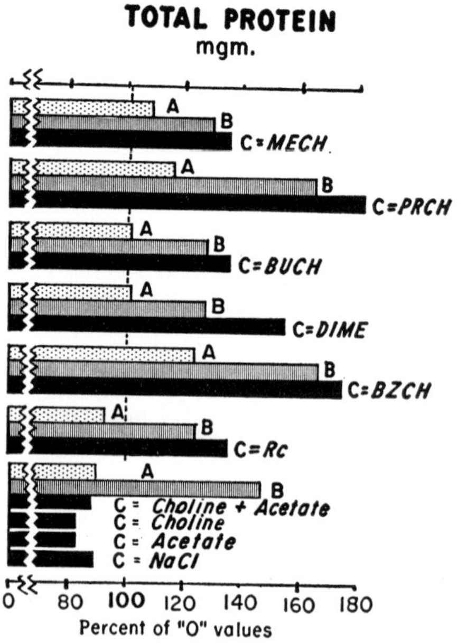

FIG. 1. Summary of data from seven experiments.

Each bar represents the total milligrams protein of the tissue in 16 roller tubes (6 roller tubes in the last experiment) expressed as a percentage of the "O" (nonincubated) group. A—incubated without added substrate. B—incubated with added ACH. C—incubated with added compound indicated. In the first 6 experiments all the C bars and all but the B bar in the mecholyl experiment are significantly higher than their corresponding A bars. In the last experiment the B bar is significantly greater than the A bar. Significance is at the 5 per cent level.

dominantly neither the classic acetylcholinesterase nor the non-specific cholinesterase (Augustinsson, 1950). The results reported in this paper show that the chick intestinal CHE was an "intermediate" type when compared with examples of the classical types of CHE's on the basis of hydrolysis of five substrates. Other cholinesterases having substrate specificities different from those of the classic enzymes have been described (Ord and Thompson, 1950; Goldstein and Goldstein, 1953). These results further support the suggestion that the cholinesterases are a family of enzymes with a wide variety of properties and that several substrates should be used for the characterization of any one cholinesterase.

In the previous paper it was reported that after eight days' incubation the CHE level was approximately 40 per cent of the original level, based upon Q_{CO_2} values, and that addition of ACH to the incubation media caused an increase in the total CHE of cells and a slight increase in the Q_{CO_2} value over that of the non-incubated controls. In the experiments reported here the CHE level after incubation was approximately 40 per cent of the non-incubated controls, based upon micromoles of ACH hydrolyzed per milligram of protein. This is in agreement with the previous work. The addition of ACH to the incubation media did not cause an increase in CHE activity per milligram of protein above the non-incubated controls, and, therefore, it appears that the ACH effect was a "protection" or "maintenance" of the original enzyme. However, preliminary experiments with cultivation of chick embryonic lung tissue, which has a very low CHE content, indicated that addition of ACH to the incubation media caused a twofold increase in CHE activity per milligram of protein and a fourfold increase in total CHE activity over non-incubated controls. Further experiments are being done in investigating this "induction" of CHE by ACH in lung tissues cultivated *in vitro*.

In the previous work with embryonic intestinal cells (Jones *et al.*, 1956) the addition of ACH to the culture medium had little influence on wet or dry weights, which were used to estimate growth. In the present investigation growth was estimated by the chemical determination of protein content, and the addition of ACH or the other ACH analogs to the culture medium apparently caused an increase in protein (figure 1, compare B and C *vs.* A bars). This observed effect of ACH and the analogs was *not* related to their ability to influence the CHE activity, as shown by the fact that BZCH and the RC analog (a non-choline ester) allowed increases in protein and did *not* affect the CHE activity. Further study must be done to characterize the proteins which seem to be formed when the quaternary ammonium compounds are present. It seems inconceivable, in view of the nonspecific nature of this effect as noted above and of the quantities of protein involved, that cholinesterase protein can be involved in the increases noted.

SUMMARY

Primary explants of chick embryo intestine, cultivated in embryo extract for eight days, lost more than one-half of their cholinesterase activity on a milligram of protein basis, although the protein content of the cultured cells was maintained.

Addition of acetylcholine, acetyl β-methylcholine, and β-dimethyl aminoethyl acetate to the cultures maintained the total cholinesterase activity of the cultured cells compared with non-incubated cells, and prevented the decrease in enzyme activity per milligram of protein although the maintained level was lower than the original enzyme level. Propionylcholine and butyrylcholine were less effective than the above compounds in maintaining the enzyme level, and benzoylcholine and the "RC" analog of acetylcholine were ineffective in preventing the decrease in enzyme activity observed after 8 days' incubation.

On the basis of a comparative study with 5 substrates, the cholinesterase of embryo chick intestine seemed to be neither the classical specific nor the non-specific type of enzyme.

REFERENCES

Augustinsson, K. B.: The Enzymes, p. 443, James B. Sumner and Karl Myrbäck, Ed. Academic Press, N. Y., 1950.

Bass, W. B., Schueler, F. W., Featherstone, R. M., and Gross, E. G.: This Journal, **100:** 465, 1950.

Bonting, S. L., and Featherstone, R. M.: Arch. Biochem. and Biophys., **61:** 89, 1956.

Bonting, S. L., and Jones, Marion: Arch. Biochem. and Biophys., **66:** 340, 1957.

Goldstein, D. B., and Goldstein, A.: J. Gen. Microbiol., **8:** 8, 1953.

Jones, Marion, Featherstone, R. M., and Bonting, S. L.: This Journal, **116:** 114, 1956.

Mather, K.: Statistical Analysis in Biology, 2nd Ed., Interscience Publishers, Inc., N. Y., 1947.

Ord, M. G., and Thompson, R. H. S.: Biochem. J., **46:** 346, 1950.

ENZYMATIC REDUCTION OF PRONTOSIL AND OTHER AZO DYES

JAMES R. FOUTS, JEROME J. KAMM AND BERNARD B. BRODIE

Laboratory of Chemical Pharmacology, National Heart Institute, National Institutes of Health, Public Health Service, U. S. Department of Health, Education, and Welfare, Bethesda, Maryland

Received for publication February 6, 1957

The biological reduction of prontosil (4′-sulfamyl-2,4-diaminoazobenzene) is a reaction of historical significance in the field of drug metabolism. This azo dye is active in the intact animal against streptococcal and other infections, but shows no activity in the test tube. It was demonstrated by Tréfouël *et al.* (1935) that prontosil underwent splitting of the azo linkage to form *para*-aminobenzenesulfonamide (sulfanilamide), the actual therapeutic agent. This was a momentous discovery and led to the development of the large range of sulfonamides with which we are familiar today. Reductive cleavage of azo dyes is also important in another direction since many azo dyes are potent carcinogens and it is important to know whether the metabolites contribute to the carcinogenicity. Finally the metabolism of azo dyes in the body is a matter of some interest because of the increasing use of synthetic coloring matters as food additives. It should be a matter of some concern to ensure that these dyes are not reduced *in vivo* to toxic or carcinogenic products before substituting them for colors from natural sources simply because they make our food and drink more attractive to the eye.

A number of studies have shown that azo compounds in general, including prontosil, 4-dimethylaminoazobenzene (butter yellow) and azobenzene are reductively split in the body to form primary amines (Sisley and Porcher, 1911; Fuller, 1937; Stevenson *et al.*, 1942; Elson and Warren, 1944). The reductive cleavage of butter yellow by rat liver homogenates has been studied by Mueller and Miller (1950), who demonstrated that the activity was mainly present in microsomes and that reduced triphosphopyridine nucleotide (TPNH) was a requirement. Their results indicated that the enzyme system was a flavoprotein having as the prosthetic group, flavin adenine dinucleotide (FAD).

The present communication deals with the biochemical mechanisms responsible for the reductive cleavage of prontosil and other azo dyes. The reductive enzyme system has been found to be TPNH dependent and to be localized mainly in the soluble fraction of the rabbit liver cell, though it also occurs in microsomes. Furthermore, it has been possible, to demonstrate that any of the three flavins, riboflavin, riboflavin-5-phosphate (FMN) and flavinadenine dinucleotide (FAD) added in excess markedly accelerate the normal rate of reduction. In spite of its similarity in a number of respects to mammalian nitro reductase (Fouts and Brodie, 1957) the system that reduces prontosil has been shown to be a different enzyme system.

MATERIALS AND METHODS. *Materials.* Riboflavin-5-phosphate (FMN), flavin adenine dinucleotide (FAD, 90 per cent purity), glucose-6-phosphate dehydrogenase, and diphosphopyridine nucleotide (DPN) were obtained from Sigma Chemical Co. Triphosphopyridine nucleotide (TPN) was obtained from Pabst Laboratories. Glucose dehydrogenase was prepared from beef liver according to the method of Strecker and Korkes (1952).

Acknowledgment is made to the Sterling-Winthrop Research Institute for the generous donation of prontosil.

Preparation of tissue samples. Male albino rabbits were killed by a blow on the head and the tissues immediately excised and homogenized in four parts of isotonic KCl with a Waring blendor at 0 to 3° C. Supernatant, (9000 × *g* supernate), soluble (72,000 × *g*), and microsomal fractions were prepared by differential centrifugation, as previously described (Fouts and Brodie, 1957).

The azo compounds were incubated with the various preparations in a Dubnoff metabolic shaking incubator at 37° C. with nitrogen as the gas phase. Substrate and cofactors were added as described in the tables and the final volume was adjusted when necessary to 5 ml. with 0.1 *M* phosphate buffer, pH 7.2.

Prontosil was used as the substrate in most experiments because its rate of reduction in the liver preparations was rapid and sulfanilamide, its reduced product, was available in a pure form. Prontosil was dissolved in alcohol; the volume of alcohol added to the incubation mixture never exceeded 0.2 ml.

Reductase activity of the enzyme preparations was determined by measuring the amount of sulfanilamide formed from prontosil. Sulfanilamide was stable in homogenates and various cell fractions. At the end of the incubation period, the reaction was stopped by the addition of 15 ml. of 6.67 per cent trichloroacetic acid. After centrifugation, suitable aliquots, usually 5 ml. of the supernate, were analyzed for sulfanilamide.

Chemical methods. Sulfanilamide was diazotized and coupled as described by Bratton and Marshall (1939) after removal of the prontosil by shaking the trichloroacetic acid filtrates with 50 to 100 mgm. of activated charcoal. The treatment with charcoal removed virtually all of the prontosil without significant loss of sulfanilamide. The colored sulfanilamide derivative was extracted into 5 to 15 ml. of isoamyl alcohol. After acidification with 25 per cent trichloroacetic acid in ethylene dichloride the optical density of the solvent was determined spectrophotometrically at 540 mμ. Aniline was determined in a similar manner. Extraction into isoamyl alcohol reduced tissue blanks to a negligible value.

The various azo dyes were determined in trichloroacetic acid filtrates by direct measurement of the optical densities at the wavelengths of maximal absorption.

Paper chromatography. Samples were chromatographed on Whatman No. 1 paper with butanol, acetic acid and water (50:15:60) as the ascending solvent. The paper was dried in air and the amines detected by spraying with nitrous acid followed by α-naphthylethylene diamine.

RESULTS. *Azo reductase activity in various tissues and species.* Prontosil was incubated for two hours with slices of a number of tissues in Krebs-Ringer phosphate buffer at pH 7.2. The drug was metabolized in a number of tissues with liver being the most active and kidney being about one-fourth as active (table 1). In general, the pattern of distribution was the same as that found for nitro reductase (Fouts and Brodie, 1957).

The reduction of prontosil was compared in liver homogenates of the guinea pig, mouse, rabbit, rat and chicken. As with nitro reductase guinea pig and mouse livers showed greater activity than those of rabbit and rat. The activity of chicken liver was about one-fifth that of the guinea pig liver (table 2).

Requirements of the enzyme system in liver homogenates. Rabbit liver homogenates after dialysis overnight against distilled water no longer reduced prontosil, but activity could be restored by the addition of glucose-6-phosphate, nicotinamide and catalytic amounts of TPN. No activity was noted even in

TABLE 1

Tissue distribution of enzyme activity

Various rabbit tissue slices (1 gm.), 7.0 micromoles of prontosil and Krebs-Ringer phosphate buffer, pH 7.2, to a final volume of 5.0 ml. were incubated at 37° C. for 2 hours with nitrogen as the gas phase.

Tissue	Sulfanilamide Formed*	Relative Activity
	μmoles	
Liver	1.56	100
Kidney	0.43	28
Lung	0.26	17
Heart	0.19	12
Brain	0.12	8
Spleen	0.0	0
Muscle	0.0	0

* Sulfanilamide was acetylated to some extent in tissue slices. The free amine was liberated by adding 1 ml. of concentrated HCl to 5 ml. of the trichloracetic acid filtrate and heating in a boiling water bath for 30 minutes.

TABLE 2

Enzyme activity in liver of various species

Supernatant fraction (9000 × *g*) equivalent to 0.4 gm. of liver, 7.0 micromoles of prontosil, 0.2 micromole of TPN, 25 micromoles of glucose-6-phosphate, 1.0 mgm. of glucose-6-phosphate dehydrogenase, 100 micromoles of nicotinamide and phosphate buffer to a final volume of 5.0 ml. were incubated for 2.5 hours at 37° C. with nitrogen as the gas phase.

Species	Sulfanilamide Formed	Relative Activity
	μmoles	
Guinea pig	4.01	100
Mouse	3.30	82
Rabbit	2.36	59
Rat	1.27	32
Chicken	0.92	23

the presence of nicotinamide and TPN, unless glucose-6-phosphate was also added.

The reduction of prontosil was inhibited by oxygen by about 30 per cent and that of azo benzene by about 50 per cent. In contrast, the reduction of butter yellow (4-dimethylaminoazobenzene) was inhibited only slightly, about 10 per cent, in the presence of oxygen.

Intracellular localization of azo reductase. The enzyme activity of a rabbit liver homogenate was found entirely in the 9000 × *g* supernate. Fractionation of this supernate into a microsomal and a soluble fraction showed that the soluble fraction contained about 70 per cent of the total activity. Microsomes were demonstrated to have activity, also, by adding a small amount of the soluble fraction (table 3). It was concluded from these observations that azo reductase was present in both the microsomes and the soluble fraction of the cell, but that

TABLE 3

Intracellular distribution of azo reductase

Various cell fractions equivalent to 1.0 gm. of rabbit liver, 7.0 micromoles of prontosil, 0.2 micromole of TPN, 100 micromoles of nicotinamide, 25 micromoles of glucose-6-phosphate and phosphate buffer to a final volume of 5.0 ml. were incubated for 1.5 hours at 37° C. with nitrogen as the gas phase.

System	Sulfanilamide Formed
	μmoles
Whole homogenate	3.44
Supernatant fraction (9000 × *g*)	3.88
Soluble fraction (72,000 × *g*)	3.12
Microsomes	0
Microsomes + 0.2 ml. soluble fraction*	0.99

* Value corrected for sulfanilamide formed by the 0.2 ml. of soluble fraction alone.

TABLE 4

Requirements for reduced TPN

Microsomes or soluble fraction of the cell (72,000 × *g* supernate) equivalent to 1 gm. of liver, 7.0 micromoles of prontosil, 100 micromoles of nicotinamide, added cofactors and phosphate buffer to a final volume of 5.0 ml. were incubated for 1 hour at 37° C. with nitrogen as the gas phase.

System	Sulfanilamide Formed
	μmoles
Microsomes + 0.5 μmole TPN + 50 μmoles glucose-6-phosphate	0
Microsomes + 0.5 μmole TPN + 50 μmoles glucose-6-phosphate + 5 mgm. glucose-6-phosphate dehydrogenase	.23
Dialyzed soluble fraction + 0.5 μmole TPN	0.74*
Dialyzed soluble fraction + 0.5 μmole TPN + 50 μmoles glucose-6-phosphate	3.88

* Residual activity presumably due to incomplete removal of glucose-6-phosphate by dialysis.

the enzyme system in microsomes also required a factor present in the soluble fraction.

Requirement for TPNH. Since the metabolism of prontosil involves reductive cleavage of the azo linkage, it was logical to consider TPNH as the hydrogen donor. This would be in accord with the requirements of dialyzed homogenates for TPN and glucose-6-phosphate, which together with glucose-6-phosphate dehydrogenase present in the soluble fraction of the cell, would constitute a potent TPNH generating system.

The TPNH requirement of both the microsomal and soluble fractions was demonstrated by the following experiments. Dialysis of the soluble fraction against distilled water for 16 hours resulted in a considerable reduction in activity that could be restored by the addition of glucose-6-phosphate and TPN. The addition of these factors to a microsomal preparation produced no activity unless glucose-6-phosphate dehydrogenase was also added (table 4). Thus, the soluble fraction is a complete enzyme system whereas the microsomes contain only the reductase and lack the cofactor TPNH.

Replacement of the TPNH generator by the DPNH generating system of glucose, glucose dehydrogenase and DPN gave no activity with either dialyzed supernate or microsomes.

TABLE 5

Reduction of various diazo compounds by rabbit liver homogenates

Supernatant fraction (9000 × *g*) equivalent to 0.75 gm. liver, 10 micromoles of azo dye, 0.2 micromole of TPN, 100 micromoles of nicotinamide, 25 micromoles of glucose-6-phosphate, and phosphate buffer to a final volume of 5.0 ml. were incubated for 1.5 hours at 37° C. with nitrogen as the gas phase.

Substrate	Structure	Dye Disappeared	Product Formed
		μmoles	*μmoles*
Neo-prontosil	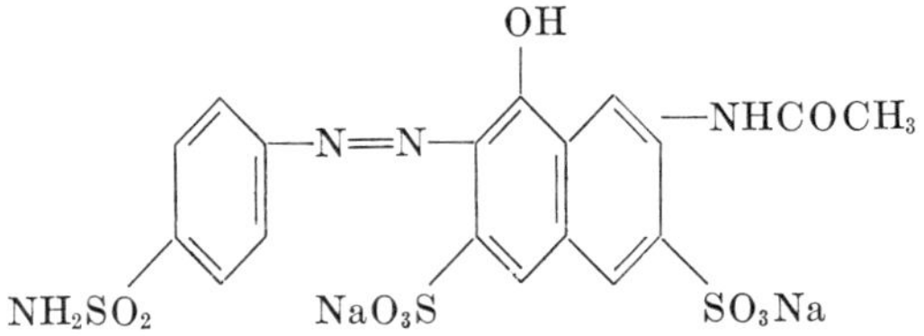	6.5	7.9
Orange III	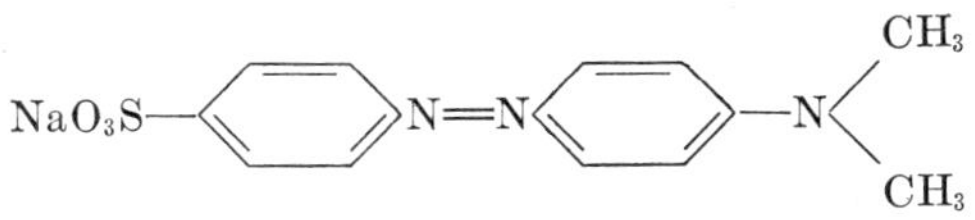	6.3	—
Prontosil	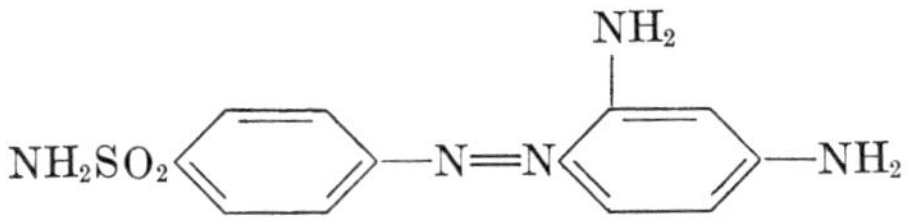	5.2	5.7
Orange IV	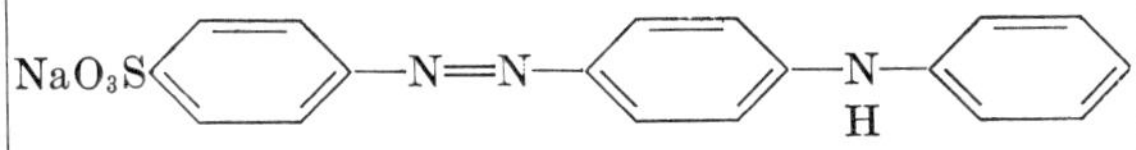	4.2	—
Scarlet R	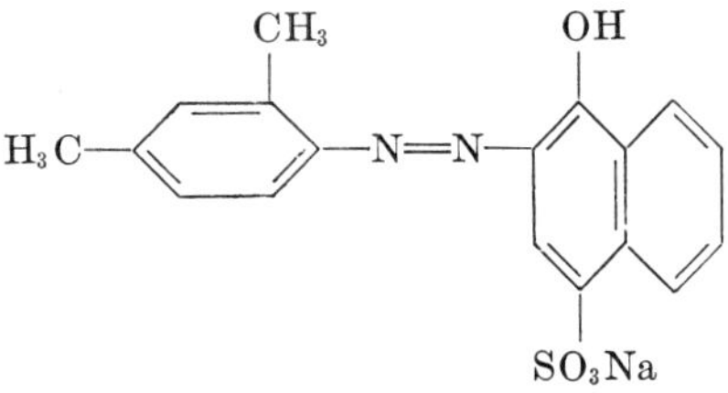	2.7	—
Butter Yellow	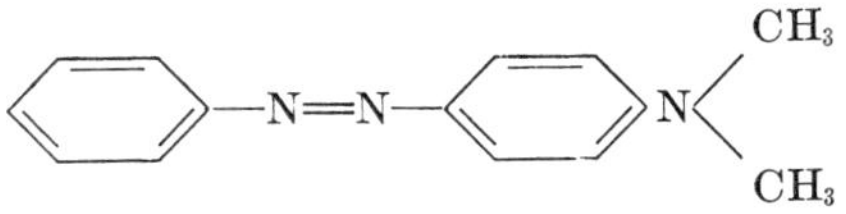	2.2	—

TABLE 5—*Continued*

Substrate	Structure	Dye Disappeared	Product Formed
		µmoles	*µmoles*
Azo Violet	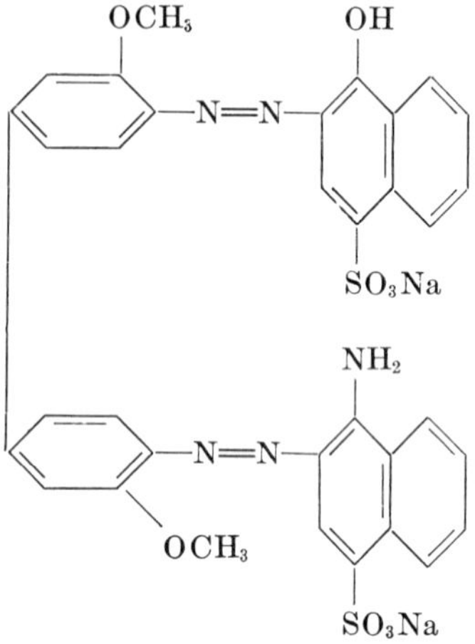	2.0	—
Azobenzene	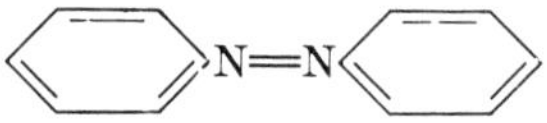	—	1.9*

* Product formed asayed by Bratton and Marshall reaction and expressed in terms of aniline.

Substrate optimum for azo reductase. When liver supernatant fraction (9000 × *g*) was incubated for one hour with various concentrations of prontosil, the amount of sulfanilamide formed was roughly proportional to all concentrations of substrate up to the maximal solubility of the drug, about 10^{-3} M. Because of the limited solubility of the drug it was not possible to measure the maximal rate of reaction, but it is evident that the affinity of the enzyme for prontosil is low.

Lack of specificity of azo reductase. Table 5 shows that a number of azo dyes are reduced by a rabbit liver homogenate. These compounds vary in structural complexity from azobenzene to a complex dye such as azo violet. Of all the substrates tested neoprontosil seems to be most rapidly reduced.

Products of reduction. The products of reduction of prontosil were identified by means of paper chromatography using the solvent system described under METHODS. An amine compound was found having the same R_f (0.74) as authentic sulfanilamide. Another spot was observed at the origin, indicating that it was a relatively basic substance, presumably triaminobenzene. This material was not identified as the reference compound was unavailable.

Separation of azo reductase from nitro reductase. Preliminary attempts to purify azo reductase led to a separation of this enzyme system from nitro reductase. As shown in table 6, the fraction that precipitated between 50 and 60 per cent ammonium sulfate could reduce prontosil to sulfanilamide but could not reduce *p*-nitrobenzoic acid to *p*-aminobenzoic acid (Fouts and Brodie, 1957) Nitro reductase activity was concentrated mainly in the precipitate produced by 40 per cent saturation with ammonium sulfate whereas most of the azo reductase activity was associated with the material that precipitated between 30 and 70 per cent saturation.

Acceleration of azo reductase by flavins. Previous studies (Fouts and Brodie, 1957) have shown that the flavins when added to rabbit liver homogenates or slices increased the activity of nitro reductase severalfold. This prompted us to determine the effect of flavins on the reduction of prontosil. As shown in table 7,

TABLE 6

Separation of azo reductase from nitro reductase by ammonium sulfate precipitation

Precipitates were obtained using ammonium sulfate at the saturations shown. Quantities of these fractions equivalent to 5.0 gm. of liver together with 7.0 micromoles of prontosil or 6.0 micromoles of *p*-nitrobenzoic acid, 0.2 micromole of TPN, 100 micromoles of nicotinamide, 25 micromoles of glucose-6-phosphate, 1.0 mgm. of glucose-6-phosphate dehydrogenase and phosphate buffer to a final volume of 5.0 ml. were incubated for three hours with nitrogen as the gas phase.

Per Cent $(NH_4)_2SO_4$	Sulfanilamide Formed	*p*-Aminobenzoic Acid Formed
	μmoles	*μmoles*
Control	3.92	1.67
0–50% saturation	1.18	0.81
50–60% saturation	0.52	0.0

TABLE 7

Acceleration of enzyme activity in rabbit liver homogenates by flavins

Supernatant fraction (9000 × *g* supernate) equivalent to 0.75 gm. of liver, 7.0 micromoles of prontosil, 0.2 micromole of TPN, 100 micromoles of nicotinamide, 50 micromoles of glucose-6-phosphate, various concentrations of riboflavin, riboflavin-5-phosphate (FMN), or flavin adenine dinucleotide (FAD) and phosphate buffer to a final volume of 5.0 ml. were incubated for 15 minutes at 37° C. with nitrogen as the gas phase.

System	Sulfanilamide Formed
	μmoles
Supernatant fraction	1.18
Supernatant fraction + riboflavin (10^{-5} *M*)	1.81
Supernatant fraction + riboflavin (10^{-4} *M*)	4.16
Supernatant fraction + riboflavin (10^{-3} *M*)	5.72
Supernatant fraction + FMN (10^{-5} *M*)	2.07
Supernatant fraction + FMN (10^{-4} *M*)	4.84
Supernatant fraction + FMN (10^{-3} *M*)	6.06
Supernatant fraction + FAD (10^{-5} *M*)	2.10
Supernatant fraction + FAD (10^{-4} *M*)	3.91
Supernatant fraction + FAD (10^{-3} *M*)	5.96

FMN, FAD or riboflavin markedly increased the rate of reduction of prontosil by rabbit liver supernate.

Flavin requirements of azo reductase. Since the mammalian nitro reductase system includes a flavoprotein and is similar in other respects to azo reductase, it was logical to consider that the latter system might also include a flavoprotein. In an attempt to demonstrate this, the soluble fraction of rabbit liver cells was subjected to mild acid treatment according to the method of Zelitch and Ochoa (1953) to remove the flavin prosthetic group from a flavoprotein. Although this treatment reduced the activity of the enzyme system, up to one-half original activity still remained. Activity could be restored by the addition of excess FAD or FMN or riboflavin; but the activity was not usually as high as that obtained by the addition of excess flavin to the untreated homogenate. It was not possible, therefore, to conclude whether the acid treatment was dissociating a flavin group or merely denaturing part of the enzyme. If the latter possibility is considered, the apparent restoration of the enzyme activity by the flavins could be due to acceleration of the activity of undenatured enzyme rather than replacement of a prosthetic group.

Alternative treatment of the liver supernatant with carbon dioxide saturated water as described by Mueller and Miller (1950) also yielded only partial loss of azo reductase activity.

DISCUSSION. Experiments described in this paper show that prontosil and other aromatic azo compounds are reductively split in mammals to amines by a biochemical mechanism found mainly in liver.

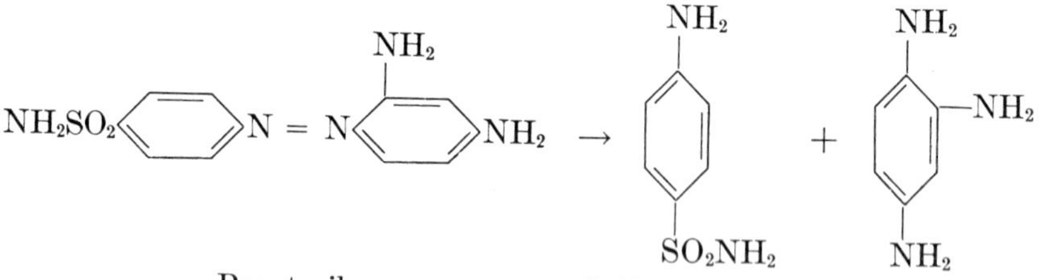

Prontosil Sulfanilamide Triaminobenzene

The splitting of the azo groups takes place presumably in two steps, the formation of a hydrazo compound, followed by reductive splitting of the nitrogen to nitrogen bond.

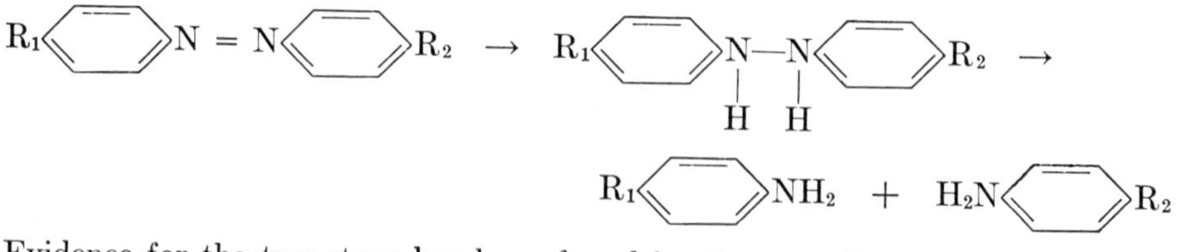

Evidence for the two steps has been found by Bray *et al.*, (1951) who showed the presence of hydrazobenzene in the urine of rabbits given azobenzene.

Azo reductase is present in rabbits mainly in the liver but it is also present in kidney, lung and other tissues. The enzyme system is localized largely in the soluble fraction of the liver cell, but some activity is also present in microsomes.

TPNH acts as a specific hydrogen donor for the azo reductase system, DPNH having virtually no action. The coenzyme is maintained in a reduced state by pyridine nucleotide dependent dehydrogenases and oxidizable substrates present in the soluble part of the cell. Although it is a reductive system, azo reductase still shows considerable activity in the presence of oxygen.

A wide variety of azo compounds are reduced by liver homogenates, indicating that the enzyme system probably requires little from its substrate excepting that it possesses an azo linkage. It must be kept in mind, however, that the data presented thus far do not indicate whether azo reductase is a single system or a composite of a number of systems.

Azo reductase, like nitro reductase, is peculiar in that its normal activity is markedly accelerated by the addition of an excess of FMN, FAD and riboflavin. This, together with the requirements for the coenzyme TPNH, suggests the possibility that azo reductase is a flavoprotein system. Rigid proof of this is lacking however, since the classical procedure for splitting off the flavin prosthetic group by acid treatment produces only partial inactivation of the enzyme. The loss of activity by acid treatment may result from denaturation of the enzyme system and the restoration of activity by the addition of FAD, FMN or riboflavin may be merely a reflection of the acceleration of the residual enzyme activity by these flavins. It is not possible to settle definitely the question of whether azo reductase is a flavoprotein, until a way is found to completely dissociate the enzyme and restore activity by the addition of a flavin.

It is probable though that, as has been postulated for nitro reductase, the flavins act in two capacities: 1) as a tightly bound prosthetic group and 2) as a loosely bound or soluble electron carrier, similar to the coenzymes TPN and DPN.

The second mechanism is in accord with the observations of a number of workers that the carcinogenicity of butter yellow is decreased in rats when the riboflavin level in hepatic tissue is elevated and correspondingly the rate of destruction of butter yellow by rat liver slices is dependent on their content of riboflavin (Kensler, 1948, 1949; Antopol and Unna, 1942; Kawai, 1952).

The question arises as to whether azo reductase and nitro reductase are one and the same system. The two systems are similar in relative tissue distribution, in relative activity among various animal species, a common requirement for a reduced pyridine nucleotide, and susceptibility to the accelerating action of riboflavin, FMN and FAD. Certain dissimilarities are evident however: 1) TPNH and DPNH can both serve as hydrogen donors for nitro reductase, but the azo system is TPNH specific, 2) treatment with mild acid completely dissociates a flavin prosthetic group from nitro reductase, but only partially dissociates the flavin from azo reductase, and 3) ammonium sulfate fractionation yields a fraction that has azo reductase activity, but not nitro reductase activity.

Mueller and Miller (1950) have made a rather thorough study of the system involved in the reduction of 4-dimethylaminoazobenzene (butter yellow) by rat liver. They reported that liver homogenates require TPNH as a coenzyme and that the activity resides predominantly in the microsomes. Furthermore, the dialysis of the acid treated liver homogenate resulted in partial inactivation of the system which can then be specifically restored with FAD. Since the rabbit azo reductase studied by us is localized mainly in the soluble part of the cell, and the loss of activity by acid treatment is restored by riboflavin and FMN as well as by FAD, it is possible that the enzymes that reduce prontosil in rabbit and butter yellow in rat are different.

SUMMARY

Prontosil and a variety of azo dyes are reductively cleaved in the rabbit by an enzyme system present predominantly in liver. The azo reductase system is localized mainly in the soluble fraction of the cell, but is also present in microsomes. TPNH serves as the hydrogen donor, DPNH having virtually no activity.

The system is markedly accelerated by an excess of riboflavin, FMN or FAD and is probably a flavoprotein. It is proposed that flavins act in at least two ways in the system: 1) as the prosthetic group and 2) as an unbound hydrogen transport system similar to a coenzyme. The accelerating effect of flavins would be due to their acting in this latter property.

Evidence is presented which shows that azo reductase and nitro reductase, though similar in many respects, are different enzyme systems.

REFERENCES

Antopol, W., and Unna, K.: Cancer Research, **2:** 694, 1942.
Bratton, A. C., and Marshall, E. K., Jr.: J. Biol. Chem., **128:** 537, 1939.
Bray, H. C., Clowes, R. C., and Thorpe, W. V.: Biochem. J., **49:** LXV, 1951.
Elson, L. A., and Warren, F. L.: Biochem. J., **38:** 217, 1944.
Fouts, J. R., and Brodie, B. B.: This Journal, **119:** 000, 1957.
Fuller, A. T.: Lancet, **232**, 194, 1937.
Kawai, K.: Med. Journal Osaka Univ., **3:** 69, 1952.
Kensler, C. J.: Cancer, **1:** 483, 1948.
Kensler, C. J.: J. Biol. Chem., **179:** 1079, 1949.
Mueller, G. C., and Miller, J. A.: J. Biol. Chem., **185:** 145, 1950.
Stevenson, E. S., Dobriner, K., and Rhoads, C. P.: Cancer Research, **2:** 160, 1942.
Sisley, P., and Porcher, C.: Compt. Rend. Acad. d. sc., **152:** 1062, 1911.
Strecker, J. H., and Korkes, S. J.: J. Biol. Chem., **196:** 769, 1952.
Tréfouël, J., Tréfouël, Mme. J., Nitti, F., and Bovet, D. Compt. rend. Soc. de Biol., **120:** 765, 1935.
Zelitch, I., and Ochoa, S.: J. Biol. Chem., **201:** 707, 1953.

EFFECTS OF DIPHENYLHYDANTOIN ON SYNAPTIC TRANSMISSION IN CAT SPINAL CORD AND STELLATE GANGLION[1, 2, 3]

DON W. ESPLIN

With the technical assistance of Dale G. Heaton and Judith Coray

Department of Pharmacology, University of Utah College of Medicine, Salt Lake City

Received for publication February 8, 1957

Prototype drugs (*e. g.*, diphenylhydantoin, trimethadione and phenacemide) representing the several important classes of antiepileptic agents have been thoroughly studied with respect to their anticonvulsant actions (Toman *et al.*, 1946; Toman and Goodman, 1948; Goodman *et al.*, 1949; Goodman and Gilman, 1955) and to their effects upon excitation and transmission in peripheral nerve (Toman, 1949, 1952; Korey, 1951). Nevertheless, the experimental results to date provide few clues concerning the mechanisms by which anticonvulsants act on complex neuronal circuits to reduce seizure activity or concerning the mechanisms underlying the distinct differences in antiepileptic properties exhibited by the various agents. Since synaptic systems necessarily exhibit functions not posessed by collections of axons, information concerning effects of anticonvulsant drugs on various aspects of synaptic function may contribute to an understanding of the mechanisms basic to the particular complex of antiepileptic properties of each agent. An investigational program which encompasses the present work is concerned with the effects of several representative anticonvulsants on synaptic transmission. It is anticipated that the information to be obtained will indicate certain correlations between specific effects on synaptic transmission and characteristics of anticonvulsant action.

METHODS. Unanesthetized spinal cats were used in all experiments. The animals were anesthetized with ether, a tracheal cannula was inserted, and the spinal cord was transsected at the atlanto-occipital junction. Artificial respiration was begun, and the anesthesia was discontinued. A minimum of one hour in stellate ganglion experiments and three hours in spinal cord experiments was allowed for elimination of the ether. Decamethonium, in doses of 0.5 mgm./kgm., was employed as needed for paralysis during the surgery.

Surgical procedures. In spinal cord experiments a laminectomy was performed in the lumbosacral region. All nerves were raised into a mineral oil pool by hook-electrodes made of platinum or silver wire. Stimuli were applied either to a peripheral nerve or to a dorsal root (L_7 or S_1). To prevent antidromic activation of motoneurons, the relevant homolateral ventral roots (L_6 to S_2) were severed (Reighard and Jennings, 1949; Jefferson and Benson, 1953; Romanes, 1953). In dorsal root-ventral root (DR-VR) preparations, intact afferent inflow was not necessary; hence both dorsal and ventral roots of the segments mentioned were cut on both sides. All reflex responses were recorded from either L_7 VR or S_1 VR.

---

[1] This investigation was supported by research grants from the National Institute of Neurological Diseases and Blindness (B-381 and B-872), National Institutes of Health.

[2] A preliminary report of this work appeared in Fed. Proc., **14:** 337, 1955.

[3] This paper is based on a thesis submitted to the faculty of the University of Utah in partial fulfillment of the requirements for the degree of Doctor of Philosophy, June, 1955.

Following transection of the spinal cord in ganglion experiments, the thoracic cavity was opened on the left side. Blunt dissection was employed to free the preganglionic sympathetic trunk and the inferior cardiac nerve for about 3 cm. from the ganglion. The inferior cardiac nerve was cut distally, ramus III was severed, and the sympathetic trunk was cut just proximal to ramus IV. Stimulating electrodes were placed on the sympathetic trunk. The proximal recording electrode was about 1 to 1.5 cm. from the ganglion.

Recording instruments. Monophasic "square-wave" stimuli were delivered by two Grass model S-4 stimulators. Recorded potentials were amplified through Grass model P-4 preamplifiers and were displayed on a dual-beam oscilloscope, either a DuMont type 322-A or Tektronix type 531. Responses on the oscilloscope were photographed by a Grass kymograph camera. The postsynaptic response was monitored continuously by an audio system as a check of background activity and interference. In some stellate ganglion experiments, responses were recorded directly on paper by means of a Brush BL-962 power amplifier and Brush BL-202 direct inking oscillograph.

Temperature control. One of the most important variables affecting the level of reflex excitability in spinal cord preparations is the temperature of the spinal cord (Koizumi *et al.*, 1954; Brooks *et al.*, 1955). Decreasing the temperature of the cord from 38°C to 25°C. causes a progressive increase in reflex excitability. All experiments were done at temperatures between 30°C. and 38°C., and in the majority of experiments the temperatures were 32°C. to 34°C. In a given experiment, spinal cord temperature selected was that which appeared to be optimum for the responses being studied, and was maintained as constant as possible by a battery of thermostatically controlled heat lamps outside of the recording cage. Temperature variation during the recording periods usually did not exceed 0.5°C.

Transmission in the stellate ganglion is not influenced as markedly by temperature changes (between 30°C. and 38°C.) as is that in the spinal cord; rectal temperature was maintained at about 35°C. during the period of recording.

Administration of diphenylhydantoin (Dilantin). Dilantin sodium dissolved in 0.9 per cent saline solution was used in all experiments. All injections were made in the cephalic vein. In some of the early experiments, Dilantin was used in a concentration of 20 mgm./ml. brought into solution by addition of a small amount of sodium hydroxide. Injections were made rapidly, and in three spinal cord experiments a profound but temporary depression of reflex excitability was observed. Since rapid intravenous injection of Dilantin produces transient hypotension (Harris and Kokernot, 1950; Harreveld and Feigen, 1950; Harreveld *et al.*, 1951) and since a rise in flexor reflex threshold accompanies a fall in blood pressure (Pedersen, 1954), it was felt that the brief areflexia following Dilantin might be secondary to hypotension and not due to a direct action of Dilantin on neurons. Accordingly, blood pressure was recorded in two spinal cats while Dilantin, in a concentration of 2 mgm./ml., was injected intravenously at various rates. It was found that Dilantin could be given intravenously at the rate of 1 mgm./kgm./minute without producing significant changes in either the blood pressure or the electrocardiogram (*cf.* Scherf, 1943). Therefore, in all subsequent spinal cord experiments and in all ganglion experiments, Dilantin sodium in a concentration of 2 mgm./ml. was administered by constant infusion at a rate not exceeding 1 mgm./kgm./minute.

In this study, intravenous doses of Dilantin from 10 to 40 mgm./kgm. were used. These values were found by Toman *et al.* (1946) to define respectively the minimally effective anticonvulsant and the minimally neurotoxic doses of Dilantin given to cats by the intraperitoneal route; similar studies after intravenous administration have not been made. However, it is probable that intravenous doses of Dilantin employed in this investigation are generally comparable to similar intraperitoneal doses, since the absorption of injected Dilantin is rapid (Swinyard *et al.*, 1952), and the experiments were of several hours duration. Destruction or excretion of Dilantin could be safely disregarded in these acute experiments since in cats the anticonvulsant effect of the drug persists for many days after a single protective dose (Toman *et al.*, 1946).

Experimental design. Each experiment consisted of 3 phases: 1) the period of stabilization following surgery, 2) the control recording period, and 3) the drug recording period. During the period of stabilization, which lasted 1 to 6 hours in spinal cord experiments and about 30 minutes in stellate ganglion experiments, tests of various aspects of synaptic transmission were made, the possibility of stimulus spread was investigated, spinal cord temperature was varied if necessary, and the stability of reflex excitability at the chosen temperature was assured. Some experiments were terminated at this point because of inability to maintain reflex excitability at a constant level. When adequate stability was attained, control records were taken of certain aspects of transmission. Dilantin was then administered and the tests were repeated at one or more levels of dosage. Control testing usually required 1 to 4 hours and testing following Dilantin was sometimes continued as long as 36 hours. At the conclusion of Dilantin testing in some experiments, pentylenetetrazol (Metrazol) or strychnine was investigated for antagonism of the effects of Dilantin.

RESULTS. I. *Effects of Dilantin on transmission in the spinal cord.* Dilantin was studied in 22 spinal cord preparations in which rigid criteia of stability were satisfied throughout the periods of control and drug testing; thus changes in synaptic transmission could reliably be ascribed to the drug.

a) Transmission of isolated impulses: Dilantin has little effect upon responses elicited at such a rate that the effects (depression, post-tetanic potentiation) of repeated stimulation do not summate. When the stimulus interval is 4 seconds or longer, the monosynaptic spike, which is most sensitive to effects of repeated stimulation, exhibits no appreciable response deficit (Jefferson and Schlapp, 1953). Table 1 shows the effects of various doses of Dilantin on monosynaptic (2N) and polysynaptic potentials of isolated responses elicited every 4 seconds in a number of experiments. It can be seen that Dilantin produced a slight reduction in 2N spike height in the majority of experiments, although there is some variation due to fluctuations in spinal cord excitability over the time necessary for these experiments and also due to random variations in spike height at a given level of excitability. Standard deviations are included in table 1 to indicate variability of responses in various representative experiments. Tests for significance would not be meaningful because of variations in excitability independent of the drug over the time of observation. The average reduction in 2N spike height produced by 30 mgm./kgm. of Dilantin for all experiments is about 10 per cent. Polysynaptic activity, however, is more markedly reduced by this dose of the drug; whether elicited by stimulation of a cutaneous nerve (*e. g.*, sural) or of the dorsal root, it is reduced about 30 per cent. It is likely that the more pronounced decrease in polysynaptic discharge is an expression of a slight depressant effect at all constituent synapses similar in magnitude to that exerted at the 2N junction (Bárány, 1947).

Dilantin does not affect 2N spike latency except for slight changes which are secondary to changes in spike amplitude. The duration of the 2N discharge is also unaffected by the drug. Measurements of 2N spike height are therefore valid indications of the number of neurons contributing to the discharge. Potentials recorded from the cord dorsum (*cf.* Bernhard, 1953) have not suggested effects of Dilantin on transmission of isolated impulses other than those noted above, namely, a slight depressant effect most noticeable in polysynaptic pathways. No rise in peripheral nerve or dorsal root threshold accompanies the decreased

TABLE 1

Effects of Dilantin on monosynaptic spike height and polysynaptic response area of isolated impulses

N.M.H.G., nerve to medial head of gastrocnemius; DR, dorsal root. Each mean is based upon about 30 responses in sequence at 4-sec. intervals.

Control		Dilantin		
Afferent	Mean ± S.D.	Dose *mgm./kgm.*	Mean ± S.D.	% Change from control
Monosynaptic				
N.M.H.G.	8.93 ± 3.19 A.U.*	10	10.90 ± 2.36 A.U.	+22
		20	7.18 ± 1.58 A.U.	−20
N.M.H.G.	0.800 ± 0.215 mv.	30	0.927 ± 0.163 mv.	+16
DR	1.25 ± 0.08 mv.	30	0.82 ± 0.48 mv.	−34
DR	0.809 ± 0.038 mv.	30	0.779 ± 0.067 mv.	−4
DR	5.53 ± 0.25 A.U.	30	4.62 ± 0.18 A.U.	−16
DR	1.30 ± 0.08 mv.	30	1.24 ± 0.11 mv.	−5
DR	1.86 ± 0.25 mv.	30	1.97 ± 0.37 mv.	+6
		40	1.56 ± 0.11 mv.	−16
DR	2.54 ± 0.08 mv.	30	2.09 ± 0.08 mv.	−18
Polysynaptic				
Sural N.	1.20 ± 0.14 mv. msec.	10	0.65 ± 0.45 mv. msec.	−46
Sural N.	1.40 ± 0.14 mv. msec.	30	1.01 ± 0.10 mv. msec.	−28
DR	10.62 ± 0.64 mv. msec.	30	6.95 ± 0.33 mv. msec.	−34
DR	7.59 ± 0.48 mv. msec.	30	5.73 ± 0.42 mv. msec.	−24

* Arbitrary units.

motoneuron discharge following Dilantin. Since the stimuli are 2 to 3 times that required to produce maximum discharge, the response depressed by Dilantin cannot be restored by an increase in stimulus voltage.

b) Facilitation and inhibition: Conceivably, spread of seizure activity could be reduced by an agent which decreases neuronal facilitation or enhances inhibition. Accordingly, the effects of Dilantin on both processes were investigated. Facilitation exerted between synergic motoneuron pools in the ankle joint myotatic unit (Lloyd, 1946) and also homosynaptic facilitation studied by conditioning and test stimuli applied to the same dorsal root were both found to be unaffected by Dilantin. Likewise inhibitory influences, either between muscle antagonists (Lloyd, 1946) or between two dorsal roots (Lloyd, 1941), were not affected by the drug.

c) Synaptic depression: Following transmission of an impulse in the 2N pathway, excitability, as tested by the second of two maximal volleys, does not recover for about 4 seconds (Brooks *et al*, 1950; Eccles and Rall, 1951a). In 5 experiments Dilantin produced a deepening of synaptic depression to orthodromic volleys similar to that illustrated in figure 1A. This effect of the drug is clearly exerted at a presynaptic site since recovery of motoneurons (figure 1B) is not influenced by Dilantin.

d) Response to repetitive stimulation: While depression following transmission of a single impulse in the 2N pathway is markedly increased by Dilantin (figure 1A), the responses to repetitive stimulation at low frequencies in 9 experiments have failed to show consistent response deficit of comparable magnitude. During stimulation at higher frequencies (5 to 25/second), depression following Dilantin is more evident. In figure 2 are shown curves representing the responses to repetitive stimulation at 4 frequencies in the same experiment. In each instance it can

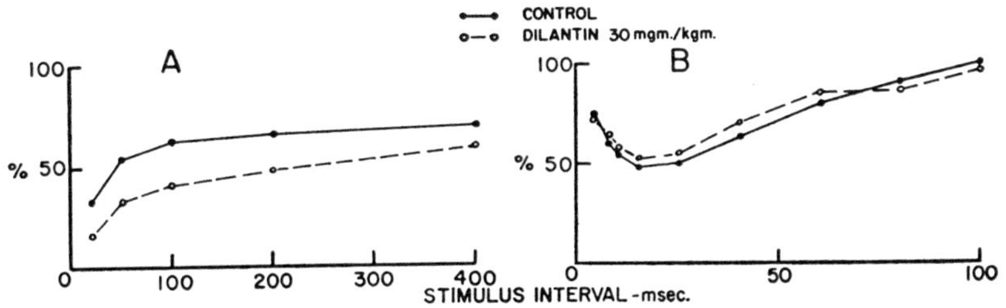

FIG. 1. Effect of Dilantin on synaptic recovery following a maximal volley in the 2N pathway.

A, orthodromic, maximal test and conditioning stimuli applied to DR. B, antidromic, maximal conditioning volley applied to sciatic nerve with relevant dorsal roots severed and all ipsilateral ventral roots intact; maximal test stimulus applied to DR. The maximum depression does not reach 100 per cent because not all the motoneurons tested by the DR volley contribute to the sciatic nerve. Ordinates, per cent synaptic recovery. Abscissae, interval between conditioning and test stimuli. Each point is an average of 9 responses. A and B, results obtained in the same experiment. See text for explanation.

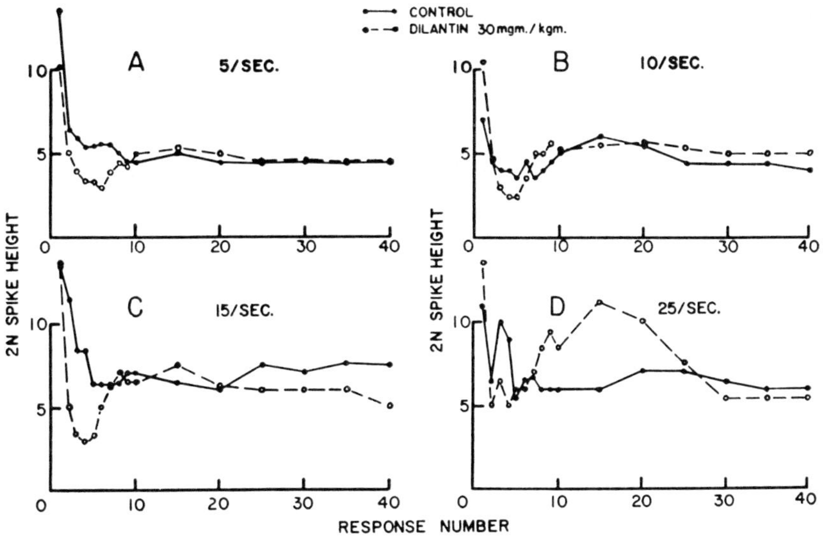

FIG. 2. Effect of Dilantin on 2N response to repetitive stimulation at various frequencies in one experiment, DR-VR preparation.

Dilantin reduced the control 2N spike by 3 per cent. In this and later figures, spike height is in arbitrary units unless voltage is specifically indicated on the ordinate. A, B, C and D, stimulation at 5, 10, 15 and 25 per sec., respectively. See text for explanation.

be seen that Dilantin causes an early increase in depression. During continued stimulation, however, transmission recovers and control and drug curves show similar response deficits. The recovery of transmission may be ascribed to cumulative facilitatory effects and to post-tetanic potentiation acting to counteract depression by recruiting neurons from the subliminal fringe (Eccles and Rall, 1951b). Examination of monosynaptic response to repetitive stimulation at frequencies of 5 to 50/second in 7 experiments has given results generally similar to the data of figure 2. In many experiments Dilantin has been observed to induce rhythmic fluctuations in 2N spike amplitude during stimulation. Occasionally, after the first few stimuli, Dilantin causes large and small spikes to alternate during continued stimulation. Such alternation in spike amplitude is occasionally seen during control stimulation but is greatly exaggerated by Dilantin. These fluctuations in amplitude may be an expression of the increased synaptic depression produced by the drug.

Repetitive stimulation of polysynaptic pathways activated selectively via the sural nerve has been studied in 3 preparations. The effect of Dilantin on poly-

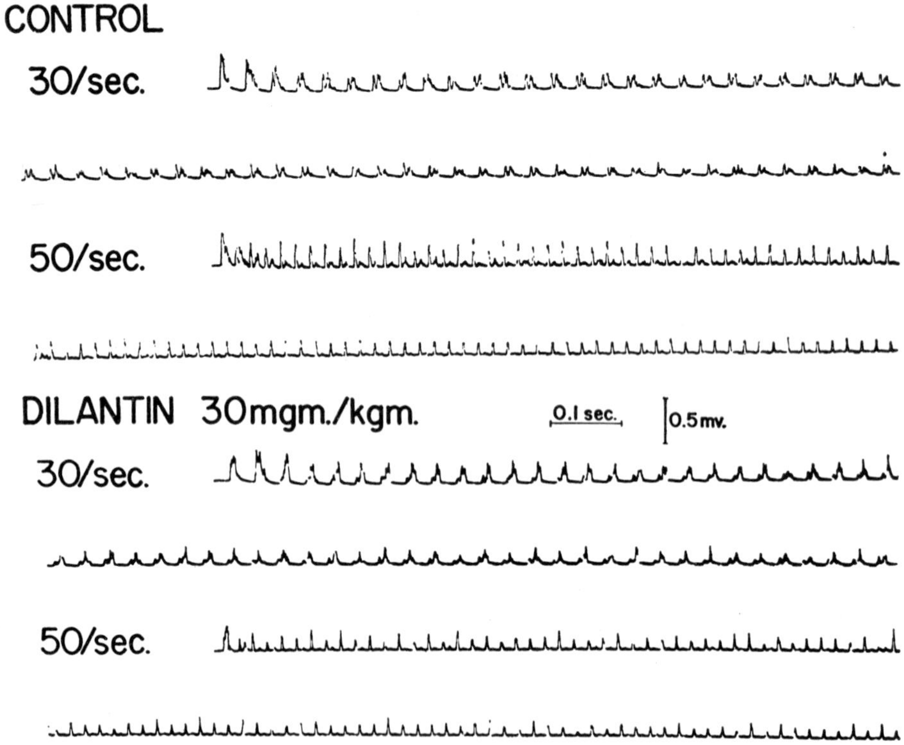

FIG. 3. Effect of Dilantin on polysynaptic responses to stimulation at 2 frequencies in the same experiment.

Supramaximal stimuli applied to the sural nerve. Dilantin (30 mgm./kgm.) reduced the control response by 28 per cent. Time and voltage calibrations apply to all 4 records. See text for explanation.

synaptic responses is similar to that on monosynaptic potentials. In figure 3 are shown responses obtained during stimulation at 30/second and at 50/second. It can be seen that in both control series the responses decrease in amplitude and duration but are quite regular. In the two Dilantin series, on the other hand, the responses show regular fluctuations in amplitude, particularly at 50/second. Since Dilantin reduces polysynaptic potentials, the initial response in each Dilantin series is smaller than the corresponding control potential. Considering this initial depression by the drug, the response deficits which occurred during stimulation are quite similar in the control and drug series. Thus, for both monosynaptic and polysynaptic responses, Dilantin has relatively little effect on the degree of transmission during repetitive stimulation.

e) Post-tetanic potentiation (PTP): The most striking effect of Dilantin upon activity in monosynaptic pathways is reduction of PTP. This effect has been studied in 18 preparations. Since at least one hour is required for a comparison of PTP before and after Dilantin, it was deemed worthwhile to determine the stability of PTP with time during control testing. In one control period extending over 3.5 hours there was only a small increase in PTP which resulted from a slight increase in level of excitability. While this was the longest study of PTP

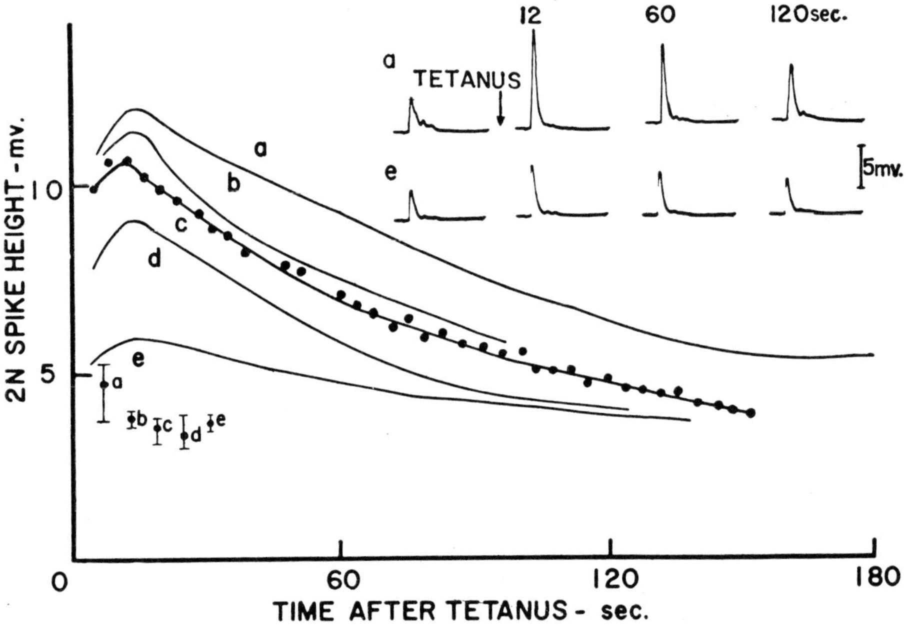

FIG. 4. Effect of various doses of Dilantin on spinal cord PTP.

DR-VR preparation, tetanus 500/sec. for 15 sec. a, control; b, c, d and e, after 10, 20, 30 and 40 mgm./kgm. Dilantin, respectively. Individual points are included for curve c to show dispersion typically observed. Upper right inset shows representative pre- and post-tetanic responses for curves a (control) and e (largest Dilantin dose). In this and later PTP curves, lower left points and brackets indicate mean and range of approximately 10 maximal pre-tetanic responses.

during control testing, it provides an adequate time control for all PTP experiments because, even though some experiments have continued for 40 hours, initial testing of PTP following Dilantin was always done within 3 hours of the control determination. Furthermore, in studies of drugs which do not affect PTP (Esplin and Curto, 1956), PTP has been observed to remain constant indefinitely at a given level of excitability.

In figure 4 are shown the effects of 4 doses (10 to 40 mgm./kgm.) of Dilantin on PTP induced by dorsal root stimulation. It can be seen that a dose of 10 mgm./kgm. produces a reduction in pre-tetanic spike height, but with higher doses the level of excitability remained essentially constant. Because of this reduction, the effect of 10 mgm./kgm. of Dilantin on PTP is equivocal; however, graded reduction in PTP was observed with successively higher doses, and potentiation was almost abolished by 40 mgm./kgm. Dilantin has a similar effect on PTP induced by muscle-nerve stimulation.

While some reduction in PTP is characteristically observed immediately following intravenous injection of Dilantin, it has been noted in a number of experiments that depression of PTP increases during the first hour after administration of the drug. Figure 5 shows three PTP determinations made 5 minutes and 1 and 13 hours after bringing the total dose of Dilantin to 30 mgm./kgm. There is a pronounced fall in PTP during the first hour and a slight decrease during the succeeding 12 hours after injection of the drug. This suggests that some time is required for full effectiveness of Dilantin. Of equal significance, however, is the lack of recovery of PTP following depression by Dilantin. In no experiment has there been any indication of recovery of PTP throughout recording periods extending up to 36 hours after injection. This suggests parallelism

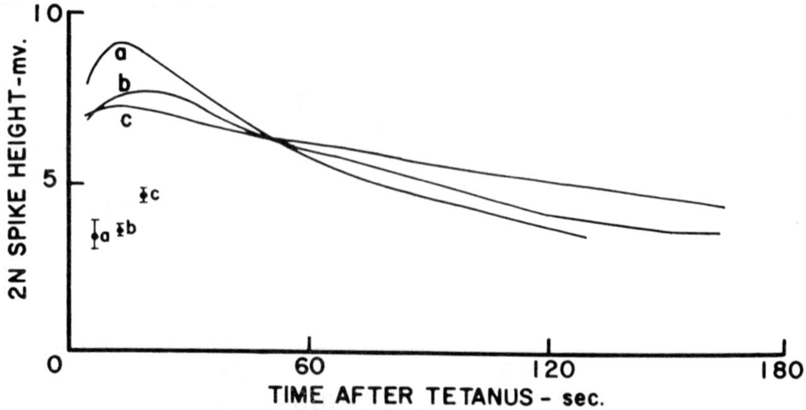

FIG. 5. Depression of spinal cord PTP as a function of time after 30 mgm./kgm. of Dilantin.

Same DR-VR experiment as that of figure 4. a, PTP determined 5 minutes after bringing total dose to 30 mgm./kgm.; b and c, 1 hour and 13 hours, respectively, after this total dose of Dilantin. Curve a is the same as curve d in figure 4. The curves cross because, as PTP wanes, each curve tends toward its own baseline. Points and bracketed lines, as explained in legend to figure 4.

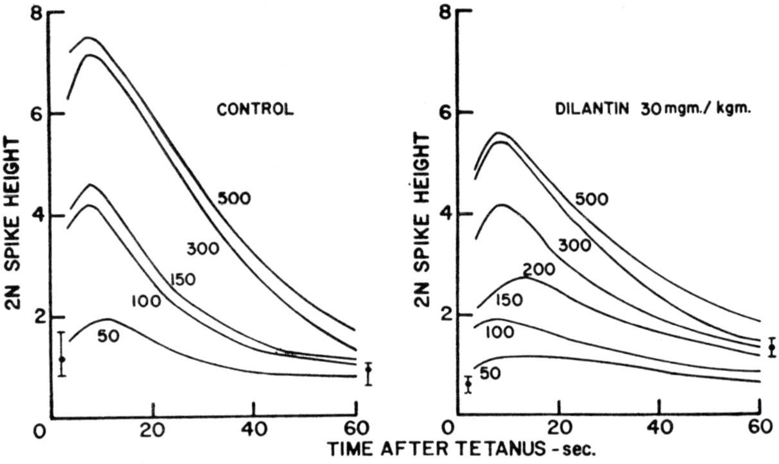

FIG. 6. Effect of Dilantin on spinal cord PTP induced by tetanic stimulation at various frequencies.

Nerve to medial head of gastrocnemius stimulated. Tetanic stimulation was of 15 sec. duration at frequencies indicated on each curve. In each series, curves were determined in order of increasing frequency with 5 to 8 minutes between tetanizations. Pre-tetanic responses (mean and bracketed range) are shown at the beginning and at the end of each series. Note the increase in pre-tetanic 2N spike height which occurred during determination of the Dilantin series. Thus, several of the curves in the Dilantin series (higher frequencies) tend toward a higher baseline than do curves for corresponding frequencies in the control series. Ordinates, arbitrary units.

between the anticonvulsant action of Dilantin and its effect on PTP, inasmuch as the anticonvulsant effect in cats is detectable for longer than 7 days following this dose of the drug (Toman *et al.*, 1946).

In all the experiments described thus far, the parameters of tetanization have been those which produce almost maximal potentiation (Lloyd, 1949). In the study of the effects of Dilantin on potentiation produced by less effective tetanization, frequency was varied and the duration of tetanization was constant at 15 seconds. It can be seen from figure 6 that the depressant effect of Dilantin on PTP is approximately the same for all frequencies. These results exclude the possibility that the effect of the drug on PTP is due to a block in the presynaptic terminals at high frequencies.

In assessing the effects of Dilantin on PTP, little attention has been given to effects on PTP ratio, that is, the ratio of the post-tetanic and the pre-tetanic discharges. PTP ratio is greatly dependent upon the level of excitability in the absence of specific modification by drugs. Jefferson and Benson (1953) have shown that following tetanization of a muscle-nerve (*e. g.*, nerve to medial head of gastrocnemius) all relevant motoneurons may be discharged. This maximum discharge may be observed at various levels of excitability, indicating that PTP ratio is not of fundamental importance. The existence of such a limit, however, may be questioned in the case of DR-VR preparations, because the motoneurons concerned are not restricted to such anatomically discrete pools. It has been

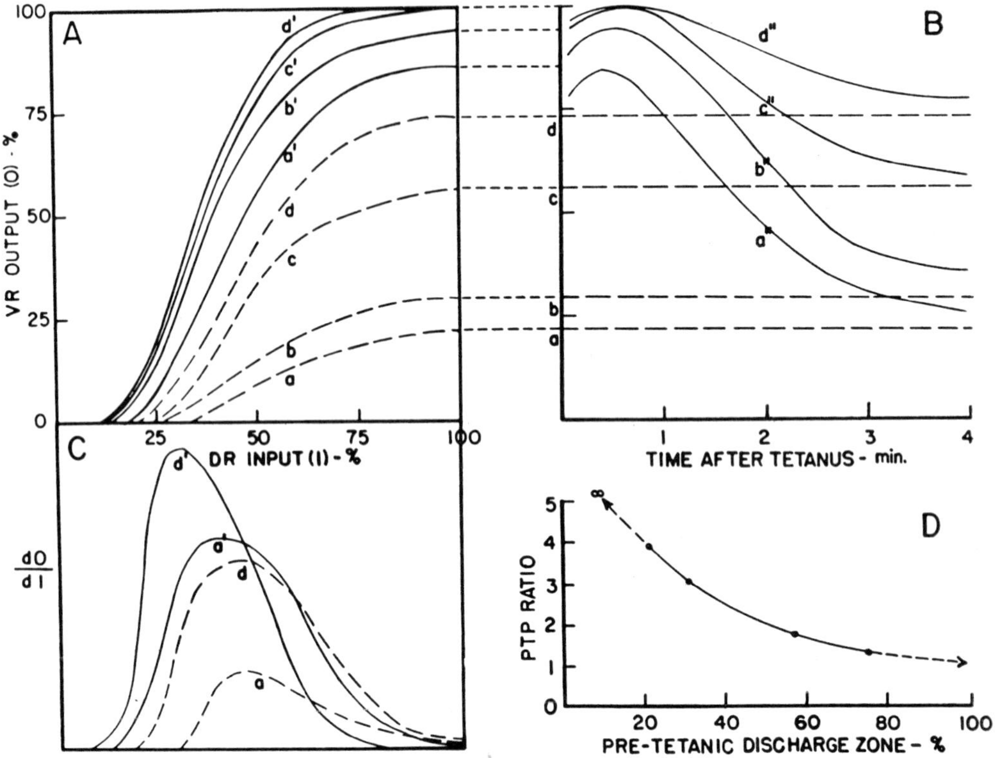

FIG. 7. Various aspects of PTP in the 2N pathway as a function of level of excitability. DR-VR (S_1) preparation. A, experimentally determined input-output curves at rest (a–d) and during the peak of PTP (a′–d′). Input-output relations represented by each pair of curves (a, a′; b, b′; etc.) were determined at a given level of excitability as controlled by varying the spinal cord temperature. Temperatures for curves a,a′–d,d′ were 36°C., 35°C., 32°C. and 30°C., respectively. B, curves illustrating the time-course of PTP at the 4 levels of excitability. C, curves illustrating distributions of synaptic thresholds for representative curves in A, obtained by graphical differentiation of corresponding input-output curves. Areas under curves are proportional to the respective maximal discharge zones in A. D, relationship between PTP ratio and discharge zone at rest. Values plotted are those obtained from the Y intercepts of A. See text for explanation.

observed in many DR-VR experiments that as level of excitability is increased the highest potentiated discharge increases to a maximum and remains constant. Such a maximum, indicating activation of all motoneurons available for the potentiated discharge, is best revealed by input-output curves (*cf.* Lloyd, 1943; Rall, 1955) which show the amplitude of post-synaptic discharge for all degrees of afferent stimulation. Figure 7A shows pairs of input-output curves at rest and during maximum PTP at 4 levels of excitability, as determined by varying the spinal cord temperature. Input-output relations during PTP were determined by testing only during the period of maximum potentiation. The 100 per cent value for the VR output is the highest potentiated discharge observed in the experiment. Observe that at the two highest levels of excitability the curves during

PTP both reach 100 per cent, and the slight increase in the potentiating process is revealed not by the size of the discharge zone but only by the decrease in threshold which is indicated by the shift to the left of the input-output curves. These relationships provide convincing evidence for the existence in DR-VR preparations of a limit to the number of postsynaptic neurons which can be discharged during potentiation. This maximum may be considered the total relevant pool (TRP) without defining its anatomical boundaries. The existence of a limit to the TRP specifies considerations which must be taken into account in assessing the effects of drugs on PTP when testing is performed in the usual manner, namely, by comparison of maximal synaptic discharges before and after tetanization. Firstly, if during the control PTP determination the potentiation is more than sufficient to lead to discharge of the TRP, then the maximum potentiated discharge fails completely to reflect increases in potentiation and is a relatively insensitive indicator of decreases in the potentiating process. Thus, reduction in potentiation revealed by the shift in the input-output curves from d′ to c′ would not be indicated in the usual determination of the time-course of PTP. Secondly, estimates of drug effect based upon PTP ratio alone are unreliable indications of drug effect. It can be seen from figure 7D that as the maximal discharge zone at rest approaches 100 per cent, PTP ratio necessarily approaches unity, and as the discharge zone falls to zero PTP ratio becomes infinite. Criteria for assessing effects of drugs on PTP in light of these considerations have been discussed elsewhere (Esplin, 1956).

Because of the slight effect of Dilantin on maximal discharge at rest, the effect on PTP is in most cases unequivocal. Where pre-tetanic discharge has been reduced, however, PTP ratio, instead of increasing, has been lowered by the drug. The specific effect of Dilantin on the potentiating process is most convincingly shown in figure 8. In this case synaptic threshold at rest, as shown by the input-output relations at rest was not influenced by the drug. The input-output curves during PTP show unequivocally the effect of Dilantin in reducing the maximum potentiated discharge. The lower portion of figure 8 shows the distributions of synaptic thresholds, in terms of the number of afferent fibers required for motoneuron discharge, for the corresponding input-output curves. It can be seen that during PTP, synaptic threshold of the motoneurons is reduced and there is greater homogeneity of the population. Dilantin partially prevents the reduction in synaptic threshold produced by tetanization.

Effects of Dilantin on PTP have been investigated in 18 experiments. In 16 of these the potentiated discharge was unequivocally reduced by the drug. In 1 experiment the potentiated discharge was not reduced; however, the input-output curves obtained during PTP were moved to the right by the drug and the potentiation, though reduced, was still sufficient to discharge the TRP (*cf.* figure 7). Input-output relations were not determined in the remaining negative experiment. In all of the PTP experiments stimuli were supramaximal for the fibers concerned in the 2N pathway. The potentiated discharge reduced by Dilantin therefore cannot be restored by increases in the strength of stimulation during testing or tetanization. Conclusive evidence that the effect of Dilantin on PTP

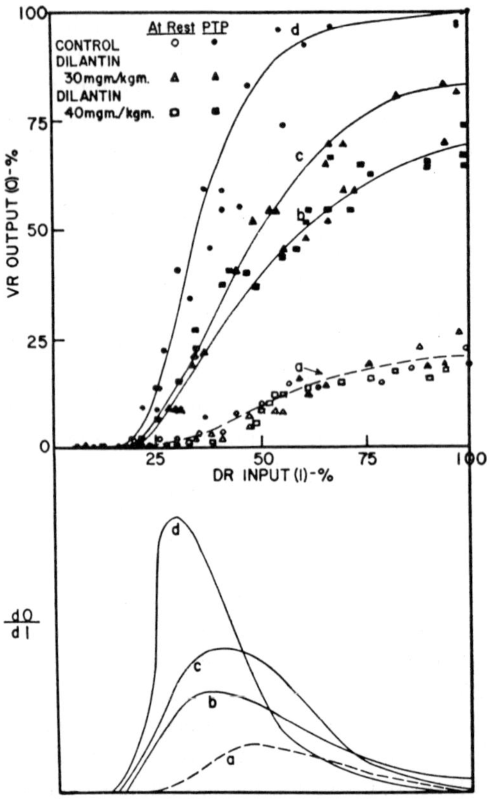

FIG. 8. Effect of Dilantin on synaptic thresholds at rest and during PTP.

Upper portion of the figure shows input-output curves and lower portion shows distributions of synaptic thresholds as in figure 7. Input-output relations at rest (open symbols) are so similar for control and drug observations that the points are adequately described by a single curve (a). At rest, each point is an average of 4 responses; during PTP, each point (closed symbol) represents a single response. PTP testing was carried out only during the peak of potentiation following tetanization at 500/sec. for 15 sec. Three series of tetanizations were required to give the points for each curve. Symbols a–d identify corresponding curves in the two portions of the figure.

is exerted at the synapse is that test and tetanic afferent volleys recorded at the dorsal root are not altered by the drug.

f) Effects of Metrazol and strychnine: In many experiments, at the conclusion of testing following Dilantin, either Metrazol (20 to 100 mgm./kgm.) or strychnine (0.05 to 0.2 mgm./kgm.) was studied for antagonism of the Dilantin effects. In the higher doses used, both excitant drugs exerted their characteristic actions on the spinal cord, and these effects did not appear to be significantly influenced by the presence of Dilantin. Neither drug restored PTP in doses which did not produce spontaneous activity. In no experiment was there evidence of antagonism of the effect of Dilantin by either agent.

II. *Effects of Dilantin on transmission in the stellate ganglion.* The stellate

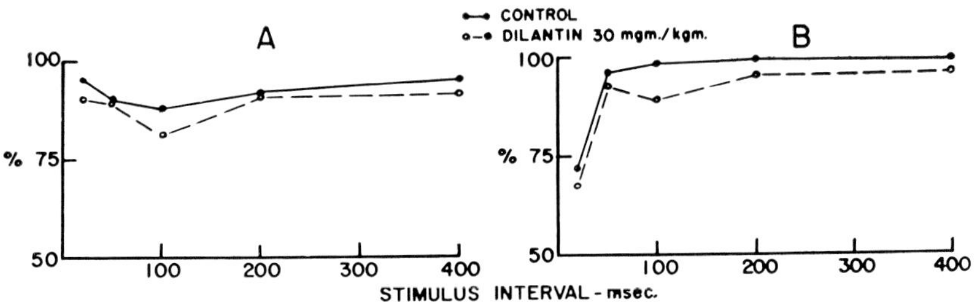

FIG. 9. Effect of Dilantin on synaptic recovery in the stellate ganglion following a maximal volley.

A, stimulating electrodes between rami II and III. B, stimulating electrodes between rami III and IV. Solid line, control; broken line, after 30 mgm./kgm. Dilantin. Ordinates, per cent synaptic recovery; abscissae, interval between two maximal volleys.

ganglion has been included in the study of the effects of Dilantin on synaptic transmission because it is a simple, accessible synaptic system. There is neither anatomical (Castro, 1951) nor physiological (*e. g.*, Eccles, 1953) evidence for interneurons in sympathetic ganglia; hence effects exerted at these sites are more easily interpreted than effects upon the monosynaptic pathways of the spinal cord. Interpretation of the results is further simplified by the absence of specific inhibitory fibers in the stellate ganglion (Eccles, 1953; Job and Lundberg, 1953). With the exception of inhibition, most aspects of synaptic transmission studied in the spinal cord can be investigated in the stellate ganglion, and this permits comparison of the effects of Dilantin on transmission in two synaptic systems which differ in certain anatomical and functional respects.

a) Transmission of isolated impulses: Dilantin (30 mgm./kgm.) produces a slight reduction in the amplitude of maximal responses elicited at 2-second intervals. For the 8 stellate ganglion experiments in which Dilantin was used, the average reduction produced by 30 mgm./kgm. of the drug was 8.6 per cent. Dilantin does not affect spike latency, except for small changes related to reduction in spike amplitude, nor is the duration of the discharge influenced by the drug.

b) Synaptic depression: As in the spinal cord, Dilantin deepens depression following transmission of an impulse in the stellate ganglion. Figure 9 illustrates the effects of Dilantin on synaptic depression observed in 2 of the 3 experiments in which this was examined.

c) Response to repetitive stimulation: Repetitive stimulation was studied in all 8 experiments. In all cases Dilantin increased the degree of transmission failure during stimulation. The records of figure 10 show a moderate effect of Dilantin during stimulation at 30/second and a very pronounced effect of the drug at 50/second. In some experiments it was noted that Dilantin caused large and small spikes to appear alternately in a manner similar to that observed in spinal cord preparations. This effect is not illustrated in figure 10, but indication of it is given in the record of tetanic stimulation shown in figure 12. It is conceivable that the increased transmission failure seen after Dilantin is attributable to depletion

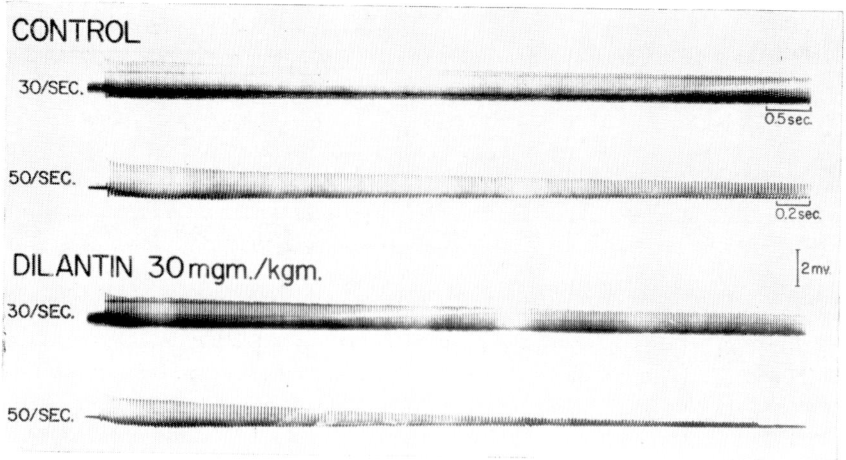

FIG. 10. Records illustrating effect of Dilantin on postganglionic response to high frequency stimulation.

Time calibrations for control records apply to the corresponding Dilantin records; voltage calibration applies throughout.

of mediator rather than to a direct effect of the drug. This is unlikely because in a number of control experiments far more prolonged and intense stimulation has been employed without any obvious effects on the response to repetitive stimulation.

d) Post-tetanic potentiation: Post-tetanic potentiation was studied in 4 experiments in which the stimulating electrodes were between rami II and III. Clear evidence of reduction in PTP by Dilantin was not obtained, though in some experiments there was suggestion of slight reduction. With application of stimuli at this point, PTP ratio is small since most of the relevant postsynaptic neurons are discharged by the maximal test volleys (Larrabee and Bronk, 1947). Because of this intense afferent stimulation it was thought that perhaps the excitatory action during PTP was greatly in excess of that required to discharge available postsynaptic neurons. If this were true, PTP would be rather insensitive to modification, and the apparent lack of effect of Dilantin would not be meaningful (*cf.* figure 7). Accordingly, stimulating electrodes were placed between rami III and IV. With this electrode placement, fewer preganglionic fibers were stimulated and hence the subliminal fringe was increased (*cf.* Larrabee and Bronk 1947). Dilantin was observed to have a pronounced effect upon PTP in this experiment as well as in another experiment in which this electrode placement was used. Figure 11 shows the effects of various doses of Dilantin (10 to 30 mgm./kgm.) on PTP rendered sensitive to testing by reduction in the afferent supply relative to the number of postsynaptic neurons. Since the pronounced effect of Dilantin on PTP which is shown in figure 11 was not detectable with stimulating electrodes between rami II and III, it is permissible to extend the criteria discussed above with reference to spinal cord PTP to include the stellate ganglion as well, and perhaps all synaptic systems in which limitations on efferent pool size exist (*cf.* Esplin, 1956).

Figure 12 contains portions of two paper records illustrating the effect of Dilantin on PTP. Also to be noted in this figure is the change in response to tetanic stimulation following Dilantin. Following initial fatigue, large and small spikes alternate. While not fully apparent at this paper speed, at higher recording speeds the presence of small spikes is clearly shown and response deficit during tetanization in the presence of the drug exceeds that of the control. Because of this it may be supposed that reduction of PTP by Dilantin is a direct consequence of reduced transmission. All the evidence indicates that PTP is due to changes produced in the presynaptic fibers by tetanization and that activation of postsynaptic neurons is not necessary for the phenomenon (Eccles, 1953; Fatt, 1954). In fact, Larrabee and Bronk (1947) have shown that antidromic tetanization of postsynaptic neurons leads to depression rather than potentiation. That PTP is not directly dependent upon transmission during tetanization can convincingly be demonstrated by pharmacological means. Figure 13A shows the pattern of PTP in the stellate ganglion at various levels of blockade (0 to 99 per cent) of transmission by tetraethylammonium (TEA). Also shown (B) are responses recorded during repetitive stimulation at several levels (0 to 50 per cent) of ganglionic blockade. It can be seen that, although transmission during stimulation falls markedly in the presence of TEA, the maximum potentiated discharge is only slightly reduced and PTP ratio (C) increases with increasing blockade as a consequence of the increased subliminal fringe. Comparison of figure 13 with figure 7 illustrates the general similarities of the two synaptic systems studied, and further emphasizes the factors which must be considered in assessing effects of drugs on PTP.

Discussion. Only doses of Dilantin between the minimally effective anticonvulsant and the minimally neurotoxic dose for cats were employed in this study. In spite of the anatomical and functional differences between the synaptic systems of spinal cord and stellate ganglion, the effects of Dilantin on transmission at these sites are qualitatively identical. The identity of effects provides

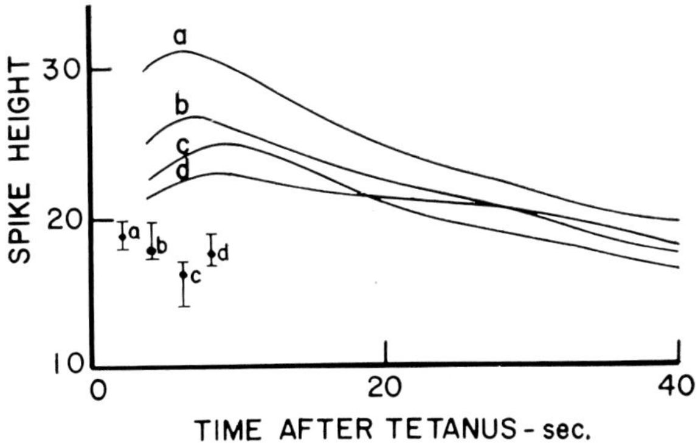

Fig. 11. Effect of Dilantin on ganglionic PTP.
Stimulating electrodes between rami III and IV. a, control; b, c and d, after 10, 20 and 30 mgm./kgm. Dilantin, respectively. Spike height in arbitrary units. Points and bracketed lines are mean and range, respectively, of about 10 pre-tetanic responses.

a basis for the assumption that such effects are exerted by Dilantin on synaptic transmission generally, and that similar effects may occur at sites concerned in initiation and propagation of epileptic discharge.

In assessing the significance of the various effects of Dilantin upon transmission in the spinal cord and stellate ganglion, the two synaptic systems will be considered together. The slight effect of Dilantin upon transmission of isolated impulses and upon overall synaptic threshold (figure 8) is in marked contrast to the effect of depressant drugs. This observation is in accord with the fact that Dilantin, even in extreme doses, produces little depression of the nervous system (Toman and Goodman, 1948). The reduction of polysynaptic potentials was approximately 3 times that of the monosynaptic spike. This depression would appear to reflect diminution of excitation at each synapse of the polyneuronal circuit (*cf.* Bárány, 1947), and there seems to be no justification for categorizing Dilantin as an "interneuron depressant" drug. The observed effects of Dilantin on monosynaptic and polysynaptic potentials parallel those of similar doses of the

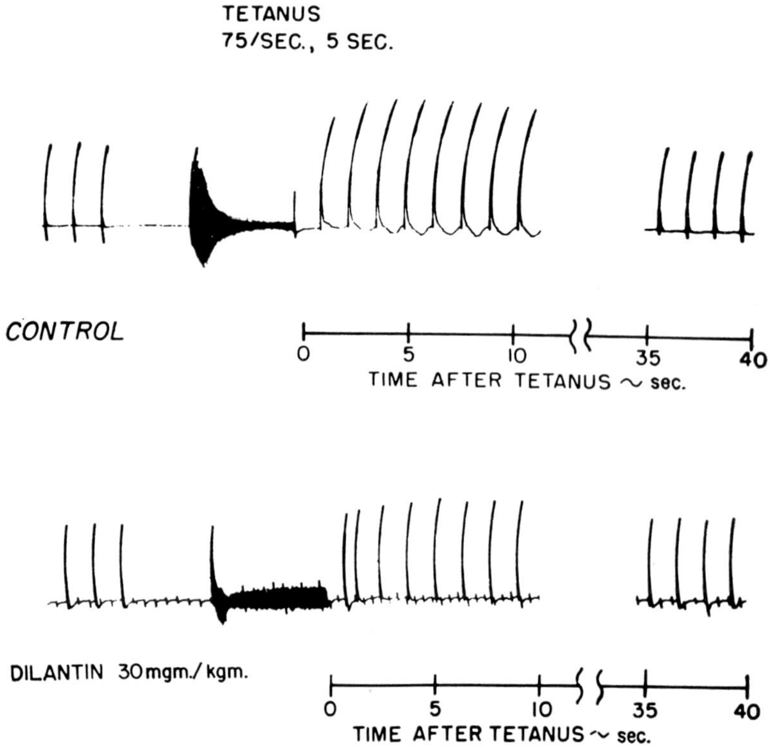

FIG. 12. Records showing effect of Dilantin on ganglionic PTP and on the postganglionic response during tetanization.

Records were obtained with an ink-writing oscillograph. Stimulating electrodes between rami III and IV. Apparent recovery of transmission during the tetanus in the presence of Dilantin is in reality alternation of small and large spikes. See text for significance. A slight change in the recording conditions caused the ECG to appear in the lower record.

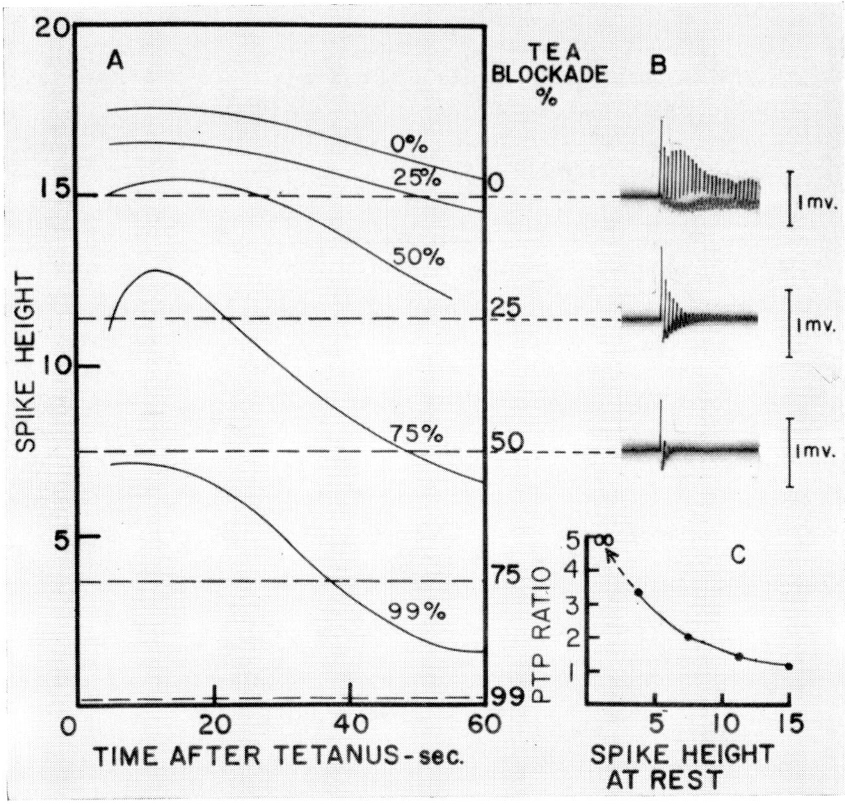

FIG. 13. Various aspects of ganglionic PTP as a function of level of excitability as determined by blockade with tetraethylammonium (TEA).

A, degree of PTP at several levels of TEA blockade. Stimulating electrodes between rami II and III. Broken lines indicate spike height in arbitrary units (left-hand ordinate) at each level of blockade (right-hand ordinate). Solid lines show the time-courses of PTP at corresponding degrees of transmission block. B, records showing degree of transmission during stimulation at 30/sec. at several levels of blockade. C, relationship between PTP ratio and spike height at rest (*cf.* figure 7D) obtaining for the data in A. See text for explanation. Responses in B retouched to improve contrast.

drug upon spinal reflexes mediated through monosynaptic and polysynaptic pathways (Stille, 1955). The relative constancy of the diminution in excitatory action, whether induced by dorsal root or muscle-nerve stimulation, provides presumptive evidence that neither facilitation nor inhibition is specifically affected by the drug. Examination of both processes apart from excitation has confirmed that neither is significantly influenced by Dilantin.

Following transmission of a single impulse, recovery of excitability in the presynaptic terminals is delayed by Dilantin. This effect may underlie the action of Dilantin in delaying recovery of CNS excitability following a maximal electroshock seizure (Tedeschi *et al.*, 1956). During repetitive stimulation the response deficit attributable to Dilantin was generally greater in the ganglion than in the spinal cord. In the spinal cord the degree of response deficit referable to the drug was generally less than the drug-induced depression following a single impulse. Thus, it appears that the rate of recovery of excitability is more affected by Dilantin than is the level of summated depression reached during repetitive stimulation. The absence of a marked effect of Dilantin to elevate synaptic threshold or to enhance transmission failure may be related to the inability of the drug significantly to raise seizure threshold (Goodman *et al.*, 1949). According to the theoretical scheme of Toman and Taylor (1952), one can assume an oscillator which is excited by the seizure stimulus. Following a drug which raises synaptic threshold, a greater stimulus would be required to excite the oscillator. Following a drug which enhances transmission failure, the oscillator, excited by a minimum stimulus, would cut-off before overt seizure activity was manifest. Support for the above argument is provided by the action of trimethadione (Tridione). This drug, in contrast to Dilantin, is quite effective in raising threshold for electrically—as well as Metrazol-induced seizures (Toman and Goodman, 1948; Goodman *et al.*, 1949). In spinal cord experiments similar to those of the present study, it has been found (Esplin and Curto, to be published) that Tridione, while without effect on synaptic threshold, profoundly increases transmission failure during repetitive stimulation.

Of particular significance is the inability of Metrazol or strychnine to antagonize any of the effects of Dilantin, and a striking contrast is provided by a comparison of Dilantin and Tridione in this respect. Metrazol specifically antagonizes all the effects of Tridione on the spinal cord (Esplin and Curto, to be published). Thus, comparison of Dilantin and Tridione with respect to Metrazol antagonism indicates complete correlation with the well-known actions of these anticonvulsants in Metrazol seizures, namely, the protective effect of Tridione but not of Dilantin (Everett and Richards, 1944; Goodman *et al.*, 1949).

The most prominent effect of Dilantin on synaptic transmission is the reduction, and in some instances almost complete suppression, of PTP. The drug specifically affects the potentiation process, and reduction in PTP is not quantitatively related to, nor dependent on, an effect on excitation. This property of Dilantin provides clues to the fundamental action of the drug on neurons and equally, to its anticonvulsant action.

Definitive studies of PTP have been made on spinal cord and autonomic ganglia, and all the results indicate that tetanization produces some change in the afferent terminals which is responsible for the prolonged potentiation (Larrabee and Bronk, 1947; Lloyd, 1949; Eccles and Rall, 1951a, b; Eccles, 1953; Fatt, 1954). Several explanations for PTP have been proposed. Lloyd (1949) observed a slight increase in intraspinal afferent spike potential which followed the same time-course as the potentiated reflex discharge. He suggested that the enhanced afferent spikes led directly to an increased postsynaptic discharge. Eccles and Rall (1951a) have suggested that activity in the presynaptic terminals alters their spatial relationship with the motoneuron and makes a given afferent impulse a more efficient excitatory agent. In view of the impressive evidence in favor of chemical mediation of transmission in the spinal cord (Eccles, 1953;

Fatt, 1954; Eccles *et al.*, 1956), Lloyd's hypothesis involving purely electrical considerations may be inadequate. However, further evidence that the increased spike in the fine afferent branches is a causal factor in PTP was recently provided by Brown and Holmes (1956) who showed that tetanization of fine nerve fibers produces an increase in both membrane and action potentials. Post-tetanically the spike amplitude is increased almost three fold in some nerves, and the time-course of the enhancement parallels that of PTP in the ganglion. This observation would appear to apply directly to PTP inasmuch as the fine fibers which show post-tetanic enhancement are assumed to be anatomically and functionally similar to the unmyelinated extensions of large afferent fibers. There is a mechanism, not expressed in any of the above explanations of PTP, whereby the hyperpolarization, which appears clearly to be implicated as a causal factor in PTP, may lead to an increased output of mediator following tetanization. Abundant evidence exists to support the generalization that sites of axon branching are regions of low safety factor and that incoming impulses may fail to invade all the ramifications. Direct evidence for the existence of such blocked branches of primary afferent fibers in the spinal cord has been supplied by Eccles and Malcolm (1946) and by Koketsu (1956). Post-tetanically the many branches previously blocked may now be invaded by the enhanced action potential (Lloyd, 1949; Brown and Holmes, 1956). The potentiation of transmission itself is then revealed as increased postsynaptic discharge as a consequence of a greater number of active presynaptic knobs. The crucial assumption in the hypothesis, namely the existence of presynaptic branches inactive at rest but capable of being activated following a tetanus, is currently being tested in this laboratory by microelectrode exploration of the dorsal horn.

Directly supporting the suggestion that post-tetanic enhancement of action potential is a causal factor in PTP is the finding (Esplin, unpublished observations) that Dilantin (10 to 40 mgm./kgm.) reduces post-tetanic enhancement of action potentials in C fibers of cat vagus nerve *in vivo*. This effect of Dilantin also provides the basis for suggestions regarding the discrete action of the drug upon neuronal processes. The enhanced action potential is due to hyperpolarization of the fibers as a result of tetanic stimulation (Brown and Holmes, 1956). This hyperpolarization (summation of positive after-potentials) appears from present evidence (Hodgkin, 1951; Eccles, 1953; Hodgkin and Keynes, 1954; Coombs *et al.*, 1955) clearly to be dependent upon transport of ions across the membrane during recovery processes. The effect of Dilantin in reducing PTP would therefore appear to be referable to an action upon ion transport processes. Evidence that Dilantin enhances activity of the sodium pump of neurons in the brain has been obtained by Woodbury (1955). An action of Dilantin upon such processes fundamental to all excitable tissue may also underlie the effects of the drug upon the heart (Harris and Kokernot, 1950) and upon intestinal motility (Druckman and Moore, 1955).

While PTP has been most studied in the monosynaptic pathways of the spinal cord and autonomic ganglia, it is clearly demonstrable in the complex polysynaptic pathways of the spinal cord (Wilson, 1955) and is assumed to be a general synaptic property (Eccles, 1953; Fatt, 1954). The phenomenon has recently been demonstrated in auditory and visual pathways of the cat (Hughes, 1956; Evarts *et al.*, 1956). PTP is most convincingly revealed by experimental technics which are rarely simulated physiologically: impulses are delivered to the synapse following abrupt cessation of an intense, maximal, synchronous afferent barrage. Although PTP is most dramatic when produced in this manner, electrical manifestations of the process are clearly evident during as well as following tetanic stimulation with only a few impulses (Eccles and Rall, 1951a). The term "post-tetanic" therefore belies the actual nature of the process; enhancement of excitability referable to PTP, such as that shown in figure 2, occurs continuously during repetitive stimulation (Eccles and Rall, 1951b; Esplin and Curto, to be published), although it is necessarily intermingled with the effects of refractoriness, depression and facilitation. Thus, PTP would appear to be a phenomenon similar to summated synaptic depression though opposite in sense; the latter process would tend to restrict synaptic activity while the former would act to extend and maintain it. Considered in this light PTP may be significantly concerned in all functions of the nervous system characterized by repetitive activity, and the magnitude of its role would seem to be in direct relation to the intensity of such activity.

Ward *et al.* (1955) have shown that neurons in cortical epileptogenic foci in monkeys may fire in prolonged bursts at frequencies as high as 500 impulses per second. There is considerable evidence also that the "centrencephalic system" (Penfield and Jasper, 1954) may be the primary seizure focus in some instances and an important relay for dispersion of seizure discharge in other cases (Faeth *et al.*, 1954; French *et al.*, 1956). It is evident, therefore, that conditions for PTP exist at seizure foci, and the result of such potentiation, including potentiation during the repetitive discharge, would be expansion of the discharge zone and increase in the output-input ratio (figures 7 and 8; *cf.*, Toman and Taylor, 1952).

According to Toman and Taylor (1952), the action of Dilantin is "predominantly on the progressive detonation mechanism which determines spread and intensity of convulsive involvement of the brain." The effect of Dilantin on PTP is therefore consistent with its anticonvulsant action; should the drug be shown to reduce PTP in pathways concerned with seizure spread, this effect would appear clearly to be implicated as one component of its anticonvulsant property. Support for the suggestion that the effect of Dilantin on PTP is related to its effect on seizure spread is again provided by the effects of Tridone. This drug, which appears to act directly on the seizure focus rather than on the spreading mechanism (Toman and Taylor, 1952), has no effect on PTP in the spinal cord (Esplin and Curto, to be published).

One of the aims of the investigation of which the present study is a part is to establish reliable correlations between anticonvulsant actions and discrete effects upon synaptic transmission for certain prototype drugs. The reported effects of Dilantin meet the necessary conditions for correlation with anticonvulsant action as regards dose, onset of effect, duration of effect, and lack of antagonism of effect by Metrazol and strychnine. Furthermore, all the effects of Dilantin on synaptic transmission can be harmoniously correlated with prominent effects of the drug as seen in intact animals, as follows: the slight effect on excitation with the absence of obvious central depression; the slight effect on synaptic threshold and on response to repetitive stimulation with the poor ability to raise seizure threshold; the deepening of synaptic depression with prolongation of recovery following a seizure; the decrease in PTP with the reduction in spread of seizure discharge. The last mentioned correlation is of the most significance inasmuch as it compares the most dramatic effect of Dilantin on synaptic transmission with the most outstanding anticonvulsant property of the drug. It is specifically suggested that PTP (as discussed above) is an important process concerned in propagation of seizure discharge and that the anticonvulsant action of Dilantin is in part attributable to a depressant effect upon this process.

SUMMARY

Diphenylhydantoin (Dilantin) has been studied for its effects on various aspects of synaptic transmission in 30 unanesthetized cats. The effects on spinal cord and stellate ganglion are qualitatively identical and will be summarized together.

Maximal isolated monosynaptic responses are reduced about 10 per cent by 30 mgm./kgm. of the drug. This dose reduces polysynaptic potentials by about 30 per cent. Dilantin does not affect either direct facilitation or inhibition in the spinal cord. The drug deepens presynaptic depression following transmission of an impulse and enhances transmission failure during repetitive stimulation. Response deficit referable to the drug is quite pronounced in the ganglion, but it is slight in both monosynaptic and polysynaptic pathways of the spinal cord.

Post-tetanic potentiation (PTP) is strikingly reduced by Dilantin. This reduction in PTP is attributable to specific suppression of the potentiating process. It is not dependent upon the parameters of tetanization, nor related to the effect of the drug on excitation or transmission during tetanization. None of the effects of Dilantin is antagonized by Metrazol or strychnine.

The doses of Dilantin employed in all experiments were in the anticonvulsant, nontoxic range for cats. The observed effects are discussed with regard to the anticonvulsant properties of the drug. It is specifically proposed that PTP, including enhancement of transmission during tetanic stimulation, is involved in spread of seizure discharge and that reduction of PTP by Dilantin is intimately related to its anticonvulsant action.

ACKNOWLEDGMENT. The writer is indebted to Drs. Robert W. Doty, Herbert L. Borison, and J. Walter Woodbury for suggestions during the course of this work. The writer is particularly grateful to Dr. Louis S. Goodman for his role in initiating this investigation and for advice throughout the study and during preparation of the manuscript.

REFERENCES

BÁRÁNY, E.: Arch. internat. pharmacodyn., **75:** 222, 1947.

BERNHARD, C. G.: In: The Spinal Cord, Malcolm, J. L. and Gray, J. A. B., Editors, Little, Brown and Co., Boston, 1953.

BROOKS, C. McC., DOWNMAN, C. B. B., AND ECCLES, J. C.: J. Neurophysiol., **13:** 157, 1950.

Brooks, C. McC., Koizumi, Kiyomi, and Malcolm, J. L.: J. Neurophysiol., **18:** 205, 1955.
Brown, G. L., and Holmes, L.: Proc. Roy. Soc., London, S. B., **145:** 1, 1956.
Castro, F., de: Arch. internat. physiol., **59:** 479, 1951.
Coombs, J. S., Eccles, J. C., and Fatt, P.: J. Physiol., **130:** 374, 1955.
Druckman, R., and Moore, F. J.: Proc. Soc. Exper. Biol. & Med., **90:** 173, 1955.
Eccles, J. C.: The Neurophysiological Basis of Mind, Clarendon Press, Oxford, 1953.
Eccles, J. C., Eccles, R. M., and Fatt, P.: J. Physiol., **131:** 154, 1956.
Eccles, J. C., and Malcolm, J. L.: J. Neurophysiol., **9:** 139, 1946.
Eccles, J. C., and Rall, W.: J. Neurophysiol., **14:** 353, 1951a.
Eccles, J. C., and Rall, W.: Proc. Roy. Soc., London, S. B., **138:** 475, 1951b.
Esplin, D. W.: Science, **124:** 1150, 1956.
Esplin, D. W., and Curto, E. M.: In preparation, 1956.
Evarts, E. V., Hughes, J. R., and Marshall, W. H.: Fed. Proc., **15:** 59, 1956.
Everett, G. M., and Richards, R. K.: This Journal, **81:** 402, 1944.
Faeth, W. H., Walker, A. E., and Andy, O. J.: Epilepsia, Third Series, **3:** 37, 1954.
Fatt, P.: Physiol. Rev., **34:** 674, 1954.
French, J. D., Gernandt, B. E., and Livingstone, R. B.: A.M.A. Arch. Neurol. & Psychiat., **75:** 260, 1956.
Goodman, L. S., and Gilman, A.: The Pharmacological Basis of Therapeutics, 2nd Ed., Macmillan Co., New York, 1955.
Goodman, L. S., Toman, J. E. P., and Swinyard, E. A.: Arch. internat. pharmacodyn., **78:** 144, 1949.
Harreveld, A. van, and Feigen, G. S.: Am. J. Physiol., **160:** 451, 1950.
Harreveld, A. van, Foster, R. J., and Fasman, G. D.: Am. J. Physiol., **166:** 718, 1951.
Harris, A. S., and Kokernot, R. H.: Am. J. Physiol., **163:** 505, 1950.
Hodgkin, A. L.: Biol. Rev., **26:** 339, 1951.
Hodgkin, A. L., and Keynes, R. D.: In: Symposia of the Society for Experimental Biology. VIII. Active Transport and Secretion, Academic Press, New York, 1954.
Hughes, J. R.: Fed. Proc., **15:** 97, 1956.
Jefferson, A., and Benson, A.: J. Neurophysiol., **16:** 381, 1953.
Jefferson, A. A., and Schlapp, W.: In: The Spinal Cord, Malcolm, J. L. and Gray, J. A. B., Editors, Little, Brown and Co., Boston, 1953.
Job, C., and Lundberg, A.: Acta physiol. scandinav., **28:** 14, 1953.
Koizumi, Kiyomi, Malcolm, J. L., and Brooks, C. McC.: Am. J. Physiol., **179:** 507, 1954.
Koketsu, K.: Am. J. Physiol., **184:** 338, 1956.
Korey, S. R.: Proc. Soc. Exper. Biol. & Med., **76:** 297, 1951.
Larrabee, M. G., and Bronk, D. W.: J. Neurophysiol., **10:** 139, 1947.
Lloyd, D. P. C.: J. Neurophysiol., **4:** 184, 1941.
Lloyd, D. P. C.: J. Neurophysiol., **6:** 111, 1943.
Lloyd, D. P. C.: J. Neurophysiol., **9:** 421, 1946.
Lloyd, D. P. C.: J. Gen. Physiol., **33:** 147, 1949.
Pedersen, E.: Acta psychiat. et neurol. scandinav., Supp. **88:** 1, 1954.
Penfield, W., and Jasper, H.: Epilepsy and the Functional Anatomy of the Human Brain, Little, Brown and Co., Boston, 1954.
Rall, W.: J. Cell & Comp. Physiol., **46:** 413, 1955.
Romanes, G. J.: In: The Spinal Cord, Malcolm, J. L. and Gray, J. A. B., Editors, Little, Brown and Co., Boston, 1953.
Reighard, J., and Jennings, H. S.: Anatomy of the Cat, Henry Holt and Co., New York, 1949.
Scherf, D.: Bull. N. Y. Med. College, Flower and Fifth Ave. Hosp., **6:** 82, 1943.
Stille, G.: Arch. exper. Path. u. Pharmakol., **226:** 172, 1955.
Swinyard, E. A., Brown, W. C., and Goodman, L. S.: This Journal, **106:** 319, 1952.
Tedeschi, D. H., Swinyard, E. A., and Goodman, L. S.: Proc. Soc. Exper. Biol. & Med., **93:** 379, 1956.

TOMAN, J. E. P.: Electroencephalog. & Clin. Neurophysiol., **1**: 33, 1949.
TOMAN, J. E. P.: Pharmacol. Rev., **4**: 168, 1952.
TOMAN, J. E. P., AND GOODMAN, L. S.: Physiol. Rev., **28**: 409, 1948.
TOMAN, J. E. P., SWINYARD, E. A., AND GOODMAN, L. S.: J. Neurophysiol., **9**: 231, 1946.
TOMAN, J. E. P., AND TAYLOR, J. D.: Epilepsia, Third Series, **1**: 31, 1952.
WARD, A. A., JR., THOMAS, L. B., AND SCHMIDT, R. P.: Fed. Proc., **14**: 158, 1955.
WILSON, V. J.: J. Gen. Physiol., **39**: 197, 1955.
WOODBURY, D. M.: THIS JOURNAL, **115**: 74, 1955.

FREQUENCY-FORCE RELATIONSHIP IN THE RABBIT AURICLE AND ITS MODIFICATION BY SOME METABOLIC INHIBITORS[1]

B. KATZUNG, H. ROSIN AND F. SCHEIDER

Department of Pharmacology, State University of New York, Upstate Medical Center, Syracuse

Received for publication February 8, 1957

The effect of previous activity or quiescence on myocardial contractility was first described by Bowditch (1871). Working with the frog heart, he noted that following a period of rest, stimulation resulted in a staircase-like series of beats of increasing force of contraction. He called this phenomenon "treppe", and its existence has been confirmed by many authors (reviewed by Szent-Gyorgyi, 1953). Most authors have observed that any increase in contraction frequency results in increased contractility. On the other hand, a few authors have observed in mammalian myocardium the opposite effect, *i.e.*, a temporary potentiation of contractility following rest (rest potentiation) (Rosin and Farah, 1955; Brooks *et al.*, 1955; Katzung and Farah, 1956). A similar and probably related reversal of the classical Bowditch treppe has been observed at very low rates in rat ventricle by McDowall *et al.* (1955) and in turtle myocardium by Katzung and Farah (1956). Another reversal of the Bowditch treppe occurs at high frequencies of contraction, where a further increase in frequency results in decreased contractility. One purpose of the present study was to further define the inotropic effects of frequency with particular reference to the low frequency boundary of the treppe phenomenon.

Although the treppe phenomenon is well known, relatively little is known concerning the relationship of frequency and drug action on cardiac contractility. Some aspects of this problem have been investigated by Szent-Gyorgyi (1953), Whitehorn (1954), Lee (1954), and Porro (1955). It was the second purpose of this investigation to emphasize the qualitative and quantitative variations in the effects of some metabolic inhibitors at different contraction frequencies.

In the third portion of this report we have included observations on the effects of these inhibitors on post-stimulation potentiation and rest potentiation as elicited by the method of Rosin and Farah (1955). We have attempted to relate these phenomena to treppe potentiation and to define the conditions favorable for post-stimulation potentiation of contractility by means of the effects of the inhibitors studied.

METHODS. Left auricles from rabbits were prepared as described in a previous paper (Rosin and Farah, 1955). The bath consisted of 50 ml. of Tyrode solution (NaCl 137 *mM*, KCl 2.7 *mM*, $CaCl_2$ 1.8 *mM*, $MgCl_2$ 0.6 *mM*, $NaHCO_3$ 12 *mM*, NaH_2PO_4 0.4 *mM*, and glucose 5.5 *mM*) maintained at 37.5° C. ± 0.5° C. and aerated with a 95 per cent oxygen, 5 per cent carbon dioxide gas mixture. A minimum equilibration period of one hour was observed in all experiments.

---

[1] Supported by a grant-in-aid from the American Heart Association, Inc.

The "standard" frequency-force relationship was determined by equilibrating the auricles at 0.2, 0.3, 0.5, 1.0, 2.0, 3.0, 4.0, and 6.0 beats per second. Three experiments were performed using low rates down to 1 per minute. In these experiments the auricles were equilibrated at 1, 3, and 6 per minute and the remainder of the rates as above. Citrate in tissue was determined by the method of Ettinger *et al.* (1952).

RESULTS. The effect of frequency on isometric contractility is shown in figure 1A which represents equilibrated contractions taken from an actual recording. Figure 1B represents the average of 20 experiments in which contractile force was plotted against frequency of stimulation. It is evident that there are three major phases in the response to increasing rate of stimulation: an initial decrease in contractility (0.2 to 0.5 per sec.), a rising phase between 0.5 and 3.0 per second which corresponds to the "classical" positive treppe, and a final decrease in contractility with rates above the optimal 3.0 to 4.0 per second. Experiments performed with very low rates of contraction showed that the first or falling phase of the rate-force relationship begins at a rate of 3 per minute, while the contractility is not greatly affected by rates between 1 and 3 per minute. We have termed this triphasic frequency force relationship the "S-shaped curve." Comparison with results obtained by Brooks *et al.* (1955) using cat papillary muscle shows that the rabbit auricle is more sensitive to changes in frequency.

Effects of some metabolic inhibitors on the S-shaped curve are shown in figures 2 and 3. Figure 2 consists of equilibrated contractions at high and low frequencies taken from an experiment in which the auricle was exposed to 6.0×10^{-4} *M* sodium fluoroacetate for one hour. It can be seen that the effect of the drug at a rate of 0.2 per second was to increase contractile force while at 2.0 per second contractile force was decreased. The results obtained for fluoroacetate and the

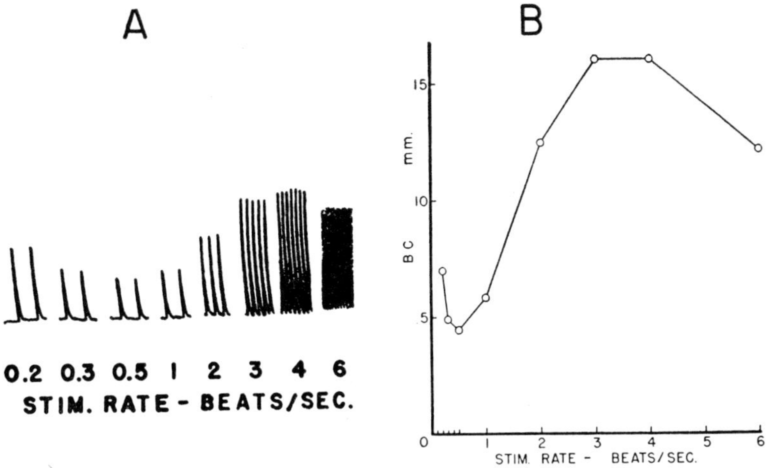

FIG. 1. Effect of frequency on contractile force of the isolated left auricle of the rabbit. 1A. Typical contractions as displayed on a recording. Only equilibrated contractions shown for the rates designated. 1B. Isometric basal contractility (BC) plotted in terms of millimeters of pen deflection on the ordinate; basal rate in beats per second on the abscissa. This is the "S-shaped curve." Average of 20 auricles.

other inhibitors studied are shown graphically in figure 3A and B. It can be seen that cyanide, dinitrophenol (DNP), and iodoacetate depressed contractility at all frequencies, while fluoroacetate and fluoride had positive inotropic effects at low frequencies, but depressed contractility at high rates. As shown in figure 4A, B and C, there were three different types of response to the various inhibitors. In the case of fluoroacetate (figure 4A) and fluoride, there was a marked frequency effect with potentiation of contractility at low rates and depression in the higher range of frequency. The positive inotropic effect of fluoroacetate has been observed by Bennett and coworkers (1951) and Reilly *et al.* (1953) using cat papillary muscle. Loewi (1955) has reported a similar effect of fluoride on the frog heart preparation.

In the second class of inhibitors (2,4-dinitrophenol, figure 4B, and cyanide) contractility was depressed slightly at low frequencies and markedly at high

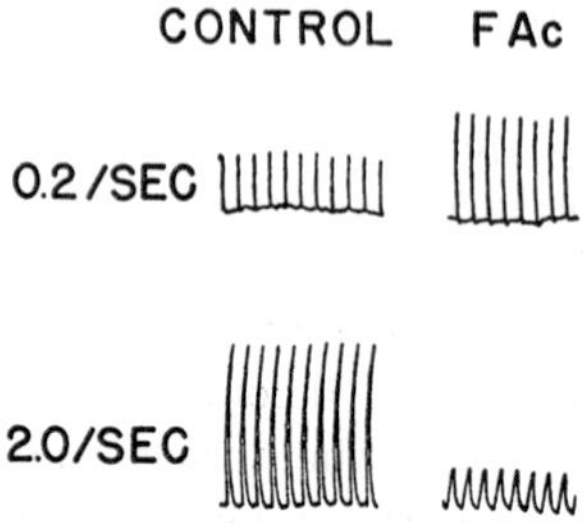

FIG. 2. Effect of fluoroacetate on auricular contractile force at slow and fast rates.
Control contractions and after exposure to 0.6 × 10^{-3} *M* sodium fluoroacetate for 60 minutes ("FAc"). Paper speed of recording increased for 2.0 per second stimulation rate.

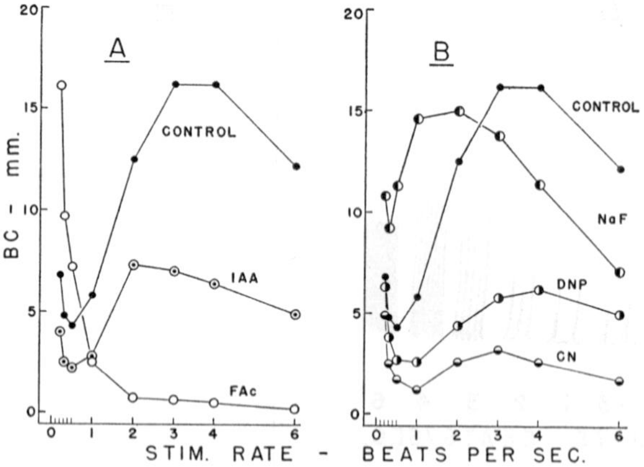

FIG. 3. Effect of inhibitors on frequency-force relationship (S-shaped curve) in the isolated left auricle.

Basal contractility (BC) in millimeters pen deflection plotted against rate. Control—average of 20 auricles. IAA—effect of iodoacetic acid, 5 × 10^{-5} *M*, after 73 minutes' exposure. FAc-effect of sodium fluoroacetate, 6.0 × 10^{-4} *M*, after 66 minutes' exposure. NaF-effect of sodium fluoride, 7.2 × 10^{-3} *M*, after 64 minutes' exposure. DNP—effect of 2,4-dinitrophenol, 3 × 10^{-5} *M*, after 64 minutes' exposure. CN—effect of sodium cyanide, 4 × 10^{-4} *M*, after 61 minutes' exposure. Each curve represents the average of 4 auricles.

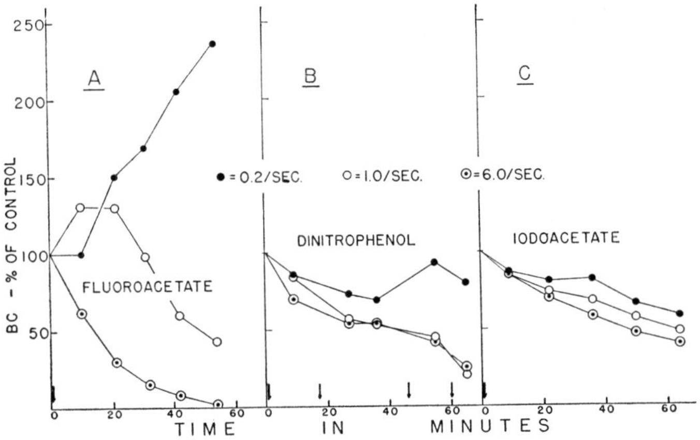

FIG. 4. Basal contractility (BC) at rates of 0.2, 1.0, and 6.0 per second, in terms of per cent of control contractility, plotted against time of exposure to the drug.

A. effect of fluoroacetate, 6×10^{-4} M, added at the arrow. Average of 4 auricles. B. effect of dinitrophenol, concentration increased by 5×10^{-6} M at each arrow. Average of 4 auricles. C. effect of iodoacetic acid, 5×10^{-5} M, added at the arrow. Average of 5 auricles.

rates. Thus the protective effect of low frequency was still present. This protective effect of low rates of stimulation may be related to the longer diastolic recovery period obtained with low frequencies.

Iodoacetate (figure 4C) produced the third type of response in which the protective frequency effect was almost completely abolished and the difference between low and high frequency depression was minimal.

It should be noted that with sufficient duration of exposure (3 to 4 hours) all the inhibitors depressed contractility at all frequencies studied. However, only fluoroacetate rapidly and completely abolished the positive treppe phenomenon. This effect was observed with all concentrations used from 0.5×10^{-4} to 1.2×10^{-3} M NaFAc. Figure 3A shows that, while the contractility at low frequencies was potentiated by exposure to fluoroacetate, the contractility curve was markedly depressed in the region of the positive treppe (above rates of 1.0 per sec.).

The effect of contraction frequency on citrate accumulation in the absence and presence of fluoroacetate has been determined in the rabbit auricle[2] using the method of Ettinger *et al.* (1952) and the results obtained are shown in table 1. It is apparent that in both control and fluoroacetate-treated auricles the rate of contraction had no effect on the accumulation of citrate. Therefore, the increase in contractility at low rates, induced by fluoroacetate, is probably not due to an increasing degree of blockade of the tricarboxylic acid cycle.

The effects of metabolic inhibitors on "rest contractions" are shown in figure 5A, B and C. In these experiments the auricles were stimulated at a constant rate of 1.0 per second with intermittent rest periods of from 2 to 20 seconds. The rest contraction (RC) was the initial contraction elicited upon resumption of stimulation following a rest period. It will be seen that the inhibitors fell into three classes. Fluoroacetate (figure 5A) produced a greater potentiation of the

[2] We are indebted to Dr. Margaret Wilson for these data.

TABLE 1

Effect of frequency of stimulation on citrate accumulation in isolated left auricular strips of the rabbit

FAc = sodium fluoroacetate, 3×10^{-4} *M*

Procedure	Microgm. Citrate per Gm. Tissue	"T Test"
Control, quiescent, 1 hour, 3 aur.	34.3 ± 3.0 S.E.	For any combination P > 0.1
Control, 1 per sec., 1 hour, 4 aur.	30.6 ± 2.5 S.E.	
Control, 3 per sec., 1 hour, 12 aur.	32.7 ± 2.5 S.E.	
FAc, quiescent, 1 hour, 5 aur.	354.4 ± 11.4 S.E.	For any combination P > 0.1
FAc, 1 per sec., 1 hour, 5 aur.	429.4 ± 60.4 S.E.	
FAc, 3 per sec., 1 hour, 10 aur.	367.7 ± 13.8 S.E.	

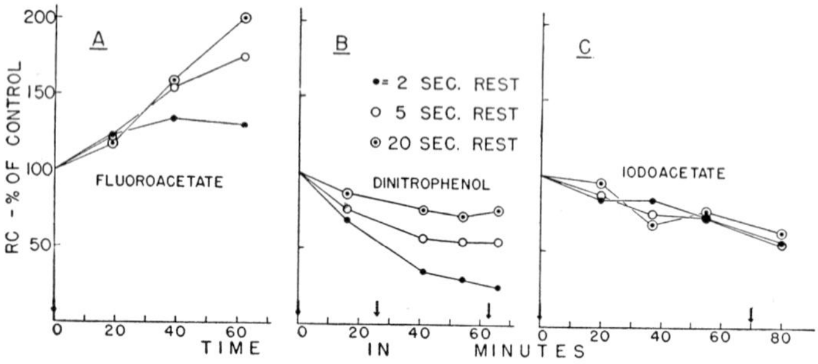

FIG. 5. Effect of varying rest period on the rest contraction after exposure to inhibitors. Basal rate 1.0 per second. Ordinate—rest contractility (RC) plotted as per cent of control rest contractility. Abscissa—time of exposure to the drug in minutes. A. effect of fluoroacetate, 6×10^{-4} *M*, added at the arrow. Average of 4 auricles. B. effect of dinitrophenol, concentration increased by 5×10^{-6} *M* at each arrow. Average of 4 auricles. C. effect of iodoacetic acid, concentration increased by 5×10^{-5} *M* at each arrow. Average of 5 auricles.

rest contraction following long rest periods than following short rest periods. In the case of dinitrophenol (figure 5B) and cyanide, RC was depressed for all rest durations but depression was much more marked following short rest periods (short diastolic interval). Iodoacetate (figure 5C) produced approximately the same degree of depression regardless of rest duration. These results further emphasize the importance of the diastolic recovery period in determining drug actions on cardiac contractility.

In studying the effects of drugs on post-stimulation potentiation it was of interest to isolate the effects of drugs on the basic contractile mechanism and on the mechanism responsible for post-stimulation potentiation. Rosin and Farah (1955) have made such an attempt by subtracting the rest (RC) from the post-stimulation (PS) contraction. In the present study we have used a basal rate of 0.1 beat per second since at this rate rest contraction was equal to the basal contraction. By interjecting a rapid stimulation period (6 per sec.) lasting 5 seconds followed by a 10-second rest period, post-stimulation (PS) potentiation could be elicited. In this experimental procedure the rest contraction (RC) was equal to the basal contraction and thus by subtracting the basal contraction from the post-stimulation contraction (PS-RC) we could partially differentiate post-stimulation potentiation from the basal contractile mechanism and study drug effects on both these mechanisms.

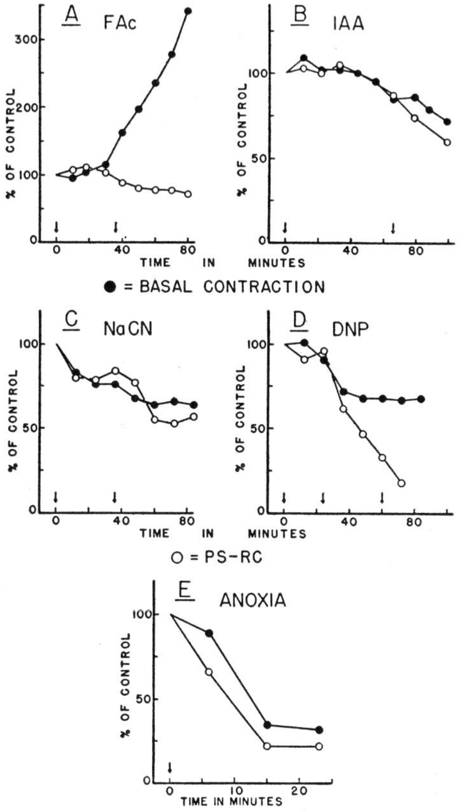

FIG. 6. Effect of inhibitors on basal contractility and post-stimulation minus rest contractility (PS-RC).

Ordinate—parameters plotted in terms of per cent of control values. Abscissa—time of exposure to the drug in minutes. Fluoroacetate—concentration increased 3×10^{-4} M at each arrow. Iodoacetate—concentration increased by 5×10^{-5} M at each arrow. Cyanide—concentration increased by 2×10^{-4} M at each arrow. Dinitrophenol—concentration increaeds by 5×10^{-6} M at each arrow. Anoxia—95 per cent nitrogen, 5 per cent carbon dioxide gas mixture substituted for 95 per cent oxygen, 5 per cent carbon dioxide at 0 time. Each plot represents the average of 4 auricles. ●——●, Basal contractility. ○——○, Post stimulation minus rest contractility (PS-RC).

The effects of a number of inhibitors are shown in figure 6. Fluoroacetate (figure 6A), although it increased the basal contractile mechanism, depressed the post-stimulation potentiation (PS-RC). Iodoacetate, cyanide and anoxia (figure 6B, C, E) produced equal depression of both the basal and post-stimulation contractility. On the other hand, 2,4-dinitrophenol depressed post-stimulation to a greater extent than basal contractility (figure 6D) and in this respect it was similar to fluoroacetate.

DISCUSSION. It is apparent from the control S-shaped curve that frequency has a complex and marked effect on isometric contractility. Previously proposed mechanisms for the classical treppe (Spadolini, 1949; Szent-Gyorgyi, 1953; Rosin and Farah, 1955; and Ritchie and Wilkie, 1955) are not applicable to the entire curve since only the midsection of the frequency range is associated with the positive inotropic effect of rate at which these explanations are directed. Since the negative or reverse treppe is seen at both extremes of the curve it seems probable that there is a single negative inotropic effect associated with increasing rate of contraction which is operative over the entire frequency range. Then one may postulate a potentiating mechanism, possibly one of those proposed by the above authors, which is dominant in the middle range of rates, producing the positive treppe.

The mechanism of negative treppe has been discussed for the turtle myocardium (Katzung and Farah, 1956) and the hypothesis presented may be equally applicable to rabbit tissues. The mechanism proposed is that the amount of energy available for contraction is dependent on the duration of energy buildup, *i. e.*, diastole, throughout the frequency range studied. Thus it follows that the lower the frequency, the longer the diastolic interval, and the greater the contractility becomes. In guinea pig auricles a ten-fold change in frequency had no significant effect on the concentration of several high energy phosphate compounds including adenosine triphosphate, adenosine diphosphate, and creatine phosphate (Furchgott *et al.*, 1954). However, recent investigations (Fleckenstein *et al.*, 1954; Mommaerts, 1955) cast doubt on the role of any of these substances as the immediate energy source for muscular contraction. Thus it is possible that, over the entire range of frequencies studied, there is a gradual and significant decrease in the energy available for contraction as diastole is shortened resulting in negative treppe except in the middle range where this process is masked. This mechanism also explains the potentiation of contractions following rest since the lengthened diastole would permit increased energy buildup with the resultant potentiation when contractions are resumed.

If this hypothesis holds, then after completely abolishing the positive treppe phenomenon, contractility should be a direct linear function of diastolic duration. Figure 7 shows that this is indeed true following exposure to fluoroacetate. In this figure the reciprocal of the rate was used to calculate the diastolic interval.

The mechanism of the positive treppe probably is related to post-stimulation potentiation. Fluoroacetate eliminated the positive treppe and depressed post-stimulation potentiation to a greater extent than the basal contractility. Dinitrophenol in the concentrations used depressed the positive treppe and the post-stimulation potentiation. On the other hand, cyanide, iodoacetate and anoxia, although they depressed the treppe phenomenon, did not produce any differential effect on the post-stimulation potentiation. It is thus likely that both fluoroacetate and dinitrophenol have, besides their action on energy production, some specific effect on the phenomenon responsible for post-stimulation potentiation and the treppe phenomenon. The mechanism of depression of post-stimulation potentiation by fluoroacetate is not known. The fact that citrate accumulation induced by fluoroacetate was the same at low and high frequencies makes it unlikely that blockade of the enzyme aconitase could be the cause of the depression of the treppe and post-stimulation potentiation. The liberation of fluoride as causative agent is also unlikely since the carbon fluoride bond is stable and the same effects could not be elicited with sodium fluoride in concentrations exceeding those of fluoroacetate. Furthermore, similar experiments with fluoropropionate resulted in only slight, non-specific depression of contractility at all rates.

The fact that DNP produced a differential depression of post-stimulation potentiation suggests that high energy phosphate bond formation may somehow be related to this phenomenon or that DNP has effects other than those on high energy phosphate production. Ellis (1955) has shown that hexose monophosphate concentration increased in rapidly beating cardiac muscle.

That drug action can be modified both qualitatively and quantitatively by rate is clearly shown in the present experiments. This relationship between rate and action of pharmacological agents has not been stressed sufficiently and this phenomenon may be of some theoretical as well as practical importance. The experiments of Benforado and Witt (1954) with veratridine have shown that heart frequency is an important factor in modifying its rate of action. Wilbrandt, Brawand and Witt (1953) have shown that, in the frog heart, frequency also influences the rate of action of Strophanthosid. These studies all emphasize the importance of rate in quantitative evaluations of drug action on cardiac activity. In the present study 3 classes of substances can be differentiated: 1) fluoroacetate which increased contractility at low and depressed it at high frequencies, 2) iodoacetate which depressed contractility about equally at all frequencies studied and 3) cyanide which produced a greater depression of contractility at high than at

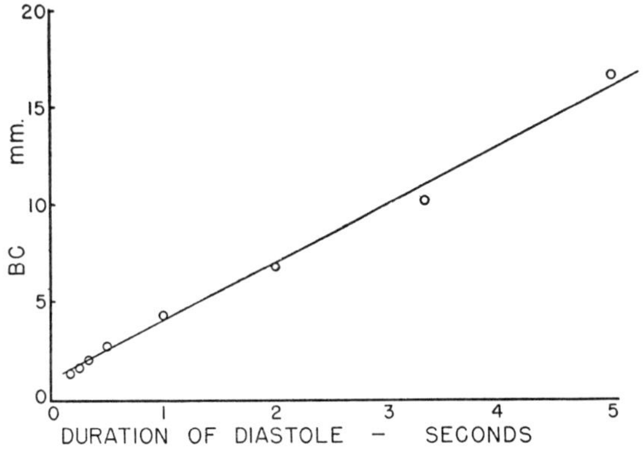

FIG. 7. Frequency force relationship following exposure to sodium fluoroacetate, 2×10^{-4} M, for 36 minutes.

Ordinate—basal contractility (BC) in millimeters of pen deflection. Abscissa—reciprocal of rate per second as an approximation of duration of diastole in seconds.

low frequencies. The differences in pharmacological action are probably related to actions of these inhibitors on energy production (cyanide), on the contractile protein (iodoacetate), and on the potentiating mechanism (fluoroacetate and DNP). It is clear that with all these substances simultaneous actions on a number of these mechanisms are operative and it would be of interest to find a substance which specifically inhibited potentiation without influencing energy production or the contractile protein. Such attempts are now in progress.

On the basis of our present knowledge little can be said concerning the biochemical nature of the potentiating process. It is sensitive to fluoroacetate and 2,4 dinitrophenol, it is inhibited by lowering temperature (Katzung and Farah, 1956), it is fairly stable and can persist for 5 to 10 minutes or more, and it is utilized by the following contractions in an exponential manner (Rosin and Farah, 1955). The relationship of potassium ion movements to the treppe phenomenon has been stressed by Szent-Gyorgyi (1953) and this relationship is probably of importance. However, the hypothesis of Szent-Gyorgyi can not explain the rest contraction nor can it explain the stability of the phenomenon. One possible modification of this hypothesis would be that potassium entry into, or exit from, the cell which may occur during activity may be operative in this phenomenon and that potassium entry during diastole is of lesser importance. Another possibility is that the contractile protein is changed by activity. Dubuisson (1949) has observed a peak in the electrophoretic pattern of skeletal muscle protein which increased greatly following stimulation. He has called the substance represented by this peak "contractin" and it is conceivable that "contractin" may be related to the treppe and post-stimulation phenomena.

SUMMARY

The effect of frequency of contraction on isometric contractility of rabbit auricular muscle has been studied over a wide range of frequencies. This frequency force relationship can be presented as a triphasic curve which has been termed the "S-shaped curve".

The action of a number of metabolic inhibitors on the isolated auricle can be modified both qualitatively and quantitatively by rate variations.

It is postulated that in cardiac muscle at least two processes influence contractility: a) energy production and b) the potentiating phenomenon elicited by high rate of stimulation. The complex actions of some inhibitors on cardiac contractility can be partially explained by differential action on these two processes.

ACKNOWLEDGMENT. We are indebted to Dr. Alfred Farah for his valuable advice and assistance.

REFERENCES

BENFORADO, J. M. AND WITT, P. N.: THIS JOURNAL, **110:** 334, 1954.

BENNETT, D., PENGSRITONG, K., WEEKS, J. R. AND CHENOWETH, M. B.: THIS JOURNAL, **101:** 2, 1951.

BOWDITCH, H. P.: Ludwigs Arb., **VI:** 139, 1871.

BROOKS, C., HOFFMAN, B., SUCKLING, E. AND ORIAS, O.: Excitability of the Heart, Grune and Stratton, N. Y., 1955.

DUBUISSON, M.: Experientia, **4:** 437, 1949.
ELLIS, S. J.: THIS JOURNAL, **113:** 17, 1955.
ETTINGER, R. H., GOLDBAUM, L. R. AND SMITH, L. H. JR.: J. Biol. Chem., **199:** 531, 1952.
FLECKENSTEIN, A. J., JAUKE, J., DAVIES, R. E. AND KREBS, H. A.: Nature, **174:** 1081, 1954.
FURCHGOTT, R. F., DE GUBAREFF, T. AND MCCAMAN, M. W.: THIS JOURNAL, **110:** 19, 1954.
KATZUNG, B. AND FARAH, A.: Am. J. Physiol., **184:** 557, 1956.
LEE, K. S.: THIS JOURNAL, **112:** 484, 1954.
LOEWI, O.: THIS JOURNAL, **114:** 90, 1955.
MCDOWALL, R. J. S., MURRO, A. F. AND ZAYAT, A. F.: J. Physiol., **130:** 615, 1955.
MOMMAERTS, W. F. M. H.: Am. J. Physiol., **182:** 585, 1955.
PORRO, A.: Arch. di Sci. Biol., **39:** 416, 1955.
REILLY, J., RIKER, W. F. JR., WHITEHOUSE, W. C. AND KURIAKI, K.: THIS JOURNAL, **108:** 393, 1953.
RITCHIE, J. M. AND WILKIE, D. R.: J. Physiol., **130:** 488, 1955.
ROSIN, H. AND FARAH, A.: Am. J. Physiol., **180:** 75, 1955.
SPADOLINI, I.: J. Physiol., **109:** 308, 1949.
SZENT-GYORGYI, A.: Chemical Physiology of Contraction in Body and Heart Muscle, Academic Press, N. Y., 1953.
WHITEHORN, W.: Proc. Soc. Exp. Biol. Med., **85:** 268, 1954.
WILBRANDT, W., BRAWAND, K. AND WITT, P. N.: Arch. Exp. Pathol. u. Pharmak., **219:** 397, 1953.

RELEASE OF SEROTONIN FROM BLOOD PLATELETS BY RESERPINE *IN VITRO*[1]

ARVID CARLSSON,[2] PARKHURST A. SHORE AND BERNARD B. BRODIE

Laboratory of Chemical Pharmacology, National Heart Institute, National Institutes of Health, Public Health Service, U. S. Department of Health, Education, and Welfare, Bethesda, Maryland

Received for publication February 11, 1957

Previous results have shown that reserpine releases serotonin (5-hydroxytryptamine) from various body depots, including intestine, platelets, and brain (review—Shore *et al.*, 1957). A wide variety of other centrally acting drugs have also been studied for their effects on brain serotonin. Of these, only the *Rauwolfia* alkaloids that cause sedation were found to liberate serotonin (Brodie *et al.*, 1956).

The present studies provide further information on the release of serotonin by showing that reserpine induces the discharge of serotonin from platelets *in vitro* by a mechanism that is not simple physical displacement from a cellular receptor. Comparison of the effects of a number of *Rauwolfia* drugs indicates that the ability to release serotonin from platelets *in vitro* is limited to alkaloids that exert a tranquilizing effect in animals.

METHODS AND MATERIALS. *Serotonin assay.* Serotonin in plasma was assayed by a method described by Sjoerdsma *et al.* (1957). In this procedure plasma proteins are precipitated with zinc hydroxide and the serotonin is determined directly in the acidified supernatant fluid by activation at 295 mμ and measurement of the resulting fluorescence at 550 mμ.[3]

Experimental procedures. Blood was taken from adult male rabbits, anesthetized with ether, by cannulation of the carotid artery with polyethylene tubing and collected in siliconed centrifuge tubes. One-ninth volume of one per cent disodium ethylenediamine tetraacetate was added to prevent clotting. Red cells were removed by centrifugation of the blood for 45 minutes at 150 × *g*. Five-ml. aliquots of the platelet-enriched plasma which contained 6 to 12 microgm. of serotonin per ml., were placed in siliconed 20-ml. beakers. Drugs were added by pipetting into the beakers 0.05-ml. aliquots of drug solution.[4] The samples were incubated at 37° C. in a Dubnoff metabolic incubator in an atmosphere of nitrogen. At the end of the incubation period samples of the platelet suspensions were taken for serotonin analysis. The remainder of the suspensions was transferred to siliconed centrifuge tubes and the platelets removed by centrifugation for 30 minutes at 1200 × *g*. Aliquots of the supernatant plasma were then taken for serotonin analysis.

Normally, virtually all the serotonin in plasma is localized in platelets and, in the ab-

---

[1] A preliminary account of this work was presented before the Society for Pharmacology and Experimental Therapeutics, Atlantic City, New Jersey, April, 1956, and the 20th International Physiological Congress, Brussels, July, 1956.

[2] Guest worker from University of Lund, Lund, Sweden.

[3] Farrand Spectrofluorometer was used in these studies.

[4] Solutions of drugs were made by dissolving various amounts of the free bases in 0.05 ml. glacial acetic acid and adding 0.5 ml. absolute ethanol, 0.5 ml. propylene glycol and 4 ml. of water. One ml. of this solution was diluted with 9 volumes of isotonic glucose solution.

We are indebted to Ciba Pharmaceutical Products, Inc., Riker Laboratories, Inc., and S. B. Penick and Co. for their liberal donations of the various *Rauwolfia* alkaloids.

sence of added drug, only a small fraction of the indole spontaneously escapes after 4 hours of incubation in the Dubnoff shaker. The release of serotonin by various drugs was therefore determined by the measurement of serotonin found in plasma after removal of platelets. Since serotonin is somewhat unstable in the presence of air, the incubations were carried out in an atmosphere of nitrogen. A number of experiments carried out in an atmosphere of air, with appropriate correction for loss of serotonin by oxidation, indicated that the rate of release was essentially the same aerobically as anaerobically.

RESULTS. *Rate of serotonin release.* One microgm. per ml. of reserpine was added to platelet suspensions and the liberation of serotonin from platelets determined after various times of incubation (fig. 1, typical of a number of experiments). Serotonin was freed slowly but continuously, and after four hours, about half the serotonin was in plasma and the rest in platelets. To establish that the release of serotonin was not due to platelet disruption, platelet counts were made in the plasma with added reserpine and found to be essentially the same as in the control plasma sample. It is of interest that the release of serotonin showed zero order kinetics; that is, a constant amount of indole passed into plasma per unit of time. The liberation of serotonin from the platelet suspensions, without added reserpine, was usually negligible, but occasionally as much as 10 per cent of the total indole appeared in plasma. When the period of incubation was longer than four hours, the spontaneous liberation of serotonin tended to increase rather sharply, presumably due to disruption of the platelets.

Serotonin release at various reserpine concentrations. Platelets were found to be extremely sensitive to the effects of reserpine and a definite release of serotonin was observed at a concentration of reserpine as low as 0.06 microgm. per ml. of plasma. With increasing concentrations of the alkaloid, the rate of serotonin liberation increased until the maximal rate was reached at a concentration of about 0.3 microgm. of reserpine per ml. of plasma. Further increase in the level of reserpine, by as much as twenty-five fold, failed to increase serotonin release beyond the limiting rate of about 40 to 50 per cent in four hours (fig. 2, typical of a number of experiments).

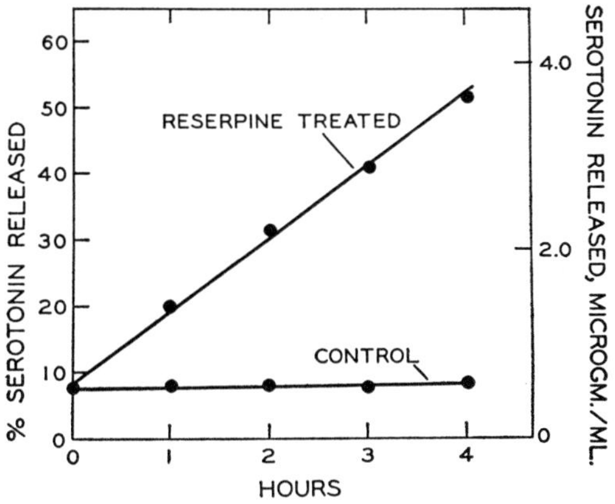

FIG. 1. Serotonin release after incubating suspension of rabbit platelets for various times with reserpine (1 microgm. per ml.).

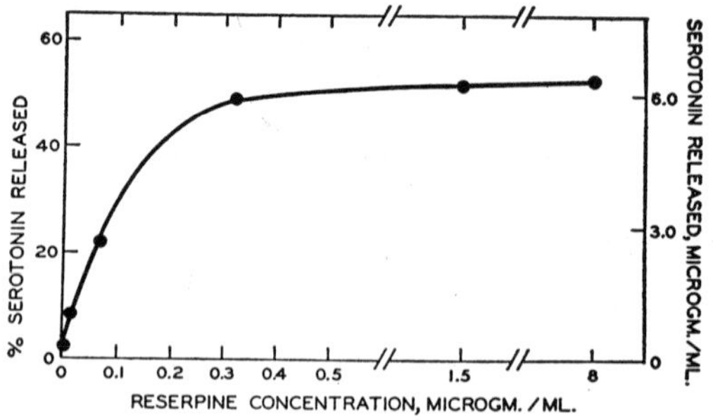

FIG. 2. Serotonin release after incubating suspensions of rabbit platelets 4 hours with various concentrations of reserpine.

TABLE 1

Release of serotonin from rabbit blood platelets in 4 hours by various drugs in vitro

Drug	Conc. of Drug	Serotonin Released
	microgm./ml.	*per cent of total**
Reserpine	1–2	47, 37, 39, 36, 47, 45
Deserpidine (Recanescine)	1–2	38, 37
Rescinnamine	1–2	37, 37
Raunescine	1–2	37, 41
11-Desmethoxyreserpine	2	39
Methyl reserpate syringate	2	47
Methyl reserpate acetoacetate	2	18
Methyl reserpate	2	8
Isoraunescine	1	6
Isoreserpine	1–2	0, 0
Reserpinine	2	0
Ajmaline	2	0
Reserpic acid	2	0
Chlorpromazine	20	5
Azacyclonol	20	2
Phenobarbital	20	0
Lysergic acid diethylamide	20	0
48/80	1	0

* Figures represent release caused solely by drug action; that is total per cent released less the small release (averaging 6 per cent) that occurred spontaneously in the control platelet suspension preparation.

The effect of various drugs on serotonin release. A number of *Rauwolfia* alkaloids were incubated with the platelet-enriched plasma preparation. The results in table 1 show that raunescine, deserpidine, rescinnamine, 11-desmethoxyreserpine and methyl reserpate syringate, all potent tranquilizing agents in the rabbit, released about 40 to 50 per cent of platelet serotonin in four hours. It cannot be concluded from this observation that these alkaloids are equally active in liberating serotonin as it is probable that the concentration of each drug was well above that required for it to exert a maximal effect. Methyl reserpate acetoacetate which exerts only a slight sedative action in rabbits dislodged only a small amount of serotonin from platelets. A number of *Rauwolfia* alkaloids that have no tranquilizing action failed to release serotonin.

Methyl reserpate and reserpic acid, hydrolytic products of reserpine, were also tested. Reserpic acid, which causes no sedative effects, released no serotonin; and methyl reserpate, which has little activity, released little or no platelet serotonin.

Several other centrally acting drugs, structurally unrelated to reserpine, were also tested: chlorpromazine and azacyclonol (Frenquel) because they have been considered to exert central effects similar to those of reserpine, LSD because it is an antagonist of reserpine and of serotonin, compound 48/80 because it has been reported to release serotonin from mast cells (Parrott and West, 1956), and phenobarbital because of its sedative action. These compounds released little or no platelet serotonin.

Effect of lowered temperature on release by reserpine. The release of serotonin from platelets was measured at room and at ice bath temperature. During a period of four hours the platelets at room temperature (25° C.) released only about 20 per cent of the serotonin, while at the temperature of the ice bath there was negligible release of the amine.

Stability of reserpine in plasma. The stability of reserpine in platelet-enriched plasma was demonstrated by incubation of the drug at a concentration of 1 microgm. per ml. for four hours. Reserpine was determined by a method which assays the parent compound, but not its hydrolytic products, methyl reserpate or reserpic acid (Hess *et al.*, 1956). The complete recovery of reserpine indicated that little if any of the alkaloid had been hydrolyzed in plasma.

Analysis of plasma before and after removal of platelets showed no significant difference in reserpine concentration. This indicates that the drug had not localized in the platelets to a significant degree.

DISCUSSION. Previous work has shown that reserpine impairs the capacity of brain and platelets *in vivo* to store serotonin (Brodie *et al.*, 1957). The present studies, which show that reserpine acts directly on platelets *in vitro* suggest that the use of platelets might be a valuable experimental procedure for study of the serotonin storage mechanism. The direct liberation of serotonin from platelets suggests that the liberation of serotonin from other tissues is also induced by a direct action of reserpine. Since reserpine releases platelet serotonin *in vitro* and *in vivo* (Shore *et al.*, 1956) at about the same rate, it is probable that the parent compound rather than a metabolic product causes release in the intact animal.

The stoichiometry of the reserpine-induced liberation of serotonin in platelets indicates that the mechanism is not simply physical displacement from a cellular receptor. Calculation of the amount of serotonin freed by 0.1 microgm. of reserpine (fig. 2) indicates that one molecule of the alkaloid effected the release of hundreds of serotonin molecules. The failure of reserpine to release serotonin at a low temperature also suggests that serotonin is released by a chemical rather than a physical action.

The mechanism of serotonin release by reserpine and the mechanism whereby tissues bind serotonin are probably different facets of the same problem. To describe serotonin as being bound is simply stating that the compound is localized and protected from monoamine oxidase which otherwise would quickly destroy it. To explain the localization, it could be assumed that the compound is anchored onto a specific constituent of the cell. Reserpine could act by "denaturing" the storage site so that it no longer localizes serotonin. The high temperature coefficient of reserpine action and the large number of serotonin molecules liberated by a single molecule of reserpine are facts compatible with the concept that serotonin is kept within the cell by chemical forces.

The close relationship between the extent of platelet serotonin release by *Rauwolfia* alkaloids and their pharmacological activity are in accord with the thesis that their tranquilizing effects are mediated through free serotonin (Shore *et al.*, 1957). Thus, isoreserpine, a pharmacologically inactive stereoisomer of reserpine, and isoraunescine, an inactive isomer of raunescine, fail to liberate serotonin. Methyl reserpate acetoacetate causes only slight though definite sedative effects and correspondingly liberates only a small amount of serotonin. Rescinnamine, which profoundly sedates rabbits, releases a great deal of brain serotonin in this species, while in the mouse it exerts considerably less pharmacologic activity and releases much less serotonin (unpublished). Amphetamine is the only compound, not a *Rauwolfia* alkaloid, that has been reported to cause the release of brain serotonin in dogs (Paasonen and Vogt, 1956). Thus far we have been unable to induce the liberation of brain serotonin in rabbits with amphetamine even in convulsive doses.

Although chlorpromazine and reserpine induce similar central effects, the former drug does not liberate serotonin *in vivo* or *in vitro*. This tranquilizing agent, therefore, does not act through serotonin, a finding that is in accord with other evidence indicating that chlorpromazine and reserpine alter central autonomic balance by different mechanisms (Brodie and Shore, 1957).

The difference in the actions of 48/80 and reserpine are of considerable interest. The former substance has been demonstrated to rupture mast cells causing an explosive release of histamine as well as a heparin and the small amount of serotonin that they contain. While serotonin is released from mast cells (Parrott and West, 1956) and other cells by reserpine, these do not appear to be ruptured by reserpine.

SUMMARY

Reserpine incubated at 37° C. with platelet-enriched plasma induces the release of serotonin from platelets. The alkaloid does not simply displace serotonin from its binding sites for one molecule of reserpine releases hundreds of serotonin molecules. The ability of reserpine to release serotonin is temperature dependent being appreciably lower at room temperature and almost negligible at 2° C.

Only those *Rauwolfia* alkaloids with reserpine-like pharmacologic properties cause the release of serotonin from platelets. In contrast, chlorpromazine, lysergic acid diethylamide, phenobarbital and 48/80 do not release serotonin.

REFERENCES

Brodie, B. B., Shore, P. A., and Pletscher, A.: Science, **123:** 992, 1956.

Brodie, B. B., and Shore, P. A.: Annals New York Academy of Sciences, **66:** 631, 1957.

Brodie, B. B., Tomich, E. G., Kuntzman, R., and Shore, P. A.: This Journal, **119:** 461, 1957.

HESS, S. M., SHORE, P. A., AND BRODIE, B. B.: THIS JOURNAL, **118**: 84, 1956.
PAASONEN, M. K., AND VOGT, M.: J. Physiol., **131**: 617, 1956.
PARROTT, J. R., AND WEST, G. B.: J. Physiol., **134**: 11P, 1956.
SHORE, P. A., PLETSCHER, A., TOMICH, E. G., KUNTZMAN, R., AND BRODIE, B. B.: THIS JOURNAL, **117**: 232, 1956.
SHORE, P. A., PLETSCHER, A., TOMICH, E. G., CARLSSON, A., KUNTZMAN, R., AND BRODIE, B. B.: Annals New York Academy of Sciences, **66**: 609, 1957.
SJOERDSMA, A., WEISSBACH, H., TERRY, L. L., AND UDENFRIEND, S.: Am. J. Med., in press, 1957.

PHARMACOLOGY OF *d*-LYSERGIC ACID MORPHOLIDE (LSM)[1]

JOHN H. GOGERTY AND JAMES M. DILLE

Department of Pharmacology, School of Medicine,
University of Washington, Seattle

Received for publication February 11, 1957

The actions of *d*-lysergic acid diethylamide (LSD) have been extensively described (Graham *et al.*, 1954; Gaddum, 1953; Rinkel *et al.*, 1952; Rinkel *et al.*, 1954). *d*-Lysergic acid morpholide (LSM) differs from LSD in that the diethylamine side chain is replaced by a morpholine group as shown in the following structures:

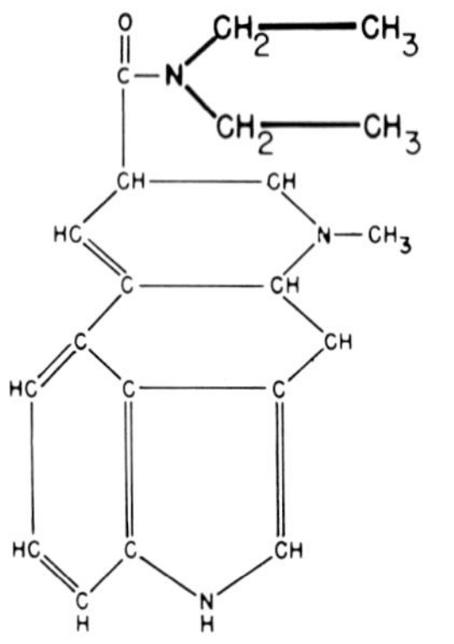

Lysergic Acid Diethylamide (LSD)

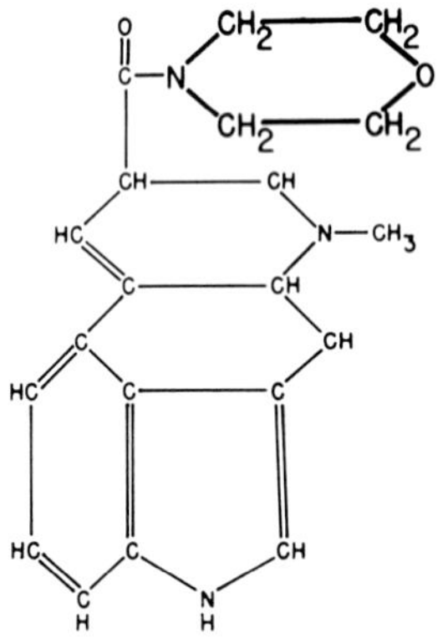

Lysergic Acid Morpholide (LSM)

LSM is a crystalline powder and is soluble in water to the extent of 8 mgm. per ml. The compound is in the form of the tartaric acid salt and all doses are expressed as such. Work in this laboratory indicates that in the more concentrated solutions this substance will remain stable for only three or four hours whereas in dilute solution (400 to 600 micrograms per ml.) the stability is maintained for approximately 7 days.

This report presents some of the pharmacological and behavioral effects of this lysergic acid derivative and compares these with those produced by LSD.

EXPERIMENTAL PROCEDURES AND RESULTS. A. *Animal studies. Acute toxicity studies.* Determinations of the LD_{50} for both LSM and LSD were made in white albino mice having an average weight of 25 grams. All injections were made intravenously by the tail vein. The results are shown in table 1. The Litchfield-Wilcoxon (1949) method for statistical analysis of dose response data was employed in the analysis of this data. It will be noted that the values for the LD_{50} differ with the rate of the injection.

[1] This work was partially supported, and the *d*-lysergic acid morpholide was furnished, by the Eli Lilly Company, Indianapolis, Indiana.

TABLE 1

Summary of LD_{50} determinations for LSM and LSD by intravenous administration to mice

Duration of Injection	Lethal Dose* 50% (LSM)	Lethal Dose* 50% (LSD)
10 sec.	55.5 mgm./kgm. (52.37–58.83 mgm./kgm.)	54 mgm./kgm. (45.29–64.26 mgm./kgm.)
30 sec.	128.0 mgm./kgm. (119–136.96 mgm./kgm.)	88 mgm./kgm. (82.2–94.16 mgm./kgm.)

* Confidence limits are shown in parenthesis.

Systematic determinations of the LD_{50} were not made in other species. However, some values were found for other species in the behavior studies reported later. These may be summarized as follows: 400 micrograms per kgm. produced death in rabbits; 6400 micrograms produced death in cats; 600 micrograms per kgm., the highest dose used in dogs, did not produce death. The special sensitivity of rabbits to LSM was also observed for LSD.

General pharmacology. Cardiovascular effects: Previous workers, while attempting to define some of the pharmacodynamic actions of LSD, found that it produced a prolonged drop in blood pressure when administered intravenously to chloralose-anesthetized cats. They tentatively ascribed this effect to a central action of LSD since the drug produced no observable effects in the spinal cat (Horita and Dille, unpublished observations). Effects of LSM on blood pressure were studied in chloralose-urethane anesthetized cats. Kymograph recordings were made by a mercury manometer attached to the left common carotid artery. Drugs were administered through the left femoral vein with the aid of an injection burette.

Single injections of 100 micrograms of LSM per kgm. over a period of 10 to 30 sec. resulted in a biphasic blood pressure response which showed a pressor-depressor sequence. This was accompanied by depression and failure of respiration. The secondary depressor response lasted approximately 20 minutes followed by a gradual return to the base level (figure 1). LSM, in this dosage, appeared to prolong the normal responses to acetylcholine and to epinephrine. However, the depressor response to LSM was not affected by previous atropinization of the animal. LSM did not affect the nicotinic response to acetylcholine nor did it alter the blood pressure response to peripheral splanchnic nerve stimulation or to peripheral vagal stimulation.

Three doses of 100 micrograms of LSM per kgm. within a period of 60 minutes resulted in a shift from a biphasic blood pressure response to a pure pressor effect. This pressor response had a duration of approximately 4 to 7 minutes. The pressor response was not abolished by previous administration of Dibenzyline or dihydroergotamine but, instead, appeared to be augmented by the previous administration of the latter.

In an attempt to elucidate the general depressor response of LSM, studies were made on the effect of LSM on the pressor response produced by carotid occlusion

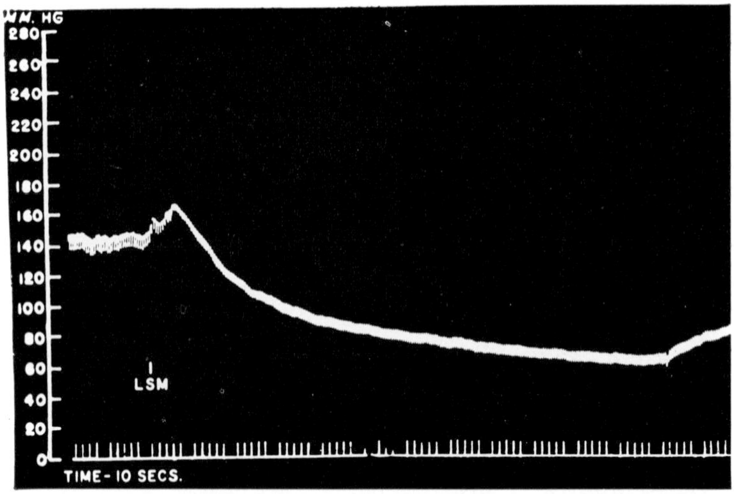

FIG. 1. Carotid blood pressure response of a cat under chloralose-urethane anesthesia to 100 micrograms per kgm. of LSM administered over 20 seconds intravenously.

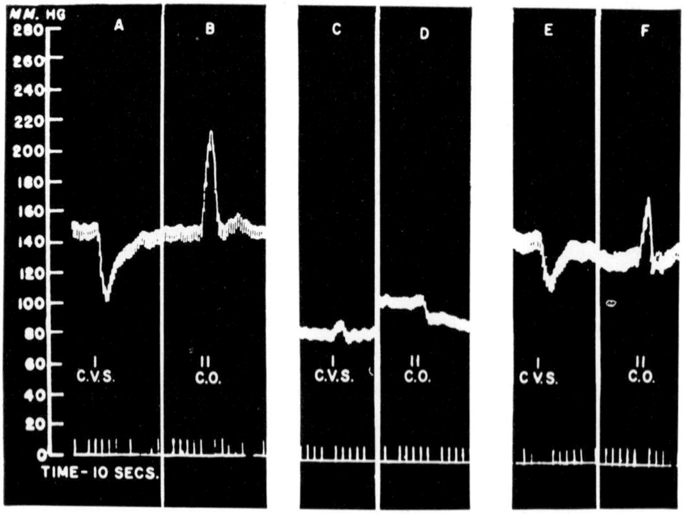

FIG. 2. Carotid blood pressure response of a cat under chloralose-urethane anesthesia. A and B, responses before administration of LSM to central vagus stimulation and carotid occlusion. C and D, abolition of these responses 20 minutes after administration of 100 micrograms of LSM intravenously. E and F, recovery of these responses 75 minutes after administration of LSM.

and on the depressor response produced by central vagal stimulation. The right vagus nerve was severed at the mid-cervical region in order to stimulate centrally without the direct peripheral effects. Shielded electrodes were used in all stimulation experiments. As is shown in figure 2, LSM, in a dose of 100 micrograms per kgm., completely abolished both of the above responses. These results compare to those obtained for LSD in a similar study (Ginzel, 1955). Although those workers found that LSD was effective only when injected intraventricularly, we were able to obtain a complete abolition of the above reflexes for both LSM and LSD for approximately 60 minutes when injections were made intravenously.

Pyretogenic effects: LSD, when administered intravenously to rabbits produces a rise in rectal temperature which varies with the dosage (Horita and Dille, 1954a). This pyretogenic effect is of interest because of possible relationships with the central effects (Horita and Dille, 1954).

Three different dose levels of LSM were used in a series of six rabbits and the resultant temperature curves compared with that produced by a standard dose of LSD (figure 3). Temperatures were taken every half hour by means of a rectal thermometer. Injections of all compounds were made intravenously into the marginal ear vein. From the figure, it can be seen that a dose of 150 micrograms per kgm. of LSM was necessary to produce a temperature curve similar to that obtained for a dose of 50 micrograms per kgm. of LSD. Also, the duration of a comparable effect of LSM was much shorter than that for LSD.

Serotonin antagonism: The fact that LSD, in minute quantities, is an effective antagonist of serotonin-induced contractions of the sensitized rat's uterus has been well demonstrated (Gaddum, 1953a; Gaddum and Hameed, 1954). This, coupled with the evidence that serotonin is present in the mammalian brain (Amin *et al.*, 1953; Twarog and Page, 1953), has resulted in the hypothesis that LSD might exert its psychotomimetic effect by a serotonin-antagonizing mechanism in the central nervous system (Gaddum, 1953b; Woolley and Shaw, 1954a, b). Therefore the relation of LSM to serotonin was investigated.

Female rats were injected subcutaneously with 0.1 mgm. per rat per day of estradiol for six days previous to removing the uterine horns. On the sixth day, the animals were killed and the uterine horns were immediately removed and mounted in constant temperature (37° C.) 50 ml. muscle baths containing the

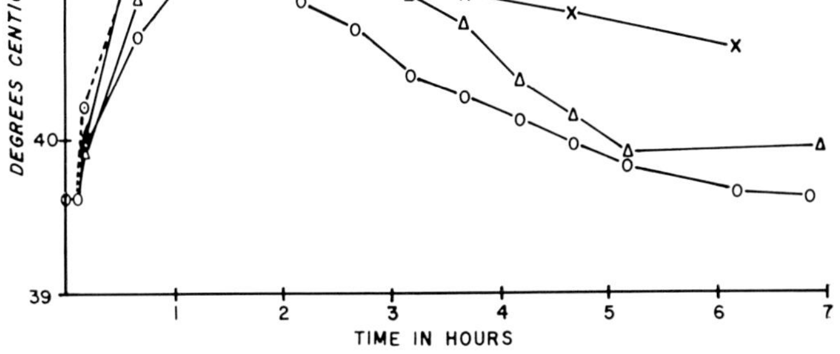

FIG. 3. Rectal temperature of the rabbit after intravenous administration of LSM in the dose levels indicated compared to the effect of 50 micrograms of LSD. Each curve represents the mean values of six rabbits.

following oxygenated modified Tyrode's solution (NaCl, 8; KCl, 0.2; $CaCl_2$, 0.18; $MgCl_2$, 0.102; NaH_2PO_4, 0.494; dextrose, 1; $NaHCO_3$, 1 gm./l.). Recording was made by means of an isotonic lever having a load of 1 gm. Control contractions to a standard dose of serotonin creatinine sulfate were established after which either LSD or LSM was added to the bath followed in one and one-half minutes by the standard dose of serotonin. In previous studies (Gaddum, 1953a), the interval between LSD administration and serotonin administration was given as ten minutes. However, we found that LSD or LSM would themselves induce contractions within the ten-minute period in the concentrations which were used by us. The serotonin was allowed to act for two minutes before being washed out. From figure 4 it may be seen that LSM must be used in more than ten times the amount of LSD to produce a comparable inhibition of contractions. A 50 per cent decrease in serotonin-induced contractions was the maximum amount of inhibition that could be demonstrated before the LSM-induced contractions interfered with the results. Also, it was observed that the serotonin control contractions returned almost immediately upon washing out of the LSM whereas with the LSD, serotonin contractions comparable to those of the control contractions did not return for approximately 60 minutes.

Observations on the effects of LSM on behavior in animals. Mice: Minimally effective intravenous doses of LSM of from 1 to 10 micrograms per kgm. produced in mice a general hyperexcitability with increased respiration and piloerection. The animals also appeared to be somewhat hyperreflexic at this dose level. As

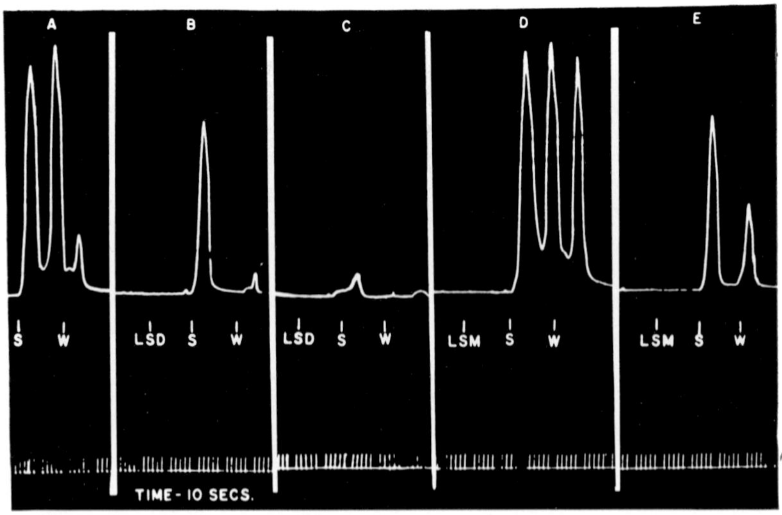

FIG. 4. Comparison of effects of LSD (A, B and C) and LSM (D and E) in serotonin induced contractions of the sensitized rat uterus.

S—indicates the addition of serotonin to the bath to make a concentration of 12 micrograms per 100 ml. W—indicates wash. A—control response to serotonin. B—response to serotonin after 1.2 micrograms per 100 ml. of LSD. C—response to serotonin after 2.3 micrograms of LSD per 100 ml. D—response to serotonin after 2.3 micrograms of LSM per 100 ml. Compare this to C. E—response to serotonin after 14 micrograms per 100 ml. Compare this to B where comparable inhibition was produced by 1.2 micrograms of LSD.

the dose was increased to 20 to 50 micrograms per kgm., a picture of generalized tremors with hyperexcitability began to appear. The animals seemed to be confused and disoriented, running purposelessly about when tactily stimulated. There was an increased sensitivity to auditory stimuli. When not being stimulated, the animals showed in some cases spontaneous backing movements similar to those described for LSD (Woolley, 1955). A stiffening of the tail resembling the Straub tail phenomena was seen. Exopthalmos and piloerection were present. The animals showed a spreading of the hind limbs with movements resembling those of swimming. Recovery from these effects took place in approximately 7 to 10 minutes at which time hyperexcitability with some evidence of prostration was seen. Further increase in dosage to 50 to 100 micrograms per kgm. resulted in convulsions, the respiration becoming irregular with gasping and anoxia evident. The mice died of respiratory failure.

Rabbits: Intravenous doses of 50 to 100 micrograms per kgm. of LSM in rabbits produced effects of autonomic stimulation evident in mydriasis and piloerection within the first five minutes. Hyperreflexia and hyperactivity were also observed within the first five minutes. Increased respiratory rate was noted within 15 minutes. The righting reflex was present at all times in the lower doses of 100 to 200 micrograms per kgm.; however, in the higher doses of 300 to 400 micrograms per kgm., the animals demonstrated a depressed righting reflex within 40 minutes after injection. The placing response was slightly depressed in the lower doses, with the depression increasing as the dosage increased. In general, lower doses produced hyperexcitability and hyper-reflexia, but no observable depression. Higher doses produced hyperactivity followed by ataxia, depressed righting reflex, depressed respiration and, finally, death from respiratory failure.

Cats: The behavior of cats under the influence of varying doses of LSM was observed. A geometrically increasing dose schedule from 100 micrograms per kgm. to 6400 micrograms per kgm. was used in a series of 14 cats. All injections were made intravenously utilizing the saphenous vein of the hind limb. It was found that the effects of LSM could be divided into three stages according to the dose level used. In a range of 400 to 600 micrograms per kgm. a behavior reaction was produced which was very similar to that described by Barger for ergometrine in doses of 2.0 to 2.5 milligrams per kgm. (Barger, 1938). This was accompanied by pronounced autonomic stimulation, chiefly sympathetic, with maximal pupillary dilatation, hypersalivation and piloerection. The behavior was especially significant. There was a marked coordinated aggression with spitting, snarling, baring of the teeth and striking with barred claws in response to auditory, visual or tactile stimuli of any kind. At this dose level it was impossible to handle the animal since it would attack upon the slightest provocation. This aggressive behavior had a duration of approximately 20 minutes at which time there was a gradual return to "normal" behavior. This coordinated, directed aggressive behavior is practically identical with that produced in cats by the intravenous administration of 200 to 400 micrograms of LSD per kgm.

In dose levels of 800 micrograms per kgm., LSM produced similar autonomic effects seen in the lower dose level except that exophthalmos was also evident.

Behavior was now changed. Instead of directed attack such as that seen in the previous dose level, the animal demonstrated a disorientation which progressed to an incoordinated aggression with signs of fearfulness and apprehension. Although the animal appeared aggressive, he was, in fact, quite fearful and any aggressive appearing movements were more in a line of defense than of attack. The animals were hypersensitive to auditory, tactile and visual stimuli. The animals demonstrated a "tracking behavior" in which they seemed to fix their gaze on something in the cage although nothing was there. During the latter part of the reaction, there was a somewhat depressed righting reflex and a slight hind limb ataxia.

In the higher dose levels, from 800 micrograms per kgm. to 6400 micrograms per kgm., LSM produced a lethargic behavior which increased as the dosage was increased. The animals showed a loss of righting reflex and placing reactions, slow, shallow, irregular respiration followed by panting with an elevated body temperature, and stupor which was similar to catalepsy. There was none of the behavior characteristic of the lower dose levels.

Dogs: An intravenous dose of 300 micrograms per kgm. of LSM produced signs of autonomic stimulation similar to those seen in cats consisting of pupillary dilatation, hypersalivation and piloerection. However, there was no aggressive rage observed; rather there was marked disorientation with fear and apprehensive behavior predominating. This was shown by whining with attempts to escape, especially from tactile stimulation. "Behavioral blindness" and a moderate ataxia were noted and the animals showed signs of great discomfort. Recovery was complete within 1 hour and 45 minutes.

By increasing the dose to 600 micrograms per kgm., the syndrome described for the preceding dose was accentuated with the fear and apprehension being greater. There was, in addition, depression marked by loss of motor coordination.

B. *Comparative effects of LSM and LSD in humans.* Two subjects served as volunteers for an exploration of dose ranges and subjective and objective effects of LSM on humans. Before the investigations of LSM both subjects took LSD in a total oral dose of 50 micrograms. Preparatory to this both subjects took the Rorschach and Thematic Apperception test which were again administered during the action of the drugs. During the effect of the drug, polygraphic records were taken on the subjects. These comprised measurements of the galvanic skin reflex, the heart rate by the means of an ECG record, respiratory rate and depth, face, and skin temperature, and muscle tension. Dr. Evan L. Frederickson, anesthesiologist and Dr. Albert Ax, clinical psychologist, both of the Medical School staff, aided in the experiments by administering the tests and making observations of the behavior responses of the subjects. Both subjects showed reactions to LSD which have been generally those already described in the literature (DeShon *et al.*, 1952; Sloane *et al.*, 1954). In one subject there was a high component of anxiety which was manifest in the polygraphic records and in the Rorschach test while the other subject showed little anxiety but depersonalization increased imagination as measured by the Rorschach test and some euphoria. Both subjects recorded their subjective experiences the following day.

With this experience of the effects of LSD as a guide, LSM administration was begun cautiously with lower doses allowing at least five days between tests. The first dose was a total oral dose of 25 micrograms. Neither subject showed any definite departures from normal subjective feeling or observable behavior changes. At a total oral dose of 50 micrograms, both subjects reported some subjective changes in feelings and attitudes but there were no observable departures from normal behavior except perhaps for a slight tendency to talkativeness. At a total oral dose of 75 micrograms the subjective feeling of the subjects and the objective observations indicated the degree of this action was approximately the same as that produced by a total oral dose of 50 micrograms of LSD. The difference lay in the shorter duration of the LSM effect. This effect required about 45 minutes to develop and lasted about an hour. By contrast, the LSD effect required about an hour to develop, had a peak effect of about four hours with residual effects from six to eight hours. These preliminary experiments with human subjects are being extended and attempts are being made to develop and make use of psychological tests which more precisely and objectively measure some of the subtleties of the action of these two phrenotropic drugs.

Discussion. Results of systemic pharmacological studies of the effect of *d*-lysergic acid morpholide (LSM) in animals may be summarized as follows:

Toxicity studies in mice and observations in other species indicate that LSM required a slightly higher dose than LSD for equivalent effects.

Cardiovascular studies demonstrate that LSM produce a biphasic response with a primary pressor effect followed by a prolonged depressor action. Simultaneous with the hypotensive response to LSM is a block of the reflex responses mediated through the vasomotor centers. These results, in addition to those demonstrating that LSM does not influence the nicotinic response to acetylcholine nor does it affect the blood pressure responses to splanchnic nerve stimulation or to peripheral vagal stimulation, would indicate that at least part of the blood pressure response to LSM is centrally determined. The fact that the responses to acetylcholine and epinephrine are prolonged after LSM might be explained by a depression of the compensatory mechanisms located in the vasomotor centers. Preliminary studies in this laboratory indicate that LSM is ineffective as a cholinesterase inhibitor *in vitro*.

Of special significance is the action of LSM in blocking the effects of serotonin. Approximately twelve times as much LSM is required to block the serotonin-induced contractions of the rat's uterus as LSD; yet, the equivalent central effects of the LSM are produced by only about one-third greater dosage. These results would seem to indicate that there is no correlation between the peripheral anti-serotonin activity of these compounds and their ability to produce changes in mental behavior. Support for this idea may also be found in the report by Cerletti and Rothlin (1955) in which the powerful serotonin blocking agent brom-lysergic acid diethylamide (BOL-148) does not produce any central effects in either animals or humans.

Generally, the systemic pharmacology of lysergic acid derivatives such as LSM and LSD may be regarded as secondary to the dominating interest in the effects of these agents on the activities of the brain as expressed in the subtle qualities of emotion, intelligence, and mentation. Because of such effects, LSD has been used in the treatment of psychoneurosis (Frederking, 1953; Sandison *et al.*, 1954; Abramson, 1956). The exact role of LSD in this regard is not yet clear but since the indications are that LSM produces the same kind of effects but with a shorter duration of action it may have a practical advantage.

SUMMARY

d-Lysergic acid morpholide (LSM) produces pharmacological effects generally similar to those produced by *d*-lysergic acid diethylamide (LSD).

Intravenous administration of LSM to anesthetized cats produces a transient rise in blood pressure followed by a fall. The fall of blood pressure is attributed to central effects.

LSM, like LSD, produces a rise in body temperature. Approximately three times the dose is required to produce equivalent increases in temperature and the duration of maximum effect is less.

LSM is approximately one-twelfth as effective as LSD in antagonizing serotonin-induced contractions of the rat uterus.

Death with lethal doses of LSM is caused, as with LSD, by respiratory failure.

Behavior modifications in animals produced by LSM are similar to those produced by LSD. The dose required for equivalent effects is about one-third greater and the duration of such effects is about one-half as long.

Preliminary studies of the effects of LSM in humans indicates that these are qualitatively similar to those of LSD. The dose required is at least a third larger and the duration of action is shorter.

REFERENCES

Abramson, H. A.: J. Psychol., **41:** 199, 1956.

Amin, A. H. T., Crawford, B. B., and Gaddum, J. H.: Intern. Physiol. Congress, Montreal, p. 165, 1953.

Barger, G.: Handbuch Exper. Pharmakol., **6:** 84, 1938.

Cerletti, A., and Rothlin, E.: Nature, **176:** 785, 1955.

Deshon, H. J., Rinkel, M., and Solomon, H. C.: Psychiat. Quart., **26:** 33, 1952.

Frederking, W.: Psyche, **7:** 342, 1953–1954.

Gaddum, J. H.: J. Physiol., **121:** 15P, 1953a.

Gaddum, J. H.: Ciba Foundation Symposium on Hypertension, J. and A. Churchill, Ltd., London, 1953b.

Gaddum, J. H., and Hameed, K. A.: Brit. J. Pharmacol., **9:** 240, 1954.

Ginzel, K. H.: J. Physiol., **129:** 61P, 1955.

Graham, J. D. P., and Alaa Iddeen Khalidi: J. Fac. Med., Iraq, **18:** 1, 1954.

Horita, A., and Dille, J. M.: Science, **120:** 1100, 1954.

Litchfield, J. T., Jr., and Wilcoxon, F.: This Journal, **95:** 99, 1949.

Rinkel, M., Deshon, H. J., Hyde, R. W., and Solomon, H. C.: Am. J. Psychiat., **108:** 572, 1952.

Rinkel, M., Hyde, R. W., and Solomon, H. C.: Dis. Nerv. Sys., **15:** 3, 1954.

Sandison, R. A., Spenser, A. M., and Whitelaw, J. D. A.: J. Ment. Sc., **100:** 491, 1954.

Sloane, B., and Doust, J. W. L.: J. Ment. Sc., **100:** 129, 1954.

Twarog, B. M., and Page, I. H.: Amer. J. Physiol., **175:** 157, 1953.

Woolley, D. W.: Proc. Nat'l. Acad. of Sci., **41:** 338, 1955.

Woolley, D. W., and Shaw, E.: Science, **119:** 587, 1954a.

Woolley, D. W., and Shaw, E.: Brit. Med. J., ii, 122, 1954b.

PREVENTION OF EXPERIMENTAL POLYARTHRITIS WITH SODIUM AUROTHIOMALATE

GAËTAN JASMIN

Institut de Médicine et de Chirurgie expérimentales, Université de Montréal, Montréal, Canada

Received for publication February 11, 1957

The use of a centrifuged exudate originating from a Murphy Rat Lymphosarcoma (MRLS) tumor pouch and injected intraperitoneally into rats, has become a standardized technique in our laboratory for the production of experimental polyarthritis (Jasmin, 1956). The joint lesions so produced lend themselves to the investigation of various anti-inflammatory drugs and it is the purpose of this communication to report on the therapeutic effectiveness of sodium aurothiomalate (Myochrysine) and the influence of corticoid hormones upon the development of the nephrocalcinosis which results from gold treatment.

Description of the syndrome. Articular changes develop within a few days after a single intraperitoneal injection of tumor exudate. The inflammatory reaction is more severe when the animals are also adrenalectomized. In their proliferative nature, the lesions differ from those seen in other experimental infectious arthritis; they involve the periarticular tissue and induce osteolysis with resulting ankylosis. Such pathological changes may be found in several joints including the dorsal spine. Treatment with cortisone has successfully prevented this polyarthritic syndrome, and it has been found that oxytetracycline (Terramycin) exerts an inhibitory effect (Jasmin, 1956).

After many fruitless attempts to cultivate the responsible agent in the exudate on various synthetic media, we finally succeeded in growing colonies on egg embryo. From these colonies we isolated a microorganism bearing the characteristics of *Nocardia asteroides.*

Since it was demonstrated by other workers that gold compounds exert therapeutic effects on polyarthritis, induced in various species of animals by an infectious agent (Sabin and Warren, 1940; Rothbard *et al.*, 1941), we decided to study the influence of Myochrysine on the syndrome described above. A preliminary experiment, in which only intact animals were used, has shown that this drug was effective in preventing the articular lesions. In order to determine to what extent the therapeutic effect was relayed by the adrenal gland, a second experiment was planned in which the gold preparation was administered to adrenalectomized rats receiving either pro- or antiphlogistic corticoids as substitution therapy. Because of the well-known nephrotoxic action of gold compounds, we were also interested to see to what degree these antagonistic corticoids would influence the renal lesions. It was observed that a syndrome of nephrocalcinosis developed in adrenalectomized rats receiving desoxycorticosterone acetate (DOC-Ac) substitution therapy, but was absent when the animals received cortisol acetate (COL-Ac) substitution therapy.

MATERIALS AND METHODS. Sixty female Sprague-Dawley albino rats with an average body-weight of 153 gm. were subdivided into six equal groups, as outlined in table 1. They received a "Purina Fox Chow" diet, and tap water as drinking fluid. Bilateral adrenalectomy was performed and hormonal therapy was started 48 hours prior to the beginning of the experiment. Corticoids were injected subcutaneously, once daily, in the form of an aqueous microcrystal suspension at a dosage of 400 microgm. of COL-Ac and 100 microgm. of DOC-Ac.

On the first day of the experiment 1 ml. of a fresh MRLS exudate obtained from a "neoplastic pouch" was injected intraperitoneally. This "neoplastic pouch" technique, which has been described elsewhere (Horava, 1954), is particularly appropriate for the production of large quantities of exudate. Essentially it consists of injecting 0.5 ml. of tumor cell suspension into 25 ml. of air space under the connective tissue of the dorsal skin.

An aqueous solution of 2.5 mgm. of sodium aurothiomalate was injected subcutaneously in a volume of 0.1 ml. once on the first day of the experiment and twice daily thereafter. The experiment lasted eight days and daily readings were made of the articular lesions according to a scale of 0 to +++. The severity of the inflammation was evaluated as regards both intensity and extent. At the end of the experiment all animals were killed and the thymus and kidney removed. The former was fixed in Susa solution and the latter in neutral formalin for weighing and histo-chemical demonstration of calcium deposits with Kossa's silver nitrate technique.

RESULTS. Comparison of intact and adrenalectomized rats, maintained either with DOC-Ac or COL-Ac, revealed that the gold salt was equally effective in all groups. However, as evidenced by the mortality rate, the DOC-Ac treated animals showed a lower resistance to the toxic effects of both exudate and gold treatment. Animals receiving COL-Ac, although having greater resistance, showed substantial loss of body-weight. From these results is may be concluded that the anti-inflammatory properties of sodium aurothiomalate is not relayed by the adrenals.

Renal lesions. At autopsy, the kidney of adrenalectomized DOC-Ac-Myochrysine-treated rats (Group V) showed slight hypertrophy. On sectioning the organ a whitish, chalky zone was readily distinguishable in the parenchyma. Histological examination showed a pronounced calcium deposit in renal tubules (in the region commonly referred to as *zona intermedia*) which corresponded to

TABLE 1

Influence of sodium aurothiomalate on MRLS experimental arthritis

Group	Number of Rats	Treatment	Articular Lesions on the 6th Day		Nephrocalcinosis	Thymus Weight *mgm.*	Final Body Weight *gm.*	Weight Gain *gm.*	Mortality
			Incidence	Mean severity					
I	10	Intact	10	+	0	200	160	+7	0
II	10	Adr-X (DOC-Ac)	8	++	0	375	146	−7	2
III	10	Adr-X (COL-Ac)	10	++	0	105	127	−26	0
IV	10	Intact, Na aurothio.	0	0	0	282	173	+20	0
V	10	Adr-X (DOC-Ac), Na aurothio.	2	±	++	330	155	+2	2
VI	10	Adr-X (COL-Ac), Na aurothio.	0	0	0	107	147	−6	0

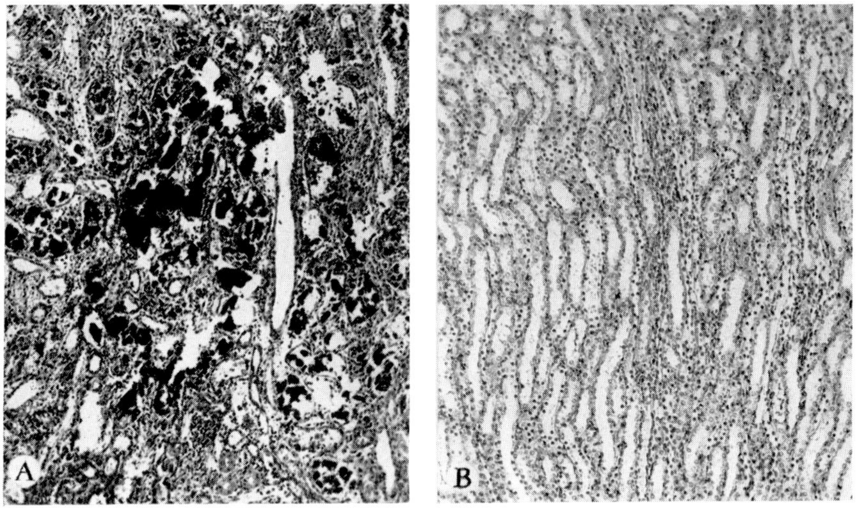

FIG. 1. a) Massive calcium deposition surrounded by imflammatory cells in the "zona intermedia" of the kidney of an adrenalectomized rat treated with DOC-Ac and sodium aurothiomalate (Kossa-stain × 100). b) Complete absence of calcium deposits in the kidney of an adrenalectomized rat treated with COL-Ac and sodium aurothiomalate (Kossa-stain × 100).

calcified cast located in Henle's loops (fig. 1). Very few calcifications were found in the cortical region; in the calcified area some inclusions were noticed which were thought to be gold deposits. No pathological changes were observed in any other groups.

DISCUSSION. The mechanism of action of gold salt is still not well understood. According to Sabin and Warren (1940), sodium aurothiomalate has no antimicrobial effect *per se*, and the blood of animals treated with large doses of the salt does not prevent the growth of the microorganism *in vitro*. Yet, Dawson and Hobby (1940) were able to demonstrate that serum from a patient subjected to gold therapy had a marked bacteriostatic effect *in vitro* against *Streptococcus hemolyticus*. Some authors suggest that gold compounds exert a therapeutic effect by their blocking action on the sulfhydryl-containing enzymes, thereby causing a lowering of the oxygen consumption of tissues (Block and Knapp, 1945). To our knowledge, very few studies have been made to evaluate the role of adrenocortical hormones in gold therapy and the present investigations suggest that the anti-inflammatory action of sodium aurothiomalate is not mediated by the adrenals.

The rather high incidence of toxic manifestations has limited the use of gold salts in rheumatoid arthritis, especially since the beneficial effect of hormonal therapy has been established. A follow-up of more than 1,000 patients treated with either gold or cortisone has proved that the hormonal therapy was definitely superior (Sebardt, 1955). On the other hand a recent study on the combined treatment of gold with cortisone, cortisol or ACTH, revealed that this combined therapy permitted control of the disease until the benefit of gold was manifest. If the hormone treatment was interrupted at that stage, it was found that the final improvement was identical with that of therapy with gold alone (Bilka and Weil, 1955).

The most common toxic manifestations of gold treatment is exfoliative dermatitis, but albuminuria may also be detected in more than 29 per cent of the cases (Freyberg *et al.*, 1942). Further, it has been reported that the nephrotoxic syndrome, occurring after prolonged gold therapy, is relieved by administration of prednisone but not by ACTH (Grégoire *et al.*, 1956).

On the basis of the present experiment, it seems that the maximum therapeutic benefit would be obtained from the conjoint administration of gold compounds and anti-inflammatory corticoids. This conclusion is substantiated by the following points:

1) That the mechanism of action of gold apparently has no relationship to the adrenal function but, since both gold and corticoids have an anti-inflammatory property, some additive effects will occur in the treatment of rheumatoid arthritis.

2) That, according to our observations, anti-inflammatory corticoids already known to prevent allergic manifestations, can also prevent renal damage resulting from the toxic effect of gold therapy. These observations have been further supported by work carried out simultaneously in this laboratory. Selye and Bois (1956, 1957) found that the pathologic deposition of calcium in the kidneys resulting from the administration of phosphate or sublimate in rats is prevented by anti-inflammatory corticoids.

SUMMARY

An experimental polyarthritis develops in rats following the intraperitoneal injection of 1 ml. of Murphy Rat Lymphosarcoma exudate. It was observed that gold therapy (Myochrysine) is equally effective in intact or adrenalectomized animals when the latter are maintained either on DOC-Ac or COL-Ac.

Nephrocalcinosis resulting from massive treatment with myochrysine was evident only in adrenalectomized rats receiving DOC-Ac. It is suggested that combined treatment of gold and COL-Ac might be beneficial as they both possess anti-inflammatory properties and the nephrotoxic action of gold is prevented by COL-Ac.

ACKNOWLEDGMENTS. These investigations were subsidized by a grant from the Canadian Arthritis and Rheumatism Society. The author is indebted to Pfizer Laboratories for the cortisol acetate (Cortril), to the Schering Corporation for the desoxycorticosterone acetate (Cortate) and to Poulenc Laboratory for the sodium aurothiomalate (Myochrysine).

REFERENCES

BILKA, P. J., AND WEIL, M. H.: Ann. Intern. Med., **42:** 638, 1955.
BLOCK, W. D., AND KNAPP, E. L.: THIS JOURNAL, **83:** 275, 1945.
DAWSON, M. H., AND HOBBY, G. L.: THIS JOURNAL, **49:** 359, 1940.
FREYBERG, R. H., BLOCK, W. D., AND WELLS, G. S.: Clinics, **1:** 537, 1942.

Grégoire, F., Malmendier, C., and Lambert, P. P.: J. d'Urol. Med. et Chir. No. 1., **28:** 34, 1956.
Horava, A.: Canad. Med. Ass. J., **70:** 676, 1954.
Jasmin, G.: Rev. can. de biol., **15:** 107, 1956.
Rothbard, S., Angevine, D. M., and Cecil, R. L.: This Journal, **72:** 164, 1941.
Sabin, A. B., and Warren, J.: J. of Bact., **40:** 823, 1940.
Sebardt, G.: Nord. Med., **54:** 1277, 1955.
Selye, H., and Bois, P.: Am. J. Physiol., **187:** 41, 1956.
Selye, H., and Bois, P.: J. Lab. and Clin. Med., **49:** 263, 1937.

STUDIES OF ANALGESIC DRUGS: DIHYDROCODEINE[1]

ARTHUR S. KEATS, JANE TELFORD AND YOSHIO KUROSU

Department of Anesthesiology, Baylor University College of Medicine and Jefferson Davis Hospital, Houston, Texas

Received for publication February 11, 1957

Dihydrocodeine was first prepared in Germany by Skita and Franck (1911). It was introduced by Fraenkel (1913) as an anti-tussive and since then has been widely used for this purpose in Europe and Japan. Analgesic properties were reported in mice (Haffner, 1929), in cats (Eddy, 1934), and in man (Dahl, 1913; Heinroth, 1926). Despite this, dihydrocodeine has never been widely used as an analgesic. Respiratory depression similar to that produced by codeine was observed in rabbits (Biberfield, 1920; Wright, 1934). Himmelsbach (1941) reported the addiction liability of dihydrocodeine in man to be between that of codeine and morphine.

Recently Gravenstein *et al.* (1956) have re-investigated the use of dihydrocodeine bitartrate in man. They reported that 30 mgm. per 70 kgm. of body weight of dihydrocodeine subcutaneously produced analgesia similar to that of 10 mgm. of morphine in postoperative patients. In normal subjects this dose of dihydrocodeine produced no greater respiratory depression than a placebo nor any greater frequency of unpleasant subjective effects than a placebo. Because of this unique and clinically important observation the following study was undertaken in order to investigate the effects of higher doses of dihydrocodeine in man.

METHODS. *Analgesia.* An estimation of analgesic potency was made in postoperative patients by the method described in detail by Keats, Beecher and Mosteller (1950). Dihydrocodeine bitartrate in doses of 30 mgm., 60 mgm. and 90 mgm. per 70 kgm. of body weight were alternated in individual patients with 10 mgm. per 70 kgm. of morphine sulfate. (These doses refer to weight of the respective salts.) Two evaluations of pain relief were made by a technician following each dose of each drug during the first 30 postoperative hours. A dose was considered analgesic when "most of the pain" was relieved at both evaluations. No attempt was made to evaluate degrees of severity of pain other than that the pain be of sufficient intensity to warrant a narcotic. No attempt was made to evaluate degrees of pain relief. No scoring system was used. Only paired doses were included in these data. Analgesic potency was expressed as the difference in the per cent of total paired doses which were analgesic.

Respiratory depression: The respiratory effects of saline, 30 mgm. and 60 mgm. of dihydrocodeine, and 10 mgm. of morphine were determined in 4 male and 3 female healthy subjects, between the ages of 20 and 30 years (mean body area of 1.69 ± 0.08 m.[2]). These doses were per 70 kgm. of body weight. All subjects received all drugs but in random order with at least five days between drug trials. Subjects breathed through a mouthpiece attached to Kirchoff non-rebreathing valve. Total dead space of this system was 25 cc. Expired gases were passed through a low resistance dry gas meter. Expired minute-volume and respiratory rate were measured for 3-minute periods. Alveolar air was sampled continuously during the 3-minute periods by means of a Rahn end-tidal alveolar-air sampler attached to the ex-

[1] This work was supported by funds generously provided by Mallinckrodt Chemical Works, St. Louis, Mo., who also supplied the dihydrocodeine as Parzone Bitartrate.

piratory tube. The sample was dried and passed through an infra-red carbon dioxide analyzer and percentage of carbon dioxide determined directly. CO_2 values were discarded if tidal volumes fell below 200 cc. Measurements were made at three intervals: before durg, 1 and 3 hours post-drug. At each period subjects first breathed room air, then 3 to 4 per cent carbon dioxide in oxygen. Data were collected during two three-minute periods on each gas mixture. The mean values of these two periods provided data for further analysis. All volumes were corrected to 37° C. at standard atmospheric pressure.

For ease in handling these data, the following transformations were made. Alveolar ventilation (V_A) was calculated from expired minute-volume and respiratory rate assuming a deadspace of 150 cc. for males and 100 cc. for females. V_A was converted to alveolar ventilation ratio (V_AR), using predrug V_A on room air as unity. Alveolar carbon dioxide tension (P_ACO_2) was converted to increase or decrease in P_ACO_2 from the pre-drug value on room air. For statistical treatment the data of each subject at each time interval on each drug were plotted as respiratory stimulus (P_ACO_2)-response (V_AR) curve. For each curve (12 curves for each subject) the V_AR at a hypothetical 4 mm. increase in P_ACO_2 from the pre-drug room air value was estimated, *eg.* V_AR at +4 mm.Hg for all three curves in fig. 1. The differences in these values between pre-drug and post-drug measurements represented drug effect in a single expression. This is primarily a measure of displacement of the curve. The significance of such changes could then be determined by the t-test for paired replicates (Snedecor, 1946). Comparisons between drugs could be similarly made. No attempt was made to evaluate differences in the slopes of these curves since only two points determined each curve.

Subjective effects. These were estimated in preoperative patients who were free of pain and awaiting elective surgery. We have found such patients to be unusually responsive to drug effects and useful for assessing subjective effects of drugs (Keats and Telford, 1957). Patients who had been hospitalized for long periods or had received narcotic or sedative drugs in the recent past were not used. On the day before operation, suitable patients were given either saline, 30 mgm. or 60 mgm. of dihydrocodeine, or 10 mgm. of morphine by the ward nurse without explanation as to the purpose of the injection. All doses were per 70 kgm. of body weight. All data were collected by technicians who were unaware of the drugs being used. Patients were interviewed prior to drug administration and at 30, 60, and 120 minutes after the drug. Three types of data were collected: 1) Subjective; the presence or absence of the following were recorded: light-headedness, drunkenness, headache, dizziness, difficulty in concentration, grogginess, shaking, palpitations, "heavy limbs," nervousness, "blue feeling," nausea, difficulty in focusing eyes, itching, and dry mouth. A check list of these symptoms was used as a guide by the technician but patients were not questioned specifically for each symptom. All data were obtained from patients' statements made in response to such questions as: "How do you feel?", "Do you feel any different?". 2) Objective, such as restlessness, hiccoughs, tremor, pallor, sweating, vomiting, or unusual behavior. A check list was also used as a guide. 3) Value judgments; the technicians estimated the following: friendly or unfriendly, groggy or clearheaded, depressed or cheerful, calm or nervous. The technician also summarized the total drug effects as sedation or stimulation or both, and as pleasant, unpleasant or extremely unpleasant drug effect. Only signs and symptoms which represented a change from the pre-drug interview were attributed to the drug. No patient received more than one drug. Estimates of the significance of the differences in frequency of these effects between drugs were made by the rank method for paired replicates of Wilcoxon (1949).

RESULTS. *Analgesia.* (table 1) The incidence of analgesia following 30 mgm. of dihydrocodeine was 8.7 per cent less than that of 10 mgm. of morphine. This is a good approximation of the 12 per cent difference found by Gravenstein *et al.* (1956) by a similar technique. The frequency of analgesia after 60 mgm. was identical to that of morphine and 90 mgm. produced no additional pain relief.

TABLE 1

Frequency of analgesia following several dose levels of dihydrocodeine compared to morphine

No. of Patients	No. of Paired Doses	Dihydrocodeine		Morphine		Differences in Per Cent Analgesic Doses
		Dose *mgm. per 70 kgm.*	Per cent analgesic dose	Dose *mgm. per 70 kgm.*	Per cent analgesic doses	
54	104	30	66.3	10	75.0	−8.7
51	96	60	72.9	10	72.9	0.0
41	81	90	72.8	10	77.8	−5.0

TABLE 2

Drug effects on mean expired minute-volume (at 37°C.), respiratory rate, and alveolar carbon dioxide tension in 7 subjects breathing room air and a carbon dioxide mixture

	Room Air			3% CO_2 in O_2		
	MV ± S.E.* *liters*	RR ± S.E.* *per min.*	pCO_2 ± S.E.* *mm. Hg*	MV ± S.E.* *liters*	RR ± S.E.* *per min.**	pCO_2 ± S.E.* *mm. Hg*
Saline						
Control	6.61 ± 0.82	12.8 ± 0.2	33.0 ± 1.9	12.49 ± 0.62	18.7 ± 1.6	35.6 ± 1.9
1 Hour	5.84 ± 0.39	13.2 ± 0.3	33.6 ± 1.7	12.22 ± 0.89	18.1 ± 1.1	36.0 ± 1.8
3 Hours	6.25 ± 0.59	12.2 ± 0.6	32.4 ± 1.8	12.73 ± 0.81	19.0 ± 1.1	35.5 ± 2.0
Dihydrocodeine 30 mgm.						
Control	5.73 ± 0.58	11.8 ± 0.4	35.4 ± 1.2	11.20 ± 0.38	16.1 ± 0.1	40.2 ± 1.1
1 Hour	5.10 ± 0.60	11.7 ± 0.4	36.4 ± 1.2	10.72 ± 0.38	16.3 ± 1.1	40.7 ± 1.4
3 Hours	5.65 ± 0.65	11.9 ± 0.6	35.4 ± 1.3	11.14 ± 0.51	16.4 ± 1.0	39.7 ± 1.0
Dihydrocodeine 60 mgm.						
Control	5.72 ± 0.56	12.2 ± 0.2	34.2 ± 0.3	13.08 ± 0.36	16.7 ± 1.0	38.8 ± 0.8
1 Hour	4.37 ± 0.34	11.2 ± 0.9	38.0 ± 1.0	10.26 ± 0.31	16.5 ± 1.0	43.2 ± 0.8
3 Hours	4.97 ± 0.37	11.8 ± 0.6	36.3 ± 1.2	11.71 ± 0.30	16.4 ± 0.2	41.7 ± 0.8
Morphine 10 mgm.						
Control	5.83 ± 0.51	12.4 ± 0.5	36.2 ± 0.9	12.01 ± 0.37	17.0 ± 0.9	39.7 ± 1.2
1 Hour	4.12 ± 0.28	12.9 ± 0.5	40.6 ± 1.2	9.76 ± 0.33	18.2 ± 1.2	44.0 ± 1.2
3 Hours	4.66 ± 0.31	13.0 ± 0.5	39.4 ± 1.4	10.29 ± 0.41	17.5 ± 1.1	42.5 ± 1.4

* Standard error of mean.

The slight decrease in analgesia at 90 mgm. compared to 60 mgm. of dihydrocodeine is of interest. We have observed this previously with other potent analgesics studied by this technique. It suggests that an optimal dose has been exceeded.

Respiration. The data as collected (table 2) and the mean carbon dioxide sensitivity curves pre-drug and post-drug are presented (fig. 1 and 2). Shift of the curve to the right represents respiratory depression. Saline did not significantly

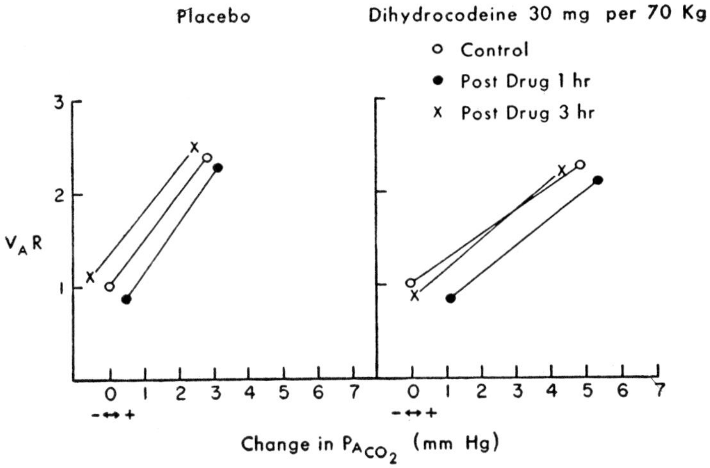

FIG. 1. Changes in respiratory stimulus-response curves following saline and 30 mgm. dihydrocodeine.

Mean values for seven subjects. Abscissa: Change in alveolar carbon dioxide tension from pre-drug room air value. Ordinate: Alveolar ventilation ratio.

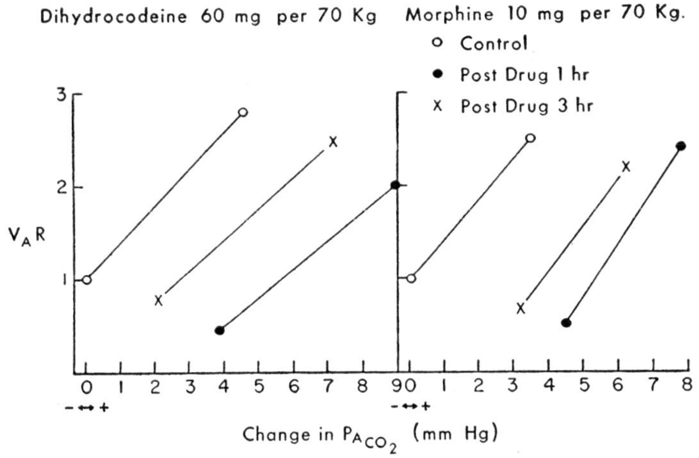

FIG. 2. Changes in respiratory stimulus-response curves following 60 mgm. of dihydrocodeine and 10 mgm. of morphine.

Mean values for seven subjects. Abscissa: Change in alveolar carbon dioxide tension from pre-drug room air value. Ordinate: Alveolar ventilation ratio.

alter respiration. Thirty milligrams of dihydrocodeine slightly depressed respiration at one hour following drug administration ($P < 0.05$) but respiration had returned to normal within three hours. Sixty milligrams of dihydrocodeine more markedly depressed respiration ($P < 0.01$), but this depression was significantly less than the depression of morphine ($P < 0.05$). The three hours post-drug data suggest that dihydrocodeine was shorter acting than morphine at both doses. These data agree well with those of Seed *et al.* (1957), who recently reported

TABLE 3

Frequency (per cent) of subjective effects produced by saline, dihydrocodeine, and morphine in hospitalized patients

	Placebo	Dihydrocodeine 30 mgm. s.c.	Dihydrocodeine 60 mgm. s.c.	Morphine 10 mgm. s.c.
Number of subjects	30	30	40	30
Per cent male	17	23	30	17
Per cent white	40	37	40	30
Per cent over 40 years	43	43	35	43
Drunkenness	7	17	25	33
Headache	0	0	5	7
Grogginess	7	10	43	47
Shakiness	0	0	0	7
Nervousness	0	0	8	10
Depression	3	0	13	20
Dizziness	23	43	43	80
Cheerfulness	7	20	10	20
Absence of cheerfulness	3	0	13	23
Nausea	7	3	13	27
Vomiting	0	3	3	17
Visual difficulties	3	3	8	20
Itching	7	0	10	13
Dry Mouth	13	20	25	40
Dislike of drug effect	6	20	55	36
Unreal dreams	0	0	3	10
Pallor	0	0	3	10
Difficulty in concentration	3	3	5	17
Heavy feeling	0	3	18	20
Technician evaluation				
"Euphoria"	10	0	8	17
Little drug effect	63	53	38	27
Sedation	53	43	46	81
Stimulation	10	17	15	7
Unpleasant drug effect	7	10	35	37
Not clearheaded	10	10	45	47

that 77 mgm. of dihydrocodeine would depress respiration as much as 10 mgm. of morphine.

Subjective effects. In table 3, some of the group characteristics of the patient samples are presented together with the frequency of the most prominent subjective effects which followed these drugs. The effects of 30 mgm. of dihydrocodeine were only slightly different from those following a placebo ($P > 0.05$), confirming the observations of Gravenstein *et al.* (1956). The primary effect of this dose was mild dizziness and a drunk feeling. The subjective effects of 60 mgm. were significantly greater than those of 30 mgm. ($P < 0.01$). They approached the effects of morphine both in type and frequency, but remained significantly less frequent than morphine ($P < 0.01$). Sixty milligrams were more unpleasant than 30 mgm. with an increased incidence of drunkenness, grogginess, psychic depression, and nausea. Dihydrocodeine at both doses differed from morphine chiefly in its lack of sedative effects and its less frequent nausea and vomiting. Patients receiving dihydrocodeine did not sleep despite the presence of such effects as dizziness, drunkenness, and grogginess.

DISCUSSION. From these data, we estimate 60 mgm. of dihydrocodeine to be the analgesic equivalent of 10 mgm. of morphine. In studies on cancer patients, Wallenstein, Seed, and Houde (1957) estimate this equivalence to be 68 mgm. of dihydrocodeine. It is significant, however, that the analgesia of 10 mgm. of morphine could not be surpassed even by 90 mgm. of dihydrocodeine. It has been possible to exceed the analgesia of 10 mgm. of morphine with all analgesics of the morphine type previously studied by this technique (Keats and Beecher, 1952). It would therefore seem that dihydrocodeine is not a morphine-like analgesic but more nearly like codeine. From studies of the analgesic effectiveness of codeine phosphate by Lasagna and Beecher (1954), dihydrocodeine bitartrate would appear to be twice as potent an analgesic as codeine on a milligram of salt basis.

Dihydrocodeine in sufficient dose is capable of producing all the undesirable actions of morphine studied here. However at 30 mgm., the respiratory and subjective effects of dihydrocodeine were minimal in contrast to those produced by 60 mgm. of codeine (Lasagna and Beecher, 1954) and 10 mgm. of morphine. At 30 mgm. significant analgesia was produced in postoperative patients. Increasing the dose of dihydrocodeine to 60 mgm. achieved only a small increase in analgesia (9 per cent) at the expense of a large increase in undesirable side actions. Thirty milligrams of dihydrocodeine promises to be a useful dose, from which adequate analgesia could be frequently obtained with minimal sedation, nausea and respiratory depression. When analgesia is not obtained by 30 mgm. or in the treatment of severe pain, it would seem advisable to use a more potent drug rather than to increase the dose of dihydrocodeine. The eventual utility of this drug in clinical medicine will depend, we believe, on an appreciation of its limitations and its intelligent use.

SUMMARY

The analgesic, respiratory and subjective effects of 30 and 60 mgm. of dihydrocodeine have been studied in hospitalized patients and normal subjects. These effects have been compared to those of a placebo and 10 mgm. of morphine.

Thirty milligrams of dihydrocodeine produced a high incidence of analgesia with slight respiratory depression and few subjective effects compared to a placebo.

Sixty milligrams of dihydrocodeine was the analgesic equivalent of 10 mgm. of morphine, but at this dose approached morphine in respiratory and subjective effects. Ninety milligrams of dihydrocodeine was no more effective an analgesic than 60 mgm.

Dihydrocodeine is not an analgesic of the morphine type, but rather a codeine of increased effectiveness. Sedation was not produced by either dose level of dihydrocodeine.

REFERENCES

Biberfield, J.: Biochem. Ztschr, **111:** 91, 1920.

Dahl, W.: Deutsche med. Wchnschr., **39:** 1304, 1913.

Eddy, N. B.: This Journal, **51:** 35, 1934.

Fraenkel, A.: Munchen med. Wchnschr., **60:** 522, 1913.

Gravenstein, J. S., Smith, G. M., Sphire, R. D., Isaacs, J. P., and Beecher, H. K.: New Eng. Jour. Med., **254:** 877, 1956.

Haffner, F.: Deutsche med. Wchnschr., **55:** 731, 1929.

Heinroth, H.: Arch. f. Exper. Path. u. Pharmakol., **116:** 245, 1926.

Hummelsbach, C. K., This Journal, **71:** 42, 1941.

Keats, A. S., Beecher, H. K., and Mosteller, F. C.: J. Appl. Physiol., **1:** 35, 1950.

Keats, A. S., and Beecher, H. K.: This Journal, **105:** 109, 1952.

Keats, A. S., and Telford, J.: This Journal, **119:** 370, 1957.

Lasagna, L., and Beecher, H. K.: This Journal, **112:** 306, 1954.

Seed, J. C., Wallenstein, S. L., Belleville, J. W., and Houde, R. W.: This Journal (abs.), **119:** 182, 1957.

Skita, A., and Franck, H. H.: Ber., **44:** 2862, 1911.

Snedecor, G. W.: Statistical Methods, p. 44, Iowa State College Press, Ames, 1946.

Wallenstein, S. L., Seed, J. C., and Houde, R. W., This Journal (abs.), **119:** 191, 1957.

Wilcoxon, F.: Some Rapid Approximate Statistical Procedures. Am. Cyanimid Co., New York, 1949.

Wright, C. I.: This Journal, **51:** 343, 1934.

COMPARATIVE EFFECTS OF EPINEPHRINE AND LEVARTERENOL (*l*-NOREPINEPHRINE) ON LEFT VENTRICULAR PERFORMANCE IN CONSCIOUS AND ANESTHETIZED DOGS[1]

THEODORE C. WEST AND ROBERT F. RUSHMER

Department of Pharmacology and Department of Physiology and Biophysics, School of Medicine, University of Washington, Seattle

Received for publication February 11, 1957

The reports of Goldenberg *et al.* (1948) and Barcroft and Starr (1951) emphasized differences between the effects of epinephrine and levarterenol (*l*-norepinephrine) on cardiac output in man. Since the time of those reports further studies comparing the cardiac stimulatory qualities of the two drugs have been made. Garb (1950) showed levarterenol to possess inotropic effects as great or greater than epinephrine in cat papillary muscle. Serin (1952) found the two drugs to be quantitatively similar with respect to positive chronotropic and inotropic action in the perfused rat heart. Lands and Howard (1952) studied frog hearts, turtle hearts, isolated rabbit auricles and the perfused rabbit heart and reported that the inotropic effect of levarterenol was less than that of epinephrine in amphibian preparations but greater in the rabbit heart. These findings did not agree with the earlier report of Ahlquist (1948) in which the inotropic and chronotropic actions of epinephrine were more marked than those of levarterenol in the perfused rabbit heart. Lee (1953) found that the two drugs were indistinguishable with regard to their effects on oxygen consumption, force of contraction and speed of action in the isolated cat papillary preparation. In the anesthetized dog, Wakim and Essex (1952) observed little difference between epinephrine and levarterenol effects on blood flow, heart rate and arterial pressure. Ahlquist *et al.* (1954) found levarterenol significantly more effective as a pressor agent and in producing vagal bradycardia in the anesthetized dog, but these studies did not include measurement of ventricular performance. Zanetti and Opdyke (1953) observed that the mean increase in stroke index after epinephrine was somewhat greater than with levarterenol, but the difference between drugs was not significant. More direct measurements of ventricular contractile force were made by Goldberg *et al.* (1953), Gazes *et al.* (1953) and Cotten and Pincus (1955) employing strain gauge arches on thoracotomized, anesthetized and conscious dogs. In these studies, epinephrine and levarterenol were shown to be qualitatively and quantitatively similar. Categorically, it appears incorrect to say that epinephrine is appreciably the greater myocardial stimulant. However, the controversy began with observations on man. Crucial human experiments in this regard still remain to be done.

The present investigation was undertaken in view of the availability of a new technique for observing various parameters of left ventricular performance in

[1] This investigation was supported in part by research grants from the National Heart Institute of the National Institutes of Health, Public Health Service; and from the American Heart Association.

either the conscious or the anesthetized dog. The effects of epinephrine and levarterenol on these parameters were studied. Constant infusion of drugs at three concentration levels was utilized. No premedication was administered to the conscious animals in order that the total effect of direct and indirect action of each drug would not be obscured. The infusion schedule was duplicated in the presence of pentobarbital anesthesia. In the present investigation it is possible to observe depression of homeostatic influence on drug effects during anesthesia.

METHODS. The experimental animals were eight male dogs of approximately ten kilograms weight. Under pentobarbital anesthesia aseptic surgery was performed. For the measurement of effective left ventricular pressure, a differential transformer pressure transducer was mounted at the apex of the heart. For continuous recording of left ventricular diameter a modified sonar technique was employed. Heart rate was recorded by means of a charged condensor interval timer. These techniques have been described elsewhere (Rushmer and West, 1957). Heart rate, pressure and diameter were recorded on a Sanborn Polyviso recorder. In addition, pressure-diameter loops were displayed continuously on an oscilloscope. The nature of these loops has been described previously (see Rushmer and West, 1957).

A minimum of four days was allowed to elapse between surgical preparation of the dog and the first experimental procedure. At the time of experiment an indwelling polyethylene catheter was inserted into the major antecubital vein of the experimental animal. The catheter was connected to a ten ml. syringe mounted in a constant infusion pump capable of delivering various calibrated infusion rates. Epinephrine and levarterenol were used in the form of *l*-epinephrine bitartrate and *l*-norepinephrine bitartrate[2] respectively. Both drugs were diluted to working concentration with physiological saline. Three infusion rates, all under 1 ml. per minute, were used in order to provide the following graded doses: 0.001, 0.002 and 0.004 micromole per kilogram per minute. The injection schedule was as follows: after a suitable control period, the infusion was begun at the lowest rate and allowed to continue for three minutes; at this time the rate was doubled and continued for the next three minutes before changing to the highest rate for the last three minutes. Following discontinuation of the infusion at least ten minutes were allowed to elapse before beginning another injection series. The order of injection of epinephrine and levarterenol was reversed with each experiment in order to minimize effects of long term changes in blood storage depots (Zanetti and Opdyke, 1953). After observing the changes evoked in conscious dogs, sodium pentobarbital was injected slowly through the catheter in order to produce surgical anesthesia. The concentration needed was between 25 and 30 milligrams per kilogram. Upon stabilization following the barbiturate injection, the infusion schedule for the adrenergic agents was repeated.

RESULTS. The methods used offer an opportunity to compare left ventricular response to epinephrine and to levarterenol in equimolar concentration at several levels, both in the conscious and in the barbiturate anesthetized dog. The following description of the experimental results refers largely to the data presented in table 1 and to figure 1, in which the data have been graphed.

Pulse rate. In the conscious animal both epinephrine and levarterenol decreased pulse rate in proportion to concentration, except when the infusion rate reached 0.004 micromole per kilogram per minute. The decreased rate and the disturbance in rhythm illustrated in figure 2 presumably were of vagal origin. Apparently the highest infusion rate partially overcame the vagal effect. Initial tachycardia

[2] Kindly supplied by Sterling-Winthrop Corporation.

TABLE 1

Changes in parameters of left ventricular performance in response to graded doses of epinephrine and levarterenol

	State of Consciousness	Drug Concentration	Direction and Degree of Mean Change				
			Pulse rate	Intraventricular systolic pressure	Ventricular diastolic diameter	Ventricular systolic diameter	Ventricular stroke
		μM/kgm./min.	*beats/min.*	*mm.Hg*	*mm.*	*mm.*	*mm.*
Epinephrine	Conscious	0.001	−11.8 (±1.49)	+7.2 (±0.80)	+1.0 (±0.03)	+0.6 (±0.05)	+0.5 (±0.01)
		0.002	−22.5 (±3.00)	+10.0 (±1.08)	+1.4 (±0.14)	+0.9 (±0.16)	+0.64 (±0.04)
		0.004	−20.5 (±2.83)	+37.5 (±2.41)	+1.2 (±0.12)	+0.5 (±0.17)	+1.0 (±0.07)
	Anesthetized	0.001	+1.9 (±0.45)	+18.0 (±0.38)	+0.4 (±0.03)	−0.06 (±0.05)	+0.74 (±0.03)
		0.002	+7.5 (±0.47)	+31.0 (±2.60)	+1.0 (±0.1)	−0.14 (±0.18)	+1.1 (±0.07)
		0.004	+7.2 (±0.71)	+65.6 (±1.62)	+1.1 (±0.06)	−0.2 (±0.09)	+1.3 (±0.05)
Levarterenol	Conscious	0.001	−20.4 (±0.68)	+16.0 (±0.62)	+0.66 (±0.02)	+0.2 (±0.02)	+0.4 (±0.02)
		0.002	−36.7 (±1.16)	+23.0 (±0.94)	+0.52 (±0.1)	−0.08 (±0.07)	+0.6 (±0.03)
		0.004	−32.0 (±0.69)	+40.4 (±1.16)	+1.05 (±0.05)	+0.03 (±0.03)	+1.0 (±0.03)
	Anesthetized	0.001	−7.4 (±0.80)	+33.8 (±1.25)	+0.45 (±0.03)	+0.23 (±0.03)	+0.32 (±0.01)
		0.002	−17.0 (±0.95)	+49.2 (±1.00)	+0.8 (±0.16)	+0.2 (±0.18)	+0.66 (±0.04)
		0.004	−23.2 (±1.74)	+80.0 (±0.86)	+1.4 (±0.12)	+0.28 (±0.15)	+0.92 (±0.04)

at the beginning of the infusion was not observed. In the presence of barbiturate anesthesia, pulse rate still was retarded by levarterenol but increased slightly after epinephrine (figure 3).

Left ventricular diastolic pressure. Diastolic pressure measurements were not consistently available and are not included in the tabular data. However, as seen in figures 2 and 3, both drugs generally increased both early and end diastolic pressure in the conscious and in the anesthetized animal. The increase in ventricular diastolic pressure accompanying atrial contraction was greatly increased by administration of both epinephrine and levarterenol. Although figure 3 indicates a drop in diastolic pressure due to levarterenol in the anesthetized dog, this is not typical.

Left ventricular systolic pressure. The level of systolic pressure was a function of drug concentration either in the conscious or anesthetized dog. Typical results are seen in figures 2 and 3 and in the pressure-diameter loops of figure 4. Although variation in the degree of response in this parameter was encountered,

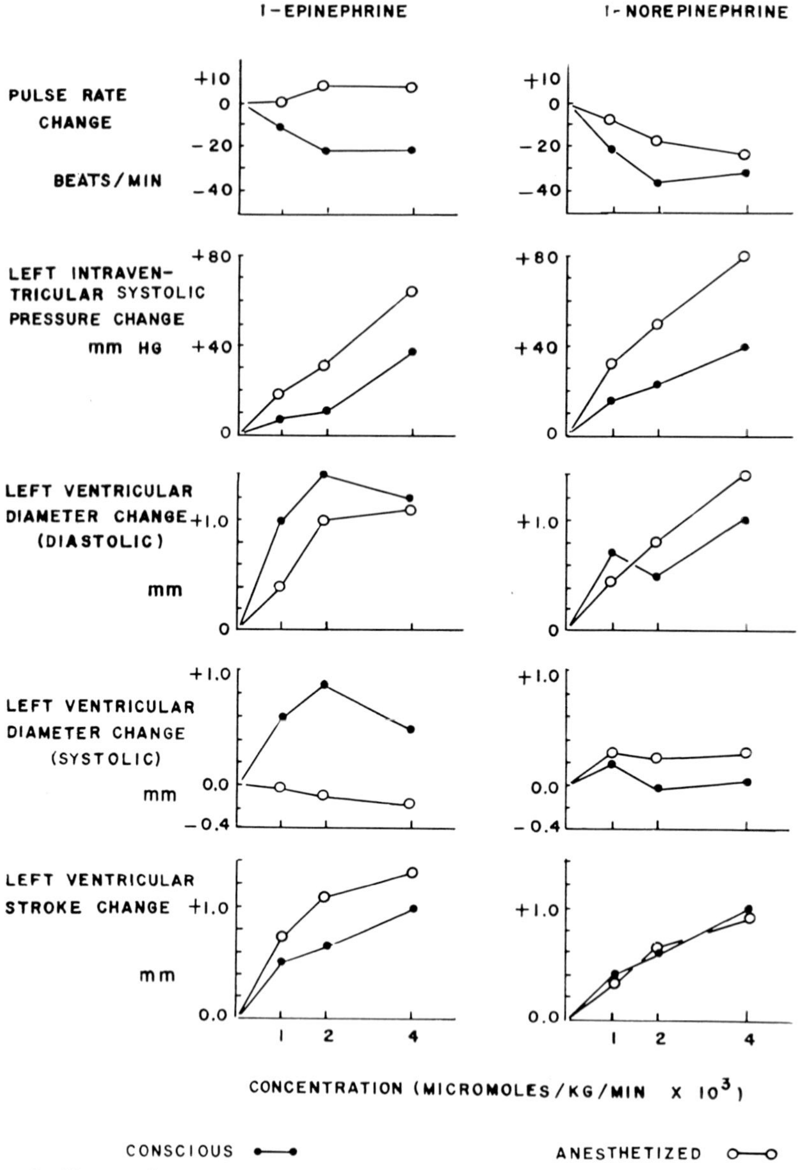

FIG. 1. Changes in parameters of left ventricular function induced by continuous IV infusion of epinephrine or levarterenol (*l*-norepinephrine) in conscious and anesthetized dogs.

Standard error of each point presented in tabular form in text.

the effect on systolic pressure at a given concentration was greatest in the anesthetized dog, particularly in response tol evarterenol. This comparison is illustrated in table 1 and in figure 1.

Left ventricular diameter. Measurable diameter increased following the administration of each of the adrenergic drugs. Changes in diastolic or systolic size

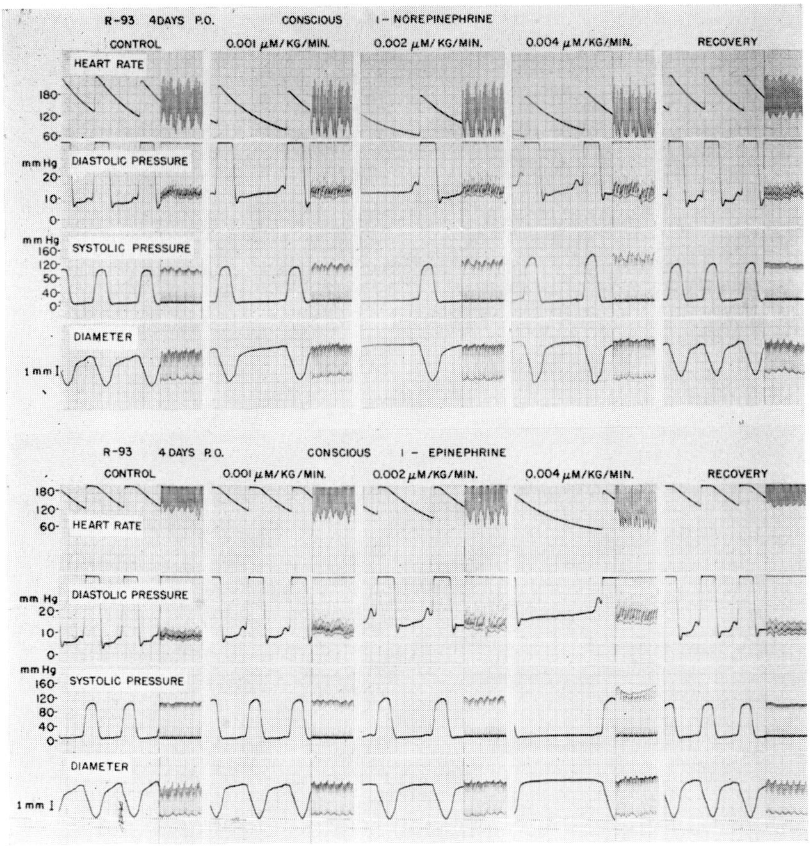

FIG. 2. Response of the conscious dog to continuous intravenous infusion of epinephrine and levarterenol (l-norepinephrine).

Portions of record during drug injection taken from final minute of three minute infusion at each concentration indicated. Downward deflection in ventricular diameter record indicates reduction in diameter. Fast record at 50 mm. per second; slow record at 1 mm. per second.

are related in part to cardiac cycle length and therefore varied considerably. The mean changes are shown in table 1 and figure 1, while fairly typical results are illustrated in figures 2 and 3.

a. Diastolic diameter: A general increase was observed in proportion to drug concentration. Differences between response to the two drugs, or in the two states of consciousness are not significant.

b. Systolic diameter: Great variation occurred in this parameter. This is reflected in table 1 where little difference exists between the mean change and the standard error. The response to levarterenol underwent little change from control values. In the case of epinephrine, systolic diameter increased in the conscious state, but decreased slightly in the anesthetized animal. Figures 2 and 3 are fairly typical of the mean data.

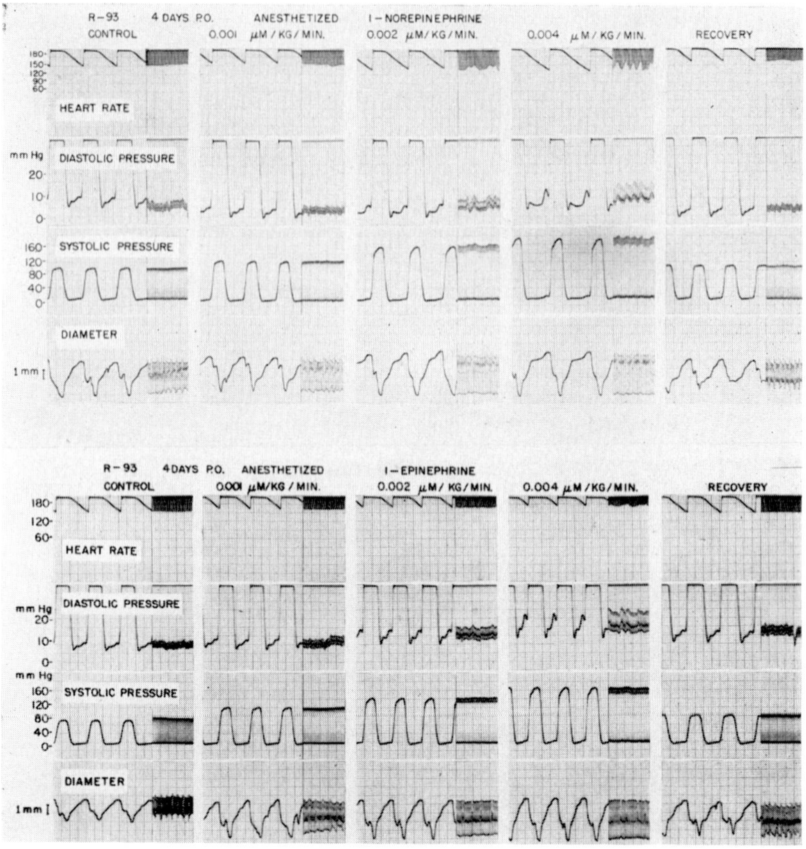

FIG. 3. Response of the pentobarbital anesthetized dog to continuous intravenous infusion of epinephrine and levarterenol (*l*-norepinephrine).

Portions of record during drug injection taken from final minute of three minute infusion at each concentration indicated. Downward deflection in ventricular diameter record indicates reduction in diameter. Fast record at 50 mm. per second; slow record at 1 mm. per second.

c. Stroke change in diameter: Stroke change in ventricular diameter increased uniformly in proportion to concentration. Little difference was seen between levarterenol in both states of consciousness and epinephrine in the conscious state. The stroke response to epinephrine in the anesthetized dog achieved a higher value than under any other experimental condition.

Pressure-diameter loops. The loops shown in figure 4 are continuous plots during a given cardiac cycle of left ventricular pressure against left ventricular diameter. The pressure baselines are not necessarily indicative of absolute values. Assuming diameter to be directly proportional to volume, the area of a loop reflects the stroke work of the left ventricle. From inspection of the figures, the proportionality between drug concentration and energy release is apparent. Again, it is seen that stroke change increase and pressure change are more evident in the

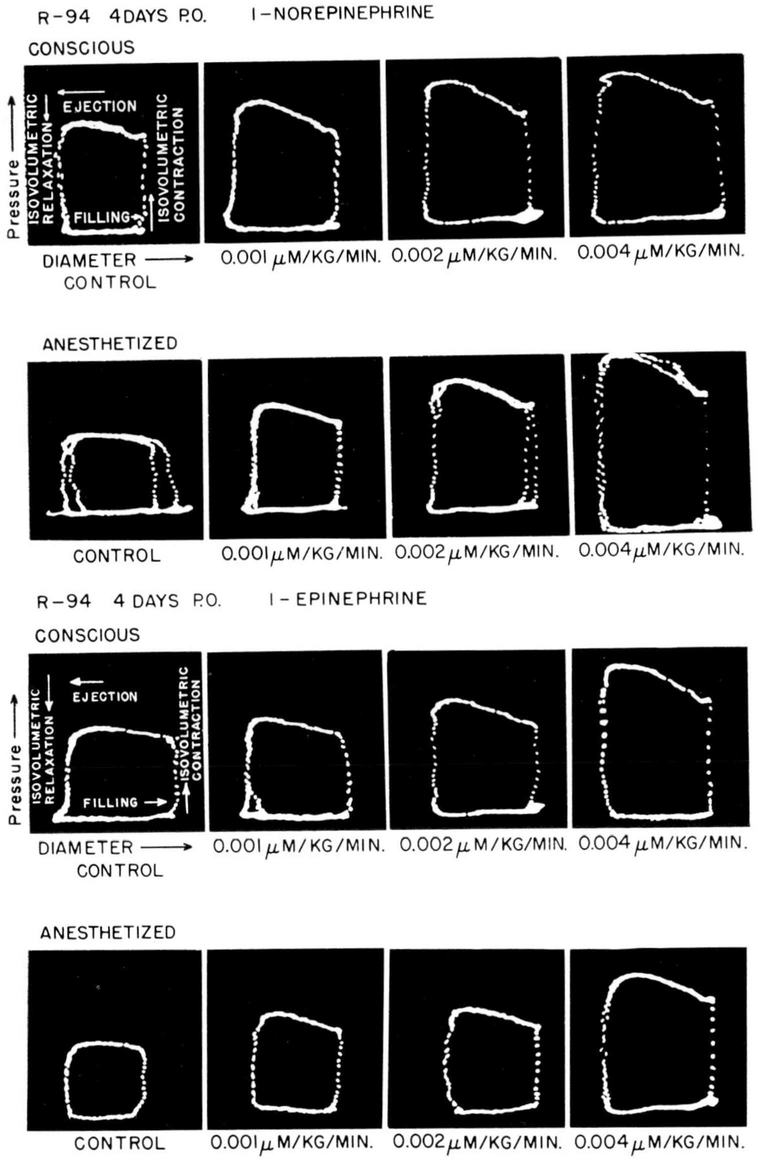

FIG. 4. Oscilloscope tracings of left ventricular pressure-diameter loops from conscious or anesthetized dog during continuous intravenous infusion of epinephrine or levarterenol (*l*-norepinephrine). Traces photographed during final minute of three minute infusion at each concentration indicated. Time pips occur once every four milliseconds.

anesthetized state. In addition, there is the suggestion that the greater stroke energy release occurs in the presence of levarterenol, regardless of state of consciousness.

Influence of neural control. The results have reaffirmed the notion that anesthe-

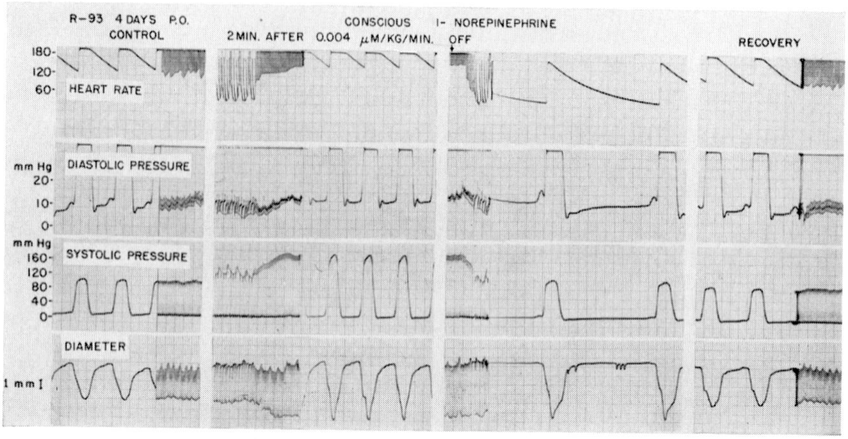

FIG. 5. Changes associated with non-sinus tachycardia in conscious dog during continuous intravenous infusion of levarterenol (*l*-norepinephrine). Downward deflection in diameter record indicates reduction in diameter. Fast record at 50 mm. per second; slow record at 1 mm. per second.

sia can profoundly modify neural control of cardiac function. For example, as shown in figure 5, routine infusion of levarterenol in a conscious dog produced the usual bradycardia and sinus arrhythmia. Suddenly, a spontaneous shift to tachycardia occurred. The atrial component of the diastolic pressure curve disappeared, indicating that the tachycardia was of AV nodal or ventricular origin. As heart rate increased, diastolic pressure, systolic pressure and stroke change also increased. Systolic diameter diminished, accounting for the increase in stroke change. It is difficult to imagine that baroreceptor mechanisms had become inoperative. Presumably, acetylcholine from the vagi continued to be released during the tachycardia, but establishment of a new pacemaker bypassed the inhibitory influence. This is reminiscent of the resistance of paroxysmal tachycardia to vagal stimulation or to the administration of cholinergic drugs. When the infusion was discontinued, reversion to bradycardia and normal ventricular pressure configuration occurred prior to recovery. It was concluded that the ventricular inotropic effect of levarterenol can be opposed by vagal reflexes only so long as normal pacemaker activity is present.

DISCUSSION. In the conscious animal, bradycardia followed the injection of either drug at any of the three concentration levels. This differs from the results of Barcroft and Konzett (1949) in which humans responded with tachycardia to epinephrine injection. However, it does agree with the observations of Cotten and Pincus (1955) who also noted in dogs that levarterenol usually resulted in a more profound bradycardia than did epinephrine. Slowing of the heart rate by levarterenol carried over into the anesthetized state in contrast to the findings of Cotten and Pincus (1955) who employed vagotomy. With anesthesia, epinephrine usually produced mild tachycardia. Using single injections of epinephrine or levarterenol, Zanetti and Opdyke (1953) observed bradycardia with both drugs in the anesthetized state as did Ahlquist *et al.* (1954). Interpretation of differences in this respect are difficult since various experimental techniques were employed in the several investigations. The heart rate response to pressor drugs will be determined in part by depth of anesthesia, a possible factor in the different results. In addition, constant infusion to the point of a steady state response, as used in the present experiments, may also produce responses differing from those following a single injection.

Ventricular pressure changes were greatest after levarterenol. Cotten and Pincus (1955) observed a similar result on arterial systolic pressure in anesthetized and vagotomized dogs. However, they felt that differences would not have existed had they administered the two drugs in equimolar concentration. Judging from the pressure-diameter loops, stroke work also was greatest in the presence of levarterenol. However, in any given state of consciousness, heart rate was more rapid in the presence of epinephrine. Consequently, the effect of epinephrine on minute-work can be expected to attain or exceed that of levarterenol. This is in agreement with the results of Goldenberg *et al.* (1948) and Barcroft and Starr (1951) on cardiac output in man.

Systolic diameter and diastolic diameter are both diminished when heart rate is experimentally accelerated by direct electrical stimulation (Rushmer, unpublished results). However, in the present experiments, when systolic size diminished, diastolic diameter generally increased. The result was augmented ventricular stroke. This may indicate increased ventricular contractility, particularly when examination of the records indicates increased rate of ejection. If so, it appears that the positive inotropic capacity of both drugs, but particularly levarterenol, can be strongly opposed by reflex neural intervention. When neural opposition is diminished, as in anesthesia, or bypassed as in the phenomenon shown in figure 5, the inherent chronotropic and inotropic effects of the two drugs are revealed. This also is apparent from those studies in which vagotomy was employed (Cotten and Pincus, 1955).

As a result of this investigation little distinction can be made between the effect of epinephrine and that of levarterenol on left ventricular performance in the dog. Many variables implicit in the conscious state were left uncontrolled in order to gain more insight into the response of the conscious animal to potent cardiovascular drugs. The influence of pentobarbital anesthesia was observed largely because so much of our teaching regarding autonomic drugs is based on laboratory experiments in which the anesthetized dog is a convenient test object. In these studies, anesthetic depression of homeostatic mechanisms modified responses to the drugs employed mainly in a quantitative sense. Exception to this was seen in the heart rate effects.

SUMMARY

Dogs were surgically prepared for continuous measurement of left ventricular pressure, left ventricular diameter and pulse rate. These and other derived parameters of left ventricular function were recorded during continuous intravenous infusion of epinephrine or levarterenol (*l*-norepinephrine) at least four days after surgery. Effects of the two drugs at three equimolar concentrations were studied in the conscious dog and again after anesthesia by sodium pentobarbital. Pulse rate was decreased by levarterenol both in the conscious and anesthetized animal. Epinephrine decreased pulse rate in the conscious state but caused tachycardia during anesthesia. Left ventricular systolic pressure was increased in proportion to concentration by both drugs in the conscious and in the anesthetized dog, but the effect of levarterenol was the more intense. Left ventricular stroke change was increased by both drugs in proportion to concentration; the most intense effect was exerted by epinephrine during anesthesia. Diastolic diameter increased in response to both drugs to about the same extent. Systolic diameter changes were more variable. Pressure-diameter loops (stroke work) were increased in area by both drugs and to a similar degree. The amount of change relative to control was greatest during anesthesia. There was no suggestion of major differences between the effects of the two drugs on ventricular contractility.

REFERENCES

AHLQUIST, R. P.: Am. J. Physiol., **153:** 586, 1948.

AHLQUIST, R. P., TAYLOR, J. P., RAWSON, C. W., JR., AND SYDOW, V. L.: THIS JOURNAL, **110:** 352, 1954.

BARCROFT, H., AND KONZETT, H.: Helv. Physiol. Pharmacol Acta, **7:** C4, 1949.

BARCROFT, H., AND STARR, I.: Clin. Sci., **10:** 295, 1951.

COTTEN, M. DEV., AND PINCUS, S.: THIS JOURNAL, **114:** 110, 1955.

GARB, S.: Proc. Soc. Exp. Biol. & Med., **73:** 134, 1950.

GAZES, P. C., GOLDBERG, L. I., AND DARBY, T. D.: Circ., **8:** 883, 1953.

GOLDBERG, L. I., COTTEN, M. DEV., DARBY, T. C., AND HOWELL, E. V.: THIS JOURNAL, **108:** 177, 1953.

GOLDENBERG, M., PINES, K. L., BALDWIN, E. DEF., GREENE, D. G., AND ROH, C. E.: Am. J. Med., **5:** 792, 1948.

LANDS, A. M., AND HOWARD, J. W.: THIS JOURNAL, **106:** 65, 1952.

LEE, L. S.: THIS JOURNAL, **109:** 313, 1953.

RUSHMER, R. F., AND WEST, T. C.: Circ. Res., (In Press).

SERIN, F.: Acta Physiol. Scand., **26:** 291, 1952.

WAKIM, K. G., AND ESSEX, H. E.: Circ., **5:** 370, 1952.

ZANETTI, M. C., AND OPDYKE, D. F.: THIS JOURNAL, **109:** 107, 1953.

A STUDY IN THE DOG OF THE RENAL CLEARANCE OF MORPHINE AND THE EFFECT OF MORPHINE ON *p*-AMINOHIPPURATE CLEARANCE[1, 2]

W. P. BAKER AND L. A. WOODS

Department of Pharmacology, University of Michigan Medical School, Ann Arbor

Received for publication February 13, 1957

Since information on the mechanism of the renal elimination of free and conjugated morphine was not available, studies in the dog were initiated to provide such data. The effect of morphine on renal filtration rate and blood flow of the dog was reinvestigated using a procedure which minimized the depressor action of this drug. The latter precaution was desirable since the marked reduction of renal filtration rate and blood flow in the dog described previously as an effect of morphine (Handley and Keller, 1950) could have resulted from the generalized vasodepressor action of the drug administered intravenously.

METHODS. *Estimation of drug.* Each sample of urine or plasma was analyzed in duplicate for each drug and the values averaged. If the duplicate determinations were not in close agreement, or if the results seemed out of line, the analyses were repeated until the results were constant. Inulin, *p*-aminohippuric acid, and morphine were determined according to the procedures described by Schreiner (1950), Smith *et al.* (1945), and Woods *et al.* (1954), respectively.

Animal experiments. Trained female mongrel dogs ranging in weight from 15 to 22 kgm. were used in these experiments. Thirty minutes before the beginning of the experiment, each animal was given 15 to 25 ml./kgm. of tap water via a stomach tube. Plasma samples were obtained from venous blood which was withdrawn at the mid-point of the clearance period of 15 minutes and mixed with oxalate. At the end of each clearance period the urine was removed via a Foley-bag indwelling catheter and the bladder rinsed three times with 15 to 20 ml. of distilled water. Hematocrit determinations performed on samples of blood selected from typical experiments gave nearly constant values.

The priming doses of inulin and sodium *p*-aminohippurate of 350 mgm. and 200 mgm., respectively, were administered intravenously in a volume of 25 ml. during a period of 5 minutes and followed immediately by a constant intravenous infusion of 36.5 mgm./kgm./hr. of inulin and 12.5 mgm./kgm./hr. of sodium *p*-aminohippurate in physiological saline (115 ml./hr.). The animal was allowed to equilibrate for 30 to 45 minutes.

After three to four consecutive control periods for the clearance of inulin and *p*-aminohippuric acid, 30 mgm./kgm. of morphine sulfate (calculated as free base) was injected subcutaneously. In most of the experiments a constant intravenous infusion of 7.5 mgm./kgm./hr. of morphine sulfate (calculated as free base), incorporated in the solution of inulin and hippurate solution, was initiated 40 minutes after the subcutaneous injection of morphine. Sixty minutes after the subcutaneous injection of the morphine sulfate, clearance values were obtained for four to five consecutive periods of 15 minutes, each.

The procedure for the determination of the maximum tubular excretion of *p*-aminohippuric acid was that utilized by Shideman *et al.* (1952).

---

[1] Supported in part by research grant B-625 from the Division of Research Grants, National Institutes of Health, United States Public Health Service.

[2] A preliminary report of some of these experiments appears in THIS JOURNAL, **116:** 4, 1956.

TABLE 1

Average renal clearance of free and conjugated morphine one hour after a subcutaneous injection (30 mgm./kgm. as free base) of morphine sulfate, followed by intravenous infusion of 7.5 mgm./kgm./hr.

Dog No. (Body Wt.)	Mean Renal Clearance (ml./min.) ± Standard Deviation			
	Free morphine	Conjugated morphine	Inulin	PAH
C-1 (18 kgm.).......	81 ± 5*	59 ± 14	79 ± 7†	217 ± 10
C-2 (16 kgm.).......	63 ± 15	56 ± 13	68 ± 4	157 ± 14
C-3 (15 kgm.).......	54 ± 12	83 ± 17	63 ± 4	134 ± 13

* Simultaneous PAH and inulin clearances were determined using priming doses of 200 mgm. and 350 mgm., respectively, followed by the intravenous infusion of 36.5 mgm./kgm./hr. of inulin and 12.5 mgm./kgm./hr. of PAH.

† Clearance values for free and conjugated morphine are the average of three consecutive determinations while the mean values for inulin and PAH are averages of four periods.

Mean blood pressure was determined in some animals by placing a cannula in the femoral artery using local anesthesia and subsequently recording pressure with a mercury manometer.

RESULTS. *Renal clearance of free and conjugated morphine.* The renal clearance of free and conjugated morphine in three dogs is compared with the values for inulin and *p*-aminohippuric acid in table 1. The averages of the clearance values for the three dogs were as follows: Free morphine, 66 ml./min.; conjugated morphine, 66 ml./min.; and inulin, 70 ml./min. The proportion of free and conjugated morphine bound to plasma protein was not determined for these experiments and accordingly the above values were not corrected for protein binding. Previous investigations have shown that at comparable plasma levels approximately 25 per cent of free morphine, but only a few per cent of conjugated morphine, is bound to plasma protein (Blaney and Woods, 1956). If the clearance values for free morphine are corrected for protein binding, the results suggest that a small amount of tubular excretion occurs. The variation of the figures for the clearance of morphine is such that a valid conclusion cannot be drawn, but the possibility of a small amount of tubular excretion certainly exists.

It is to be noted that in table 1 the clearance values for *p*-aminohippuric acid in two of the animals are less than would be expected. The significance of these observations will be discussed subsequently.

Effect of morphine on the renal clearance of inulin and p-aminohippuric acid. A single subcutaneous injection of 30 mgm./kgm. of morphine to each of four dogs did not result in a consistent alteration of the renal clearance of either inulin or *p*-aminohippuric acid. However, a combination of the above administration with intravenous infusion of morphine (7.5 mgm./kgm./hr.) produced an 11 to 45 per cent decrease in the clearance values for *p*-aminohippuric acid, although the clearance values for inulin were not altered significantly (table 2).

The effect of the combination of subcutaneous injection and intravenous infusion of morphine on maximum tubular excretion of *p*-aminohippuric acid was

TABLE 2

Average renal clearance of inulin and PAH preceding and following a subcutaneous injection (30 mgm./kgm. as free base) and intravenous infusion (7.5 mgm./kgm./hr. as free base) of morphine sulfate*

Dog No. (Body Wt.)	Control			One Hour After Morphine		
	Mean B.P. *mm. of Hg*	Renal clearance *ml./min. ± S.D.*		Mean B.P. *mm. of Hg*	Renal clearance *ml./min. ± S.D.*	
		Inulin	PAH		Inulin	PAH
C-8 (17.0 kgm.)....	94	52 ± 4†	209 ± 20	90	69 ± 7	186 ± 9
C-9 (16.0 kgm.)....	120	79 ± 5	203 ± 14	115	71 ± 7	158 ± 8
C-10 (21.5 kgm.)...	110	59 ± 6	302 ± 35	80	58 ± 2	195 ± 18
C-11 (17.0 kgm.)...	—	72 ± 4	261 ± 28	—	72 ± 5	143 ± 13

* Clearance values for PAH and inulin were determined using priming doses of 200 mgm. and 350 mgm., respectively, followed by the intravenous infusion of 36.5 mgm./kgm./hr. of inulin and 12.5 mgm./kgm./hr. of PAH.

† Values in above table are averages computed from four consecutive clearance determinations.

investigated in two dogs and the following results were obtained: Mean Tm PAH (mgm./min.) ± S.D.; control—18.2 ± 0.6 (dog C-12), 15.5 ± 2.5 (dog C-13); after morphine—15.2 ± 3.0 (dog C-12), 15.4 ± 1.1 (dog C-13). The absence of a significant alteration of Tm PAH by morphine is noteworthy.

Discussion. The renal clearance values for free and conjugated morphine suggest that these two forms are excreted primarily by glomerular filtration although a small amount of free morphine may be removed by tubular excretion. Agents which inhibit tubular excretion would therefore not be expected to interfere appreciably with the elimination of morphine and accordingly would not potentiate the pharmacologic action of this drug.

Handley and Keller (1950) described a prominent reduction in glomerular filtration rate, renal plasma flow and maximum tubular reabsorption of glucose in dogs for a considerable period following the intravenous injection of 2 mgm./kgm. of morphine. Indeed, morphine eliminated all renal function for ten to forty minutes in some animals, as measured by clearance techniques. These investigators noted a fall in systemic blood pressure following the administration of morphine. Shideman and Johnson (1948) investigating the effects of the above dose of morphine in unanesthetized and anesthetized dogs described a marked hypotensive effect lasting for many minutes.

Since the hypotensive action of morphine administered intravenously might explain the changes in renal clearance values described by Handley and Keller (1950), it was considered important to study the renal effects of significant plasma concentration of morphine in the absence of any marked changes in systemic blood pressure. It has been observed in these laboratories that neither the subcutaneous injection of 30 mgm./kgm. of morphine nor the combination of this administration with intravenous infusion of low concentrations of the alkaloid has any appreciable effect on systemic blood pressure. The subcutaneous injection of morphine did not result in any significant change in the clearance of inulin or *p*-aminohippuric acid, although the combination with intravenous infusion effected an 11 to 45 per cent reduction in the clearance of *p*-aminohippuric acid. This reduction could be a result of either a metabolic inhibition of renal tubular excretory mechanisms or a decrease in renal blood flow. If metabolic inhibition of the tubular excretory mechanism were the correct explanation, then a reduction in the maximum tubular excretion of *p*-aminohippuric acid by morphine might be expected. However, the latter was not observed. An alternative explanation is that local vascular changes in the kidney result in decreased renal blood flow without reduction in glomerular filtration, a suggestion which is rather difficult to accept and even more difficult to prove as fact.

SUMMARY

In normal unanesthetized female dogs the primary mechanism by which free and conjugated morphine are removed from plasma by the kidney appears to be glomerular filtration although a small amount of free morphine may be eliminated by tubular excretion. Neither subcutaneous injection of 30 mgm./kgm. of morphine nor the combination with intravenous infusion of 7.5 mgm./kgm. of morphine, both of which have minimal effects on systemic blood pressure, has any effect on the renal clearance of inulin and accordingly glomerular filtration rate. However the combination of the subcutaneous injection with the intravenous infusion of morphine produces an 11 to 45 per cent reduction in the clearance of *p*-aminohippuric acid and accordingly in apparent renal plasma flow. The maximum tubular excretion of *p*-aminohippuric acid is not altered by the combination of subcutaneous injection and intravenous infusion of morphine.

ACKNOWLEDGMENT. The authors are indebted to Miss Beverly Waterman for performing the morphine analyses and to Mr. Victor Bloom for assisting in some of the animal experiments.

REFERENCES

BLANEY, D. J., AND WOODS, L. A.: THIS JOURNAL, **116**: 7, 1956.
HANDLEY, C. A., AND KELLER, A. D.: THIS JOURNAL, **99**: 33, 1950.
SCHREINER, G. E.: Proc. Soc. Exper. Biol. & Med., **74**: 117, 1950.
SHIDEMAN, F. E., AND JOHNSON, H. T.: THIS JOURNAL, **92**: 414, 1948.
SHIDEMAN, F. E., RATHBUN, R. C., AND STONEMAN, F.: Am. J. Physiol., **170**: 31, 1952.
SMITH, H. W., FINKELSTEIN, N., ALIMINOSA, L., CRAWFORD, B., AND GRAVER, M.: J. Clin. Investigation, **24**: 388, 1945.
WOODS, L. A., COCHIN, J., FORNEFELD, E. G., AND SEEVERS, M. H.: THIS JOURNAL, **111**: 64, 1954.

A COMPARISON OF SOME PHENOTHIAZINE DERIVATIVES IN INHIBITING APOMORPHINE-INDUCED EMESIS

HERBERT ROSENKILDE AND WILLIAM M. GOVIER

Department of Pharmacology, Research Division, Schering Corporation, Bloomfield, New Jersey

Received for publication February 26, 1957

One of the numerous effects of chlorpromazine, shown by few other drugs, is the suppression of vomiting, experimentally induced or occurring spontaneously in humans in the course of various diseases. Following the original report of Courvoisier *et al.* (1953), other workers have demonstrated the efficacy of chlorpromazine in antagonizing emesis elicited by apomorphine in the dog (Boyd *et al.*, 1953; Cook and Toner, 1954; Brand *et al.*, 1954; Boyd *et al.*, 1955; Glaviano and Wang, 1955), as well as in human volunteers (Isaacs and MacArthur, 1954). Chlorpromazine has been shown to be a valuable agent in the treatment of nausea and vomiting, occurring as a symptom in a multitude of diseases, during pregnancy or as an undesired therapeutic side effect (Friend and Cummins, 1953, 1954; Kent *et al.*, 1954; Moyer *et al.*, 1954; Chinn and Sheldon, 1954; Marks, 1954; Stephan *et al.*, 1955; Fink and Winslow, 1955; Amols and Merritt, 1955). Complications in the treatment, such as drowsiness, orthostatic hypotension, or dryness of the mouth, were usually observed only at higher doses. Since rather large initial doses of chlorpromazine are required in some patients to suppress vomiting, other phenothiazine derivatives were investigated to determine whether any were active at a lower dose level or would specifically inhibit vomiting without showing other marked central nervous system effects. Four compounds were thus compared with chlorpromazine for their activity in blocking apomorphine-induced emesis in the dog (table 1).

METHOD. Apomorphine hydrochloride was used as the emetic agent in a group of seven healthy mongrel dogs, weighing from 10 to 14 kgm. A preliminary apomorphine dose-emetic response curve was obtained by administering four doses of apomorphine intravenously at weekly intervals to a group of seven dogs. Each week the animals were rotated between the four doses so that no dog received the same dose three weeks in succession. This process was continued until eight or nine observations had been collected. The percentage vomiting at each dose was transformed to probits and the weighted probit-log dose regression line computed (Finney, 1952) together with the ED_{95} of apomorphine. This value was 22.7 microgm./kgm. The compound to be evaluated, dissolved in distilled water, was injected intravenously one hour after the dogs were fed, and followed thirty minutes later by the challenging dose of apomorphine. The dogs were observed for about one hour after the last injection for neurological and behavioral changes. Emesis usually occurred 1.5 to 3 minutes after the administration of apomorphine. Only the ejection of gastric contents was taken as a sign of vomiting. Experiments were repeated once a week only in order to prevent any development of tolerance towards the emetic in these animals. Saline controls did not show a conditioning of the vomiting reflex. The probable dose range of the phenothiazine derivatives under study was estimated in the initial trials. Their antiemetic potencies were evaluated against chlorpromazine as the reference standard in a four-square factoral assay (Cochrian and Cox, 1950) in which the drugs were each tested at four levels

TABLE 1

Structural formulas of compounds investigated in the prevention of apomorphine-induced emesis

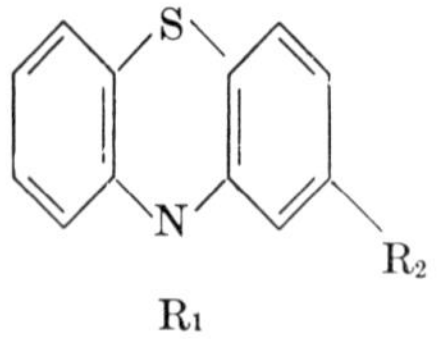

Compound	R_1	R_2
Promazine 10-(3-dimethylaminopropyl)-phenothiazine	CH_2—CH_2—CH_2—N(CH_3)(CH_3)	H
Chlorpromazine 10-(3-dimethylaminopropyl)-2-chlorophenothiazine	CH_2—CH_2—CH_2—N(CH_3)(CH_3)	Cl
Mepazine 10-(1-methyl-3-piperidyl-methyl)-phenothiazine	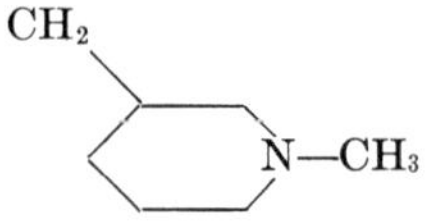	H
Proclorperazine 10-[3-(1-methyl-4-piper-azinyl)-propyl]-2-chloro-phenothiazine	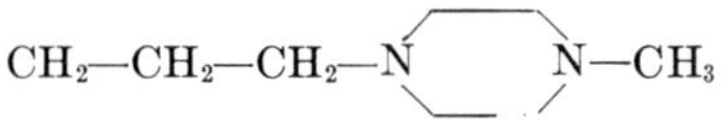	Cl
Sch 3940* 10-{3-[1-(2-hydroxyethyl)-4-piperazinyl]-propyl}-2-chlorophenothiazine	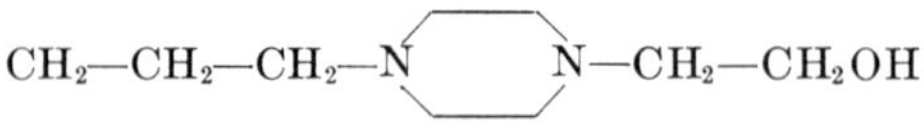	Cl

* Sch 3940 is now known by the generic name of perphenazine and is marketed under the trade name, Trilafon.

with a total three dogs per drug level. The data were analyzed by several iterations with weighted probits and the relative potencies and PD_{50}'s estimated. The latter is the dose of drug which will protect fifty per cent of the animals from vomiting after administration of an ED_{95} of apomorphine.

RESULTS. Sch 3940 was the most potent of all the compounds tested (table 2). By comparison it was approximately twenty-four times as active as chlorpromazine, whereas proclorperazine was three times more effective than chlorpromazine. This last figure compares favorably with the data given by Ducrot and Koetschet (1956), who reported that in the apomorphine test proclorperazine was four times more potent than chlorpromazine.

TABLE 2

The antiemetic PD_{50} and the potency ratios of three phenothiazine derivatives active in inhibiting apomorphine-induced emesis

Compound	PD_{50} *microgm./kgm.*	90 Per Cent Confidence Limits	Potency Ratio	90 Per cent Confidence Limits
Chlorpromazine	78.1	39.1–132.0	1	
Proclorperazine	25.2	15.2– 44.7	3.0	1.2– 6.0
Sch 3940	3.2	1.6– 5.5	24.2	10.7–56.0

Promazine and mepazine were excluded from quantitative experiments, since they showed little or no activity during the preliminary trial. Mepazine failed to protect the dogs from vomiting in doses of 1.5, 3 or 6 mgm./kgm. Promazine was inactive at 1.5 or 3 mgm./kgm., but suppressed vomiting at 6 mgm./kgm.

Central nervous system effects could not be seen, except at the high doses of mepazine and promazine, in which case the dogs exhibited signs of sedation and slight ataxia.

DISCUSSION. Glaviano and Wang (1955) conclude from the results of their experiments that chlorpromazine exerts its antiemetic activity by way of two different mechanisms, depending upon the dose used. In small amounts, chlorpromazine assumedly blocks the apomorphine-sensitive receptors in the chemoceptive emetic trigger zone. Larger amounts may depress the medullary emetic center directly. The mechanism of action of the highly potent antiemetic Sch 3940 has not yet been determined, but it is conceivable that it acts similarly to chlorpromazine by competition with the emetic at the site of the chemoceptive emetic trigger zone.

The question arises as to the relationship of the tranquilizing properties of these compounds to their antiemetic activity. Freedman and Giarman (1956) propose to utilize the apomorphine test as one of the screening procedures for tranquilizing agents. This is a very valuable suggestion and the results of our experiments lend some support to the idea that there may be a rough correlation between tranquilizing and antiemetic effect. However, it should be pointed out that in some instances there may be a wide dissociation between the antiemetic and the tranquilizing component of a drug. Some compounds, particularly those of a non-phenothiazine character, may be overlooked, since even in the case of reserpine the evidence that it possesses anti-emetic properties is equivocal. Thus, Malhutra and Sidhu (1956) reported that reserpine is an effective inhibitor in the apomorphine-induced vomiting response, whereas Ballinger and Borison (1956) found it to be ineffective.

SUMMARY

Four phenothiazine derivatives were compared with chlorpromazine for their inhibitory potencies in apomorphine-induced emesis in dogs. On intravenous injection, Sch 3940 was about twenty-four times, and proclorperazine three times more active than chlorpromazine. With the small doses used, no side effects could be observed. Two other compounds, mepazine and promazine, showed little or no activity in the doses used.

ACKNOWLEDGMENT. We wish to acknowledge the help of Mr. Gordon Thomas, Schering Corporation, Bloomfield, New Jersey for the statistical analysis as well as the valuable technical assistance of Miss Elizabeth Ogilvy and Miss Mary Sawyer.

REFERENCES

AMOLS, W., AND MERRITT, H. H.: Neurology, **5:** 645, 1955.

BALLINGER, C. M., AND BORISON, H. L.: Meeting of the Am. Soc. for Pharmacol. and Exper. Therap., French Lick, Indiana, November 1956.

BOYD, E. M., CASSELL, W. A., AND BOYD, C. E.: Fed Proc., **12:** 303, 1953.

BOYD, E. M., CASSELL, W. A., BOYD, C. E., AND MILLER, J. K.: THIS JOURNAL, **113:** 299, 1955.

BRAND, E. D., HARRIS, T. D., BORISON, H. L., AND GOODMAN, L. S.: THIS JOURNAL, **110:** 86, 1954.

CHINN, H. I., AND SHELDON, G. L.: Proc. Soc. Exper. Biol. & Med., **86:** 293, 1954.

COCHRIAN, W. G., AND COX, G. M.: Experimental Design. John Wiley, New York, p. 215, 1950.

COOK, L., AND TONER, J. J.: THIS JOURNAL, **110:** 12, 1954.

COURVOISIER, S., FOURNEL, J., DUCROT, R., KOLSKY, M., AND KOETSCHET, P.: Arch. internat. de pharmacodyn., **92:** 305, 1953.

DUCROT, R., AND KOETSCHET, P.: Abstr. of Communications, 20th Internat. Physiological Congress, Brussels, p. 258, 1956.

FINK, S., AND WINSLOW, W. A.: Gastroenterology, **28:** 731, 1955.

FINNEY, D. J.: Statistical Methods in Biological Assay. Hafner Publishing Co., New York, p. 468, 1952.

FREEDMAN, D. X., AND GIARMAN, N. J.: Science, **124:** 264, 1956.

FRIEND, D. G., AND CUMMINS, J. F.: J.A.M.A., **153:** 480, 1953.

FRIEND, D. G., AND CUMMINS, J. F.: New England J. Med., **250:** 997, 1954.

GLAVIANO, V. V., AND WANG, S. C.: THIS JOURNAL, **114:** 358, 1955.

ISAACS, B., AND MACARTHUR, J. G.: Lancet, **2:** 570, 1954.

KENT, B., MORRIS, G., ROGERS, S., AND KNIGHT, R.: THIS JOURNAL, **110:** 29, 1954.

MALHUTRA, C. L., AND SIDHU, R. K.: THIS JOURNAL, **116:** 123, 1956.

MARKS, J. H.: New England J. Med., **250:** 999, 1954.

MOYER, J. H., KENT, B., KNIGHT, R. W., MORRIS, R., DIZON, M., ROGERS, S., AND SPURR, C.: Am. J. Med. Sci., **228:** 174, 1954.

STEPHEN, C. R., DENT, S., AND BOURGEOIS-GAVARDIN, M.: Arch. Int. Med., **96:** 794, 1955.

THE EFFECT OF CHLORPROMAZINE ON FEAR-MOTIVATED BEHAVIOR IN RATS[1]

ROBERT E. MILLER, JOHN V. MURPHY AND I. ARTHUR MIRSKY

Department of Clinical Science, School of Medicine, University of Pittsburgh

Received for publication February 27, 1957

A number of pharmacological agents are now in rather widespread clinical use for the purpose of alleviating emotional disturbances, especially those characterized by fear and/or anxiety. These "tranquilizing agents" appear to reduce tension and anxiety without markedly affecting the patients' cognitive or motor behavior. The present experiments were designed to quantify the effects of one such agent, chlorpromazine, on a fear-motivated response in rats.

Mowrer (1950) has developed a theoretical system in which fear and anxiety are of prime importance. According to this theory, a stimulus which occurs contiguously with a noxious stimulus acquires the property of eliciting anticipation of the noxious stimulus. This anticipation of pain is what Mowrer defines as fear or anxiety. One well-standardized technique for presenting such stimulus combinations is avoidance conditioning. The conditioned avoidance stimulus elicits fear in the conditioned subject since it is followed by punishment. The only way the subject can avoid the noxious stimulation is to perform a response arbitrarily designated by the experimenter as the "correct response." If the subject performs this response, the "conditioned response", each time the conditioned avoidance stimulus is presented, he avoids the noxious stimulus. Thus, in avoidance learning, the subject at first is motivated by pain but later learns to avoid this pain by responding appropriately when the fear-eliciting stimulus is presented.

The first of three studies to be reported was designed to determine the effects of various dosage levels of chlorpromazine[2] on the extinction of a conditioned avoidance response. Single treatments of the drug were administered and the effects were determined for nine consecutive hours. Since this initial experiment clearly indicated that chlorpromazine administration reduced fear-motivated behavior as a function of dosage, a second experiment was performed to determine whether the obtained results could be attributed simply to a motor and/or sensory deficit consequent to chlorpromazine administration or to an effect of the agent on the motivation of fear. Finally, the third investigation which utilized the information obtained from the other two experiments was designed in a bioassay framework, thus enabling more precise determinations of the effects of chlorpromazine on the fear motivated response.

[1] This research was supported in part by a grant (M487C2) from the National Institute of Mental Health, National Institutes of Health, Public Health Service, and in part by a grant from the Foundations' Fund for Research in Psychiatry.

[2] We are indebted to Smith, Kline, and French Laboratories for generous supplies of Thorazine.

METHOD. *Experiment I.* Male rats of the Carworth strain, weighing from 300 to 350 grams were used. The animals were first conditioned to avoid a painful electric shock. This was accomplished by placing the animals in a modified two-compartment conditioning apparatus (Murphy and Miller, 1955). On each conditioning trial a buzzer was activated and, in the event that the animal did not perform the appropriate instrumental response within five seconds, an electric shock was delivered through a grid floor. In order to escape the shock the animal was required to cross a two-inch barrier which separated the two compartments in the apparatus. If the rat made a barrier-crossing response during the initial five seconds when the buzzer was sounding but shock was not present, the conditioned stimulus was immediately terminated and the subject avoided the shock completely. Fifteen conditioning trials were presented each day for fifteen consecutive days. The intertrial intervals were progressively diminished over the fifteen day conditioning period since such a procedure has been found to produce rapid conditioning with significantly prolonged extinction while tripling the number of subjects which can be tested in any given time interval (Murphy and Miller, 1956).

On the day following completion of conditioning trials the tests with chlorpromazine were begun. An extinction procedure was used throughout, that is, the buzzer was not followed by electric shock regardless of whether or not the animal made a barrier-crossing response to the buzzer. In the event that the animal failed to cross the barrier within five seconds, the buzzer was terminated. Each rat was first given a ten-trial control test in the apparatus. Animals which did not perform at least eight conditioned responses were excluded from further participation in the experiment as they did not evidence satisfactory avoidance conditioning. Thirty-six animals which met this criterion were divided randomly into four groups. Group I (N = 7) received an injection of 0.75 ml. of normal saline per kgm. of body weight. The remaining groups were injected with chlorpromazine as follows: Group II (N = 9) with 0.25 mgm. per kgm.; Group III (N = 10) with 0.75 mgm. per kgm.; and Group IV (N = 10) with 1.25 mgm. per kgm. All injections were administered subcutaneously. Each animal was tested for ten trials on an extinction procedure one hour following the injection and received an additional ten trials each hour for the next eight hours.

Experiment II. The apparatus used to assess motor deficits following drug administration was an escape runway. This runway was eight feet long, six inches wide, and 18 inches high. The floor was an electrifiable grid constructed of ⅛ inch stainless steel rods. A wooden goal box was located at one end of the runway and was accessible to the rat through a three inch opening in the end of the runway located three inches above the grid floor. A shock (110 volts with 85,000 ohms in series with the animal) was on the grid continuously.

Groups of gentled rats were trained on the escape runway. The animal was placed at the end of the runway facing the goal box eight feet away. Since the grid was constantly electrified and the rat had no other possibilities for escape, it was strongly motivated to run the length of the alley and jump into the goal box which was not electrified. The latency of running was measured to the nearest $\frac{1}{10}$ second from placement on the grid to entrance into the goal box. After each trial the animal was placed in a carrying cage for at least four minutes before the next trial. Ten trials were administered each day. The training period was continued for five days. Determinations were then made of deficit in running speed following treatment with chlorpromazine and phenobarbital. A dosage level of one of the agents was injected two hours prior to the daily testing session in the escape runway. On alternate days the injection was always saline solution so that any interaction or residual effects of drug administration were minimized. As an additional precaution, the animals were divided into two groups with counterbalanced treatment and saline control runs to insure that day effects were controlled.

The initial determinations were made for 1.2 mgm. per kgm. of chlorpromazine and for a comparable volume of normal saline solution. When the escape time deficit attributable to that dosage of chlorpromazine had been ascertained, the dosage level of phenobarbital sodium required to produce an equivalent deficit was determined. On succeeding tests 25

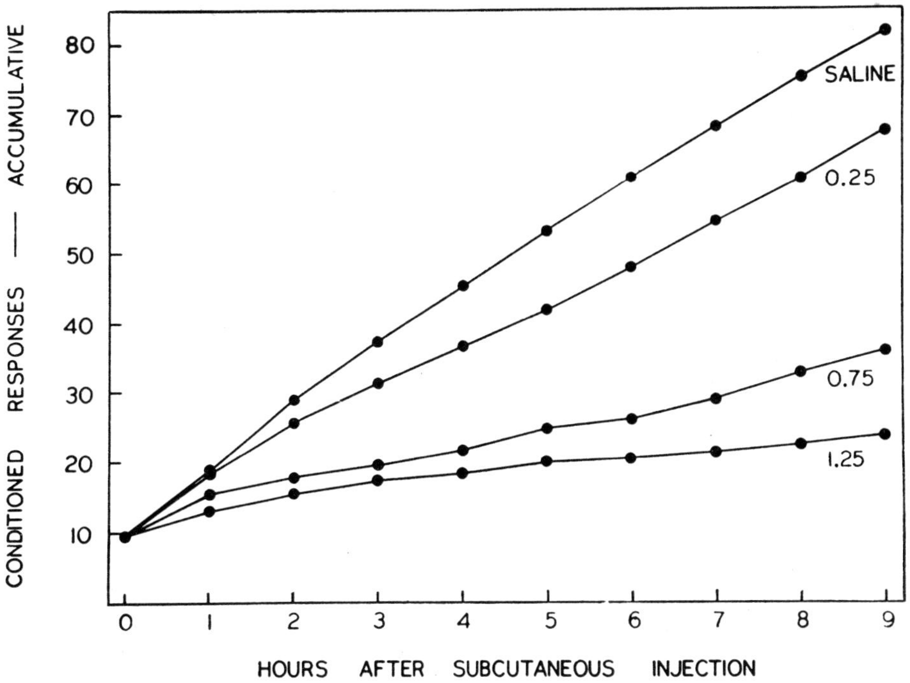

FIG. 1. The effect of chlorpromazine on an avoidance conditioned response. Numerals refer to dosage levels of chlorpromazine in mgm. per kgm. of body weight.

mgm., 40 mgm., and 50 mgm. of phenobarbital were tested. As before, each determination was followed the next day by a saline control run.

Next, an additional group of 25 animals were avoidance conditioned in the two compartment conditioning apparatus as described in Experiment I. The only procedural change in conditioning was that 10 rather than 15 trials were given daily for the 15-day conditioning period.

After conditioning was completed the assay procedure was begun. As before, a ten-trial control test was given with the criterion that animals making fewer than 80 per cent of the responses were excluded from further participation. The remaining animals (N = 19) were divided randomly into two groups. One group was given injections of 40 mgm. per kgm. of phenobarbital while the other group received 1.2 mgm. per kgm. of chlorpromazine. At periods of two and four hours after administration of the agents the animals were given ten trial tests in the two compartment apparatus using an extinction procedure.

Experiment III. Forty-eight Carworth rats were avoidance conditioned in the two compartment apparatus. The conditioning trials were conducted at the rate of 10 trials per day for 15 days using the diminishing interval procedure.

On the day following completion of conditioning a control test of ten trials was run on an extinction procedure. As before, any animal not performing at least 80 per cent avoidance responses was discarded. The 40 animals which met this criterion were randomly divided into four treatment groups of ten animals each. These groups were then injected with 0.3, 0.6, and 1.2 mgm. per kgm. of chlorpromazine; and 0.6 ml. per kgm. of normal saline respectively. Tests in the two compartment avoidance apparatus were conducted at two and four hours after injection.

RESULTS. *Experiment I.* The results are summarized in figure 1. It can be seen that there was an effect of chlorpromazine on avoidance responding. Further, there appeared to be a relationship between the dosage level of the drug and the subsequent decrement in avoidance responding. A repeated measures analysis of variance (Edwards, 1950) indicated that these differences between dosage levels were statistically significant ($p < 0.001$).

The number of avoidance responses were then transformed by $\sqrt{Y + 0.5}$. The relationships between these transformed data and the log of the dosage administered were determined for each of the nine hourly samples by the method of Bliss (1952). In addition, homogeneity of variance was tested for each sample (Bartlett, 1937). It was found that the variances were homogeneous for the range 2 to 6 hours after administration of the chlorpromazine. The log dose and the amount of avoidance responding were found to be linear throughout these same samples.

Experiment II. The rapidity of learning in the escape runway testified to the simplicity of the task. Within a very few training trials the animals had eliminated random behavior and were running directly to the goal box when placed on the grid. The latency curve approached the asymptote on the third training day.

The mean latency of escape two hours after injection of normal saline was 2.12 seconds for the entire group of 20 rats. The running time for these same animals two hours after treatment with 1.2 mgm. per kgm. of chlorpromazine was 2.85 seconds. The retardation in running time following injection of chlorpromazine was found to be significant beyond the 0.01 level with a "t" test.

It was found that 40 mgm. per kgm. of phenobarbital most closely approximated the deficit in running time obtained with 1.2 mgm. per kgm. of chlorpromazine. The mean escape time two hours after treatment with the 40 mgm. level of phenobarbital was 3.09 seconds as compared to 2.85 seconds with the 1.2 mgm. level of chlorpromazine. The difference between these means was not significant.

The tests in the two-compartment conditioning apparatus (figure 2) clearly indicated that chlorpromazine inhibited the avoidance response while the comparable dosage of phenobarbital did not affect the response. A repeated measures analysis of variance indicated that the difference in rate of avoidance responding between the two groups was significant beyond the 0.001 level.

Thus, while the dosage levels of 1.2 mgm. per kgm. of chlorpromazine and 40 mgm. per kgm. of phenobarbital were equivalent in terms of amount of deficit which they produced in the escape runway, they were significantly different in terms of their effect on avoidance responding. The escape task was selected for study because it required little from the animal in terms of discrimination learning; it minimized to a very great extent the anticipatory and orienting responses; and presumably was largely dependent on motor coordination. If motor effects or sedation were important factors in the effect of chlorpromazine on avoidance behavior, the phenobarbital group should have exhibited a comparable decrement in avoidance responding. Since no such decrement was observed it seems logical to conclude that the chlorpromazine effect was primarily mediated by altering the response to a fear-eliciting stimulus.

Experiment III. The results of this experiment are shown in figure 3. A re-

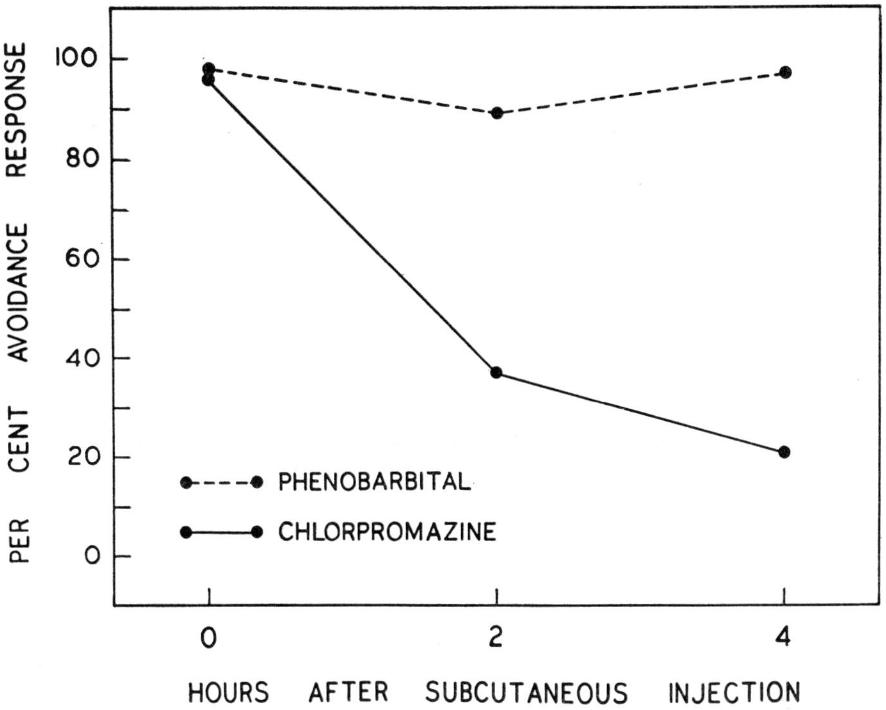

FIG. 2. The effects of chlorpromazine and phenobarbital on a conditioned avoidance response.

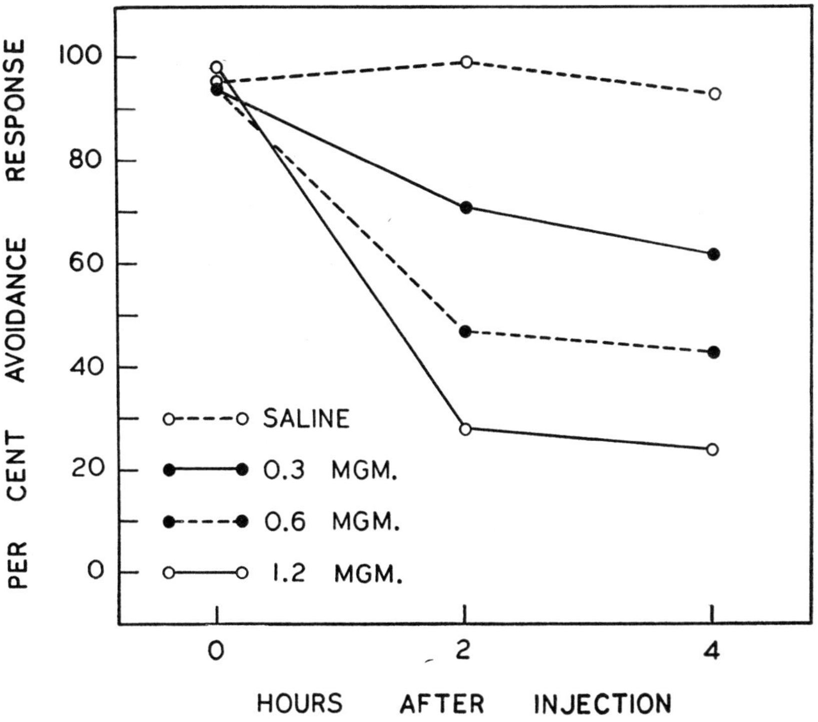

FIG. 3. The effect of subcutaneous injection of chlorpromazine on conditioned avoidance behavior.

Dosage levels are in terms of mgm. per kgm. of body weight.

TABLE 1

The relationships between the log of the dose of chlorpromazine and the amount of avoidance responding in an assay procedure with determinations two and four hours after administration

Number of avoidance responses have been transformed by $\sqrt{Y + 0.5}$.

Hours after Administration	Formula of Best-fit Line		Slope	λ	Homogeneity of Variance?
2	Y = 1.7325	−1.64 X	−1.64	0.52	Yes
4	Y = 1.666	−1.279 X	−1.279	0.75	Yes
2 and 4 combined	Y = 2.337	−2.11 X	−2.11	0.60	Yes

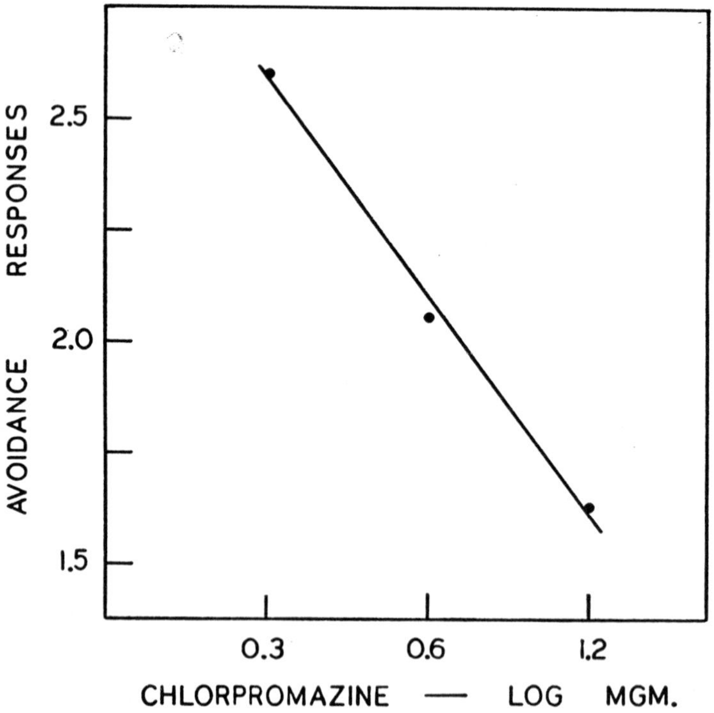

FIG. 4. The relationship between the log of the dose of chlorpromazine and the amount of avoidance behavior two hours after administration.

The number of avoidance responses have been transformed by $\sqrt{Y + 0.5}$.

peated measures analysis of variance (Edwards, 1950) indicated that the differences in avoidance responding resulting from dosage levels were significant beyond the 0.01 level. The data were then analyzed using the Bliss procedure. As in Experiment I, the avoidance data were transformed by $\sqrt{Y + 0.5}$. The formula of the best-fit line, index of precision, and slope are presented in table 1 for the test periods at two hours, four hours, and two and four hours combined. In each analysis Bartlett's Test indicated that the variances were homogeneous. The analysis of variance of the log dose-response data showed that the relationship was linear (figure 4) for each test separately and for both tests combined.

DISCUSSION. The results of these experiments have indicated that chlorpromazine has an effect on extinction of a fear-motivated response in rats. The administration of chlorpromazine produced significant decrements in the amount of avoidance responding within one hour after treatment (figure 1) and these effects were maintained for the higher dosage levels throughout the succeeding nine hours of tests.

The second experiment was perhaps the most significant of the three investigations. While the results of Experiment I clearly demonstrated that conditioned rats treated with chlorpromazine did diminish their avoidance responding to the conditioned stimulus, it was not known whether this decrement was attributable to a specific effect of the agent on the fear elicited by the conditioned stimulus or to an effect on some other system. This kind of problem has been discussed by Brady (1953) with regard to tetraethylammonium.

The second experiment was designed, therefore, to determine whether the previous results might be attributable to motor effects or to general sedative or debilitating effects of the drug. One premise which we have accepted is that fear and/or anxiety is invariably reflected in motor behavior. It follows that any alteration in the affective level will likewise be accompanied by a change in motor behavior. According to this assumption, then, an effective tranquilizer would be expected to alter motor responsivity as well as emotional responsivity. However, it must be shown that the decrement in avoidance responding was not a direct sedative or motor effect that there was, in addition, a decrement in the affective response to the buzzer.

The plan of attack on this problem was to determine quantitatively the amount of deficit induced by a given amount of chlorpromazine in a highly motivated task which involved primarily motor behavior. When this deficit had been determined, another pharmacological product which also produces sedative and motor effects was tested. The agent selected for this purpose was sodium phenobarbital which sedates and produces motor incoordination but is not generally regarded as a tranquilizer. The phenobarbital was tested at several dosage levels until a dosage was determined which disrupted motor behavior in an amount commensurate with a given level of chlorpromazine. These dosages of chlorpromazine and phenobarbital were then considered empirically equivalent in terms of motor and/or sedative effect.

The comparable levels of the two materials were then tested on the fear-motivated behavior in the avoidance apparatus. Since it was found (figure 2) that chlorpromazine administration produced significant decrements in avoidance responding while the comparable dosage of sodium phenobarbital had no effect on avoidance behavior, it was concluded that the motor deficits consequent to chlorpromazine treatment were not sufficient to account for the obtained decrement in the fear-motivated responses.

The simple avoidance conditioning method was found to be quite efficient in the determinations of chlorpromazine effect. Experiment III demonstrated that sufficient numbers of animals could be tested within a relatively short time and that the data obtained were amenable to analysis with bio-assay statistics which provided an index of the precision of the test as well as the log-dosage relationships. It would appear that this method might prove useful in comparisons between various tranquilizing agents. If two or more such agents were empirically equated for motor deficits in the straight runway test, subsequent determinations of the comparable dosage levels in the conditioned avoidance situation would enable comparisons of relative potency of the agents in alleviating fear-motivated behavior.

Several other techniques have been used for the determination of psychological effects of pharmacological treatment. A method deriving from Estes and Skinner (1941) has been used by Brady (1953) and by Hill *et al.* (1954). In this procedure measures of the inhibition of an operant feeding response by a "conditioned emotional response" (CER) are obtained. Variables which affect the emotional responsivity of the animal are detectable in terms of rate of operant responding during the period when the conditioned emotional stimulus is present. An advantage of this method is that some quantitative indication as to impairment of motor and/or motivational systems is available on every test session. However, this method involves intensive testing of single animals and is subject therefore to the limitations inherent in small sample research. The data are customarily presented in terms of response rate curves for a single animal tested under a number of treatment conditions. The generality and predictive power of data derived from one subject are, of course, considerably less than that of large sample data.

Other investigators have reported studies in which the effect of "tranquilizing" agents on avoidance conditioning were determined (Cook *et al.*, 1955; Weiskrantz and Wilson, 1955). In these experiments the tranquilizers were administered during the conditioning of the animals. If the animal failed to respond to the avoidance stimulus the painful unconditioned stimulus was presented. The determination of effects of "tranquilizing" agents during the conditioning phase is complicated by the confounding of both conditioned fear to the conditioned stimulus and pain upon presentation of the unconditioned stimulus. The use of an extinction procedure (shock disconnected) as in the present technique eliminates the painful stimulus. Accordingly, the effects of the agents are related to the psychological meaning of the conditioned stimulus, *i.e.*, to fear or anxiety.

SUMMARY AND CONCLUSIONS

The relationships between chlorpromazine and fear-motivated behavior were investigated. Rats were conditioned to fear a buzzer in an avoidance conditioning situation. Then chlorpromazine was administered at several dosage levels to groups of conditioned animals and samples of avoidance behavior were measured at specified time intervals. The data were analyzed by means of bio-assay statistics. The log of the dosage of chlorpromazine administered and the amount of avoidance behavior were found to be linearly related. A procedure was described which demonstrated that the observed decrements in avoidance behavior were not attributable to motor and/or sedative effects of the drug.

REFERENCES

Bartlett, M. S.: J. Roy. Stat. Soc. Supplement, **4:** 137, 1937.
Bliss, C. I.: The Statistics of Bioassay, Academic Press, New York, 1952.

BRADY, J. V.: J. Comp. Physiol. Psychol., **46:** 307, 1953.
COOK, L., WEIDLEY, E. F., MORRIS, R. W., AND MATTIS, P. A.: THIS JOURNAL, **113:** 11, 1955.
EDWARDS, A. L.: Experimental Design in Psychological Research, Rinehart, New York, 1950.
ESTES, W. K., AND SKINNER, B. F.: J. Exp. Psychol., **29:** 390, 1941.
HILL, H. E., BELLEVILLE, R. E., AND WIKLER, A.: Proc. Soc. Exper. Biol. & Med., **86:** 881, 1954.
MOWRER, O. H.: Learning Theory and Personality Dynamics, Ronald Press, New York, 1950.
MURPHY, J. V., AND MILLER, R. E.: J. Comp. Physiol. Psychol., **48:** 47, 1955.
MURPHY, J. V., AND MILLER, R. E.: J. Exp. Psychol., **52:** 77, 1956.
WEISKRANTZ, L., AND WILSON, W. A.: Ann. N. Y. Acad. Sci., **61:** 36, 1955.

USE OF DIFFERENTIAL BAR-PRESSING RATES OF RATS FOR SCREENING ANALGESIC DRUGS. I. TECHNIQUES AND EFFECTS OF MORPHINE

HARRIS E. HILL, FRANK T. PESCOR, RICHARD E. BELLEVILLE AND ABRAHAM WIKLER

U. S. Department of Health, Education, and Welfare, Public Health Service, National Institute of Mental Health, Addiction Research Center, Lexington, Kentucky

Received for publication February 28, 1957

The results of a number of investigations on human subjects in this laboratory support the hypothesis that one important action of potent analgesic drugs such as morphine is reduction of pain-anticipatory anxiety. It was shown that a) an analgesic dose (15 mgm. of morphine) reduces the overestimation of intensities of painful shock which occurs when anxiety is not allayed in the experimental situation (Hill *et al.*, 1952), and b) morphine reduces the disrupting effects of anticipation of painful shock penalties upon visuo-manual reaction time, an action not shared by a sedative dose (250 mgm.) of pentobarbital (Hill *et al.*, 1955). It was hypothesized further that reduction of pain-anticipatory anxiety is a necessary, though perhaps not a sufficient, action that a drug must exert in order to be a potent analgesic. Further confirmation of this hypothesis would require that all known potent analgesic agents share this action in common, and that at least some, if not all, new drugs which reduce pain-anticipatory anxiety should prove to be potent analgesics.

Because of difficulties inherent in human experimentation, it appeared advisable to develop an animal-testing technique based on similar principles. Escape or avoidance conditioning techniques were considered unsuitable since one characteristic of "clinical" pain is that the sufferer can neither escape from nor avoid the noxious stimulus. On the other hand, the method of Estes and Skinner (1941) seemed to provide a suitable model of pain-anticipatory anxiety, since in this situation the animal can neither escape nor avoid the electric shock which is used to induce the "conditioned emotional response" (anxiety). Accordingly, a modified form of this technique was employed (Hill *et al.*, 1954), and it was found that shock-conditioned inhibition of bar-pressing was reduced to a degree proportional to the dose of morphine. The inference that such restoration of bar-pressing rate was due to direct reduction of pain-anticipatory anxiety was based upon certain additional observations and a number of assumptions. Thus, it was noted that such restoration occurred even though morphine slowed the bar-pressing rates of hungry animals motivated by a food reward. If reduction of "hunger" were a determining factor, intensification, rather than attenuation of conditioned inhibition of bar-pressing would be expected. In addition, since some influence of the conditioned stimulus (tone) was found under all doses of morphine, it was assumed that, as in man (Hill *et al.*, 1952; Wikler *et al.*, 1945), simple discrimination was not impaired; if this were not the case, decreased inhibition might occur through auditory impairment.

The objectives of the present series of studies were to determine to what extent such actions of morphine are reproducible, and to what extent they are shared by other analgesics, as well as by compounds with little or no analgesic properties. In addition to the measures already described (Hill *et al.*, 1954) two other measures were utilized to delineate further the differential actions of all drugs studied, in the expectation that they might reveal effects of these agents other than reduction of pain-anxiety, which might enhance the usefulness of the method as a "screening" procedure for the detection of analgesics. These included "time-action" curves (the effects of a given drug upon food-rewarded bar-pressing rates as a function of time after administration of the agent), and "operant level" curves (the effects of a given drug upon the unrewarded bar-pressing rates of untrained animals as a function of time spent in the Skinner Box). The present report is concerned only with the details of the apparatus and procedures and the results obtained with morphine. The data obtained with the other drugs will be presented in subsequent papers.

METHODS AND MATERIALS. *Subjects.* The 128 Wistar rats utilized were four months old when the experiment began. They were housed in a quiet air-conditioned room in individual cages. Food and water were available at all times for one month, after which food was limited to amounts which would gradually reduce the animals to 70 per cent of their individual satiation weights. Thereafter, the animals were weighed daily and fed according to their gain or loss. This procedure stabilized the animal at 70 ± 1 per cent of their satiation weight.

Apparatus.[1] A Skinner Box (Skinner, 1938) modified to accommodate animals working under drug conditions was employed. A conditioning chamber (8 x 7 x 10 inches) was mounted in a partially soundproof box (14 x 14 x 18 inches). The bar was similar to that described by Skinner and was constructed to depress at approximately 9 grams. Because the higher doses of several drugs produce some neuromuscular impairment, the bar in the "up" position was lowered to 2½ inches from the grid floor. Because it had to be depressed a certain distance to set the feeder mechanism for food delivery, the presentation of a click was synchronized with the "setting" mechanism to provide a discriminative stimulus. To prevent holding of the bar in a depressed position, the automatic feeding device was set to deliver a food pellet (0.1 gm.), after the appropriate elapsed time, only when the bar was released. Food was dispensed automatically by a rotary disc feeder at aperiodic intervals with a two-minute mean.

The floor of the inner chamber was a grid, consisting of $\frac{3}{16}''$ brass rods, spaced $\frac{11}{16}''$ from center to center, running at a 45° angle. The shock was delivered to the grid by means of a variable auto-transformer within a range of 40 to 80 volts with a duration of 0.5 second. A small speaker fastened to the inside of the lid 12 inches from the bar was used as a sound source for the conditioned auditory stimulus. Facilities were not available for direct measurement of this stimulus (tone generated by a 50 to 60 cycle, irregular wave input). However, the intensity of the tone used throughout the present studies was one which just failed to produce a "driving" effect (increased bar-pressing rate due to presentation of the tone *per se*) in control and morphine rates under food reinforcement prior to pairing of the tone with electric shock.

[1] Acknowledgment is gratefully made for assistance rendered by Mr. H. G. Flanary and Mr. W. M. Procop in the construction and maintenance of the apparatus used in these investigations.

Experiment A. Unconditioned bar-pressing. The animals utilized for this part of the study had been maintained on the stabilized feeding schedule and had not been used previously on any test procedure. They were deprived of food for twenty-four hours. No training was given. Each animal was tested in the apparatus for one hour and responses were cumulated on counters for the first and second 30-minute periods. This measurement gave the rate of unconditioned bar pressing, since no food reinforcement was given. Different groups of animals were tested on control (no injection), a morphine placebo (pH 6.45) subcutaneously, and 9 mgm./kgm. of a 0.5 per cent solution of morphine subcutaneously (N's were 30, 20, and 14 respectively). Reported rates were recorded after the animals had had three previous trials in the apparatus under morphine and control conditions. At this time the initially high operant rates had decreased and were at a rather stable level. Testing was begun 60 minutes after injection. Differences in the rates obtained on the three conditions were evaluated by the Rank Test (Edwards, 1955).

Experiment B. Time-action effects of morphine on conditioned bar pressing. Bar pressing for food pellets was conditioned to high and consistent rates (approximately 14 to 16 depressions per minute). The animals were maintained at 70 per cent of satiation weight and were deprived of food for approximately twenty-four hours. Time-action effects were obtained on 9 mgm./kgm. of morphine, the morphine placebo and control.

Responses during a 12-minute control period were recorded on automatic counters. The placebo or morphine was then injected and the rats were immediately returned to the Skinner Box and a second 12-minute count was made. Successive measures of rate were obtained in this manner every 24 minutes thereafter, two animals being alternately tested in each experimental box over a period of 108 minutes from time of injection. A mean was calculated for each 12-minute interval and these were expressed as 4-minute means. The statistical significance of drug effects at each time interval were computed by the Rank Test.

Experiment C. Conditioned inhibition of bar pressing. A new group of animals was employed using the controlled weight and feeding schedule already described. After 10 to 15 daily sessions in the apparatus the animals were trained on tone-shock inhibition three days a week. After an animal had been bar-pressing for several minutes a tone was sounded which was terminated at the time shock was applied to the grid. Until inhibition was fairly well established the shock was applied manually to avoid direct punishment of the bar-pressing response. Three tone-shock pairings were used for the first two conditioning days, with tone intervals of 5, 10 and 15 seconds. For the next two conditioning days two tone-shock pairings of 10 and 30 seconds were used. Subsequently, the tone interval was gradually lengthened to four minutes using only one pairing at each daily session. The shock was controlled automatically for the remainder of the study. Inhibition of bar pressing was achieved in 10 to 12 days. Shock intensity was set at 40 volts for initial conditioning but was later adjusted to a value which maintained each animal at an optimal level of bar-pressing and conditioned inhibition.

These procedures resulted in a high rate of response for approximately eight minutes followed by nearly complete cessation during the 4-minute tone, with immediate resumption of the high rate following shock. These procedures were repeated three times weekly, on Monday, Wednesday and Friday. Each Monday constituted a reconditioning of the tone-shock effect. Control data were obtained on Wednesday and drugs were tested on Friday. Three 4-minute counts of rate were obtained; the first covered the period immediately preceding the tone, the second covered the four minutes of tone presentation, and the third covered the period following the shock.

The earlier study of the effects of morphine on conditioned inhibition (Hill *et al.*, 1954) was repeated to verify the dose-effect curves. The doses used were 3, 5, 7, 9, 1, and 11 mgm./kgm. given in this order. To prevent the development of tolerance these doses were tested at weekly intervals; no animal received drugs more than once per week. This phase of the study was followed by the concurrent testing of eight other drugs using a randomized experimental design. Five, 7, and 9 mgm./kgm. of morphine were again included in the series to further verify the morphine effect.

When a high dose (7 to 11 mgm./kgm.) of morphine was administered for the first time, a large proportion (50 to 100 per cent) of the animals failed to operate the bar during the pretone period. Subsequently, the incidence of such failures was greatly reduced; nevertheless, the records of animals that did not attain at least ten responses in the pretone period were discarded for that particular day. The t-test was used for calculating the significance of the differences between means. Drug-produced changes were determined by expressing pretone rate under drug conditions as a per cent of that on the control day, using each animal as its own control.

Calculations of per cent restoration during the tone-shock period were based on performance during the 4-minute pretone period, since most drugs produce some change in rate of response. Results are presented both as mean percentages and mean rates. No animals were included in final tabulations if their control tone-shock values exceeded 25 per cent of the pretone rate. Only very occasionally was it necessary to eliminate an animal for this reason; actually, very few exceeded 10 per cent. Tests of significance were applied to demonstrate range of effect and the reliability of measures obtained for the randomized and non-randomized experimental designs.

Post-shock data were treated in the same manner as were those of the tone-shock period. Both absolute rate and percentages of pretone rate were calculated. The differences between means under various drug conditions were evaluated by the t-test (Edwards, 1955).

Patterning effects. In utilizing patterns of effects for screening purposes, the dose of each drug was used that produced the greatest restoration without at the same time producing hypnosis or marked neuromuscular impairment. With morphine, this appears to be from 9 to 10 mgm./kgm. Thus, for the purposes of this study only pattern effects of 9 mgm./kgm. are presented (table 1, figure 1).

RESULTS. *Experiment A. Unconditioned bar pressing.* The results on unconditioned bar-pressing under control, placebo, and 9 mgm./kgm. of morphine are presented in table 1 and figure 1. A substantial drop of about two-thirds of the operant rate occurred on both control and placebo conditions from the first to the second half-hour period. Morphine administration resulted in an extreme reduction of this unconditioned bar-pressing; the mean rate during the entire hour period was less than one response. However, the bar-pressing rates during the first half-hour were quite similar to those in the second.

Experiment B. Time-action effects of morphine on conditioned bar pressing rate. During control determinations, a mean of 67 responses per 4-minute period was recorded for the first 12 minutes. A similar rate was maintained across the time dimension although several slight, non-significant changes appeared (figure 1). The placebo group showed an initially lower rate than the control animals, but no significant differences were found on any of the time-periods. Rate of responding diminished rapidly following administration of morphine. This decrease in rate continued to a maximal effect which held for 36 to 84 minutes after injection. Comparisons of control and placebo with morphine revealed significant differences at the 0.01-level for all time periods. The point of greatest action of morphine corresponds quite closely to the time when this drug was tested for its anxiety reducing potency. Reduction of the unconditioned rate (Experiment A) was much greater than the reduction of the conditioned bar pressing rate. The mean for the latter was 30.7 per cent of the control rate, whereas the unconditioned rate at the same time interval after injection was 3.7 per cent of control.

Experiment C. Conditioned inhibition of bar pressing. Dose-effect relationships of these measures are shown in table 2 and figure 2. Results of the first tests in

TABLE 1

Mean response rates under three drug conditions for operant level, time-action, and pattern of inhibition

Operant level

Drug Condition	Period 1 (30 minutes)	Period 2 (30 Minutes)	N
Control	16.7	7.5	30
Placebo	11.9	5.7	20
Morphine	0.3	0.6	12

Time action

Drug Condition	Before Injection	Minutes After Injection					N
		12	36	60	84	108	
Control	66.5	70.8	68.2	63.2	62.7	62.6	12
Placebo	53.5	60.9	59.2	64.8	66.8	63.9	12
Morphine	54.3	26.5	13.3	9.6	18.2	24.6	12

Pattern of inhibition

(Combined "consecutive" and "randomized" order studies)

Drug Condition	Pre-Tone	Tone-Shock	Post-Shock	N
Control	42.7	2.2 (5.2%)*	52.6 (123%)*	27
Placebo	35.3	2.8 (7.9%)*	42.0 (119%)*	12
Morphine	27.0	22.4 (83%)*	20.5 (75%)*	27

* Per cent of pre-tone rate.

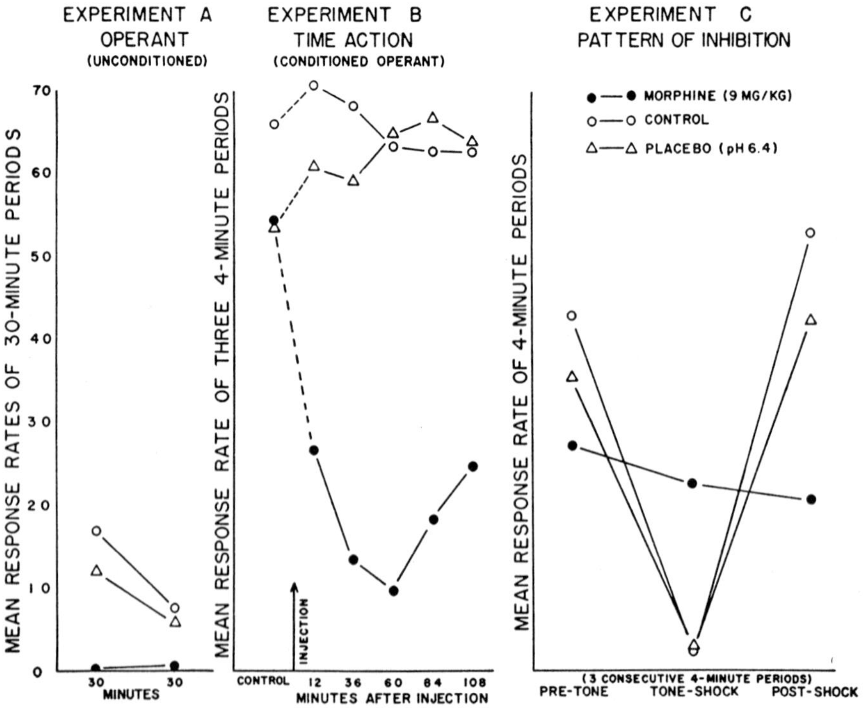

FIG. 1. The effects of 9 mgm./kgm. of morphine upon response-patterns obtained in three experimental procedures.

TABLE 2

Comparison of the effects of various morphine dosages on pre-tone, tone-shock, and post-shock response rates ("consecutive order" study)

Pre-tone

Drug Condition	Control Rate	Drug Rate	S.E. Diff.	N	P	% of Control (Charted Value)
Placebo	35.3	35.3	3.88	12	>0.05	100
Morphine (mgm./kgm.)						
1	27.8	33.2	4.59	10	>0.05	119
3	42.5	32.5	6.81	12	>0.05	77
5	46.2	35.2	6.79	11	>0.05	76
7	46.3	28.4	4.38	14	<0.01	61
9	40.0	25.8	3.29	11	<0.01	65
11	39.0	24.8	3.83	11	<0.01	62

Tone-shock

Drug Condition	Tone Rate Control	Tone Rate Drug	*	N	P	% of Pre-tone (Charted value)
Placebo	1.9	2.8		12	>0.05	9
Morphine (mgm./kgm.)						
1	1.6	3.0		10	>0.05	10
3	2.0	7.6		12	<0.05	20
5	6.8	14.6		11	>0.05	44
7	2.4	22.1		14	<0.01	75
9	5.1	22.5		11	<0.01	88
11	1.6	20.6		11	<0.01	84

Post-shock

Drug Condition	Pre-Tone Rate	Post-Shock Rate	S.E. Diff.	N	P	% of Pre-tone (Charted Value)
Placebo	35.2	42.0	4.91	12	>0.05	123
Morphine (mgm./kgm.)						
1	33.2	31.9	7.19	10	>0.05	107
3	32.5	26.7	5.13	12	>0.05	97
5	35.2	13.0	3.95	11	<0.01	35
7	28.4	22.2	2.32	14	<0.05	75
9	25.8	12.9	2.72	11	<0.01	54
11	24.8	14.0	2.58	11	<0.01	60

* Calculated by non-parametric technique.

which only morphine was used are labeled "Consecutive" order; "Randomized" order refers to results obtained when morphine doses were tested with eight other drugs. Pretone rates on both orders were reduced progressively by increasing doses of morphine. The reductions in rate on 7, 9, and 11 mgm./kgm. were statistically significant (P = <0.01, <0.01, <0.01, respectively).

The results shown in figure 2 for the tone-shock period were obtained by averaging the results when each animal was used as its own control; percentage and

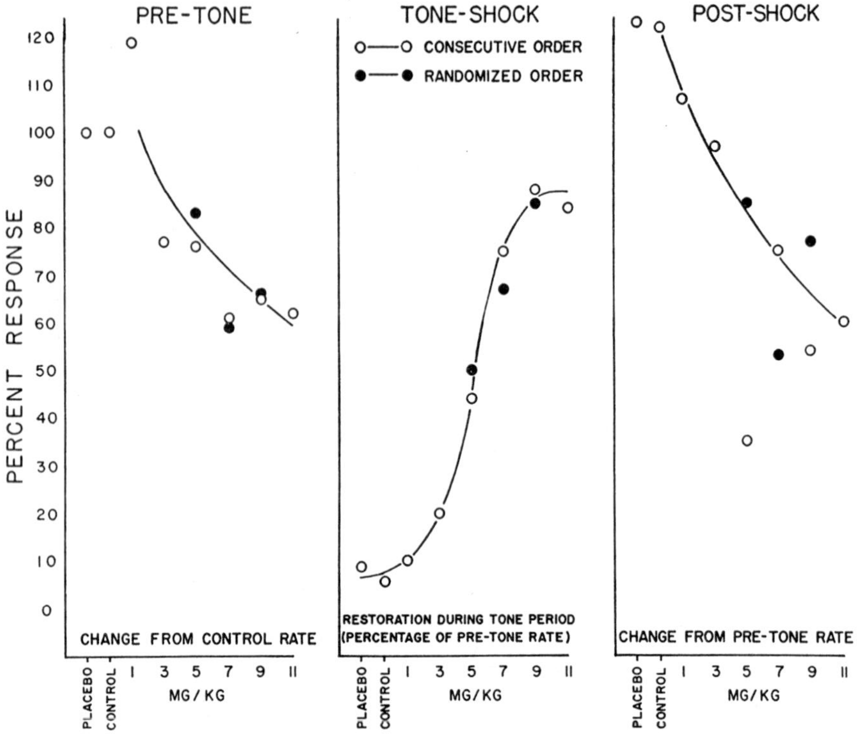

FIG. 2. Dose-effect relationships obtained on pretone, tone-shock, and post-shock conditions.

raw score means are presented in table 2. The data were quite similar to those obtained in the previous study (Hill *et al.*, 1954). The peak restoration was 88 per cent on 9 mgm./kgm., which is slightly higher than that found earlier, whereas the control value of 5.5 ± 1.0 per cent is considerably less. This latter value, which is the mean of the controls for all doses of morphine, is very close to the mean control value for the entire series of studies on all drugs (4.4 ± 0.59 per cent). Results on the morphine-placebo were also quite close to this figure.

Progressive increments in restoration of inhibited bar pressing by increasing doses of morphine were quite regular. Although a slight increase over control was found for 1 mgm./kgm., the lowest dose that could be statistically differentiated from control at the 5 per cent level was 3 mgm./kgm. Five mgm./kgm. produced significantly less restoration than 7 and, although a substantial increase occurred from 7 to 9 mgm./kgm., it was not significant. Analysis of variance showed that the slight differences between the consecutive and randomized orders of 5, 7, and 9 mgm./kgm. were not statistically significant. This indicates that morphine can be tested individually or in alternation with other drugs at weekly intervals without materially affecting the results.

Figure 2 and table 2, also, show that a progressive decrease in post-shock rates occurred that was significant at doses of 5 mgm./kgm. and higher.

Patterning effects. The results on control and on morphine shown as Pattern of Inhibition in table 1, figure 1, are based on 27 animals. Control and morphine means were significantly different for all three periods ($P = <0.001, <0.001, <0.001$). Placebo rates were quite similar to those of control except for pretone rate which was somewhat lower than that for control and nonsignificantly higher than morphine pretone. The three periods under morphine produced similar rates even though those for the tone and post-shock periods were significantly lower than that for pretone ($P = <0.01, <0.01$).

DISCUSSION. The restoration of inhibited bar-pressing by graded doses of morphine reported in the previous study (Hill *et al.*, 1954) was reproduced in the present investigation. Reliability of the method was demonstrated in several ways. The control rate for the period of inhibition was reduced to nearly zero. As shown, the control mean for individual doses of morphine, as well as the results on placebo, closely approximate this control value. A close correspondence was also seen between placebo and control values for pretone, tone-shock, and post-shock rates. Further evidence of reliability is gained from inspection of the morphine data. The two orders of testing the higher doses of morphine showed only minor differences, none of which were statistically significant. This was also true for the effects of 9 mgm./kgm. when tested over an interval of several months. The validity of the technique will be given consideration in subsequent papers, when the pattern of effects for 9 mgm./kgm. of morphine will be compared with the patterns produced by other drugs in doses which are optimal for restoring bar pressing.

Unconditioned and time-action response rates can be obtained quite easily. Although procedures for testing the effects of drugs on conditioned inhibition are somewhat more difficult and time consuming, animals can be prepared in about 30 days, and they are then available for repeated testing over a period of months. The method for developing patterns of effect, while reliable and valid to date, might be improved, especially when testing drugs with psychotomimetic effects, if a measure of discrimination were included.

Knowledge concerning psychological effects of drugs in animals is growing rapidly. At present, however, there is little information available which might be useful in constructing systematic theories of drug actions. Although the present study raised more theoretical problems than it answered it has provided some additional information on the effects of morphine. A depressive action of 9 mgm./kgm. was shown by all measures obtained. Both reinforced and non-reinforced bar-pressing rates were decreased by this dose, which was optimal for restoration during the tone-shock period. Also, this restoration of inhibited bar-pressing shows that the effects of the tone-shock conditioning were depressed to the point of being almost eliminated. These findings indicate that the depressive action is selective: the effect of morphine is much greater on responses that are under control of noxious stimuli than it is on responses under control of a food-reward schedule.

In the present study it was also found that animals under morphine tend to continue executing a response once it is begun. Although the non-reinforced rate was very low, animals responded consistently over the experimental period, in contrast to those under control conditions. Such constancy of rate, although at a higher level, held for the time-action curves within any one period. The pattern of inhibition also demonstrated this effect to a marked degree since 9 mgm./kgm. of morphine practically eliminated the influence of the tone-shock conditioning. Similar results for maze running and extinction of a conditioned escape response were found by Simon and Eddy (1935) and Collins and Myers (1957), respectively. Thus, in addition to showing a reduced effect of both rewarding and penalizing conditions, data are available which strongly suggest that perseveration, or stereotypy of behavior, frequently occurs in rats under morphine.

It appears reasonable to assume, at least in part, that the depressive effects of morphine on food-reinforced bar-pressing rate are due to reduction of hunger, and that its restorative effects on inhibited bar-pressing are due to a much greater reduction of pain-conditioned anxiety. These explanations, however, do not seem to account in any simple manner for the "perseveration" produced by morphine. To account for this action, other experimental approaches, perhaps designed to deal with possible effects of morphine on discrimination, response hierarchies, and reactive inhibition, may have to be undertaken. From the standpoint of empirical "screening" procedures, however, the results obtained with morphine have been used primarily to serve as a basis for comparing its patterns of action with those of other drugs. Data bearing on the latter will be presented in subsequent publications.

SUMMARY AND CONCLUSIONS

A behavioral "screening" procedure is described for detecting drugs that have potent analgesic actions similar to those of morphine. Measurements of the relationship between bar-pressing rates of rats in a Skinner Box under various conditions imposed by the experimenters constituted the "screen." These measurements included: a) "operant level" curves, representing the performance of untrained animals without reinforcements of any kind, b) "time action" curves, representing the performance of animals trained with food-reinforcement over a continuous 108-minute period, and c) "inhibition" curves, representing the inhibition of bar-pressing for food produced by tone-shock conditioning.

Under control and placebo conditions the operant level was found to decrease as a function of time, whereas, after 9 mgm./kgm. of morphine the animals operated the bar at a greatly reduced rate. Time action curves showed no significant changes under control or placebo conditions. Morphine (9 mgm./kgm.) caused a significant, early decrease in rate which continued throughout the testing periods.

The nearly complete inhibition of bar pressing that occurred under control and placebo conditions following the pairing of tone and shock was practically eliminated by 9 mgm./kgm. of morphine. This dose produced a marked restoration of previously inhibited performance, as well as "perseveration" or "stereotypy" of response. The "restoration" effect was also shown to be proportional to the dose of morphine.

Technical problems inherent in the method and the theoretical significance of the results are discussed. While the pattern of morphine actions on the measures used supports the inference that morphine reduces pain-conditioned "anxiety", this explanation does not appear sufficient to account for the "stereotypy" of performance which was observed. Some areas for further investigation are suggested.

REFERENCES

Collins, G., and Meyers, E.: Proc. Soc. Exper. Biol. & Med. in Press, 1957.

Edwards, A. L.: Statistical Methods for the Behavioral Sciences, Rinehart & Co., New York City, 1955.

Estes, W. K., and Skinner, B. F.: J. Exp. Psychol., **29:** 390, 1941.

Hill, H. E., Kornetsky, C. H., Flanary, H. G., and Wikler, A.: J. Clin. Invest., **31:** 473, 1952.

Hill, H. E., Belleville, R. E., and Wikler, A.: Proc. Soc. Exper. Biol. & Med., **86:** 881, 1954.

Hill, H. E., Belleville, R. E., and Wikler, A.: Arch. Neurol. & Psychiat., **73:** 602, 1955.

Simon, A. K., and Eddy, N. B.: Am. J. Psychol., **47:** 597, 1935.

Skinner, B. F.: The Behavior of Organisms, Appleton-Century-Crofts, Inc., New York City, 1938.

Wikler, A., Goodell, H., and Wolff, H. G.: This Journal, **83:** 294, 1945.

CHEMOREFLEX ACTIVITY OF DEXTROMETHORPHAN (ROMILAR), DEXTRORPHAN, CODEINE AND MORPHINE IN THE CAT AND THE DOG[1, 2]

CARL C. GRUHZIT

Department of Physiology and Pharmacology, Graduate School of Medicine, University of Pennsylvania, Philadelphia

Received for publication February 27, 1957

Various investigators have suggested that a portion of the cardiovascular and respiratory effects of morphine might involve the stimulation of chemoreflex mechanisms. The marked central depression and tachyphylaxis associated with repeated injections of morphine have interfered with the adequate testing of this hypothesis. The morphinan analogues, dextrorphan[3] and dextromethorphan,[3] however, have been shown to be comparatively weak central nervous system depressants (Fromherz, 1950; Randall and Lehmann, 1950; Benson *et al.*, 1953; Randall *et al.*, 1953). Experiments were designed, therefore, to test the chemoreflex activity of these compounds. In addition in several experiments the responses to codeine and morphine were analyzed for evidence of possible participation of chemoreflexes.

METHODS. The respiratory and cardiovascular effects of dextrorphan, dextromethorphan, codeine and morphine were measured in 24 cats and 5 dogs. Anesthesia in cats was induced with chloroform and was maintained with 25 to 55 mgm./kgm. of α-chloralose i.v. In dogs 15 to 20 mgm./kgm. of thiopental sodium i.v. and 50 to 75 mgm./kgm. of α-chloralose i.v. were used to induce and maintain anesthesia. Respiration was measured by means of a modified Donald-Christie apparatus (Donald and Christie, 1949) in which pressure changes were recorded by a strain gauge-Grass EEG ink writing system and volume changes were calculated from these. The duration of the longest respiratory cycle, the smallest tidal volume and the minimum 10-second respiratory ventilation during the response period were measured for comparison with the values obtained during the control period. The latent period was measured from the beginning of the injection to the onset of observable change. The injection time was less than 0.5 second. Injections of physiological saline were employed as controls. Data obtained during periods of gross respiratory irregularities were not included in the quantitative analysis of the results.

Femoral or carotid arterial blood pressure was recorded on the EEG by means of a Statham strain gauge connected to an appropriately placed polyethylene or radio-opaque catheter. Vena caval, right atrial, right ventricular or pulmonary arterial pressure was recorded in a similar manner. Injections into the left ventricle were made by a catheter passed via the left common carotid artery. Localization of the tip of the catheters was determined during the experiment by pressure recordings and fluoroscopic visualization and was confirmed at autopsy.

---

[1] Presented in part at the Fall meetings of the American Society for Pharmacology and Experimental Therapeutics, Iowa City, September, 1955.

[2] This work was supported (in part) by research grant USPHS H406 from the National Heart Institute of the National Institutes of Health, Public Health Service.

[3] Dextrorphan (*d*-3-hydroxy-N-methyl morphinan) tartrate and dextromethorphan (*d*-3-methoxy-N-methyl morphinan) hydrobromide (Romilar) were kindly supplied by Hoffmann-La Roche Inc. through the courtesy of Dr. W. A. Davis.

The effect of bilateral vagal cooling on the responses to dextromethorphan, dextrorphan and codeine was tested in 6 cats according to the method described by Dawes *et al.* (1951). Cold alcohol was passed through specially designed, standardized vagal thermodes;[4] the temperature of the thermodes was measured by means of thermocouples and galvanometers. As employed, the effects of serotonin, phenyl diguanide and veratridine were blocked at temperatures similar to those described by Dawes and his associates.

RESULTS. *Dextromethorphan.* Respiration: All initial intravenous or right atrial injections of 1.0 to 2.0 mgm./kgm. of dextromethorphan in 14 cats and 4 dogs anesthetized with chloralose and with intact vagi produced a decrease in tidal volume and respiratory ventilation. The respiratory depression was usually characterized by a period of expiratory apnea followed by several slow shallow breaths and a gradual return to control values within ten minutes (fig. 1 and 2). In about a third of the responses, however, a marked decrease in tidal volume was accompanied by an increase in respiratory rate. The injection of similar doses at 15-minute or greater intervals produced comparable respiratory alterations. In the initial experiments it was noted that when injections of dextromethorphan were repeated at more frequent intervals, the respiratory response frequently showed evidence of tachyphylaxis. In all subsequent experiments, therefore, injections were made at intervals of greater than fifteen minutes.

In chloralose-anesthetized animals with intact vagi, the latent period of the respiratory response following right atrial injections of dextromethorphan was three seconds or less in approximately two-thirds of the 24 trials in 10 cats and the 8 trials in 4 dogs. Comroe *et al.* (1953) have shown that the right ventricular to aortic valve circulation time in chloralose-anesthetized cats is approximately 3.4 seconds; Rahn *et al.* (1952) and Nordenstrom (1954) have obtained similar values in the dog. The short latent period suggested, therefore, that the respiratory depression induced by this morphinan analogue was, in part at least, reflex in nature and involved the stimulation of receptors located between the point of injection and the aortic valve orifice. In an effort to localize these receptors more precisely, a comparison was made in three experiments of the responses to right atrial, right ventricular, pulmonary arterial and left ventricular injections of dextromethorphan. Left ventricular injections failed to produce significant respiratory alterations although similar injections into the right atrium, right ventricle or pulmonary artery produced marked expiratory apnea (fig. 1).

Since the pulmonary respiratory-depressor chemoreflex (Dawes and Comroe, 1954) elicited by serotonin, phenyl diguanide and other drugs has been shown to involve vagal receptors, the effect of bilateral cervical vagal section on the response to dextromethorphan was tested in three experiments. Following vagotomy, the respiratory depression induced by the intravenous or right atrial injection of 1.0 to 2.0 mgm./kgm. of dextromethorphan was abolished or markedly reduced (fig. 1). The injection of 4.0 mgm./kgm. still produced respiratory depression in a vagotomized animal, but only after a latent period of approximately 18 seconds.

Although injections were made at intervals greater than 15 minutes, the

[4] The thermodes were kindly supplied by Dr. G. S. Dawes.

possibility exists that the marked decrease in the respiratory response seen after vagotomy may be associated with tachyphylaxis. The effects of dextromethorphan were compared, therefore, in three experiments before, during and after bilateral cervical vagal cooling (fig. 2). The respiratory depression induced by the intravenous or right atrial injection of 1.0 to 2.0 mgm./kgm. of dextromethorphan was not significantly altered by cooling the vagi to between 4 and 12°C. for two minutes but was abolished by vagal cooling to 0 to 3°C. The pulmonary respiratory depressor chemoreflex response to serotonin and phenyl diguanide is also blocked in this temperature range. In each case, after removing the cold block, the typical response to dextromethorphan reappeared.

In approximately half of the experiments, the ratio *tidal volume/respiratory intrathoracic pressure change* was diminished during the response to dextromethorphan. This indicates that this morphinan analogue may produce alterations in lung compliance or airway resistance in a chloralose-anesthetized cat or dog similar to those observed by Randall *et al.* (1953) in the spinal cat. Qualitatively similar changes were also produced occasionally by dextromethorphan following vagotomy or during bilateral cooling of the cervical vagi to 0 to 3°C., even though the respiratory depression was prevented by these procedures. It appears therefore that dextromethorphan may produce bronchial constriction by a

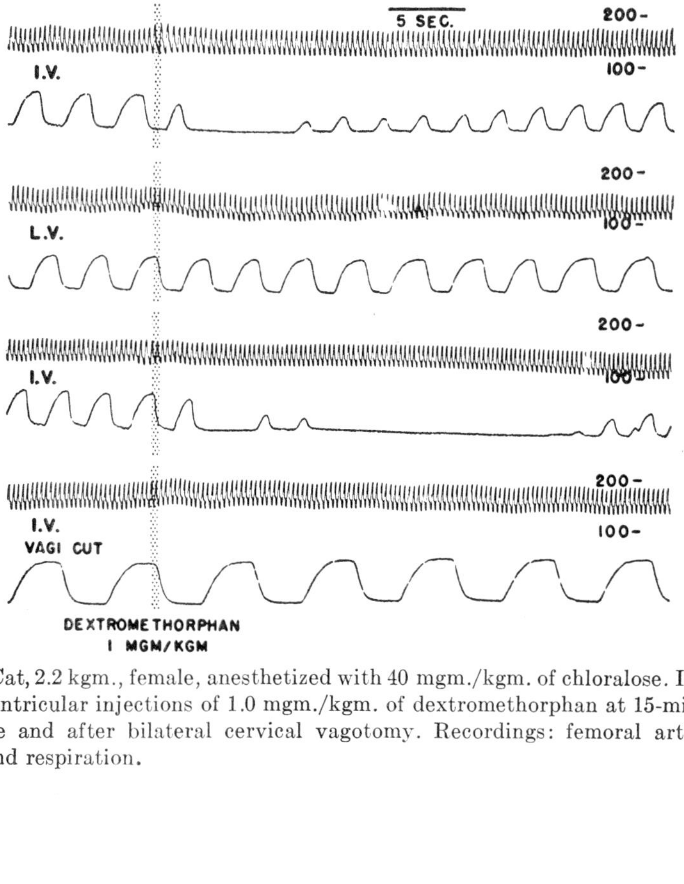

FIG. 1. Cat, 2.2 kgm., female, anesthetized with 40 mgm./kgm. of chloralose. Intravenous and left ventricular injections of 1.0 mgm./kgm. of dextromethorphan at 15-minute intervals before and after bilateral cervical vagotomy. Recordings: femoral arterial blood pressure and respiration.

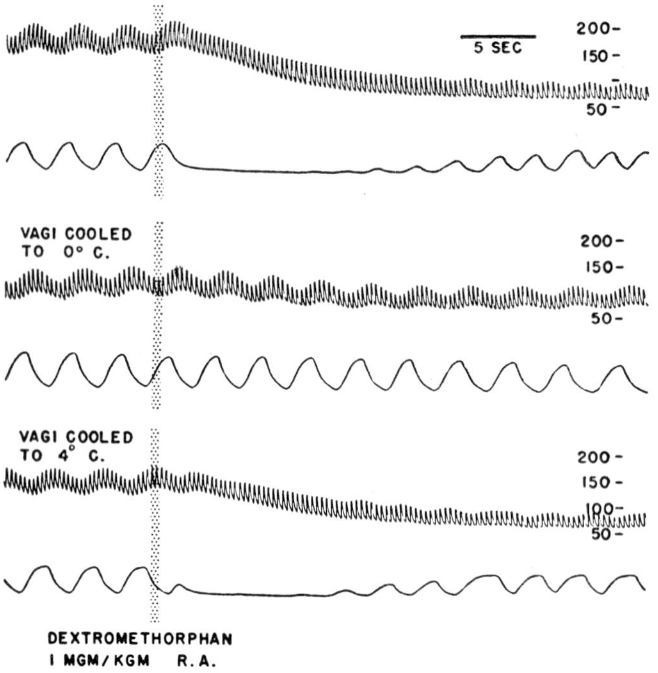

FIG. 2. Cat, 3.7 kgm., female, anesthetized with 30 mgm./kgm. of chloralose. Right atrial injections of 1.0 mgm./kgm. of dextromethorphan at 15-minute intervals before and during bilateral cervical vagal cooling. Recordings: femoral arterial blood pressure and respiration.

direct action on smooth muscle, though more subtle changes in pulmonary compliance or resistance cannot be ruled out by these studies.

In order to determine the effect of a barbiturate upon the respiratory response, in two experiments, 5.0 mgm./kgm. of sodium thiopental was administered intravenously. In these experiments dextromethorphan failed to elicit respiratory depression ten minutes after the administration of the barbiturate although twenty minutes later dextromethorphan again produced responses similar to those observed during the control period.

Systemic arterial blood pressure: The administration of 1.0 to 2.0 mgm./kgm. of dextromethorphan produced, after a latent period greater than 4.5 seconds, a decrease in both systolic and diastolic arterial blood pressures in 40 out of 46 injections. The fall in mean blood pressure varied considerably, the magnitude varied from a few mm. of Hg in some animals to more than 100 mm. of Hg in others and the duration varied between several minutes and one hour. In general, the hypotensive effect was greatest with the initial injection and, although still present, was usually diminished in both duration and degree with repeated injections even though sufficient time elapsed between injections for the blood pressure to return to control values.

The blood pressure response to dextromethorphan was not abolished by vagotomy or vagal cooling to 0 to 3°C. and could be demonstrated with left ventricular injections. The long latent period and the persistence of a significant hypotensive response following vagal blockade indicates that the fall in blood pressure produced by dextromethorphan, unlike that elicited by phenyl diguanide and serotonin in the cat, is not primarily dependent on vagal reflexes.

Since morphine is known to cause the liberation of histamine, it was thought possible that the fall in blood pressure induced by dextromethorphan might involve a similar mechanism. Comparisons were therefore made in three experiments of the responses to right atrial injections of dextromethorphan, histamine, acetylcholine and glyceryl trinitrate before and after the administration 0.5 to 2.5 mgm./kgm. of promethazine (Phenergan). Following the intravenous injection of this antihistaminic, the hypotensive effect of histamine and dextromethorphan was markedly reduced or abolished. Although the response to acetylcholine was also reduced by promethazine, it is unlikely that its blockade of the cardiovascular effects of dextromethorphan involves anticholinergic action, since atropine (0.5 mgm./kgm., i. v.) failed to alter the hypotensive effect of this morphinan analogue. It is also unlikely that the ability of promethazine to prevent the fall in blood pressure induced by dextromethorphan represents a non-specific depressant effect since the response to glyceryl trinitrate is unaltered by this antihistaminic. The intracutaneous injection of dextromethorphan affords additional evidence that dextromethorphan may liberate histamine. The intracutaneous injection of 0.05 ml. of dextromethorphan (1:500) produced a triple response indistinguishable from that elicited by 0.02 ml. of 1:1000 histamine phosphate.

Cardiac rate: Dextromethorphan did not alter heart rate significantly in about two-thirds of the trials. With the remaining injections, heart rate usually decreased moderately after a latent period of between four seconds and two minutes. With one injection, however, cardiac arrest followed the administration of dextromethorphan. The decrease in rate was not dependent on the integrity of the vagi thus suggesting that the bradycardia, when it occurred, might involve, in part at least, the direct action of dextromethorphan on the cardiac pacemaker.

Dextrorphan. The right atrial injection of 1.0 to 2.0 mgm./kgm. of dextrorphan in chloralose-anesthetized cats and dogs with intact vagi produced a decrease in tidal volume and respiratory ventilation in ten out of eleven animals. The response was usually characterized by expiratory apnea lasting up to 18 seconds, but on occasion the decrease in tidal volume was associated with rapid, shallow breathing; there was not significant tachyphylaxis when injections were repeated at twenty- to thirty-minute intervals. The latent period of the respiratory change was approximately four to six seconds in the majority of the responses and was greater than 3 seconds in all but one of 39 injections. The long latent period does not necessarily rule out the participation of chemoreflexes in the respiratory response to dextrorphan since slow diffusion or other physical-chemical actions could retard the response. The effects of dextrorphan were measured, therefore, in three experiments before and after cervical vagotomy. Vagal section prevented the respiratory depression induced by dextrorphan in these experiments. The administration of sodium thiopental also inhibited the respiratory responses in two additional experiments.

The heart rate and blood pressure responses to dextrorphan were similar to those elicited by dextromethorphan.

Codeine. The effects of repeated right atrial injections of 1.0 mgm./kgm. of codeine sulfate were measured in two cats. The initial injection of codeine produced a period of expiratory apnea lasting up to thirty seconds. Subsequent injections at intervals up to one hour produced diminished respiratory responses. The latent period of the respiratory responses was as short as 2.6 seconds in one trial but was between three and seven seconds in seven of the eight responses. Injections made before, during and after bilateral cervical vagal cooling to 1°C. for two minutes demonstrated that this procedure markedly diminished the respiratory response in one experiment but failed to alter the degree of respiratory depression induced by this dose of codeine in the second experiment.

Heart rate and blood pressure decreased in about one-third of the trials during the periods of expiratory apnea but were unaltered in the remainder of the responses.

Morphine. The respiratory and cardiovascular effects of repeated right atrial injections of 1.0 to 2.0 mgm./kgm. of morphine sulfate were measured in four experiments. The initial injections produced marked respiratory depression with periods of expiratory apnea lasting up to 25 seconds. Subsequent injections at intervals of up to one hour produced only slight effects in comparison with the initial response. The latent period of the respiratory response was consistently less than 2.5 seconds in one experiment but was between 3.5 and 8 seconds in the remaining experiments.

The initial right atrial injections of morphine produced, after a latent period greater than five seconds, slight to moderate decreases in blood pressure and heart rate greater than fifteen minutes in duration. Subsequent injections at one hour or shorter intervals did not alter blood pressure significantly.

Discussion. There appears to be no doubt that dextromethorphan and dextrorphan may produce expiratory apnea, a large part of which appears to arise from thoracic chemoreflexes, mediated over the vagus nerves. Injections of radioactive saline solutions have demonstrated that the right ventricular-aortic valve circulation time is approximately 3.4 seconds in chloralose-anesthetized cats (Comroe *et al.*, 1953), and similar values have been obtained in dogs by a variety of techniques (Rahn *et al.*, 1952; Nordenstrom, 1954). The short latent period of the respiratory response following right atrial injections of dextromethorphan strongly suggests that this action involves pulmonary or endocardial receptors. Unless simultaneous measurements of the circulation time and latent period are made, however, the possibility exists that an accelerated circulation time may be present which would preclude the localization of the site of drug action on the basis of latent period alone.

A comparison of the responses obtained with injections into different portions of the heart or pulmonary circulation affords additional information regarding the localization of the site of drug action. The failure of the left ventricular administration of 1.0 to 2.0 mgm./kgm. of dextromethorphan to elicit significant respiratory depression in comparison with that produced by the pulmonary arterial injection of the same dose indicates that left ventricular endocardial receptors and receptors at or distal to the aortic valve do not play a significant role in the response to this dose. It appears likely, therefore, that the respiratory depression induced by right atrial injections of dextromethorphan is due, in part at least, to the stimulation of receptors located in the lungs. On the basis of the experiments which have been performed, it is not possible to localize the receptors more precisely. An analysis of the effect of dextromethorphan on single vagal nerve fiber action potentials might offer additional information regarding the localization and nature of the receptor sites.

Although the respiratory responses induced by serotonin, phenyl diguanide and dextromethorphan in the cat are blocked by similar degrees of vagal cooling, the failure of dextromethorphan to induce vagal mediated reflex hypotension and bradycardia suggests that more than one type of receptor is involved in the responses to these drugs. Occasionally small doses of serotonin or phenyl diguanide may elicit respiratory depression without significant cardiovascular response. This dissociation of the cardiovascular and respiratory responses suggests that the cardiovascular-depressor reflex and the pulmonary respiratory-depressor reflex involve at least two types of receptors. It is possible that dextromethorphan stimulates the receptors which participate in the expiratory apnea produced by serotonin and phenyl diguanide in the cat; if so, additional information is required to explain the ability of dextromethorphan to induce expiratory apnea in the dog while larger doses of serotonin or phenyl diguanide injected into the pulmonary circulation fail to do so, even when opposing carotid and aortic body respiratory reflexes are not stimulated.[5] It is possible that the receptors involved are identical with a portion of those affected by hydrazine hydrate (Comroe, 1952) which, when stimulated, produce expiratory apnea in both the cat and dog without significant cardiovascular actions.

The failure of a compound to produce a respiratory response within three seconds following right atrial injection does not necessarily preclude the involvement of pulmonary receptors. The phasic nature of respiratory activity may obscure the actual onset of chemoreflex stimulation; if an injection is given during the expiratory phase of respiration it will be necessary to wait until the next inspiratory effort to evaluate properly respiratory depressant effects. If the inspiratory rate is 15 per minute for example, inhibition might be observable on the first breath following the injection but the measurable latent period may be greater than three seconds. In addition, other physical-chemical factors, such as slow diffusion of the drug, could delay the onset of observable drug activity following right atrial injections, even though pulmonary receptors were involved. Although the latent period of the respiratory response to dextrorphan was usually greater than three seconds, an abolition of the respiratory responses

[5] Serotonin and phenyl diguanide were injected into the right or left pulmonary circulation in which stasis had been produced by inflation of a balloon proximal to the catheter tip located in the right or left pulmonary artery.

following bilateral cervical vagotomy indicates that the respiratory depression involves reflex actions. The failure of previous investigators (Fromherz, 1950; Randall and Lehmann, 1950; Benson *et al.*, 1953), to observe significant respiratory depressant effects of dextrorphan and dextromethorphan in cats and dogs may be attributed to the barbiturates employed as anesthetics in these animals. Thiopental, for example, may obtund chemoreflex activity elicited by other drugs such as serotonin, phenyl diguanide, and nicotine (Gruhzit, 1957). The responses to the morphinan analogues were also markedly inhibited by this barbiturate. The effects of anesthesia on chemoreflex activity make it difficult to predict accurately the significance of the reflex component in the respiratory responses to these morphinan analogues in the unanesthetized animal or intact human.

The short latent period for the respiratory responses to morphine and codeine in some animals also indicates that a portion of the respiratory depression produced by these narcotics may be due to chemoreflex activity. The tachyphylaxis observed with repeated injections of these compounds and the central depressant activity preclude the accurate evaluation of the relative significance of the chemoreflex component in the respiratory response to morphine and codeine. It is possible, however, that such an action may contribute to the respiratory depression induced by morphine and codeine in patients. It is also possible that the antitussive activity of dextromethorphan may involve alterations in reflexes which participate in the normal cough mechanisms.

SUMMARY AND CONCLUSIONS

In chloralose-anesthetized cats and dogs with intact vagi, right atrial and pulmonary arterial, but not left ventricular, injections of 1.0 to 2.0 mgm./kgm. of dextromethorphan produced, after a latent period usually less than three seconds, respiratory depression frequently characterized by brief periods of expiratory apnea. This respiratory response was blocked by bilateral cervical vagotomy or cooling to 0 to 3°C. for two minutes. The short latent period, the blockade by vagotomy and the failure of left ventricular injections to produce significant respiratory alterations indicates that the expiratory apnea produced by dextromethorphan at this dosage level is reflex and is caused by stimulation of pulmonary receptors.

An analysis of the latent periods and the effects of vagotomy or vagal cooling suggests that a portion of the respiratory depression produced by dextrorphan probably, and codeine and morphine possibly, may be due to the stimulation of similar pulmonary chemoreflexes.

The hypotension and bradycardia produced by these compounds were not dependent on the integrity of the vagi and could be elicited with left ventricular injections as well as with injections into the right ventricle. The cardiovascular responses showed marked tachyphylaxis with repeated injections and may be due in part to histamine release.

REFERENCES

BENSON, W. M., STEFKO, P. L., AND RANDALL, L. D.: THIS JOURNAL, **109:** 189, 1953.
COMROE, J. H., JR.: THIS JOURNAL, **106:** 378, 1952.
COMROE, J. H., JR., VAN LINGEN, B., STROUD, R. C., AND RONCORONI, A.: Am. J. Physiol., **173:** 379, 1953.
DAWES, G. S., AND COMROE, J. H., JR.: Physiol. Rev., **34:** 167, 1954.
DAWES, G. S., MOTT, J. C., AND WIDDICOMBE, J. G.: J. Physiol., **115:** 258, 1951.
DONALD, K. W., AND CHRISTIE, R. V.: Clin. Sci., **8:** 21, 1949.
GRUHZIT, C. C.: Fed. Proc., **16:** 303, 1957.
FROMHERZ, K.: Arch. internat. pharmacodyn., **85:** 387, 1950.
NORDENSTROM, B.: Acta Radiol., **41:** 209, 1954.
RAHN, H., STROUD, R. C., AND MEIER, H.: J. Appl. Physiol., **5:** 308, 1952.
RANDALL, L. O., KRUGER, J., CONROY, C., KAPPELL, B., AND BENSON, W. M.: Arch. Exper. Path. u. Pharmakol., **220:** 26, 1953.
RANDALL, L. O., AND LEHMANN, G.: THIS JOURNAL, **99:** 163, 1950.

INFLUENCE OF pH AND ATROPINE ON THE RESPONSE OF SUPERFUSED TISSUES TO 5-HYDROXYTRYPTAMINE AND ACETYLCHOLINE[1]

JAMES L. LEITCH, D. MARYN, V. G. DEBLEY AND THOMAS J. HALEY

Division of Pharmacology and Toxicology, Atomic Energy Project, School of Medicine, University of California at Los Angeles

Received for publication March 2, 1957

There is some disagreement among investigators concerning the effect of atropine on the responses of isolated tissues to 5-hydroxytryptamine. Erspamer (1954) reported that atropine had little or no effect on the response of the rat uterus to 5-hydroxytryptamine. Feldberg and Toh (1953), Gaddum (1953a) and Gaddum and Hameed (1954) observed that atropine concentrations which abolish the response of the guinea pig ileum to acetylcholine had little effect on the 5-hydroxytryptamine response. Conversely, Robertson (1953), Rocha e Silva *et al.* (1953) and Cambridge and Holgate (1955) reported that such responses were markedly affected by atropine. On the other hand, Edlung (cited by Rocha e Silva *et al.*, 1953) stated that gut sensitivity to atropine was increased at a more acid pH. Rocha e Silva *et al.* (1953) therefore suggested that a variable relationship between atropine and 5-hydroxytryptamine might result from variations in the pH of the solutions bathing the isolated tissues.

In the present investigation, a study has been made of the relationships between a) the pH of the superfusate and b) the concentration of atropine and the responses of both the rat uterus and the guinea pig ileum to acetylcholine and 5-hydroxytryptamine.

METHODS. The superfusion method of Gaddum (1953b) was used with two pieces of tissue studied simultaneously in separate units of a constant temperature bath. At a constant flow rate of 4 ml./min., one tissue was studied with the perfusate adjusted to pH 8.1 and the second to pH 6.5. Tyrode's solution at 37.5 ± 0.5°C. was used for the guinea pig ileum and Gaddum-Peart-Vogt (1949) solution at 29.5 ± 0.5°C. for the rat uterus. Only those rat uteri showing the characteristics of Stage II of the estrous cycle were used. This was assured by administration of 50 microgm. of estradiol 24 hours prior to use along with examination of the vaginal smears according to the method of Long and Evans (1922). The body weight range of the rats was 150 to 200 gm. The male guinea pigs weighed 400 to 600 gm. Tension on both tissues was 0.4 gm. The ileal strips were 30 mm. in length. Drug doses were prepared by diluting concentrated stock solutions with the appropriate superfusate adjusted to the required pH and given in a constant volume of 0.5 ml. The time interval between successive doses was kept constant at 5 minutes for the 5-hydroxytryptamine experiments and at 4 minutes for those with acetylcholine. All doses are reported in terms of the respective base. A series of doses of each spasmogen, each double that of the preceding one and varying from 1 to 16,384 nanograms (1 nanogram equalling 10^{-9} gm.), was given in any one experiment. Ten experiments were completed for each set of experimental conditions. The concentration of atropine in the superfusate varied from 0.004 to 1.0 microgm./ml. The results obtained were analyzed statistically by the least squares method of Croxton (1953), using the linear portion of the curve (20 to 80 per cent response).

[1] This article is based on work performed under Contract No. AT-04-1-GEN-12 between the Atomic Energy Commission and the University of California at Los Angeles.

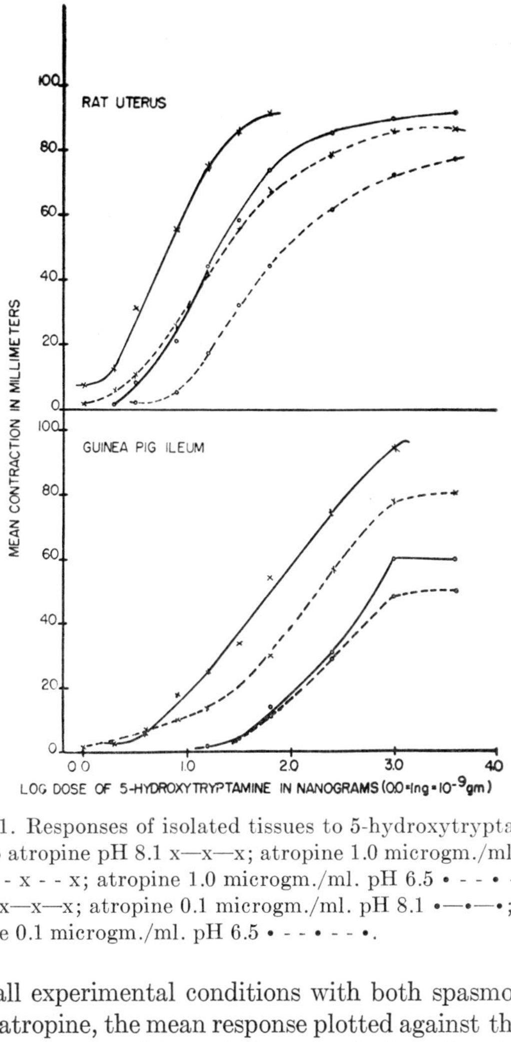

FIG. 1. Responses of isolated tissues to 5-hydroxytryptamine

Upper curves: no atropine pH 8.1 x—x—x; atropine 1.0 microgm./ml. pH 8.1 •—•—•; no atropine pH 6.5 x - - x - - x; atropine 1.0 microgm./ml. pH 6.5 • - - - • - - - •. Lower curves: no atropine pH 8.1 x—x—x; atropine 0.1 microgm./ml. pH 8.1 •—•—•; no atropine pH 6.5 x - - x - - x; atropine 0.1 microgm./ml. pH 6.5 • - - - • - - - •.

RESULTS. For all experimental conditions with both spasmogens and various concentrations of atropine, the mean response plotted against the log-dose showed the same sigmoid-type curve. Figure 1 shows typical results obtained with 5-hydroxytryptamine at pH values of 6.5 and 8.1 with both tissues. It is quite evident that the rat uterus is much more sensitive than the guinea pig ileum to this spasmogen. With the rat uterus, the lower pH value appears to reduce the slope over the middle range significantly. At both pH levels the concentration of atropine used appears to reduce the maximal response of the guinea pig ileum. This latter observation agrees with the observations of Cambridge and Holgate (1955). Furthermore, both tissues appear to have their sensitivity to 5-hydroxytryptamine decreased by atropine although the responses of the guinea pig ileum are influenced by much lower concentrations of the latter drug (0.01 microgm./ml. *vs.* 0.1 microgm./ml.). Analysis of the results by the least squares method, see table 1, indicate that a decrease in pH alone tends to decrease the sensitivity of the rat uterus to both 5-hydroxytryptamine and acetylcholine and the sensi-

TABLE 1

Effect of pH and atropine on spasmogen responses of tissues

Tissue	Drug	pH	Atropine Microgm./ml.*	Least square data			Response (y) in mm. for	
				a	b	S_{yx}	x = 100 ngm.	x = 1000 ngm.**
Rat uterus	5-HT†	8.1	0.0	3.79	53.0	5.5	109.8	—
			0.1	−6.00	49.5	6.5	92.9	—
			1.0	−12.80	44.1	5.6	75.5	—
		6.5	0.0	−8.76	43.7	5.4	78.7	—
			0.1	−12.2	42.1	5.8	72.0	—
			1.0	−18.8	32.1	3.7	45.4	—
	Ac‡	8.1	0.000	−69.7	47.8	2.5	—	73.7
			0.004	−74.8	43.4	4.5	—	55.4
			0.01	−145.8	43.1	5.4	—	0.0
		6.5	0.000	−40.1	32.3	4.6	—	56.8
			0.004	−41.2	26.9	2.5	—	39.5
			0.01	−137.2	41.8	6.2	—	0.0
Guinea pig ileum	5-HT	8.1	0.0	−17.2	37.5	4.4	57.8	95.3
			0.1	−5.16	16.5	3.7	27.7	44.2
			1.0	−32.3	28.5	6.1	24.6	53.0
		6.5	0.0	−14.7	28.7	5.1	42.7	71.4
			0.1	−10.8	20.8	1.6	30.8	51.5
			1.0	−17.4	17.9	5.1	18.4	36.3
	Ac	8.1	0.0	−6.61	31.0	6.8	55.5	86.5
			0.01	−38.3	32.2	7.2	26.1	58.3
			0.05	−72.9	31.4	6.3	0.0	21.2
			0.10	−99.6	36.5	5.2	0.0	9.9
		6.5	0.0	4.03	16.8	5.1	37.7	54.5
			0.01	−12.0	20.7	7.9	29.3	49.9
			0.05	−27.1	16.2	5.9	5.2	21.3
			0.10	−37.8	17.2	5.2	2.6	19.8

* Microgm. = 10^{-6} gm.

† 5-HT = 5-hydroxytryptamine.

‡ Ac = acetylcholine.

** ngm. = nanograms = 10^{-9} gm. These doses represent actual concentrations whose log-doses are 2 and 3 respectively.

tivity is further decreased with increasing atropine concentration. It can also be seen that the acetylcholine responses of the rat uterus are affected by much lower concentrations of atropine than the 5-hydroxytryptamine responses. Furthermore, the rat uterus can be used for the estimation of 5-hydroxytryptamine through the dosage range studied at both pH levels in the presence of 16,384 nanograms of acetylcholine, if the concentration of atropine is 0.1 microgm./ml. Under our conditions the guinea pig ileum does not appear to be suitable for the estimation of 5-hydroxytryptamine in the presence of acetylcholine. In order to block the response to acetylcholine, the concentration of atropine must be raised to 1 microgm./ml. This results in such a great decrease in the response to 5-hydroxytryptamine as to make quantitative estimation impractical. In no instance did we observe tachyphylaxis with either tissue following the higher doses of 5-hydroxytryptamine.

DISCUSSION. Contrary to the report of Cambridge and Holgate (1955) we have found that the superfused rat uterus was suitable for the estimation of 5-hydroxytryptamine. The differences in results may be due to our selection of only those animals whose vaginal smears were in Stage II of the estrous cycle and the exclusion of all animals weighing more than 200 gm. Our results support the suggestion of Rocha e Silva *et al.* (1953) that the variability of the effect of atropine on 5-hydroxytryptamine response is related to the variation in pH of the bathing solution. Moreover, the data show that pH itself is one factor concerned with decreasing the sensitivity of both the rat uterus and the guinea pig ileum to acetylcholine and 5-hydroxytryptamine. The rat uterus appears to be more sensitive to atropine at a more acid pH. Contrary to Edlund (cited by Rocha e Silva *et al.*, 1953) the guinea pig ileum was not more sensitive to atropine at a more acid pH. It also appears that the effects of pH and atropine concentration in the rat uterus are additive because there is a generalized shift in the dose-response curve requiring larger doses to produce the same degree of response. This did not occur with the guinea pig ileum. Our results support the statement of Cambridge and Holgate (1955) that the guinea pig ileum is unsuitable for the estimation of 5-hydroxytryptamine in the presence of acetylcholine. On the other hand our results point out the utility of the rat uterus for this purpose because concentrations of atropine which block acetylcholine do not materially affect the 5-hydroxytryptamine response.

SUMMARY

A study has been made of the effects of pH of the superfusate and atropine concentration on the responses of the superfused rat uterus and the guinea pig ileum to 5-hydroxytryptamine and acetylcholine. The rat uterus is more sensitive to 5-hydroxytryptamine and acetylcholine than the guinea pig ileum. It is possible to estimate the amount of 5-hydroxytryptamine in the presence of acetylcholine by the selection of a concentration of atropine which blocks the latter and only slightly diminishes the responses to the former. It has been shown that a more acid pH decreases the sensitivity of the rat uterus to both acetylcholine and 5-hydroxytryptamine and increases its sensitivity to atropine.

ACKNOWLEDGMENT. The authors wish to thank Sandoz Pharmaceuticals for the 5-hydroxytryptamine used in this study.

REFERENCES

CAMBRIDGE, G. W., AND HOLGATE, J. A.: Brit. J. Pharmacol., **10:** 326, 1955.
CROXTON, F. E.: Elementary Statistics with Applications in Medicine, pp. 109–143, Prentice-Hall, Inc., New York, 1953.
ERSPAMER, V.: Pharmacol. Rev., **6:** 425, 1954.
FELDBERG, W., AND TOH, C. C.: J. Physiol., **119:** 352, 1953.
GADDUM, J. H.: J. Physiol., **119:** 363, 1953a.
GADDUM, J. H.: Brit. J. Pharmacol., **8:** 321, 1953b.
GADDUM, J. H., PEART, W. S., AND VOGT, M.: J. Physiol., **108:** 467, 1949.
GADDUM, J. H., AND HAMEED, K. A.: Brit. J. Pharmacol., **9:** 240, 1954.
LONG, J. A., AND EVANS, H. M.: Memoirs Univ. of Calif., **6:** 1922.
ROBERTSON, P. A.: J. Physiol., **121:** 54P, 1953.
ROCHA E SILVA, M., VALLE, J. R., AND PICARELLI, Z. P.: Brit. J. Pharmacol., **8:** 378, 1953.

STUDIES ON VERATRUM ALKALOIDS XXVI. COMPARISON OF THE CARDIAC ACTION OF VARIOUS TERTIARY AMINE ESTER ALKALOIDS [1]

J. M. BENFORADO

Department of Pharmacology, Harvard Medical School, Boston, Massachusetts

Received for publication March 4, 1957

The direct effects of the veratrum alkaloids on the heart permits their division into two pharmacological groups dependent on chemical structure. The tertiary alkamines and their esters have cardiac actions similar to those of the cardiac glycosides (Krayer and Acheson, 1946; Krayer *et al.*, 1953). The secondary alkamines and their glycosides exert a negative chronotropic and antiaccelerator effect on cardiac pacemaker tissue (Krayer, 1954). The subject of the present communication is a comprehensive comparative investigation, hitherto lacking, of the direct cardiac action of a representative series of the tertiary amine ester alkaloids. The substances studied, their botanical origin and their chemical relations are given in table 1.

METHODS. Using mongrel dogs of both sexes ranging in weight from 7 to 15 kgm., the dog heart-lung preparation (HLP) was set up as described by Krayer (1931). Sodium pentobarbital, 35 mgm./kgm. intraperitoneally, was used for anesthesia. The arterial resistance was set to give a mean arterial pressure of 100 to 110 mm. Hg. The right atrial pressure (RAP) was recorded with a water manometer and the systemic outflow (left ventricular output minus coronary flow) was measured with a Weese Stromuhr and initially set between 600 and 800 ml./min. The blood volume varied between 1000 and 1300 ml. at the start of the experiment, and the blood temperature was kept between 38°C. and 39°C. Direct cardiac leads for the EKG were taken from the right atrium and across the pericardium. This procedure allowed independent recording of atrial and ventricular electrical activity which proved useful in the analysis of cardiac arrhythmias. The advantage is illustrated in figure 1A which shows a simultaneous recording of atrial P waves and ventricular fibrillatory complexes just after the onset of ventricular fibrillation in an experiment with veratridine. The term *average heart rate* in this paper refers to the value derived by dividing the total beats during a whole experiment by the experimental time. The averaging of heart rate in this manner was suggested by the fact that the rate of the ventricular beat during an experiment was not constant but varied because of cardiac arrhythmias produced by the substances studied.

Stock solutions of the veratrum alkaloids[2] containing 1 mgm./ml. were prepared by dissolving the free bases with an equivalent amount of $N/10$ hydrochloric acid and diluting with distilled water to the concentration of 1:1000. For purposes of infusion, stock solutions were diluted to the desired concentration and the infusion made into the venous cannula by means of a syringe with motor driven plunger. The rate of infusion was constant

[1] This work was supported by funds obtained from the Eugene Higgins Trust, the U. S. Public Health Service (H-2205), and the American Heart Association.

[2] The veratridine and cevadine were prepared from a batch of veratrine generously supplied by S. P. Penick and Co., N. Y. The veratroylzygadenine, vanilloylzygadenine, germidine and neogermitrine were from the same samples used by Krayer *et al.*, 1953. The germitetrine B, protoveratrine A and protoveratrine B were generously supplied by Dr. H. A. Nash of Pitman-Moore and Co., Indianapolis, Ind.

TABLE 1

Origin and chemistry of various veratrum ester alkaloids

Plant source	Ester alkaloid	Alkamine	Acids
Schoenocaulon officinale	Veratridine	veracevine	veratric
	Cevadine	veracevine	tiglic
Zygadenus venenosus	Veratroylzygadenine	zygadenine	veratric
	Vanilloylzygadenine	zygadenine	vanillic
	Germidine	germine	acetic 2-methylbutyric
	Neogermitrine	germine	acetic acetic 2-methylbutyric
Veratrum album	Germitetrine B	germine	acetic acetic 2-methylbutyric 2-methyl-2,3-hydroxybutyric
	Protoveratrine A	protoverine	acetic acetic 2-methylbutyric 2-methyl-2-hydroxybutyric
	Protoveratrine B	protoverine	acetic acetic 2-methylbutyric 2-methyl-2,3-hydroxybutyric

during a single experiment but varied from experiment to experiment. Doses refer to the base. Drug infusions were started after a control period of one-half hour following the isolation of the heart and lungs.

In some experiments, in order to increase the range of average heart rates, the hearts were stimulated at a rate of 190 to 200 stimuli per minute by a Grass stimulator set to deliver square waves of 8 volts and 1 msec. duration. The supramaximal stimulus was transmitted to the right atrial appendage through small electrode clamps clipped to the muscle. On the assumption that the mass of heart muscle would influence the lethal dose, rates of administration and lethal doses were expressed per kgm. heart. To correct for increases in weight due to edema accumulation during the course of an experiment, the "true heart weight" was determined by using the chloride method of Wood and Moe (1942), which estimates the edema by measuring the increase in extracellular chloride. The corrected heart weight was employed in all calculations.

The natural life span of the HLP is limited since progressive failure of the heart and lungs develops with time. The deterioration is materially hastened by the toxic effect of drugs. Experiments in which the preparation failed before the onset of ventricular fibrillation have been excluded from the portion of this report dealing with calculations of lethal dose.

The terms therapeutic dose, irregularity dose and lethal dose refer to the doses of drug producing the first detectable fall in RAP, the first EKG abnormality, and ventricular fibrillation, respectively.

As is true for the cardiac glycosides, marked therapeutic action of the tertiary amine veratrum ester alkaloids can be seen best in a failing heart. In the HLP, barbiturates or other hypnotic agents can readily produce severe heart failure. This was not attempted in these experiments because of the possible complicating effects of cardiac depressants on parameters, such as cardiac irregularity and lethal dose, that were to be measured. The appearance of a fall in RAP during drug infusion, at constant heart rate and constant reservoir level, therefore, represents cardiac compensation following that degree of spontaneous cardiac failure which occurs during the setting up of the HLP and within the thirty-minute control period prior to the start of drug administration.

In consideration of cardiac arrhythmias noted in this study, the term ventricular tachycardia has been arbitrarily limited to include only those cases where a unifocal ventricular tachycardia persisted for one minute duration or longer. This allowed a distinction (which became apparent during the course of the study) to be made between experiments for which this criterion was satisfied, and others in which only short bursts of ventricular ectopic beats, usually multifocal, were noted.

In most experiments terminating in ventricular fibrillation, the end point was sharp. However, in the experiments with neogermitrine, germitetrine B, protoveratrine A, and protoveratrine B, the preparations often exhibited repeated transient episodes of ventricular flutter-fibrillation (see, for example, figure 1B) lasting from a few seconds to one minute. In these experiments, the final episode was taken as the lethal end point.

The regressions of lethal dose on rate of infusion and on average heart rate were calculated by the method of multiple regression according to Mather (1947), and were assumed to be linear.

RESULTS. Under conditions of continuous infusion, all of the compounds studied showed effects in the HLP which were qualitatively similar to those observed with various cardiac glycosides (Farah and Maresh, 1948). First noted during infusion, at constant heart rate and constant reservoir level, is a fall in RAP. This is followed, after a variable interval of time, by cardiac irregularities terminating in ventricular fibrillation. The alkaloids studied showed great variability in the types of cardiac irregularity produced, in minimal lethal dose, in therapeutic range and in the relationship of lethal dose to rate of infusion and average heart rate. Table 2 gives a breakdown of the experiments in terms of therapeutic effect and irregularities of cardiac rate and rhythm. The most important of the various irregularities observed are illustrated in figures 1 and 2.

1. *Therapeutic action*. In all experiments with the esters of veracevine and zygadenine, with the exception of three out of thirty-five experiments with veratridine, a fall in RAP was the first sign of drug action noted. Among the esters of germine and protoverine this was observed in all experiments with the diester germidine but, as is shown in table 2, in only varying numbers of experiments with the tri- and tetraesters of germine and the tetraesters of protoverine. The experiments in which a therapeutic effect was not observed were usually those in which the rate of infusion was very low although in occasional experiments this effect was absent when the infusion rate was medium or high. The decreases in RAP were usually of small magnitude when compared to changes in RAP following the administration of these agents in the HLP during severe cardiac failure.

A negative inotropic effect, as reflected by a decrease in cardiac output or by

TABLE 2

Therapeutic, irregularity and lethal effects of various veratrum ester alkaloids in the heart-lung preparation of the dog

	Veratridine	Cevadine	Veratroylzygadenine	Vanilloylzygadenine	Germidine	Neogermitrine	Germitetrine B	Protoveratrine A	Protoveratrine B
1. Total no. experiments	**35**	**9**	**11**	**9**	**7**	**8**	**15**	**11**	**10**
a. experiments ending in ventricular fibrillation	26*	6	10	9	7	6	15	8	8
b. others**	9	3	1***	0	0	2	0	3	2
2. Experiments starting with normal sinus rhythm†	16	9	10	8	7	8	15	11	10
3. No. exp. of the total (see line 1) which showed the following:									
therapeutic effect	32	all	all	all	all	4	11	9	6
irregularity effects	all	all	all	all	all	7	all	all	6
electrical alternans of the QRS	all	1	all	all	6	0	0	0	0
2:1 heart block	25	0	5	6	0	0	0	0	0
bigeminal rhythm	0	0	0	0	all	6	8	8	3
ventricular tachycardia (one minute duration or greater)	0	1	0	0	3	1	10	7	2
4. No. exp. of those ending in ventricular fibrillation (see line 1a) which showed irregularity effects	all	all	all	all	all	5	all	all	5
5. No. exp. of those starting with normal sinus rhythm (see line 2) which showed the following:									
decrease in sinus rate (10 beats/min. or more)	4	5	2	2	2	0	1	0	0
increase in sinus rate†† (10 beats/min. or more)	4	1	0	0	2	0	0	0	1
sinus tachycardia	0	7	0	0	0	0	0	0	0

* Two experiments in this group were not included in calculations involving lethal dose because corrected heart weights were not available.

† Experiments (of the total no. see line 1) not included in this group were artificially stimulated at high rates and therefore did not start with normal sinus rhythm.

†† Not including sinus tachycardias.

** These experiments, at low infusion rates, terminated with failure of the heart and lungs. Ventricular fibrillation did not occur. These experiments were not used for calculation of therapeutic, irregularity or lethal dose.

*** This experiment terminated in ventricular fibrillation coincidental with mechanical failure of the stromuhr resulting in an elevated arterial pressure. The experiment was not used for calculation of lethal dose.

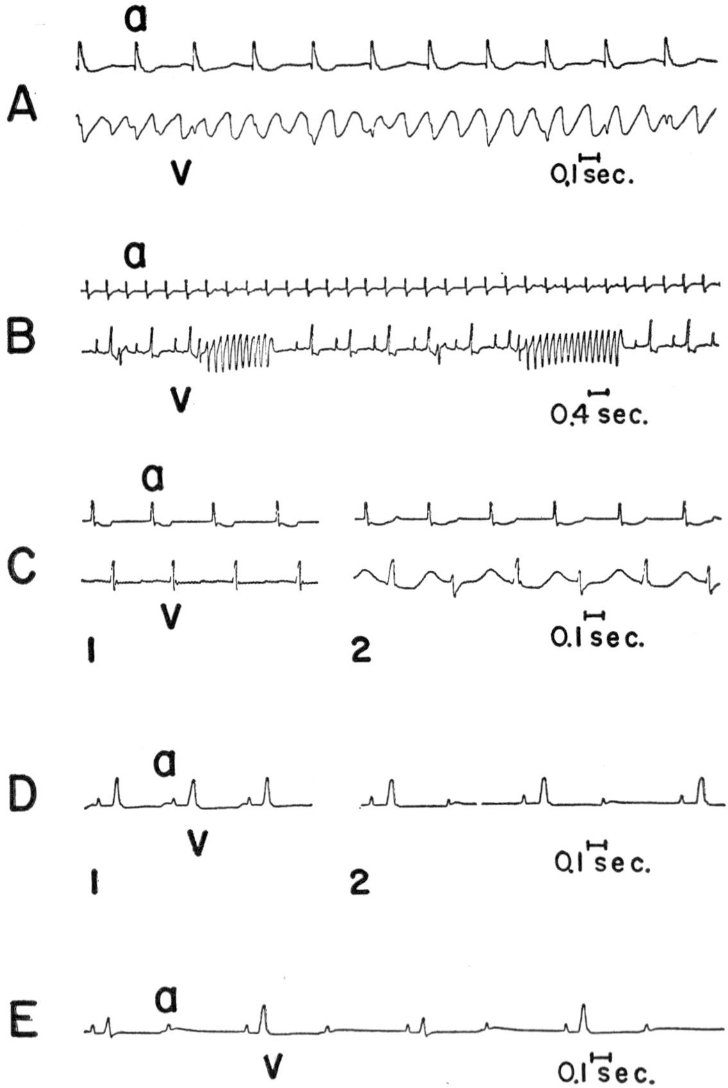

FIG. 1. Cardiac irregularities caused by veratrum ester alkaloids.

Dogs. Heart-lung preparations. EKG tracings taken with Grass inkwriting oscillograph. The veratrum alkaloids were administered by continuous infusion until the lethal effect was reached. In A, B and C the upper tracings were taken with direct atrial leads while the lower tracings represent pericardial leads. In D and E pericardial leads alone were used. a signifies an atrial complex; v signifies a ventricular complex. A. veratridine: atrial P waves recorded simultaneously with fibrillatory complexes from the ventricles. B. germitetrine B: transient flutter-fibrillation complexes from the ventricles. C. veratroylzygadenine: 1. sinus rhythm; 2. sinus rhythm with electrical alternation of the QRS. D. veratridine: 1. sinus rhythm; 2. 2:1 heart block. E. veratridine: electrical alternation of the QRS in the presence of 2:1 heart block.

an increase in RAP, prior to the onset of cardiac irregularities was not seen with any of the alkaloids studied.

2. *Cardiac irregularities.* a. Esters of veracevine and zygadenine: Irregularity effects were noted in all experiments. These followed the therapeutic effect when it was present. In experiments terminating in ventricular fibrillation, irregularity effects were always present at some time prior to the terminal event. Figure 1C shows an example of the electrical alternation of the QRS complex of the EKG which was the characteristic first sign of irregularity in every experiment with veratridine, veratroylzygadenine and vanilloylzygadenine. In thirty-six out of sixty-four experiments with these drugs, the electrical alternation was followed later during infusion by the onset of 2:1 heart block (figure 1D) which occasionally proceeded to 3:1 and 4:1 block. In the experiments in which 2:1 heart block occurred, persistence of the electrical alternation (figure 1E) was noted in nineteen of twenty-five experiments with veratridine, in four of five experiments with veratroylzygadenine, and in all of six experiments with vanilloylzygadenine.

Cevadine differed from the other alkaloids in this group in various ways. First, electrical alternation was observed in only one out of nine experiments. Second, in the presence of sinus rhythm 2:1 heart block did not occur in any of the experiments. Third, in one of the nine experiments ventricular tachycardia, not seen with the other alkaloids, was noted.

b. Esters of germine and protoverine: Irregularities of rate and rhythm were not observed in all experiments with the germine esters and the protoverine esters. Ventricular fibrillation, unheralded by previous cardiac irregularities, was seen in one of six neogermitrine experiments and in three of eight experiments with protoveratrine B. In one further experiment with protoveratrine B, at a low rate of infusion and in which ventricular fibrillation did not occur, no cardiac irregularities were recorded up to the time of failure of the HLP more than three hours after the start of drug infusion. The types of cardiac irregularities observed were varied (see figure 2A-D). Only germidine produced electrical alternation. Out of a total of seven experiments, it occurred in six, and in these it was the first evidence of irregularity. Electrical alternation was later followed by the onset of bigeminal rhythm (figure 2A) in which ventricular premature beats alternated with, and showed a constant coupling to, sinus beats. This type of bigeminal rhythm was noted in all germidine experiments. In varying numbers of experiments with the other germine esters and protoverine esters this type of bigeminal rhythm, when it was present, was the first sign of irregularity.

In the entire group of the germine esters and protoverine esters, with the exception of germidine, the onset of irregular bursts of ventricular or nodal ectopic beats (figure 2B) was the first sign of irregularity in about one-half of the experiments. In one experiment with protoveratrine A, a gradual migration of the pacemaker from the S-A node to the A-V node, without a change in rate, was observed. Figure 2C illustrates the gradual shift of the unaltered P wave to a position simultaneous in time with an altered QRS and, finally, to a position some milliseconds after the QRS. The P-P and Q-Q intervals are identical and

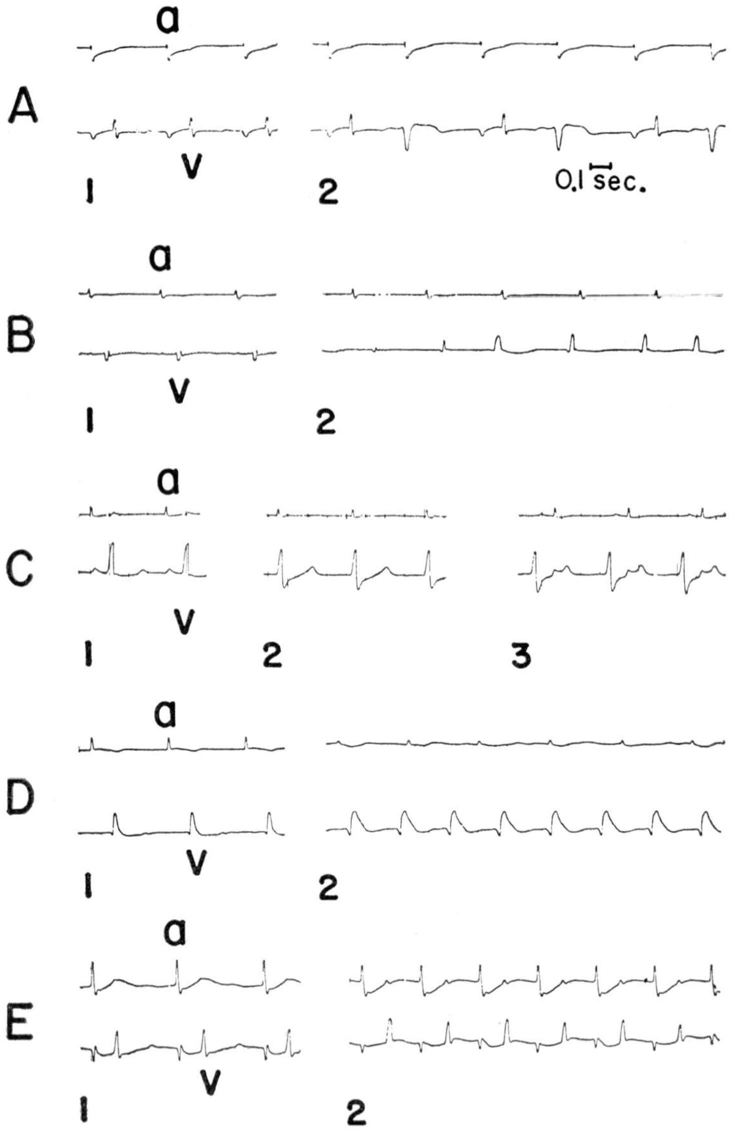

FIG. 2. Cardiac irregularities caused by veratrum ester alkaloids.

Dogs. Heart-lung preparations. EKG tracings taken with Grass inkwriting oscillograph. The veratrum alkaloids were administered by continuous infusion until the lethal effect was reached. Upper tracings were taken with direct atrial leads while the lower tracings represent pericardial leads. a signifies an atrial complex; v signifies a ventricular complex. A. germitetrine B: 1. sinus rhythm; 2. ventricular bigeminal rhythm. B. neogermitrine: 1. sinus rhythm; 2. ventricular ectopic beats. C. protoveratrine A: Form of the P wave remains unchanged throughout (thin vertical lines are time lines). 1. sinus rhythm; 2. A-V nodal pacemaker discharging at the same rate as the S-A node; P wave written simultaneously with nodal complex; 3. shift of the P wave to 0.1 second after nodal complex; the S-A node and the A-V node discharging independently at the same rate with only a shift in phase. D. protoveratrine A: 1. sinus rhythm; 2. ventricular tachycardia. E. cevadine: 1. sinus rhythm; 2. sinus tachycardia.

remain unaltered throughout. Periods of ventricular tachycardia (figure 2D), of more than one minute duration and usually occurring just prior to the onset of ventricular fibrillation, were observed in varying numbers of experiments. They were most pronounced with germitetrine B.

3. *Chronotropic effects.* In the HLP, even at constant temperature, spontaneous variations in sino-atrial rate, during the periods of time involved in these experiments, are of the order of less than ten beats per minute. A direct action on the rate of discharge of the S-A node, causing a decrease in heart rate of ten or more beats per minute, was observed in sixteen of a total of ninety-four experiments which started with normal sinus rhythm. The sixteen experiments comprise occasional experiments with the veracevine esters and zygadenine esters and with germidine and germitetrine B. This negative chronotropic effect occurred during the period following the onset of the therapeutic effect but prior to the beginning of cardiac irregularities. The decrease in rate amounted to less than ten per cent of the initial heart rate.

A true sinus bradycardia was observed in only one experiment among all the alkaloids studied. This was an experiment with veratridine in which, prior to drug infusion, the atrial rate was elevated by electrical stimulation from a sinus rate of 130 beats per minute to 180 beats per minute. After forty-five minutes of drug infusion, the atrium failed to follow the stimulator over a wide range of voltages, and stimulation was discontinued. The spontaneous atrial rate at this time was again 130 beats per minute. With the continuing drug infusion, it gradually decreased to eighty beats per minute, when 2:1 heart block supervened.

In eight of the total of ninety-four experiments, increases in sinus rate up to

TABLE 3

Lethal cardiac action of various veratrum ester alkaloids in the heart-lung preparation of the dog

	Veratridine	Cevadine	Veratroylzygadenine	Vanilloylzygadenine	Germidine	Neogermitrine	Germitetrine B	Protoveratrine A	Protoveratrine B
Regression coefficient (lethal dose on rate of infusion)	27.07*	1.96	13.98*	11.61	2.23	8.17	2.04	3.18	3.84
Regression coefficient (lethal dose on average heart rate)	−0.341*	+3.51	+0.018	−0.756*	+0.096	+0.006	−0.009	−0.006	−0.003
Minimal lethal dose (μmol./kgm. at average heart rate 143 beats/min.)	28.4	196.8	15.1	22.0	34.5	3.0	1.5	1.5	2.5

* Significant at the 1% level (none of the other regression coefficients were significant at the 5% level).

fifteen per cent were noted. The eight experiments comprise experiments with veratridine, cevadine, germidine and protoveratrine B, but do not include those experiments with cevadine in which sinus tachycardia occurred.

Only cevadine, of all the alkaloids studied, evoked sinus tachycardia (figure 2E). It occurred in seven out of nine experiments; the range of sinus rates observed was 215 to 268 beats/min. In one of these experiments, in which a sinus rate of 268 beats/min. was recorded, 2:1 heart block ensued.

4. *Rate of infusion, average heart rate and lethal dose.* For each alkaloid, in separate experiments, the rate of infusion and in some cases the heart rate were varied in an attempt to assess the dependence of lethal dose on these variables. The absolute values for rates of infusion varied with the potencies of the different alkaloids. For the mono-, di-, and triesters the infusion rates varied over a six- to thirteen-fold range; for the tetraesters, over a forty-seven to seventy-fold range. The range of average heart rates in all experiments was 67 to 227 beats per minute. In the groups of experiments carried out with the individual drugs the variation was much less, averaging about one and one-half fold. Lethal doses were calculated only for those experiments which terminated in ventricular fibrillation. The regression coefficients relating rate of infusion and average heart rate with lethal dose are listed in table 3.

a. Esters of veracevine and zygadenine: Among the esters of veracevine and zygadenine a significant relationship between rate of infusion and lethal dose was found only for veratridine and veratroylzgadenine. The regression coefficients of +27.07 and +13.98, respectively, are significant at the 1 per cent level. Significance for the inverse relation between average heart rate and lethal dose was found only for veratridine and vanilloylzygadenine with regression coefficients of −0.341 and −0.756, respectively. These are significant at the 1 per cent level.

b. Esters of germine and protoverine: Significance, at the 5 per cent level, for relationships between lethal dose and rate of infusion or average heart rate was not established for any of the germine esters and protoverine esters over the ranges of infusion rate and heart rate studied.

TABLE 4

Therapeutic and irregularity cardiac action of various ester alkaloids in the heart-lung preparation of the dog

Drug	Mean Therapeutic Dose in % of Lethal Dose ± S.E. (Range)	Mean Irregularity Dose in % of Lethal Dose ± S.E. (Range)	Mean Therapeutic Index* ± S.E. (Range)
Veratridine	4.6 ± 0.7 (1.4–15.2)	34.5 ± 2.5 (12.0–51.6)	8.9 ± 0.9 (2.8–18.7)
Cevadine	2.8 ± 0.5 (1.1–4.1)	84.0 ± 5.9 (58.2–97.5)	39.2 ± 10.9 (14.2–86.0)
Veratroylzygadenine	4.9 ± 0.6 (2.2–8.7)	44.1 ± 4.0 (26.1–68.4)	9.7 ± 0.9 (7.1–15.8)
Vanilloylzygadenine	4.8 ± 0.7 (1.9–7.9)	31.8 ± 5.7 (12.2–53.3)	7.2 ± 1.1 (2.6–12.5)
Germidine	5.4 ± 1.3 (1.6–10.7)	28.5 ± 3.9 (12.6–42.1)	7.3 ± 1.8 (2.0–14.1)
Neogermitrine	2.9 ± 0.4 (1.9–3.7)	35.6 ± 6.1 (15.3–50.0)	13.5 ± 4.8 (4.4–20.8)
Germitetrine B	17.0 ± 1.4 (10.5–26.4)	49.6 ± 3.7 (27.3–84.2)	3.1 ± 0.4 (1.8–6.0)
Protoveratrine A	7.8 ± 1.4 (4.8–14.3)	46.6 ± 4.6 (30.8–75.0)	6.1 ± 0.8 (3.5–9.3)
Protoveratrine B	22.4 ± 5.0 (5.6–37.0)	58.6 ± 6.7 (46.9–78.6)	2.5 ± 0.6 (1.9–3.7)

* The therapeutic index for each experiment was obtained by dividing the irregularity dose by the therapeutic dose.

5. *Minimal lethal dose and therapeutic range.* The minimal lethal doses (see table 3) were derived by obtaining the Y intercept in the regression of lethal dose on rate of infusion. All minimal lethal doses were corrected to an average heart rate of 143 beats per minute, which was the mean average heart rate in the experiments with veratridine. The minimal lethal doses spread over an approximately hundred-fold range, from 1.5 micromol./kgm. heart for germitetrine B and protoveratrine A to 197 micromol./kgm. heart for cevadine.

Mean therapeutic doses and mean irregularity doses, expressed in per cent of the lethal dose, are listed in table 4. Only experiments terminating in ventricular fibrillation were used for this evaluation. There was no apparent relation between rate of infusion or average heart rate (these varied from experiment to experiment) and the fraction of the lethal dose required for the appearance of therapeutic or irregularity effects, when these effects were present. This allowed the averaging of these parameters. Table 4 also lists the mean therapeutic indices derived from the therapeutic and irregularity doses. The variability, in terms of standard error, is in many instances quite marked.

DISCUSSION. The finding of a therapeutic action, in the HLP, of the veratrum tertiary amine ester alkaloids is in agreement with previously published reports (Krayer and Acheson, 1946). There have been suggestions in the recent literature that the characteristic hypotensive response to the veratrum alkaloids may result in part from the decrease in cardiac output associated with cardiac depressant effects (Waud *et al.*, 1955). Positive and negative inotropic effects in the rabbit heart have been reported by Stearns and Maison (1950). In the experiments reported here, no evidence of negative inotropic effects was seen at doses smaller than those required to produce cardiac irregularities. For protoveratrine, the minimal cardiac irregularity dose in the HLP is approximately two to five times that required in the intact dog to produce a 25 to 40 per cent decrease in blood pressure. This makes it unlikely that any direct cardiac depression is involved in the hypotensive response.

In a study of ventricular arrhythmias evoked by various agents in the intact dog, veratrine[3] was found to produce electrical alternans, sinus tachycardia and ventricular ectopic beats but no true extrasystoles, in the sense of ventricular beats accurately coupled to preceding sinus beats (Scherf *et al.*, 1952). The results of the present investigation suggest that of the arrhythmias found with veratrine, the electrical alternans is ascribable to its veratridine component while sinus tachycardia is probably due to the presence of cevadine. The ability of some veratrum alkaloids to produce true extrasystoles is evidenced by the ventricular bigeminal rhythm characteristic of the di- and polyacyl esters of germine and protoverine.

The electrical alternation noted with veratridine in the intact dog has been ascribed to skeletal muscle spasm and to respiratory movements (Cotton and Walton, 1951). However, its occurrence in the heart-lung preparation indicates that this effect can be explained by a direct cardiac action and presumably results

[3] A mixture of alkaloids derived from *Schoenocaulon officinale* containing mainly veratridine and cevadine.

from changes in intraventricular conduction (Lepeschkin, 1950). Of particular interest is the fact that, in most experiments in the present series in which 2:1 heart block followed the electrical alternation, the alternation persisted. This raises the question of some relationship between the altered QRS complex and either the preceding nonconducted or the preceding conducted beat or both.

The characteristic sinus bradycardia evoked by systemic administration of tertiary amine veratrum alkaloids to intact animals has been ascribed to reflex vagal discharge and to possible inhibition of accelerator tone (Jarisch and Richter, 1939; Krayer, 1954). The report of a sinus rate decrease from 148 to 52 beats per minute in one experiment in the isolated dog heart with veratrine suggested the possibility of an additional direct negative chronotropic effect (Krayer and Mendez, 1942). In one experiment with veratridine, in the present series, true sinus bradycardia of 80 beats per minute was observed in a heart with an original sinus rate of 130 beats per minute. With the exception of this single experiment, the data here reported indicate that bradycardia is rarely seen and, when present, is of the order of less than 10 per cent. It is, therefore, improbable that the sinus bradycardia seen in the intact animal has any direct cardiac component.

On the basis of the cardiac arrhythmias produced, the agents studied fall into two groups: 1) veratridine and the zygadenine esters, which produce electrical alternation and 2:1 block, and 2) the germine and protoveratrine esters, which produce ventricular bigeminal rhythm and ventricular tachycardias. Germidine, which causes electrical alternation and bigeminal rhythm, possesses characteristics of both groups; and it is interesting that in its veratrinic action on skeletal muscle it resembles veratridine rather than neogermitrine or the protoverine esters (Krayer *et al.*, 1953). Unique arrhythmias were seen with some of the substances studied, *i.e.*, sinus tachycardia with cevadine, sinus bradycardia with veratridine, and the presence of two independently discharging pacemakers (S-A node and A-V node) with protoveratrine A. How these differences in the nature of the arrhythmias are related to the differences between the alkamines and to the character, number, and position of the acyl groups of the alkaloids is not known.

In studying the lethal dose following intravenous administration of various cardiac glycosides in the cat, Maresh and Farah (1947) found that the rate of infusion affected the lethal dose when the drugs were given by continuous infusion at a constant rate. The same situation obtained in similar studies on the dog HLP (Farah and Maresh, 1948). The relationship observed indicated that, as the rate of infusion (starting at high rates) is reduced, the lethal dose decreases until at very low rates it tends to become constant. This relatively constant value has been designated the minimal lethal dose. The highest rate of infusion at which the minimal lethal dose was obtained has been called the optimal rate of infusion. The relationships could be best accounted for by assuming a maximal rate of uptake of drug by the heart equivalent to the optimal rate of infusion.

The significant regressions of lethal dose on rate of infusion obtained with veratridine and veratroylzygadenine suggest that, as for the cardiac glycosides, the rate of uptake of drug is a limiting factor. In the case of veratridine, the variability of the data is only partially narrowed by considering the influence of average heart rate. For the substances in which no significant relationship of lethal dose and rate of infusion was obtained, it is probable that over the range studied the access of drug to the myocardium is not a limiting factor. The absence of increases of lethal dose at low rates of infusion suggest that the alkaloids are not destroyed within the experimental periods.

In a study of the effect of heart rate on the lethal dose of veratridine in the dog heart-lung preparation, Benforado and Witt (1954) reported an inverse relationship between lethal dose and average heart rate. In their experiments the rate of infusion was constant and the criteria for lethal dose allowed the inclusion of experiments which did not terminate in ventricular fibrillation. In the experiments here reported, in which lethal doses were determined only for experiments terminating in ventricular fibrillation, the effect of heart rate, as well as rate of infusion, on lethal dose was examined. Differences in average heart rate (as defined under METHODS) are attributable to at least two factors: first, the initial rate of the isolated heart at the start of an experiment; and second, the action of the infused drug resulting in various arrhythmias which alter the rate of the ventricular beat. The initial rate was either the inherent sinus rate or a high rate arbitrarily imposed by electrical stimulation of the right atrium (twelve experiments with veratridine, one experiment with veratroylzygadenine, and one experiment with vanilloylzygadenine). The inherent sinus rate of the isolated dog heart in the HLP at temperatures between 38 and 39°C. varies and has been reported as 141.7 beats/min. with a standard deviation of 12.8 (Krayer and Benforado, 1955).

In the case of veratridine and vanilloylzygadenine, these factors resulted in a wide range of average heart rates (2.2 to 2.4 fold) and only for these alkaloids a significant inverse relationship between lethal dose and average heart rate was obtained. For the remaining substances the ranges of average heart rates were only 1.3 to 1.7 fold and no significant relationship was observed. A hypothesis concerning the possible importance of a critical number of beats for lethal action, accounting for the inverse relationship between lethal dose and average heart rate, has been presented in a previous paper (Benforado and Witt, 1954).

The minimal lethal doses (see table 3), determined by the technique of continuous infusion, indicate that, on a molar basis, highest cardiac potency is to be found in the triesters and tetraesters. In general, this relationship holds for the hypotensive potency as well. With the exception of cevadine, the minimal (molar) lethal doses are in the same range as those reported for various cardiac glycosides (Farah and Maresh, 1948).

The studies of Farah and Maresh (1948) on the therapeutic ranges of cardiac glycosides in the dog HLP are remarkable for the constancy of response observed at varying rates of infusion and in the presence of differences in potency. The therapeutic and irregularity doses, when expressed in per cent of lethal dose, were about 18 per cent and 62 per cent, respectively. The therapeutic indices for the cardiac glycosides, calculated as irregularity dose divided by therapeutic dose, are about three. The variation in these data, though not analyzed by the authors, was surprisingly small. Comparable data on the veratrum alkaloids indicate that the relative therapeutic and irregularity doses vary from substance to substance and that, with the same substance, the variability is high as evidenced by high standard errors. It is to be remembered that positive inotropic effects and EKG irregularities prior to ventricular fibrillation were not seen in some experiments with the tri- and tetraesters (see table 2). The mean therapeutic indices listed in table 4 suggest that, for the veratrum alkaloids, the values may be three to four times higher than those for the cardiac glycosides, but that the dose range in which a specific response can be expected is subject to wide variation.

Therapeutic ranges of veratridine and protoveratrine when administered in divided doses to the dog HLP have been reported by Krayer, Moe and Mendez (1944). Protoveratrine has since been separated into two components, protoveratrines A and B. The values for minimal therapeutic and minimal irregularity doses of veratridine and of the individual protoveratrine alkaloids obtained in the present experiments by the technique of continuous infusion and expressed in mgm. per heart (average heart weight 66.8 gm.) agree in general with those reported by Krayer, Moe and Mendez (1944). They are probably better estimates because of the manner in which they were obtained.

SUMMARY

When administered by continuous infusion into the dog heart-lung preparation, the veracevine, zygadenine, germine and protoverine ester alkaloids studied produced effects qualitatively similar to those reported for the cardiac glycosides. A therapeutic action on cardiac contractility was first noted; this was followed by the onset of cardiac irregularities terminating in ventricular fibrillation. The character of the irregularities produced varied with the number and nature of the acids as well as with the nature of the alkamine. Sinus tachycardia was the characteristic irregularity with cevadine while veratridine and the other closely related zygadenine esters produced electrical alternation and 2:1 heart block. The germine and protoverine esters, on the other hand, evoked ventricular premature contractions with bigeminal rhythm and ventricular tachycardia. Germidine, a diester of germine, possesses characteristics of both groups in that it produced first an electrical alternation followed by bigeminal rhythm. The negative chronotropic effect of these alkaloids, if present, is of the order of less than ten per cent. This makes it improbable that the marked bradycardia seen following their administration in the intact animal has any appreciable direct cardiac component. A significant relationship between lethal dose and rate of infusion, established for the cardiac glycosides, was observed only for veratridine and veratroylzygadenine. A significant inverse relationship between lethal dose and average heart rate, not apparent with the cardiac glycosides, was established for veratridine and vanilloylzygadenine. With the exception of cevadine, for which the minimal lethal dose was about 200 micromol./kgm., the minimal lethal doses were in the range of 1 to 30 micromol./kgm. This is of the same order reported for the cardiac glycosides. Highest molar potency was found in the tri- and tetraesters. The therapeutic ranges for some of the veratrum alkaloids studied were three to four times greater than those reported for various cardiac glycosides. However, the variability from experiment to experiment with the same alkaloid, as well as the variability between different alkaloids, was much greater than with the cardiac glycosides.

ACKNOWLEDGMENTS. I wish to thank Professor O. Krayer for his help and encouragement throughout this work. Thanks are also due to Mrs. Steffi Hunger, Mrs. Ursula Henderson, Miss Brigitte Hofheinz, and Mr. Douglas Ruane for technical assistance.

REFERENCES

BENFORADO, J. M., AND WITT, P. N.: THIS JOURNAL, **110:** 334, 1954.
COTTEN, M. DEV., AND WALTON, R. P.: Arch. int. Pharmacodyn., **87:** 473, 1951.
FARAH, A., AND MARESH, G.: THIS JOURNAL, **92:** 32, 1948.
JARISCH, A., AND RICHTER, H.: Arch. f. exper. Path. u. Pharmakol., **193:** 347, 1939.
KRAYER, O.: Arch. f. exper. Path. u. Pharmakol., **162:** 1, 1931.
KRAYER, O., AND MENDEZ, R.: THIS JOURNAL, **74:** 350, 1942.
KRAYER, O., MOE, G. K., AND MENDEZ, R.: THIS JOURNAL, **82:** 167, 1944.
KRAYER, O., AND ACHESON, G. H.: Physiol. Rev., **26:** 383, 1946.
KRAYER, O., KUPCHAN, S. M., DELIWALA, C. V., AND ROGERS, B. H.: Arch. f. exper. Path. u. Pharmakol., **219:** 371, 1953.
KRAYER, O.: Pharmacology in Medicine, Chapter 33, ed., Victor A. Drill, McGraw-Hill, N. Y., 1954.
KRAYER, O., AND BENFORADO, J. M.: Pflügers Arch. ges. Physiol., **260:** 177, 1955.
LEPESCHKIN, E.: Cardiologia, **16:** 278, 1950.
MARESH, G. J., AND FARAH, A. E.: THIS JOURNAL, **90:** 304, 1947.
MATHER, K.: Statistical Analysis in Biology, Interscience Pub., N. Y., 1947.
SCHERF, D., BLUMENFELD, S., MUELLER, P., AND TERRANOVA, R.: Proc. Soc. Exper. Biol. & Med., **81:** 701, 1952.
STEARNS, N. S., AND MAISON, G. L.: THIS JOURNAL, **100:** 238, 1950.
WAUD, R. A., LANSING, A. M., AND LEWIS, R. A.: THIS JOURNAL, **114:** 271, 1955.
WOOD, E. H., AND MOE, G. K.: Am. J. Physiol., **136:** 506, 1942.

THE EFFECTS OF RELAXIN-CONTAINING OVARIAN EXTRACTS ON VARIOUS TYPES OF SMOOTH MUSCLE[1]

JACK W. MILLER, ANTHONY KISLEY[2] AND WILLIAM J. MURRAY

Department of Pharmacology and Toxicology, The University of Wisconsin, Service Memorial Institutes, Madison

Received for publication March 4, 1957

Aqueous extracts of ovaries containing relaxin are known to produce a variety of actions on the genitourinary system and the pubic symphysis. Certain of these actions have been discussed in a review by Frieden and Hisaw (1953). These extracts have been found to inhibit the spontaneous uterine motility of the guinea pig, rat, mouse (Sawyer *et al.*, 1953) and human (Posse and Kelly, 1956), and to relax the cervix of the cow (Graham and Dracy, 1953) and sow (Zarrow *et al.*, 1956). The extracts have also been employed to inhibit the uterine contractions associated with premature labor (Abramson and Reid, 1955; Eichner *et al.*, 1956; Folsome *et al.*, 1956). The component which inhibits the uterus may be identical with relaxin, although a "uterine relaxing factor" in similar ovarian extracts has been described. The latter factor inhibits the uterine motility of guinea pigs (Felton *et al.*, 1953) and has been employed for premature labor (Majewski and Jennings, 1955) and dysmenorrhea (Jones and Smith, 1954; Jones, 1955). Recently, Frieden *et al.* (1956) have presented evidence indicating that the "uterine relaxing factor" and the substance which relaxes the pubic symphysis are two different materials; however, neither factor has been isolated. It is likely that the known actions of the water soluble extracts of ovaries are due to more than one component. The present study was undertaken to obtain further information concerning the general pharmacology of relaxin-containing extracts, particularly with respect to various types of smooth muscle.

METHODS. The potencies of the relaxin-containing extracts[3] employed in the present studies are expressed in guinea-pig pubic-symphysis units (GPU) and were stated by the supplier to be as follows: Releasin Standard Powder (B-37-348/8 alpha) 150 GPU/mgm. and Releasin Powder (80516, M-43) 18 GPU/mgm. These extracts will be referred to as relaxin standard and M-43, respectively.

A total of 26 dogs of mixed sexes, 80 rats and 15 rabbits were employed in the present study. Dogs were anesthetized with pentobarbital (33 mgm./kgm., intraperitoneally) and the carotid blood pressure was followed by means of a recording mercury manometer; ureteral motility was measured by perfusion techniques and a drop recorder (Abrahams and Pickford, 1956). Drugs were injected into the femoral vein. The histamine content of plasma was estimated by means of an assay utilizing the atropinized guinea pig ileum and specificity established with diphenhydramine. Blood was obtained from the carotid arteries of dogs

[1] Supported in part by the Research Committee of the Graduate School from funds supplied by the Wisconsin Alumni Research Foundation. The results of this study were presented at the meeting of the American Society for Pharmacology and Experimental Therapeutics, French Lick, Indiana, November 8, 1956. THIS JOURNAL, **119**: 170, 1957.

[2] Research Fellow supported by a grant from the National Science Foundation for medical students.

[3] Kindly supplied by Warner-Chilcott Laboratories.

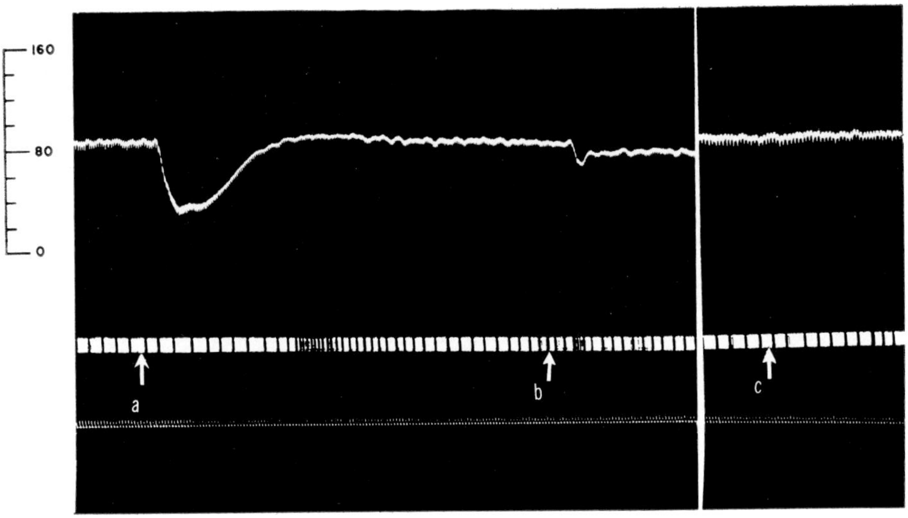

FIG. 1. The carotid blood pressure (upper) and ureteral motility (drop record of ureteric flow) of the dog; time (lower) at 5 sec. intervals. (A) M-43, 15 mgm./kgm., (B) M-43, 30 mgm./kgm. and (C) M-43, 15 mgm./kgm., 22 min. after (B). Extract given intravenously.

which were not employed for blood pressure measurements; heparin was employed to prevent clotting.

Segments of each uterine horn were suspended in constant temperature baths (37° C.) containing 50 ml. of Locke's solution (Sawyer *et al.*, 1953) aerated with 95 per cent oxygen and 5 per cent carbon dioxide and spontaneous motility recorded isotonically. Drug concentrations are expressed as the quantity of agent added.

Uterine motility *in vivo* was measured by recording the pressure changes within a uterine horn or segment which was filled with saline, cannulated, and connected to a recording tambour. Rats were anesthetized with pentobarbital (50 mgm./kgm. subcutaneously); rabbits were anesthetized with urethane (2 gm./kgm. subcutaneously).

The changes in capillary permeability to trypan blue in rats were judged by the degree of bluing in skin areas where agents were administered intradermally. Three days following chemical depilation of the backs of rats, 10 mgm. of trypan blue was administered intravenously. Following dye administration, drugs dissolved in 0.9 per cent sodium chloride were injected intradermally in a volume of 0.1 ml. The animals were killed 10 minutes later and the skin removed for viewing or photographing (Miles and Miles, 1952).

The compositions of the solutions employed in studies concerning the effect of proteolytic enzymes on the hypotensive and uterine inhibitory actions of M-43 were as follows: salt free chymotrypsin (General Biochemicals, Inc.) 0.5 mgm./ml. and M-43, 10 mgm./ml. of Locke's solution; and pepsin (Merck) 2 mgm./ml. and M-43, 30 mgm./ml. in dilute HCl (pH 1.4). The effect of solutions containing a) enzyme, b) enzyme plus extract, and c) boiled enzyme plus extract were studied. When pepsin was employed, all solutions were boiled and cooled just prior to injection.

RESULTS. The effect of the low potency extract (M-43) on the blood pressure and ureteral motility of the dog is shown in figure 1. The material produced a marked hypotension approximately twenty seconds after intravenous administration. This effect was greatly diminished or absent on subsequent administration indicating development of tachyphylaxis. The extract also produced an apparent constriction of the ureters for short periods of time, during which the passage of perfusion fluid was greatly diminished. The ureteral inhibition usually occurred during the hypotension, although occasionally as shown in figure 1, the inhibition occurred later. Tachyphylaxis also developed to the action on the ureters. The effects of the extract on blood pressure and the ureters were observed in both male and female dogs. In additional studies it was found that the relaxin standard (4 mgm./kgm. intravenously) produced a fall in blood pressure about half as great as that produced by 15 mgm./kgm. of M-43. Further comparison of the hypotensive actions of M-43 and the relaxin standard were not made due to the limited supply of the latter extract.

The delayed hypotension and subsequent tachyphylaxis that was noted suggested that a component in the extract caused the release of histamine (Macintosh and Paton, 1949; Paton, 1951). In preliminary studies it was found that histamine was released and that maximum concentrations occurred one to two minutes following M-43. The average plasma concentration of histamine in 4 dogs one to two minutes following the intravenous administration of M-43 is shown in table 1. Histamine was not detected in control plasma samples. The sensitivity of the assay was sufficient to detect approximately 0.02 microgm. of histamine/ml. of plasma. The histamine released resulted in plasma concentrations the same as that detected immediately after intravenous administration of 10 microgm./kgm. of histamine phosphate (table 1). This dose of histamine produced a hypotension comparable to that produced by M-43, but was of shorter duration. The hypotension could therefore be accounted for mainly through the release of histamine. The changes in hematocrit following administration of M-43 or histamine are also shown in table 1. The hematocrit appeared to be slightly increased in both instances, which would be consistent with an increase in capillary permeability and hemoconcentration. Other histamine releasers are known to produce such an action (Macintosh and Paton, 1949). It should be mentioned that the extract did not contain histamine as determined by direct assay employing the guinea pig ileum. Further, the hypotension was not prevented by prior administration of atropine sulfate (0.2 mgm./kgm.) or diphenhydramine (5 mgm./kgm.). This dosage of antihistamine either prevented or greatly diminished the hypotension produced by 1 and 10 microgm./kgm. of

TABLE 1

The effect of M-43 on the histamine content of plasma one to two minutes after its intravenous administration to dogs

The values obtained following intravenous histamine phosphate are those immediately after drug administration. The mean and standard error of the mean (±) for 4 dogs are shown.

	Control	M-43 *15 mgm./kgm.*	Histamine Phosphate *10 microgm./kgm.*
Histamine base equivalent microgm./ml. plasma	Not detected	0.084 (±0.025)	0.084 (±0.033)
Hematocrit	46 (±2.8)	49 (±3.0)	50 (±3.9)

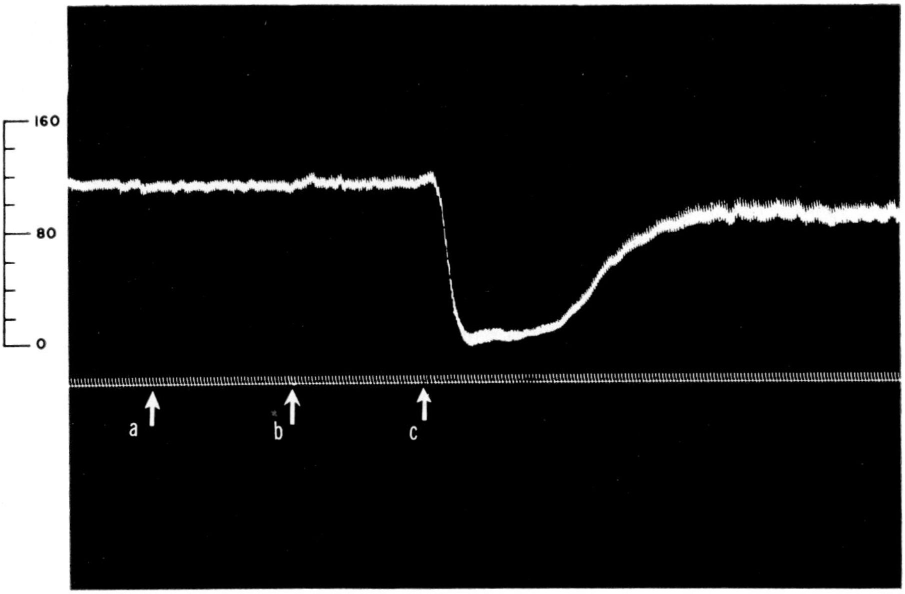

FIG. 2. The carotid blood pressure of the dog; time at 5 sec. intervals. (A) incubation medium plus chymotrypsin, (B) same as (A) but including M-43 (equivalent to 15 mgm./kgm.) after 2 hours incubation, (C) same as (B) except enzyme boiled.

histamine phosphate, respectively. The failure of diphenhydramine to antagonize the vascular actions of M-43 may be related to the dose of the latter. Macintosh and Paton (1949) found that while the vascular effects of small doses of a histamine releaser could be antagonized by prior administration of antihistamines, only the rate at which blood pressure fell could be altered when larger doses of the releaser were employed.

The mechanism of inhibitory action of M-43 on the ureters is difficult to explain. It was observed that administration of histamine produced a similar action on the ureters. However, as figure 1 shows, the ureteral inhibition may occur after the period of hypotension (and release of histamine). It is possible that the delayed action in certain experiments is related to a decrease in blood flow to the ureters during the hypotension and a failure of the material to gain access to this area as rapidly as to vascular smooth muscle. Abramson *et al.* (1953) concluded that periodic administration of relaxin-containing extracts to rabbits produced an atonicity of the ureteral musculature. The duration of action appears to be much longer in the rabbit when compared to the present experiments with dogs. The results obtained by Eichner *et al.* (1956) indicate that administration of relaxin does not result in any consistent action on the ureters of women.

In electrocardiographic studies it was noted that doses of M-43 which produced hypotension, caused a bradycardia rather than the usual reflex tachycardia associated with a fall in blood pressure. This change in heart rate is not evident in the kymographic tracings shown in figures 1 and 2 due to the slow drum speed employed. The bradycardia like the hypotension was delayed and hyperpnea often occurred. Tachyphylaxis to the action of the extract on heart rate can also develop. Other than the changes in heart rate, no consistent changes in the ECG were noted.

The substance(s) responsible for the hypotensive action of M-43 was found to be heat stable (30 min. at 100° C.), non-diffusible through a dialysis sack (Visking), rapidly destroyed by incubation with chymotrypsin (figure 2) but not with pepsin. In parallel studies it was noted that the component which inhibited the motility of the rat uterus had similar properties except that it was also inactivated by peptic digestion. Thus both materials exhibit properties of a protein or polypeptide but differ with respect to their susceptibility to destruction by pepsin.

The effect of the relaxin standard on the permeability of capillaries in rat skin to trypan blue is illustrated in figure 3. The darker areas of the photograph are sites of bluing and indicate an increase in capillary permeability to trypan blue. It may be seen that 100 microgm. of the reference standard produced a bluing slightly greater than that caused by 10 microgm. of histamine phosphate. The injections of saline produced essentially no bluing. These results, as well as those obtained with dogs, are consistent with the view that the relaxin standard also contains the component which releases histamine.

The relaxin standard (1.0 to 1.5 mgm.) produced a constriction of the perfused vessels of the hinder portion of the rat. Tachyphylaxis developed to this action. The constriction may be due to the release of histamine, although it was difficult

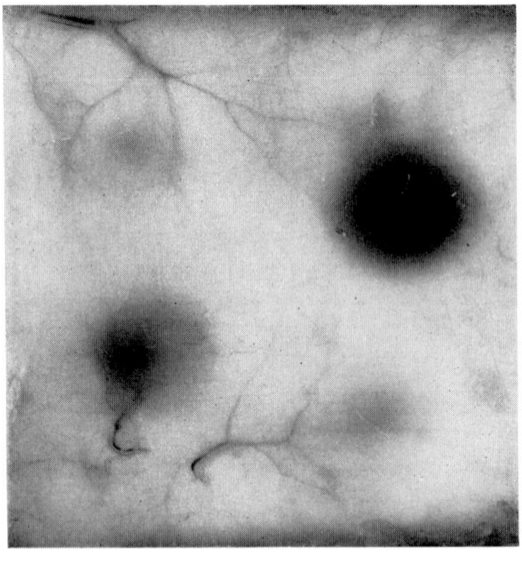

FIG. 3. Photograph of skin from the back of a rat given trypan blue intravenously followed by intradermal injections of various agents.

Dark areas indicate bluing. Upper right, relaxin standard, 100 microgm.; upper left and lower right, saline; lower left, histamine phosphate, 10 microgm.

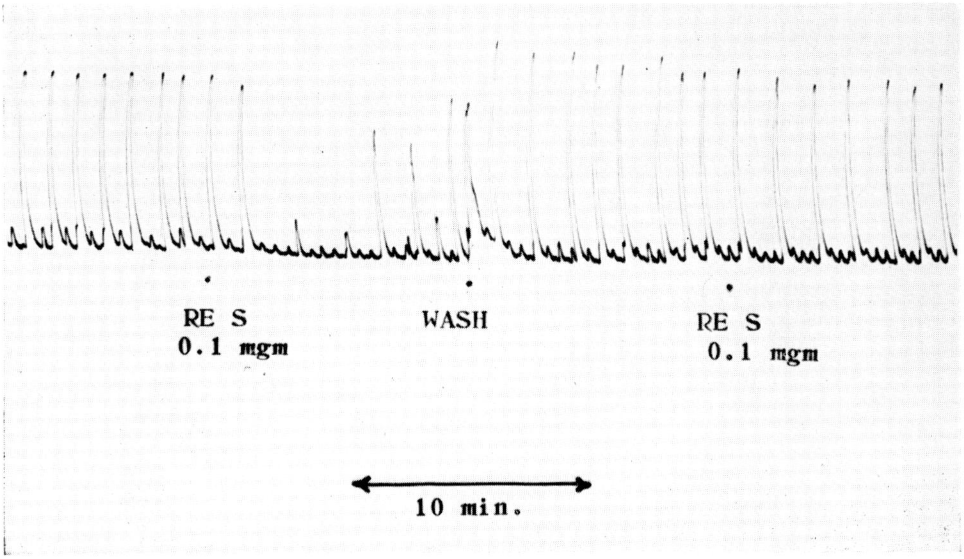

FIG. 4. Spontaneous contractions of the isolated uterus of the rat illustrating development of tachyphylaxis to the relaxin standard (RE S).
The animal was castrated and a diethylstilbestrol pellet (15 mgm.) implanted 2 months previously.

to produce a vascular constriction even with large amounts of histamine phosphate (1 to 2 gm.) in this preparation.

Administration of M-43 produced no consistent alteration in the motility of the gastrointestinal tract of the anesthetized dog. Further, the relaxin standard did not affect the rate of propulsion of a carbon black meal through the gastrointestinal tract of the mouse (Miller *et al.*, 1955) and did not alter the motility of the guinea pig ileum *in vitro*. Sawyer *et al.* (1953) found that relaxin-containing extracts were without action on the rat intestine *in vitro*. The muscle of the gall bladder of the rat *in vitro* was not affected by the extracts; contractions were, however, produced by histamine. It was also noted that the contractile amplitude of the isolated atria of the rat but not of the rabbit was increased by relaxin standard.

The inhibitory effect of relaxin standard on the spontaneous motility of the rat uterus is shown in figure 4. It can be seen that the inhibitory action was reversed by washing. Sawyer *et al.* (1953) have reported similar results. In addition, however, figure 4 also shows that a second addition of the extract failed to produce inhibition, indicating the development of tachyphylaxis. The rate of development of tachyphylaxis was variable and in certain instances inhibition could be produced several times. Further, it was noted that uterine motility usually returned without washing the preparation if sufficient time were allowed (figure 4). The inhibition usually was quantal, although on occasion it was possible to obtain an intermediate response for short periods of time. The fact that tachyphylaxis may develop places limitations on the use of this type of preparation for bioassay purposes.

The sensitivity of the rat uterus to the extracts depended to a large extent on prior estrogen treatment. Sensitivity was enhanced by administration of alpha estradiol dipropionate (0.15 mgm./day) for two or three days to previously castrated animals (100 gm.). Under these circumstances responses were obtained with amounts as small as one microgm. of relaxin standard; in untreated animals doses as large as one milligram were often required to produce inhibition. Suitable preparations were also obtained from castrated or unoperated rats which had received ethinyl estradiol (0.15 mgm./day for 1 to 10 days) or an implanted stilbestrol pellet (15 mgm.) 2 to 12 weeks previously.

The inhibitory effect of the relaxin standard on the motility of the rat uterus *in vitro* was reversed by a number of agents which normally cause contraction of the uterus of this species (figure 5). Such agents as acetylcholine, 5-hydroxytrypta-

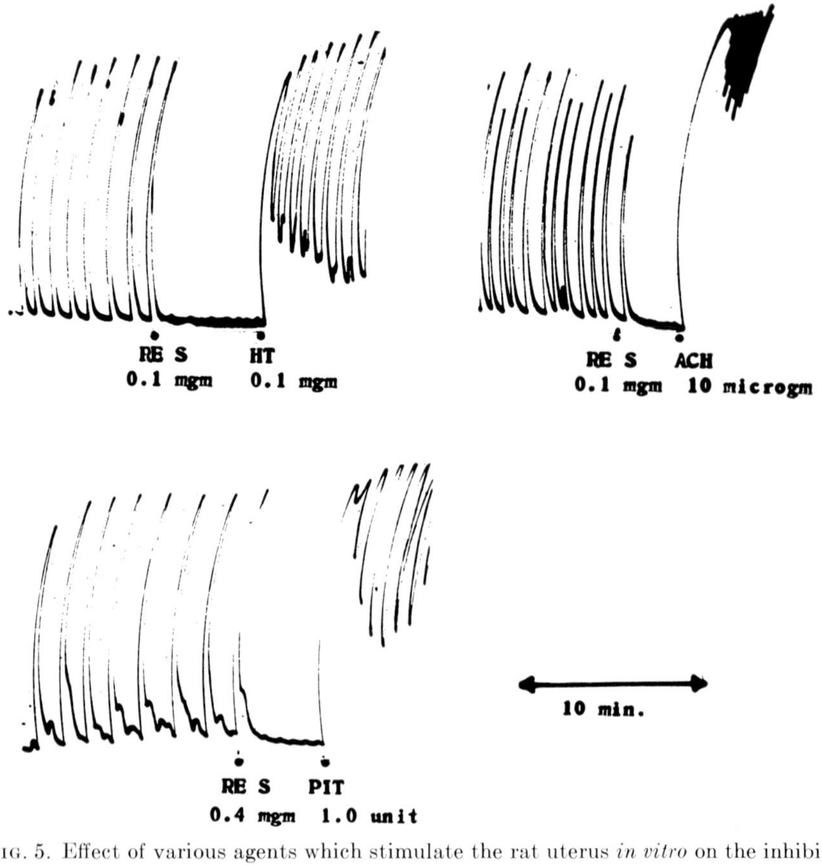

FIG. 5. Effect of various agents which stimulate the rat uterus *in vitro* on the inhibition produced by relaxin standard (RE S).

5-Hydroxytryptamine (HT), acetylcholine (ACH), oxytocin (PIT). Ethinyl estradiol (0.15 mgm.) daily for 2 days.

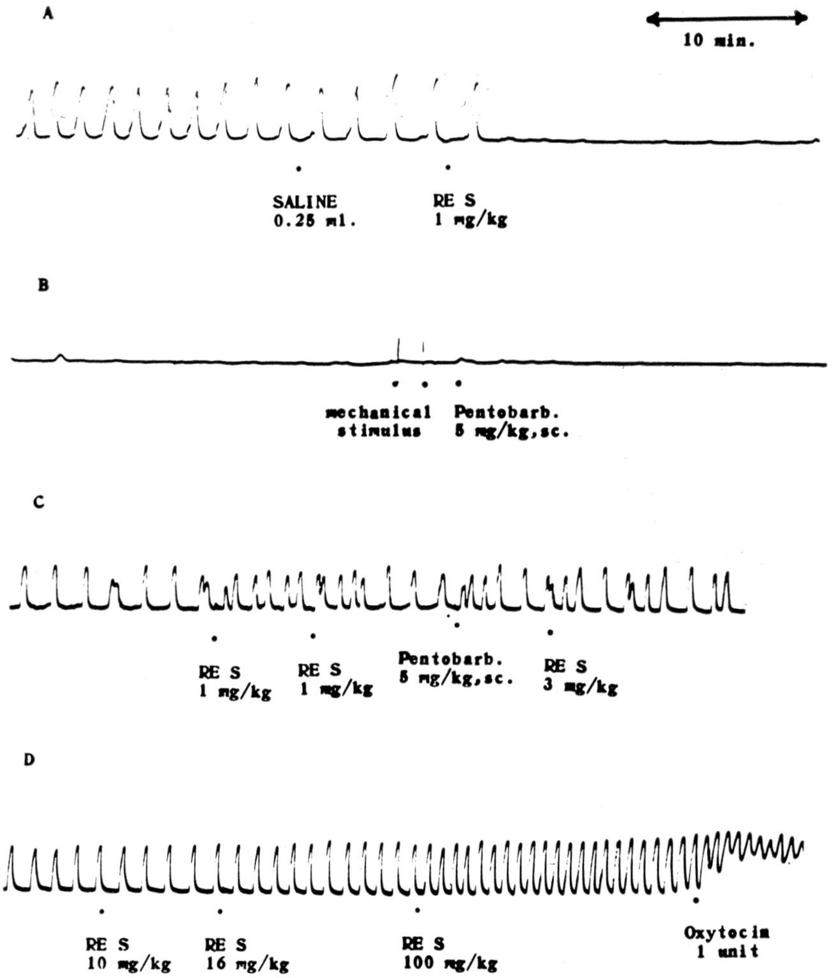

FIG. 6. The effect of relaxin standard (RE S) on uterine motility of the rat *in vivo* Record is continuous except between (B) and (C) where motility was induced by a series of mechanical stimuli that are not shown. Ethinyl estradiol (0.15 mgm.) daily for 6 days.

mine, oxytocin and bradykinin (not shown) readily antagonized this action of the extract. Sawyer *et al.* (1953) also noted that reversal was produced by oxytocin and acetylcholine.

The component in M-43 which inhibited the motility of the rat uterus was destroyed by chymotrypsin and pepsin. In several experiments it was noted that destruction by pepsin, with the concentrations employed, was incomplete after two hours; chymotrypsin, however, produced inactivation in as little time as 30 minutes. Felton *et al.* (1953) found that relaxin and the "uterine relaxing factor" were destroyed by pepsin and trypsin within 24 hours.

The effect of the relaxin standard on the motility of the rat uterus *in vivo* is shown in figure 6. It may be seen that the intraperitoneal administration of 1.0 mgm./kgm. abolished uterine contractions for about one hour. During this period of time, mechanical stimulation (a brief increase in pressure inside the uterus) failed to induce a contraction. However, after one hour, mechanical stimulation initiated contractions and motility was restored. At this time various doses of the relaxin standard were again administered but failed to produce inhibition. Figure 6 demonstrates that under these circumstances, doses as large as 100 mgm./kgm. failed to inhibit motility, whereas sensitivity to oxytocin was retained. Data from one experiment suggest that the period of inhibition of an effective dose can be shortened by prior administration of several subthreshold doses. Usually inhibition was of several hours duration and the motility which eventually developed was irregular. Administration of oxytocin always antagonized the inhibition of uterine motility.

It may be noted that since histamine inhibits the rat uterus, the results of the present study might be explained on the basis of the histamine-releasing action of the extracts. The tachyphylaxis which was observed might then be related to a depletion of endogenous histamine. However, as previously mentioned, other investigators have reported that the uterus of guinea pigs is also inhibited by similar extracts and histamine is known to stimulate the uterus of this species. Additional evidence that histamine release is not a factor in the observed results derives from the fact that pepsin destroyed the factor which inhibited the rat uterus but not the histamine releaser present in the extracts.

The extracts failed to alter uterine motility in the rabbit. Prior administration of diethylstilbestrol did not affect this lack of responsiveness; intravenous doses as large as 26.4 mgm./kgm. of the relaxin standard were employed. In addition, the motility of the rabbit uterus *in vitro* was not inhibited by the extracts; indeed, on occasion, increased contractile amplitude developed. Thus, the rabbit appears to be an exception to the inhibitory action of the extracts on the uterus. Krantz *et al.* (1950) indicated that the aqueous ovarian extracts which they studied inhibited the motility of the rabbit uterus. This difference might be regarded as evidence for several different inhibitory factors.

The motility of strips prepared from 8 human uteri obtained either after hysterectomy or during cesarean section was also studied *in vitro*. The states of the nonpregnant uteri were as follows: 2 menstrual, 1 proliferative, 2 secretory and 1 menopausal. Strips from 2 pregnant uteri were obtained during the 39th week of gestation. The strips prepared from the menopausal uterus were contracted by the relaxin standard; in every other preparation the standard (1 to 4 mgm.) failed to alter motility. Thus, although the extracts are known to inhibit the human uterus *in vivo*, this effect was not produced *in vitro*. The time for motility to develop and the response to epinephrine of the strips of human uteri were essentially the same as reported by Garrett (1955).

DISCUSSION. The results of the present study indicate that tachyphylaxis can develop to the inhibitory action of relaxin-containing ovarian extracts on the uterus of the rat. The presence of a component in these extracts which is capable of causing a release of histamine also has been demonstrated. These observations may have a bearing on the use of similar extracts in man and offer an explanation for certain findings of other investigators.

The majority of clinical studies employing a parenteral preparation containing relaxin have been made with the commercial product, Releasin.[4] This product is standardized in terms of the relaxin standard which was employed in the present study and supplied by the same company. Another commercial product which is administered orally, Lutrexin,[5] also contains relaxin although potency is stated in terms of "uterine relaxing factor" units (Felton *et al.*, 1953).

It has been noted that pain at the site of injection (Perkoff *et al.*, 1954; Eichner *et al.*, 1956) is associated with the administration of Releasin. In addition, Perkoff *et al.* (1954) observed local edema following subcutaneous infusions of the material. Our findings suggest a local release of histamine as an explanation for the foregoing observations. However, there is little evidence that histamine is released systemically following administration of Releasin to man. Only in certain isolated instances has administration of the extract resulted in hypotension. Folsome *et al.* (1956) reported one case in which hypotension developed during the course of continuous intravenous infusion, and it was stated that the vehicle might have been a factor. In the same study, the authors reported that a decline in blood pressure occurred in two patients with toxemia of pregnancy. Kelly and Posse (1956) and Posse and Kelly (1956) reported that intravenous administration of Releasin sometimes was followed by chills but no changes in blood pressure or urticaria were noted.

Several factors may be responsible for the apparent differences in action of these extracts on the vascular system of man and the dog. In studies of other histamine releasers, activity has been found in certain instances to depend on the species employed. Dextran is stated to release histamine only in the albino rat and polyvinylpyrrolidone has a specific action in the dog (Halpern, 1956). Thus, it is conceivable that ovarian extracts cause histamine release in the dog, such activity being limited or absent in other species. Dosage may be another factor which is important in determining whether sufficient histamine is released to produce an observable effect. The concentration of Releasin at an injection site may be sufficient to cause histamine release locally but be too low when distributed throughout the body to produce a systemic response. The possibility also exists that a series of sub-threshold doses may lead to a refractory state similar to that described by Slomka and Goth (1956) for the action of 48/80 in dogs. Finally it is known that the ability of serum from pregnant women to inactivate histamine increases with gestation (Ahlmark, 1944, Kapeller-Adler, 1949). Thus it might be possible that a histamine releaser would produce little or no action in pregnant women due to the increased histaminolytic activity observed in serum at this time. However, there is evidence against this possibility since Janowitz and Grossman (1949) have shown that the threshold dose of histamine to produce vascular responses is not decreased in pregnant women. It

[4] Releasin, Warner-Chilcott Laboratories, brand of relaxin.
[5] Lutrexin, Hynson, Westcott and Dunning, Inc., brand of lututrin, N.N.R.

may be added that other actions of histamine are not altered during pregnancy in women and these findings have been discussed by Kahlson (1956).

The observation in the present study that tachyphylaxis can develop to the inhibitory action of the extracts on the rat uterus may have important implications in their clinical usage. Posse and Kelly (1956) have recently reported that rapid tolerance or tachyphylaxis also develops to the uterine effects of Releasin in non-pregnant women. Kelly and Posse (1956) noted that the uterine contractions in one patient in her 39th week of pregnancy were initially abolished by Releasin but when motility returned one hour later, further administration of the extract was without effect. In other clinical studies, previously mentioned, the extracts have stopped premature labor and extended pregnancy. However, abortion or premature delivery still occurred in many patients but it is not clear whether tachyphylaxis developed or other factors were involved.

The physiological function of endogenous relaxin is poorly understood at the present time. The relaxing action on the pubic symphysis, particularly in certain rodents, appears to be one important function. It also may play a role in inhibiting uterine motility during pregnancy. However, since the blood concentrations of relaxin increase throughout pregnancy and fall only after parturition (Zarrow *et al.*, 1955) it might, at least theoretically, interfere with labor at term. It should be pointed out, however, that extracts containing relaxin do not prevent the actions of oxytocin on the uterus and labor could therefore progress as a result of the latter hormone.

The reason for the apparent failure of the relaxin-containing extracts to prevent or interrupt premature labor in certain patients is unknown. The development of a partial or absolute refractory state as a result of endogenously released relaxin might be one explanation. Noall and Frieden (1956) found that when relaxin was administered to guinea pigs for a period of three to six months, a refractory state developed to its action on the pubic symphysis. Additional studies are necessary to assess the possible physiological significance of tachyphylaxis development to the uterine inhibitory action of endogenously released relaxin.

SUMMARY

The effects of ovarian extracts containing relaxin on various types of smooth muscle have been investigated. Administration of the extracts to dogs produced hypotension, bradycardia and inhibition of ureteral motility; tachyphylaxis developed to these actions. A component in the extracts caused the release of histamine in quantities sufficient to account for the hypotension. The extracts inhibited the spontaneous uterine motility of the rat but not that of the rabbit or human (*in vitro*). Tachyphylaxis developed to the uterine inhibitory action *in vitro* and *in vivo*. The component which produced hypotension differed from the factor which inhibited the uterus in not being inactivated by pepsin. The results of these studies have been discussed in relation to the effects of relaxin-containing extracts in man.

ACKNOWLEDGMENT. The authors wish to acknowledge the cooperation of the Department of Obstetrics and Gynecology of the University of Wisconsin in obtaining the human material and to thank Dr. R. L. Kroc of Warner-Chilcott Laboratories for his assistance in supplying the relaxin-containing extracts employed in this study.

REFERENCES

ABRAHAMS, V. C., AND PICKFORD, M.: Brit. J. Pharmacol., **11:** 44, 1956.

ABRAMSON, D., CATON, W. L., JR., AND ROBY, C. C.: Am J. Obst. & Gynec., **65:** 654, 1953.

ABRAMSON, D., AND REID, D. E.: J. Clin. Endocrinol. & Metabolism, **15:** 206, 1955.

AHLMARK, A.: Acta Physiol. Scand., **9:** suppl. 28, 1944.

EICHNER, E., WALTNER, C., GOODMAN, M., AND POST, S.: Am. J. Obst. & Gynec., **71:** 1035, 1956.

FELTON, L. C., FRIEDEN, E. H., AND BRYANT, H. H.: THIS JOURNAL, **107:** 160, 1953.

FRIEDEN, E. H., AND HISAW, F. L.: The Biochemistry of Relaxin, Recent Progress in Hormone Research, p. 333, Academic Press Inc., New York, 1953.

FRIEDEN, E. H., NOALL, M. W., AND DEFLORIDA, F. A.: J. Biol. Chem., **222:** 611, 1956.

FOLSOME, C. E., HARAMI, T., LAVIETES, S. R., AND MASSELL, G. M.: Obst. & Gynec., **8:** 536, 1956.

GARRETT, W. J.: Brit. J. Pharmacol. & Chemotherapy, **10:** 39, 1955.

GRAHAM, E. F., AND DRACY, A. E.: J. Dairy Science, **36:** 772, 1953.

HALPERN, B. N.: Histamine, Ciba Foundation Symposium, p. 92, Little, Brown and Company, Boston, 1956.

JANOWITZ, H., AND GROSSMAN, M. I.: Amer. Jour. Physiol., **157:** 94, 1949.

JONES, G. S., AND SMITH, F.: Am. J. Obst. & Gynec., **67:** 628, 1954.

JONES, S. S.: Northwest Med., **54:** 1253, 1955.

KAHLSON, G.: Histamine, Ciba Foundation Symposium, p. 248, Little, Brown and Company, Boston, 1956.

KAPELLER-ADLER, R.: Lancet, **2:** 745, 1949.

KELLY, J. V., AND POSSE, N.: Obst. & Gynec., **8:** 531, 1956.

KRANTZ, J. C., BRYANT, H. H., AND CARR, C. J.: Surg. Gynec. & Obst., **90:** 372, 1950.

MACINTOSH, F. C., AND PATON, W. D. M.: J. Physiol., **109:** 190, 1949.

MAJEWSKI, J. T., AND JENNINGS, T.: Obst. & Gynec., **5:** 649, 1955.

MILES, A. A., AND MILES, E. M.: J. Physiol., **118:** 228, 1952.

MILLER, J. W., GEORGE, R., ELLIOTT, H. W., SUNG, C. Y., AND WAY, E. L.: THIS JOURNAL, **114:** 43, 1955.

NOALL, M. W., AND FRIEDEN, E. H.: Endocrinology, **58:** 659, 1956.

PATON, W. D. M.: Brit. J. Pharmacol., **6:** 499, 1951.

PERKOFF, G. T., SALHANICK, H. A., ZARROW, M. X., NELSON, D. H., AND TYLER, F. H.: J. Clin. Endocrinol. & Metabolism, **14:** 531, 1954.

POSSE, N., AND KELLY, J. V.: Surg. Gynec. & Obst. **103:** 687, 1956.

SAWYER, W. H., FRIEDEN, E. H., AND MARTIN, A. C.: Am. J. Physiol., **172:** 547, 1953.

SLOMKA, M. B., AND GOTH, A.: Proc. Soc. Exper. Biol. & Med., **93:** 30, 1956.

ZARROW, M. X., HOLMSTROM, E. G., AND SALHANICK, H. A.: J. Clin. Endocrinol. & Metabolism, **15:** 22, 1955.

ZARROW, M. X., NEHER, G. M., SIKES, D., BRENNAN, D. M., AND BULLARD, J. F.: Am. J. Obst. & Gynec., **72:** 260, 1956.

PHARMACOLOGY OF SOME NEW UNSYMMETRICAL BISQUATERNARY HYPOTENSIVE AGENTS—SUBSTITUTED PYRIDINE AND PIPERIDINE DERIVATIVES

THOMAS B. O'DELL AND MARTHA D. NAPOLI [1]

Research Laboratories, Irwin, Neisler & Co., Decatur, Illinois

Received for publication March 4, 1957

Previous publications from this laboratory have described some novel chemical and pharmacological features of hypotensive agents which are unsymmetric bisquaternary ammonium compounds (O'Dell *et al.*, 1955a, b; Cavallito *et al.*, 1955; Gray *et al.*, 1955a, b). The most interesting biological property of these agents is that their abilities to lower blood pressure are unrelated to, and usually greater than, the degree of peripheral autonomic blockade which they produce. Some evidence was presented which permitted the suggestion that these compounds had a central component of activity. Recent independent observations appear to support this view (Lape *et al.*, 1956). The present work describes some pharmacological properties of substituted pyridine and piperidine unsymmetrical bisquaternary compounds (Gray *et al.*, 1957). Several of these compounds were of particular interest because of their high degree of specificity of hypotensive activity as compared with other much less prominent pharmacological properties.

RESULTS AND DISCUSSION. Except where specifically noted, the methods used throughout these investigations have been previously described (O'Dell *et al.*, 1955a, b).

Hypotensive action. The hypotensive activity, acute toxicity and sympathetic ganglionic blocking activity of the compounds described in this report are summarized in tables 1 and 2. In the anesthetized dog, intravenous administration of the more active compounds produced a hypotensive effect which was characterized by having a relatively slow onset. In general, the blood pressure fall occurred over a 30 to 45-minute period. The complete duration of the hypotensive action was usually not determined, for in most cases the blood pressure was still lowered several hours after administration of the compound. Compound XIII (IN 391) also was administered orally (in a capsule) to dogs immediately prior to anesthesia using doses of 0.5 to 1.0 mgm./kgm. After a lag period of approximately 45 minutes, the usual slow sustained hypotensive effect was seen[2] (fig. 1).

[1] The authors wish to acknowledge the valuable aid of Dr. C. J. Cavallito, Director of Research, whose comments and suggestions contributed much to the work reported here, and the technical assistance of Mrs. Lenore Foutch and Mrs. Loretta Wilson.

[2] In an attempt to increase the absorption after oral administration, IN 391 was administered in combination with 1,3-bis-(trimethylammonium) propane dichloride. While this compound proved to be inactive when administered alone, it did enhance the hypotensive action of IN 391 when the two compounds were administered in combination orally. For example, IN 391 at 0.5 mgm./kgm. orally produced a blood pressure fall of 30 per cent, but when administered at this same dose in combination with the above compound (1.0 mgm./kgm.), IN 391 produced a 55 per cent blood pressure fall.

TABLE 1

Hypotensive activity, ganglionic blocking activity and toxicity of some substituted pyridine unsymmetrical bisquaternary compounds

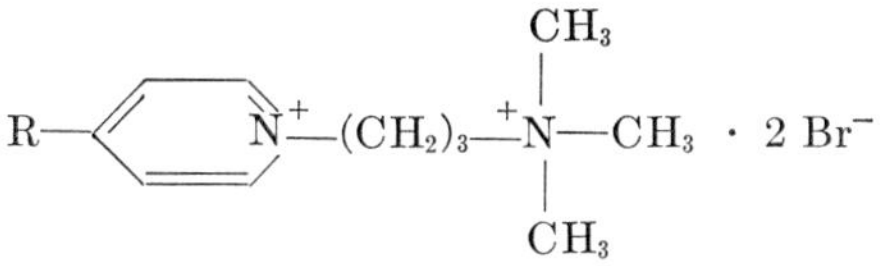

No.	R	Position	Acute Toxicity,* Mouse I.V. LD_{50} *mgm./kgm.*	Hypotensive Activity† Dose/% Fall/Duration	No. dogs	Sympathetic Gang. Block‡ Dose/Degree/Duration	No. cats
I	H—	—	180.	0.25/25/0.1 0.5/35/0.1 2.0/50/0.1	3	—	
II	CH_3—	4	>212.	0.25/10/0.1 0.5/15/0.1 1.0/30/0.1	3	—	
III	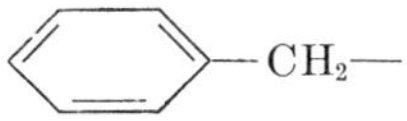	4	40.	0.25/15/? 0.5/30/2 1.0/35/2.5	6	—	
IV	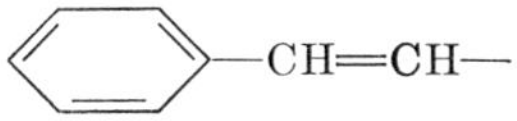	4	16.5	0.25/—/— 0.5/15/1 1.0/15/1	4	—	
V	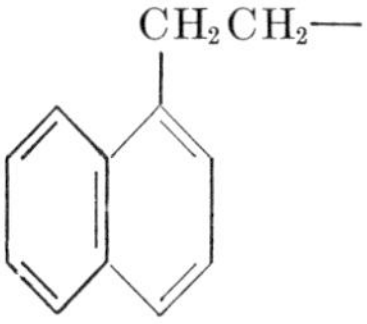	2	5.2	0.01/25/>2 0.025/50/>3 0.1/65/>4	9	0.05/—/— 0.1/+/0.2 0.25/+++/0.75	2
VI	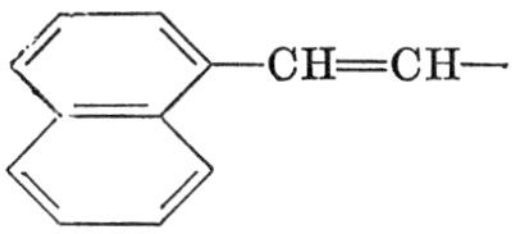	4	1.2	0.05/15/? 0.1/20/>2 0.25/20/>2	4	—	
VII	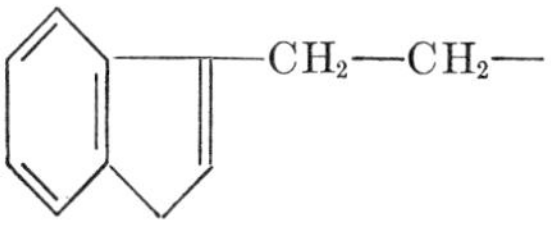	2	11.5	0.025/25/>1.5 0.05/45/>4 0.1/55–75/>4	14	0.1/—/— 0.25/+/0.7 0.5/++/2 1.0/+++/>2	6
VIII	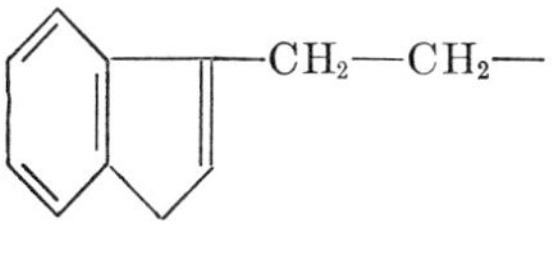	4	8.2	0.1/40/>2 0.25/40/>2	5	0.1/—/— 0.25/+/0.4 0.5/++/0.75	2
IX	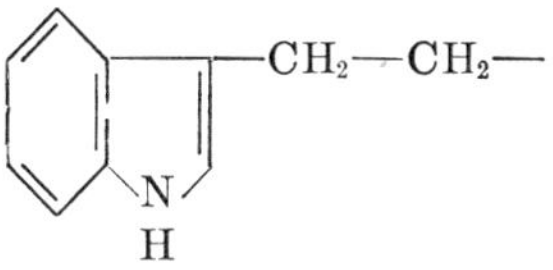	2	12.	0.025/25/2 0.05/65/>4 0.1/65/>4 1.0/65/>4	6	0.05/—/— 0.1/+/0.5 0.25/+++/1 0.5/++++/2	2

TABLE 1—*Continued*

No.	R	Position	Acute Toxicity,* Mouse I.V. LD_{50} *mgm./kgm.*	Hypotensive Activity†		Sympathetic Gang. Block‡	
				Dose/% Fall/Duration	No. dogs	Dose/Degree/Duration	No. cats
X	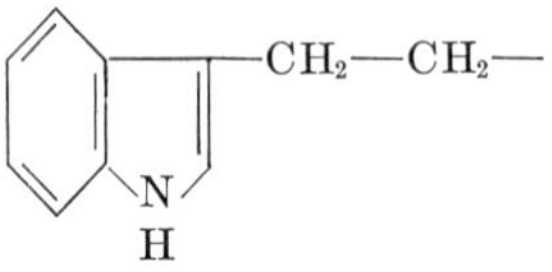	4	9.	0.05/15/0.5 0.1/40/>3 0.25/45/4 0.5/40–65/>4	8	0.05/—/— 0.1/+/0.5 0.25/+++/1	2
XI	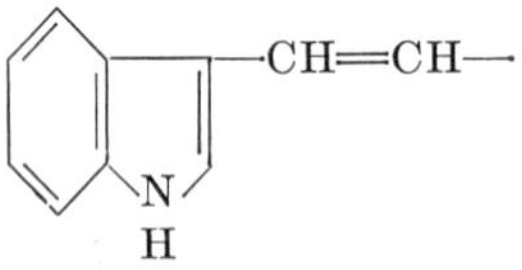	4	10.	0.1/—/— 0.25/20/0.5 0.5/40/3	7	0.5/—/— 1.0/++/0.5 2.0/++++/?	2
XII	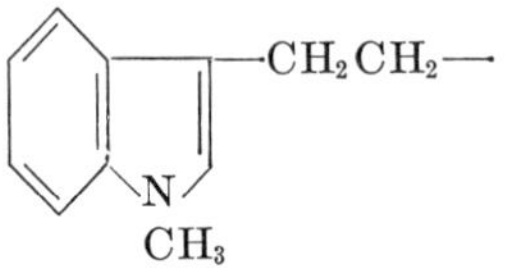	2	7.6	0.025/10/0.4 0.05/40/>2 0.1/45/>4	7	0.05/—/— 0.1/+/0.1 0.25/++/0.75	2
XIII (391)	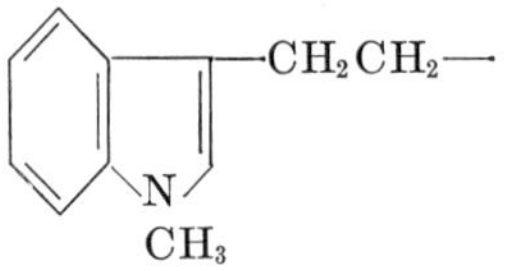	4	13.2	0.01/0–20/>2 0.02/25/>3 0.025/50/4 0.05/50/>2 0.1/55/>3	12	0.05/—/— 0.1/+/0.2 0.25/++/0.75 0.5/++/? 1.0/+++/2	2
XIV	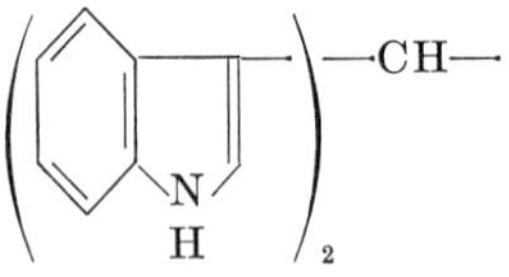	4	6.4	0.1/—/— 0.25/30–55/0.4 0.5/60–90/>1.5	5	—	
XV	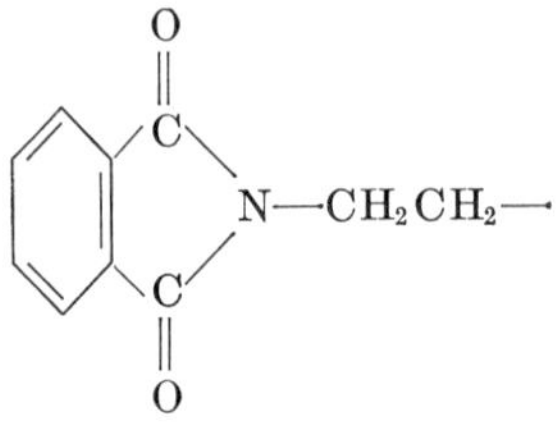	4	27.5	0.1/5/0.15 0.25/25/? 0.5/40/1.5 1.0/45/2	4	—	
XVI	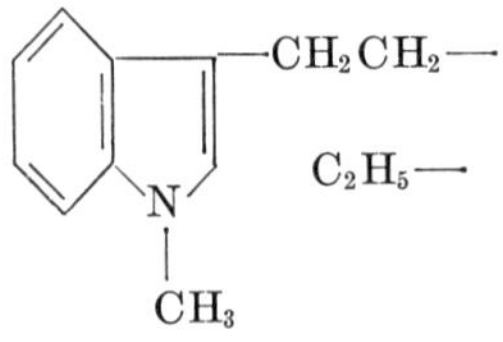	2 5	7.1	0.01/55/>3 0.025/55/>3 0.05/55/>3 0.1/50–65/>3	2	0.25/—/— 0.5/+/0.25 1.0/++/0.4 2.0/+++/0.5	3

TABLE 1—*Concluded*

No.	R	Position	Acute Toxicity,* Mouse I.V. LD_{50} *mgm./kgm.*	Hypotensive Activity†		Sympathetic Gang. Block‡	
				Dose/% Fall/Duration	No. dogs	Dose/Degree/ Duration	No. cats
XVII	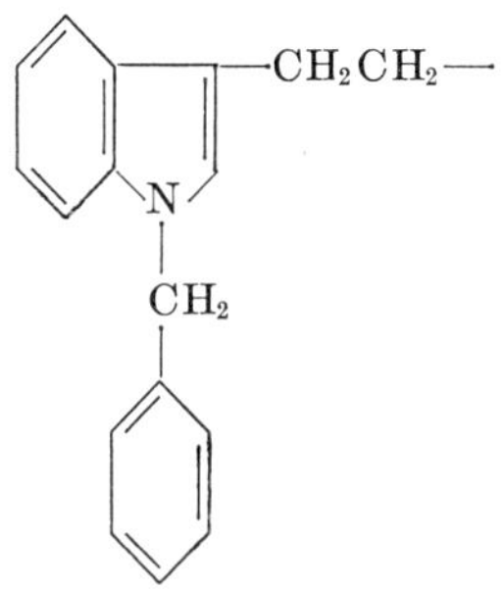	4	3.5	0.05/—/— 0.1/20/2 0.25/35-60/>4 0.5/55/>4	5	—	
XVIII	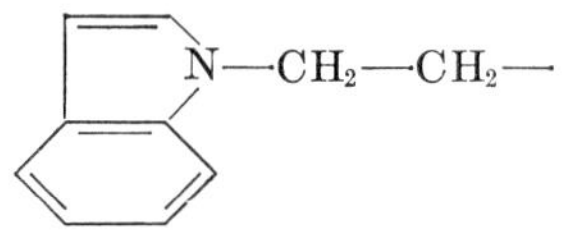	4	8.5	0.005/10/1 0.01/65/>2 0.05/65/>2 0.1/70/>2	7	0.05/—/— 0.1/+/0.25 0.25/+++/1	2
XIX	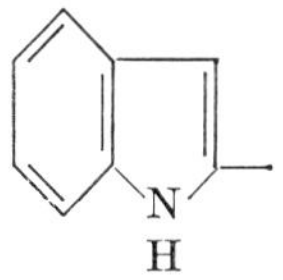	3	32.8	0.25/—/— 1.0/10/0.1 2.0/25/0.1	2	—	
XX	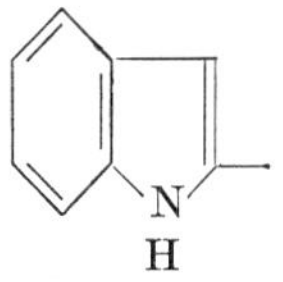	4	33.	0.1/15/>1 0.25/40/>1.5	3	0.1-1.0/—/— 2.0/++/2	1
XXI	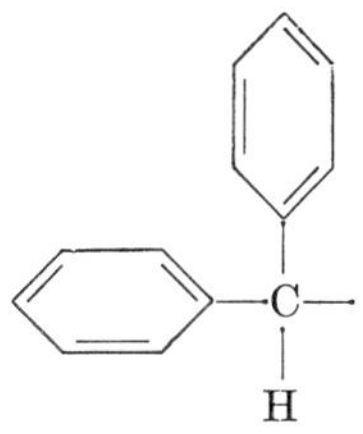	4	2.5	0.1/—/— 0.25/60/0.5	2	0.1/—/— 1.0/++/0.4	1

* Calculated using the method of Behrens (Behrens and Kärber, 1934).

† Dose—mgm./kgm., i.v./% maximum blood pressure fall/duration (hours) before return of blood pressure to pre-drug level.

‡ Cat, superior cervical ganglion. Dose—mgm./kgm., i.v./degree of block (0-4+)/duration (hours) before recovery. ++++ = complete blockade.

TABLE 2

Hypotensive activity, ganglionic blocking activity and toxicity of some substituted piperidine unsymmetrical bisquaternary compounds

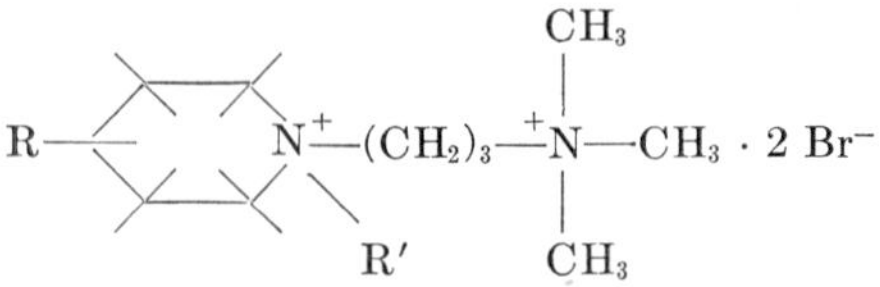

No.	R′	R	Position of R	Acute Toxicity,* Mouse I.V. LD_{50} *mgm./kgm.*	Hypotensive Activity†		Sympathetic Gang. Block‡	
					Dose/% Fall/Duration	No. dogs	Dose/Degree/ Duration	No. cats
XXII	CH_3	H	—	162.5	0.1/5/0.1 0.25/5/0.1 1.0/40/0.1	2	—	
XXIII	CH_3	 —CH_2—	4	50.5	0.25/—/— 0.5/30–70/>3 1.0/40–70/>3	12	0.25/—/— 0.5/++/0.5	2
XXIV	H	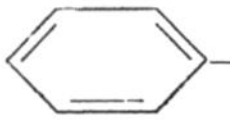 —CH_2—§	4	47.3	0.25/5/0.1 0.5/10/0.1 2.0/15/0.1	2	—	
XXV	CH_3	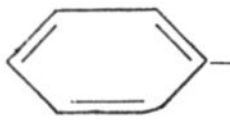 —CH_2—§	4	71.	0.1/0–35/? 0.25/35/2 0.5/45/>2	5	0.1/—/— 0.25/+/0.3 0.5/++/0.5 1.0/+++/0.5	2

* Calculated using the method of Behrens (Behrens and Kärber, 1934).

† Dose—mgm./kgm., i.v./% maximum blood pressure fall/duration (hours) before return of blood pressure to pre-drug level.

‡ Cat, superior cervical ganglion. Dose—mgm./kgm., i.v./degree of block (0–4+)/duration (hours) before recovery. ++++ = complete blockade.

§ Length of connecting methylene chain = 2.

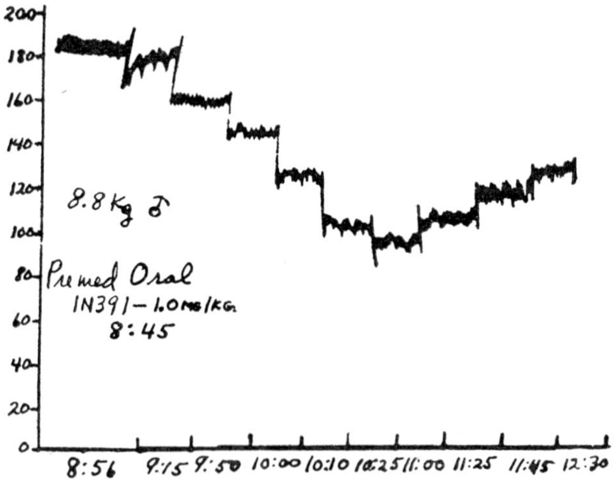

FIG. 1. Effect of IN 391 when administered orally to a dog just prior to anesthesia and set-up. Kymograph stopped except at times indicated.

In unanesthetized dogs, onset of hypotensive response, after intravenous administration of IN 391, was slower, and approximately four times the dose used in the anesthetized animals was required to obtain the same fall in blood pressure. This finding was not too surprising since in the doses employed, IN 391 has no effect on the sympathetic reflexes and thus any apprehension or excitement on the part of the dog would tend to keep the blood pressure elevated.

The effect of relatively minor structural variations on the hypotensive potency is evident from table 1 (Compounds IX, X, XII, XIII and XVIII). Although the sympathetic ganglionic blocking activity of these compounds is of the order of that of hexamethonium, their effectiveness in lowering blood pressure is evident at dramatically smaller doses as low as 10 to 25 microgm./kgm. This group of compounds particularly well demonstrates that the hypotensive action is not directly correlated with the peripheral effects of these compounds, but could involve an action at some central site as previously suggested (O'Dell *et al.*, 1955a, b, and Cavallito *et al.*, 1955). A more complete discussion of the mechanism of hypotensive action follows.

Mechanism of action. The compound used to carry out these studies was XIII (IN 391), the sustained hypotensive effect of which appears to involve some central site. This conclusion is based on both direct and indirect evidence obtained using dogs and cats. The procedures employed and the results obtained are summarized below.

Direct effect on the smooth muscle of the blood vessels: To determine this effect, the flow rate was measured in a dog's femoral artery using a Shipley-Wilson rotameter and the compound was administered directly into the artery. The administration of IN 391 in total doses ranging from 0.05 to 0.25 mgm. caused no significant increase in the rate of blood flow. As would be expected, nitroglycerin in a total dose of 0.01 mgm. caused a marked increase in the blood flow (105 per cent). The lack of a direct effect of IN 391 on the blood vessel musculature was also borne out by the observation that sodium nitrite (4.0 mgm./kgm., i.v.) produced essentially the same hypotensive effect when administered before and after IN 391 (0.1 mgm./kgm., i.v.).

Sympatholytic or adrenergic blocking action: When IN 391 was administered in greater than effective hypotensive doses, *e.g.*, 0.1 mgm./kgm., i.v., it showed no blockade of the blood pressure effects of injected epinephrine or arterenol.

Reflex action, such as the von Bezold reflex: Since this type of action is mediated by way of the afferent vagus, double vagotomy and/or atropinization should block the blood pressure fall. Intravenous administration of IN 391 to dogs after both double vagotomy and atropinization resulted in the usual sustained blood pressure fall.

Ganglionic blockade: The superior cervical ganglion (cat) may be partially blocked with IN 391 but the quantities required are appreciably greater than those needed to lower blood pressure. This difference or the ratio between these effects is best seen in table 1. It is appreciated that considerable differences in sensitivity to blocking agents exist among various sympathetic ganglia but in our experience, the superior cervical ganglion has best reflected the degree of side reactions from sympathetic blocking effects that one observes upon intravenous administration in man.

Direct effect on the carotid sinus areas: If a compound produces an effect on or by way of the carotid sinus areas, denervation of these areas should eliminate this effect. After such denervation in the dog, the hypotensive action of compounds such as IN 391 was not blocked, but possibly was enhanced.

Cross circulation: Four pairs of dogs were used for cross circulation experiments. The procedure used has been described previously (O'Dell *et al.*, 1955a, b). When IN 391, at a total dose of 0.1 mgm., was administered intraarterially into the circulation going from the body of the donor dog to the head of the recipient dog and back to the body of the donor dog, the systemic blood pressure of the recipient dog was lowered while the blood pressure of the donor dog remained constant. Thus the hypotensive action was evident in the recipient (head) dog but not in the donor (peripheral) dog.

Central vagus (C.V.) stimulation: If the central (cephalic) stump of the sectioned vagus nerve is stimulated electrically, there is a blood pressure rise reportedly due to a direct stimulation of central vasomotor centers. Thus a compound acting centrally could tend to block this blood pressure rise due to C.V. stimulation. Administration of IN 391 (0.025 to 0.05 mgm./kgm., i.v.) to 4 anesthetized dogs resulted in a progressive blockade of the blood pressure effect of C.V. stimulation. This progressive blockade followed very well the gradual blood pressure fall produced by this compound. Sodium nitrite was used as a control compound and did not show any evidence of blockade of C.V. stimulation effects.

Stimulation of the greater splanchnic nerve of dogs: Recently Maxwell *et al.* (1956) reported the lack of blocking effects of several ganglionic blocking agents on the pressor responses induced by peripheral splanchnic nerve stimulation. It was of interest to note that in our preliminary studies, IN 391 (0.1 mgm./kgm., i.v.) did block the pressor response to splanchnic nerve stimulation. In confirmation of the report of Maxwell *et al.*, hexamethonium (0.5 mgm./kgm., i.v.) did not block this response. The full significance of this effect of IN 391 is not known as yet.

As further indirect evidence for the central action of these compounds it was reasoned that the combination of an unsymmetrical bisquaternary compound with a different type of hypotensive agent, where complementary mechanisms are involved, could result in a synergistic or potentiating effect. To explore this possibility, IN 391 and cryptenamine, an alkaloid preparation from *Veratrum viride*, were used. The amount of each drug used was approximately one-fourth of the usually effective dose. The procedure employed was to administer either of the drugs, wait 30 to 60 minutes and then administer the other drug. As may be seen from fig. 2, there was little, if any hypotensive effect from these small individual doses until the second drug was administered, regardless of which was administered initially. Also, it may be noted that the type of blood pressure fall produced was similar to that found with IN 391 rather than that usually ob-

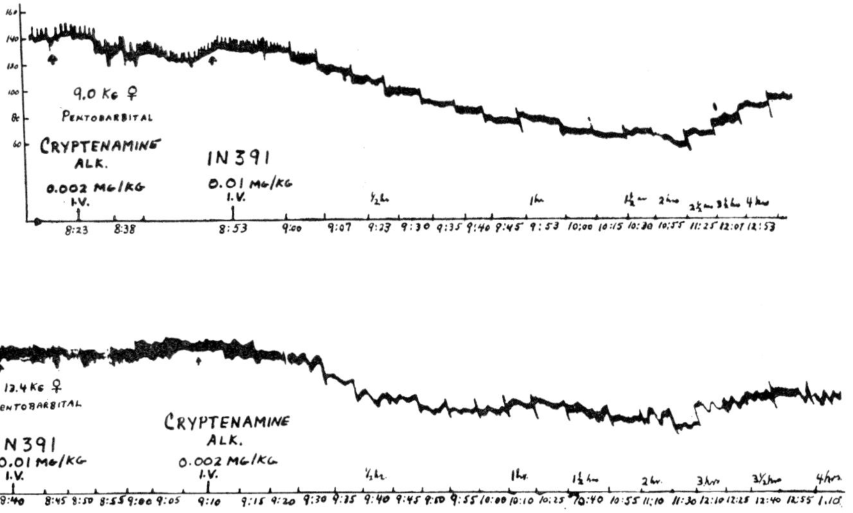

FIG. 2. Kymograph tracings illustrating the potentiating effect of cryptenamine on the hypotensive action of IN 391. Kymograph stopped except at times indicated.

served with the cryptenamine or other *Veratrum* alkaloids. This was interpreted to indicate that the cryptenamine potentiates the hypotensive effect of IN 391 and not *vice versa*. Such results are not unreasonable when the mechanisms involved are taken into consideration. If, as postulated, IN 391 is active at some central site with a lesser effect on the peripheral ganglia, then the normal "buffer" or reflex pressor systems should be intact to antagonize this action. The *Veratrum* alkaloids have been postulated to have a component of action at, or by way of, the carotid sinus areas. Thus, the action of small amounts of these alkaloids on the carotid sinus areas would tend to partially overcome the compensatory pressor effect of this buffer area to the hypotensive effect of IN 391.

Hypotensive agents having a primary mechanism of action at more peripheral sites should not necessarily produce such a synergistic effect with IN 391 in the doses used, and this was found to be the case. Following the same procedures outlined above, hexamethonium (0.25 mgm./kgm.), tolazoline HCl (Priscoline HCl) (0.1 mgm./kgm.), and sodium nitrite (1.0 mgm./kgm.) were combined separately with IN 391. None of these drugs showed evidence of synergism or potentiation such as that seen with cryptenamine, although combination with hexamethonium or sodium nitrite did appear to produce a moderate additive effect.

The mechanism studies with IN 391 thus show it to be a very potent hypotensive agent with a marked degree of selectivity of action. As earlier postulated (Cavallito *et al.*, 1955), it is believed that the unsymmetric bisquaternaries include compounds with sufficient degrees of specificity of action to permit demonstration of influence at a central site as a principal component of activity. This component may be present in many quaternaries but usually subordinate to, or masked by, more prominent peripheral actions. The central action may well involve penetration of the blood-brain barrier (Cavallito *et al.*, 1955) by these quaternaries and might also involve autonomic afferent receptors located in the blood vessels of the head region.

Several of the compounds and combinations described in this report are currently undergoing extensive clinical trials.

SUMMARY

Pharmacological studies on some new substituted pyridine and piperidine unsymmetrical bisquaternary compounds have been described. Several of these compounds are potent hypotensive agents with such action being found in some cases with intravenous doses as low as 10 to 25 microgm./kgm. It was found that relatively minor structural modifications can markedly alter the degree of hypotensive activity and to a lesser extent the degree of sympathetic ganglionic blockage or acute toxicity. Mechanism studies are described and the results indicate that the sustained hypotensive effect of these compounds involves primarily an action at some central site.

REFERENCES

Behrens, B., and Kärber, G.: Arch. f. exper. Path. u. Pharmakol., **177:** 379, 1934.
Cavallito, C. J., Gray, A. P., and O'Dell, T. B.: Arch. internat. pharmacodyn., **101:** 38, 1955.
Gray, A. P., Archer, W. L., Schlieper, D. C., Spinner, E. E., and Cavallito, C. J.: J. Am. Chem. Soc., **77:** 3533, 1955a.
Gray, A. P., Archer, W. L., Schlieper, D. C., Spinner, E. E., and Cavallito, C. J.: J. Am. Chem. Soc., **77:** 3536, 1955b.
Gray, A. P., Archer, W. L., Spinner, E. E., and Cavallito, C. J.: J. Am. Chem. Soc., in press, 1957.
Lape, H. E., Fort, D. J., and Hoppe, J. O.: This Journal, **116:** 462, 1956.
Maxwell, R. A., Plummer, A. J., Ross, A. D., and Osborne, M. W.: Proc. Soc. Exp. Biol. & Med., **92:** 225, 1956.
O'Dell, T. B., Luna, C., and Napoli, M. D.: This Journal, **114:** 306, 1955a.
O'Dell, T. B., Luna, C., and Napoli, M. D.: This Journal, **114:** 317, 1955b.

THE ABSORPTION AND METABOLISM OF ANILERIDINE,[1] ETHYL-1-(4-AMINOPHENETHYL)-4-PHENYLISONIPECOTATE

CURT C. PORTER

Merck Institute for Therapeutic Research, Rahway, New Jersey

Received for publication March 9, 1957

Anileridine (I, figure 1) is structurally related to, but more potent as an analgesic than meperidine (Orahovats *et al.*, 1956). Metabolically, anileridine would be expected to undergo deesterification to yield anileridine acid (II), as meperidine yields meperidine acid (Burns *et al.*, 1955; Way *et al.*, 1949; Plotnikoff, Elliott and Way, 1952). Further, acetylation of the aromatic amino group in anileridine and its acid would be anticipated in species other than the dog (Williams, 1947). Consequently, techniques for the separation and estimation of anileridine, anileridine acid, and the respective acetyl derivatives (III, IV) were developed and applied to urine. Blood plasma and tissues were examined for anileridine and its analgesically active acetyl derivative.

ANALYTICAL METHODS. *Anileridine and acetyl anileridine.* Plasma (3 ml.), tissue homogenate (10 ml. containing 1 to 2 gm. of tissue) or urine were twice extracted, at pH 7 to 8 with 2 volumes of ethylene chloride. Emulsions were broken by freezing in dry ice-ethanol, then thawing and centrifuging. The extracts were evaporated to dryness in a stream of air and the residues dissolved in 2.5 ml. of 1 *N* H_2SO_4. Two 1-ml. aliquots of the acid solution were taken, and one of them autoclaved (15 lb. pressure, 30 min.). To each was added 1 ml. of water, then at 3-min. intervals, 0.5 ml. of 0.1 per cent sodium nitrite, 0.5 per cent ammonium sulfamate and 0.5 per cent *N*-(1-naphthyl)-ethylenediamine · 2 HCl (Bratton *et al.*, 1939). Absorbencies at 510 mμ were determined about 30 minutes after the final addition of reagent.

Anileridine acid and acetyl anileridine acid. Urine samples, which had been extracted with ethylene chloride, then were extracted at pH 7 to 11 with benzyl alcohol. Samples were also hydrolyzed (1 *N* H_2SO_4, 15 lb. pressure, 30 min.), then extracted similarly. Benzyl alcohol extracts were diluted with an equal volume of chloroform, and extracted with 1 *N* H_2SO_4. Application of the diazotization and coupling reactions to the acid extracts from unhydrolyzed urine yielded the amount of anileridine acid present. The procedure applied to hydrolyzed urine revealed the sum of anileridine acid and acetyl anileridine acid.

The addition of solid sodium sulfate (20 per cent w/v) to aqueous solutions facilitated the separation of layers upon extraction with benzyl alcohol, but did not influence the recovery of anileridine acid. Less sodium sulfate (10 per cent w/v) was added to urine. Benzyl alcohol was equilibrated with 20 per cent aqueous sodium sulfate before use.

The hydrolysis procedure used did not destroy anileridine or anileridine acid, and adequately hydrolyzed the acetyl derivatives. Recovery of anileridine and acetyl anileridine from aqueous solutions was 93 to 99 per cent, while recovery of the acid forms was about 87 per cent. Analytical values for the acid forms reported in the following sections have been corrected to 100 per cent recovery. In all analyses, control material was processed similarly and the data from dosed animals corrected accordingly.

EXPERIMENTAL AND RESULTS. *Blood and tissue concentrations of anileridine in rats.* Concentrations of anileridine in rat plasma were too low to be detected by

[1] 'Leritine', Merck & Co., Inc.

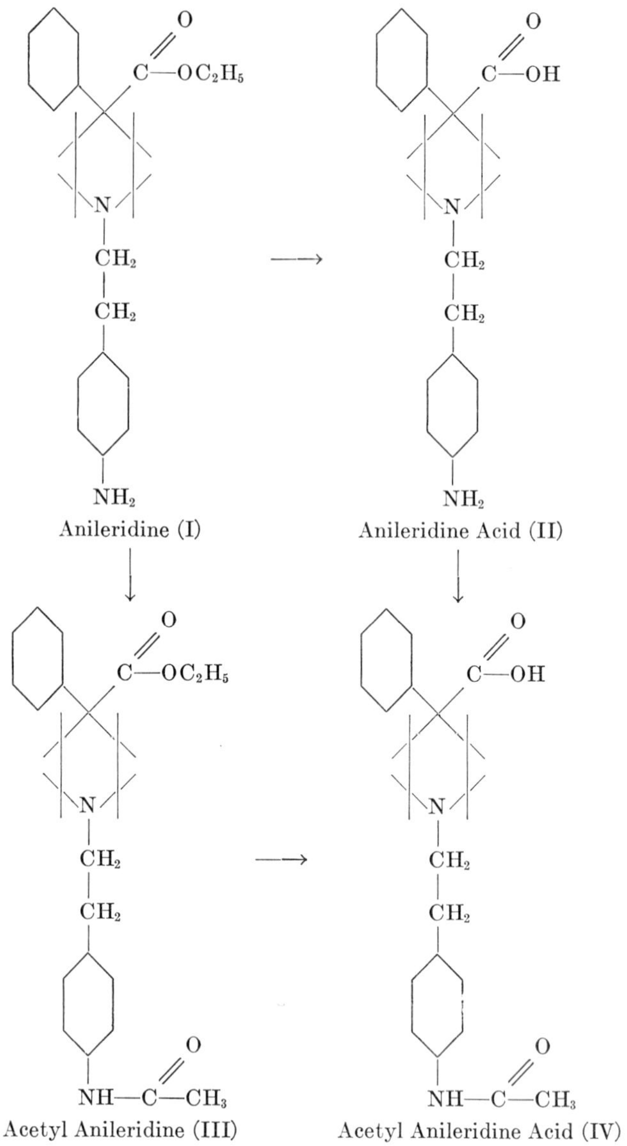

FIG. 1. The Metabolism of anileridine

the method used, with one exception. If a rat was given an intravenous dose of the drug and then sacrificed by decapitation immediately, anileridine was found in the plasma. Intravenously administered anileridine was rapidly taken up in the brain; peak concentrations were found 2 to 4 min. after the injection (table 1). Thirty minutes after injection, brain anileridine concentrations had fallen to about 11 per cent of the peak values.

Following subcutaneous administration of anileridine, anileridine and acetyl anileridine were found widely distributed in the rat (figure 2). In this species,

TABLE 1

Anileridine in rat brain after i.v. injection of 8 mgm./kgm.

Time After Injection *min.*	Anileridine Concentration in Brain *microgm./gm.*				
	Individual rats				Average
0.5	0	7.25			3.63
1	0	8.02	7.34		7.68
2	6.78	6.37	13.80		8.98
3	6.35	7.57	8.14		7.35
4	5.73	8.82	9.55		8.03
8	4.03	4.33	5.52		4.63
15	2.38	2.94			2.66
30	0.75	1.04	1.22	1.37	1.09

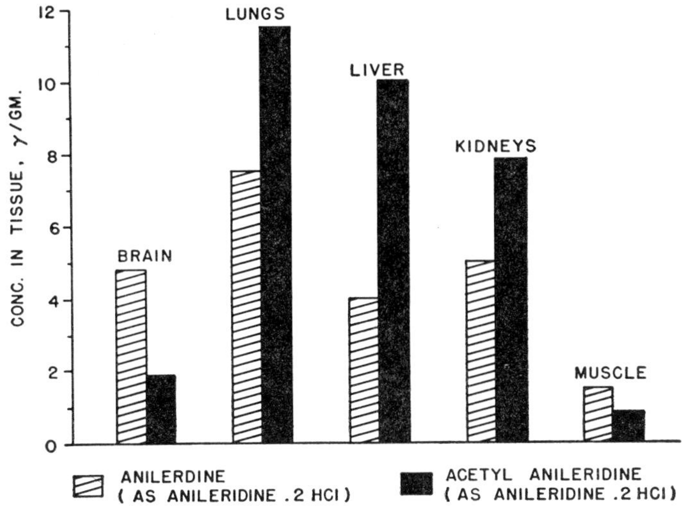

FIG. 2. Distribution of anileridine and acetyl anileridine in rat tissues 1 hr. after subcutaneous doses of 16 mgm./kgm. of anileridine dihydrochloride.

anileridine was picked up most readily by the lungs, followed by brain and kidneys, then liver and finally muscle. Relatively large concentrations of acetyl anileridine appeared in the lungs, liver and kidneys, while brain acetyl anileridine accumulated more slowly and to a lesser extent. Peak concentrations of both compounds were found approximately one hour after dosing. Twenty-four hours after the dose, only the liver contained a detectable amount of anileridine.

The concentration of anileridine in the brain is a linear function of the subcutaneous dose given. With doses of 2 to 32 mgm./kgm., brain anileridine (microgm./gm.) 45 min. after dosing plotted against the dose yielded a straight line which passed through the origin and whose slope was 0.349 ± 0.02 (s.e.). Acetyl anileridine (1 to 2 microgm./gm.) was found only in the brains of animals which had received 16 or 32 mgm. of anileridine per kgm.

The concentration of anileridine in rat brain can be directly correlated with degree of analgesia. Rats were given single subcutaneous doses of anileridine dihydrochloride, 8 mgm./kgm. Degree of analgesia (reaction time, tailflick method) was determined at various intervals thereafter. The animals then were sacrificed immediately, and concentrations of anileridine in the brain were determined (table 2). It is clear that in this experiment concentrations of anileridine in the brain exceeding about 2 microgm./gm. resulted in reaction times greater than 10 seconds. The dividing line was not sharp, however. With brain levels between 1.8 and 2, analgesia had definitely declined below the peak; this may show that rapid development of "tolerance" to the drug is more important in recovery from analgesia than is decreasing concentration of the drug in the brain.

The metabolism of anileridine. The anticipated metabolites of anileridine were detected in the urine of rats, guinea pigs and men. Only a trace of unchanged drug was excreted by the two animal species (0.2 to 0.5 per cent of the dose), while two human subjects excreted about 5 per cent of the oral dose unchanged. Burns *et al.* (1955) reported a similar excretion of unchanged meperidine by men.

The largest fraction of identified anileridine metabolites excreted by all three species studied was composed of the deesterified derivatives. In the rat and guinea pig, about 17 per cent of the dose of anileridine was excreted as the acetylated derivative and only 2 per cent as free anileridine acid. However, men excreted 1 to 2 per cent as the acetyl compound and 7 to 14 per cent as anileridine acid. A small fraction, *i.e.* 0.5 to 2 per cent, of the dose was identified as acetyl anileridine in the urine of these species.

About 20 per cent of the doses administered was excreted in the urine as identified metabolites. This is less than the 34 per cent recovery reported by Burns *et al.* (1955) after the administration of meperidine to men. The smaller recovery of anileridine metabolites may be related to the smaller doses employed (*i.e.*, 150 mgm. in 20 hours), in comparison to 400 to 600 mgm. of meperidine per day used by Burns *et al.* (1955).

Some 15 to 35 per cent of the dose of anileridine could be accounted for as

TABLE 2

Correlation of concentration of anileridine in rat brain with degree of analgesia (3 rats/group; dose, 8 mgm./kgm.)

Time After s.c. Dose *hr.*	Control Reaction Time *sec.*	Reaction Time After Dose* *sec.*			Anileridine in Brain *microgm./gm.*
0.25	4.1	C	C	8.4	5.14
0.5	4.5	C	C	8.7 (C)	2.86
0.75	4.0	C	7.5	C	2.22
1.0	4.1	10.6	10.5	9.5	3.37
1.5	4.1	10.3	5.0	9.9	1.98
2.0	3.8	4.7	4.9	7.5	1.85
3.0	3.8	5.0	5.4	4.0	0.40
4.0	4.1	3.8	4.5	4.0	0.28

* C indicates reaction time greater than 10–11 sec.

unidentified diazotizable substances, which were present principally in a free state in human urine and in a bound form, *i.e.* released by hydrolysis, in rat and guinea pig urine. Countercurrent distribution studies with this fraction from rat urine indicated that *p*-acetylaminophenylacetic acid or a very closely related compound was present. This type of compound would be produced by metabolic degradation of the isonipecotic portion of the anileridine molecule. Plotnikoff *et al.* (1952) found 8 to 17 per cent of subcutaneously administered methyl C^{14}-meperidine and about 45 per cent of intravenously administered compound as expired CO_2 in the rat. Since demethylation plays only a minor role in the metabolism of meperidine (Burns *et al.*, 1955) and physiological scission in the nitrogen-ethylaniline portion of anileridine is unlikely, it appears that extensive degradation of the isonipecotic moiety of these drugs must occur.

The metabolism of anileridine is thus quite similar to that of meperidine in many respects; it is interesting to note that although acetylation plays an important role in the rat and guinea pig, this mechanism is of minor importance in the metabolism of anileridine in man.

SUMMARY

Anileridine, 1-(4-aminophenethyl)-4-phenylisonipecotate, was rapidly taken up by the tissues of rats following parenteral administration. Highest concentrations of the drug were found in the lungs, kidneys and brain. Concentrations of anileridine in rat brain bear a linear relationship to degree of analgesia.

Anileridine is acetylated in the rat and guinea pig, probably in the liver, possibly also in the lungs, to produce another analgesic, acetyl anileridine. This derivative was found in rat liver, kidneys and lungs in concentrations greater than that of anileridine after administration of the unacetylated compound. It appeared in the brain in smaller amounts.

The metabolism of anileridine resembles that of meperidine in that the major pathways involve saponification and destruction of the isonipecotic acid moiety. Acetylation of the aromatic amino group in anileridine is a major pathway in rats and guinea pigs, but is of minor importance in man.

ACKNOWLEDGMENTS. The clinical material was supplied by Dr. Elmer Alpert, First (Columbia) Medical Division, Bellevue Hospital, New York. Dr. P. D. Orahovats and Mr. E. G. Lehman performed the analgesia measurements in rats, and Mr. J. L. Gilfillan rendered valuable technical assistance.

REFERENCES

BRATTON, A. C., MARSHALL, E. K., JR., BABBITT, D., AND HENDRICKSON, A. R.: J. Biol. Chem., **128:** 537, 1939.

BURNS, J. J., BERGER, B. L., LIEF, P. A., WOLLACK, A., PAPPER, E. M., AND BRODIE, B. B.: THIS JOURNAL, **114:** 289, 1955.

ORAHOVATS, P. D., LEHMAN, E. G., AND CHAPIN, E. W.: THIS JOURNAL, **119:** 26, 1957.

PLOTNIKOFF, N. P., ELLIOTT, H. W., AND WAY, E. L.: THIS JOURNAL, **104:** 377, 1952.

WAY, E. L., GIMBLE, A. I., MCKELWAY, W. P., ROSS, H., SUNG, C-Y, AND ELLSWORTH, H.: THIS JOURNAL, **96:** 477, 1949.

WILLIAMS, R. T.: Detoxication Mechanisms, John Wiley & Sons, N. Y., 1947.

THE CURARIFORM ACTION OF STREPTOMYCIN

OSWALDO VITAL BRAZIL AND ALEXANDRE PINTO CORRADO[1]

Department of Pharmacology, University of São Paulo Faculty of Medicine, São Paulo, Brazil

Received for publication March 9, 1957

Molitor and collaborators (1946, 1949, 1950) investigated the acute toxicity of streptomycin on several animal species (pigeons, frogs, mice, rats, guinea-pigs, rabbits, cats and dogs), following the administration of the drug by different routes. In all warmblooded animals which had received a lethal dose of the antibiotic, they found that death occurred by respiratory paralysis since the heart continued to beat for several minutes after respiration had ceased. It was observed that prompt initiation and maintenance of artificial respiration could often prevent an otherwise fatal outcome. They reported in addition that frogs, which do not depend solely upon pulmonary respiration, survived doses of streptomycin many times larger than those tolerated by mice, provided they were kept partially submerged in frequently changed water. As signs of acute poisoning caused by venous and subcutaneous administration of streptomycin, they reported restlessness, labored respiration, loss of consciousness and coma. In larger animals such as cats and dogs, besides these symptoms, nausea, vomiting and ataxia were also observed.

The mechanism through which streptomycin produces motor effects and respiratory arrest was not clear. Some of the observations of Molitor and his collaborators (1946, 1949, 1950) seem to suggest participation of the neuromuscular junction in the genesis of these effects. The results reported in this paper indicate that streptomycin exerts a neuromuscular blocking action which we assume to be responsible for the motor effects of the acute streptomycin intoxication and death of the animal.

MATERIAL AND METHODS. The investigation was carried out on a neuromuscular preparation of the dog and on intact unanesthetized dogs and pigeons.

a) Sciatic-tibialis anticus preparation. Experiments were performed on 30 dogs anesthetized with pentobarbital (33 mgm./kgm.) injected intravenously. One of the legs was immobilized by drills through the tibia. The sciatic nerve was sectioned and silver-silver chloride-saline electrodes were attached to the peroneal nerve. In some experiments needle electrodes were also attached to the tibialis anticus muscle. Contractions were recorded on smoked paper, a steel spring myograph being employed for this purpose. The trachea was systematically cannulated. In most experiments a François Franck cannula was inserted into one of the carotids in order to record also the arterial blood pressure through a Ludwig's manometer. All injections were made intravenously into one of the radial veins, previously cannulated. Nerve and muscle stimulation was performed with square wave pulses of one-millisecond duration delivered from an electronic stimulator. Supramaximal stimuli of several frequencies (50 per minute, 70 or 100 per second) were used for nerve stimulation. For direct stimulation, single shocks delivered at a rate of 50 per minute were applied.

[1] Present Address: Department of Pharmacology, Faculty of Medicine, Ribeirão Preto, State of São Paulo, Brazil.

In the majority of experiments (25 dogs) streptomycin was injected while the nerve was uninterruptedly stimulated with shocks delivered at a rate of 50 per minute. When the tibialis anticus responses to the indirect stimulation were abolished, the direct excitability of the muscle was tested in some experiments. In other experiments, tetanizing stimuli at frequencies of 70 or 100 per second were applied to the nerve for 10 or 20 second periods, after which the nerve was again stimulated with low frequency stimuli. In some experiments neostigmine (0.15 mgm. per kgm.) or calcium chloride (0.5 ml. per kgm. of 10 per cent solution) was injected.

In five dogs, the nerve was stimulated with tetanizing frequencies (70 or 100 per second) for 5 second periods, repeated each 3 or 5 minutes. The streptomycin was injected between the excitation periods. Low frequency stimuli were also tried before and after the tetanization (10 or 20 seconds duration) of the nerve in some experiments.

b) Experiments on intact unanesthetized animals. Ten dogs and 12 pigeons were used. Dogs were given 110 mgm. of streptomycin base per kgm. of body weight intravenously (v. saphena). Calcium chloride (0.5 ml. per kgm. of body weight of a 10 per cent solution) or neostigmine (0.15 mgm. per kgm.) was injected intravenously into 6 dogs, while the animals presented signs of acute streptomycin intoxication. Pigeons, weighing from 200 to 300 gm., were given streptomycin intramuscularly. A 25 per cent solution of streptomycin and a single dose of 580 mgm. of the base per kgm. of body-weight were used. Calcium chloride (5 ml. per kgm. of body weight of a 1 per cent solution) or neostigmine (0.1 mgm.) was injected intravenously into 10 animals.

Drugs used. Streptomycin sulphate[2] from two different manufacturers was employed: Rhône Poulenc and Bristol. Doses were calculated as the free base and were dissolved in 5 to 10 ml. of distilled water immediately before injection. For pigeons, a 25 per cent solution was prepared in distilled water. Other drugs used were: neostigmine methylsulphate (Prostigmine Roche, 0.05 per cent solution), and calcium chloride (10 per cent or 1 per cent solution in distilled water).

RESULTS. Streptomycin injected in the dose of 110 mgm. per kgm. of body weight abolished in some dogs the contractions of the tibialis anticus indirectly stimulated with shocks delivered at a rate of 50 per minute (fig. 1). In other dogs, it reduced markedly the amplitude of the tibialis anticus contractions. Our results are shown in table 1. The muscle responded always to direct stimulation. Respiration became diaphragmatic; in a few dogs the respiratory movements stopped. When this occurred, artificial respiration secured the animal's survival in almost all cases. Arterial blood pressure fell after the injection of the antibiotic, in general between 80 and 40 mm. Hg. In most dogs the pressure rose slowly after three or four minutes without attaining its previous level. (fig. 1). The neuromuscular block persisted for ten to twenty minutes.

When isolated volleys of impulses were blocked, high frequency (70 or 100 per second) stimulation of the nerve elicited tetanic contraction of still strong tension (fig. 1 and 2). The tetanic stimulation of the nerve being stopped, the muscle was found to respond to single volleys of impulses (post-tetanic decurarization). The post-tetanic twitches were maximum immediately after the tetanus in some experiments (fig. 2). In other experiments, there was a very brief delay of two or four seconds. The decurarization was transient and the twitches declined progressively.

Complete neuromuscular block to tetanic impulses was attained through administration of doses over 200 mgm. of streptomycin base per kgm. of body weight

[2] Kindly supplied by Dr. José Inácio Lobo, Laborterápica, S/A São Paulo, Brazil.

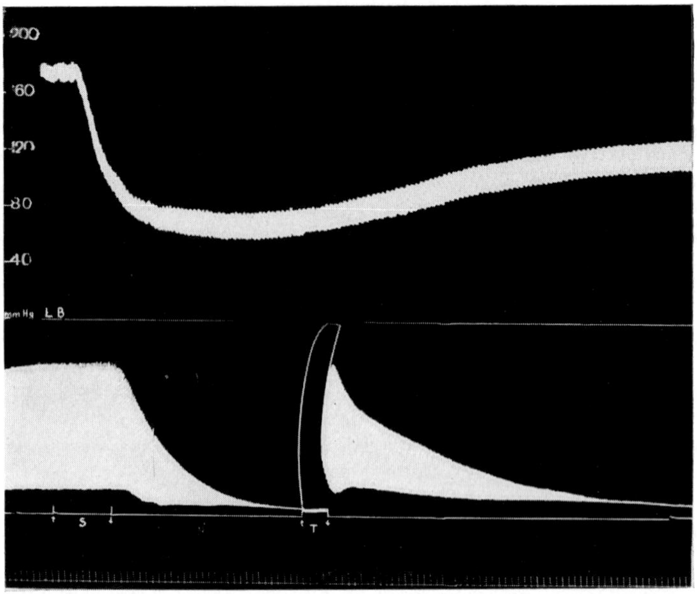

FIG. 1. Neuromuscular blocking action of streptomycin and antagonism by nerve tetanization.

Arterial blood pressure and contractions of tibialis anticus in response to indirect stimulation with shocks delivered at a rate of 50 per minute; at *T*, indirect stimulation with a tetanizing frequency (100 per second) for a 20-second period. At *S*, streptomycin,was injected (110 mgm./kgm. of body weight). Dog under pentobarbital anesthesia. Time: 6/6 seconds.

TABLE 1

Neuromuscular blocking potency of streptomycin in dogs (sciatic-tibialis anticus preparation)

Dose of Streptomycin Base per Kgm.	Maximal Reduction of the Amplitude of the Tibialis Anticus Contractions		
	<50%	>50%	100%
74 mgm.	2/5	2/5	1/5
110 mgm.	2/20	12/20	6/20

Numerator: number of animals which presented block of intensity registered at the vertical column. Denominator: number of animals injected with the dose indicated in the horizontal column.

(fig. 3). During partial block, tetanic stimulation of the nerve elicited an initial abrupt rise of the muscle tension which did not change greatly (fig. 2 and 3c), or increased gradually throughout the stimulation period (five to twenty minutes).

Calcium chloride antagonized the neuromuscular block produced by streptomycin (fig. 4). The effect of calcium chloride injections upon respiration was also striking: spontaneous respiratory movements were restored with normal amplitude and rhythm. Arterial blood pressure in most experiences rose to the level prior to the administration of the antibiotic.

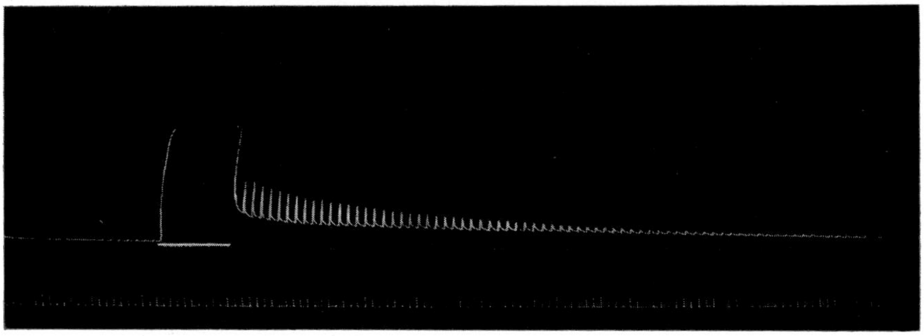

FIG. 2. Antagonism of streptomycin blockade by nerve tetanization.
Peroneal nerve stimulated with shocks delivered at a rate of 50 per minute before and after its excitation with a tetanic frequency (100 per second) for a 10-second period (at signals). Neuromuscular block was produced by 110 mgm. of streptomycin per kgm. of body weight. Dog under pentobarbital anesthesia. Recording of tibialis anticus contractions. Time: 1/1 second.

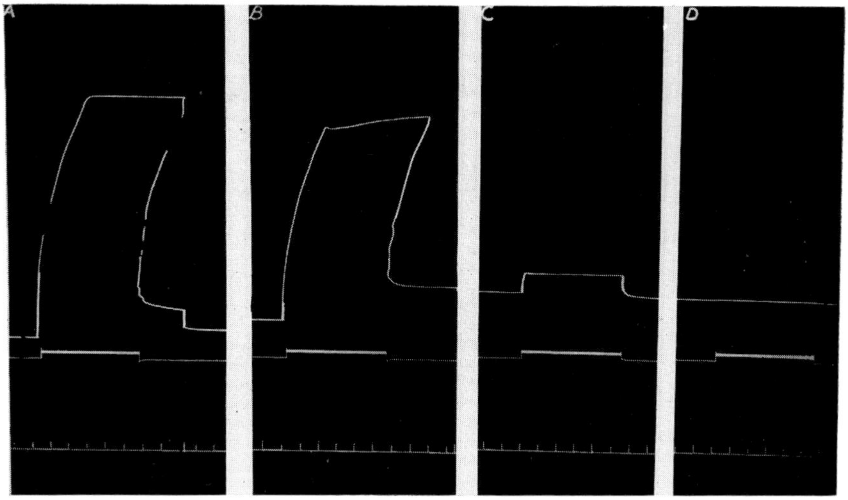

FIG. 3. Tibialis anticus responses to nerve stimulation with tetanic frequency (70 per second) during progressive streptomycin neuromuscular blockade.
Peroneal nerve was stimulated for 5-second periods. Between *A* and *B*, 165 mgm. of streptomycin per kgm. of body weight were injected; between *C* and *D*, 55 mgm. of streptomycin per kgm. of body weight were given. Dog under pentobarbital anesthesia. Time: 1/1 second.

Neostigmine was also able to antagonize the neuromuscular block produced by streptomycin (fig. 5). Indirect excitability, however, was restored more slowly. In some experiments the antagonistic effect was slight.

On the intact unanesthetized dog, streptomycin in the dose of 110 mgm. per kgm. of body weight induced muscular hypotonia, ataxia, flaccid paralysis, nausea and vomiting. In some dogs muscular hypotonia and incoordination of movements were the only motor effects observed. In addition to these signs,

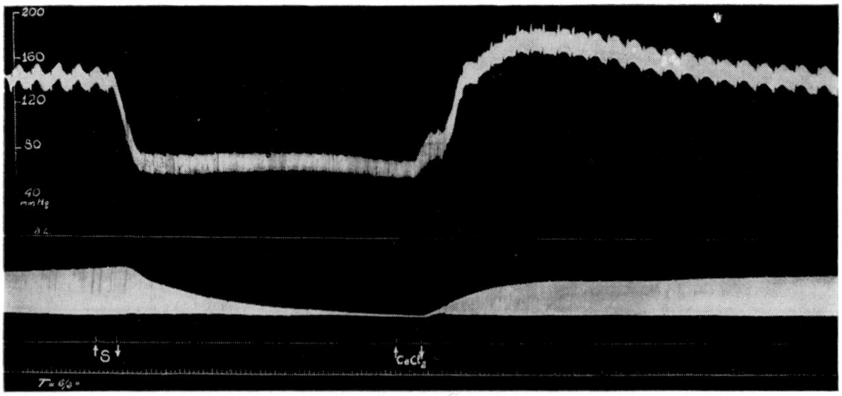

FIG. 4. Neuromuscular blocking action of streptomycin and the antagonistic effects of calcium.

Arterial blood pressure and contractions of tibialis anticus in response to indirect stimulation with shocks delivered at a rate of 50 per minute. At *S*, streptomycin (110 mgm./kgm. of body weight) and at $CaCl_2$, 0.5 ml. of a 10 per cent solution of calcium chloride were given. Time: 6/6 seconds.

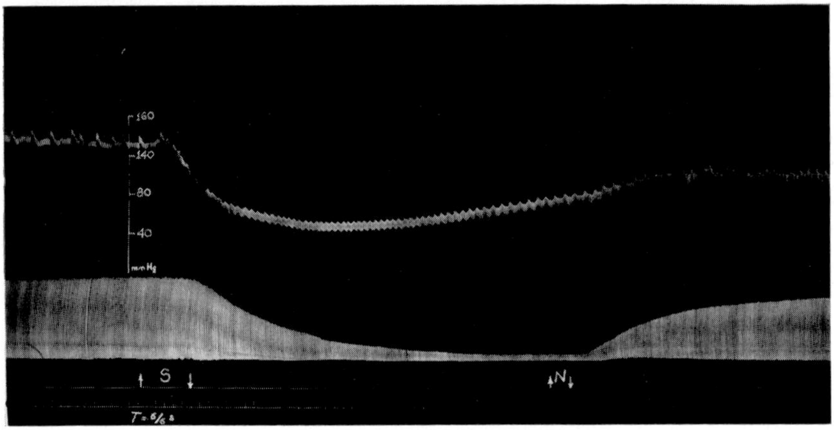

FIG. 5. Neuromuscular blocking action of streptomycin and the antagonistic effects of neostigmine.

Arterial blood pressure and contractions of tibialis anticus in response to indirect stimulation with shocks delivered at a rate of 50 per minute. At *S*, streptomycin (110 mgm./kgm. of body weight) and at *N*, neostigmine (0.15 mgm./kgm. of body weight) were given. Time: 6/6 seconds.

flaccid paralysis occurred in other dogs. Animals with severe degrees of paralysis suffered from respiratory impairment. Corneal reflex was unaltered.

Calcium chloride suppressed all motor signs produced by streptomycin administration. Following calcium chloride injection, the antagonistic effect appeared very promptly and was striking. Dogs with a severe degree of paralysis and respiratory impairment could stand up and move as freely as before the streptomycin injection thirty seconds after the administration of calcium chloride.

On the other hand, calcium chloride did not abolish nausea and vomiting; these signs were apparently more severe in those dogs injected with calcium chloride.

The antagonistic effect produced by neostigmine was similar to that of calcium chloride, but it occurred more slowly and gradually: recuperation of muscular tonus and motility was complete only four to five minutes after the neostigmine injection. Dogs which received neostigmine presented nausea and vomiting.

Following streptomycin injection in pigeons, vomiting, muscular hypotonia and flaccid paralysis occurred. This last effect persisted for an extremely long period. As in dogs, calcium chloride and neostigmine antagonized the motor signs produced by streptomycin. The antagonistic effect of calcium chloride persisted for four to six minutes and that of neostigmine for six to ten minutes.

DISCUSSION. The characteristics of neuromuscular blockade by streptomycin and by magnesium are surprisingly alike. During neuromuscular blockade with magnesium sulphate, when isolated volleys of impulses were blocked, Łubinska (1935) observed that indirect stimulation with tetanizing frequencies still evoked a tetanus. This behavior of the muscle is observed also under streptomycin. With the use of *d*-tubocurarine or decamethonium there is only an initial twitch (*d*-tubocurarine) or no contraction at all (decamethonium).

Post-tetanic enhancement of single volleys occurs during neuromuscular blockade produced by curare (Boyd, 1932) and by magnesium (Lubinska, 1935); it is not observed during neuromuscular blockade with decamethonium (Paton, 1951). Under curare, the first post-tetanic twitches are relatively feeble but become progressively stronger until a maximum is reached. During neuromuscular blockade with magnesium, the post-tetanic twitches are maximum immediately after stopping nerve tetanization (Boyd, Brosnan and Maaske, 1938). Under streptomycin, in some experiments, maximal twitches occurred immediately after tetanic stimulation of the nerve was stopped, exactly as when magnesium is employed. In other experiments, there was a very brief delay, invariably much smaller than that observed under curare.

The sharp antagonism of streptomycin blockade by calcium reveals a very striking similarity between neuromuscular blockade produced by streptomycin and that produced by magnesium, although an antagonistic effect is also produced by calcium during curare neuromuscular block (Feng, 1936). Under neuromuscular blockade produced by *d*-tubocurarine, however, the anti-curare effect in most experiences is very feeble. Calcium does not antagonize decamethonium neuromuscular blockade (Vital Brazil and Corrado, unpublished observations).

Neostigmine-streptomycin antagonism is similar to neostigmine-magnesium antagonism. Neostigmine does not antagonize neuromuscular block produced by decamethonium (Paton, 1951).

Tetanic stimulation of the nerve under progressive neuromuscular blockade by magnesium evokes an initial abrupt rise of muscle tension followed by a secondary rise which surpasses the first (Boyd, Brosnan and Maaske, 1938). During partial block with *d*-tubocurarine there is also an abrupt rise of tension of the muscle which is followed, however, by Wedensky inhibition. In some streptomycin experiments the muscle behaviour was similar to that observed under magnesium; in other experiments it differed slightly from this pattern: the muscle tension increased abruptly but did not change as long as the nerve was stimulated.

Table 2 summarizes some of the characteristics of neuromuscular blockade by decamethonium, *d*-tubocurarine, magnesium and streptomycin here discussed.

The similarity between the neuromuscular blockade produced by magnesium and that produced by streptomycin suggests that streptomycin neuromuscular blockade is produced by the same mechanism. Magnesium decreases the sensitivity of the endplate to the depolarizing action of applied acetylcholine and the direct excitability of the muscle fibres. The main effect, however, of magnesium (Del Castillo and Engbaeck, 1954) is to decrease the amount of acetylcholine liberated by a nerve impulse. Other similarities between the pharmacodynamic actions of streptomycin and magnesium are plain muscle depression and ganglionic transmission blockade. Ganglionic transmission is restored by calcium under magnesium (Hutter and Kostial, 1954) and streptomycin block (Corrado, to be published) but not when the blockade is produced by hexamethonium or *d*-tubocurarine (Vital Brazil and Corrado, unpublished observations). Ganglionic blockade produced by magnesium is due to a lessening of effectiveness of acetylcholine at the ganglion cells and to a reduction of the output of acetylcholine from the nerve endings (Hutter and Kostial, 1954).

TABLE 2

Test	Decamethonium	*d*-Tubocurarine	Mg^{++}	Streptomycin
Stimulant effects on muscle	Spontaneous fasciculations. Increase of amplitude of muscle contractions to isolated volleys of impulses prior to blockade	Absent	Absent	Absent
Effects on pigeons	Spastic paralysis	Flaccid paralysis	Flaccid paralysis	Flaccid paralysis
Response to indirect stimulation with tetanizing frequency when isolated volleys of impulses are blocked	Absent	Initial twitch	Tetanus	Tetanus
Post-tetanic facilitation	Absent	Present; post-tetanic twitches initially very weak, increase gradually	Present; post-tetanic twitches are maximum immediately after tetanus	Present; post-tetanic twitches are maximum immediately after tetanus or after a brief delay.
Neostigmine	Little effect, occasionally feeble potentiation or antagonism	Antagonism	Antagonism	Antagonism
Ca^{++}	No effect	Partial antagonism	Complete or almost complete antagonism	Complete or almost complete antagonism
Response to indirect stimulation with tetanizing frequency	Abrupt rise of tension which does not change as long as the nerve is stimulated	Abrupt rise of tension followed by Wedensky inhibition	Abrupt rise of tension followed by a secondary rise which transcends the first	As under Mg^{++} or as under decamethonium

The motor signs of acute streptomycin intoxication were identical to those produced by curare or magnesium sulphate. The ataxia which was observed prior to paralysis seemed to be due to the reduction of muscular tone and strength. It did not differ from the incoordination observed under curare. Motor symptoms should be imputed to the neuromuscular block produced by streptomycin since neostigmine injection abolished them. Death of the animals—dogs and pigeons—should also be attributed to the neuromuscular blocking action of streptomycin.

SUMMARY

Streptomycin possesses neuromuscular blocking properties. When injected intravenously in the dose of 110 mgm. per kgm. of body weight, the contractions of the tibialis anticus indirectly stimulated with shock delivered at a rate of 50 per minute were abolished in some dogs. In others, streptomycin reduced markedly the amplitude of the tibialis anticus contractions. When administered in larger doses, streptomycin induced complete myoneural blockade to tetanizing impulses. The muscle responded always to direct stimulation. Nerve tetanization, neostigmine and calcium were shown to antagonize streptomycin blockade.

Under neuromuscular blockade produced by streptomycin and that produced by magnesium, some effects such as the response to tetanic indirect stimulation when isolated volleys of impulses are blocked, post-tetanic facilitation, the responses to tetanic stimulation of the nerve during progressive neuromuscular blockade and the effect of calcium chloride administration are surprisingly alike. This seems to suggest the same mechanisms of action in both cases.

On intact unanesthetized dogs and pigeons, streptomycin induced muscular hypotonia, flaccid paralysis and vomiting. Calcium and neostigmine suppressed the motor effects of the acute streptomycin intoxication.

The motor signs of the acute streptomycin poisoning should be imputed to neuromuscular blockade since neostigmine abolished them. Death of the animals, dogs and pigeons, should be also attributed to the neuromuscular blocking action of streptomycin.

REFERENCES

Boyd, T. E.: Am. J. Physiol., **100:** 569, 1932.

Boyd, T. E., Brosnam, J. J., and Maaske, C. A.: J. Neurophysiol., **1:** 497, 1938.

Del Castillo, J., and Engbaek, L.: J. Physiol., **124:** 370, 1954.

Feng, F. P.: Chinese J. Physiol., **10:** 513, 1936.

Hutter, O. F., and Kostial, K.: J. Physiol., **124:** 234, 1954.

Lubinska, L.: Arch. Internat. Physiol., **41:** 456, 1935.

Molitor, H., and Graessle, O. E.: Pharmacol. Rev., **2:** 1, 1950.

Molitor, H., Graessle, O. E., Kuna, S., Mushett, C. W., and Silber, R. H.: This Journal, **86:** 151, 1946.

Molitor, H.: in Waksman, S. A.: Streptomycin, Nature and Practical Application. The Williams & Wilkins Comp., Baltimore, 1949.

Paton, W. D. M.: Ann. N. Y. Acad. Sci., **54:** 347, 1951.

THE DIFFERENTIAL EFFECT OF QUINIDINE AND PYRILAMINE ON THE MYOCARDIAL ACTION POTENTIAL AT VARIOUS RATES OF STIMULATION

E. A. JOHNSON AND M. G. McKINNON

Department of Pharmacology, University of Sydney, Sydney, Australia

Received for publication March 16, 1957

It has already been reported that quinidine and quinidine-like agents produce a pronounced reduction in the maximum rate of depolarization of the myocardial action potential as recorded with intracellular microelectrodes (Weidmann, 1955b; Johnson, 1956). However, we have since observed that even in the presence of relatively large doses of quinidine there is no reduction in the maximum rate of depolarization if the rate of stimulation is sufficiently slow. This is of interest in view of the hypothesis put forward by Weidmann for the mechanism by which quinidine reduces the maximum rate of depolarization of action potentials derived from Purkinje tissue. His suggestion is that quinidine acts on the mechanism responsible for transporting sodium ions through the fiber membrane during depolarization. We have examined the dependence of the effects of quinidine and pyrilamine on the frequency of stimulation of guinea pig ventricular fibers with a view of gaining further information on the manner by which these drugs interfere with the transport of sodium ions during depolarization.

METHODS. Preparations of guinea pig right ventricle were obtained in the manner previously described and the same microelectrode recording equipment was used (Johnson, 1956). The usual method of examining the effects of drugs on the membrane resting and action potentials is to make a number of penetrations into different fibers, to record the data which is required at each preparation, and to take the mean of the values so obtained before administration of the drug, during its administration, and after washout. In view of the relatively large variation of membrane properties seen in this type of experiment, it was decided that fine changes in membrane behaviour could better be ascertained if the same fiber were kept under observation throughout each experiment. In spite of the mechanical activity of the muscle it was possible to keep the microelectrode in one fiber for periods up to four and one-half hours. Several such experimental runs were made on each preparation. The results are from seven preparations, only one drug being tested on each. If accidental withdrawal of the microelectrode occurred, comparisons were made between results obtained from one fiber before, and another after administration of the drug. Some results were obtained from the same fiber during the administration and after partial recovery from the drug. As the quinidine-like agents tend to depress the mechanical activity of the preparation, withdrawal of the microelectrode during such circumstances is far less common than in actively beating tissue.

When it was considered that the microelectrode was securely lodged in a fiber, the threshold for stimulation at the external electrodes was found. Measurements were then made of the amplitude of the action potential and of the maximum rate of depolarization (maximum rate of rise of the action potential) in the arbitrary units provided by the oscilloscope grille. These measurements were carried out over a wide range of stimulation frequencies (usually 0 1 to 10/sec.), and the increases in threshold for stimulation at the external electrodes at high frequencies were noted. Whenever a change in action potential amplitude occurred, we determined whether this was due to an alteration of the diastolic resting potential or of membrane reversal (overshoot). Quinidine sulphate (10 microgm./ml.) or pyrilamine maleate (7.5 microgm./ml.) was then introduced into the bath by changing over from the inflow of normal Krebs-Henseleit to Krebs-Henseleit solution containing the drugs in the above concentrations. After five to ten minutes the above experimental procedure was repeated and finally the drug was removed by washing out the bath with fresh Krebs-Henseleit solution.

RESULTS. *The effect of frequency of stimulation on the membrane resting and low action potentials of the normal fiber.* As the rate of stimulation was increased from low values (0.1/sec.) there was no discernible change in the amplitude or maximum rate of rise of the action potential until a frequency of 2 to 4/sec. was reached. Above this frequency the maximum rate of rise of the action potential progressively declined as the frequency of stimulation was increased such that at 10/sec. the value was 10 to 50 per cent less than below 2 to 4/sec. This was consistently observed.

It is known that a reduction in the membrane diastolic resting potential will cause a decrease in the maximum rate of depolarization of Purkinje fibers (Weidmann, 1955a). We were able to show that there was no significant change in the diastolic resting potential with a sudden increase in rate of stimulation (from 0.4 to 4/sec.) sufficient to cause a substantial fall in the maximum rate of rise of the action potential. Any change which might have occurred was within the short term spontaneous drift of the amplifier, contact potentials and membrane noise ($\pm$1.5 mV).

The amplitude of the action potential also declined with increase in frequency of stimulation, the decline commencing at approximately the same frequency (2 to 4/sec.) as that of the maximum rate of depolarization. At a frequency of 10/sec. the amplitude of the action potential was 10 to 25 per cent less than at frequencies below 2 to 4/sec. As no concurrent reduction in diastolic resting potential was observed, these changes in action potential amplitude represent alterations in the degree of overshoot.

All these changes, including the increases in stimulation threshold with increasing frequency of stimulation, are illustrated in fig. 1, 2 and 3 which are the results of typical experiments displayed in graphical form.

The effect of quinidine sulphate and pyrilamine maleate. The addition of 10 microgm./ml. of quinidine sulphate to the bathing solution had the following effects. At low rates of stimulation (0.1/sec.) the maximum rate of rise of the action potential and its amplitude approached closely to values obtained prior to the administration of the drug. However, the maximum rate of rise declined steeply and the threshold for stimulation increased at a much lower frequency of stimulation than in the absence of the drug. No difference was observed between the declines in action potential amplitude with increasing rate of stimulation in the normal and in the quinidine-treated preparation. These changes are illustrated in fig. 1 and 2. In fig. 1, data from a normal fiber and one affected by quinidine are presented graphically. The action potential amplitude and maximum rate of depolarization are almost identical in the two fibers at a stimulation rate of 0.1/sec. The maximum rate of depolarization of the fiber affected by quinidine is reduced drastically at rates of stimulation at and above 0.5/sec.

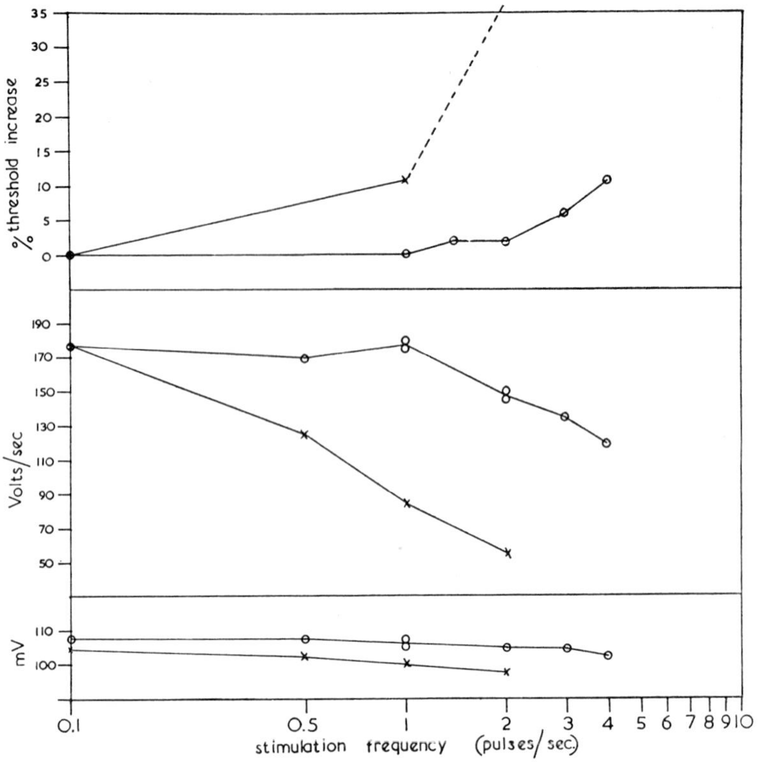

FIG. 1. The percentage increase in stimulation threshold, the amplitude (mV) and maximum rate of rise (Volts/sec.) of action potentials from guinea pig ventricular fibers plotted against frequency of stimulation.

X——X in the presence of 10 microgm./ml. of quinidine sulphate; O——O after washout and partial recovery from the drug. All the data obtained from one fiber.

compared with no change until 3/sec. in the normal fiber. Quinidine produced no significant alteration from the normal in the decline in action potential amplitude at high frequencies of stimulation. Data in fig. 2 were obtained from one fiber in the presence of and following the removal of quinidine sulphate (10 microgm./ml.). This clearly shows that at a frequency of stimulation of 0.1/sec. the maximum rate of depolarization of the fiber in contact with quinidine remains unchanged after the drug is removed; at frequencies higher than 0.1/sec., the maximum rate of depolarization is considerably lower in the presence of quinidine. Pyrilamine maleate had essentially the same effects as quinidine on the preparation. The results displayed in fig. 3 were obtained from one fiber before and during the administration of 7.5 microgm./ml. of pyrilamine maleate.

When the tissue was exposed to either drug no change in the diastolic membrane potential could be detected as the frequency of stimulation was increased. If the frequency of stimulation was suddenly increased or decreased, the maximum rate of depolarization did not change immediately but there was a time lag of approximately 5 sec. during which the new value was

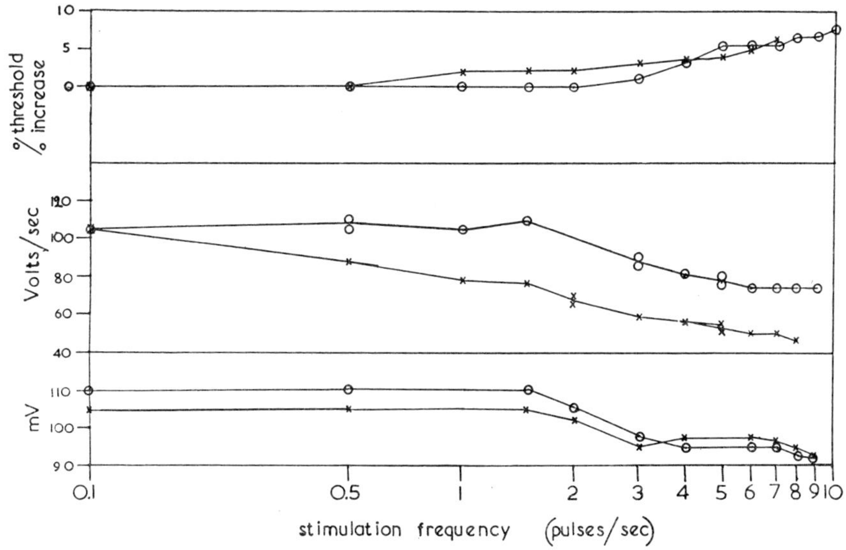

FIG. 2. The percentage increase in stimulation threshold, the amplitude (mV) and maximum rate of rise (Volts/sec.) of action potentials from guinea pig ventricular fibers plotted against frequency of stimulation.

O——O data from one fiber before the administration of quinidine and X——X data from another fiber in the presence of 10 microgm./ml. of quinidine sulphate.

gradually assumed. It was difficult to detect such a time lag in the untreated tissue as it was not always possible to produce a sufficiently large reduction in maximum rate of depolarization to enable the phenomenon to be clearly seen. The time lag is illustrated in fig. 4 where successive action potentials and their first differentials from a fiber affected by quinidine are recorded on the one exposure following a sudden increase in frequency of stimulation from 0.4 to 4/sec. The maximum rate of depolarization gradually falls with each successive action potential at the high rate of stimulation until it becomes stable at a lower level after several beats.

The lower frequency at which the stimulation threshold began to increase, as compared with the normal fiber, is almost certainly due to an increase in the time for the return of resting excitability after excitation. Observations made throughout the present work indicate that the resting excitability may not have completely returned by the end of the repolarization phase of the action potential. By recording as close to the stimulating electrodes as possible in order to minimize the conduction time of the propagated action potential from the stimulating electrodes to the recording electrode, and as there were no serious differences in the duration of the action potential throughout the tissue (confirmed by experiment). we were able to show that even when stimuli were falling some 100 msec. after the completion of the repolarization phase, an increase in stimulation threshold was observed. In one extreme case, in the presence of 50 microgm./ml. of quinidine sulphate the tissue was absolutely refractory to stimulation at a rate of 1/40 sec. yet the action potential at frequencies slightly below this was completed within

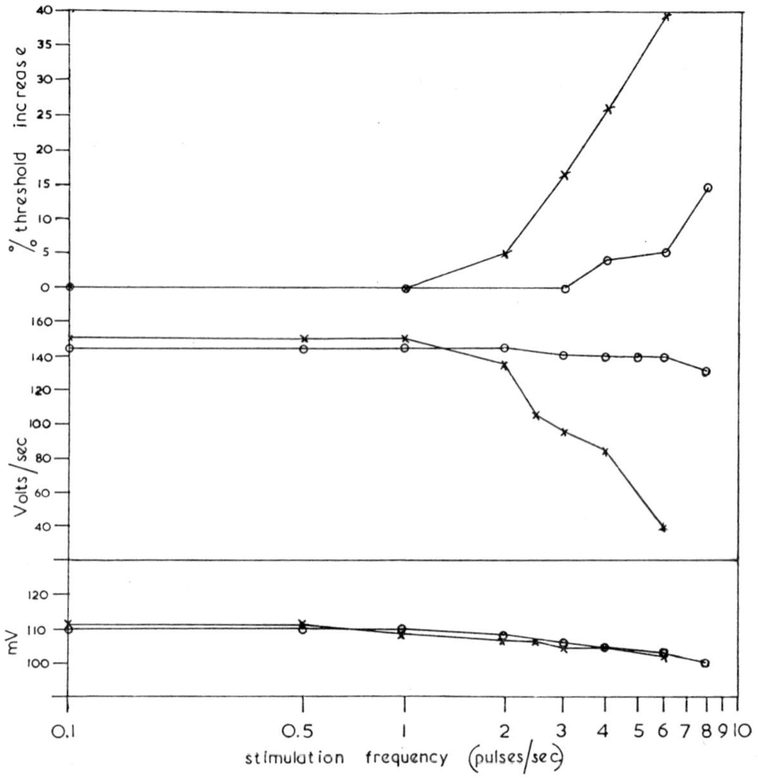

FIG. 3. The percentage increase in stimulation threshold, the amplitude (mV) and maximum rate of rise (Volts/sec.) of action potentials from guinea pig ventricular fibers plotted against frequency of stimulation.

○——○ before the administration of pyrilamine; ×——× in the presence of 7.5 microgm./ml. of pyrilamine maleate. All the data were recorded from one fiber.

approximately 500 msec. Furthermore, at frequencies above 1/40 sec. the tissue would not respond to any of the stimuli, showing that the subthreshold responses produced by these stimuli were sufficient to so exhaust the excitatory mechanism as to render the tissue completely inexcitable.

DISCUSSION. There is evidence that the depolarization phase of the membrane action potential is associated with a selective increase in the permeability of the membrane to sodium ions and a consequent net flux of sodium ions into the fiber down an electroconcentration gradient. Further evidence exists that the passage of sodium ions into the fiber is not a simple diffusion process but is associated with a "sodium carrying" mechanism consisting of "sodium carrying units", (Weidmann, 1955a). According to Hodgkin and Huxley (1952) these sodium carrying units exist in three states: the *resting* state where they may be converted into *active* units when the fiber is depolarized, the *active* state where they are engaged in transporting sodium ions into the fiber and finally the *inactive* state where they are neither carrying nor are capable of carrying sodium ions. Weidmann (1955b) has suggested that these three states may be connected as shown in expression (1).

$$\text{Resting} \rightleftharpoons \text{Active} \rightarrow \text{Inactive.} \tag{1}$$

(Inactive $\xrightarrow{?}$ Active; Inactive $\xrightarrow{?}$ Resting)

A satisfactory explanation of the effects of quinidine and pyrilamine described in the present work must account for a) the frequency selective nature of the decline in maximum rate of depolarization that the drugs produce, b) the fact that "normal" values of maximum rate of depolarization can be obtained in the presence of the drugs if the tissue is driven at a sufficiently low rate, c) the time lag experienced before the maximum rate of depolarization assumes its new value upon a sudden increase or decrease in rate of stimulation, and d) the failure to observe a paralleled decline in action potential amplitude with the fall in maximum rate of depolarization in the presence of the drugs. The maximal rate

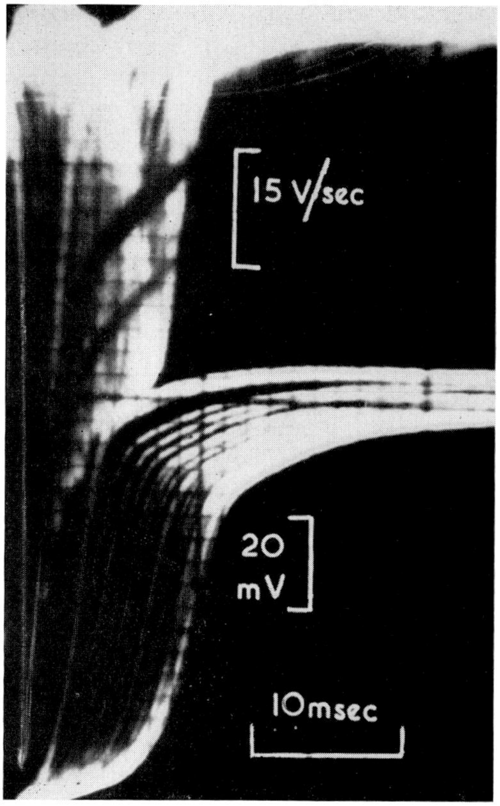

FIG. 4. Record showing successive action potentials and their first derivatives from one fiber exposed to quinidine sulphate immediately following a sudden change in stimulation frequency from 0.4 to 4/sec.

The maximum rate of rise progressively declines and reaches its final value after several beats. Upper trace: first differentials of the action potentials. Lower trace: action potentials. The upper trace is displaced to the left in order to avoid interference with the lower trace.

of depolarization can be considered as proportional to the sodium current or rate of entry of sodium ions during depolarization (Hodgkin and Katz, 1949). There are a number of possible ways by which quinidine and pyrilamine could reduce the rate of entry of sodium ions during depolarization. However, any mechanism which involves a reduction in the number of resting units available at the start of the action potential, either by a direct action or one involving a reduction in the rate of reactivation of inactive to resting units, and any mechanism which interferes with the movement of the carrier through the membrane would require that there be a reduction in the peak value of sodium permeability as well as the rate of entry of sodium ions during depolarization. Unless the sodium permeability normally rose to a value sufficient to swamp the permeability of the membrane to other ions (K^+ and Cl^-), a reduction in peak value of the sodium permeability would be reflected in a reduction in the magnitude of overshoot. It seems unlikely that the sodium permeability rises to a value sufficient to swamp the permeabilities of the membrane to other ions; if this were the case the potential attained at the peak of depolarization should approach that of the sodium equilibrium potential for a sodium concentration cell and would be relatively insensitive to further increases in sodium permeability. Neither of these conditions appears to be satisfied as the degree of overshoot, in Purkinje tissue, for example, falls some 20 mV short of that required for a membrane exclusively permeable to sodium ions (Draper and Weidmann, 1951) and, more convincingly, the overshoot can be increased in Purkinje fibers if the membrane is hyperpolarized prior to the initiation of an action potential. Unless guinea pig ventricular fibers, unlike Purkinje fibers, become exclusively permeable to sodium ions during depolarization, the failure to observe any concurrent reduction in action potential amplitude with the reduction in maximum rate of depolarization in the fiber exposed to quinidine or pyrilamine indicates that under the conditions existing in the present work the drugs reduce the rate of entry of sodium ions without affecting the peak level to which sodium permeability rises during depolarization. The drugs appear therefore to slow the rate of production of active units (slow the rate of rise of sodium permeability during depolarization) without affecting the final number in the active state (peak sodium permeability). In such circumstances a reduction in maximum rate of depolarization would be observed without a decline in action potential amplitude. The drugs do not appear to have a direct effect on the rate of production of active units; provided that the tissue is driven at a sufficiently low frequency the maximal rate of depolarization returns to a value close to that of the fiber unaffected by the drugs. Obviously some subsidiary mechanism is affected as is further suggested by the existence of a time lag before the maximum rate of depolarization assumes its new value after a sudden change in rate of stimulation. Comment on the possible nature of this mechanism is not at present justified.

The increase in stimulation threshold at the higher rates of stimulation shows that the stimuli are falling in the relative refractory period of the tissue beneath the stimulating electrode. As this increase in threshold often commenced at the same frequency as the decline in maximum rate of depolarization, it might be suggested that there is a direct causal relationship between the two. One piece of evidence appears to be against this view. The change in maximum rate of depolarization which results from a sudden increase in stimulation rate is effected over several beats; the first action potential at the new rate has a slightly lower value than the previous beat, and every succeeding action potential for a few seconds shows a progressively lower maximum rate of rise. This is contrary to what one would expect were it directly connected with the decrease in refractory period which is known to accompany an increase in stimulation rate. The first action potential at the higher rate should show the lowest rate of depolarization as presumably the refractory period is longest at this moment and the stimulus would have fallen further into the relative refractory period than subsequent stimuli.

Weidmann (1955b) has shown that quinidine reduces the maximum rate of rise and overshoot of action potentials derived from Purkinje tissue driven at a constant rate. He found that "normal" values of the maximum rate of rise could be obtained in the presence of quinidine if the fiber were hyperpolarized prior to the initiation of an action potential. He concluded that the effect of hyperpolarization was to increase the number of resting units available at the start of the action potential and that quinidine affected the sodium transport mechanism by shifting the reactions shown in (1) to the right. However, our findings show that quinidine can cause a decline in the maximum rate of rise without producing a concurrent decrease in overshoot. This finding is incompatible with such a hypothesis which requires a concurrent reduction in the amplitude of the action potential as well as a decline in maximum rate of rise. One explanation of this difference may be that in Weidmann's experiments the tissue was exposed to the action of quinidine for one hour prior to the taking of measurements whereas the equivalent time in the present experiments was five to ten minutes. Perhaps the results of Weidmann refer to later effects of quinidine.

SUMMARY

The maximum rate of depolarization and amplitude of action potentials from guinea pig ventricular fibers together with the threshold for stimulation have been measured over a range of stimulation frequencies (0.1 to 10/sec.) in the presence of quinidine sulphate or pyrilamine maleate.

In the normal fiber, a progressive reduction in amplitude and maximum rate of depolarization of the action potential, and increase in stimulation threshold (external electrodes) commence at approximately 2 beats/sec. while no change in membrane resting potential could be detected at this or higher rates.

In the presence of quinidine sulphate (10 microgm./ml.) or pyrilamine maleate (7.5 microgm./ml.) a) the progressive decline in the maximum rate of depolarization and increase in stimulation threshold which occur commence at a much lower rate of stimulation and were more pronounced than in the normal fiber, b) at sufficiently low rates of stimulation the threshold for excitability and the maximum rate of depolarization were unchanged, c) compared with the normal fiber there was no significant change in the decline in action potential amplitude with increasing frequency of stimulation and d) when the rate of stimulation was suddenly increased or decreased there was a time lag occupying several beats during which the maximum rate of depolarization progressively changed to a new stable value.

These findings are discussed in relation to some possible ways by which the drugs could affect the transport of sodium ions into the fiber during depolarization.

Acknowledgment. One of us (E. A. J.) wishes to acknowledge a grant from the Life Insurance Medical Research Fund of Australia and New Zealand, which provided animals and all equipment, and our thanks are due to Professor R. H. Thorp for constant advice and encouragement.

REFERENCES

Draper, M. H., and Weidmann, S.: J. Physiol., **115:** 74, 1951.
Hodgkin, A. L., and Huxley, A. F.: J. Physiol., **117:** 500, 1952.
Hodgkin, A. L., and Katz, B.: J. Physiol., **108:** 37, 1949.
Johnson, E. A.: This Journal, **117:** 237, 1956.
Weidmann, S.: J. Physiol., **127:** 213, 1955a.
Weidmann, S.: J. Physiol., **129:** 568, 1955b.

TOLERANCE TO SOME EFFECTS OF BARBITURATES

RICHARD E. BELLEVILLE AND H. F. FRASER

U. S. Department of Health, Education, and Welfare, Public Health Service, National Institute of Mental Health, Addiction Research Center, Lexington, Kentucky

Received for publication March 20, 1957

The present study was undertaken to describe certain changes which occur during the course of continuous administration of secobarbital and pentobarbital in doses of 0.4 gram per day. Of particular interest was the development of tolerance which may be defined operationally as follows: 1) the dosage of a drug must be increased to maintain the initial degree of effect, or 2) the initial degree of effect is observed to decrease when the same dose is administered repeatedly. The latter defines tolerance as it is used in the present study. When such definitions are used, no inferences need be made concerning the nature of the mechanisms underlying its development. Although it is generally agreed that tolerance to barbiturates does occur (Seevers, 1931; Fraser and Isbell, 1954), attempts toward quantitative demonstrations of this phenomena in man have met with little success. Isbell and associates (1950) found that it was very difficult to determine whether tolerance developed during the course of experimental addiction to barbiturates, because of the marked fluctuation in the effects of the drugs from day to day. They concluded, however, that tolerance must occur since patients withdrawn from barbiturates show much greater intoxication when replaced on the same dosages which they had attained gradually during addiction. Ideström (1954), however, succeeded in demonstrating tolerance to the effects of phenobarbital on flicker-fusion and obtained suggestive evidence that cross tolerance to phenobarbital and amobarbital may exist.

Intoxication, with its attendant impairment of performance, may be classified as an undesirable effect of barbiturates, whereas sedation and hypnosis, under appropriate circumstances, are desirable effects. The major purpose of the present study was to obtain quantitative data on the rate and degree of development of tolerance to both classes of effects of barbiturates.

METHODS AND MATERIALS. *Subjects.* Eighteen physically healthy subjects ranging in age from 25 to 57 years volunteered for the experiment. All were male postaddicts who were serving sentences for violations of the Harrison Narcotic Act and who were completely recovered from the debilitating effects of opiate withdrawal.

Clinical observations. Patients were housed in a closed ward and were observed continually by specially trained attendants for a preliminary period of 30 days without drugs, for 90 days during administration of barbiturates, and for 10 days after barbiturates were abruptly discontinued. The observations were as follows: 1) rectal temperature, systolic and diastolic blood pressures, pulse and respiratory rates were taken three times daily after resting in bed for 20 to 30 minutes, 2) body weight and caloric intake were measured daily, 3) hours of sleep were recorded at one-half hour intervals throughout each day, and 4) degree of intoxication was rated every eight hours on a four-point scale as follows: 0, no evidence of intoxication; 1+, mild intoxication; 2+, moderate intoxication; and 3+, marked intoxication.

Definitions of these grades and criteria for rating have been specified by Isbell *et al.*, (1955).

Psychomotor performance. Simple visuo-manual reaction times, using foreperiods of 1, 2, 4 and 7 seconds presented in randomized order, were recorded by means of a chronoscope and supplementary instruments which have been described in an earlier paper (Hill *et al.*, 1955). Forty responses were taken at each session.

The vertical tracing path described by Hill and Belleville (1953) was used as a simple measure of muscular coordination. Subjects were required to negotiate the path with a stylus and were given 10 trials on this test, with no rest periods.

The pursuit rotor device consisted of a small metal disk (2 cm. in diameter) set 8 cm. off center in a phonographlike turntable which rotated at the rate of 1 cycle per second. Subjects were instructed to keep a stylus in contact with the disk. They were given one practice trial and 10 test trials. A perfect score for any one trial was 20 seconds on the target disk.

Experimental phases. A. Preliminary: During this phase control observations and measurements were obtained under the general conditions which prevailed during the entire course of the experiment. Although this phase lasted for at least 30 days, in order to allow for some adaptation to the experimental environment, the clinical data obtained during the last 10 days only were analyzed. All subjects were given two days practice on reaction time and vertical tracing. Only 8 of the subjects were tested with the rotary pursuit apparatus. They were given four practice series on each of five consecutive days; control measures were then obtained for five days. Thus, on each day subjects were given two series of reaction times (20 reactions per series), one series on the tracing path (10 trials) and, in the case of 8 subjects, one series on the rotary pursuit apparatus (10 separate 20-second trials).

B. Chronic drug administration. Secobarbital group: Ten subjects were given 0.4 gram of secobarbital daily for 90 days. Medication was divided into four doses of 0.1 gram each which were given orally at 6:00 a.m., 11:00 a.m., 5:00 p.m., and 11:00 p.m. On days when psychomotor tests were given, the first medication of the day was given at 8:00 a.m., 30 minutes before the psychomotor tests. No coffee or breakfast was given until after completion of the tests. The tasks were performed each day for the first five days of medication, and during the last five days before withdrawal. The tests on this drug included reaction time and vertical tracing.

C. Chronic drug administration. Pentobarbital group: Eight subjects received 0.4 gram of pentobarbital per day for 90 days in the same dosage and at the same time of day as the secobarbital group. However, tests were made 45 minutes after ingestion of the drug. Subjects receiving pentobarbital were tested on the first seven consecutive days of medication, and for the last five days prior to withdrawal. Rotary pursuit, reaction time and tracing measurements were obtained on these subjects.

D. Withdrawal: Withdrawal of barbiturates was abrupt and complete in all patients. Tests were run on both groups during the first five days after discontinuing the drugs. The last dose was given at 11:00 p.m. the night before withdrawal tests were begun. Daily clinical observations were discontinued 10 days after withdrawal of the drug.

E. Recovery: During the sixth week following the last dose of the drug, the psychomotor tests were administered in the same manner as they had been under control (preliminary observation) conditions. No clinical observations were made at this time.

Treatment of data. Analysis of variance using a mixed two-factor design (Lindquist, 1953) was applied to the data obtained on reaction time, vertical tracing and hours of sleep. Since pursuit rotor performance was obtained under only one drug (pentobarbital), a "treatments x subjects" analysis was applied to these data. Where significant F-ratios were found, it was possible to compute critical differences to test the significance of differences between individual pairs of means, since the number of subjects was equal for all comparisons. Comparisons involving days 6 and 7 were evaluated by t-tests, since they were not included in the analysis of variance.

In arriving at mean scores for psychomotor tests during control, the last week of intoxi-

TABLE 1

Summary of analysis of variance

Item	Source	Items Compared	Reaction Time			Vertical Tracing		Sleep		
			df	Mean squares	F-ratio	Mean squares	F-ratio	df	Mean squares	F-ratio
(1)	Between-Subjects		17	2807.06		21.43		17	11.40	
(2)	Drugs	2/3	1	925.38	0.32	51.10	2.61	1	11.12	0.97
(3)	Error		16	2924.66		19.57		16	11.42	
(4)	Within-Subjects		144	1331.11		8.02		180	0.67	
(5)	Periods	5/7	8	15264.13	29.14*	89.26	27.63*	10	4.29	9.33*
(6)	Drugs × Periods (Interaction)	6/7	8	313.58	0.60	3.46	1.07	10	0.42	0.91
(7)	Error		128	523.89		3.23		160	0.46	
(8)	Total		161	1486.96		9.43		197	1.60	

* P <0.01.

cation, withdrawal, and recovery, each individual's performance on 5 consecutive days was averaged to obtain a mean for each of these periods. During the first week of intoxication, each of the first 5 days was treated as a separate period. In analyzing sleep, caloric intake, weight, and intoxication scores, the data were segmented into consecutive 5- or 10-day periods and the means for each period obtained.

RESULTS. Analysis of variance applied to reaction time, vertical tracing, and hours of sleep (table 1, item 2) revealed no significant differences between the two drugs on any of these measures. Likewise, clinical measurements showed no apparent differences between drugs. Data on both drugs, therefore, were combined for subsequent presentation.

Significant F-ratios, however, were found for the reaction time, vertical tracing and sleep measures obtained during different periods of the experiment (table 1, item 5). Similar differences were also found on the pursuit rotor scores, which were obtained only under pentobarbital (F = 36.12; df 10, 70; P = <0.01).

Psychomotor performance. Means for the combined data on both drugs and differences between means on reaction time as well as the level of significance for each of the experimental periods are presented in table 2 and illustrated in figure 1. Table 2 shows that the slowing of reaction time that occurred on day 2 was significantly different from control. This trend continued and became more pronounced on day 3. The difference between days 1 and 2 shows a cumulative effect. It should be noted, however, that the subjects had received only the early morning dose (0.1 gram) on day 1 at the time the tests were performed. Although improvement occurred between days 3 and 5, there was no significant decrease in reaction time between days 5, 6 and 7, and in addition day 7 remained significantly poorer than control (P = <0.05). The failure to find differences between the control phase and days 86 through 90 of intoxication demonstrates that tolerance to this effect is complete by this time. Similarly, following with-

TABLE 2

Reaction time (in milliseconds): differences between means of various conditions†

	Means	Intoxication						With-drawal	Recovery
		Day 1	Day 2	Day 3	Day 4	Day 5	Days 86–90	Days 1–5	Days 35–40
Control	198.44	10.45	49.56*	69.33*	60.73*	36.06*	4.39	1.95	−7.00
Intoxication									
Day 1	208.89	—	39.11*	58.88*	50.28*	25.61*	−6.06	−8.50	−17.45
Day 2	248.00	—	—	19.77*	11.17	−13.50	−45.17*	−47.61*	−56.56*
Day 3	267.77	—	—	—	−8.60	−33.27*	−64.94*	−67.38*	−76.33*
Day 4	259.17	—	—	—	—	−24.67*	−56.34*	−58.78*	−67.73*
Day 5	234.50	—	—	—	—	—	−31.67*	−34.11*	−43.06*
Days 86–90	202.83	—	—	—	—	—	—	−2.44	−11.39
Withdrawal									
Days 1–5	200.39	—	—	—	—	—	—	—	−8.95
Recovery									
Days 35–40	191.44	—	—	—	—	—	—	—	—

* Significant at the 0.01 level of confidence.

† The difference between any pair of conditions can be obtained by finding the intersect of any period in the left column and the desired period in the top row.

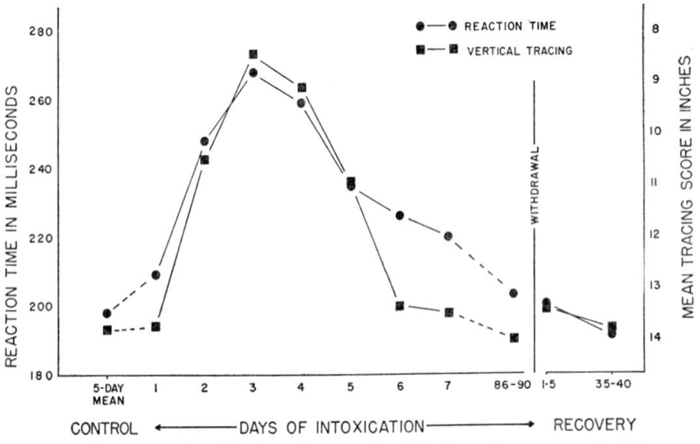

FIG. 1. Tolerance to secobarbital and pentobarbital as demonstrated by reaction time and tracing measures.

drawal of drugs no significant differences were obtained among control, withdrawal, and recovery phases. These findings are illustrated in figure 1.

Since the results on the vertical tracing test are substantially the same as those obtained on reaction time, they are presented only in graphic form (figure 1). However, tracing scores showed a significant improvement on days 6 and 7 as compared with day 5, and no significant difference between control and day 7. Although pursuit rotor performance was measured only on pentobarbital subjects, the results were quite similar to those of tracing and reaction time measurements. On this test, some improvement was seen between days 5 and 7, but the rate of improvement had decreased and day 7 remained significantly poorer

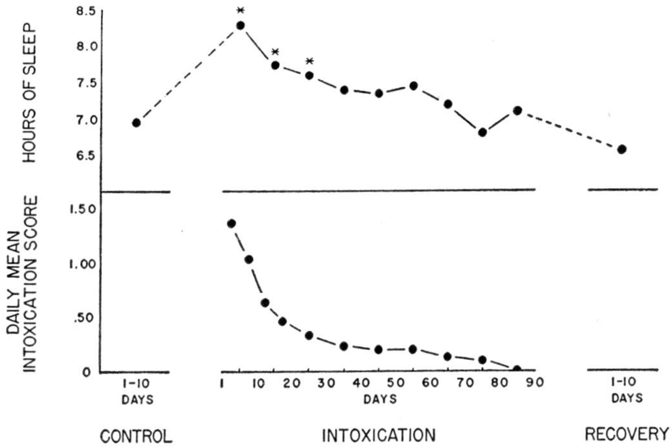

FIG. 2. Tolerance to the effects of secobarbital and pentobarbital on hours of sleep and degree of intoxication.
* Indicates a significant difference from control ($P < 0.01$).

than control. Comparisons between day 7 and days 86 through 90 showed that the degree of tolerance to the effect on this test was as great after one week as it was after three months of continuous medication.

Clinical observations. A significant increase in hours of sleep as compared with control appeared during the first 10 days of intoxication and remained significant through the 30th day of intoxication (figure 2). Although the differences are not significant after 30 days, the subjects slept more from the 30th to the 70th day of intoxication than they did during the control period. Some tolerance to the hypnotic effect occurred early, since a significant drop in hours of sleep was observed between days 1 through 10 and days 21 through 30. This trend continued throughout 70 days; the number of hours of sleep decreasing rather consistently throughout the intoxication phase.

As noted in previous reports from this laboratory (Isbell *et al.*, 1950; Fraser *et al.*, 1954), differences in susceptibility to the intoxicating effects of barbiturates exist among subjects. In the present study the maximum degree of intoxication recorded during the experiment was as follows: 12 subjects were estimated 3+, 4 were 2+, and 2 were 1+. These differences could not be accounted for entirely by differences in body weight. The changes from higher to lower intoxication scores as the experiment continued are illustrated in figure 2. For the first 20 days of intoxication, intoxication scores recorded during successive 5-day periods were compared with each preceding 5-day period. All of these comparisons showed significant decreases in the estimated degree of intoxication ($P = <0.01$).

No appreciable changes in temperature, blood pressure, pulse or respiratory rate, caloric intake or body weight were observed during the experiment.

DISCUSSION. The development of tolerance is clearly demonstrated by all measures which showed an initial barbiturate effect. The tolerance curve obtained on the sleep measure is of special interest since inferences based on these findings may be made concerning the clinical utility of barbiturates. These drugs, of course, are used widely for the purpose of inducing sleep, and are often administered over extended periods of time. In the doses tested in the present study and under these particular conditions, they were no longer effective for this purpose after 70 consecutive days of medication. Actually, there was no statistically significant increase in sleep over control beyond the 30th day of administration and, furthermore, a substantial decrease in the effect on sleep occurred during the second 10-day period of administration.

Although the therapeutic value of barbiturates is well recognized, various effects were demonstrated which would be undesirable under certain conditions. It is quite apparent from the results on psychomotor tests and clinical estimates of intoxication that substantial impairment was produced during the early periods of medication. The extent of behavioral impairment produced by the dosages used in the present study was not nearly as severe as that produced by larger doses of barbiturates (Hill and Belleville, 1953; Kornetsky, 1951); nevertheless, somewhat similar conclusions may be drawn. During the first week of medication, this dosage would interfere with normal occupational and social pursuits if administered under ordinary environmental conditions. Obviously, more appropriate dosages and schedules could be arranged which would minimize the deleterious effects and maximize the therapeutic effects of barbiturates.

SUMMARY

Eighteen healthy male postaddicts who volunteered to take barbiturates for 90 days were studied by means of clinical observation and performance on psychomotor tests under control and chronic drug administration conditions, and following withdrawal of drugs. Ten men received 0.4 gram of secobarbital daily divided among four equal doses, and 8 men received pentobarbital in the same dose schedule.

The effects of both drugs were found to be quite similar. No appreciable effects on temperature, blood pressure, pulse, respiratory rate, caloric intake or body weight were observed during the course of the experiment. Tolerance was demonstrated on all measures showing an initial barbiturate effect, including hours of sleep, intoxication scores and psychomotor test performance.

REFERENCES

Fraser, H. F., and Isbell, H.: This Journal, **112:** 261, 1954.

Fraser, H. F., Isbell, H., Eisenman, A. J., Wikler, A., and Pescor, F. T.: Arch. Int. Med., **94:** 34, 1954.

Hill, H. E., and Belleville, R. E.: Arch. Neurol. & Psychiat., **70:** 180, 1953.

Hill, H. E., Belleville, R. E., and Wikler, A.: Arch. Neurol. and Psychiat., **73:** 602, 1955.

Ideström, C. M.: Acta Psychiat. et Neurol. Supp., **91:** 1954.

Isbell, H., Altschul, S., Kornetsky, C. H., Eisenman, A. J., Flanary, H. G., and Fraser, H. F.: Arch. Neurol. & Psychiat., **64:** 1, 1950.

Isbell, H., Fraser, H. F., Wikler, A., Belleville, R. E., and Eisenman, A. J.: Quart. J. Stud. on Alcohol, **16:** 1, 1955.

Kornetsky, C. H.: Arch. Neurol. & Psychiat., **65:** 557, 1951.

Lindquist, E. F.: Design and Analysis of Experiments in Psychology and Education, Houghton, Mifflin, New York, 1953.

Seevers, M. H., and Tatum, A. L.: This Journal, **42:** 217, 1931.

SOME FACTORS AFFECTING THE BIOLOGICAL DISPOSITION OF SMALL DOSES OF MORPHINE IN RATS [1]

T. K. ADLER, H. W. ELLIOTT AND R. GEORGE[2]

Departments of Pharmacology and Experimental Therapeutics, and Anesthesiology, University of California Medical Center, San Francisco

Received for publication March 25, 1957

The analgesic response to morphine in normal rats has been found to parallel concentration of C^{14} in brain after injection of morphine-N-$C^{14}H_3$ (Miller and Elliott, 1955). It has been shown that the analgesic response can be modified by pretreatment with either adrenalcortical hormones or ACTH (Winter and Flataker, 1951), or by adrenalectomy (Miller *et al.*, 1955). We have, therefore, elected to investigate the relationship between modification of pituitary-adrenal hormonal activity in rats and the concentrations of morphine in tissues after injection of morphine at dosage levels comparable to the ED_{50} (Miller *et al.*, 1955). These studies were facilitated by using morphine-N-$C^{14}H_3$ and applying appropriate techniques to identify the tissue C^{14}-compounds. In some cases the data include values for absorption of the dose and for urinary morphine excreted during the time of the experiment.

METHODS. Adult male rats of the Long-Evans and Sprague-Dawley strains were divided into four groups. Group I acted as untreated controls. Animals in group II were adrenalectomized under light ether anesthesia and maintained for 7 to 9 days postoperatively on Purina chow and 1 per cent saline. Those in group III were pretreated with vasopressin (Pitressin, Parke, Davis) injected intraperitoneally 10 minutes before the morphine injection, using 100 milliunits/kgm. for Long-Evans rats and 200 milliunits/kgm. for Sprague-Dawley rats. Group IV was pretreated with ACTH (Armour) according to the schedule described by Winter and Flataker (1951).

Three dosage levels of morphine were used: 2.0 mgm./kgm., 5.0 mgm./kgm. and 8.0 mgm./kgm. Alkaloid morphine-N-$C^{14}H_3$ (specific activity 3.7 microcuries/mgm., Rapoport *et al.*, 1951) was converted to the hydrochloride salt for injection but all calculations refer to the anhydrous alkaloid content.

The animals were injected either subcutaneously or into the popliteal space[3]. In the latter case it was possible to determine the amount of unabsorbed drug by removing *en masse* the muscles in the sciatic sheath surrounding and enclosing the popliteal space, and subtracting the value obtained for C^{14} content of the uninjected leg from that of the injected leg.

Sixty minutes after injection the animals were decapitated and the blood collected in an oxalated beaker. In certain cases the experiment was terminated 30 minutes after in-

---

[1] This investigation was supported in part by research grants B-570 and RG-1839 from the Division of Research Grants of the National Institutes of Health, Public Health Service; part of the work was carried out during the tenure of a Lederle Medical Faculty award to H. W. Elliott.

[2] Present address, Institute of Psychiatry, Maudsley Hospital, London SE5, England.

[3] The popliteal space is entered through the skin at the fascial junction just medial to the biceps femoris, lateral to the semitendinosus, and superior to the gastrocnemius muscles. Approximately 0.5 ml. of solution can be injected into the space of a 100 gm. rat without perceptible distention. No muscle mass will be encountered if a # 24⅜ inch needle is used.

jection. Red blood cells were separated from plasma by centrifugation followed by carefully layering 10 per cent sucrose over the undisturbed cells. In some experiments aliquots of whole blood were analyzed separately and the red blood cell C^{14} content calculated from hematocrit values and plasma and whole blood C^{14} concentrations.

The tissues were prepared for C^{14} determination by the direct plating method following acid-pepsin digestion as described by Miller and Elliott (1955). Volumes for plasma determination were modified as follows: 0.1 ml. plasma, 0.1 ml. acid-pepsin, 0.5 ml. ethanol. An estimate of the residual blood trapped in the cerebrum and spinal cord was obtained by determining the amount of hemoglobin present in the individual tissues of 4 untreated rats. The tissues were weighed and then homogenized with 5 or 10 ml. water and aliquots of the supernate treated with benzidine as described by Creditor (1953). Aliquots of suitably diluted homologous blood served as standards for calculating the volume of blood present in the tissue. (A slight turbidity was easily removed by filtering through Whatman #5 paper.) Lipid content of brain and spinal cord was determined after continuous petroleum ether extraction of pooled samples of dried tissues.

Free morphine-N-$C^{14}H_3$ present in tissues was determined by the isotope dilution technique, adding known amounts of commercial morphine sulfate to an aliquot of the ethanol-HCl-pepsin digest containing a known amount of C^{14}. Since preliminary tests showed that all the C^{14} remained in the supernate after centrifuging, an aliquot of this was taken for extraction of morphine. The ethanol was allowed to evaporate and the aqueous residue was then saturated with KOH and extracted with n-butanol according to the method of Fujimoto, Way and Hine (1954). The butanol layer was in turn extracted with a small volume of 3 N H_2SO_4 to which was then added 15 to 20 volumes of absolute ethanol to precipitate inorganic salts. After filtering, the ethanol solution of morphine sulfate was slowly evaporated and the residue dissolved in 30 per cent methanol preparatory to isolation as 2:4-dinitrophenylmorphine as previously described (Adler and Shaw, 1952). After purification and drying, a homogenous slurry was prepared with hot ethanol and transferred to an aluminum disc for counting as described by Calvin *et al.* (1949) for C^{14} determination. The process of purification was repeated to establish a constant specific activity, after which several samples were subjected to powder X-ray diffraction pattern analysis (chromium Kα) for verification of structure as previously described (Adler and Shaw, 1952; Adler *et al.*, 1955)[4].

Separate determinations for total morphine-N-$C^{14}H_3$ in plasma were made in two experiments where sufficient amounts were obtained to permit further analysis. After adding carrier morphine, an aliquot was subjected to acid pressure hydrolysis (Gross and Thompson, 1940) prior to extraction.

When determinations were made on urine, the animals were injected and immediately placed on filter paper covering the bottom of a one-liter beaker. Urine voided during the course of the experiment was caught on the paper and subsequently eluted with 95 per cent ethanol acidified with a few drops of conc. HCl. The contents of the bladder were aspirated and added to the eluate in a volumetric flask of either 50- or 100-ml. capacity. Urine adhering to the walls of the bladder was washed into the flask by rinsing cut strips of the bladder with acidified ethanol. The final volume represented a dilution of approximately 200 times the original volume of urine. An aliquot was taken for direct C^{14} determination as described by Calvin *et al.* (1949).

Free morphine-N-$C^{14}H_3$ present in urine was determined by adding carrier morphine to an aliquot of the alcoholic solution of urine which was then diluted with H_2O to make a final concentration of 33 per cent ethanol. This solution was used without further treatment for reaction with dinitrochlorbenzene to isolate dinitrophenylmorphine-N-$C^{14}H_3$. Other acid-stable, urinary C^{14} compounds were differentiated by descending paper partition chromatography using Whatman #1 filter paper and the butanol-acetic acid-H_2O solvent

[4] We are indebted to Mrs. Helena Ruben of the Department of Chemistry, Berkeley Campus, for determination and interpretation of the powder X-ray diffraction patterns.

mixture recommended by Seibert *et al.* (1954). Radioautograms were prepared from the paper chromatograms using Dupont X-ray film, X-trafast, Medical type 508.

Carbon-14 counts were determined by using conventional automatic scalers in conjunction with either a windowless helium-alcohol gas-flow Geiger counter having an efficiency of 52.5 per cent, or a thin mica end-window[5] Geiger counter having an efficiency of 17.5 per cent. Thickness corrections were made from empirically derived self-absorption curves determined separately for the different counters. (It was noted that the self-absorption curve for dinitrophenylmorphine-N-$C^{14}H_3$ was essentially the same as that for tissue-C^{14}). No thickness correction was necessary for urine samples plated directly since the mass was well below 0.1 mgm. per cm^2.

Counting errors were combined with those arising from other manipulations such as weighing and volume sampling in order to calculate the resultant experimental error involved in each individual determination. In view of the small numbers of animals contained within any one experimental regimen no statistical treatment of the data was attempted. Errors reported in the tables represent the resultant experimental error associated with the particular datum.

RESULTS AND DISCUSSION. *Characterization of C^{14} compounds in tissue and urine.* All but small amounts of the C^{14} in urine and plasma could be accounted for by the free and bound forms of morphine-N-$C^{14}H_3$. In the case of urine excreted by Sprague-Dawley rats the results obtained with paper-partition chromatography indicated the presence of only two radioactive substances: a compound with an R_f = 0.2, characteristic of morphine glucuronide (bound morphine) and a compound with an R_f = 0.6, characteristic of morphine for the solvent system used (Seibert *et al.*, 1954; Fujimoto and Way, 1957). However, urine obtained from Long-Evans rats showed an additional spot representing a small amount of radioactivity at R_f = 0.4. Figure 1 presents a typical radio-autogram obtained from chromatographed urine of a Long-Evans rat (column A) and a Sprague-Dawley rat (column C). Column B in figure 1 shows intensification of the spot at R_f = 0.6 due to the addition of 0.40 microgm. of authentic morphine-N-$C^{14}H_3$ to an aliquot of the sample used in column A. With this particular chromatogram the film was exposed for 36 days and the volume of urine used for analysis in each column contained an amount of C^{14} equivalent to 1.0 microgm. of morphine. It can be seen from the relative intensities of the spots that the ratio of bound to free morphine is two to three times greater in

[5] It was found necessary to use the end-window counter for those samples of dinitrophenylmorphine-N-$C^{14}H_3$ with specific activities greater than approximately 500 dis./min./mgm. since such samples when placed in the gas-flow counter caused a continuous discharge of the tube as well as abolishment of the Geiger plateau. This occurred both in the helium-ethanol gas-flow counter and in a Q-gas-flow counter. Since such behavior is characteristic of ineffective quenching, the possibility that trace amounts of NO gas are released which inactivates the quenching agent has been suggested by Dr. B. M. Tolbert of the University of California Radiation Laboratory. Reliable and valid counts, determined by preparing authentic samples of dinitrophenylmorphine-N-$C^{14}H_3$ of various known specific activities, were obtained by mounting a plastic film (Saran Wrap) directly over the compound on the aluminum disc, or by using an end-window counter. Under these conditions consistent counts were obtained with plates prepared as long as 15 months previously. Since no measurable change in activity occurs with storage, it is possible that the break-down of trace amounts of the compound occurs as a result of radiation self-damage accentuated by the high voltage encountered only during the time of counting.

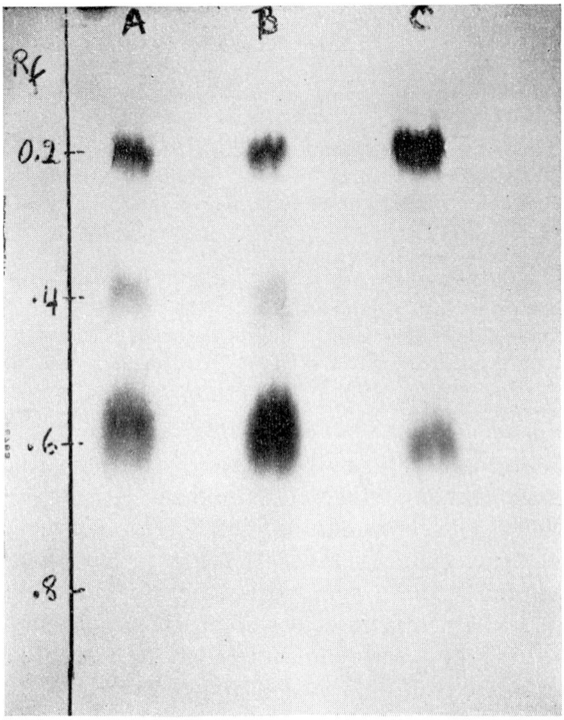

FIG. 1. Radioautogram of chromatographed urine from rats after morphine-N-$C^{14}H_3$ injection.

(A) urine from a Long-Evans rat; (B) known morphine-N-$C^{14}H_3$ added to urine from Long-Evans rat; (C) urine from a Sprague-Dawley rat.

the Sprague-Dawley than in the Long-Evans strain. This finding was substantiated by results obtained using the isotope dilution technique and will be discussed later together with other results obtained in control rats. It can also be seen from figure 1 that the unidentified compound (R_f = 0.4) represents only a small part of the total radioactivity in column A. However, sufficient amounts of this material could be isolated from pooled urine samples to permit some preliminary experiments; these indicate that the compound is a phenolic alkaloid which does not form an ether in the presence of 2,4-dinitrochlorbenzene under conditions appropriate for the formation of the morphine ether (Adler and Shaw, 1952).

Attempts to differentiate C^{14} compounds in plasma, brain or muscle by paper partition chromatography gave inconclusive results owing to extremely low tissue concentrations of C^{14} which required overloading the paper in order to achieve a satisfactory number of counts. This led to streaking of the spots and the method was abandoned in favor of the isotope dilution technique applied to non-hydrolyzed and hydrolyzed samples of tissue. The results obtained with plasma from a Sprague-Dawley rat and a Long-Evans rat showed that, respectively, 89 ± 7 per cent and 95 ± 3 per cent of the acid-stable C^{14} content was recovered as morphine-N-$C^{14}H_3$ after hydrolysis of the samples. Recoveries of morphine-N-$C^{14}H_3$ from non-hydrolyzed aliquots of these same samples were, respectively, 4.6 per cent and 5.1 per cent of the C^{14} content. It thus appears that although the presence of free and bound morphine accounts for most of the radioactivity in plasma, small amounts of acid-stable C^{14} may be due to some unidentified metabolite.

In contrast to results obtained with plasma, the results of analyses of muscle or brain indicated that a considerable portion of the C^{14} present could not be recovered as morphine-N-$C^{14}H_3$ from hydrolyzed aliquots of the tissues. Thus, after adding carrier morphine to pooled samples of muscles obtained from the Sprague-Dawley rats the recovery of C^{14} as morphine-N-$C^{14}H_3$ was as follows: in the control rats, 34 per cent before hydrolysis, 63 per cent after hydrolysis; in the adrenalectomized rats, 33 per cent before, 43 per cent after hydrolysis; in the vasopressin-treated rats, 23 per cent before, 27 per cent after hydrolysis; in the ACTH-treated rats, 40 per cent before, 66 per cent after hydrolysis. It should be noted that although the non-recoverable C^{14} in muscle forms a fairly substantial fraction of the radioactivity present in the tissue, it represents, nonetheless, only a small part of the dose. Assuming that skeletal muscle comprises 40 per cent of the body weight, calculations based on mean concentration values indicate that approximately five per cent of the dose is present as unidentified C^{14} in the muscles of control rats.

In brain the concentration of C^{14} in most cases was too low to permit addition of amounts of carrier required for a manageable yield. However, in 8 individual analyses of brains containing suitable amounts of radioactivity we found that only 10 to 20 per cent of the C^{14} could be recovered as free morphine. Since the complete sample of tissue had to be used in these analyses, we resorted to a pooled sample obtained in another series of experiments, where the animals were sacrificed at shorter intervals and after higher doses, in order to establish the relation between free and total recoverable morphine in brain. Under these conditions 51 per cent of the C^{14} was recovered as free morphine-N-$C^{14}H_3$ (*i.e.* before hydrolysis) and 58 per cent was recovered after hydrolysis. It would appear, therefore, that although the brain contains practically no "bound" morphine if this term is defined as free alkaloid released by hydrolysis, it does contain some compound either wholly or partially derived from morphine.

It is, of course, possible that the unidentified C^{14}-fraction results from N-demethylation of morphine-N-$C^{14}H_3$ (March and Elliott, 1954) with subsequent incorporation of labeled "C_1 fragments" into normal tissue constituents. Alternately, it may represent simply a more firmly bound morphine molecule which is not released by acid pressure hydrolysis. Inasmuch as the sole evidence for these assumptions rests upon the fact that the specific activity of dinitrophenylmorphine-N-$C^{14}H_3$ obtained from hydrolyzed samples is less than expected, it was necessary to establish that there is no contamination of the compound by extraneous substances (*e.g.* amino compounds) which might have formed similarly insoluble dinitrophenyl derivatives. This was done by examination of the powder X-ray diffraction pattern which showed that the isolated material was, indeed, pure dinitrophenylmorphine. Since the dinitrophenyl ethers of even such closely related congeners as dihydromorphine and normorphine result in identifiable but uniquely different patterns, it must be concluded that the unidentified C^{14}-fraction in muscle and brain is associated with a molecule the chemical properties of which differ markedly from those of morphine. However, in the absence of further information it is convenient to consider the quantitative data for C^{14} determinations as representing the maximum morphine concentrations in the respective tissues.

Absorption, distribution and urinary excretion in control rats. By 60 minutes after injection between 92 and 99 per cent of the dose has been absorbed from the popliteal space. It may be assumed that these figures represent absorption after subcutaneous injection as well since the same plasma and tissue concentrations are obtained for the two routes (tables 1, 2 and 3).

At the 2.0-mgm. dosage level the plasma concentrations of free morphine are essentially the same for the two strains of rats (tables 1 and 2) but a difference is seen in the bound morphine levels which are approximately three times higher in Sprague-Dawley rats than in Long-Evans rats. The mean plasma bound morphine concentration (*i.e.*, total minus free) for the 4 Sprague-Dawley rats in table 1 is 1.79 microgm. per ml., and for the 4 Long-Evans rats in table 2 is 0.56 microgm. per ml. This same strain difference is seen in the urinary excretion of bound morphine. Since no difference was found in the urinary excretion of free morphine (approximately fifteen per cent of the dose in both strains) it may mean that extensive intestinal excretion of bound morphine in the Long-Evans rats is responsible for the low plasma and urine values.

The brain levels after 2 mgm. of morphine indicate maximally a concentration of the order of magnitude of the free morphine plasma values although the free (*i.e.*, extractable) morphine content in brain may be as little as one- to two-tenths of the amounts reported in the tables. Moreover, especially in the Sprague-Dawley rats of table 1, the residual blood content of the cerebrum may contribute a considerable fraction of the morphine content at this low dosage level. In these studies, on analyzing 14 samples of either whole blood or red blood cells separately, we have found that whole blood contained between 66 per cent and 78 per cent (mean = 72 per cent) of the C^{14} concentration of plasma. (These values were always inversely correlated with the hematocrit.) This would mean that the cerebral values in table 1 could be achieved by the trapping of between 30 to 67 microl. of blood per gm. of tissue. Actual analysis of residual blood content of 4 control rats showed that between 5.5 and 25.2 microl. of blood (mean = 15.7 microl.) per gm. of cerebrum are trapped. In the Long-Evans rats, on the other hand, the relatively low C^{14} blood levels recorded in table 2 would require between 110 and 330 microl. of blood per gm. of cerebrum to account for the cerebral C^{14} values. This appears to be far in excess of the actual amounts of blood trapped in our dissected tissues.

Even stronger evidence that the CNS contains morphine in excess of any possible contribution of blood is gained from the data on spinal cord values at the 5.0 mgm. dosage level in Long-Evans rats. The spinal cord C^{14} concentration of

TABLE 1

Data obtained on Sprague-Dawley rats 60 minutes after injection of 2.0 mgm. of morphine per kgm.

Pretreatment	Route of injection	Absorption % dose	Plasma*		Cerebrum* Total morphine max. γ per gm.	Muscle* Total morphine max. γ per gm.	Urine	
			Total morphine γ per ml.	Free morphine γ per ml.			% dose	Ratio Bound/Free
Control #1	popliteal	96.5 ± 0.2	1.56 ± 2%	0.032 ± 100%	0.075 ± 38%	0.690 ± 4%	55.2	2.84
Control #2	popliteal	99.1 ± 0.1	1.99 ± 2%	0.085 ± 25%	0.085 ± 30%	0.860 ± 4%	>29.8†	2.80
Control #3	subcutaneous	—	1.91 ± 1%	0.086 ± 35%	0.084 ± 35%	0.675 ± 5%	36.6	1.07
Control #4	subcutaneous	—	2.03 ± 2%	0.122 ± 14%	0.042 ± 69%	0.645 ± 5%	43.8	2.26
[Mean value]			[1.87]	[0.081]	[0.072]	[0.717]		[2.28]
Adrenalectomy #1	popliteal	91.6 ± 0.2	2.95 ± 1%	0.342 ± 20%	0.137 ± 22%	0.805 ± 5%	39.6	2.60
Adrenalectomy #2	subcutaneous	—	2.22 ± 1%	0.557 ± 30%	0.111 ± 25%	0.905 ± 4%	42.3	3.76
Adrenalectomy #3	subcutaneous	—	1.92 ± 1%	0.174 ± 30%	0.107 ± 28%	0.790 ± 4%	53.1	2.54
[Mean value]			[2.36]	[0.356]	[0.118]	[0.833]		[2.96]
Vasopressin #1	popliteal	93.6 ± 0.2	1.63 ± 2%	0.112 ± 50%	0.023 ± 100%	0.540 ± 6%	55.0	2.86
Vasopressin #2	popliteal	97.2 ± 0.2	1.53 ± 2%	0.185 ± 69%	0.066 ± 50%	0.440 ± 7%	>31.2†	2.21
Vasopressin #3	popliteal	98.8 ± 0.2	1.13 ± 3%	0.058 ± 100%	—	0.352 ± 9%	47.0	2.68
[Mean value]			[1.43]	[0.118]	[0.044]	[0.444]		[2.58]
ACTH #1	popliteal	98.2 ± 0.2	1.10 ± 2%	0.030 ± 100%	0.086 ± 33%	0.340 ± 10%	46.8	3.03
ACTH #2	popliteal	94.0 ± 0.2	1.68 ± 1%	0.160 ± 30%	0.068 ± 41%	0.470 ± 7%	38.7	2.66
[Mean value]			[1.39]	[0.095]	[0.077]	[0.405]		[2.84]

* Resultant experimental errors are expressed as per cent of the individual datum.

† Part of sample lost.

TABLE 2

Data obtained on Long-Evans rats 60 minutes after injection of 2.0 mgm. of morphine per kgm.

Pretreatment	Route of injection	Absorption % *dose*	Plasma* Total morphine γ *per ml.*	Plasma* Free morphine γ *per ml.*	Cerebrum* Total morphine *max.* γ *per gm.*	Spinal cord* Total morphine *max.* γ *per gm.*	Liver* Total morphine *max.* γ *per gm.*	Urine % dose	Urine Ratio Bound/Free
Control #1	popliteal	92.0 ± 0.2	0.575 ± 9%	0.130 ± 13%	0.136 ± 20%	—	—	26.0	0.875
Control #2	popliteal	97.2 ± 0.2	1.083 ± 2%	0.102 ± 5%	0.088 ± 33%	—	—	25.1	0.677
Control #3	subcutaneous	—	0.458 ± 5%	0.028 ± 16%	0.051 ± 41%	0.048 ± 100%	2.42 ± 2%	—	—
Control #4	subcutaneous	—	0.546 ± 4%	0.140 ± 5%	0.081 ± 42%	0.097 ± 55%	1.66 ± 2%	—	—
[Mean value]			[0.665]	[0.100]	[0.089]	[0.072]	[2.04]		0.776
Adrenalectomy #1	subcutaneous	—	1.62 ± 2%	—	0.145 ± 24%	0.258 ± 22%	1.82 ± 2%	—	—
Adrenalectomy #2	subcutaneous	—	1.35 ± 2%	—	0.154 ± 22%	0.168 ± 30%	1.74 ± 2%	—	—
Adrenalectomy #3	subcutaneous	—	1.34 ± 2%	—	0.130 ± 23%	0.177 ± 30%	1.75 ± 2%	—	—
[Mean value]			[1.44]		[0.143]	[0.201]	[1.77]		
Vasopressin #1	popliteal	95.2 ± 0.2	0.645 ± 5%	0.090 ± 7%	0.076 ± 43%	—	—	27.4	0.327
Vasopressin #2	popliteal	91.4 ± 0.2	0.860 ± 3%	0.189 ± 5%	0.082 ± 40%	—	—	19.9	0.504
[Mean value]			[0.752]	[0.140]	[0.079]				

* Resultant experimental errors are expressed as per cent of the individual datum.

the three control rats of table 3 would require between 107 and 137 microl. of blood per gram of tissue, whereas the actual volumes of blood trapped (4 animals) ranged between 5.8 and 13.6 microl. per gm. of cord tissue. The values for C^{14} in cerebrum and spinal cord confirm previous findings (Miller and Elliott, 1955) that compared with cerebrum the cord concentration is higher when calculations are made on a per gm. of wet tissue basis. However, calculations on the basis of lipid content indicate a lower concentration with a mean of 2.7 microgm. per gm. of cerebrum lipid compared with a mean of 1.9 microgm. per gm. of cord lipid (lipid content of cerebrum = 7.14 per cent, of cord = 18.9 per cent of the wet weight).

With regard to the CNS content of C^{14} an interesting difference can be seen between the values obtained in these studies where the animals remained quiescent during the course of the experiment and those obtained by Miller and Elliott (1955) in their studies where the animals were periodically subjected to a thermal stimulus for the purpose of determining reaction times. Thus, at sixty minutes after injection of 5 mgm. of morphine the mean cord concentrations per gram in these studies is about one-half that obtained by Miller and Elliott and the cerebrum C^{14} content is about three-quarters that obtained for the same strain in the earlier study. It is not possible to say at this time whether the higher CNS values in the thermally stimulated animals result from vascular changes or from true permeability changes occurring during a stressful situation.

Effect of adrenalectomy. At the 2.0-mgm. dosage level, somewhat higher concentrations are found in the plasma and CNS of the operated rats of both strains compared with the corresponding controls (table 1 and 2). The effect of adrenalectomy is more marked at the 5.0-mgm. dosage level where all tissues studied show elevated C^{14} concentrations (table 3). It can be seen that the higher plasma and brain values in adrenalectomized rats cannot be attributed to any decreased uptake by either muscle, liver or kidney. Nor does it seem probable that the higher concentrations result from dehydration of the tissues since it has been shown that muscle and plasma of adrenalectomized rats maintained on NaCl contain normal amounts of water (Buell and Turner, 1941; Davenport, 1949). Moreover, in view of the overlap of the range of values obtained for urinary morphine at the 2.0 mgm. dose level, it appears unlikely that there is an interference with urinary excretion of the drug after adrenalectomy. Other possible factors which have not as yet been explored, but which may contribute to these results are a) decreased biliary excretion or b) enhanced intestinal reabsorption. Although the mechanism responsible for the increased tissue concentration of morphine is obscure, there appears to be some correlation between the increased sensitivity to morphine and the brain and plasma levels of the drug in adrenalectomized rats. It is of interest to note that, judging from the plasma levels of bound morphine, there appears to be no impairment in the ability of these animals to conjugate morphine. In support of this hypothesis, Way *et al.* (1954) reported that the integrity of the adrenals is not essential for conjugation of morphine. These results are in contrast to those obtained by Zauder (1952) who showed that *in vitro* conjugation of morphine does not occur at all in the presence of liver

TABLE 3

Data obtained on Long-Evans rats 60 minutes after injection of 5.0 mgm. of morphine per kgm.

Pretreatment	Route of injection	Absorption % dose	Plasma*		Cerebrum* Total morphine *max. γ per gm.*	Spinal cord* Total morphine *max. γ per gm.*	Muscle* Total morphine *max. γ per gm.*	Liver* Total morphine *max. γ per gm.*	Kidney* Total morphine *max. γ per gm.*
			Total morphine *γ per ml.*	Free morphine *γ per ml.*					
Control #1	popliteal	90.7 ± 0.2	4.55 ± 1%	0.247 ± 15%	0.143 ± 20%	0.348 ± 15%	1.82 ± 2%	4.13 ± 1%	26.0 ± 1%
Control #2	subcutaneous	—	3.42 ± 1%	0.252 ± 25%	0.204 ± 15%	0.338 ± 15%	1.54 ± 2%	4.80 ± 1%	17.6 ± 1%
Control #3	subcutaneous	—	3.32 ± 1%	—	0.195 ± 16%	0.330 ± 10%	1.41 ± 3%	2.78 ± 2%	23.2 ± 1%
[Mean value]			[3.76]	[0.250]	[0.180]	[0.338]	[1.59]	[3.90]	[22.3]
Adrenalectomy #1	popliteal	88.1 ± 0.3	6.70 ± 1%	0.603 ± 5%	0.288 ± 11%	0.660 ± 9%	2.61 ± 2%	3.50 ± 1%	60.5 ± 1%
Adrenalectomy #2	subcutaneous	—	5.05 ± 1%	0.661 ± 15%	0.323 ± 10%	0.625 ± 8%	2.58 ± 2%	6.50 ± 1%	18.5 ± 1%
Adrenalectomy #3	subcutaneous	—	5.62 ± 1%	0.410 ± 30%	0.228 ± 15%	0.695 ± 8%	2.46 ± 2%	5.16 ± 1%	49.0 ± 1%
[Mean value]			[5.79]	[0.558]	[0.309]	[0.660]	[2.55]	[5.05]	[42.6]
Vasopressin #1	popliteal	92.0 ± 0.2	2.23 ± 2%	0.402 ± 6%	0.288 ± 15%	—	1.52 ± 2%	—	—
ACTH #1	popliteal	97.6 ± 0.2	1.62 ± 2%	0.136 ± 2%	0.154 ± 21%	0.271 ± 20%	1.07 ± 3%	4.55 ± 1%	4.5 ± 1%
ACTH #2	popliteal	94.5 ± 0.2	1.70 ± 2%	0.188 ± 2%	0.188 ± 17%	0.247 ± 20%	1.53 ± 2%	4.27 ± 1%	4.8 ± 1%
[Mean value]			[1.66]	[0.162]	[0.171]	[0.259]	[1.30]	[4.41]	[4.6]

* Resultant experimental errors are expressed as per cent of the individual datum.

slices obtained from adrenalectomized rats during the same post-operative period as in this study.

Effect of pretreatment with vasopressin or ACTH. Since indirect evidence indicates that in adrenalectomized animals there is slow inactivation of antidiuretic hormone (Birnie, 1953; Mirsky *et al.*, 1954) it is possible that in such animals, quite apart from adrenal-cortical insufficiency *per se*, the antidiuretic hormone released by morphine might be important in the general biological response to the drug. For this reason the vasopressin-pretreated group was included in this study, especially since a preliminary screening indicated that such pretreated rats were more sensitive to morphine (Adler *et al.*, 1956). From the results obtained, however, it appears that the distribution of the drug after vasopressin pretreatment is quite different from that observed after adrenalectomy. Although slightly elevated free morphine values are seen in plasma, the concentrations in other tissues are either reduced or relatively unaffected as contrasted with the generally increased values seen in the adrenalectomized animals (tables 1, 2 and 3). The tendency toward lower concentrations after vasopressin pretreatment was observed also in one experiment terminated 30 minutes after injection of 8.0 mgm. morphine per kgm. (table 4).

Although it has been demonstrated that a decreased response to morphine occurs after ACTH pretreatment (Winter and Flataker, 1951), the results obtained in both strains of rats indicate that this effect is not reflected in decreased brain levels of C^{14}. The major effects seen at the 2.0-mgm. dose level in Sprague-Dawley rats are a reduction in the levels of plasma bound morphine and muscle-C^{14} (table 1). In the Long-Evans rats at the 5.0-mgm. dose level markedly decreased values for plasma bound morphine and kidney-C^{14} are seen and only slight reductions are observed in muscle or spinal cord values (table 3). In general, the profile of results obtained after ACTH pretreatment resembles that obtained after vasopressin pretreatment and it is quite possible that the experimental results observed in the latter group should be attributed to the presence of the ACTH-releasing factor found in commercial vasopressin (Swingle *et al.*, 1956).

Even though neither of these hormones appears to affect either absorption of the dose or urinary excretion at 60 minutes after morphine injection, it is possible that a more complete distribution study may reveal the factors responsible for

TABLE 4

Data obtained on Long-Evans rats 30 minutes after subcutaneous injection of 8.0 mgm. of morphine per kgm.

Pretreatment	Plasma*		Cerebrum*		Urine*	
	Total morphine γ *per ml.*	Free morphine γ *per ml.*	Total morphine *max.* γ *per gm.*	Free morphine γ *per gm.*	Total morph. *% dose*	Free morph. *% dose*
	%	%	%	%		
Control	3.92 ± 1	2.02 ± 7	0.372 ± 10	0.060 ± 12	5.07 ± 0.5	3.00 ± 5
Vasopressin	2.77 ± 1	1.55 ± 30	0.319 ± 10	0.063 ± 15	2.79 ± 0.5	2.54 ± 3

* Resultant experimental errors are expressed as per cent of the individual datum.

the reduced levels observed in these experiments. An investigation of the effect of adrenocortical hormones and of adrenocortical insufficiency on the biliary excretion and intestinal reabsorption of morphine will be initiated when an additional supply of C^{14}-labeled morphine becomes available.

SUMMARY

The metabolic fate of small doses of C^{14}-labeled morphine in rats as influenced by adrenalectomy or pretreatment with ACTH or vasopressin has been studied utilizing isotope dilution and paper chromatography techniques. The principal findings were as follows:

The ratio of bound to free morphine is 2 to 3 times greater in the urine and plasma of Sprague-Dawley rats than in Long-Evans rats on the same dose.

The C^{14} content of plasma can be almost completely accounted for as free and bound morphine but a substantial fraction of that present in brain and muscle remains unidentified as does a very small fraction in urine of Long-Evans rats.

The tissues of adrenalectomized rats, of both strains, contain higher concentrations of C^{14} after morphine-N-$C^{14}H_3$ administration than do control rats. Plasma bound morphine levels indicate no impairment in the ability of these animals to conjugate morphine.

Although vasopressin increases the sensitivity of rats to morphine, tissue concentrations after pretreatment with vasopressin are either reduced or relatively unaffected in marked contrast to the increased values after adrenalectomy.

Tissue C^{14} levels after ACTH are similar to those after vasopressin. Thus decreased sensitivity to morphine due to ACTH is not reflected in lower brain C^{14} concentrations.

None of the treatments appear to affect the absorption of the dose or urinary excretion at sixty minutes after injection.

ACKNOWLEDGMENT. We wish to express our sincere thanks to Dr. E. Leong Way of this department for his many helpful suggestions.

REFERENCES

ADLER, T. K., AND SHAW, F. H.: THIS JOURNAL, **104:** 1, 1952.

ADLER, T. K., FUJIMOTO, J. M., WAY, E. L., AND BAKER, E. M.: THIS JOURNAL, **114:** 251, 1955.

ADLER, T. K., GEORGE, R., AND ELLIOTT, H. W.: Fed. Proc., **15:** 393, 1956.

BIRNIE, J. H.: Endocrinol., **52:** 33, 1953.

BUELL, M. V., AND TURNER, E.: Am. J. Physiol., **134:** 225, 1941.

CALVIN, M., HEIDELBERGER, C., REID, J. C., TOLBERT, B. M., AND YANKWICH, P. F.: Isotopic Carbon, p. 113, John Wiley and Sons, Inc., New York, 1949.

CREDITOR, M. C.: J. Lab. Clin. Med., **41:** 307, 1953.

DAVENPORT, V. D.: Am. J. Physiol., **156:** 322, 1949.

FUJIMOTO, J. M., AND WAY, E. L.: THIS JOURNAL, **121:** 000, 1957.

FUJIMOTO, J. M., WAY, E. L., AND HINE, C. H.: J. Lab. Clin. Med., **44:** 627, 1954.

GROSS, E. G., AND THOMPSON, V.: THIS JOURNAL, **68:** 413, 1940.

MARCH, C. H., AND ELLIOTT, H. W.: Proc. Soc. Exper. Biol. & Med., **86:** 494, 1954.

MILLER, J. W., AND ELLIOTT, H. W.: THIS JOURNAL, **113:** 283, 1955.

Miller, J. W., George, R., Elliott, H. W., Sung, C. Y., and Way, E. L.: This Journal, **114:** 1, 1955.
Mirsky, A. I., Paulisch, G., and Stein, M.: Endocrinol., **54:** 691, 1954.
Rapoport, H., Lovell, C. H., and Tolbert, B. M.: J. Am. Chem. Soc., **73:** 5900, 1951.
Seibert, R. A., Williams, C. E., and Huggins, R. A.: Science, **120:** 222, 1954.
Swingle, W. W., Brannick, L. J., Parlow, A. F., and Barrett, W.: Proc. Soc. Exper. Biol. & Med., **92:** 540, 1956.
Way, E. L., Sung, C. Y., and Fujimoto, J. M.: This Journal, **110:** 51, 1954.
Winter, C. A., and Flataker, L.: This Journal, **103:** 93, 1951.
Zauder, H. L.: This Journal, **104:** 11, 1952.

HISTOCHEMICAL DEMONSTRATION OF REVERSIBLE ANTICHOLINESTERASE ACTION AT SELECTIVE CELLULAR SITES *IN VIVO*[1]

GEORGE B. KOELLE

With the technical assistance of Priscilla Smart

Department of Physiology and Pharmacology, Graduate School of Medicine, University of Pennsylvania, Philadelphia 4

Received for publication March 25, 1957

The anticholinesterase (anti-ChE) agents constitute one of the few classes of drugs for which a mechanism of action has been defined in terms of inhibition of a specific enzyme. The demonstration by Mackworth and Webb (1948) that diisopropylfluorophosphate (DFP) produces irreversible inactivation of cholinesterases (ChE's) permitted quantitative correlation between this effect and the pharmacological actions of DFP and related agents. Such studies have indicated that fifty to eighty per cent of the total acetylcholinesterase (AChE) of nervous tissue or effector organs must be inactivated before pharmacological actions are noted (Mazur and Bodansky, 1946; Koelle and Gilman, 1946; Nachmansohn and Feld, 1947; Riker and Wescoe, 1949; Kamijo and Koelle, 1952).

Of the large number of drugs which inhibit AChE reversibly, only the limited number which are relatively potent in this respect are generally considered to produce their major effects by AChE-inhibition (Koelle and Gilman, 1949). Certain reversible inhibitors, which by their nature do not permit direct quantitation of the degree of inhibition obtained *in vivo*, produce cholinomimetic responses at doses which are estimated to cause relatively little AChE-inhibition. Consequently, their primary effects have been ascribed chiefly to a direct action at cholinoceptive sites (Randall and Lehmann, 1950; Wescoe *et al.*, 1950).

If the distributions of both the AChE and an anti-ChE agent of either type are considered at the cellular level, then it becomes apparent that there are important limitations to the significance of the aforementioned inferred causal relationships. The neuronal membrane is a relatively impermeable lipoid-like or porous structure (Mullins, 1956) which probably separates the total AChE into external and internal portions (Burgen and Chipman, 1952), just as in the axonal trunk (Nachmansohn, 1950; Berkowitz, 1955). The external, or "functional", AChE is probably involved directly in the hydrolysis of acetylcholine (ACh) during the process of cholinergic transmission, whereas the internal, or "reserve", AChE probably represents more recently synthesized enzyme which may be formed within the endoplasmic reticulum and transported eventually to the cell membrane (Koelle and Steiner, 1956). A highly lipoid-soluble compound, such as diisopropylfluorophosphate (DFP), would be expected to reach and

[1] This investigation was supported by research grants (B-282 (C3 and C4)) from the National Institute of Neurological Diseases and Blindness, National Institutes of Health, Public Health Service.

react with AChE at both sites; hence, the percentage inactivation of total AChE, which is measured by the usual homogenate techniques, probably reflects approximately the proportionate inactivation of the functional AChE. A poorly penetrating compound, in contrast, might produce equivalent inhibition of the functional enzyme without affecting the internal AChE; the overall percentage AChE-inhibition at which cholinomimetic effects occur would therefore be proportionately lower. This consideration, and the partial reversal of inhibition which occurs on dilution of a reversible inhibitor-enzyme complex (Strauss and Goldstein, 1943), could account for the failure to detect significant inhibition in tissues which are removed and subsequently assayed.

A recent drug which appears to illustrate this situation is N,N′-bis (2-diethylaminoethyl) oxamide bis-2-chlorobenzyl chloride (WIN 8077, ambenonium chloride, Mytelase chloride). As a bisquaternary compound of high molecular weight (538 for the active cation) it would be expected to penetrate membranes poorly; *in vitro,* it has six times the potency of neostigmine as a reversible inhibitor of AChE. It produces cholinomimetic effects in various species in doses ranging upward from 0.3 to 3.0 microgm./kgm., yet AChE-inhibition could be detected by subsequent analysis only after doses greater than 20 (dog brain) or 100 (cat muscle) microgm./kgm. (Karczmar and Howard, 1955; Lands *et al.*, 1955). Its 2-methoxybenzyl analog, WIN 8078, is a considerably weaker anti-ChE agent, and requires higher doses to produce equivalent effects.

The histochemical approach to determination of the anti-ChE actions of WIN 8077 and WIN 8078 *in vivo* was based on the observation that the reversible inhibitor, physostigmine, can protect cats from the lethal action of the irreversible anti-ChE agent, DFP (Koster, 1946), by transient competitive combination with the enzyme (Koelle, 1946). Therefore, if a similarly acting reversible inhibitor were given immediately before a dose of DFP sufficient, if given alone, to cause practically complete inactivation of the AChE of a given tissue, and the excess DFP and all the reversible inhibitor were subsequently removed, then any residual AChE-activity should represent that which was inhibited by the reversible inhibitor at the time the DFP was given.

In the present study, the concentration-inhibition curves of WIN 8077 and WIN 8078 were determined with the AChE of cat brain homogenate. Their protective actions against DFP were determined quantitatively with the same homogenate, and semi-quantitatively with sections of cat autonomic ganglia, using the histochemical technique. Cats were then given various doses of the two reversible inhibitors prior to DFP, and after a sufficient interval tissues were removed, sectioned, washed and stained for AChE-activity. The results indicate that WIN 8077 and WIN 8078 cause inhibition of AChE at the motor endplate and at selective ganglionic sites in the dosage range reported as the threshold for the production of pharmacological effects.

MATERIALS AND METHODS. The inhibitory activities of WIN 8077 and WIN 8078[2] on the AChE of a homogenate of whole cat brain (1 part wet weight brain plus 3 parts distilled

---

[2] WIN 8077 and WIN 8078 were kindly provided by Dr. A. M. Lands, Sterling-Winthrop Research Institute, Rensselaer, New York.

H_2O, prepared with a Teflon-glass homogenizer) were determined with the Warburg apparatus. The main wells of the vessels contained the enzyme, inhibitor, and final concentrations of 0.03 *M* $NaHCO_3$ and 0.033 *M* $MgCl_2$; the final volume was 3.0 ml., and the pH 7.6 after equilibrating with 5 per cent CO_2–95 per cent N_2. The substrate, methacholine chloride (MeCh), was tipped in from the sidearm to a final concentration of 0.03 *M*. Activity was calculated on the basis of CO_2 liberated during the 30-minute period starting 10 minutes after the addition of substrate. Corrections were made for CO_2-liberation in the absence of substrate and of homogenate; all determinations were conducted in duplicate.

The protective effects of WIN 8077 and WIN 8078 against inactivation of cat brain AChE by DFP[3] were determined quantitatively as follows. To a portion of the same cat brain homogenate was added four volumes of water; the mixture was centrifuged for 15 min. at approximately 11,000 r.p.m. in a Servall centrifuge, the supernatant discarded, and the sediment resuspended in H_2O to the original diluted volume. This "washed" homogenate represented approximately sixty-five per cent of the AChE activity of the original diluted homogenate. To each of three centrifuge tubes were added 3.0 ml. of washed homogenate, 3.0 ml. of 0.09 *M* $NaHCO_3$, H_2O to bring the final volume (after all additions) to 9.0 ml., 0.3 ml. of *M* $MgCl_2$, and 0.9 ml. of a dilution of WIN 8077 or WIN 8078. (The last was omitted from the control.) The contents, which, excepting for substrate, were essentially the same as those present in the Warburg flasks when the inhibition measurements were made, were mixed thoroughly and allowed to stand for five minutes at room temperature. To one of the tubes containing the reversible inhibitor was then added 0.9 ml. of 10^{-3} *M* DFP. The tubes were kept at 37°C. for thirty minutes, with frequent agitation, then 21.0 ml. of H_2O was added to each, and they were centrifuged for fifteen minutes as before. The supernatant was removed and discarded, and the sediment in each tube was resuspended in 30 ml. of the following solution, and allowed to stand for fifteen minutes at room temperature: 0.03 *M* $NaHCO_3$, 0.033 *M* $MgCl_2$, and 0.03 *M* AChBr. Preliminary determinations showed that this step brought about complete reversal of the inhibition of the AChE by WIN 8077 or WIN 8078 (see RESULTS). The tubes were centrifuged as before, the supernatant removed and discarded, and the sediment in each tube resuspended in 30 ml. of 0.03 *M* $NaHCO_3$. After standing fifteen minutes in the refrigerator, the tubes were again centrifuged as before, the supernatant discarded, and the sediment from each tube transferred quantitatively to a graduated tube and brought to a volume of 4.5 ml. with H_2O. Acetylcholinesterase activity was determined in duplicate on aliquots from each tube in the manner described above, and was expressed as a percentage of the control tube to which no reversible inhibitor or DFP had been added. The tube from which DFP had been omitted served as a check for the reversal of inhibition by WIN 8077 or WIN 8078. The activity of the controls was equivalent to approximately seventy-five per cent of that of the original washed homogenate. No measurable AChE-activity was present in similarly treated preparations to which had been added DFP but no reversible inhibitor.

The same principle was employed for the semi-quantitative histochemical demonstration of the protection of the AChE of cat tissue slices against DFP *in vitro*. Ten-micron fresh-frozen sections of cat ciliary and stellate ganglia were placed on slides and kept for 5 minutes in Coplin jars containing solutions of the following composition: 24 per cent Na_2SO_4, 0.033 *M* $MgCl_2$, and WIN 8077 (pI 6.4, 7.0, 7.6 and 8.2) or WIN 8078 (pI 4.4, 5.0, 5.6 and 6.2); the reversible inhibitors were omitted from two sets of controls. All slides excepting one set of controls were then transferred to a series of solutions which contained the same components as above plus 10^{-4} *M* DFP. After 30 minutes' incubation at 37°C., the slides were placed in a rinse solution (24 per cent Na_2SO_4, 0.033 *M* $MgCl_2$) in which they were kept for 30 minutes at room temperature. The last step was repeated. All slides (including the first set of controls) were then placed in acetylthiocholine incubation solution (Koelle, 1951), in which one of each set was incubated for 10, 20, 40 and 80 minutes at 37°C. They were then developed with $(NH_4)_2S$, gold-toned, dehydrated and mounted. The intensities

[3] DFP was kindly provided by Dr. William C. Summerson, Army Chemical Center, Maryland.

and patterns of staining of the WIN 8077 or WIN 8078-treated slides were compared with those of the controls and the DFP-controls. Two such experiments were conducted with each inhibitor, using the full concentration-range each time.

The inhibition of AChE (or protection against DFP) by WIN 8077 and WIN 8078 *in vivo* was demonstrated as follows. Cats were anesthetized (35 mgm. of sodium pentobarbital/kgm., i.p.) and atropinized (3 mgm./kgm., i.p.), and a femoral vein was exposed. An intravenous injection of WIN 8077 or WIN 8078 was given, which was followed five minutes later by an intravenous injection of 3.68 mgm. (20 micromol.) of DFP/kgm. Thirty to forty minutes after the injection of DFP, cats were sacrificed by i.v. air, and the stellate and ciliary ganglia and a portion of intercostal muscle were removed and placed in chilled saline solution. Fresh frozen sections were cut immediately (ganglia at 10 micra, muscle at 20), placed on slides, and washed by standing for thirty minutes each in three changes of 24 per cent Na_2SO_4 solution. The slides were then incubated in AThCh medium for 5, 10, 20, 40 and 80 minutes, developed, gold-toned and mounted. Each of the following doses of reversible inhibitor, followed by the dose of DFP, was given to two cats: WIN 8077: 0.3, 3.0, 30, 300 microgm. (0.0005 to 0.5 micromol.)/kgm.; WIN 8078: 3.0, 30, 300 microgm. (0.005 to 0.5 micromol.)/kgm. Tissues from four cats which received only DFP and four control cats which received no AChE-inhibitor were sectioned, washed and stained similarly.

Results. The anti-AChE potency of WIN 8077 was found to be one hundred times that of WIN 8078, when cat brain homogenate was employed as the source of enzyme and MeCh as substrate; the pI_{50}'s are 7.6 and 5.6, respectively (fig. 1). Although the inhibition is reversible, the reversibility is highly dependent upon the other constituents of the reaction-mixture. This was investigated particularly with WIN 8077 as a preliminary step to the determination of its protective action against DFP *in vitro*. When the homogenate and inhibitor were incubated in aqueous medium or with 0.03 *M* $NaHCO_3$, then washed twice with water or the same concentration of $NaHCO_3$, as described under Methods, little or no reversal occurred (table 1). The addition of 0.033 *M* $MgCl_2$ or 0.03 *M* AChBr to the first wash solution resulted in approximately fifty per cent reversal; one-tenth this concentration of AChBr was considerably less effective. When 0.033 *M* $MgCl_2$ was included in the initial incubation mixture, as is done customarily in determinations of AChE-activity, the addition of the same concentration of $MgCl_2$ or of 0.03 *M* AChBr to the first wash solution brought about complete reversal; the lower concentration of AChBr or 0.03 *M* $NaHCO_3$ alone was less effective. In all these determinations, the percentage recovery is expressed in terms of a matching control which was treated identically excepting for the addition of WIN 8077; differences between the recovered activities of the controls were small.

The mechanism by which the presence of $MgCl_2$ along with the inhibitor promotes the subsequent reversal of the inhibition is not apparent at present. When Warburg determinations were conducted, as described above, in the presence and absence of 0.033 *M* $MgCl_2$, there was no significant difference in the control AChE-activities or in the inhibition (fifty per cent) in the presence of WIN 8077, pI 7.6. One might speculate that the Mg^{++} ion interferes with binding forces between the quaternary groups of the inhibitor and the anionic sites of the enzyme, without modifying the number of active enzymatic sites "covered." In order to insure uniformly complete reversal in the protection

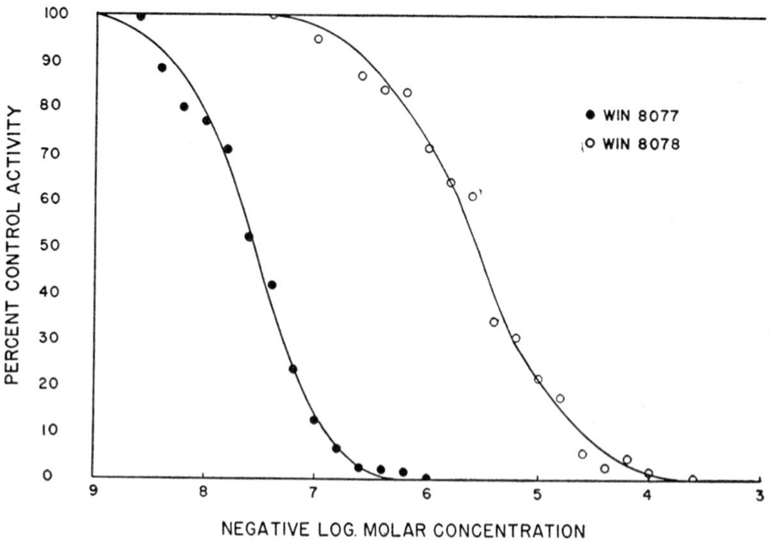

FIG. 1. Inhibition of AChE activity of cat brain homogenate by WIN 8077 and WIN 8078

TABLE 1

Reversibility of inhibition of cat brain AChE by WIN 8077 (10^{-6} M) in vitro

Incubation Solution 30 *min.*	Wash No. 1 15 *min.*	Wash No. 2 15 *min.*	Per Cent Recovery
1. $NaHCO_3$, 0.03 *M*	$NaHCO_3$, 0.03 *M*	$NaHCO_3$, 0.03 *M*	4
2. $NaHCO_3$, 0.03 *M*	$NaHCO_3$, plus $MgCl_2$, 0.033 *M*	$NaHCO_3$, 0.03 *M*	53
3. $NaHCO_3$, 0.03 *M*	$NaHCO_3$, plus AChBr, 0.03 *M*	$NaHCO_3$, 0.03 *M*	49
4. $NaHCO_3$, 0.03 *M*	$NaHCO_3$, plus AChBr, 0.003 *M*	$NaHCO_3$, 0.03 *M*	34
5. $NaHCO_3$, 0.03 *M*, plus $MgCl_2$, 0.033 *M*	$NaHCO_3$, 0.03 *M*	$NaHCO_3$, 0.03 *M*	73
6. $NaHCO_3$, 0.03 *M*, plus $MgCl_2$, 0.033 *M*	$NaHCO_3$, plus $MgCl_2$, 0.033 *M*	$NaHCO_3$, 0.03 *M*	109
7. $NaHCO_3$, 0.03 *M*, plus $MgCl_2$, 0.033 *M*	$NaHCO_3$, plus AChBr, 0.03 *M*	$NaHCO_3$, 0.03 *M*	103
8. $NaHCO_3$, 0.03 *M*, plus $MgCl_2$, 0.033 *M*	$NaHCO_3$, plus AChBr, 0.003 *M*	$NaHCO_3$, 0.03 *M*	63

studies, both 0.03 *M* AChBr and 0.033 *M* $MgCl_2$ were included in the first wash solution.

Under the conditions employed, WIN 8077 exhibited remarkably efficient protection against inactivation by DFP (table 2). At each of the four concentrations of WIN 8077 tested, the percentage of AChE activity recovered corresponded with the percentage inhibition determined previously, within the limits of reproducibility of the methods. WIN 8078 likewise competed effectively against DFP for the active sites of the enzyme during the thirty-minute incubation period.

In the earlier protection studies mentioned in the introduction (Koelle, 1946), in which reversible inhibitors and excess of DFP were removed by dialysis, physostigmine and neostigmine afforded protection of relatively small fractions of the percentage of activity which they inhibited initially, indicating that they were largely displaced from the enzyme by DFP. The difference in techniques

TABLE 2

Protection of cat brain AChE by WIN 8077 and WIN 8078 against irreversible inactivation by DFP (10^{-4} M, 30 min.)

Reversible Inhibitor	pI	Per Cent Inhibition	Per Cent Protection against DFP	Per Cent Recovery in Absence of DFP
WIN 8077	6.4	98	92	111
WIN 8077	7.0	88	74	93
WIN 8077	7.6	48	48	100
WIN 8077	8.2	20	28	101
WIN 8078	4.4	97	78	110
WIN 8078	5.0	78	74	99
WIN 8078	5.6	49	40	96
WIN 8078	6.2	16	4	106

does not, of course, permit a direct comparison with the results with the present reversible inhibitors.

Comparable results were obtained with the histochemical technique when sections of cat ciliary ganglion and stellate ganglion were incubated with WIN 8077 or WIN 8078 plus DFP *in vitro*. Slides incubated in AThCh medium for the longest period (80 minutes) were chosen for the photomicrographs[4] to permit demonstration of low residual activity, hence the cytological localization of AChE activity is poorly depicted in the control sections. However, it can be seen that in the ciliary ganglion, the heaviest staining occurred both in the peripheral zones and throughout the cytoplasm of the ganglion cells (fig. 2 and 3). In the stellate ganglion, only the occasional cholinergic neurons show heavy staining, but high AChE-activity is present in the intercellular plexuses, or protoplasmic tracts, representing the terminal arborizations of the cholinergic preganglionic fibers. Incubation with DFP alone produced complete loss of detectable AChE-activity in both ganglia. With the addition, prior to and during incubation with DFP, of concentrations of WIN 8077 and WIN 8078 which had caused nearly complete reversible inhibition in the Warburg measurements, subsequent staining was nearly as intense as in the controls. As the concentrations of the reversible inhibitors were decreased, staining was progressively lighter. The gradations are more striking in the WIN 8078-treated sections (fig. 3). It can be seen, however, that the distribution of staining in each ganglion is qualitatively nearly identical with that of the corresponding control. The chief difference is due to the relatively light staining for non-specific ChE activity seen in the glial cells of the controls. Since DFP inactivates this enzyme at a lower concentration than is required for the inactivation of AChE, and the reverse selectivity occurs with WIN 8077 and WIN 8078, only AChE activity is represented in the protected sections.

The dose of DFP (20 micromol./kgm., i.v.) employed in the *in vivo* studies

[4] Photomicrographs were taken by Mr. E. F. Glifort.

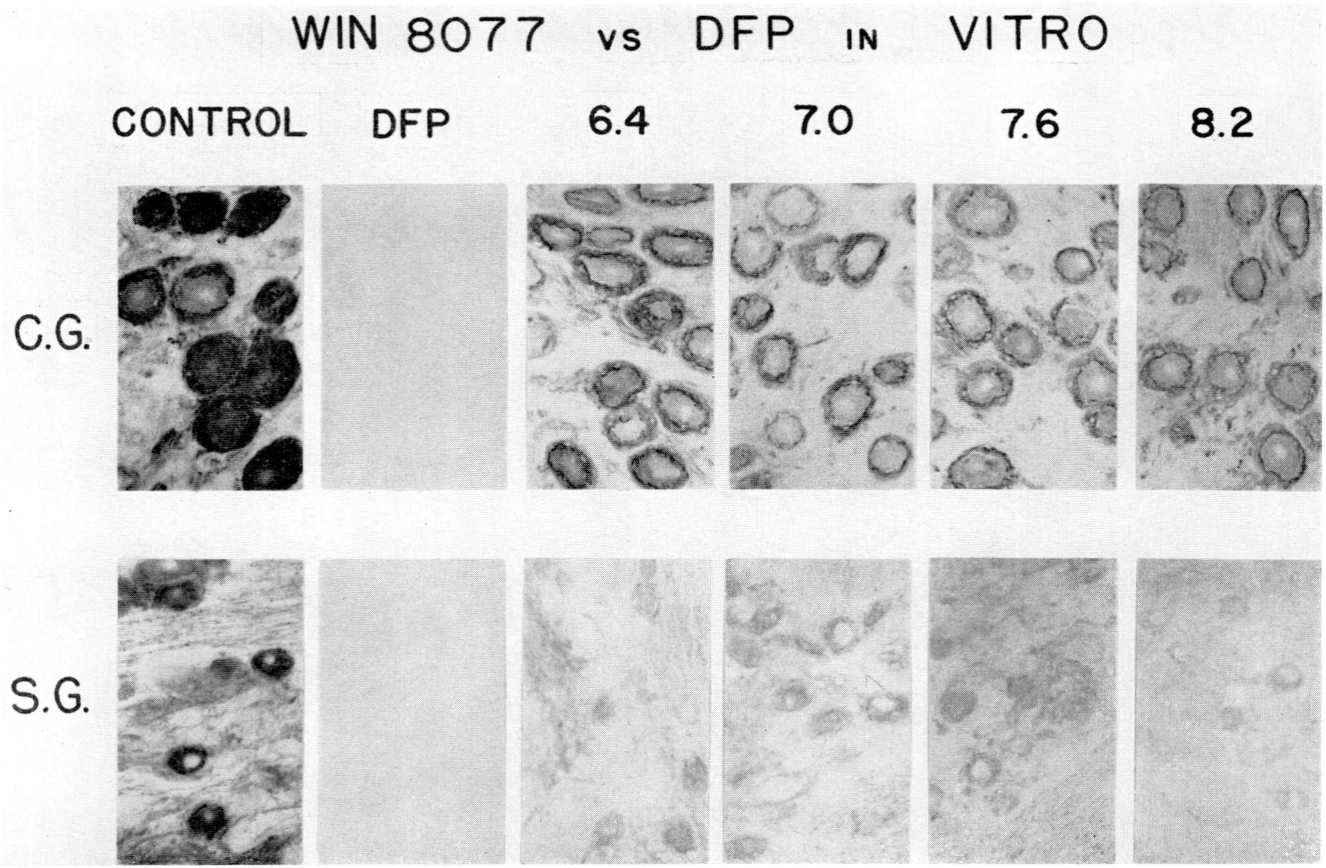

FIG. 2. Sections (10μ) of cat ciliary ganglion (C.G.) and stellate ganglion (S.G.) incubated with DFP ($10^{-4}M$, 30 min.) in presence of WIN 8077 in concentrations indicated (negative log. mol.), then washed and stained for AChE activity by 80 miuntes' incubation in AThCh medium. Magnification 200×.

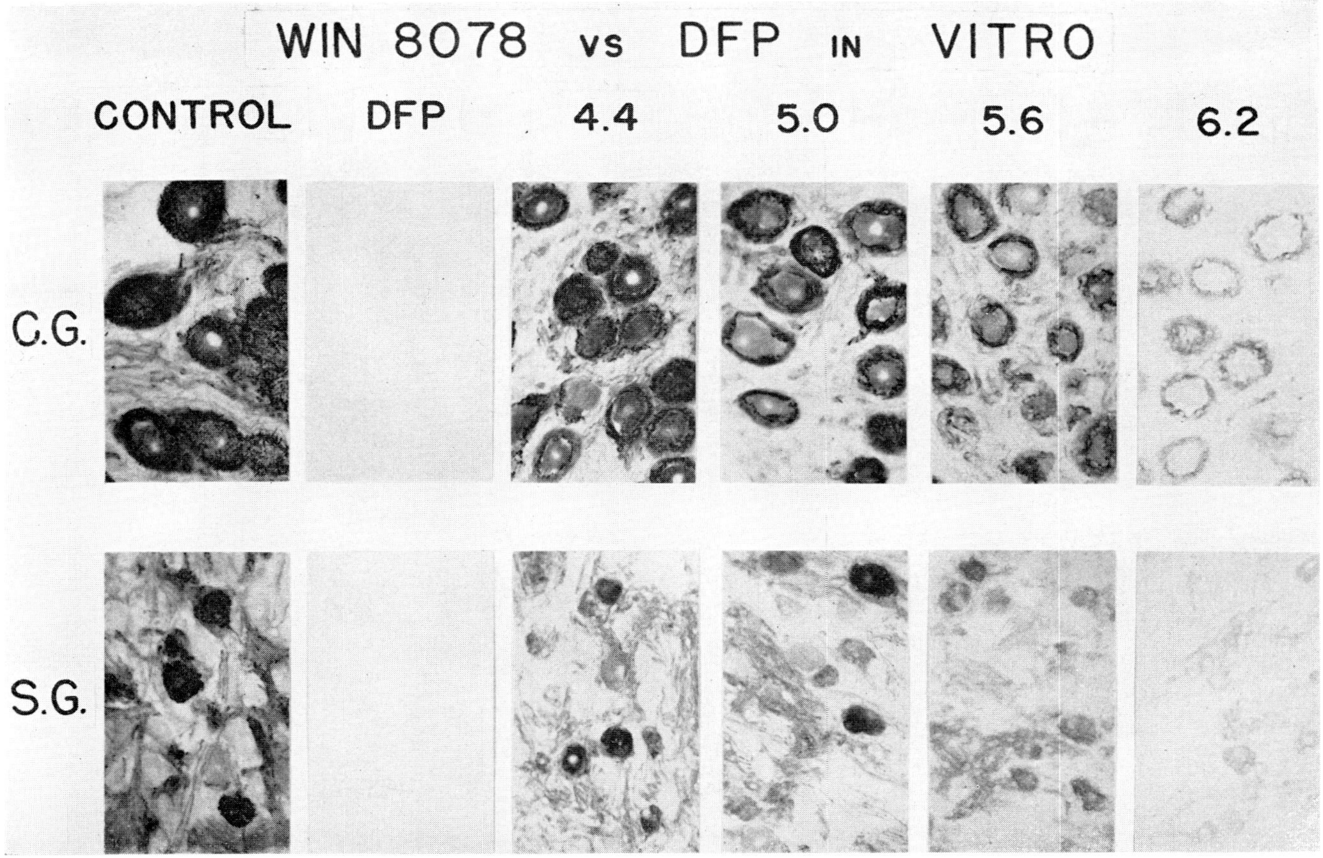

FIG. 3. Sections (10μ) of cat ciliary ganglion (C.G.) and stellate ganglion (S.G.) incubated with DFP ($10^{-4}M$, 30 min.) in presence of WIN 8078 in concentrations indicated (negative log. mol.), then washed and stained for AChE activity by 80 minutes' incubation in AThCh medium. Magnification 200×.

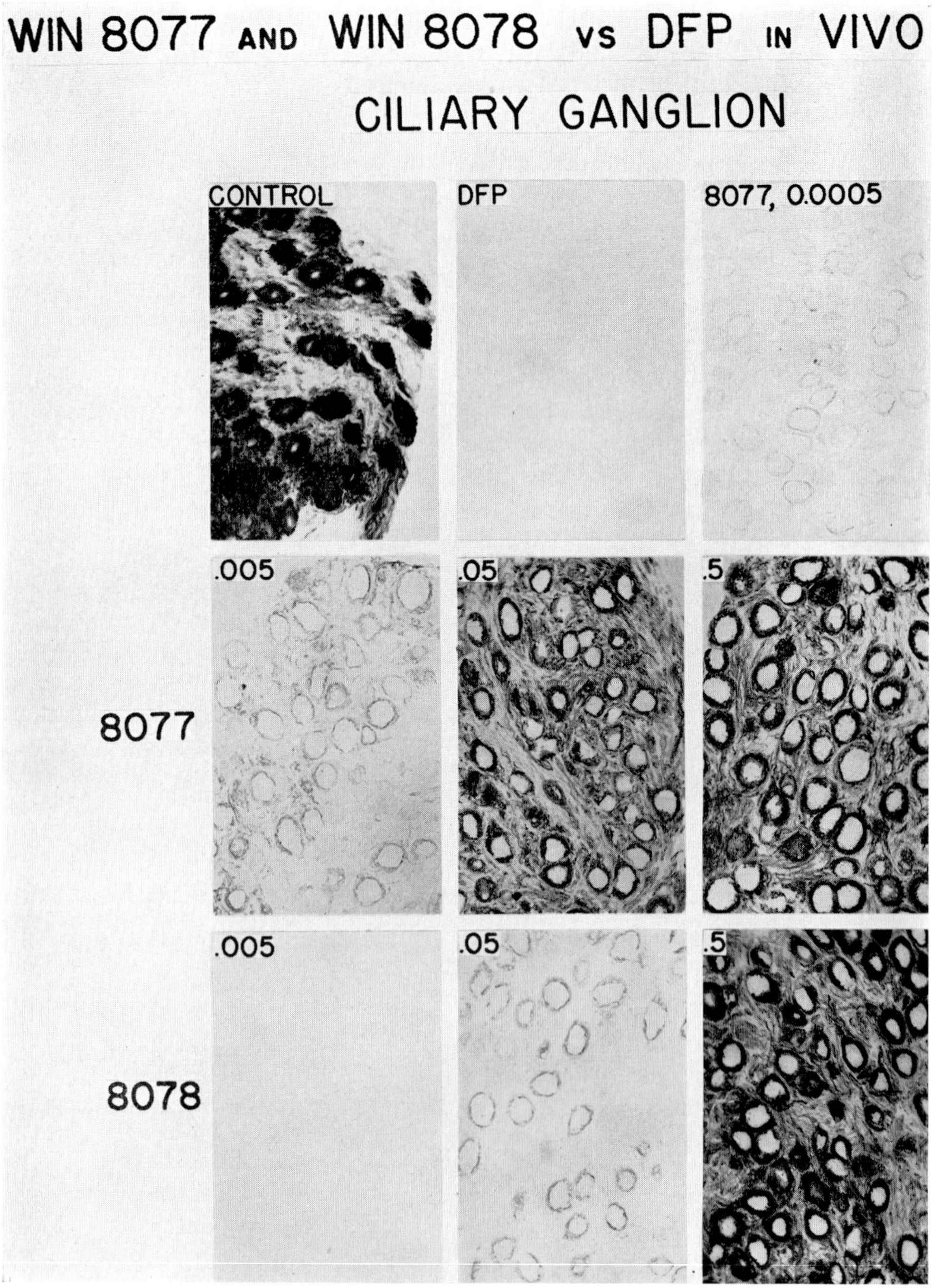

FIG. 4. Sections (10μ) of ciliary ganglia from cats injected i.v. with doses of WIN 8077 or WIN 8078 indicated (micromol./kgm.), followed five min. later by DFP (20 micromol./kgm.). Sections washed, stained for AChE by incubation for 80 min. in AThCh medium. Magnification 120×.

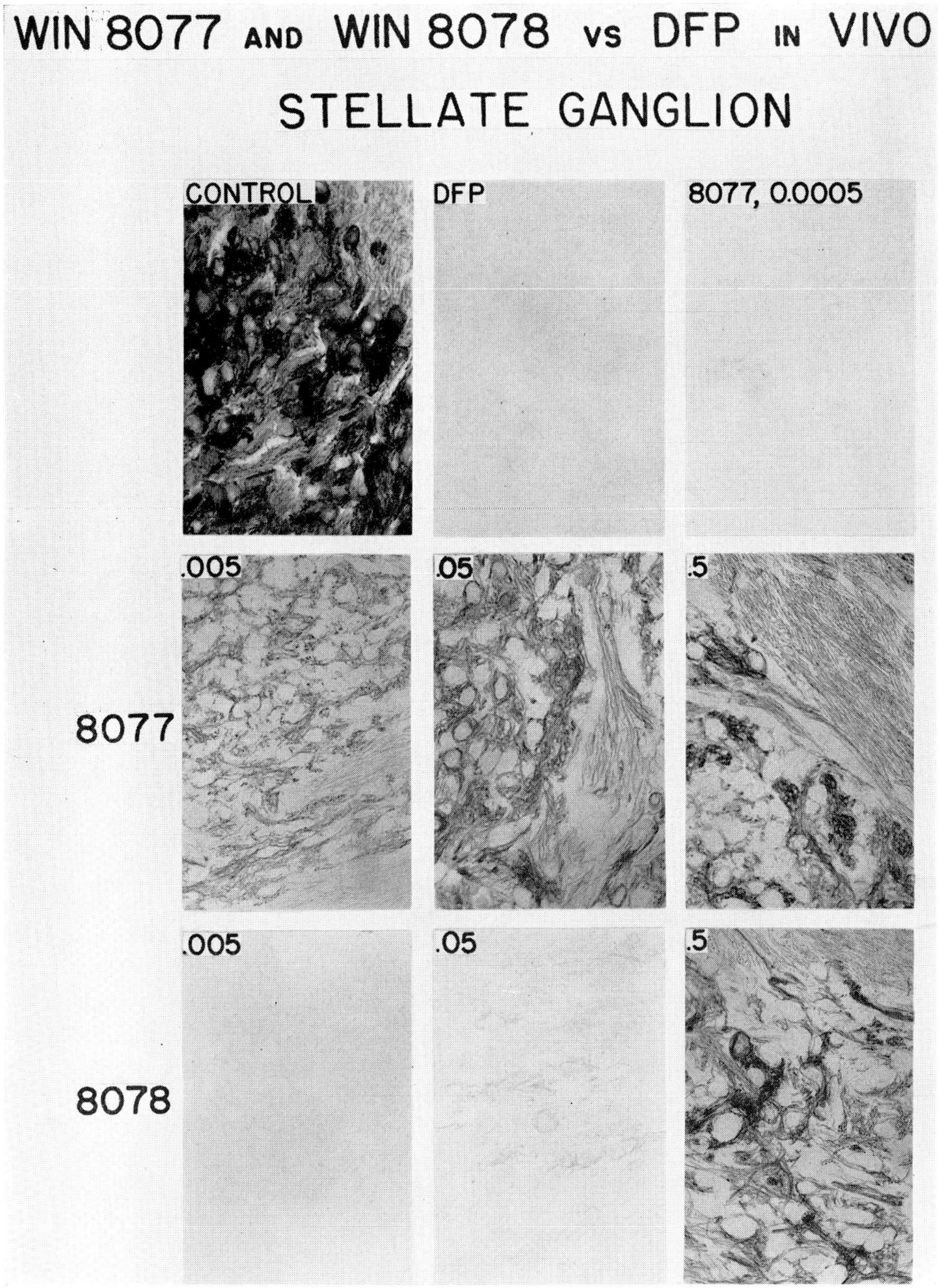

FIG. 5. Sections (10μ) of stellate ganglia from cats injected i.v. with doses of WIN 8077 or WIN 8078 indicated (micromol./kgm.), followed five min. later by DFP (20 micromol./kgm.). Sections washed, stained for AChE by incubation for 80 min. in AThCh medium. Magnification 120×.

resulted in the practically complete absence of detectable AChE in the sections of ciliary and stellate ganglia which were incubated for 80 minutes in AThCh-medium (fig. 4 and 5). The AChE-activity of the motor endplates of intercostal muscle was markedly reduced, but still detectable with 20 minutes' incubation (fig. 6). With the lowest dose of WIN 8077 (0.0005 micromol./kgm., i.v.) injected five minutes prior to DFP, no ganglionic staining was detectable in one cat; in the other, there was faint staining in both the ciliary and the stellate ganglion. In the former, this was restricted to a thin band at the periphery of each ganglion cell; the stellate ganglion showed traces of fibers in the intercellular plexus. The intensity of the motor endplates of the same animal did not appear significantly different from that of the DFP-controls. The ciliary and stellate ganglia of both cats which had received 0.005 micromol. of WIN 8077/kgm. prior to DFP were stained distinctly. The ciliary ganglion cells all showed considerably heavier peripheral bands of staining than in the previously mentioned animal, but the cytoplasm remained completely clear. Occasional fibers between the cells were also stained. In the stellate ganglia, there was definite staining of the intercellular plexuses and of the borders of scattered ganglion cells; the fibers of the entering preganglionic trunk were faintly stained. The motor endplates of these animals were decidedly more heavily stained than in the DFP-controls. In the ganglia and motor endplates of the two cats which had received the next higher dose of WIN 8077 (0.05 micromol./kgm.), the intensity of staining was considerably greater, but the cytoplasm of the ganglion cells remained unstained. The axons of the preganglionic trunks of the stellate ganglia and numerous fibers throughout the ciliary ganglia were distinctly stained. Only in the two animals which had been given the highest dose (0.5 micromol./kgm.) did the central cytoplasm of occasional ganglion cells show faint staining. At the other sites described, the intensity of staining for AChE approached or equaled that of the controls.

Similar results were obtained with WIN 8078 followed by DFP, although higher doses were required. At the lowest dose of WIN 8078 (0.005 micromol./kgm.), the ganglia remained unstained, and the motor endplates appeared indistinguishable from the DFP-controls. After 0.05 micromol. of WIN 8078/kgm., the two ganglia from both cats were stained with the same patterns as in the WIN 8077-DFP series. Their intensities were between those of the cats which had received one-one hundredth and one tenth this dose of the latter compound. The motor endplates also showed greater activity than in the DFP-controls. The three tissues from both cats which had been given 0.5 micromol. of WIN 8078/kgm. were practically indistinguishable from those of the cats which had received the same dose of WIN 8077.

Discussion. It has been shown in the present study that the inhibition of AChE by the reversible agent WIN 8077 or WIN 8078 protects the enzyme against irreversible inactivation by DFP *in vitro*. When various doses of WIN 8077 and WIN 8078 were given intravenously to cats, five minutes prior to an i.v. dose of DFP which if given alone would have been sufficient to cause inactivation of all detectable ganglionic AChE and most of the enzyme at motor end-

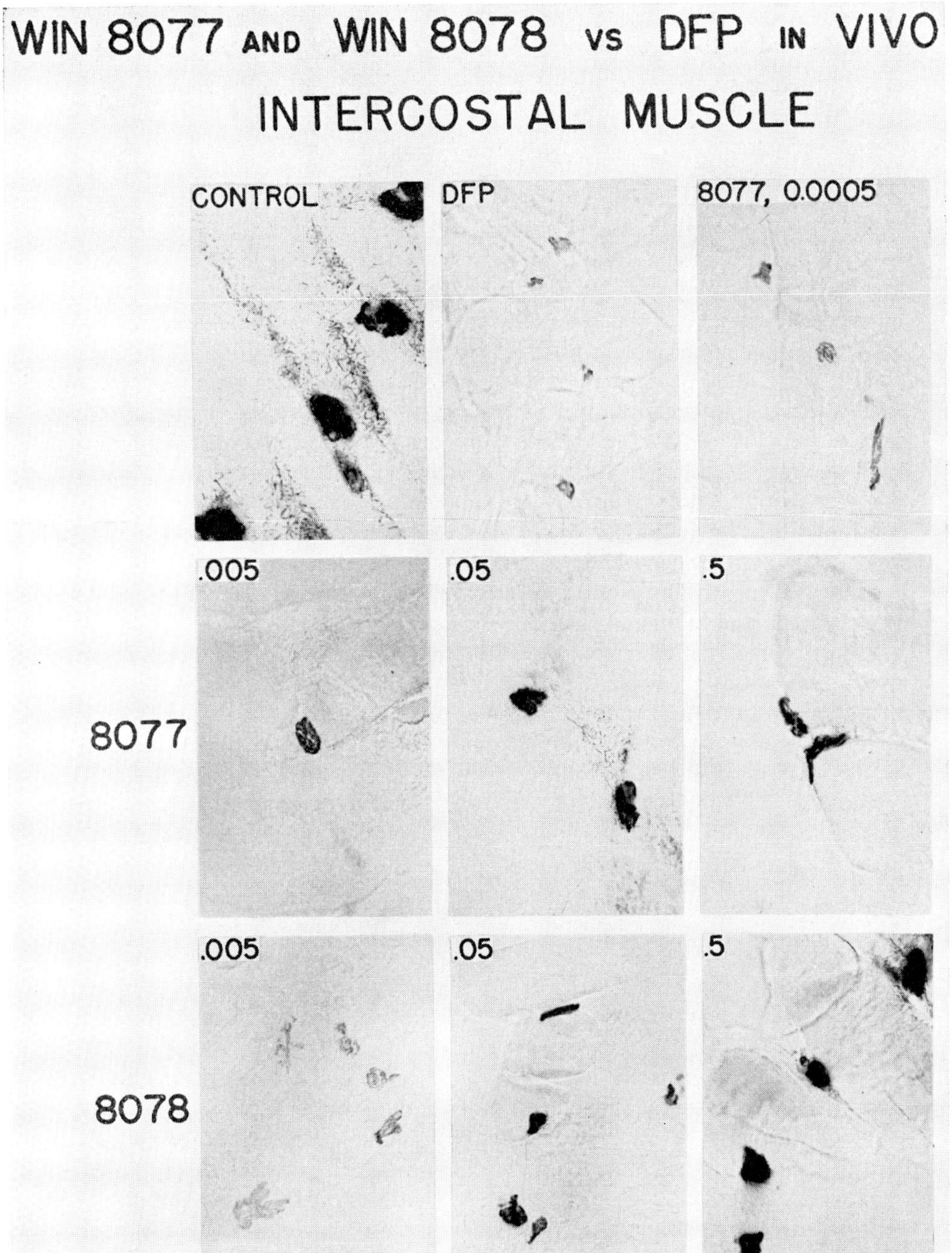

FIG. 6. Sections (20μ) of intercostal muscle from cats injected i.v. with doses of WIN 8077 or WIN 8078 indicated (micromol./kgm.), followed five min. later by DFP (20 micromol./kgm.). Sections washed, stained for AChE by incubation for 20 min. in AThCh medium. Magnification 350×.

plates, and the tissues were subsequently sectioned, washed and stained, AChE was found to be present in concentrations proportional to the doses and potencies of the reversible inhibitors. It is reasonable to assume, therefore, that the stained sites represent AChE that was inhibited *in vivo* by WIN 8077 or WIN 8078 at the time DFP was given.

The general distribution of AChE-staining in the ganglia of this series is in accordance with the initial assumption that WIN 8077 and WIN 8078, unlike DFP, do not penetrate readily certain cell membranes. This is demonstrated most graphically by the cholinergic neurons of the ciliary ganglion, where there was no evidence of protection (or, hence, of inhibition) of cytoplasmic AChE by the quaternary compounds, with the exception of the faint staining which occurred in occasional neurons after the highest dose of WIN 8077 (0.5 micromol./kgm.). In the histochemical studies conducted *in vitro*, where membrane-barriers were disrupted by freezing and sectioning prior to exposure to the anti-ChE agents, cytoplasmic AChE appeared to be protected to the same extent as that at the periphery of the neurons. The exception mentioned probably illustrates the principle that impermeability of a membrane to a given substance is a relative term, depending upon the concentration and other factors. This situation was encountered previously in a study of the penetration of the blood-brain barrier and the membranes of cerebral neurons by a quaternary anti-ChE agent (Koelle and Steiner, 1956).

The interpretation of enzymatic histochemical results requires consideration of the sequence of events that occurs during the staining process (Friedenwald, 1955). In the initial period of incubation, precipitation of the mercaptide takes place at the sites of highest activity, and probably permits the localization of such sites with fairly high accuracy. As incubation continues, precipitation develops at sites of lower activity, but accretion of more precipitate at the initial sites probably continues. This is shown in fig. 4 by the increasing widths of the peripheral bands around the cells of the ciliary ganglia with increasing doses of WIN 8077 and WIN 8078. The same sequence was seen in sections of a given ganglion with increasing incubation-time, from 5 to 80 minutes. Hence, it cannot be stated at present whether the increase in the widths of the bands represents wider zones of protected AChE, or the protection of higher concentrations of enzyme within a fixed zone. Another point which is still indefinite is the relative distribution of protected AChE between the pre- and postsynaptic sites in the ciliary ganglion. From study of a large number of sections it appears that both the terminations of the preganglionic fibers and the borders of the ganglion cells were stained. Most of the synapses in the ciliary ganglion are known to occur subcapsularly, in the immediate vicinity of the ganglion cells, which are surrounded individually by the preganglionic arborizations. In the stellate ganglion, on the other hand, the terminal ramifications of the preganglionic fibers synapse chiefly within the intercellular plexus with prolonged extracapsular dendrites of the ganglion cells (Ranson and Billingsley, 1918; de Castro, 1932). Both the plexuses and the peripheral regions of occasional ganglion cells in the latter ganglion were stained after the reversible inhibitors and DFP in the present series, indicating the presence there of both pre- and postsynaptic external AChE.

Studies with denervated ganglia are now in progress to permit a more accurate description of these relationships.

With the histochemical method it has thus been possible to detect AChE-inhibition at selective sites by two reversible bisquaternary agents at threshold pharmacologically active doses, where inhibition cannot be shown by the usual homogenate techniques. It has not been determined quantitatively, in terms of percentage of total AChE, how much inhibition occurred after each dose. Judging from the intensity of staining in the controls and in the ganglia of cats which received the lower doses of the reversible inhibitors, the figures for inhibition would probably be quite small. However, if the concept of "functional" and "reserve" AChE, as discussed in the introduction, is true, the significance of such figures for total AChE is questionable. Even with an agent such as DFP, which apparently penetrates readily all extra- and intracellular membranes, the same percentage inhibition of functional AChE might be associated with wide variations in reserve AChE-inhibition, depending upon the dose and rate of administration or absorption of the agent.

While the histochemical findings demonstrate that AChE-inhibition might account for the pharmacological actions of WIN 8077 and WIN 8078 at the regions examined, they do not exclude the possibility of a direct action at the receptor sites as well. As indicated in the introduction, either explanation can be offered for the actions of many drugs of the same general class. Both mechanisms appear to contribute to the action of neostigmine at the motor endplate (Riker and Wescoe, 1946), whereas the drug's local miotic effect seems dependent solely upon ChE-inhibition (Leopold and Comroe, 1945). Župančič (1953, Majcen and Župančič, 1956) has advanced the interesting hypothesis that AChE itself may be the receptor-protein at the post-synaptic or effector site, a possibility which has also been discussed by others (Riker, 1953; Nachmansohn, 1955; Mullins, 1956). If this should be the case, the question of direct or enzyme-inhibitory action of the anti-ChE drugs would resolve itself. Along somewhat broader lines, Cohen (1956) has speculated that the catalytic actions of AChE and other enzymes, by means of which they are characterized *in vitro*, may be frequently incidental to their functions at some sites in the body. Thus, while it is generally assumed that AChE has certain chemical groupings in common with the post-synaptic receptor and the protein to which ACh is bound at the pre-synaptic site prior to its release (Nachmansohn, 1955; Cohen and Posthumus, 1955), in terms of this suggestion all three moieties might be essentially identical. At the latter site, local factors *in vivo* might suppress the hydrolytic action of a portion of the AChE without interfering with its capacity to bind ACh. The concept could explain the function of AChE at many locations, observed histochemically, where its role is not clear (Koelle, 1955). It also suggests modifications of the currently accepted theories of the sites and mechanisms of action of the cholinomimetic and cholinergic blocking drugs.

SUMMARY

N,N′-bis (2-diethylaminoethyl) oxamide bis-2-chlorobenzyl chloride (WIN 8077) and the corresponding bis-2-methoxybenzyl chloride salt (WIN 8078) are reversible, selective inhibitors of acetylcholinesterase (AChE), which have been shown previously to produce cholinomimetic effects in doses (0.0005 to 0.02 micromol./kgm.) far below those which cause measurable AChE-inhibition *in vivo*. In the present study, their pI_{50}'s for inhibition of the AChE of cat brain homogenate were found to be 7.6 and 5.6 respectively. When the same homogenate was incubated with varying concentrations of the two inhibitors, over ranges producing twenty to nearly one hundred per cent inhibition, the equivalent percentages were protected against a concentration ($10^{-4}M$) of diisopropylfluorophosphate (DFP) which produced complete inactivation of the enzyme in the absence of the reversible inhibitors. The protective effect against DFP was also demonstrated histochemically: sections of ciliary and stellate ganglia which were incubated with WIN 8077 or WIN 8078 plus DFP, then washed and stained for AChE, showed the presence of increasing enzymatic activity with increasing concentrations of the two reversible inhibitors, whereas no activity was present after DFP alone. This principle was then employed to determine the sites of AChE-inhibition produced by various doses of WIN 8077 and WIN 8078 *in vivo*. Anesthetized, atropinized cats were given intravenous injections of WIN 8077 (0.0005 to 0.5 micromol./kgm.) or WIN 8078 (0.005 to 0.5 micromol./kgm.), and five minutes later received 20.0 micromol. of DFP/kgm., i.v.; thirty to forty minutes after DFP, they were sacrificed. The stellate and ciliary ganglia and a portion of intercostal muscle were removed, and the tissues were sectioned and stained for AChE-activity. Sections of ganglia from cats which had received only DFP were completely blank; motor endplates were stained faintly. The ciliary and stellate ganglia of one of the two cats which had received 0.0005 micromol. of WIN 8077/kgm. showed faint staining. Both ganglia of all cats which had received 0.005 micromol. of WIN 8077, or 0.05 micromol. of WIN 8078, or more were stained, with increasing intensity at higher doses or longer periods of incubation. Staining was most marked at the borders of the neurons of the ciliary ganglia, and in the intercellular plexuses of the stellate ganglia; the cytoplasm of the ciliary ganglion cells, which stains intensely in untreated controls, remained blank. Motor endplates showed evidence of AChE-inhibition over the same dosage ranges of WIN 8077 and WIN 8078. Results are discussed with respect to correlation between AChE-inhibition and pharmacological action, the concept of "functional" and "reserve" AChE, and possible physiological roles of AChE other than enzymatic.

REFERENCES

Berkowitz, E. C.: Proc. Soc. Exper. Biol. and Med., **89:** 394, 1955.

Burgen, A. S. V., and Chipman, L. M.: Quart. J. Exper. Physiol., **37:** 61, 1952.

Cohen, J. A.: De Plaats van het Enzym in de Biologische Wetenschap (Address delivered at Univ. of Leiden, 1956).

Cohen, J. A., and Posthumus, C. H.: Acta Physiol. Pharmacol. Neerl., **4:** 17, 1955.

de Castro, F.: Sympathetic Ganglia, Normal and Pathological. In W. Penfield's Cytology and Cellular Pathology of the Nervous System, Paul B. Hoeber, Inc., New York, **1:** 317, 1932.

Friedenwald, J. S.: Pharmacol. Rev., **7:** 83, 1955.

Kamijo, K., and Koelle, G. B.: This Journal, **105:** 349, 1952.

Karczmar, A. G., and Howard, J. W.: This Journal, **113:** 30, 1955.
Koelle, G. B.: This Journal, **88:** 232, 1946.
Koelle, G. B.: This Journal, **103:** 153, 1951.
Koelle, G. B.: This Journal, **114:** 167, 1955.
Koelle, G. B., and Gilman, A.: This Journal, **87:** 421, 1946.
Koelle, G. B., and Gilman, A.: This Journal, **95:** Part 2 (Pharmacol. Rev.): 166, 1949.
Koelle, G. B., and Steiner, E. C.: This Journal, **118:** 420, 1956.
Koster, R.: This Journal, **88:** 39, 1946.
Lands, A. M., Karczmar, A. G., Howard, J. W., and Arnold, A.: This Journal, **115:** 185, 1955.
Leopold, I. H., and Comroe, J. H., Jr.: Proc. Soc. Exper. Biol. and Med., **60:** 382, 1945.
Mackworth, J. F., and Webb, E. C.: Biochem. J., **42:** 91, 1948.
Majcen, A., and Župančič, A. O.: Arch. Internat. Pharmacodyn., **108:** 232, 1956.
Mazur, A., and Bodansky, O.: J. Biol. Chem., **163:** 261, 1946.
Mullins, L. J.: Molecular Structure and Functional Activity of Nerve Cells, Publ. No. *1*, Am. Inst. Biol. Sci.: 123, 1956.
Nachmansohn, D.: Biochim. et. Biophys. Acta, **4:** 78, 1950.
Nachmansohn, D.: Harvey Lect., Ser. **49** (1953–54): 57, 1955.
Nachmansohn, D., and Feld, E. A.: J. Biol. Chem., **171:** 715, 1947.
Randall, L. O., and Lehmann, G.: This Journal, **99:** 16, 1950.
Ranson, S. W., and Billingsley, P. R.: J. Comp. Neurol., **29:** 313, 1918.
Riker, W. F., Jr.: Pharmacol. Rev., **5:** 1, 1953.
Riker, W. F., Jr., and Wescoe, W. C.: This Journal, **88:** 58, 1946.
Riker, W. F., Jr., and Wescoe, W. C.: This Journal, **95:** 515, 1949.
Strauss, O. H., and Goldstein, A.: J. Gen. Physiol., **26:** 559, 1943.
Wescoe, W. C., Riker, W. F., Jr., and Beach, V. L.: This Journal, **99:** 265, 1950.
Župančič, A. O.: Acta Physiol. Scand., **29:** 63, 1953.

IN VITRO OXIDATION OF MORPHINE BY RAT TISSUE HOMOGENATES[1]

EIKICHI HOSOYA[2] AND THEODORE M. BRODY

Dept. of Pharmacology, University of Michigan Medical School, Ann Arbor

Received for publication March 28, 1957

Pseudomorphine is a dimer formed by the oxidation of two molecules of morphine. Early investigators regarded this compound as a product of the metabolism of morphine. Marme (1883a, b) claimed to have found pseudomorphine in the tissues of the tolerant dog and implicated it in the production of physical dependance. Others have failed to substantiate this early observation (Schmidt and Livingston, 1933). The present study will show that rat tissue homogenates in the presence of cytochrome c are capable of oxidizing morphine to a compound which is indistinguishable from pseudomorphine on the basis of chromatographic analysis.

METHODS. Diphosphopyridine nucleotide, triphosphopyridine nucleotide and cytochrome c (horse-heart) were obtained from the Sigma Chemical Co. Adenosine triphosphate was obtained from Pabst Laboratories and sodium azide from the Eastman Chemical Co. All other materials were reagent grade.

Homogenates and tissue fractions. Either 10 or 20 per cent homogenates from rat tissues were prepared in 0.15 *M* KCl by using a Potter-Elvehjem homogenizer. For the fractionation of the rat liver, a 10 per cent homogenate was prepared in 0.25 *M* sucrose. The homogenate was centrifuged for 10 minutes at 700 × *g* in an International Refrigerated Centrifuge. The supernatant fluid was removed for further centrifugation and the residue resuspended in a known volume of 0.15 *M* KCl by rapid homogenization. This residue represents the nuclear fraction, and is essentially nuclei contaminated with some red blood cells, residual whole cells and some mitochondria. The supernatant fluid from the first centrifugation was transferred to Lusteroid tubes and centrifuged for 15 minutes at 12,000 × *g*. The residue was redispersed by homogenization in an appropriate volume of 0.15 *M* KCl and was recentrifuged at the same speed. The resulting sediment was the mitochondrial fraction. The supernatant fluid obtained from the isolation of the mitochondria was not fractionated further. This "supernatant" contained microsomal particles as well as soluble enzymes. Resuspension in KCl was necessary since sucrose seemed to interfere in the morphine determinations.

Morphine determinations. Incubation of morphine and tissue preparations was carried out in beakers in a Dubnoff Metabolic Shaker at 37°C. in oxygen. Incubation time varied from 60 to 180 minutes. In some experiments the conventional manometric Warburg apparatus was used at the same temperature in air. In the latter experiments several flasks were usually combined prior to analysis. The constituents of the media are indicated in the appropriate tables and figures. The flask or beaker contents were acidified with 1 *N* HCl and the mixture precipitated with 20 per cent trichloroacetic acid. After shaking, centrifuging and filtering, 5 ml. of the TCA filtrate was taken for analysis of "free" morphine.

Total morphine was estimated after acidification and autoclaving an aliquot of the TCA tissue filtrate. The "bound" or conjugated morphine is the difference between the total

---

[1] A preliminary report was presented at the Fall Meeting of the American Society for Pharmacology and Experimental Therapeutics, Charlottesville, Va., Sept. 6–8, 1954, (THIS JOURNAL, **113:** 8, 1955).

[2] Present address: Dept. of Pharmacology, Keio University Medical School, Tokyo.

and the free morphine. These analyses were carried out by the method described by Woods *et al.* (1954). In all experiments morphine was calculated as the free base. All determinations were run in duplicate and paired controls were analyzed after inactivation at zero time. The latter was used to indicate the amount of morphine in all vessels prior to incubation.

Paper chromatography. Aliquots of TCA filtrates prepared after incubation of the reaction mixtures were set aside for paper partition chromatography studies. The filtrates were placed in suitable dishes and evaporated to dryness in air for approximately 20 hours. The residues were washed several times with 3-ml. portions of ether to remove the trichloroacetic acid. The final residues were acidified with 1 *N* HCl and a suitable amount placed on 18 x 22½" sheets of Whatman No. 1 filter paper for chromatography. Descending chromatograms were developed for 15 to 18 hours at 25°C. in a solvent mixture of n-butanol (40 vol.), glacial acetic acid (10 vol.) and water (20 vol.). Several chromatograms were also developed in a solvent mixture of n-butanol (40 vol.), ammonia (10 vol.) and water (20 vol.). All chromatograms were placed in a Chromatocab[3] previously equilibrated with the solvent mixture for 24 hours. The compounds isolated on the chromatograms were visualized with an ultraviolet lamp.[4] R_f values were calculated from the origin to the center of the spot of each particular compound.

RESULTS. *Homogenate fortification, morphine conjugation and recovery of morphine.* The first suggestion that morphine was being converted to a product other than a conjugated compound appeared in experiments where attempts were made to obtain maximum conjugating activity. In these studies a basic medium, Krebs-Ringer phosphate, was fortified by the addition of various cofactors and metabolic intermediates. A 20 per cent rat liver homogenate with glucose as substrate was used in most of these experiments. Table 1 shows the effect of the addition of cytochrome c on the conjugating activity and also on the subsequent recovery of total morphine. After incubation, analysis by the method of Woods *et al.* (1954) was used to obtain the amount of free morphine and that which was conjugated and released after acid hydrolysis. It may be observed in table 1 that in the absence of cytochrome c about 25 per cent of the morphine initially present was conjugated and that all was recovered after acid hydrolysis. This would indicate that the only metabolic transformation occurring in this experiment was a conversion of morphine to its conjugated product. However, when $1 \times 10^{-4}M$ cytochrome c (final concentration) was added to the incubation medium with morphine, there was a significant fall in the conjugase activity, only 11 per cent of the morphine appeared to be bound under these conditions. Furthermore, only 72 per cent of the morphine could be recovered after acid hydrolysis, indicating that in addition to conjugation morphine was being either transformed or degraded in the presence of cytochrome c.

Table 2 shows the effect of various concentrations of cytochrome c on the disappearance of morphine by rat liver homogenates. The values shown in this table are for total morphine recovered after acid hydrolysis. The optimum activity was obtained with a final cytochrome c concentration of $2 \times 10^{-4}M$. Higher concentrations did not further increase the disappearance of morphine. In the absence of cytochrome c, 97 per cent of the morphine added could be recovered. When the homogenate was omitted in the cytochrome c fortified medium all the

[3] Research Equipment Corporation, Oakland, Calif.

[4] Mineralight Lamp, Model R-51, Ultraviolet Products, Inc., S. Pasadena, Calif.

TABLE 1

The effect of homogenate fortification on morphine conjugation

Each vessel contained: 0.054 *M* KCl, 0.054 *M* NaCl, 0.006 *M* $MgCl_2$, and 0.04 *M* Na phosphate buffer, pH 7.4 and 1.0 ml. of a 20 per cent rat liver homogenate in 0.15 *M* KCl. Morphine, 250 microgm., made up in buffer was added to each experimental flask. The total volume was 3.0 ml., the gas phase 95 per cent O_2, 5 per cent CO_2. The incubation time was 180 minutes and temperature was 37°C.

Cyto. c 1×10^{-4} *M*	Micrograms Morphine*			Per cent Conjugated	Per cent Recovery of Total Morphine
	Initial (zero time)	3-hr. incub. (free morphine)	After acid hydrolysis (total morphine)		
−	252	181	252	28	100
−	247	194	252	22	102
+	247	150	180	12	73
+	249	148	173	10	70

* Calculated as the free base.

TABLE 2

Effect of cytochrome c concentration on the disappearance of morphine by rat liver homogenates

Reactants same as table 1, except as indicated above.

Cytochrome c Conc. $\times 10^{-6}$*M*	Micrograms Total Morphine Recovered*	Per cent Morphine Disappeared
none	294	3
5	280	7
10	255	16
50	233	23
100	208	31
200	185	39
400	189	38
200 (no homogenate)	310	0

* zero time morphine = 303 micrograms.

morphine was recoverable, indicating that this metabolic conversion of morphine was an enzymic one. Additions of compounds other than cytochrome c failed to influence the disappearance of morphine. Diphosphopyridine nucleotide (DPN), triphosphopyridine nucleotide (TPN) or adenosine triphosphate (ATP) separately or in combination could not replace cytochrome c. Nor did the addition of any of these agents together with cytochrome further enhance the effect.

Table 3 demonstrates that a number of rat tissues have the capacity of oxidizing morphine in the presence of cytochrome c. The figures in parentheses indicate the number of experiments. Of the tissues studied, the greatest percentage of morphine transformation was obtained with rat liver. Kidney and brain caused a lesser but significant disappearance of morphine. In a few experiments it was also demonstrated that a similar effect could be observed with skeletal or cardiac muscle.

Effect of some inhibitors on morphine transformation by tissue homogenates. A

TABLE 3

Effect of cytochrome c addition on morphine disappearance by various rat tissues
Reactants and conditions same as table 1.

Tissue Preparation*	Cyto. c $2 \times 10^{-4} M$	Per cent Free Morphine Recovered†	Per cent Total Morphine Recovered after Acid Hydrolysis
Rat liver homogenate (3)	−	81	99
Rat liver homogenate (12)	+	63	70
Rat kidney homogenate (3)	−	95	96
Rat kidney homogenate (5)	+	80	82
Rat brain homogenate (3)	−	98	96
Rat brain homogenate (6)	+	90	88

* equivalent to 200 mgm. tissue wet weight
† zero time vessels contained 200 micrograms morphine.

TABLE 4

The effect of cyanide and azide on morphine oxidation

Reactants same as table 1. Incubation time 120 minutes, gas phase air. Inhibitors added in concentrations indicated. $2 \times 10^{-4}M$ cytochrome c added to all vessels.

Inhibitor	Micrograms Total Morphine		Per cent Morphine Transformed
	zero time	3-hr. incub.	
none	306	197	36
$1 \times 10^{-4}M$ KCN	310	278	10
$2.5 \times 10^{-4}M$ KCN	290	292	0*
$1 \times 10^{-3}M$ sod. azide	302	248	17
$5 \times 10^{-3}M$ sod. azide	298	302	0

* The effectiveness of KCN in depressing morphine oxidation was confirmed by paper chromatographic techniques (see METHODS). No pseudomorphine could be detected after chromatographing and visualizing TCA filtrates which had contained this concentration of KCN in the original reaction mixture.

variety of inhibitors were used in an attempt to localize the site of metabolic transformation of morphine by tissue preparations. In these studies a 20 per cent rat liver homogenate was utilized and fortified by the addition of $2 \times 10^{-4}M$ cytochrome c. The results of such experiments are shown in table 4. A concentration of $2.5 \times 10^{-4}M$ potassium cyanide completely depressed the disappearance of morphine. A concentration of sodium azide, $5 \times 10^{-3}M$, produced the same effect. Incubation in an atmosphere of nitrogen completely inhibited the transformation. A number of other agents, $1 \times 10^{-2}M$ malonate, $1 \times 10^{-2}M$ fluoroacetate, $1 \times 10^{-4}M$ 2,4-dinitrophenol, $1 \times 10^{-3}M$ quinacrine and $2 \times 10^{-3}M$ *p*-chloromercuribenzoate failed to influence this disappearance of morphine.

Fractionation studies. From the above it appeared that terminal oxidation and more specifically the cytochrome enzyme system was responsible for the observed metabolic transformation of morphine. Since the cytochrome activity resides primarily in the mitochondria of mammalian tissues, it was decided to

TABLE 5

Capacity of various liver fractions to oxidize morphine

Reactants as in table 1, $2 \times 10^{-4} M$ cytochrome c added to all vessels. Gas phase air, incubation time 60 minutes, temperature 37°C.

Fraction	Per cent Morphine Oxidized*	Per cent activity per fraction
Homogenate	36 (33–39)†	100
Nuclei	6 (4–7)	17
Mitochondria	22 (20–26)	61
Supernatant and microsomes	2 (1–3)	5

* Average of 3 separate experiments.

† Range is indicated in parentheses.

fractionate a rat liver homogenate and determine the capacity of each fraction to oxidize morphine. Homogenates of rat liver were fractionated into three parts, the nuclear, the mitochondrial and a combined supernatant and microsome fraction. The nuclear, and mitochondrial fractions after isolation and washing were resuspended in 0.15 M KCl to a suitable volume and an amount added to each vessel to give a final concentration equivalent to 200 mgm. of the wet weight of the tissue. The supernatant fluid was used undiluted. In each tissue preparation the only other addition to the Krebs-Ringer phosphate buffer was $2 \times 10^{-4} M$ cytochrome c. Total morphine was determined after incubation and the per cent morphine oxidized by comparison of these values with zero time controls. The results of such studies are shown in table 5. Each value reported is the average of three separate experiments. These data confirm the previous observation that this conversion of morphine is catalyzed by those enzymes concerned with terminal oxidative processes in tissues.

Chromatographic studies. Chromatograms were prepared from TCA filtrates (see METHODS) in an attempt to isolate the oxidation product of morphine. Figure 1 is a reproduction of a typical chromatogram and demonstrates the isolation of a compound which has been tentatively identified as pseudomorphine (also called oxidimorphine). This chromatogram was developed for 17 hours at 25°C. and after air-drying was visualized under an ultraviolet lamp. A chromatogram developed from a filtrate of morphine and the rat liver homogenate incubated without cytochrome c was resolved into 2 compounds. The slower migrating compound having an R_f value of 0.23 is probably the glucuronide of morphine (Woods, 1954) while the compound with an R_f value of 0.69 is free morphine. In the majority of experiments with no added cytochrome c, we were able to obtain a spot comparable to the morphine glucuronide. When $2 \times 10^{-4} M$ cytochrome c was added no spot having an R_f value of 0.23 was discernable, which confirmed our earlier observations that when morphine was oxidized, glucuronide synthesis was concomitantly depressed. In addition to the free morphine, a spot was visible which was intensely fluorescent when excited by ultraviolet light and had an R_f value of 0.31. This latter spot was indistinguishable from that obtained from an acid-solution of pseudomorphine prepared

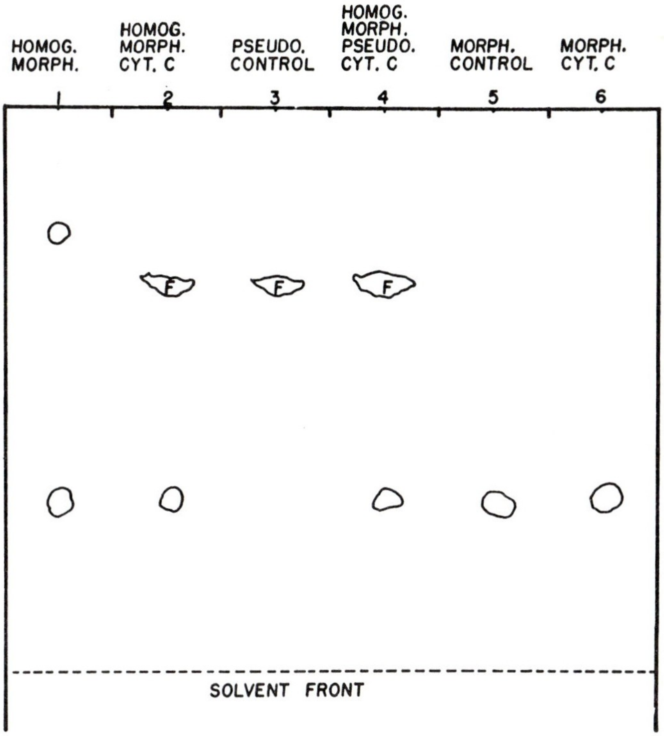

FIG. 1. Reproduction of chromatogram demonstrating isolation of pseudomorphine from tissue filtrates.

1—Filtrate from vessels containing 200 microgm. morphine, rat liver homogenate, no cytochrome c. Other reactants and conditions as in table 1. 2—Homogenate, morphine, 2×10^{-4} M cytochrome c. 3—Pseudomorphine prepared chemically. 4—Homogenate, morphine, cytochrome c, pseudomorphine. 5—Morphine. 6—Morphine, cytochrome c.

chemically.[5] When pseudomorphine was added to a mixture containing morphine, cytochrome c and homogenate, a single spot having the same R_f value and same intense blue fluorescence as pseudomorphine was obtained. Control chromatograms indicated the necessity of enzyme catalysis for this transformation. Chromatograms shown in figure 1 are for the butanol-water-acetic acid solvent system. Similar studies were performed using a butanol-water-ammonia system and essentially identical data were obtained through the R_f values obtained with each compound differed from those in the acidic solvent system. No further work was done to characterize the product. Relatively minute amounts of pseudomorphine could be detected by the chromatographic technique and although no studies were performed to determine the limit of pseudomorphine detectable, as little as 0.02 microgram was readily visualized on paper using ultraviolet light.

We have also demonstrated that other compounds chemically related to morphine can be oxidized by tissue homogenates in the presence of cytochrome c.

[5] Kindly supplied to us by Dr. L. A. Woods.

Nalorphine (Nalline) could be oxidized to a fluorescent compound in the presence of homogenate and cytochrome c. The oxidation product of nalorphine has an R_f value of 0.37 and can be separated from pseudomorphine. A chemically prepared "pseudonalline" had the same partition coefficient as the product obtained by incubating nalorphine with liver homogenate and cytochrome c.

Several other compounds were investigated to determine whether they would yield fluorescent oxidation products under these conditions. No such product could be obtained with codeine, but was observed with heterocodeine and dihydromorphinone, compounds having a free phenolic hydroxyl group in the same position as does morphine.

Attempts to isolate pseudomorphine from tissues of morphinized animals. Several attempts have been made to isolate pseudomorphine from the livers of morphinized animals using the chromatographic method described. Thus far, these attempts have been unsuccessful.

DISCUSSION. There have been a number of studies indicating that morphine can be oxidized *in vitro*. Perhaps the earliest work of this nature was that of Babel (1905) who was studying the absorption of morphine and related alkaloids by brain tissue. He added measured amounts of drug to a brain brei and then analyzed for morphine prior to and after incubation. From his studies he concluded that brain could oxidize morphine but not codeine. Although his methods of analysis may be open to question, his findings are interesting in the light of the present study. Abood and Kun (1949) reported that the phenolic hydroxyl group of morphine was oxidized to a quinone in the presence of muscle, brain, liver or kidney obtained from the rabbit, rat and guinea pig. This oxidation could be inhibited by the addition of cyanide or selenite, again implicating the cytochrome system in this metabolic transformation.

In our investigation we could demonstrate the conversion of about 30 per cent of the added morphine to pseudomorphine by 200 mgm. of rat liver. This occurred only if a sufficient amount of cytochrome c were added, a concentration of $2 \times 10^{-4}M$ cytochrome c giving optimium oxidation. These studies would indicate that cytochrome c is acting as the electron acceptor in this reaction and suggests that morphine has a redox potential which is close to that of the cytochromes. This is in agreement with previous work on the non-enzymatic cytochrome c reductase activity of morphine (Wang and Bain, 1953).

Does this oxidation occur *in vivo?* Several experiments by us, analyzing the livers from acutely morphinized animals, failed to reveal the presence of pseudomorphine. This approach should however be explored more thoroughly. Liver probably is not the tissue of choice, although our studies indicate that the oxidative rates are highest in liver. This organ is the primary site of conjugating activity and perhaps some other tissue might be more suitable. Since the capacity to conjugate morphine probably resides in the microsomal fraction of the liver, the morphine would have less opportunity of being transported unchanged to the mitochondria, which is the site of the oxidation to pseudomorphine. Brain, muscle or kidney might therefore be a more suitable tissue. It is also possible that our extraction method failed to recover the pseudomorphine, which is an extremely insoluble substance.

The concentration of cytochrome c used in our study is not unusually high. Analyses of cytochrome c in various rat tissues (Drabkin, 1950) reveal from 0.38 to 1.94 microgm. per mgm. of tissue. If one assumes the molecular weight of cytochrome c to be 16,000, then these concentrations would be from 0.25 to $1.18 \times 10^{-4}M$. Since cytochrome c is localized in the mitochondria, concentrations there would be considerable higher than this value.

SUMMARY

Morphine, in the presence of cytochrome c, is oxidized by rat tissue homogenates to a compound which is indistinguishable from pseudomorphine by chromatographic analysis. The addition of cytochrome c to these homogenates causes a concomitant fall in glucuronide synthesis. The capacity to oxidize morphine is intimately associated with the cytochrome enzymes. Nalorphine, heterocodeine and dihydromorphinone, compounds having free phenolic hydroxyl groups, are oxidized under similar conditions, codeine is not transformed in this manner. The pharmacological implications of these findings are discussed.

Acknowledgment. The authors wish to express their gratitude to Dr. L. A. Woods for his suggestions during the course of this work and to Mrs. Monica Blumenthal and Dr. L. B. Mellett for assistance in some of the experiments.

REFERENCES

ABOOD, L. G., AND KUN, E.: Fed. Proc., **8:** 270, 1949.
BABEL, A.: Arch. exp. Path. M. Pharmakol., **52:** 262, 1905.
DRABKIN, D. L.: J. Biol. Chem., **182:** 317, 1950.
MARMÉ, W.: Centralbl. F. Klin. Med., **4:** 241, 1883a.
MARMÉ, W.: Deutsche Med. Wchnschr., **9:** 33, 1883b.
SCHMIDT, C. F., AND LIVINGSTON, A. E.: THIS JOURNAL, **47:** 473, 1933.
WANG, R. I. H., AND BAIN, J. A.: THIS JOURNAL, **108:** 354, 1953.
WOODS, J. A., COCHIN, J., FORNEFELD, E. G., AND SEEVERS, M. H.: THIS JOURNAL, **111:** 64, 1954.
WOODS, L. A.: THIS JOURNAL, **112:** 158, 1954.

EFFECTS OF SYMPATHOMIMETIC DRUGS ON PULMONARY CIRCULATION: WITH SPECIAL REFERENCE TO A NEW PULMONARY VASODILATOR[1]

DOMINGO M. AVIADO, Jr. and CARL F. SCHMIDT

With the technical assistance of Sage E. Rosen

Laboratory of Pharmacology, University of Pennsylvania School of Medicine, Philadelphia

Received for publication March 29, 1957

Most of the available information on the pulmonary vascular effects of sympathomimetic amines is limited to epinephrine and levarterenol. There is considerable evidence that both these amines, which are direct constrictors for most systemic vessels, are also vasoconstrictors of the perfused lungs (Daly, 1933; Gaddum and Holtz, 1933; Konzett and Hebb, 1949; Edwards, 1951; Tyrer, 1953; Mikio, 1954; Rose *et al.*, 1955). In the intact animal or human subject they produce pulmonary arterial hypertension; which some investigators attribute to constriction of the lung vessels, because an increase in pulmonary vascular resistance is indicated by the concomitant changes in pulmonary arterial pressure and cardiac output (Jimenez-Vargas and Vidal, 1949; Baxter and Pearce, 1951; Fowler *et al.*, 1951; Bartorelli *et al.*, 1954). Others ascribe the pulmonary arterial hypertension to a primary action of the drug outside of the lung vessels: an increase in cardiac output by stimulation of the heart (Witham and Fleming, 1951), damming of blood in the lungs from a rise in left auricular pressure (Hamilton *et al.*, 1939; Nelson *et al.*, 1955), and shifting of blood from the constricted peripheral vessels to the lungs (Friedberg *et al.*, 1943).

A few scattered observations emphasize the similarities of the other pressor amines to epinephrine and levarterenol. A rise in pulmonary arterial pressure has been described for ephedrine (Nelson *et al.*, 1955), pholedrine (Buhr, 1954), methamphetamine (Cournand, 1947; Ewing *et al.*, 1954; Nelson *et al.*, 1955), mephentermine (Brofman *et al.*, 1952), hydroxyamphetamine (Friedberg *et al.*, 1943), metaraminol (Sarnoff *et al.*, 1954, Livesay *et al.*, 1954; Ewing *et al.*, 1954), and phenylephrine (Horvath and Knapp, 1954). Almost all of these drugs increase cardiac output except phenylephrine, which reduces it. The major cause for pulmonary arterial hypertension produced by this drug apparently is a local vasoconstriction in the lung. Only ephedrine has been tested in the perfused lung, where it elicits vasoconstriction (Sai, 1954).

Isoproterenol and methoxamine are strikingly different from the above mentioned drugs. Isoproterenol, a systemic depressor amine, reduces pulmonary arterial blood pressure (Buhr, 1953) and dilates the perfused lung vessels (Hebb and Konzett, 1949). Methoxamine, a systemic pressor drug, either has no effect on pulmonary arterial pressure (Ewing *et al.*, 1954) or causes a significant reduc-

[1] This study was aided by a grant from the Surgeon General, Department of Defense under contract No. DA-49-007-MD-200, and by a grant from Burroughs-Wellcome & Co. (U. S. A.) Inc.

tion (Aviado, 1957). The difference in effect of methoxamine on systemic and pulmonary blood pressures suggests a difference between the responses of the lung and systemic vessels to this sympathomimetic drug, and this suggestion is borne out by the experiments reported below.

The present study was undertaken to compare the effects of the various sympathomimetics on the lung circulation. The experiments were made on anesthetized dogs with open chests, and included measurements of pulmonary arterial pressure, left auricular pressure, pulmonary blood flow, and pulmonary vascular resistance of both intact and perfused lungs. The derivatives of methoxamine that were synthesized by the Wellcome Research Laboratories have been included in this study (Hjort *et al.*, 1948; Baltzly and Buck, 1940ab; Ardis *et al.*, 1946; Ide and Baltzly, 1948; Baltzly *et al.*, 1950). One such derivative (β-hydroxyl-β-(2,5-diethoxyphenyl) isopropylamine) is interesting because its pulmonary vasodilator action is accompanied by a reduction in pulmonary blood flow and systemic vasoconstriction. This compound (also referred to as 45–50) theoretically fulfills the requirements of an ideal drug for the treatment of burns of the respiratory tract in which there are systemic hypotension, pulmonary hypertension and pulmonary edema (Aviado and Schmidt, 1952).

METHODS. Dogs under morphine (2 mgm./kgm. s.c.) and chloralose (70 mgm./kgm. i.v.) anesthesia were used. The following procedures were routinely performed in all animals: a) cannulation of trachea to allow the use of a Starling Ideal Pump; b) cannulation of femoral vein for drug injection; c) cannulation of femoral artery for recording of systemic blood pressure by the usual mercury manometer or Statham transducer; d) opening of chest in the left fifth intercostal space to allow measurements of pressures (by saline manometers or transducers) in the pulmonary artery and left auricle from glass cannulae or plastic catheters tied into the vessels of the left upper lobe.

The additional procedures consisted of collection of lobar venous outflow (Aviado, Ling and Schmidt, 1957), inflow perfusion of the left lower lobe (Aviado *et al.*, 1952) and complete perfusion of the left lower lobe (Aviado, Ling and Schmidt, 1957). These methods are depicted in figure 1 and are briefly described with their results. Manuronate (10 mgm./kgm. intravenously) was routinely used as the anticoagulant.

Almost all of the commercially available sympathomimetic amines were included in the present study. Their generic names, commercial names and chemical structures are summarized in table 1. The derivatives of methoxamine are also listed in table 1 and are represented by their code numbers.

RESULTS. The sympathomimetic amines that are used clinically because of a desired cardiovascular action were investigated more thoroughly than the others. Such drugs include levarterenol, metaraminol, phenylephrine, hydroxyamphetamine, ephedrine, phenylpropanolamine, methylaminoheptane, methoxamine, methamphetamine, mephentermine, epinephrine and isoproterenol. A prototype of a desirable pulmonary hypotensive drug (compound 45–50) has been similarly investigated. Their effects are summarized in figures 2 to 5 as per cent changes in systemic arterial blood pressure, pulmonary arterial blood pressure, pulmonary venous outflow, vascular resistance of the intact lungs and vascular resistance of the perfused lobe. Each point in the graph represents the maximum change elicited following one injection of the drug (intravenously or directly into the perfused lobe). Since the duration of effects on the lung circulation was not

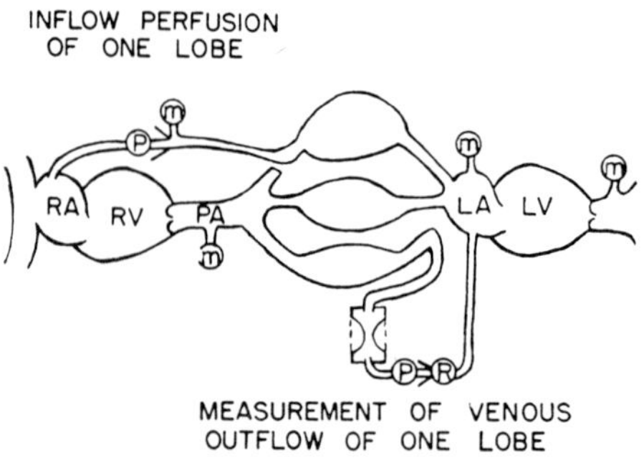

FIG. 1. Inflow and outflow perfusion of left lower lobe.

RA = right auricle; RV = right ventricle; PA = pulmonary artery; LA = left auricle; LV = left ventricle; P = Dale-Schuster pump; M = manometer; R = Shipley-Wilson rotameter. See text for details. Note that both techniques were not utilized in the same dog but were used separately.

longer than three minutes, it was possible to repeat the drug injection and to administer three or more other drugs in the same dog. The testing of more than one drug in the same animal was intentional and allowed comparison. This did not appear to influence the effects of the drug on the pulmonary circulation because the results were similar whether the drug was the first or the subsequent one used.

As far as the systemic blood pressure is concerned, the repetition of a drug injection converted the pressor response to a depressor response for some amines (see figure 2). This did not happen with levarterenol, epinephrine, metaraminol, phenylephrine, methoxamine and compound 45–50.

Pulmonary arterial blood pressure. The most outstanding features of the pulmonary arterial pressure responses to sympathomimetic amines were their variability and their lack of correspondence with the concomitant systemic arterial pressure effects (figure 2). Most of the drugs might cause a rise, a fall or no change of pulmonary blood pressure. The most intense pulmonary hypertensive response (up to 50 per cent increase) was encountered with levarterenol, epinephrine and ephedrine and this was accompanied by an excessively great rise in systemic blood pressure (5 to 100 per cent increase). This was the only correlation encountered between both pressures. For methoxamine and compound 45–50, the rise in systemic pressure was characteristically accompanied by a fall in pulmonary arterial pressure.

The variability of effect of most drugs on pulmonary arterial pressure was accompanied by primary changes in left auricular pressure, pulmonary blood flow and pulmonary vascular resistance. The changes in left auricular pressure were even more variable and did not appear to account for the pulmonary arterial pressure response. The other two measurements offer sufficient explanation and they are described in the succeeding paragraphs.

Pulmonary venous outflow. Because of the various objections to the indirect methods of measuring cardiac output, we decided to measure pulmonary venous outflow by a direct and unequivocal method (see figure 1). A glass cannula was

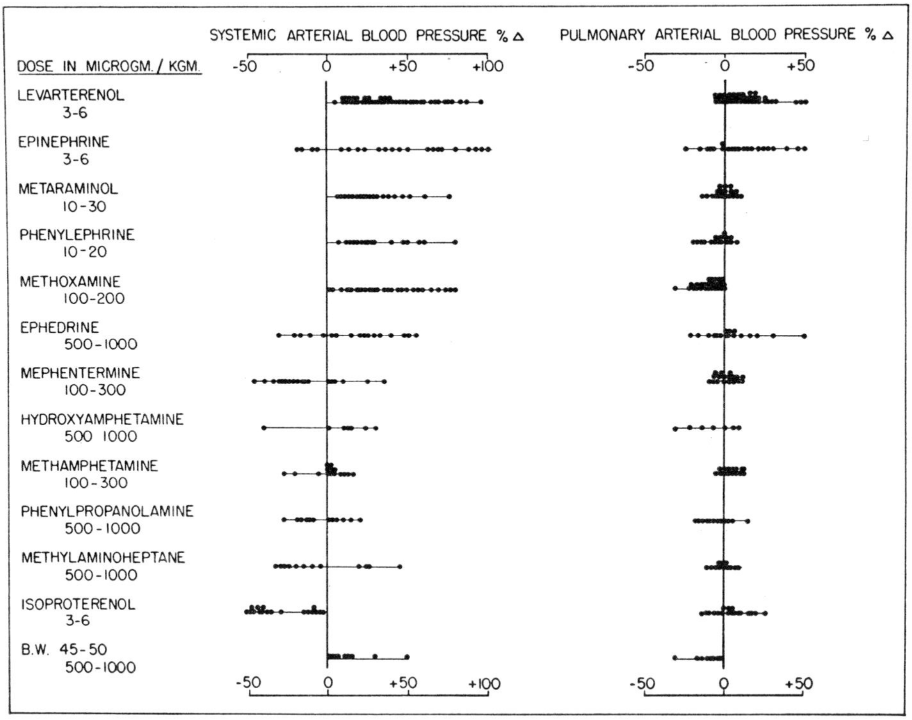

FIG. 2. Effects of intravenous injections on systemic arterial blood pressure and pulmonary arterial blood pressure.

The mean pulmonary pressure ranged from 10 to 25 mm. Hg (in 65 dogs).

inserted into the vein of the left lower lobe. All the effluent blood was collected in a collapsible rubber reservoir at the same horizontal level as the cannula. The blood was instantaneously returned by means of a Dale-Schuster pump to the animal's own left atrium or femoral vein. The pump was set to empty the reservoir continuously so that pressure between the lobar vein and the reservoir was never allowed to increase. A Shipley-Wilson rotameter was inserted into the outflow side of the pump to obtain a graphic recording of the rate of blood flowing from the pulmonary vein. Although the pulmonary venous outflow measured by this method represents only one lobe, we feel that it can be regarded as a reasonable criterion of flow in all lobes and of cardiac output (Aviado, Ling and Schmidt, 1957).

The effects of intravenous injections of the various sympathomimetic amines are summarized in figure 3. The directional change in pulmonary venous outflow brought about by the same drug was dependent on the state of the vagi. Cervical vagotomy was performed to reduce the bradycardia which often accompanies the systemic pressor response (Aviado and Wnuck, 1957). This procedure also altered the response in pulmonary venous outflow to levarterenol, epinephrine, hydroxyamphetamine and methamephetamine, which might either increase or decrease outflow when the vagi were intact but which consistently increased it

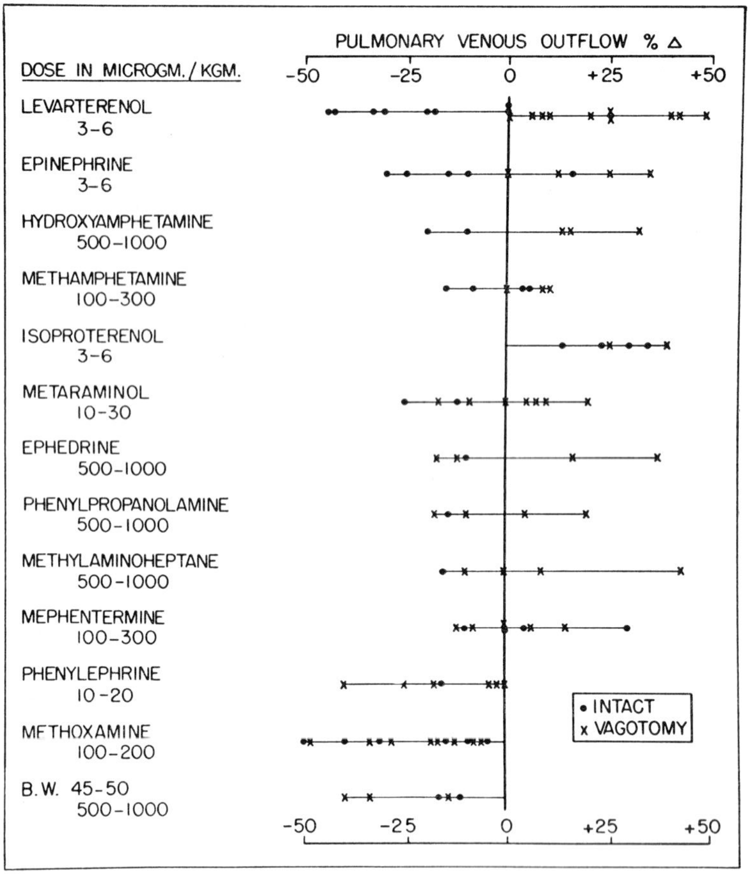

FIG. 3. Effects of intravenous injections on pulmonary venous outflow of left lower lobe. The control values in 35 dogs ranged from 60 to 350 ml./min.

after vagotomy. Metaraminol, ephedrine, phenylpropanolamine, methylaminoheptane and mephentermine continued to have variable effects even after vagotomy. Vagotomy did not alter the reduction in blood flow by methoxamine, phenylephrine and compound 45–50, nor did it alter the increase in blood flow by isoproterenol.

It is thus evident that the cardiac slowing brought about reflexly by systemic hypertension serves to reduce blood flow and to mask a primary increase produced by levarterenol, epinephrine, hydroxyamphetamine and methamphetamine. The identification of other mechanisms (myocardial stimulation or depression, alteration in venous return, *etc.*) involved in the pulmonary vascular effects of such drugs and other amines are currently being investigated. The change in pulmonary venous outflow accounts partly but not entirely for the calculated pulmonary vascular resistance, which is described in the next paragraph.

Pulmonary vascular resistance of intact dogs. This was calculated by dividing pulmonary arterial pressure by pulmonary venous outflow (of the same dogs described above) and expressing the effect of the drug as the per cent change in

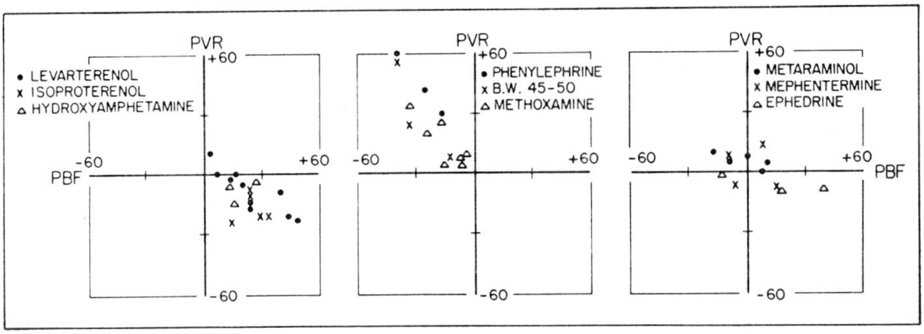

FIG. 4. The pulmonary vascular resistance (PVR) is calculated by dividing pulmonary arterial pressure by the corresponding pulmonary blood flow (PBF).
Such values are included in figures 2 and 3.

this ratio. Some of these changes are represented in figure 4 and they serve to emphasize one general feature of the lung circulation: the calculated vascular resistance can be influenced passively by primary changes in blood flow, *i.e.*, resistance is passively increased by a reduction in flow and *vice versa* (Edwards, 1951; Williams, 1954; Borst *et al.*, 1956; Aviado, Ling and Schmidt, 1957). The sympathomimetic amines that increase pulmonary blood flow when the vagi are cut (levarterenol, isoproterenol and hydroxyamphetamine) are usually accompanied by a reduction in calculated pulmonary vascular resistance. Drugs that reduce flow (phenylephrine, methoxamine, compound 45–50) are accompanied by an increase in resistance. Drugs that have variable effects on blood flow (metaraminol, mephentermine and ephedrine) also have variable effects on resistance. The differences in intensity of change in resistance among the different drugs can be explained by direct constriction or dilatation of the lung vessels by the drug and this will be discussed below under DISCUSSION. Suffice it to mention here that the absolute change in calculated pulmonary vascular resistance of intact dogs usually reflects changes in pulmonary blood flow and is not a good indicator of direct action of the drug on the lung vessels.

Pulmonary vascular resistance of the perfused lobe. The most satisfactory method for investigating local action of a drug on the lung vessels independently of changes in pulmonary blood flow is to perfuse one lobe at a constant flow. This was performed in one of two ways: 1) complete perfusion of the left lower lobe of one dog with mixed venous blood from a donor dog, the outflow from the lobar vein being returned to the donor dog by a second Dale-Schuster pump and 2) inflow perfusion of the left lower lobe without using a donor dog. In method 2, one pump is used to feed mixed venous blood from the animal's own right atrium into the lobar artery but corresponding lobar vein remains intact (see figure 1). The result of intraarterial injection of a drug is seen immediately as a rise in perfusion pressure (indicating vasoconstriction) or a fall (indicating vasodilatation). The response of perfusion pressure is the same whether the drug is not allowed to reach the systemic circulation (method 1) or is allowed to reach it (method 2).

The most powerful pulmonary vasoconstrictors demonstrable in the perfused

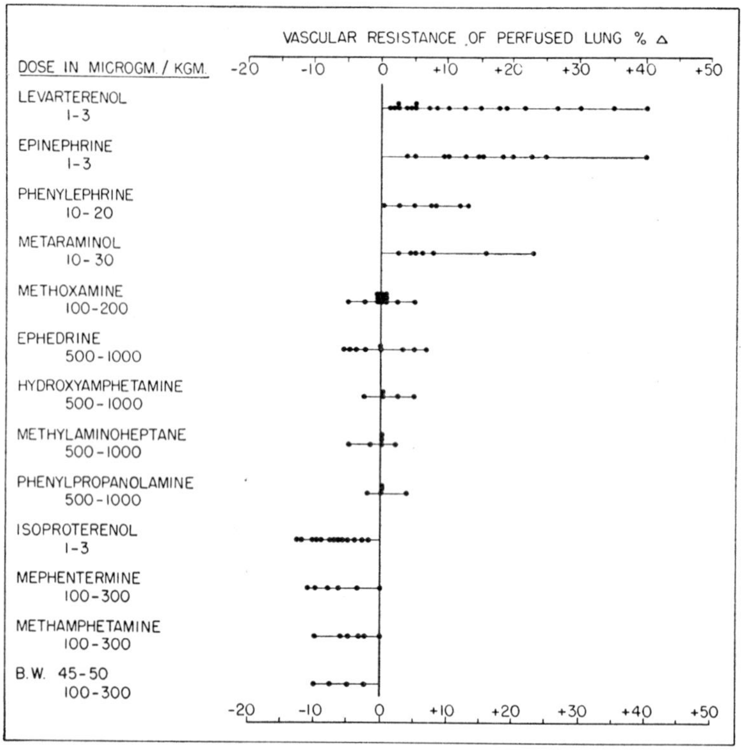

FIG. 5. Effects of intraarterial injections into the perfused lobe. The control perfusion pressures in 30 inflow perfusion and 15 complete perfusion experiments ranged from 20 to 40 mm. Hg.

lung experiments were levarterenol, epinephrine, phenylephrine and metaraminol (see figure 5). Among the pulmonary vasodilators, only isoproterenol equalled the potency of the mentioned drugs. The other vasodilators (mephentermine, methamphentamine and compound 45–50) required much larger doses.

One disappointing feature of the perfused lung experiments was that a number of amines had variable effects. Methoxamine, ephedrine, hydroxyamphetamine, methylaminoheptane and phenylpropanolamine usually had no effect but occasionally constricted or dilated the perfused vessels. The reasons for such variability are not completely known. The accompanying bronchomotor changes (to be reported elsewhere) were not significant and could not have been responsible. One possibility that is being investigated is that the drug might be acting on more than one pulmonary vascular area. Constriction or dilatation may involve the arterioles, capillaries, venules and/or shunts and perfusion may inactivate one or more of these areas.

The sensitivity of the lung vessels as compared to systemic vessels was derived from the inflow experiments (method 2). It was conspicuous that the minimum effective dose injected directly into the left lower lobe affected systemic arterial blood pressure without affecting perfusion pressure. The dose necessary to constrict or dilate the lung vessels was of the order of the usual intravenous systemic pressor dose injected entirely into the left lower lobe. This meant that the intravenous dose that would normally be distributed to all the six lobes had to be entirely injected into the left lower lobe (about one-fourth of the total lung weight) to successfully demonstrate pulmonary vasoconstriction or vasodilatation. This apparent insensitivity of the perfused lobe must be considered in evaluating the results.

Table 1 summarizes the results obtained from the 13 amines that were described in the preceding paragraphs, plus 67 other compounds. The latter group was studied in a limited number of experiments: at least three inflow perfusion experiments to elicit changes in perfused lung resistance (PLR) and at least three venous outflow experiments after cervical vagotomy to elicit changes in pulmonary blood flow (PBF). In both types of experiments, changes in systemic arterial blood pressure were also observed (SBP). The results for each measurement are summarized as: + (increased), − (decreased) or v(variable). An examination of the chemical structure of the 80 compounds permits the following generalizations:

1) *Local pulmonary vasoconstrictors.* The most potent pulmonary vasoconstrictors possess hydroxyl substitutions in the *beta* carbon atom, and in the number 3 and 4 positions of the benzene ring (lines 1 and 2). The reduction of such substitutions to two or one reduces the potency of pulmonary vasoconstriction (lines 3, 4, 10–16). All of these compounds are systemic pressor drugs suggesting that constriction of some systemic vessels is one of their important actions. The two compounds that cause local pulmonary vasoconstriction but systemic depression (lines 9 and 17) are chemically unrelated.

2) *Local pulmonary vasodilatation.* The most potent vasodilator compound possesses isopropyl substitution in the nitrogen atom, plus all the essential substitutions for a potent vasoconstrictor described above (line 45). Most of the other vasodilators contain one or two of the following three substitutions: methyl on nitrogen, (lines 47–54, 59–62, 74); diethoxy in 2 and 5 of the benzene ring (lines 63, 76, 79, 80), mono-methyl, methoxy or ethoxy substitution in 2, 3, 4 or 5 positions of the benzene ring (lines 50, 51, 54, 55, 66, 75). Most of these vasodilators are systemic depressor compounds except 8 of them. Five consistently increase pulmonary blood flow (lines 55 to 59) whereas 3 reduce or have no effect on flow (lines 68, 69, 80). Compound 45–50 (line 80) is one prototype of this group of 8 pulmonary vasodilators that are also systemic pressor agents.

3) *Increased pulmonary blood flow.* Most of the drugs that increase pulmonary blood flow contain one or more hydroxy substitutions in the *beta* carbon, 3 and 4 positions of the benzene ring (lines 1–4, 18, 19, 21, 45, 46). The other compounds that increase pulmonary blood flow have varied chemical structures, probably because the mechanisms for increasing flow are varied.

4) *Decreased pulmonary blood flow.* Most of the compounds that decrease pulmonary blood flow possess hydroxy substitution in the *beta* carbon combined with either of the following substitutions on the benzene ring: 3-OH substitution (lines 13, 43); 2, 5 disubstitutions with methyl, OH, methoxy or ethoxy radicals (lines 14–16, 38–42, 44, 76–80). The other compounds that have a similar action have varied chemical structures, again probably because the mechanisms for decreasing flow are varied.

DISCUSSION. So far, the effects of the sympathomimetic amines on the pulmonary circulation have been described as a group. Each drug will now be considered in detail, following the classification suggested in table 1 of grouping them according to their local pulmonary vascular action.

Sympathomimetic amines that constrict pulmonary vessels. Levarterenol, epinephrine, metaraminol, phenylephrine, tuaminoheptane, epinine and tyramine (see groups A, B and C, table 1)

TABLE 1

*Correlation of chemical structure of sympathomimetic amines to their effects on pulmonary circulation**

(Line No.), Name or compound no.†	Dose *mgm./kgm.*	Chemical structure  —CH—CH—NH					PLR	PBF	SBP
Group *A*. Vasoconstrictor and increased blood flow:									
(1) Levarterenol bitartrate	0.001–0.003	3-OH	4-OH	OH	H	H	+	+	+
(2) Epinephrine	0.001–0.003	3-OH	4-OH	OH	H	CH_3	+	+	+
(3) Epinine	0.05–0.1	3-OH	4-OH	H	H	CH_3	+	+	+
(4) Tyramine	0.2–0.5	4-OH		H	H	H	+	+	+
(5) Tuaminoheptane sulfate*	0.2–0.5	(n-butyl)		H	CH_3	H	+	+	+
(6) 849	0.05–0.1	3,4-diacetoxy		H	H	CH_3	+	+	+
(7) 28	0.2–0.5	3-CH_3O		H	H	CH_3	+	+	v
(8) 648	0.2–0.4	2-C_2H_5O	3-CH_3O	H	H	H	+	+	v
(9) 655	0.2–0.5	2-C_2H_5O	3-CH_3O	H	H	CH_3	+	+	−
Group *B*. Vasoconstrictor and variable or no effect on blood flow:									
(10) Metaraminol bitartrate	0.01–0.03	3-OH		OH	CH_3	H_3	+	v	+
(11) 44–55	0.2–0.5	2-OH	5-CH_3	OH	H	CH_3	+	v	+
(12) 47–26	0.2–0.5	2-OH	5-C_2H_5O	OH	H	H	+	v	v
Group *C*. Vasoconstrictor and decreased blood flow:									
(13) Phenylephrine	0.01–0.02	3-OH		OH	H	CH_3	+	−	+
(14) 45–29	0.2–1.0	2-OH	5-CH_3O	OH	H	H	+	−	+
(15) 45–16	0.5–1.0	2-OH	5-CH_3O	OH	H	CH_3	+	−	+
(16) 992	0.1–0.5	2-OH	5-CH_3O	OH	CH_3	H	+	−	+
(17) 851	0.4–1.0	4-acetoxy		H	H	CH_3	+	−	−
Group *D*. Variable or no effect on lung vessels and increased blood flow:									
(18) Pholedrine sulfate	0.2–0.4	4-OH		H	CH_3	CH_3	v	+	v
(19) Synephrin	0.1–0.2	4-OH		OH	H	CH_3	v	+	v
(20) 646	0.2	3-C_2H_5O		H	H	H	v	+	v
(21) Hydroxyamphetamine hydrobromide	0.5–1.0	4-OH		H	CH_3	H	v	+	v
(22) 37	0.4	3,4-methylenedioxy		H	H	CH_3	v	+	+
(23) 850	0.1–0.2	3,4-dicarbethoxy		H	H	CH_3	v	+	+
(24) 669	0.1–1.0	4-CH_3O		H	H	H	v	+	+
(25) 27	0.1–0.2	2-CH_3O		H	H	CH_3	v	+	−

TABLE 1—*Continued*

(Line No.), Name or compound no.†	Dose *mgm./kgm.*	Chemical structure —CH—CH—NH					PLR	PBF	SBP
Group *E*. Variable or no effect on lung vessels and blood flow:									
(26) Ephedrine sulfate	0.5–1.0			OH	CH_3	CH_3	v	v	v
(27) Amphetamine sulfate	0.1–0.5			H	CH_3	H	v	v	v
(28) Phenylpropanolamine	0.5–1.0			OH	CH_3	H	v	v	v
(29) Phenylethylamine	0.4–1.0			H	H	H	v	v	v
(30) Methylaminoheptane*	0.5–1.0	(n-butyl)		H	CH_3	H	v	v	v
(31) 32	0.2–0.5	4-OH		H	H	CH_3	v	v	v
(32) 827	0.2–0.5	2-CH_3O	5-CH_3O	H	CH_3	H	v	v	v
(33) Naphazoline*	0.05–0.1	2-(l-naphthyl-methyl)imidazoline					v	v	+
(34) 45–2	0.1–1.0	2-CH_3O	5-CH_3	OH	H	H	v	v	+
(35) 36	0.4–1.0	3-CH_3O	4-CH_3O	H	H	CH_3	v	v	+
(36) 902	0.4–1.0	3-CH_3O	4-CH_3O	H	CH_3	H	v	v	+
(37) 828	0.4–1.0	2-CH_3O	5-CH_3O	H	CH_3	CH_3	v	v	−
Group *F*. Variable or no effect on lung vessels and decreased blood flow:									
(38) Methoxamine	0.1–0.2	2-CH_3O	5-CH_3O	OH	CH_3	H	v	−	+
(39) 840	0.1–0.2	2-CH_3O	5-CH_3O	OH	CH_3	CH_3	v	−	+
(40) 819	0.2–1.0	2-CH_3O	5-CH_3O	H	H	H	v	−	+
(41) 832	0.2–0.5	2-CH_3O	5-CH_3O	OH	H	CH_3	v	−	+
(42) 45–15	0.1–0.5	2-OH	5-CH_3	OH	H	H	v	−	+
(43) 31	0.1–0.2	3-OH		H	H	CH_3	v	−	+
(44) 35	0.2–1.0	2-CH_3O	5-CH_3O	H	H	CH_3	v	−	v
Group *G*. Vasodilator and increased blood flow:									
(45) Isoproterenol	0.001–0.003	3-OH	4-OH	OH	H	C_3H_7	−	+	−
(46) Nylidrin	0.01–0.02	4-OH		OH	CH_3	3-phenyl-propyl	−	+	−
(47) 34	0.2–0.4	2-CH_3O	4-CH_3O	H	H	CH_3	−	+	−
(48) Methamphetamine	0.1–0.3			H	CH_3	CH_3	−	+	−
(49) 45	0.2–0.4			H	H	CH_3	−	+	v
(50) 652	0.2–0.4	2-C_2H_5O		H	H	CH_3	−	+	v
(51) 653	0.4–0.5	3-C_2H_5O		H	H	CH_3	−	+	v
(52) 33	0.4	2-CH_3O	3-CH_3O	H	H	CH_3	−	+	v
(53) 995	0.4–0.5	2-OH	5-CH_3	OH	CH_3	CH_3	−	+	v
(54) 29	0.4–1.0	4-CH_3O		H	H	CH_3	−	+	v
(55) 647	0.2–0.4	4-C_2H_5O		H	H	H	−	+	+
(56) 650	0.2–1.0	3-C_2H_5O	4-CH_3O	H	H	H	−	+	+
(57) 671	0.4–1.0	3-CH_3O	4-CH_3O	H	H	H	−	+	+
(58) 670	0.4	2-CH_3O	3-CH_3O	H	H	H	−	+	+
(59) 857	0.1–0.4	3,4-dibenzoyloxy		H	H	CH_3	−	+	+

TABLE 1—*Concluded*

(Line No.), Name or compound no.†	Dose *mgm./kgm.*	Chemical structure —CH—CH—NH					PLR	PBF	SBP
Group H. Vasodilator and variable or no effect on blood flow:									
(60) Mephentermine sulfate*	0.1–0.3			H	$(CH_3)_2$	CH_3	—	v	v
(61) Phenylpropylmethylamine	0.3–0.6			CH_3	H	CH_3	—	v	v
(62) Cyclopentamine*	0.2–0.5	(Cyclopentyl)		H	CH_3	CH_3	—	v	v
(63) 46–100	0.4–1.0	2-C_2H_5O	5-C_2H_5O	OH	H	H	—	v	v
(64) 43–1	0.2–0.5	2-CH_3O	5-CH_3	OH	H	CH_3	—	v	v
(65) 989	0.2–1.0	2-CH_3O	5-CH_3	OH	CH_3	H	—	v	v
(66) 654	0.2–1.0	4-C_2H_5O		H	H	CH_3	—	v	v
(67) 657	0.2–1.0	3-C_2H_5O	4-CH_3O	H	H	CH_3	—	v	v
(68) 46–57	0.2–1.0	2-OH	5-C_2H_5O	OH	H	CH_3	—	v	+
(69) 45–41	0.1–1.0	2-OH	5-CH_3O	OH	CH_3	CH_3	—	v	+
(70) 991	0.2–1.0	2-OH	5-CH_3	OH	CH_3	H	—	v	—
(71) 43–12	0.1–1.0	2-CH_3O	5-CH_3	OH	CH_3	CH_3	—	v	—
(72) 46–82	0.4–1.0	2-CH_3O	6-CH_3O	OH	H	CH_3	—	v	—
(73) 651	0.2–1.0	3-C_2H_5O	4-C_2H_5O	H	H	H	—	v	—
Group I. Vasodilator and decreased blood flow:									
(74) 658	0.2–1.0	3-C_2H_5O	4-C_2H_5O	H	H	CH_3	—	—	—
(75) 50–102	0.2–0.5	2-CH_3O		OH	CH_3	C_3H_7	—	—	—
(76) 46–83	0.2–1.0	2-C_2H_5O	5-C_2H_5O	OH	CH_3	CH_3	—	—	—
(77) 46–105	0.4–1.0	2-OH	5-C_2H_5O	OH	CH_3	CH_3	—	—	—
(78) 46–89	0.4–1.0	2-OH	5-C_2H_5O	OH	CH_3	H	—	—	v
(79) 45–63	0.2–1.0	2-C_2H_5O	5-C_2H_5O	OH	H	CH_3	—	—	v
(80) 45–50	0.1–0.3	2-C_2H_5O	5-C_2H_5O	OH	CH_3	H	—	—	+

* The abbreviations used are explained in the text. The following line numbers do not possess the basic chemical structure of the other compounds: 5, 30, 33, 60 and 62.

† All compounds were used as hydrochloride salts, except where indicated otherwise. The commercial names for some compounds are as follows: (1) Levophed; (5) Tuamine; (10) Aramine; (13) Neosynephrine; (18) Paredrinol; (19) Sympatol; (21) Paredrine; (27) Benzedrine; (28) Propadrine; (30) Oenethyl; (33) Privine; (38) Vasoxyl; (45) Isuprel; (46) Arlidin; (48) Methedrine; (60) Wyamine; (61) Vonedrine; and (62) Clopane.

Epinephrine: The local constrictor action reported here confirms the observations by others utilizing perfused lungs of the dog (Wiggers, 1909; Tribe, 1914; Daly, 1933; Konzett and Hebb, 1949; Edwards, 1951; Mikio, 1954; Rose *et al.*, 1955), cat (Gaddum and Holtz, 1933), rabbit (Beresin, 1914; Braga and Gianni, 1934; Ettinger and Hall, 1935; Suetuna, 1954) and sheep (Tyrer, 1953). The reduction in pulmonary blood flow when the vagi are intact is new but this appears to be not as important as the increase in pulmonary blood flow seen when the vagi are cut. Measurements in human subjects reveal a consistent increase in cardiac output utilizing the direct Fick method (Goldenberg *et al.*, 1948), dye dilution technique (Witham and Fleming, 1951) and ballistocardiography (Starr *et al.*, 1937; Barcroft and Starr, 1951). The fundamental question as to the relative importance of primary alterations in pulmonary blood flow, caliber of lung vessels, shifting of blood from periphery to lungs, *etc.*, remains unanswered because the present experiments have been performed entirely on dogs with open chests. Additional experiments, preferably on unanesthetized dogs, similar to those of Hamilton, Woodbury and Vogt (1939) are necessary to clarify this point.

Levarterenol: The similarities in pattern of action between levarterenol and epinephrine (local pulmonary vasoconstriction and increased pulmonary blood flow after vagotomy) confirm the following similarities observed by others: local pulmonary vasoconstriction (Konzett and Hebb, 1949; Tyrer, 1953; Rose *et al.*, 1955); increased cardiac output in dogs (Delaunois and Vanderberghen, 1954; Fowler *et al.*, 1956); increased force of myocardial contraction (Serin, 1952; Goldberg *et al.*, 1953: Baker, 1953; Hilton, 1955; Cotten *et al.*, 1955). In the human subject, there is indication that cardiac output is reduced by levarterenol but increased by epinephrine (Goldenberg *et al.*, 1948; Fowler *et al.*, 1951; Barcroft and Starr, 1951). The observed rise in pulmonary arterial pressure in humans is probably due to pulmonary vasoconstriction, but this is uncertain in dogs since a rise in pulmonary arterial pressure can be accompanied by a rise in pulmonary blood flow. There was one instance (out of 9 injections of epinephrine represented in figure 4) in which an increase in pulmonary blood flow was accompanied by an increase in pulmonary vascular resistance, indicating that local vasoconstriction can overshadow the passive effect of increase in blood flow.

Tuaminoheptane, epinine and tyramine: The similarities of the pulmonary circulatory effects of these amines to those of epinephrine have not been described previously. Goldberg *et al.* (1953) reported an increase in myocardial contractile force by tuaminoheptane.

Metaraminol: This relatively newer amine has been reported to increase pulmonary arterial blood pressure (Ewing *et al.*, 1954). Alteration in pulmonary blood flow is not a dependable cause for a number of reasons. Cardiac output is either increased (Sarnoff *et al.*, 1954), unchanged (Livesay *et al.*, 1954) or variable (reported above). The calculated pulmonary vascular resistance in the intact dogs (figure 4) and the vascular resistance of the perfused lobe (figure 5) are usually increased. The most important effect of this drug is therefore local pulmonary vasoconstriction.

Phenylephrine: This is one of the most interesting drugs because pulmonary blood flow and vascular resistance are affected in opposite directions. The local pulmonary vasoconstriction described here is new, but the reduction in cardiac output has been previously reported by Horvath and Knapp (1954). With this combination, it is not surprising that the observed response of pulmonary arterial pressure is variable. Likewise, the calculated pulmonary vascular resistance is usually increased (figure 4) but this cannot be interpreted to mean that local vasoconstriction is the major cause because the increased resistance could also be a manifestation of decreased blood flow.

Sympathomimetic amines that have variable or no effect on pulmonary vessels (see groups D, E and F). Hydroxyamphetamine, ephedrine, methoxamine, pholedrine, *synephrin*, *amphetamine*, *phenylpropanolamine*, *methylaminoheptane*, *naphazoline* and *phenylethylamine*. The effects of the last six drugs have not been described previously. The probable reasons for the variability of their local effects have been discussed above (see RESULTS) and do not require further comments.

Hydroxyamphetamine: Its pulmonary arterial hypertensive action was first described in unanesthetized dogs by Friedberg, Katz and Steinitz (1943). Since cardiac output was not measured by them, the mechanism for hypertension was not known. The present experiments indicate that the major cause for the hypertension is the observed increase in pulmonary blood flow and that a local action is unimportant.

Pholedrine: The situation here is like that of hydroxyamphetamine. Buhr (1954) described its pulmonary arterial hypertensive effect which is now explained by an increase in pulmonary blood flow.

Ephedrine: The variable effects on the lung vessels are combined with variable effects on pulmonary venous outflow. The latter is probably related to observations of Walton and Brodie (1949) that ephedrine may increase or decrease myocardial contractile force. The pulmonary hypertensive effect of ephedrine encountered by Nelson *et al.* (1955) in human subjects and by Sai (1954) in the dog heart-lung preparation is difficult to explain because of such variability.

Methoxamine: This is another interesting compound because it is the only commercially available adrenergic drug that causes systemic hypertension but pulmonary hypotension. The major cause for the latter is reduction in pulmonary blood flow which is mostly but not entirely due to cardiac slowing. The reason why the pulmonary hypotensive response was not encountered by Ewing *et al.* (1954) is probably because vagotomized dogs were used. One surprising feature of methoxamine is its local constricting action in almost all systemic vascular beds (unpublished observations) but no or variable effect on the lung vessels. As a pulmonary hypotensive agent, its unpredictable local action is unsatisfactory so that the group of dependable pulmonary vasodilators is more desirable.

Sympathomimetic amines that dilate pulmonary vessels (see groups G, H and I). Isoproterenol, methamphetamine, mephentermine, compound 45–50, *nylidrin*, *cyclopentamine* and *phenylpropylmethylamine*. The information on the pulmonary circulatory effects of the last three compounds is new and will not be discussed any further since their characteristics are similar to those of the other four dilators.

Isoproterenol: The pulmonary dilator action reported above confirms the perfusion experiments of Hebb and Konzett (1949) and of Kadatz (1950). Pulmonary blood flow is increased which also confirms the observations of Kaufman *et al.* (1951) and of Meyers *et al.* (1956). Although only pulmonary hypotension has been described (Buhr, 1953), the above pattern of action (diametrically opposite to that of phenylephrine) does not exclude the occurrence of a rise in pulmonary pressure and this is borne out by the above experiments.

Methamphetamine: The results obtained from this drug are similar to those of isoproterenol, namely, pulmonary vasodilatation and increased pulmonary blood flow. The pulmonary hypertensive action of methamphetamine has been described by several investigators (Cournand, 1947; Ewing *et al.*, 1954; Nelson *et al.*, 1955). When this occurs, the most important cause suggested by the present experiments is increased pulmonary blood flow.

Mephentermine: The available information on this drug is confusing because the reported pulmonary hypertensive effect is accompanied by no significant rise in Fick cardiac output (Brofman *et al.*, 1952). Yet this drug dilates the lung vessels and has variable effects on pulmonary blood flow. Additional experiments are necessary to clarify its effect on intact animals and humans.

Compound 45–50: This prototype of a desirable pulmonary hypotensive drug has the following features: 1) pulmonary vasodilatation, more dependable than methoxamine, 2) reduction in pulmonary blood flow, unlike methamphetamine, and 3) systemic pressure rise, unlike isoproterenol. These actions are the most desirable ones indicated in the drug therapy of burns of the respiratory tract in which there are pulmonary hypertension and edema combined with systemic hypotension. This compound and the other derivatives of methoxamine that are also pulmonary vasodilator and systemic pressor compounds are being tried in experimental lung burns and in other forms of experimental pulmonary hypertension to determine if the results presently obtained in dogs with open chests utilizing perfusion techniques can be repeated in intact dogs with damaged or diseased lungs. One undesirable feature of compound 45–50 is its low potency in dilating the lung vessels as compared to isoproterenol. Synthesis of more potent pulmonary vasodilators can be guided by the structure-activity relationships derived from the present experiments.

SUMMARY

The pulmonary circulatory effects of various sympathomimetic amines were compared in anesthetized dogs with open chests. Measurements of vascular resistance of the perfused lobe and of pulmonary venous outflow in vagotomized animals revealed nine patterns of action: 1) pulmonary vasoconstriction and increased blood flow by levarterenol, epinephrine, tuaminoheptane, epinine and tyramine; 2) vasoconstriction and variable effect on blood flow by metaraminol; 3) vasoconstriction and decreased blood flow by phenylephrine; 4) variable effect on lung vessels and increased blood flow by hydroxyamphetamine, pholedrine and synephrin; 5) variable effect on both lung vessels and blood flow by ephedrine, amphetamine, phenylpropanolamine, methylaminoheptane and naphazoline; 6) variable effect on lung vessels and decreased blood flow by methoxamine; 7) vasodilator and increased blood flow by isoproterenol, nylidrin and methamphetamine; 8) vasodilator and no effect on blood flow by mephentermine, phenylpropylmethylamine and cyclopentamine; and 9) vasodilator and decreased blood flow by compound 45–50 (β-hydroxyl-β(2,5-diethoxyphenyl) isopropylamine). The last compound is a pulmonary hypotensive but systemic hypertensive drug which suggests its suitability for the drug therapy of pulmonary hypertension and systemic hypotension accompanying heat injury to the lungs.

ACKNOWLEDGMENT. The authors are grateful to Dr. John R. Wood, Dr. Edwin J. de Beer, and the other members of the Wellcome Research Laboratories for their advice and for the availability of their compounds. They wish to acknowledge the valuable suggestions and assistance, at various phases of the study, of Drs. Albert H. Niden, Charles Quimby, Richard Matzen, Johnson S. L. Ling, Aldo N. Corbascio and Horacio Estrada.

REFERENCES

ARDIS, A. E., BALTZLY, R., AND SCHOEN, W.: J. Am. Chem. Soc., **68:** 591, 1946.
AVIADO, D. M., JR.: Ann. N. Y. Acad. Sc., **66:** 998, 1957.
AVIADO, D. M., JR., CERLETTI, A., ALANIS, J., BULLE, P. H., AND SCHMIDT, C. F.: Am. J. Physiol., **169:** 460, 1952.
AVIADO, D. M., JR., LING, J. S., AND SCHMIDT, C. F.: Am. J. Physiol., In press, 1957.
AVIADO, D. M., JR., AND SCHMIDT, C. F.: Circulation, **6:** 666, 1952.
AVIADO, D. M., JR., AND WNUCK, A. L.: THIS JOURNAL, **119:** 99, 1957.
BAKER, J. B. E.: J. Physiol., **120:** 122, 1953.
BALTZLY, R., AND BUCK, J. S.: J. Am. Chem. Soc., **62:** 161, 1940a.
BALTZLY, R., AND BUCK, J. S.: J. Am. Chem. Soc., **62:** 164, 1940b.
BALTZLY, R., BUCK, J. S., AND IDE, W. S.: J. Am. Chem. Soc., **72:** 382, 1950.
BARCROFT, H., AND STARR, I.: Clin. Sc., **10:** 295, 1951.
BARTORELLI, C., FOLLI, G., RUMOLO, R., AND AGOSTONI, E.: Cuore e Circolazione, **38:** 65, 1954.
BAXTER, I. G., AND PEARCE, J. W.: J. Physiol., **115:** 410, 1951.
BERESIN, W. J.: Arch. f. d. ges. Physiol., **158:** 219, 1914.
BORST, H. G., MCGREGOR, M., WHITTENBERGER, J. L., AND BERGLUND, E.: Circulation Res., **4:** 393, 1956.
BRAGA, C., AND GIANNI, O.: Riv. di pat. sper., **13:** 75, 1934.
BROFMAN, B. L., HELLERSTEIN, H. K., AND CASKEY, W. H.: Am. Heart J., **44:** 396, 1952.
BUHR, G.: Ztschr. Kreislaufforsch., **42:** 669, 1953.
BUHR, G.: Ztschr. Kreislaufforsch., **43:** 601, 1954.
COTTEN, M. DEV., AND PINCUS, S.: THIS JOURNAL, **114:** 110, 1955.
COURNAND, A.: Bull. New York Acad. Med., **23:** 27, 1947.
DALY, I. DEBURGH: Physiol. Rev., **13:** 149, 1933.
DELAUNOIS, A. L., AND VANDERBERGHEN, C.: Arch. internat. de pharmacodyn. et de therap., **99:** 435, 1954.
EDWARDS, W. S.: Am. J. Physiol., **167:** 756, 1951.
ETTINGER, G. H., AND HALL, G. E.: Quart. J. Exper. Physiol., **25:** 259, 1935.
EWING, P. L., ATKINSON, G., AND SEAGER, L. D.: Federation Proc., **13:** 353, 1954.
FOWLER, N. O., FRANCH, R. H., AND DUCHESNE, E. R.: Circulation, **14:** 937, 1956.
FOWLER, N. O., WESTCOTT, R. N., SCOTT, R. C., AND MCGUIRE, J.: J. Clin. Investigation, **30:** 517, 1951.
FRIEDBERG, L., KATZ, I. N., AND STEINITZ, F. S.: THIS JOURNAL, **77:** 80, 1943.
GADDUM, J. H., AND HOLTZ, P.: J. Physiol., **77:** 139, 1933.
GOLDBERG, L. I., COTTEN, M. DEV., DARBY, T. D., AND HOWELL, E. V.: THIS JOURNAL, **108:** 177, 1953.
GOLDENBERG, M., PINES, K. L., BALDWIN, E. DEF., GREENE, D. G., AND ROH, C. E.: Am. J. Med., **5:** 792, 1948.
HAMILTON, W. F., WOODBURY, R. A., AND VOGT, E.: Am. J. Physiol., **125:** 130, 1939.
HEBB, C. O., AND KONZETT, H.: THIS JOURNAL, **96:** 228, 1949.

HILTON, J. G.: Am. J. Physiol., **180:** 371, 1955.
HJORT, A. M., RANDALL, L. D., AND DE BEER, E. J.: THIS JOURNAL, **92:** 283, 1948.
HORVATH, S. M., AND KNAPP, D. W.: Am. J. Physiol., **178:** 387, 1954.
IDE, W. S., AND BALTZLY, R.: J. Am. Chem. Soc., **70:** 1084, 1948.
JIMINEZ-VARGAS, J., AND VIDAL, SEVILLE, S.: Rev. espan. fisiol., **5:** 19, 1949.
KADATZ, R.: Pfluger's Arch. f. d. ges. Physiol., **252:** 1, 1950.
KAUFMAN, J., IGLAUER, A., AND HERWITZ, G. K.: Am. J. Med., **11:** 442, 1951.
KONZETT, H., AND HEBB, C. O.: Arch. internat. de pharmacodyn. et de therap., **78:** 210, 1949.
LIVESAY, W. R., MOYER, J. H., AND CHAPMAN, D. W.: Am. Heart J., **47:** 745, 1954.
MEYERS, F. H., COLLIER, H. D., AND SCHMITT, G. H.: THIS JOURNAL, **116:** 43, 1956.
MIKIO, S.: Igaku Kenkyuu, **24:** 46, 1954.
NELSON, R. A., MAY, L. G., BENNETT, A., KOBAYASHI, M., AND GREGORY, R.: Am. Heart J., **50:** 172, 1955.
ROSE, J. C., FREIS, E. D., HUFNAGEL, C. A., AND MASSULLO, E. A.: Am. J. Physiol., **182:** 197, 1955.
SAI, Y.: Igaku Kenkyuu, **24:** 165, 1954.
SARNOFF, S. J., CASE, R. B., BERGLUND, E., AND SARNOFF, L. C.: Circulation, **10:** 84, 1954.
SERIN, F.: Acta physiol. Scandinav., **26:** 291, 1952.
STARR, I., GAMBLE, C. J., MARGOLIES, A., DONAL, J. S., JOSEPH, N., AND EAGLE, E.: J. Clin. Investigation, **16:** 799, 1937.
SUETUNA, M.: Igaku Kenkyuu, **24:** 46, 1954.
TRIBE, E. M.: J. Physiol., **48:** 154, 1914.
TYRER, J. H.: Quart. J. Exper. Physiol., **38:** 169, 1953.
WALTON, R. P., AND BRODIE, O. J.: THIS JOURNAL, **96:** 343, 1949.
WIGGERS, C. J.: THIS JOURNAL, **1:** 341, 1909.
WILLIAMS, M. H.: Am. J. Physiol., **179:** 243, 1954.
WITHAM, A. C., AND FLEMING, J. W.: J. Clin. Investigation, **30:** 707, 1951.

ABSORPTION OF DRUGS FROM THE STOMACH I. THE RAT[1]

LEWIS S. SCHANKER, PARKHURST A. SHORE, BERNARD B. BRODIE AND C. ADRIAN M. HOGBEN

Laboratory of Chemical Pharmacology and Laboratory of Kidney and Electrolyte Metabolism, National Heart Institute, National Institutes of Health, Public Health Service, U. S. Department of Health, Education and Welfare, Bethesda, Maryland

Received for publication April 4, 1957

A number of investigations in the past have indicated that the stomach is capable of absorbing drugs. Karel, reviewing gastric absorption in 1948, was able to conclude only that "while the stomach is definitely not an absorptive organ in the same sense as the intestine and cannot be considered of especial importance in supplying the nutritional needs of the organism, its absorptive ability, particularly as regards substances physiologically active in minute quantities, has been grossly underestimated." The available fragmentary evidence does not provide a discernible pattern of absorption nor indicate the extent to which the stomach can absorb drugs.

The secretion of drugs into gastric juice is dependent on their ionization constants (Shore, Brodie and Hogben, 1957). This observation can be explained by postulating a lipoid barrier between plasma and gastric juice which allows passive transfer of drugs in their lipid-soluble unionized form, but not in their lipid-insoluble ionized form. On the basis of this model, a discernible pattern of gastric absorption would be expected; organic acids should be readily absorbed from acidic gastric juice while organic bases should not be appreciably absorbed.

The following report is a quantitative study of the absorption by the rat stomach of a large number of organic acids and bases having widely differing chemical structures, physical properties and pharmacologic activities. The observed rapid absorption of most acidic drugs and absence of absorption of most basic drugs will be interpreted in terms of the lipoid barrier hypothesis and the importance of the ionization constants.

METHODS AND MATERIALS. *Experimental procedure in rats.* Male Sprague-Dawley rats weighing 150 to 220 gm. were fasted for about twenty hours prior to the experiments. Water was given *ad libitum* and coprophagy was prevented by using cages with wide-mesh floors. The stomach was exposed under pentobarbital anesthesia and the cardia ligated. The pylorus was ligated around a short polyvinyl cannula equipped with a stopcock. Care was taken to exclude major blood vessels from the ligatures.

The gastric lumen was washed with saline until the washings were clear and then three times with drug solution warmed to body temperature. The drug solution was either 0.1 *M* HCl, 0.15 *M* NaCl or 0.15 *M* $NaHCO_3$ containing 200 microgm. of drug per ml. The abdominal incision was then closed. Ten ml. of the drug solution were drawn into a syringe and 4 ml. were introduced into the stomach and then withdrawn into the syringe. When this procedure had been repeated several times to insure thorough mixing, four to five ml. of the mixed drug solution (about 2.5 ml. per 100 gm. of body weight) were introduced into the stomach

[1] A preliminary report on this work was presented before the American Society for Pharmacology and Experimental Therapeutics, Charlottesville, Virginia, September 1954.

and the stopcock closed. The solution remaining in the syringe was called the initial solution. The drug solution was withdrawn from the stomach after 1 hour and this was called the final solution.

Phenol red or inulin-C^{14}, which were expected to be unabsorbed, were dissolved in the drug solution to indicate any volume change. After 1 hour, 98 ± 2 per cent of phenol red and 100 ± 2 per cent of inulin were recovered from the stomach whether these "indicators" were dissolved in the HCl, NaCl or $NaHCO_3$ solutions.

The concentrations of the drug and indicator were determined in the initial and final solutions. If C is concentration, the extent of drug absorption, appropriately corrected by the change of concentration of the indicator, is given by the following equation:

$$\text{Per cent absorbed} = 100 - 100\left(\frac{C_{\text{drug final}}}{C_{\text{drug initial}}} \times \frac{C_{\text{indicator initial}}}{C_{\text{indicator final}}}\right).$$

The magnitude of the correction due to dilution of phenol red or inulin was five to ten per cent.

The pH of the 0.1 *M* HCl drug solutions within the stomach remained constant at 1. The initial and final pH values of the $NaHCO_3$ solutions were between 8.0 and 8.3. The initially neutral saline solutions became distinctly acid (pH < 2) after 1 hour within the stomach because of the continuous secretion of acid by the rat stomach (Friedman, 1943).

Aniline secretion into the stomach, during D_2O and salicylic acid absorption, was determined by intravenously injecting 110 mgm. per kgm. of aniline. Fifteen minutes after this injection, the stomach was washed with a 0.1 *M* HCl solution of radioinulin, 10 per cent D_2O and 200 microgm. per ml. of sodium salicylate. The initial solution was obtained from the stomach as described above. The final solution was removed from the stomach at a specified interval. The difference in concentration of aniline between the final and initial solutions removed from the stomach was multiplied by the mean fluid volume within the stomach to give the amount of aniline secreted into the stomach. The mean plasma aniline concentration was approximated by correcting the terminal concentration for the rate of decline of plasma aniline, 15 per cent per 10 minutes.

Except where specified, ± will signify the range of values. No correction was made for body weight; inspection of the data did not suggest any bias attributable to this source.

Analytical methods. All spectrophotometric analyses were performed with a Beckman DU spectrophotometer.

A. Aniline, *m*-nitroaniline, *p*-toluidine and procaine amide ethobromide: A 0.1-ml. aliquot of the gastric solution containing 15 to 20 microgm. of the drug was diluted to 5 ml. with 0.1 *N* HCl and the drug determined by the Bratton and Marshall method (1939). Plasma aniline was determined according to the method of Brodie and Axelrod (1948).

B. Mecamylamine (3-methylaminoisocamphane): Five-tenths ml. of 2.5 *N* NaOH and 15 ml. of benzene[2] containing 1.5 per cent isoamyl alcohol[2] were added to a 1-ml. aqueous sample containing 5 to 50 microgm. of drug. The mixture was shaken for 15 minutes and then centrifuged. A 10-ml. aliquot of the benzene phase was shaken with 0.6 ml. of methyl orange reagent[3] for 5 minutes and the mixture was then centrifuged. Five ml. of the benzene phase were then transferred to a test tube containing 1 ml. of 2 per cent H_2SO_4 in absolute ethanol and optical density determined at 540 mμ. Standards were run concurrently with the unknown samples and the optical densities were proportional to concentration. An optical density of about 0.150 was obtained when 15 microgm. of mecamylamine hydrochloride were assayed by this procedure.

---

[2] The solvents were purified by successive washings with 1 *N* NaOH, 1 *N* HCl and two washings with water.

[3] A stock solution of methyl orange reagent is made by dissolving 500 mgm. of methyl orange in 100 ml. of warm water. The solution is washed several times with chloroform. An aliquot of the resulting solution is diluted with an equal volume of saturated boric acid solution immediately before use.

C. Salicylic acid, benzoic acid and 5-nitrosalicylic acid: One-tenth ml. of concentrated HCl and 20 ml. of chloroform[2] were added to a 1- to 2-ml. aqueous sample of the drug. The mixture was shaken for 15 minutes and then centrifuged. A 15-ml. aliquot of the chloroform phase was shaken with 3 ml. of 0.1 *N* NaOH for 10 minutes. Two ml. of the aqueous phase were added to 1 ml. of 0.5 *N* HCl and the optical density of the resulting solution was determined at 300 mμ for salicylic acid, 273 mμ for benzoic acid or 310 mμ for 5-nitrosalicylic acid. Each drug was recovered with satisfactory precision: salicylate, 96 ± 3 per cent; benzoate 98 ± 3 per cent; 5-nitrosalicylate, 96 ± 3 per cent.

D. Acetylsalicylic acid or mixtures of acetylsalicylic acid and salicylic acid: Acetylsalicylic acid or mixtures of acetylsalicylic acid and salicylic acid were extracted into chloroform as described above for salicylic acid. The drugs were returned to an aqueous phase by shaking 15 ml. of this chloroform phase with 5 ml. of phosphate buffer (0.2 *M* Na_2HPO_4, pH 6.7) for 10 minutes. This buffer was chosen because acetylsalicylic acid would be rapidly hydrolyzed in an alkaline solution. Three ml. of the buffer phase were then added to 0.1 ml. of concentrated HCl and the optical density of the resulting solution was determined at 277 mμ and at 300 mμ. Since the ultraviolet absorption of acetylsalicylic acid at 300 mμ is negligible (less than 0.030 optical density at a concentration of 70 microgm. per ml.), the reading at 300 mμ is due to salicylic acid only. The corresponding optical density for salicylic acid at 277 mμ is read from a standard curve and is subtracted from the determined optical density at 277 mμ to give the value for acetylsalicylic acid alone. Recoveries of acetylsalicylic acid and salicylic acid from mixtures of the two were satisfactory: acetylsalicylic acid, 95 ± 3 per cent; salicylic acid, 96 ± 3 per cent.

E. 5-Sulfosalicylic acid: Aliquots of gastric solutions containing 5-sulfosalicylic acid were diluted with 20 to 30 volumes of 0.1 *N* HCl and the optical densities determined at 300 mμ. The blank due to biological material was negligible at these dilutions.

F. Phenol red: Samples of the gastric solution containing phenol red were appropriately diluted with 1 *N* NaOH and their optical densities determined at 550 mμ.

G. Isotopes: The Na^{22} content of liquid samples containing both radiosodium and radiochloride was measured with a well-type scintillation counter employing a glass vial thick enough to absorb Cl^{36} *beta* particles. These samples were then dried on planchets and counted with a thin window Geiger-Müller tube. The concentration of Na^{22} was subtracted from the total count measured by the Geiger-Müller tube to give the Cl^{36} content. The C^{14}-labeled materials, inulin and phenol, were measured by the liquid counting technique of Cotlove (1955). Total counts, several times background, exceeded 10,000 and the principle source of error was sample preparation (±2 per cent or less). Deuterium oxide samples were measured at the National Bureau of Standards (Broida *et al.*, 1954).[4]

H. Previously described methods: The following compounds were analyzed by previously described methods: *p*-hydroxypropiophenone (Shore *et al.*, 1957); acetanilide (Brodie and Axelrod, 1948); antipyrine (Brodie *et al.*, 1949); aminopyrine (Brodie and Axelrod, 1950); quinine (Josephson *et al.*, 1947); dextrorphan and levorphan (*d* and *l*-Dromoran) (Shore *et al.*, 1955); tolazoline (benzazoline, Priscoline) (Brodie *et al.*, 1952); thiopental (Brodie *et al.*, 1950); barbital and secobarbital (Goldbaum, 1948); caffeine (Axelrod and Reichenthal, 1953); tetraethylammonium (Mitchell and Clark, 1952); mepiperphenidol (Darstine) (Tillson *et al.*, 1954); *d*-α-acetylmethadol (Sung and Way, 1954); ephedrine (Axelrod, 1953); ethanol (Bucher and Rodetski, 1951).

Dissociation constants. The dissociation constants for mecamylamine and caffeine were determined by distribution between an organic solvent and 0.1 *M* aqueous buffers of various hydrogen ion concentrations as described by Butler (1953). Microtitration in 0.1 *M* saline was used for 5-nitrosalicylic acid and α-acetylmethadol. The spectrophotometric method of Flexser *et al.* (1935) was used for secobarbital. The following dissociation con-

[4] The authors wish to express their appreciation to Dr. Herbert Broida and Mrs. Margaret W. Chapman of the National Bureau of Standards for their invaluable help in the analysis of deuterium oxide.

stants, determined in aqueous media, have been previously reported: aminopyrine, levorphan, acetanilide, quinine, antipyrine, thiopental, barbital, *p*-hydroxypropiophenone, tolazoline and salicylic acid (Shore *et al.*, 1957); benzoic acid, phenol, *m*-nitroaniline, aniline and *p*-toluidine (Vandenbelt *et al.*, 1954); ephedrine (Leffler *et al.*, 1951); acetylsalicylic acid (Edwards, 1950). All values are expressed as pKa.

The pKa of phenolsulfonphthalein (phenol red) is usually accepted in biological literature as 7.9. However, White and Acree (1919) clearly demonstrated that this compound, like other sulfonic acids, is a very strong acid. That is, phenolsulfonphthalein has a pKa_1 below 1.0 due to the strong sulfonic acid group; it also has a secondary pKa of 7.9 which is associated with the weak phenolic group. Therefore, phenolsulfonphthalein is almost completely ionized in solutions having a pH of 1.0 or above.

In vitro incubation. The entire stomach of a fasted, anesthetized rat was excised, split open along the greater curvature, weighed and incubated with 5 ml. of Krebs-Henseleit Ringer's bicarbonate solution containing 1 mgm. of drug. The incubation was carried out in a Dubnoff metabolic shaker for 1 hour at 37°C. in an atmosphere of 5 per cent CO_2-95 per cent O_2. Aliquots of the solution were analyzed for drug at zero time and after 1 hour of incubation. At the end of some experiments, the incubated stomach was homogenized and analyzed for drug content.

RESULTS. *Absorption from an acidic medium.* The gastric absorption of organic acids during one hour is shown in table 1. It is evident that, with the exception of barbital, those acids having pKa values greater than 2 were generally well absorbed (30 to 61 per cent) from 0.1 *M* HCl. On the other hand, the strong sulfonic acids, phenolsulfonphthalein and 5-sulfosalicylic acid, were not absorbed from this strongly acidic solution.

The gastric absorption values for organic bases are shown in table 2. All bases having pKa's greater than 2.5 were very poorly absorbed from 0.1 *M* HCl, the values being 0 to 7 per cent. Very weak bases (pKa < 2.5), however, were absorbed to the extent of 14 to 36 per cent, the weakest base having the largest absorption value.

TABLE 1

Absorption of organic acids from the rat stomach

The per cent absorbed in one hour is expressed as the mean ± the range followed by the number of experiments in parentheses.

Acid	pKa	Per cent absorbed in 1 hour		
		0.1 *M* HCl	Saline	$NaHCO_3$, pH 8
5-Sulfosalicylic	(strong)	0 ± 0 (2)	—	0 ± 0 (2)
Phenolsulfonphthalein	(strong)	2 ± 2 (3)	2 ± 1 (2)	2 ± 1 (2)
5-Nitrosalicylic	2.3	52 ± 3 (2)	—	16 ± 2 (2)
Salicylic	3.0	61 ± 7 (4)	35 ± 5 (4)	13 ± 1 (2)
Acetylsalicylic	3.5	35 ± 4 (3)	25 ± 2 (3)	—
Benzoic	4.2	55 ± 3 (2)	48 ± 3 (2)	—
Thiopental	7.6	46 ± 3 (2)	—	34 ± 2 (2)
p-Hydroxypropiophenone	7.8	55 ± 3 (2)	—	—
Barbital	7.8	4 ± 3 (4)	4 ± 3 (4)	—
Secobarbital	7.9	30 ± 2 (2)	—	—
Phenol	9.9	40 ± 5 (3)	—	40 ± 5 (3)

TABLE 2

Absorption of organic bases from the rat stomach

The per cent absorbed in one hour is expressed as the mean ± the range followed by the number of experiments in parentheses.

Base	pKa	Per cent absorbed in 1 hour		
		0.1 *M* HCl	Saline	$NaHCO_3$, pH 8
Acetanilide	0.3	36 ± 3 (2)	—	—
Caffeine	0.8	24 ± 3 (2)	—	—
Antipyrine	1.4	14 ± 3 (4)	22 ± 1 (2)	—
m-Nitroaniline	2.5	17 ± 0 (2)	—	—
Aniline	4.6	6 ± 4 (3)	12 ± 3 (2)	56 ± 3 (2)
Aminopyrine	5.0	2 ± 2 (3)	18 ± 3 (2)	—
p-Toluidine	5.3	0 ± 0 (2)	—	47 ± 4 (2)
α-Acetylmethadol	8.3	0 ± 0 (4)	—	—
Quinine	8.4	0 ± 0 (2)	7 ± 2 (2)	18 ± 2 (2)
Dextrorphan, Levorphan	9.2	0 ± 2 (8)	—	16 ± 1 (2)
Ephedrine	9.6	3 ± 3 (2)	—	—
Tolazoline	10.3	7 ± 2 (4)	—	—
Mecamylamine	11.2	0 ± 0 (2)	—	—
Darstine	(strong)	0 ± 0 (2)	3 ± 1 (2)	—
Procaine amide ethobromide	(strong)	0 ± 0 (2)	—	5 ± 1 (2)
Tetraethylammonium	(strong)	0 ± 1 (2)	—	—

Some early experiments indicated absorption of acetylmethadol and dextrorphan. These results have been omitted from table 2 because they could not be confirmed.

Absorption from an alkaline medium. The above results suggest that the unionized form of a drug is being absorbed. Because acidic drugs would be less unionized and basic drugs more unionized in an alkaline solution, absorption was measured from a $NaHCO_3$ solution. When acidic drugs having pKa values below 8 were dissolved in 0.15 *M* bicarbonate, absorption was significantly less than when they were dissolved in HCl (table 1). The depression was greatest for the stronger acids such as salicylic and 5-nitrosalicylic where the values dropped from 61 to 13 and from 52 to 16 per cent respectively. Depression of absorption was less marked for thiopental (pKa 7.6) and was not apparent at all in the case of phenol (pKa 9.9).

A marked increase in absorption was observed when bases were dissolved in the bicarbonate solution (table 2). This increase was greatest for the weaker bases such as aniline and *p*-toluidine where the absorption values rose from 6 to 56 and from 0 to 47 per cent respectively. The change in absorption was less marked for stronger bases such as quinine (pKa 8.4) and dextrorphan (pKa 9.2) whose values rose from 0 to about 17 per cent. The very strong base, procaine amide ethobromide, exhibited little if any increase in absorption.

Absorption from saline. When acidic and basic drugs were dissolved in normal saline, their absorption values were intermediate between those observed with the acidic and alkaline media (tables 1 and 2).

The pH of the saline solution, though initially near to neutral, became distinctly acid (pH < 2) after one hour within the stomach, but the rate at which the pH declined was certainly variable. Thus absorption in these experiments occurred from a solution whose pH, though poorly defined, was intermediate between the extremes of pH of the other experiments.

Absorption related to concentration. All absorption values shown in tables 1 and 2 were obtained using a concentration of 200 microgm. per ml. of drug. Several drugs were also studied at other concentrations: aminopyrine, 1000; antipyrine, 2000; barbital, 1000; dextrorphan, 400; salicylic acid, 100; secobarbital, 50; thiopental, 20 microgm. per ml. The per cent absorption of these drugs at the designated concentrations was the same as that observed at a concentration of 200 microgm. per ml. Since the per cent absorbed was constant, the absolute quantity of the drug absorbed was proportional to the concentration.

Absorption related to lipid solubility. Because the three barbituric acids are members of a homologous series, their relative rates of absorption have been compared to the lipid:water partition of their undissociated forms. The distribution of each acid between 0.1 *M* HCl and two lipid solvents, chloroform and heptane, is given in table 3. For this homologous series, there is a correlation between absorption and lipid solubility.

Absorption of one drug in the presence of another. In order to determine whether or not very high or very low absorption values were attributable to mucosal damage by the drug or to local vascular effects, a series of experiments was performed in which two drugs were studied simultaneously. If rapid absorption were due to mucosal damage, a poorly absorbed drug would be well absorbed in the presence of a rapidly absorbed drug. Conversely, if poor absorption resulted from local ischemia, a rapidly absorbed drug would be less well absorbed in the presence of a poorly absorbed drug. The data of table 4 clearly indicate that the presence of one drug had no significant effect on the absorption of the other, each being absorbed to its usual extent.

In vitro observations. Two techniques have been commonly employed to investigate gastric absorption. The determination of absorption by appearance of material in plasma is complicated by the intricate kinetics of disposition within the body. Determining the disappearance of a drug from the gastric lumen, the technique employed in this investigation, gives a direct measure of absorption provided that degradation and adsorption of the drug are negligible.

Metabolic degradation and adsorption were investigated *in vitro*. All drugs listed in tables 1 and 2 having absorption values greater than 5 per cent were incubated with the entire rat stomach for 1 hour. The concentration of all drugs, except aniline and *m*-nitroaniline[5], decreased by 9 to 13 per cent which is less than that expected from dilution in the water content of the stomach wall. Thus

[5] The following observations are not especially pertinent to this study of gastric absorption but they are of interest. The concentration of aniline and *m*-nitroaniline in the stomach wall, after incubation, was about twice that of the bathing solution. The total recovery of these drugs from the incubated stomach and the bathing solution was 95 per cent. The isolated frog stomach preferentially accumulates aniline as well as some other bases from the solution which bathes its serosal surface (Hogben, unpublished observations). During absorption *in vivo*, such an accumulation of drug within the epithelium would be restricted by the low plasma concentration of the drug.

determining drug absorption by disappearance from the gastric lumen is a valid technique.

Gastric blood flow during absorption. The possibility that gastric blood flow might limit those rates of absorption which are most rapid was examined by simultaneously comparing the absorption of D_2O and salicylic acid from the stomach with the secretion of aniline into the stomach. The results are presented in table 5. After aniline had been injected intravenously, the 0.1 *M* HCl solution of D_2O, salicylic acid and radioinulin was introduced into the stomach. In these experiments, the absorption period and the volume introduced into the stomach were varied as indicated. The mean per cent absorption of D_2O and salicylic acid was respectively 33 and 30 in 20 minutes and 48 and 45 in 40 to 50 minutes.

In order to undertake a comparison of absorption and secretion, it is desirable to express the results in terms of clearance. The amount of aniline which is secreted into the stomach (microgm. per hr.) divided by the mean plasma concentration (microgm. per ml.) is the gastric clearance of aniline (ml. per hr.). Aniline clearance must represent the minimal gastric mucosal blood flow and may be a very close estimate (Shore *et al.*, 1957).

In order to calculate the rate of absorption as a clearance, it is necessary to correct for the change of concentration that occurs during absorption. This correction is applied in the following equation:[6]

$$\text{Clearance} = \frac{\text{Volume}}{\text{time}} \cdot \ln\left(\frac{\text{initial concentration}}{\text{final concentration}}\right).$$

The clearances of D_2O and salicylic acid were calculated using the mean volumes within the stomach and the concentration changes corrected for radioinulin dilution.

Clearly blood flow plays only a minor role in limiting absorption as the gastric mucosal blood flow is at least 10 times greater than the most rapid rate of absorption that we have observed (table 5).

[6] The following assumptions can be applied to gastric absorption (Berggren and Goldberg, 1940). The rate of absorption is proportional to the concentration gradient across the mucosa. During most of the period of absorption, the plasma concentration will be insignificant. Then, the amount disappearing from the stomach, $\frac{dc}{dt} \cdot V$, will be proportional to the concentration within the stomach, or

$$-\frac{dc}{dt} \cdot V = \alpha \cdot c$$

where c = concentration, t = time, V = volume and α is the proportionality constant or the clearance factor. On integration this yields:

$$\ln c = -\frac{t}{V}\alpha + k$$

The integration constant, k, can be substituted using c = initial c at t = 0 to give the equation presented in the text. This equation should be considered only a good working approximation. Integration of diffusion equations are usually more complex, *e.g.* for diffusion out of a sphere.

TABLE 3

Comparison between gastric absorption of barbiturates and lipid:water partition of the undissociated barbiturates

Each compound was distributed between equal volumes of 0.1 *M* HCl and an organic solvent. The concentration of barbiturate in the organic phase divided by the concentration of barbiturate in the aqueous phase is expressed as K.

Barbiturate	pKa	Per cent absorbed from 0.1 *M* HCl	$K_{chloroform}$	$K_{heptane}$
Barbital	7.8	4	0.7	<0.001
Secobarbital	7.9	30	23.3	0.10
Thiopental	7.6	46	>100.0	3.30

TABLE 4

Gastric absorption of one drug in the presence of a second drug

Drug 1	Drug 2	Per cent absorbed from 0.1 *M* HCl in 1 hour			
		Drug 1		Drug 2	
		Alone	In presence of drug 2	Alone	In presence of drug 1
Dextrorphan	Phenol	0	0	40	38
Dextrorphan	5-Nitrosalicylic acid	0	0	52	55
Phenol	Acetylmethadol	40	40	0	0
Acetylsalicylic acid	Salicylic acid	35	38	61	60
Aniline	Salicylic acid	6	0	61	53

TABLE 5

Relative gastric clearance of aniline, deuterium oxide and salicylic acid by the rat

The absorption from the stomach of D_2O and salicylic acid and the secretion of aniline into the stomach were measured simultaneously. These results have been expressed as clearance. The procedure for calculating clearance is given in the text.

Rat	Weight	Time interval	Volume recovered	Inulin ratio $\frac{\text{final}}{\text{initial}}$	Terminal plasma aniline	Clearance *ml. per hour*		
						D_2O	Salicylic acid	Aniline
	gm.	*min.*	*ml.*		*microgm. per ml.*			
1	276	20	3.8	0.96	94	5.3	4.7	70
2	244	20	4.3	0.96	86	4.1	3.0	59
3	233	20	3.8	0.94	85	4.7	4.5	78
4	282	40	7.6	0.94	66	8.4	6.5	98
5	246	40	6.8	0.94	67	5.3	6.2	63
6	235	50	6.8	0.96	60	5.2	4.7	78
Mean	253					5.5	4.9	74

Absorption of other substances. For comparative purposes, gastric absorption was determined for several materials that are not weak electrolytes. Ethanol, in a concentration of 200 microgm. per ml., was absorbed from 0.1 *M* HCl to the extent of 25 ± 2 per cent in 2 animals. The unidirectional movement, *i.e.* flux, from gastric lumen to blood was determined for water, sodium and chloride by measuring the disappearance of the respective isotopes from the gastric lumen during 1 hour. A normal saline solution of D_2O, 10 per cent by volume, lost heavy water to the extent of 61 $\pm$ 2 per cent in 2 animals whose mean weight was 116 gm. The change of concentration of Na^{22} and Cl^{36} was determined with the isotopes incorporated in a solution having an ionic composition of Na^+ 1 *mM*, Cl^- 101 *mM* and H^+ 100 *mM*. Phenol red was used as the dilution indicator. In 10 animals, mean weight 154 $\pm$ 7 gm., the per cent decrease in concentration of Na^{22} was 2.2 per cent $\pm$ 1.3 (standard error of mean). Cl^{36} disappeared to the extent of 14.4 per cent $\pm$ 2.7 (standard error of mean) in 6 animals whose mean weight was 160 $\pm$ 12 gm.

Discussion. The absorption of drugs by the rat stomach is recognizably determined by the pKa of the drug. The relative concentrations of the undissociated and the dissociated forms of a drug are given by the Henderson-Hasselbach equation:

$$pH = pKa + \log \frac{[\text{unionized basic drug}]}{[\text{ionized basic drug}]}$$

$$pH = pKa + \log \frac{[\text{ionized acidic drug}]}{[\text{unionized acidic drug}]}.$$

The rapid absorption from an acidic medium of those acids whose pKa is greater than 2, the absence of absorption of two very strong acids and the negligible absorption of all bases except those that are very weak (pKa $<$ 2.5), are clearly consistent with the hypothesis that the gastric mucosa is selectively permeable to the undissociated form of a drug. When the pH of the gastric lumen was 1.0, appreciable absorption only occurred if a drug was largely undissociated.

The concept of the gastric mucosa as a barrier selectively permeable to the undissociated form of a drug was formulated by Travell in 1940. She was able to show that absorption of a base such as strychnine would occur from an alkaline solution while absorption was difficult to demonstrate from the normally acid contents of the stomach. Previously, Bradley *et al.*, (1936) had found that the absorption of salicylic and acetylsalicylic acids from the dog stomach was greatest at lower pH values.

If the gastric mucosa were selectively permeable to the undissociated drug, increasing the pH within the gastric lumen should depress absorption of an acid and facilitate absorption of a base. The contrast between absorption from solutions of pH 1 and 8 confirms this expectation. Absorption from initially neutral saline was intermediate between absorption at these two extremes of pH.

We have assumed that gastric absorption of drugs is simply a matter of passive diffusion of the unionized moiety. If this were so, absorption should be proportional to concentration, or the per cent absorbed independent of concentration. In those instances where absorption was measured at two different concentrations, the per cent absorbed did not change. Thus, it is not necessary to postulate specific transport mechanisms to account for the gastric absorption of drugs.

The evidence considered so far supports only the contention that the gastric mucosa is selectively permeable to undissociated weak electrolytes. We would like to go further and suggest that this selective permeability is attributable to a lipoid character of the gastric membrane. The striking difference in absorption of the three barbituric acids correlates with their lipid:water partition coefficients. The only exception encountered to a generalization that all but the strongest acids are rapidly absorbed is barbital. Its poor absorption can be explained by its lipid insolubility. Ethanol is absorbed significantly more slowly than most of the weak acids even though it has a smaller molecular volume. This can be attributed to the more polar nature of ethanol. Thus, the gastric absorptive surface is similar to many other biological membranes which are considered to have a lipoid structure (Höber, 1945).

The pH at the interface across which absorption occurs is well defined when the pH of the bulk solution within ths stomach is one. When the bulk solution is less acid, the pH within the tubules of the gastric mucosa will be poorly defined due to the continuous secretion of acid by the rat stomach (Friedman, 1943). Consequently, when the pH of the solution within the stomach is varied, the rate of drug absorption will not be quantitatively proportional to the concentration of the unionized moiety in this solution. This is illustrated by a salicylic acid absorption of 61 per cent from HCl and 13 per cent from $NaHCO_3$ despite a 10^5 difference in the concentration of unionized salicylic acid.

While the predominantly lipoid character of the gastric mucosa is most important for drug absorption, the gastric mucosa is not an exception to Collander and Bärlund's lipoid-sieve model of cell membranes. The observed rapid rate of deuterium oxide movement can be attributed to small holes, not much larger than the diameter of the water molecule, which puncture the much more extensive lipoid area. Such aqueous pores would account for the slow escape of radiosodium and the disappearance of radiochloride from the gastric cavity, though chloride also moves by active transport (Hogben, 1955). The passage of larger organic ions through narrow pores would occur at a much slower rate and our present technique did not demonstrate absorption of either very strong acids or bases which are essentially completely ionized. This relative impermeability to organic ions is also confirmed by the concentration of drugs secreted into gastric juice (Shore *et al.*, 1957).

Finally, it is pertinent to consider the upper limit of absorption exhibited by D_2O and many of the weak acids, namely 50 to 60 per cent from 5 ml. in one hour. One of the following factors must impose this limit on absorption: the restraint imposed by the mucosa; the rate of gastric mucosal blood flow; or diffusion within the lumen. The experiments contrasting clearance of D_2O, salicylic acid and aniline clearly indicate that gastric mucosal blood flow is not the limiting step.[7] Until more is known, it is necessary to consider that the highest rates of

[7] The gastric absorption of D_2O by the dog and the human subject is apparently not blood-flow limited. The clearance of D_2O by the canine gastric pouch approximates the rate of gastric juice secretion (Cope *et al.*, 1943) but the clearance of aniline into the stomach is forty times greater (Shore *et al.*, 1957). The human D_2O clearance is not much more rapid than the normal maximum secretory rate (Hogben *et al.*, 1957) while the basic dye neutral red is much more concentrated in gastric juice than it is in plasma (Kolm *et al.*, 1945).

absorption obtained in this study may be only an indication of diffusion and mixing within the stomach lumen and that the gastric epithelium is no longer the limiting factor.

The rat stomach is recognizably different from the human or dog stomach in at least one important respect. The proximal third of the rat stomach is lined not by typical gastric mucosa but by keratinized squamous epithelium. In spite of this anatomical difference, absorption from the rat stomach is both qualitatively and quantitatively similar to absorption from the human stomach (Hogben *et al.*, 1957).

SUMMARY

When gastric contents are acid, the rat stomach rapidly absorbs most acidic drugs. In contrast, all but the very weakest basic drugs are poorly absorbed. When gastric contents are alkaline, absorption of acidic drugs is impeded and that of basic drugs facilitated. These observations have been presented in terms of the hypothesis that the gastric mucosa is predominantly a lipoid barrier. Gastric absorption of drugs can be explained by the diffusion of the unionized form of a weak electrolyte across such a barrier.

The unionized forms of drugs traverse the mucosa at rates approaching deuterium oxide movement and usually more rapidly than ethanol.

Rapid absorption by the stomach is not limited by gastric mucosal blood flow. When absorption is rapid, diffusion and mixing within the gastric lumen may become the limiting factors.

REFERENCES

Axelrod, J.: This Journal, **109:** 62, 1953.
Axelrod, J., and Reichenthal, J.: This Journal, **107:** 519, 1953.
Berggren, S. M., and Goldberg, L.: Acta Physiol. Scand., **1:** 246, 1940.
Bradley, W. B., Schnedorf, J. G., and Ivy, A. C.: Am. J. Digest. Dis., **3:** 415, 1936.
Bratton, A. C., and Marshall, Jr., E. K.: J. Biol. Chem., **128:** 537, 1939.
Brodie, B. B., Aronow, L., and Axelrod, J.: This Journal, **106:** 200, 1952.
Brodie, B.,B., and Axelrod, J.: This Journal, **94:** 22, 1948.
Brodie, B. B., and Axelrod, J.: This Journal, **99:** 171, 1950.
Brodie, B. B., Axelrod, J., Soberman, R., and Levy, B. B.: J. Biol. Chem., **179:** 25, 1949.
Brodie, B. B., Mark, L. C., Papper, E. M., Lief, P. A., Bernstein, E., and Rovenstine, E. A.: This Journal, **98:** 85, 1950.
Broida, H. P., Morowitz, H. J., and Selgin, M.: J. Research Natl. Bur. Standards, **52:** 293, 1954.
Bucher, T., and Rodetski, M.: Klin. Wchnschr., **29:** 615, 1951.
Butler, T. C.: This Journal, **108:** 474, 1953.
Cope, O., Blatt, H., and Ball, M. R.: J. Clin. Invest., **22:** 111, 1943.
Cotlove, E.: Fed. Proc., **14:** 32, 1955.
Edwards, L. J.: Trans. Faraday Soc., **46:** 723, 1950.
Flexser, L. A., Hammett, L. P., and Dingwall, A.: J. Am. Chem. Soc., **57:** 2103, 1935.
Friedman, M. H. F.: Proc. Soc. Exp. Biol. & Med., **54:** 42, 1943.
Goldbaum, L. R.: This Journal, **94:** 68, 1948.
Höber, R.: Physical Chemistry of Cells and Tissues, Blakiston, Philadelphia, 1945.
Hogben, C. A. M., Schanker, L. S., Tocco, D. J., and Brodie, B. B.: This Journal, **120:** 540, 1957.

HOGBEN, C. A. M.: Am. J. Physiol., **180:** 641, 1955.
JOSEPHSON, E. S., UDENFRIEND, S., AND BRODIE, B. B.: J. Biol. Chem., **168:** 341, 1947.
KAREL, L.: Physiol. Rev., **28:** 433, 1948.
KOLM, R., KOMAROV, S. A., AND SHAY, H.: Gastroenterology, **5:** 302, 1945.
LEFFLER, E. B., SPENCER, H. M., AND BURGER, A.: J. Am. Chem. Soc., **73:** 2611, 1951.
MITCHELL, R., AND CLARK, B. B.: Proc. Soc. Exp. Biol. & Med., **81:** 105, 1952.
SHORE, P. A., AXELROD, J., HOGBEN, C. A. M., AND BRODIE, B. B.: THIS JOURNAL, **113:** 192, 1955.
SHORE, P. A., BRODIE, B. B., AND HOGBEN, C. A. M.: THIS JOURNAL, **119:** 361, 1957.
SUNG, C., AND WAY, E. L.: THIS JOURNAL, **110:** 260, 1954.
TILLSON, E. K., PAULSON, S. F., AND BEYER, K. H.: J. Lab. Clin. Med., **44:** 880, 1954.
TRAVELL, J.: THIS JOURNAL, **69:** 21, 1940.
VANDENBELT, J. M., HENRICH, C., AND VANDENBERG, S. G.: Anal. Chem., **25:** 726, 1954.
WHITE, E. C., AND ACREE, S. F.: J. Am. Chem. Soc., **41:** 1190, 1919.

ABSORPTION OF DRUGS FROM THE STOMACH. II. THE HUMAN[1]

C. ADRIAN M. HOGBEN, LEWIS S. SCHANKER, DOMINICK J. TOCCO AND BERNARD B. BRODIE

Laboratory of Kidney and Electrolyte Metabolism and Laboratory of Chemical Pharmacology, National Heart Institute, National Institutes of Health, Public Health Service, U. S. Department of Health, Education and Welfare, Bethesda, Maryland

Received for publication April 4, 1957

It has been customary to regard the stomach as an inconsequential site of drug absorption. As a result, little attention has been paid to the gastric absorption of drugs other than ethanol. A previous report (Schanker *et al.*, 1957) demonstrated that the undissociated form of a drug is readily absorbed by the rat stomach. The following study extends the examination to man and indicates that the human stomach can absorb most acidic drugs as well as very weakly basic drugs. These results are consistent with the hypothesis that the human gastric mucosa is essentially a lipoid barrier selectively permitting the passive diffusion of the unionized lipid soluble form of a drug.

METHODS AND MATERIALS. The experiments were performed on three normal male subjects. The ages and body weights of the subjects were: subject 1, 35 years, 70 kgm.; subject 2, 26 years, 83 kgm.; subject 3, 28 years, 74 kgm. The subjects fasted for 15 to 17 hours prior to the experiments but drank water *ad libitum*. A Levine tube (number 12 French) was passed and then left in place throughout the experiment. The subject rested quietly in the left supine position.

A. *Absorption from 0.1 M HCl.* Following aspiration of the fasting gastric contents, 220 ml. of a 0.1 *M* HCl drug solution were introduced into the stomach. The solution was then partially withdrawn and reintroduced into the stomach a number of times to mix it thoroughly with the residual gastric fluid. Immediately following the one-minute mixing period, a 10-ml. aliquot was removed from the stomach. This aliquot was called the initial sample. Ten-ml. aliquots were then removed after 10, 20, 30 and 40 minutes. Immediately following withdrawal of the 40-minute sample, the residual drug solution was removed as completely as possible. The stomach was then washed five times with 100-ml. portions of water and these washings were combined with the previously withdrawn residual solution. The volume of this combined recovery was recorded.

The 0.1 *M* HCl drug solutions had the following compositions: solution A; sodium salicylate, 100 microgm. per ml., acetylsalicylic acid, quinine hydrochloride and phenol red, 200 microgm. per ml. each: solution B; secobarbital sodium, antipyrine, ephedrine hydrochloride and phenol red, 200 microgm. per ml. each: solution C; thiopental sodium, 80 microgm. per ml., D_2O, 50 mgm. per ml., aminopyrine and phenol red, 200 microgm. per ml. each. Deuterium oxide, which was used as a reference substance, was also included in solutions A and B for subject 3.

The concentrations of drugs and phenol red were determined in the initial sample and in the 10-, 20-, 30- and 40-minute samples. The concentration of phenol red was also determined in the original drug solution and in the combined recovery.

Phenol red, which is neither absorbed nor adsorbed by the human stomach (Penner *et al.*, 1938; Shay *et al.*, 1939) or the rat stomach (Schanker *et al.*, 1957), was included in the drug solutions for two purposes: it allowed correction for the change in drug concentration due to dilution by gastric secretion and swallowed saliva; and it provided a means

[1] A preliminary account of this work has appeared previously, Fed. Proc., **16:** 334, 1957.

of estimating the volume of drug solution within the stomach at the beginning and end of the experimental period.

If C_o is the concentration of the initial sample and C_n is the concentration of a sample withdrawn after *n* minutes, then the per cent of drug absorbed is given by the following equation:

$$\text{Per cent absorbed in n minutes} = 100 - 100\left(\frac{C_{n\ \text{drug}}}{C_{O\ \text{drug}}} \times \frac{C_{O\ \text{phenol red}}}{C_{n\ \text{phenol red}}}\right).$$

The mean phenol red corrections (C_o/C_n) and their ranges for the nine experiments were progressively: 10 minutes, 1.11 ± 0.11; 20 minutes, 1.18 ± 0.07; 30 minutes, 1.36 ± 0.14; 40 minutes, 1.65 ± 0.31.

The initial volume in the stomach was calculated from the initial dilution of phenol red. The final volume was calculated from the phenol red recovered from the stomach.

B. *Absorption from distilled water.* Following aspiration of the fasting gastric contents, 110 ml. of an aqueous solution of drugs were introduced into the stomach. An initial 10-ml. sample was removed after one minute of mixing. A single 10-ml. sample was withdrawn after 20 minutes and the per cent absorption calculated as described above.

Drugs were administered in 2 combinations: solution 1; aspirin, sodium salicylate, quinine hydrochloride, D_2O and phenol red: solution 2; secobarbital sodium, antipyrine, ephedrine hydrochloride, ethanol, D_2O and phenol red. The compounds were dissolved in distilled water and the concentrations were the same as described above. The concentration of ethanol was 10 mgm. per ml.

All of the analytical methods have been reported previously (Schanker *et al.*, 1957)[2] and the dissociation constants are cited in the same report. The designation ± signifies the range of the data.

RESULTS. The gastric absorption of drugs administered in 0.1 *M* HCl is shown in table 1. All of the acidic drugs (pKa values > 3) were absorbed more rapidly than the basic drugs. At the end of 40 minutes, the mean concentration change due to absorption ranged from 86 per cent for salicylic acid to 31 per cent for secobarbital. Antipyrine, which is very weakly basic (pKa 1.4), was the only basic drug appreciably absorbed after 40 minutes, its mean absorption being 23 per cent. No absorption was observed for the three stronger organic bases, aminopyrine, ephedrine and quinine (pKa values > 5). Deuterium oxide, which was used as a reference material, was absorbed to the extent of 74 per cent in 40 minutes. These results are graphically summarized in figure 1.

The above experiments provide additional support for the previously reported observation (Penner *et al.*, 1938; Shay *et al.*, 1939) that the very strong sulfonic acid, phenol red, is not absorbed by the human stomach. After correction for the concentration change of phenol red, the concentration changes of all three stronger bases were consistently zero. If there had been absorption of phenol red, at least one of these dissimilar compounds might have had a calculated final concentration greater than its initial concentration. Since the calculated absorption values for these bases were 0 ± 2 per cent, it is probable that the absorption of phenol red was also 0 ± 2 per cent.

During the 40-minute period of observation, there was a substantial loss of

[2] The authors again take pleasure in expressing their appreciation to Dr. Herbert Broida and Mrs. Margaret W. Chapman of the National Bureau of Standards for their help in the analysis of deuterium oxide.

TABLE 1

Human gastric absorption of drugs dissolved in 0.1 M HCl

On different days, each subject received 210 ml. of solution A, B or C. Absorption was determined at 10, 20, 30 and 40 minutes.

Solution	Subject	Cumulative per cent concentration change due to absorption												Gastric volume	
		minutes 10	20	30	40	*minutes* 10	20	30	40	*minutes* 10	20	30	40	initial *ml.*	final *ml.*
		Salicylic acid, pKa 3.0				*Aspirin, pKa 3.5*				*Quinine, pKa 8.4*					
	1	64	73	89	98	45	60	70	81	0	0	0	0	228	63
A	2	27	50	69	75	9	19	35	50	0	0	0	0	222	75
	3	36	51	72	85	18	29	40	60	0	0	0	0	243	69
		Secobarbital, pKa 7.9				*Antipyrine, pKa 1.4*				*Ephedrine, pKa 9.6*					
	1	4	10	16	22	1	6	13	19	0	0	0	0	218	54
B	2	10	20	26	40	6	13	20	31	0	0	0	0	232	89
	3	5	14	24	30	0	6	14	20	0	0	0	0	222	88
		Thiopental, pKa 7.6				*Deuterium oxide*				*Aminopyrine, pKa 5.0*					
	1	19	35	47	65	28	36	47	66	0	0	0	0	250	103
C	2	20	40	55	65	28	48	67	78	0	0	0	0	235	80
	3	19	41	59	71	26	49	66	79	0	0	0	0	244	69

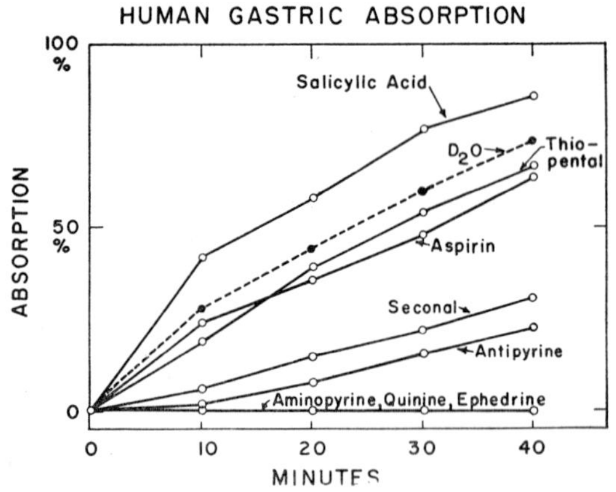

FIG. 1. Summary of human gastric absorption of drugs from 0.1 *M* HCl.

The per cent concentration changes due to absorption are the mean values from three individuals.

drug solution from the stomach by escape into the intestine. Of the mean initial volume of 233 ± 16 ml., 126 ml. escaped from the stomach into the intestine and 30 ml. were removed for analysis, resulting in a mean final volume of 77 ± 24 ml.

Since drugs are normally taken with a glass of water, absorption was determined for several drugs administered in 100 ml. of distilled water (table 2). For

TABLE 2

Human gastric absorption of drugs dissolved in distilled water

Each subject received 100 ml. of solution 1 or 2 on separate occasions. The extent of absorption was determined at the end of 20 minutes.

Drug	Per cent concentration change due to absorption	
	Mean	Individual values Subject 1 2 3
Solution 1		
Salicylic acid	62	67, 70, 49
Aspirin	30	31, 42, 16
Quinine	2	0, 5, 0
Deuterium oxide	59	59, 69, 49
Solution 2		
Secobarbital	16	15, 16, 18
Antipyrine	17	23, 12, 17
Ephedrine	6	6, 6, 5
Ethanol	40	34, 42, 43
Deuterium oxide	59	54, 60, 62

these experiments, the period of observation was 20 minutes. Again, acidic drugs were found to be rapidly absorbed by the human stomach. The slight absorption of the stronger bases, quinine and ephedrine, was so close to the limits of analysis that it does not deserve emphasis.

Ethanol was included in these experiments as a second reference material. The absorption of ethanol, 40 per cent in 20 minutes, was less rapid than that of salicylic acid and deuterium oxide but more rapid than that of aspirin and secobarbital.

In these experiments, the spontaneous basal gastric secretion made the gastric contents acidic and at the end of 20 minutes the mean pH was 1.8 ± 0.4. The initial dilution of phenol red indicated that absorption began from a volume of 125 ± 14 ml. in the six experiments. The final volumes, determined in only two of these experiments, were 101 ml. and 144 ml.

DISCUSSION. The absorption of drugs by the human stomach presents a comprehensible pattern. If a drug is partially unionized in the acid gastric contents, it is absorbed. If the drug is almost completely ionized, it is not absorbed because the lipid insoluble ionic form is unable to diffuse across the gastric mucosa. Thus those acids with a pKa of 3 or greater, which are undissociated in acidic gastric juice, were rapidly absorbed. The very weak base antipyrine (pKa 1.4), which is significantly undissociated at pH 1, was also absorbed to an appreciable extent. In contrast, the very strong sulfonic acid, phenol red, and the stronger bases (pKa > 5), which are ionized in the acidic gastric contents, were not detectably absorbed. Therefore the human gastric mucosa, like the rat gastric mucosa (Schanker *et al.*, 1957), is selectively permeable to the undissociated form of drugs.

TABLE 3

Comparison of human and rat gastric absorption

Clearance values are based on the human data of table 1 and the rat data of Schanker *et al.* (1957). Absorption has been calculated as a clearance employing the equation given in the text. These clearance values are expressed per square meter of body surface area assuming that m.^{2} = 0.1 (kgm. of body weight)$^{2/3}$.

Drug	Clearance (ml. of gastric content cleared/hr./m.^{2})		
	Human		Rat
	Observed	Relative to D_2O	
Salicylic acid	283	225	174
Deuterium oxide	173	173	198
Thiopental	152	152	108
Aspirin	138	110	89
Ethanol	101	99	52
Secobarbital	47	72	53
Antipyrine	35	46	27

The pattern of gastric absorption of drugs from distilled water was essentially the same as that from 0.1 *M* HCl. This is what would be expected since the normal basal gastric secretion made the gastric contents distinctly acid in these experiments.

These experiments show that the human stomach is potentially an important site of absorption. In actual practice however, three factors will determine the relative amount of a drug absorbed by the stomach after oral administration. The first and certainly the most important factor is the ability of a drug to dissolve in the gastric contents. For example, Dicumarol is so insoluble that no appreciable absorption can be expected from the stomach. On the other hand, a moderately soluble acid such as aspirin would be readily absorbed by the stomach. The second factor determining the extent of gastric absorption is the time that the drug remains in the stomach. This factor is extraordinarily variable; a glass of water may empty into the intestine in several minutes while a meal of ordinary food may remain in the stomach for three to four hours. Though it is true that drugs are often taken after a meal when gastric emptying is delayed, the third factor, the volume of gastric contents, must also be considered. The concentration of any given dose of a drug within the stomach will be inversely proportional to the volume of gastric contents. If the human stomach is similar to the rat stomach, the absolute rate of absorption will be proportional to the concentration (Schanker *et al.*, 1957) and thus inversely proportional to the gastric volume. The delayed gastric emptying after a meal, which favors gastric absorption, will be partially balanced by the larger volume from which absorption must take place.

In order to be able to express gastric absorption independently of the variables of time and gastric volume, we have calculated the rates of absorption as a clearance using the following equation (Schanker *et al.*, (1957):

$$\text{Clearance} = \frac{\text{Volume}}{\text{time}} \cdot \ln\left(\frac{\text{initial concentration}}{\text{final concentration}}\right).$$

The clearance of drugs by the human stomach is given in table 3. These clearances have also been calculated relative to the simultaneously measured clearance of deuterium oxide in order to correct for individual variation.

Table 3 also presents the clearances of the same drugs from 0.1 *M* HCl by the rat stomach, calculated from the data of Schanker *et al.*, (1957). The similarity between the gastric clearances of drugs by the human and rat stomach is impressive.[3]

While the design of the experiments in this study may have exaggerated gastric emptying, it is apparent that drugs may be absorbed directly from the stomach as rapidly or more rapidly than ethyl alcohol which is often considered to be the unusual example of a drug which is absorbed by the stomach.

SUMMARY

The human stomach is capable of absorbing most acidic drugs and the very weakly basic drugs. Salicylic acid, aspirin, thiopental, secobarbital and antipyrine, which are undissociated in the acidic gastric contents, were readily absorbed. Phenol red, quinine, ephedrine and aminopyrine, which are almost completely ionized in acid solution were not absorbed. These results are compatible with the hypothesis that drugs are absorbed by passive diffusion of their lipid soluble undissociated form. Many drugs may be absorbed by the human stomach as rapidly or more rapidly than ethyl alcohol.

REFERENCES

Berggren, S. M., and Goldberg, L.: Acta Physiol. Scand., **1:** 246, 1940.

Bradley, W. B., Schnedorf, J. G., and Ivy, A. C.: Am. J. Digest. Dis., **3:** 415, 1936.

Cope, O., Blatt, H., and Ball, M. R.: J. Clin. Invest., **22:** 111, 1943.

Karel, L., and Fleisher, J.: Am. J. Physiol., **153:** 268, 1948.

Lee, P.R., Code, C. F., and Scholer, J. F.: Gastroenterology, **29:** 1008, 1955.

Penner, A., Hollander, F., and Saltzman, M.: Am. J. Digest. Dis., **5:** 657, 1938.

Schanker, L. S., Shore, P. A., Brodie, B. B., and Hogben, C. A. M.: This Journal, **120:** 528, 1957.

Shay, H., Gershon-Cohen, J., and Fels, S. S.: Am. J. Digest. Dis., **6:** 361, 1939.

Sollmann, T., Hanzlik, P. J., and Pilcher, J. D.: This Journal, **1:** 409, 1910.

[3] The following clearances in ml. per hour per $m.^2$ can be calculated from data in the literature assuming $m.^2 = 0.1$ (kgm. body weight)$^{2/3}$ and using other assumptions as indicated: ethanol, rat, 48 (Karel and Fleisher, 1948); ethanol, human, no allowance for dilution, 153 (Berggren and Goldberg, 1940); ethanol, cat, 137 (Berggren and Goldberg, 1940); D_2O, dog, assuming gastric pouch equal to one-half of stomach, 390 (Cope *et al.*, 1943); D_2O, human, assuming a gastric volume of 100 ml. and disregarding the possible error due to hepatic clearance, 130 (Lee *et al.*, 1955); salicylic acid and aspirin, dog, assuming body weight of 15 kgm., 420 and 277 respectively (Bradley *et al.*, 1936). While Sollmann *et al.* (1910) demonstrated that the weak acid phenol was readily absorbed by the stomach of the cat and dog, the data are insufficient for calculating a clearance.

INDEX

Absorption of drugs from the stomach, 528, 540
Acetanilide, gastric absorption of, 528
Acetylcholine, auricular fibrillation by, 38
derivatives, effect on cholinesterases of chick embryo, 285
effect of pH and atropine on tissue response to, 408
effect on cardiac ventricular conductions, 137
effect on cholinesterases of chick embryo, 285
potentiation by endrophonium, 215
potentiation by neostigmine, 215
potentiation by pyridostigmin, 215
Acetylcholinesterase, inhibition of, at selective cellular sites *in vivo*, 488
Acetyl-β-methylcholine, effect on cholinesterase content, 285
Acetylsalicylic acid, gastric absorption of, in rats, 528
Acids, organic, gastric absorption of, 528, 540
Adenine and K transport in red cells, 9
Adler, T. K., Elliott, H. W., and George, R. Some factors affecting the biological disposition of small doses of morphine in rats, 475
Adrenal cortical hormones, effect on experimental polyarthritis, relation to aurothiomalate, 349
Adrenal-pituitary activating agents, effect of CNS depressants on, 261
Amethopterin, fluorometric determination of, 1
Aminopyrine, gastric absorption of, in man, 540
Amphetamine, effect on EEG, 160
effect on pulmonary circulation, 512
d-Amphetamine, effects on judgment, 33
Analgesics, screening method for, based on differential bar-pressing rates, 388
Andromedotoxin, effect upon cardiac ventricular conduction, 137
Anileridine, absorption and metabolism of, 447
analgesic action and concentration in brain of, 447
Aniline, gastric absorption of, 528
Antagonism of tubocurarine, edrophonium, 215
neostigmine, 215
pyridostigmin, 215
Anticholinergic agents, structure-activity relationship of, 46
Anticholinesterase, action at selective cellular sites *in vivo*, 488
treatment of poisoning by, 276
Antipyrine, gastric absorption of, 528, 540
Antiveratrinic response, 63
Apnea, after succinylcholine, 203
logarithmic distribution, 203
Apomorphine-induced emesis, effect of phenothiazine derivatives on, 375
Arthritis, experimental, effect of adrenal corticoids and aurothiomalate on, 349
Aspirin, and pituitary-adrenal activation, 261
Atropine, effect of on tissue response to serotonin and acetylcholine, 408
Auricles, effect of metabolic inhibitors on frequency-force relationships in, 324
frequency-force relationships in, 324
Auricular fibrillation, after glucose and acetylcholine, 38
after insulin and acetylcholine, 38
Aurothioglucose, gold distribution and obesity after, 84
Aviado, Domingo M., Jr., and Schmidt, Carl F. Effects of sympathomimetic drugs on pulmonary circulation: with special reference to a new pulmonary vasodilator, 512
Avoidance behavior, and chlorpromazine, 379
Azo dyes, enzymatic reduction of, 291
Azo reductase, 291

Baker, W. P., and Woods, L. A. Study in the dog of the renal clearance of morphine and the effect of morphine on *p*-aminohippurate clearance, 371
Barbiturate oxidation, in various tissues, 75
Barbiturates, effect on chemoreflexes, 399
enzymatic oxidation of, 75
gastric absorption of, in man, 540
gastric absorption of, in rats, 528
tolerance to, 469
Bases, organic gastric absorption of, 528, 540
Belleville, R. E., and Fraser, H. F. Tolerance to some effects of barbiturates, 469
see Hill, H. E., 388

Benforado, J. M. Studies on veratrum alkaloids XXVI. Comparison of the cardiac action of various tertiary amine ester alkaloids, 412
Benzoylcholine, effect on cholinesterase content, 285
Bioassay, for cardioactive principles based on staircase phenomenon, 90
Bisquaternary hypotensive agents, 438
Blood platelets, release of serotonin from, by reserpine, 334
Bogdanski, D. F., see Mitoma, C., 188
see Udenfriend, S., 255
BOL, effects of, on potentiated hexobarbital hypnosis, 20
Borreson, R. E., see Ford, R. V., 247
Brain, comparative distribution of morphine and nalorphine in dog, 58
Brodie, B. B., see Carlsson, A., 334
see Cooper, J. R., 75
see Fouts, J. R., 291
see Hogben, C. Adrian M., 540
see Schanker, Lewis S., 528
see Udenfriend, S., 255
Brody, T. M., see Hosoya, E., 504
Brown, R. V., Kunkel, A. M., Somers, L. M., and Wills, J. H. Pyridine-2-aldoxime methiodide in the treatment of sarin and tabun poisoning, with notes on its pharmacology, 276
Bufotenine, effects of, on potentiated hexobarbital hypnosis, 20
Burke, J. C., see Rubin, B., 125
Burkhalter, A., Featherstone, R. M., Schueler, F. W., and Jones, M. Effects of some acetylcholine derivatives on the cholinesterases of chick embryo intestine cultured *in vitro*, 285
Busulfan, S^{35}-labeled, see Myleran, S^{35}-labeled
Butyrylcholine, effect on cholinesterase content, 285

Caffeine, gastric absorption of, 528
Calcium, antagonism of, to curariform action of streptomycin, 452
Cardiac active principle, bioassay of, 90
isolation of, from mammalian tissue, 99
Carlsson, A., Shore, P. A., and Brodie, B. B. Release of serotonin from blood platelets by reserpine *in vitro*, 334
Cations, effect upon cardiac ventricular conduction, 137
Cations, transport in erythrocytes, 9
Central nervous system, effects of ganglionic blocking agents, 147
Cerletti, A., see Taeschler, M., 179
Cevadine, cardiac action of, 412
Chemoreflexes, effect of morphinan analogues on, 399
Chick embryo, cholinesterase as affected by acetylcholine analogs, 285
Chlorpromazine, antiemetic action of, 375
effect on avoidance behavior, 379
effect on pituitary-adrenal activation, 261
Cholinesterase, and action of succinylcholine, 203
as affected by substrates, 285
human serum, 203
inhibition of, at selective cellular sites *in vivo*, 488
of chick embryo intestine, 285
Cholinesterase inhibition, time course of action of neostigmine, pyridostigmin, and edrophonium, 215
Cholinesterase inhibitors, treatment of poisoning by, 276
Cholinolytic agents, structure-activity relationship of, 46
CNS depressants, effect of, on pituitary-adrenal activating agents, 261
Codeine, respiratory chemoreflex activity, 399
Cohen, S. B., see Kahn, J. B., Jr., 9
Conditioned response, and chlorpromazine, 379
Conduction, cardiac, 137
Cook, D. L., Lawler, C. A., and Cusic, J. W. Relation of peripheral vasodilator activity to chemical structure of 1,2,3,4-tetrahydroisoquinoline derivatives, 269
Cooper, J. R., and Brodie, B. B. Enzymatic oxidation of pentobarbital and thiopental, 75
Corrado, A. P., see Vital Brazil, O., 452
Curare, on veratrine response, 63
Cusic, J. W., see Cook, D. L., 269
Cyanide, effect on rabbit auricles, 324

Darstine, gastric absorption of, 528
Debley, V. G., see Leitch, J. L., 408
Decamethonium, on veratrine response, 63
Depressants, effect on pituitary-adrenal activating agents, 261
Deserpidine, in patients, 247
11-Desmethoxyreserpine, bioassay of, in mice, 125
Dexadrine, see *d*-Amphetamine

Dextromethorphan, respiratory chemoreflex activity, 399
Dextrorphan, respiratory chemoreflex activity, 399
Dibenzyline, effect of, on pituitary-adrenal activation, 261
Dibucaine number, and action of succinylcholine, 203
Dihydrocodeine, analgesic action of, 354
Dilantin, see Diphenylhydantoin
Dille, J. M., see Gogerty, J. H., 340
β-Dimethylaminoethyl acetate, effect on cholinesterase content, 285
Dinitrophenol, effect on rabbit auricles, 324
  effect on veratrinized muscle, 63
Diphenylhydantoin, effect on synaptic transmission, 301
  possible basis of anticonvulsant action of, 301
DNA, and 6-mercaptopurine in *E. coli*, 195
DOCA, effect of, on experimental polyarthritis, 349
Dontas, A. S., and Nickerson, M. Central and peripheral components of the action of "ganglionic" blocking agents, 147
Duchesne, E. R., see Fowler, N. O., 115
Duggan, D. E., see Udenfriend, S., 26

E. coli, effect of 6-mercaptopurine on, 195
Edrophonium, antagonism to tubocurarine, 215
Elliott, H. W., see Adler, T. K., 475
Emesis, effect of phenothiazine derivatives on, 375
Ephedrine, effect of, on pulmonary circulation, 512
  gastric absorption of, in man, 540
  gastric absorption of, in rats, 528
Epileptics, comparison of primidone and phenobarbital in, 184
Epinephrine, and pituitary-adrenal activation, 261
  effect on cardiac ventricular conduction, 137
  effect on left ventricular function, 361
  effect on pulmonary circulation, 512
Erythrocytes, potassium transport in, 9
  transport of P^{32} in, 239
Eserine, effect on EEG, 160
Esplin, D. W. Effects of diphenylhydantoin on synaptic transmission in cat spinal cord and stellate ganglion, 301
Ethanol, absorption of, from stomach in man, 540

Featherstone, R. M., see Burkhalter, A. 285
Fluoroacetate, effect on rabbit auricles, 324
Fluorometry, spectro-, of organic compounds, 26
Ford, R. V., Borreson, R. E., Lindley, G. R., and Moyer, J. H. Comparative study of the effects of four different *Rauwolfia* preparations administered parenterally, 247
Fouts, J. R., Kamm, J. J., and Brodie, B. B. Enzymatic reduction of prontosil and other azo dyes 291
Fowler, N. O., Duchesne, E. R., and Franch, R. H. Hemodynamic effects of levarterenol infusion during pulmonary stenosis 115
Franch, R. H., see Fowler N. O., 115
Fraser, H. F., see Belleville, R. E., 469
Freeman, M. V. Fluorometric method for the measurement of 4-amino-10-methyl pteroylglutamic acid (amethopterin) in plasma, 1
Friedman, G., and Tepperman, J. Distribution of gold following the injection of obesity-inducing doses of aurothioglucose in the mouse, 84
Frog heart, staircase phenomenon, and bioassay of cardioactive principles, 90

Ganglionic blocking agents, central and peripheral actions, 147
  effects on splanchnic nerve activity, 147
  effects on temporal summation in ganglia, 147
Gastric absorption of drugs, in man, 540
  in rats, 528
George, R., see Adler, T. K., 475
Germidine, cardiac action of, 412
Germitetrine B, cardiac action of, 412
Glucose, auricular fibrillation after, 38
Gogerty, J. H., and Dille, J. M. Pharmacology of *d*-lysergic acid morpholide (LSM), 340
Gold, distribution after aurothioglucose, 84
Govier, W. M., see Rosenkilde, H., 375
Grant, P., see Gruber, C. M., Jr., 184
Gruber, C. M., Jr., Mosier, J. M., and Grant, P. Objective comparison of primidone and phenobarbital in epileptics, 184
Gruhzit, C. C. Chemoreflex activity of dextromethorphan (Romilar), dextrorphan, codeine and morphine in the cat and the dog, 399
Gunn, D. R., see Kalow, W., 203

Hajdu, S. Bioassay for cardiac active principles based on the staircase phenomenon of the frog heart, 90
Hajdu, S., Weiss, H., and Titus, E. Isolation of a cardiac active principle from mammalian tissue, 99
Haley, T. J., see Leitch, J. L., 408
Hauty, G. T., and Payne, R. B. Effects of *dextro*-amphetamine upon judgment, 33
Heart, effect of epinephrine and levarterenol on, 361
frequency-force relationships in, 324
staircase phenomenon of, in bioassay of cardioactive principles, 90
ventricular conduction, 137
Heart-lung preparation, isolation of a necessary factor in, 99
Hexamethonium, effects on central nervous system, 147
Hexobarbital hypnosis, potentiated, 20
Highman, B., see Webster, S. H., 171
Hill, H. E., Pescor, F. T., Belleville, R. E., and Wikler, A. Use of differential bar-pressing rates of rats for screening analgesic drugs. I. Techniques and effects of morphine, 388
Histamine, and pituitary-adrenal activation, 261
Hogben, C., Adrian M., Schanker, Lewis S., Tocco, Dominick J., and Brodie, Bernard B. Absorption of drugs from the stomach. II. the human, 540
see Schanker, Lewis S., 528
Hosoya, E., and Brody, T. M. *In vitro* oxidation of morphine by rat tissue homogenates, 504
Hydroxyamphetamin, effect of, on pulmonary circulation, 512
Hypotensive agents, 438
Hypoxanthine and K transport in red cells, 9

Ibogaine, effects of, on potentiated hexobarbital hypnosis, 20
Inscoe, J. K., see Mandel, H. G., 195
Insulin, auricular fibrillation after, 38
Intestine, acetylcholine derivatives, effects on, 285
enzymes, 285
Iodates, acute toxicities of, 171
Iodides and iodates, acute toxicities of, 171
Iodoacetate, effect on rabbit auricles, 324
Iodoacetic acid, on veratrinized muscle, 63
Iproniazid, effect of, on serotonin metabolism, 255
Isopropylamine, β-hydroxyl-β(2,5-diethoxyphenyl, (45–50), 512
Isoproterenol, effect of, on pulmonary circulation, 512
Isoquinoline derivatives, vasodilator action of, 269

Jasmin, G. Prevention of experimental polyarthritis with sodium aurothiomalate, 349
Johnson, E. A., and McKinnon, M. G. The differential effect of quinidine and pyrilamine on the myocardial action potential at various rates of stimulation, 460
Jones, M., see Burkhalter A., 285

Kahn, J. B., Jr. Effects of ribosides and related compounds on phosphate transport in incubated fresh and cold-stored human erythrocytes, 239
and Cohen, S. B. Effects of ribosides and related compounds on cation transport in cold-stored human erythrocytes, 9
Kalow, W., and Gunn, D. R. Relation between dose of succinylcholine and duration of apnea in man, 203
Kamm, J. J., see Fouts, J. R., 291
Katzung, B., Rosin, H., and Scheider, F. Frequency-force relationship in the rabbit auricle and its modification by some metabolic inhibitors, 324
Keats, A. S., Telford, J., and Kurosu, Y. Studies of analgesic drugs: dihydrocodeine, 354
Kisley, A., see Miller, J. W., 426
Koelle, George B. Histochemical demonstration of reversible anticholinesterase action at selective cellular sites *in vivo*, 488
Kunkel, A. M., see Brown, R. V., 276
Kurosu, Y., see Keats, A. S., 354

Lactones, effect on P^{32} transport in erythrocytes, 239
Lands, A. M., see Long, J. P., 46
Lawler, C. A., see Cook, D. L., 269
Leitch, J. L., Maryn, D., Debley, V. G., and Haley, T. J. Influence of pH and atropine on the response of superfused tissues to 5-hydroxytryptamine and acetylcholine, 408
Levarterenol, effect on cardiac output, 115
effect on left ventricular function, 361

effect on pulmonary circulation, 512
hemodynamic effects of, 115
Leveque, P. E. Auricular fibrillation by acetylcholine injection during hypopotassemia, 38
Lindley, G. R., see Ford, R. V., 247
Long, J. P., and Lands, A. M. Influence of various spatial groups on cholinolytic activity, 46
Longo, V. G., and Silvestrini, B. Action of eserine and amphetamine on the electrical activity of the rabbit brain, 160
LSD, effects of, on potentiated hexobarbital hypnosis, 20
d-Lysergic acid morpholide (LSM), comparison with *d*-lysergic acid diethylamide, 340
pharmacology of, 340
Lysergic acid diethylamide, interaction with reserpine, 179
Lysolecithin, β-palmitoyl, a cardioactive factor in mammalian tissue, 99

Maling, H. M., see Mandel, H. G., 195
Malone, M. H., see Rubin, B., 125
Mandel, H. G., Inscoe, J. K., Maling, H. M., and Smith, P. K. Effect of 6-mercaptopurine on nucleic acid biosynthesis in *Escherichia coli*, 195
Maryn, D., see Leitch, J. L., 408
McKinnon, M. G., see Johnson, E. A., 460
Mead, J. C., see Smith, C. M., 215
Mecamylamine, gastric absorption of, 528
Mepazine, antiemetic action of, 375
6-Mercaptopurine, effect on nucleic acids, 195
Mescaline, effects of on potentiated hexobarbital hypnosis, 20
Metaraminol, effect of, on pulmonary circulation, 512
Methamphetamine, effect of, on pulmonary circulation, 512
Methoxamine derivatives, effect of, on pulmonary circulation, 512
Methyl reserpate, bioassay of, in mice and rats, 125
Methyl β-trimethylammonium propionate, effects on cholinesterase content, 285
Microsomes, and barbiturate oxidation, 75
Miller, J. W., Kisley, A., and Murray, W. J. Effects of relaxin-containing ovarian extracts on various types of smooth muscle, 379
Miller, R. E., Murphy, J. V., and Mirsky, I. A. Effect of chlorpromazine on fear motivated behavior in rats, 379
Mirsky, I. A., see Miller, R. E., 379
Mitoma, C., Posner, H. S., Bogdanski, D. F., and Udenfriend, S. Biochemical and pharmacological studies on *o*-tyrosine and its *meta* and *para* analogues, 188
Morphinan analogues, respiratory chemoreflex activity, 399
Morphine, analgesic action of, 388, 354
and dihydrocodeine, comparative analgesic action of, 354
and pituitary-adrenal activation, 261
biological disposition of, in rats, 475
distribution in dog brain, 58
effect of adrenalectomy on biological disposition of, 475
effect on the clearance rate of *p*-aminohippuric acid in the dog, 371
effect on differential bar-pressing rates, 388
in vitro oxidation of, 504
lack of effect of ACTH on biological disposition of, 475
lack of effect of pitressin on biological disposition of, 475
renal clearance of free and conjugated in the dog, 371
respiratory chemoreflex activity, 399
species difference in metabolism of, 475
Mosier, J. M., see Gruber, C. M., Jr., 184
Moyer, J. H., see Ford, R. V., 247
Muehlenbeck, H. E., see Woods, L. A., 52
Murphy, J. V., see Miller, R. E., 379
Murray, W. J., see Miller, J. W., 426
Myleran, S^{35}-labeled, distribution and metabolic fate in normal and tumor-bearing rats, 229
S^{35}-labeled, synthesis, 229

Nalorphine, distribution in dog brain, 58
effect of on pituitary-adrenal activation, 261
free and conjugated, distribution of in dogs and rats, 52
oxidation of, *in vitro*, 504
plasma levels in dogs, 52
Napoli, Martha, see O'Dell, T. B., 438
Neogermitrine, cardiac action of, 412
Neostigmine, antagonism to curariform action of streptomycin, 452
antagonism to tubocurine, 215
Nickerson, M., see Dontas, A. S., 147

Norepinephrine, see Levarterenol
Nucleic acid synthesis, effect of 6-mercaptopurine on, 195

Obesity, and gold distribution after aurothioglucose, 84
O'Dell, T. B., and Napoli, Martha. Pharmacology of some new unsymmetrical bisquaternary hypotensive agents—substituted pyridine and piperidine derivatives, 438
Ouabain, effect on cardiac ventricular conduction, 137
  effect on K transport in red cells, 9
Ovarian extracts, relaxin-containing, effect of, on smooth muscle, 426
  relaxin-containing, tachyphylaxis with, 426
Oxidation of morphine, *in vitro*, 504

Page, I. H., see Salmoiraghi, G. C., 20
Palmitoyl lysolecithin, a cardioactive factor in mammalian tissue, 99
Payne, R. B., see Hauty, G. T., 33
Peng, C. Distribution and metabolic fate of S^{35}-labeled Myleran (Busulfan) in normal and tumor-bearing rats, 229
Pentobarbital, effect on pituitary-adrenal activation, 261
  enzymatic oxidation of, 75
  tolerance to, 469
Pentylenetetrazol, effect on EEG, 160
Pescor, F. T., see Hill, H. E., 388
pH, effect of, on tissue response to serotonin and acetylcholine, 408
Phenobarbital, comparison of, with primidone, in epileptics, 184
  effect on avoidance behavior, 375
Phenol red, gastric absorption of, in rats, 528
Phenylephrine, effect of, on pulmonary circulation, 512
Phenylketonuria, and *o*-tyrosine, 188
Phosphorus (P^{32}), transport of in erythrocytes, 239
Piperidine derivatives, hypotensive action of, 438
Pituitary-adrenal activating agents, effect of CNS depressants on, 261
Porter, C. C. Absorption and metabolism of anileridine, ethyl-1-(4-aminophenethyl)-4-phenylisonipecotate, 447
Posner, H. S., see Mitoma, C., 188
Post-tetanic potentiation, by diphenylhydantoin, 301
Potassium, arrest of auricular fibrillation by, 38
  transport in erythrocytes, 9
Primidone, comparison of, with phenobarbital, in epileptics, 184
Proclorperazine, antiemetic action of, 375
Promazine, entiemetic action of, 375
Prontosil, enzymatic reduction of, 291
Protoveratrine A & B, cardiac action of, 412
  effect upon cardiac ventricular conduction, 137
Pseudomorphine, as oxidation product of morphine *in vitro*, 504
Pulmonary stenosis, and levarterenol, 115
Pulmonary vascular system, effect of sympathomimetic drugs on, 512
Purine, and K transport in red cells, 9
Purines, effect on P^{32} transport in erythrocytes, 239
Pyridine-2-aldoxine methiodide, in treatment of sarin and tabun poisoning, 276
Pyridine derivatives, hypotensive action of, 438
Pyridostigmin, antagonism to tubocurine, 215
Pyrilamine, effect of, on myocardial action potential, 460

Quinidine, effect on cardiac ventricular conduction, 137
  effect on myocardial action potential, 46
Quinine, gastric absorption of, in man, 540
  gastric absorption of, in rats, 528
  on veratrinized muscle, 63

Raunormine (deserpidine), in patients, 247
Rauwolfia alkaloids, comparative antihy pertensive action of in patients, 247
  comparative study of, in patients, 247
  comparison of side reactions with, 247
  release of serotonin from blood platelets by, 334
Rauwolfia, bioassay of, in mice, rats and dogs, 125
  whole root, potency relative to reserpine, in mice, rats and dogs, 125
Relaxin, action on blood pressure, 426
  action on isolated uterus in presence of uterine stimulants, 426
  action on smooth muscle, 426
  action on ureteral motility, 426
Rescamine (rescinnamine), in patients, 247
Rescinnamine, bioassay of, in mice, rats and dogs, 125
  in patients, 247

Reserpine, bioassay of, in mice, rats and dogs, 125
clinical comparison of with other *Rauwolfia* alkaloids, 247
effect of, on pituitary-adrenal activation, 261
interaction with lysergic acid diethylamide, 179
release of serotonin from blood platelets by, 334
Reserpine-like alkaloids, bioassay of, in mice, rats and dogs, 125
Ribosides, effect on P^{32} transport in erythrocytes, 239
effect on K transport in red cells, 9
Ribotides, effect on P^{32} transport in erythrocytes, 239
Rice, M. E., see Webster, S. H., 171
RNA, and 6-mercaptopurine in *E. coli*, 195
Rosenkilde, H., and Govier, W. M. Comparison of some phenothiazine derivatives in inhibiting apomorphine-induced emesis, 375
Rosin, H., see Katzung, B., 324
Rubin, B., Malone, M. H., Waugh, M. H., and Burke, J. C. Bioassay of *Rauwolfia* roots and alkaloids, 125
Rushmer, R. F., see West, T. C., 361

Salmoiraghi, G. C., and Page, I. H. Effects of LSD 25, BOL 148, bufotenine, mescaline and ibogaine on the potentiation of hexobarbital hypnosis produced by serotonin and reserpine, 20
Sarin poisoning, treatment of, 276
Sch 3940, antiemetic action of, 375
Schanker, Lewis S., Shore, Parkhurst A., Brodie, Bernard B., and Hogben, C. Adrian M. Absorption of drugs from the stomach. I. the rat, 528
see Hogben, C. Adrian M., 540
Scheider, R., see Katzung, B., 324
Schmidt, Carl F., see Aviado, Domingo M., 512
Schueler, F. W., see Burkhalter, A., 285
Scopolamine, effect on EEG, 160
Secobarbital, tolerance to, 469
Serotonin, effect of pH and atropine on tissue response to, 408
metabolism of, effect of iproniazid on, 255
release of, from blood platelets by reserpine, 334
Serpentine, in patients, 247
Shore, P. A., see Carlsson, A., 334
see Schanker, Lewis S., 528
Silvestrini, B., see Longo V. G., 160
Smith, C. M., Mead, J. C., and Unna, K. R. Antagonism of tubocurarine III: time course of action of pyridostigmin, neostigmine, and edrophonium *in vivo* and *in vitro*, 215
Smith, P. K., see Mandel, H. G., 195
Sodium aurothiomalate, effect on experimental polyarthritis, 349
effect on kidney, 349
Somers, L. M., see Brown, R. V., 276
Spectrofluorometry, of organic compounds, 26
Staircase phenomenon, bioassay of cardioactive principles based on, 90
Streptomycin, curariform action of, 452
neuromuscular blockade with, 452
Strophanthin, on veratrinized muscle, 63
Succinylcholine, dose and duration of action, 203
Swain, H. H., and Weidner, C. L. Study of substances which alter intraventricular conduction in the isolated dog heart, 137
Swaine, C. R., see Witt, P. N., 63
Sympathomimetic drugs, effects of, on pulmonary circulation, 512
Synaptic transmission, effect of diphenylhydantoin on, 301
Synephrin, effect of, on pulmonary circulation, 512

Tabun poisoning, treatment of, 276
Taeschler, M., and Cerletti, A. Some observations on the interaction of reserpine and LSD, 179
Telford, J., see Keats, A. S., 354
Tepperman, J., see Friedman, G., 84
Tetraethylammonium, effects on central nervous system, 147
gastric absorption of, 528
Tetrahydroisoquinoline derivatives, vasodilator action of, 269
Thiopental, effect on chemoreflexes, 399
enzymatic oxidation of, 75
Tissue culture, chick embryo intestine, 285
cholinesterase changes during, 285
Titus, E., see Hajdu, S., 99
Tocco, Dominick J., see Hogben, C. Adrian M., 540
Tolazoline, gastric absorption of, 528
Toxicities, acute, of iodates, 171
TPNH, and barbiturate oxidation, 75
TPNH, in reduction of azo dyes, 291

Tranquilizers, effect of on serotonin of blood platelets, 334
Transport processes, in erythrocytes, 239
Tuaminoheptane, effect of, on pulmonary circulation, 512
Tumor-bearing rat, distribution and metabolic fate of S^{35}-labeled Myleran in, 229
o-, *m*-, and *p*-Tyrosine, studies of, 188
o-Tyrosine, biochemical and pharmacological studies on, 188
metabolism and action of, 188
possible relation to phenylketonuria, 188

Udenfriend, S., Duggan, D. E., Vasta, B. M., and Brodie, B. B. Spectrophotofluorometric study of organic compounds of pharmacological interest, 26
Udenfriend, S., see Mitoma, C., 188
Udenfriend, S., Weissbach, H., and Bogdanski, D. F. Effect of iproniazid on serotonin metabolism *in vivo*, 255
Unna, K. R., see Smith, C. M., 215
Uterus, action of relaxin on, 426

Vanilloylzygadenine, cardiac action of, 412
Van Peenen, P. F. D., and Way, E. L. Effect of certain central nervous system depressants on pituitary-adrenal activating agents, 261
Vasodilator activity, of tetrahydroisoquinoline derivatives, 269
Vasta, B. M., see Udenfriend, S., 26
Ventricle, effect of epinephrine and levarterenol on, 361
Veratridine, cardiac action of, 412
Veratridine response, in frog muscle, 63
Veratrine, effect upon cardiac ventricular conduction, 137
Veratrine response, in frog muscle, 63
Veratroylzygadenine, cardiac action of, 412
Veratrum alkaloids, comparison of cardiac action of, 412
Vital Brazil, O., and Corrado, A. P. Curariform action of streptomycin, 452
von Oettingen, W. F., see Webster, S. H., 171

Waugh, M. H., see Rubin, B., 125
Way, E. L., see Van Peenen, P. F. D., 261
Webster, S. H., Rice, M. E., Highman, B., and von Oettingen, W. F. Toxicology of potassium and sodium iodates: Acute toxicity in mice, 171
Weidner, C. L., see Swain, H. H., 137
Weiss, H., see Hajdu, S., 99
Weissbach, H., see Udenfriend, S., 255
West, T. C., and Rushmer, R. F. Comparative effects of epinephrine and levarterenol (*l*-norepinephrine) on left ventricular performance in conscious and anesthetized dogs, 361
Wikler, A., see Hill, H. E., 388
Wills, J. H., see Brown, R. V., 276
Witt, P. N., and Swaine, C. R. Studies in veratrum alkaloids, XXV. Veratrine response and antiveratrinic action in frog sartorius muscle, 63
Woods, L. A. Comparative distribution of morphine and nalorphine in dog brain, 58
and Muehlenbeck, H. E. Distribution and fate of nalorphine in the dog and rat, 52
see Baker, W. P., 371